Key case-law extracts

European Court
of Human Rights

Gilles Dutertre

Council of Europe Publishing

French version:

Extraits clés de jurisprudence – Cour européenne des Droits de l'Homme

ISBN 92-871-5054-0

Cover design: Graphic Design Workshop, Council of Europe
Layout: Desktop Publishing Unit, Council of Europe
Edited by Council of Europe Publishing
http://book.coe.int

Council of Europe Publishing
F-67075 Strasbourg Cedex

ISBN 92-871-5055-9
© Council of Europe, December 2003
Printed in Germany

Preface

It is with pleasure that I welcome this publication of *Key case-law extracts*, a project begun by Gilles Dutertre when he was a trainee with the Directorate of Human Rights in the mid-1990s.

The years since then have seen an immense increase in the number of applications under the European Convention on Human Rights, first to the Commission and, since the entry into force of Protocol No. 11 in November 1998, to the new Court. Between 1995 and 2001 there has been approximately a three-fold increase in both the number of provisional files opened and the number of applications registered; while even in the relatively short life of the new Court the number of judgments has risen from 177 in 1999 (its first full year of functioning) to 844 in 2002.

Key case-law extracts sets out to provide a rational approach to understanding the ever-growing mass of case-law handed down by the Court. Rather than seeking to be an exhaustive analysis of the Convention jurisprudence, it presents the principal case law illustrating each substantive provision of the Convention and its protocols. The primary source is the judgments of the Court, but decisions of the Commission are also cited where there was no relevant Court ruling.

The arrangement by article, the extensive extracts from the case-law, the detailed table of contents and the index give the reader different ways of approaching the book, making it a useful tool for both the newcomer to Convention law and the more experienced researcher.

Pierre-Henri Imbert

Director General of Human Rights
Council of Europe, 2003

The published case-law
of the European Convention on Human Rights

European Commission of Human Rights

"Collection of Decisions of the European Commission of Human Rights",
Vols. 1-46, 1959-74, Council of Europe

Decisions and Reports, vols. 1-94, 1975-98, Council of Europe

European Court of Human Rights

Series A: *Judgments and Decisions,* Vols. 1-338, 1961-95, Carl Heymanns
Verlag, Cologne

Series B: *Pleadings, Oral Arguments and Documents,* Vols. 1-104, 1961-95,
Carl Heymanns Verlag, Cologne

Reports of Judgments and Decisions, 1996-I to 1998-VIII, 1996-98, Carl
Heymanns Verlag, Cologne

Committee of Ministers

"Collection of resolutions adopted by the Committee of Ministers in application of Articles 32 and 54 of the European Convention on Human Rights",
1959-89, 1993, Council of Europe

Yearbook of the European Convention on Human Rights

Vols. 1-40, 1959-98, Martinus Nijhoff Publishers, The Hague/London/Boston.
Contains selected decisions of the European Commission of Human Rights;
summaries of the judgments of the European Court of Human Rights; and
the human rights (DH) resolutions of the Committee of Ministers.

Contents

Foreword

"The Convention is a living instrument which [...] must be interpreted in the light of present-day conditions" (see, among other authorities, the Tyrer v. the United Kingdom judgment of 25 April 1978, Series A No. 26, pp. 15-16, paragraph 31, the Soering judgment, p. 40, paragraph 102, and the Loizidou v. Turkey judgment of 23 March 1995, Series A No. 310, pp. 26-27, paragraph 71).

It is now more that six years since the first steps to compile the present *Key case-law extracts* were taken. Since that time, the Court has had the opportunity to amend its case-law on certain points, such as the concept of "torture" referred to in Article 3. It has supplemented its case-law on other points, such as the concept of "alcoholic" within the meaning of Article 5, paragraph 1.*e*.

The increase in the number of States Parties to the Convention has allowed the Court to deal with an ever greater number of cases, while the entry into force of Protocol No. 11 provided it with more resources and enabled it to deal with cases more effectively. Note that the quantity of judgments pronounced has increased considerably. Moreover, the present work needed to be revised and brought up to date.

The aim in updating the work has been the same as that which inspired the first edition, completed with the collaboration of Jakob van der Velde: to provide, in a single document, both practitioners and students in all member states with the maximum number of citations from the judgments of the Court, while reducing, so far as reasonably possible, the place given to commentaries: thus, as it were, providing synthetic access to the "raw material" that is the Strasbourg case-law.

One point should be noted: I have endeavoured to keep the work to a reasonable size. For that reason, I have included only judgments in the strict sense, as opposed to the Court's decisions on the admissibility of applications, even though certain of these are of particular interest, like the decision of the admissibility of the application in the Papon case.

I hope that this work will shed useful light on the scope of the Convention and its Protocols, whose influence in our domestic legal orders is manifest and whose role in the protection of human rights is of the utmost importance.

Gilles Dutertre

Part 1. The European Convention on Human Rights

Article 1 ECHR – The obligation to respect human rights

Article 1 is worded as follows:

> The High Contracting Parties shall secure to everyone within their jurisdiction the rights and freedoms defined in Section I of this Convention.

In this Article, the European Convention on Human Rights (ECHR) defines the scope of Section I. Section I applies to "everyone", provided that the person concerned comes within the "jurisdiction" of a Contracting State.

1. The Convention applies to "everyone"

According to Article 1, the Contracting States must guarantee the rights and freedoms provided for in Section I to "everyone". No restriction is formulated. A person's nationality, age, race, domicile or capacity is therefore irrelevant.

However, in the Lithgow v. the United Kingdom case (8 July 1986, Series A No. 102, p. 48, paragraph 116), the following reservation is expressed:

> As to Article 1 (art. 1) of the Convention, it is true that under most provisions of the Convention and its Protocols nationals and non-nationals enjoy the same protection but this does not exclude exceptions as far as this may be indicated in a particular text (see, for example, Articles 5, paragraph 1.f, and 16 (art. 5-1-f, art. 16) of the Convention, Articles 3 and 4 of Protocol No. 4 (P4-3, P4-4)).

2. The Convention applies to everyone within the "jurisdiction of the States"

Article 1 then defines the link that must exist between a person and a member state if the Convention is to apply to him. The person in question must come within the "jurisdiction" of the State Party to the Convention. This condition is quite flexible. "Jurisdiction" is given a wide interpretation and is not limited, for example, to classic territorial competence. It encompasses any situation in which a person comes within the power or the control of a State. It is thus not so much a restrictive condition as a comprehensive criterion. The concept of jurisdiction will be examined in the form of its two components: jurisdiction *ratione loci* and jurisdiction *rationae materiae*.

Jurisdiction rationae loci

The leading decision is to be found in the Soering v. the United Kingdom judgment (7 July 1989, Series A No. 161, paragraphs 85-86, 88 and 90-91). That case concerned proceedings for extradition to the United States, where the applicant was facing a possible death sentence and the "death row syndrome". Was Article 3 of the Convention, which prohibits inhuman treatment, applicable? The Court held:

> As results from Article 5, paragraph 1.*f* (art. 5-1-f), which permits "the lawful [...] detention of a person against whom action is being taken with a view to [...] extra-dition", no right not to be extradited is as such protected by the Convention. Nevertheless, in so far as a measure of extradition has consequences adversely affecting the enjoyment of a Convention right, it may, assuming that the conse-quences are not too remote, attract the obligations of a Contracting State under the relevant Convention guarantee (see, *mutatis mutandis,* the Abdulaziz, Cabales and Balkandali judgment of 25 May 1985, Series A No. 94, pp. 31-32, paragraphs 59-60 – in relation to rights in the field of immigration). What is at issue in the present case is whether Article 3 (art. 3) can be applicable when the adverse consequences of extradition are, or may be, suffered outside the jurisdiction of the extraditing State as a result of treatment or punishment administered in the receiving State.
>
> Article 1 (art. 1) of the Convention, which provides that "the High Contracting Parties shall secure to everyone within their jurisdiction the rights and freedoms defined in Section I", sets a limit, notably territorial, on the reach of the Convention. In particular, the engagement undertaken by a Contracting State is confined to "securing" (*"reconnaître"* in the French text) the listed rights and freedoms to persons within its own "jurisdiction".
>
> Further, the Convention does not govern the actions of States not Parties to it, nor does it purport to be a means of requiring the Contracting States to impose Convention standards on other States. Article 1 (art. 1) cannot be read as justifying a general principle to the effect that, notwithstanding its extradition obligations, a Contracting State may not surrender an individual unless satisfied that the conditions awaiting him in the country of destination are in full accord with each of the safeguards of the Convention. Indeed, as the United Kingdom Government stressed, the beneficial purpose of extradition in preventing fugitive offenders from evading justice cannot be ignored in determining the scope of application of the Convention and of Article 3 (art. 3) in particular.
>
> In the instant case it is common ground that the United Kingdom has no power over the practices and arrangements of the Virginia authorities which are the subject of the applicant's complaints.
>
> These considerations cannot, however, absolve the Contracting Parties from responsibility under Article 3 (art. 3) for all and any foreseeable consequences of extradition suffered outside their jurisdiction.
>
> It would hardly be compatible with the underlying values of the Convention, that "common heritage of political traditions, ideals, freedom and the rule of law" to which the Preamble refers, were a Contracting State knowingly to surrender a fugitive to another State where there were substantial grounds for believing that

he would be in danger of being subjected to torture, however heinous the crime allegedly committed. Extradition in such circumstances, while not explicitly referred to in the brief and general wording of Article 3 (art. 3), would plainly be contrary to the spirit and intendment of the Article, and in the Court's view this inherent obligation not to extradite also extends to cases in which the fugitive would be faced in the receiving State by a real risk of exposure to inhuman or degrading treatment or punishment proscribed by that Article (art. 3).

It is not normally for the Convention institutions to pronounce on the existence or otherwise of potential violations of the Convention. However, where an applicant claims that a decision to extradite him would, if implemented, be contrary to Article 3 (art. 3) by reason of its foreseeable consequences in the requesting country, a departure from this principle is necessary, in view of the serious and irreparable nature of the alleged suffering risked, in order to ensure the effectiveness of the safeguard provided by that Article (art. 3) (see paragraph 87 above).

In sum, the decision by a Contracting State to extradite a fugitive may give rise to an issue under Article 3 (art. 3), and hence engage the responsibility of that State under the Convention, where substantial grounds have been shown for believing that the person concerned, if extradited, faces a real risk of being subjected to torture or to inhuman or degrading treatment or punishment in the requesting country The establishment of such responsibility inevitably involves an assessment of conditions in the requesting country against the standards of Article 3 (art. 3) of the Convention. Nonetheless, there is no question of adjudicating on or establishing the responsibility of the receiving country, whether under general international law, under the Convention or otherwise. In so far as any liability under the Convention is or may be incurred, it is liability incurred by the extraditing Contracting State by reason of its having taken action which has as a direct consequence the exposure of an individual to proscribed ill-treatment.

In the Loizidou v. Turkey case, the applicant, who lived in the southern part of Cyprus, complained that she was denied access to her possessions in the northern part of Cyprus. She therefore claimed that there had been an interference with her right to the peaceful enjoyment of her assets (judgment of 23 March 1995, Preliminary objections, Series A No. 310, pp. 23-24, paragraph 62). The Court gave the following summary of the concept of "jurisdiction":

In this respect the Court recalls that, although Article 1 (art. 1) sets limits on the reach of the Convention, the concept of "jurisdiction" under this provision is not restricted to the national territory of the High Contracting Parties. According to its established case-law, for example, the Court has held that the extradition or expulsion of a person by a Contracting State may give rise to an issue under Article 3 (art. 3), and hence engage the responsibility of that State under the Convention (see the Soering v. the United Kingdom judgment of 7 July 1989, Series A No. 161, pp. 35-36, paragraph 91 ; the Cruz Varas and Others v. Sweden judgment of 20 March 1991, Series A No. 201, p. 28, paragraphs 69-70, and the Vilvarajah and Others v. the United Kingdom judgment of 30 October 1991, Series A No. 215, p. 34, paragraph 103). In addition, the responsibility of Contracting Parties can be involved because of acts of their authorities, whether performed within or outside national boundaries, which produce effects outside their own territory (see the Drozd and Janousek v. France and Spain judgment of 26 June 1992, Series A No. 240, p. 29, paragraph 91).

Bearing in mind the object and purpose of the Convention, the responsibility of a Contracting Party may also arise when as a consequence of military action – whether lawful or unlawful – it exercises effective control of an area outside its national territory. The obligation to secure, in such an area, the rights and freedoms set out in the Convention derives from the fact of such control whether it be exercised directly, through its armed forces, or through a subordinate local administration.

There remained the basic problem of the imputability of the restriction of the rights in which the applicant relied. In the same judgment, the Court held (18 December 1996, *Reports of Judgments and Decisions* 1996-VI, pp. 2235-2236, paragraphs 54 and 56) that:

It is important for the Court's assessment of the imputability issue that the Turkish Government have acknowledged that the applicant's loss of control of her property stems from the occupation of the northern part of Cyprus by Turkish troops and the establishment there of the "TRNC" (see the above-mentioned preliminary objections judgment, p. 24, paragraph 63). Furthermore, it has not been disputed that the applicant has on several occasions been prevented by Turkish troops from gaining access to her property (see paragraphs 12-13 above).

However, throughout the proceedings the Turkish Government have denied State responsibility for the matters complained of, maintaining that its armed forces are acting exclusively in conjunction with and on behalf of the allegedly independent and autonomous "TRNC" authorities.

It is not necessary to determine whether, as the applicant and the Government of Cyprus have suggested, Turkey actually exercises detailed control over the policies and actions of the authorities of the "TRNC". It is obvious from the large number of troops engaged in active duties in northern Cyprus (see paragraph 16 above) that her army exercises effective overall control over that part of the island. Such control, according to the relevant test and in the circumstances of the case, entails her responsibility for the policies and actions of the "TRNC" (see paragraph 52 above). Those affected by such policies or actions therefore come within the "jurisdiction" of Turkey for the purposes of Article 1 of the Convention (art. 1). Her obligation to secure to the applicant the rights and freedoms set out in the Convention therefore extends to the northern part of Cyprus.

In view of this conclusion the Court need not pronounce itself on the arguments which have been adduced by those appearing before it concerning the alleged lawfulness or unlawfulness under international law of Turkey's military intervention in the island in 1974 since, as noted above, the establishment of State responsibility under the Convention does not require such an enquiry (see paragraph 52 above). It suffices to recall in this context its finding that the international community considers that the Republic of Cyprus is the sole legitimate government of the island and has consistently refused to accept the legitimacy of the "TRNC" as a State within the meaning of international law (see paragraph 44 above).

Jurisdiction **rationae materiae**

Jurisdiction rationae materiae *covers rules of all types*

In the United Communist Party of Turkey and Others v. Turkey judgment (30 January 1998, *Reports of Judgments and Decisions* 1998-I, pp. 17-18, paragraphs 29-31), the Court stated expressly that all legal rules, even constitutional rules, come within the "jurisdiction" of the member states for the purposes of Article 1 of the Convention. The respondent State contended that the States Parties to the Convention had "at no stage intended to submit their constitutional institutions, and in particular the principles they considered to be the essential conditions of their existence, to review by the Strasbourg institutions". The case concerned the dissolution of a political party ordered by the Constitutional Court of the respondent country on account of statutes which were held to be contrary to the Turkish Constitution. The European Court of Human Rights stated:

> Article 1 requires the States Parties to "secure to everyone within their jurisdiction the rights and freedoms defined in Section I of this Convention". That provision, together with Articles 14, 2 to 13 and 63, demarcates the scope of the Convention *ratione personae, materiae* and *loci* (see the Ireland v. the United Kingdom judgment of 18 January 1978, Series A No. 25, p. 90, paragraph 238). It makes no distinction as to the type of rule or measure concerned and does not exclude any part of the member States' "jurisdiction" from scrutiny under the Convention. It is, therefore, with respect to their "jurisdiction" as a whole – which is often exercised in the first place through the Constitution – that the States Parties are called on to show compliance with the Convention.

> The political and institutional organisation of the member States must accordingly respect the rights and principles enshrined in the Convention. It matters little in this context whether the provisions in issue are constitutional (see, for example, the Gitonas and Others v. Greece judgment of 1 July 1997, *Reports of Judgments and Decisions* 1997-IV) or merely legislative (see, for example, the Mathieu-Mohin and Clerfayt v. Belgium judgment of 2 March 1987, Series A No. 113). From the moment that such provisions are the means by which the State concerned exercises its jurisdiction, they are subject to review under the Convention.

> Moreover, it may on occasion prove difficult, even artificial, in proceedings before the Court, to attempt to distinguish between what forms part of a State's institutional structures and what relates to fundamental rights in the strict sense. That is particularly true of an order for dissolution of the kind in issue in the present case. In view of the role played by political parties (see paragraph 25 above), such measures affect both freedom of association and, consequently, democracy in the State concerned.

The particular case of transfers of competence and international treaties

The fact that a State transfers powers to an international organisation does not exempt it from responsibility under the Convention. In the Prince Hans-Adam II of Liechtenstein v. Germany judgment (12 July 2001, paragraphs 46-48), the Court recalled:

> Article 1 makes no distinction as to the type of rule or measure concerned, and does not exclude any part of the Contracting States' "jurisdiction" from scrutiny under the Convention (see the United Communist Party of Turkey and Others v. Turkey judgment of 30 January 1998, *Reports of Judgments and Decisions* 1998-I, pp. 17-18, paragraph 29).

> Thus the Contracting States' responsibility continues even after their having entered into treaty commitments subsequent to the entry into force of the Convention or its Protocols in respect of these States (see, *mutatis mutandis*, Matthews v. the United Kingdom [GC], No. 24833/94, paragraphs 29 and 32-34, ECHR 2000-I).

> The Court recalls in this respect that where States establish international organisations in order to pursue or strengthen their co-operation in certain fields of activities, and where they attribute to these organisations certain competences and accord them immunities, there may be implications as to the protection of fundamental rights. It would be incompatible with the object and purpose of the Convention, however, if the Contracting States were thereby absolved from their responsibility under the Convention in relation to the field of activity covered by such attribution.

It was from that aspect that the Court reiterated the fundamental principles that emerge from its decisions on the interpretation and application of domestic law (ibid., paragraphs 49-50):

> While the Court's duty, according to Article 19 of the Convention, is to ensure the observance of the engagements undertaken by the Contracting Parties to the Convention, it is not its function to deal with errors of fact or law allegedly committed by a national court unless and in so far as they may have infringed rights and freedoms protected by the Convention.

> Moreover, it is primarily for the national authorities, notably the courts, to interpret and apply domestic law. This also applies where domestic law refers to rules of general international law or international agreements. The Court's role is confined to ascertaining whether the effects of such an interpretation are compatible with the Convention (see Waite and Kennedy v. Germany, cited above, paragraph 54; and, as recent authority, Streletz, Kessler and Krenz v. Germany [GC], Nos. 34044/96, 35532/97 and 44801/98, paragraph 49, ECHR 2000).

In the case before it, the applicant claimed that he had been deprived of his right to effective access to a tribunal in relation to his action for restitution of a painting confiscated by the former Czechoslovakia. The German courts had declared his action inadmissible on the basis of the Convention on the Settlement of Matters Arising out of the War and the Occupation, signed on 23 October 1954, which excluded the jurisdiction of Germany. The Court stated (paragraphs 58-59, 65 and 69):

> The Court finds that when half a century after the end of the second world war, a final settlement with respect to Germany and the unification of the two German States were within reach, the position of the Federal Republic of Germany had

not changed. In the negotiations with the Three Powers, the Federal Republic of Germany had to accept that this specific limitation on its jurisdiction was not abolished.

In the Court's view, the exclusion of German jurisdiction under Chapter 6, Article 3, of the Settlement Convention is a consequence of the particular status of Germany under public international law after the second world war. It was only as a result of the 1954 Paris Agreements with regard to the Federal Republic of Germany and the Treaty on the Final Settlement with respect to Germany of 1990 that the Federal Republic secured the end of the Occupation Regime and obtained the authority of a sovereign State over its internal and external affairs for a united Germany. In these unique circumstances, the limitation on access to a German court, as a consequence of the Settlement Convention, had a legitimate objective.

In the light of these findings and having regard to the limited power of review exercisable by the Court (see paragraphs 49-50 above), it cannot be said that the German courts' interpretation of Chapter 6, Article 3, of the Settlement Convention was inconsistent with previous German case-law or that its application was manifestly erroneous or was such as to reach arbitrary conclusions.

In view of the above, the Court considers that the applicant's interest in bringing litigation in the Federal Republic of Germany was not sufficient to outweigh the vital public interests in regaining sovereignty and unifying Germany. Accordingly, the German court decisions declaring the applicant's ownership action inadmissible cannot be regarded as disproportionate to the legitimate aim pursued and they did not, therefore, impair the very essence of the applicant's "right of access to a court" within the meaning of the Court's case-law (see paragraphs 43-44 above).

It should be made clear, in the interest of a proper understanding of that passage, that the "right of access to a tribunal" guaranteed by Article 6 of the Convention admits of implicit limitations (see above). The Court so stated at paragraphs 43-44 of the judgment. It was therefore in the light of its case-law on Article 6, and not solely on the basis of a treaty excluding the jurisdiction of Germany, that the Court accepted such a limit in that particular case.

In an earlier case (Matthews v. the United Kingdom [GC], No. 24833/94, paragraphs 30-34, ECHR 2000-I), the Court had held that there had been a violation of Article 3 of Protocol No. 1 by the United Kingdom on the ground that it had not organised an election to the European Parliament in Gibraltar.

The Court notes that the parties do not dispute that Article 3 of Protocol No. 1 applies in Gibraltar. It recalls that the Convention was extended to the territory of Gibraltar by the United Kingdom's declaration of 23 October 1953 (see paragraph 19 above), and Protocol No. 1 has been applicable in Gibraltar since 25 February 1988. There is therefore clearly territorial "jurisdiction" within the meaning of Article 1 of the Convention.

The Court must nevertheless consider whether, notwithstanding the nature of the elections to the European Parliament as an organ of the EC, the United Kingdom can be held responsible under Article 1 of the Convention for the absence of elections to the European Parliament in Gibraltar, that is, whether the United Kingdom is required to "secure" elections to the European Parliament notwithstanding the Community character of those elections.

The Court observes that acts of the EC as such cannot be challenged before the Court because the EC is not a Contracting Party. The Convention does not exclude the transfer of competences to international organisations provided that Convention rights continue to be "secured". Member States' responsibility therefore continues even after such a transfer.

In the present case, the alleged violation of the Convention flows from an annex to the 1976 Act, entered into by the United Kingdom, together with the extension to the European Parliament's competences brought about by the Maastricht Treaty. The Council Decision and the 1976 Act (see paragraph 18 above), and the Maastricht Treaty, with its changes to the EEC Treaty, all constituted international instruments which were freely entered into by the United Kingdom. Indeed, the 1976 Act cannot be challenged before the European Court of Justice for the very reason that it is not a "normal" act of the Community, but is a treaty within the Community legal order. The Maastricht Treaty, too, is not an act of the Community, but a treaty by which a revision of the EEC Treaty was brought about. The United Kingdom, together with all the other parties to the Maastricht Treaty, is responsible *ratione materiae* under Article 1 of the Convention and, in particular, under Article 3 of Protocol No. 1, for the consequences of that Treaty.

In determining to what extent the United Kingdom is responsible for "securing" the rights in Article 3 of Protocol No. 1 in respect of elections to the European Parliament in Gibraltar, the Court recalls that the Convention is intended to guarantee rights that are not theoretical or illusory, but practical and effective (see, for example, the above-mentioned United Communist Party of Turkey and Others judgment, pp. 18-19, paragraph 33). It is uncontested that legislation emanating from the legislative process of the European Community affects the population of Gibraltar in the same way as legislation which enters the domestic legal order exclusively via the House of Assembly. To this extent, there is no difference between European and domestic legislation, and no reason why the United Kingdom should not be required to "secure" the rights in Article 3 of Protocol No. 1 in respect of European legislation, in the same way as those rights are required to be "secured" in respect of purely domestic legislation. In particular, the suggestion that the United Kingdom may not have effective control over the state of affairs complained of cannot affect the position, as the United Kingdom's responsibility derives from its having entered into treaty commitments subsequent to the applicability of Article 3 of Protocol No. 1 to Gibraltar, namely the Maastricht Treaty taken together with its obligations under the Council Decision and the 1976 Act. Further, the Court notes that on acceding to the EC Treaty, the United Kingdom chose, by virtue of Article 227, paragraph 4, of the Treaty, to have substantial areas of EC legislation applied to Gibraltar (see paragraphs 11-14 above).

It follows that the United Kingdom is responsible under Article 1 of the Convention for securing the rights guaranteed by Article 3 of Protocol No. 1 in Gibraltar regardless of whether the elections were purely domestic or European.

Article 2 ECHR – The right to life

Article 2, paragraph 1

Article 2, paragraph 1, is worded as follows:

> 1. **Everyone's right to life shall be protected by law. No one shall be deprived of his life intentionally save in the execution of a sentence of a court following his conviction of a crime for which this penalty is provided by law.**

1. The spirit and scope of Article 2

The spirit of Article 2

In the McCann and Others v. the United Kingdom judgment (27 September 1995, Series A No. 324, paragraphs 146-147), the Court explained how it conceives the interpretation of Article 2.

> The Court's approach to the interpretation of Article 2 (art. 2) must be guided by the fact that the object and purpose of the Convention as an instrument for the protection of individual human beings requires that its provisions be interpreted and applied so as to make its safeguards practical and effective (see, *inter alia*, the Soering v. the United Kingdom judgment of 7 July 1989, Series A No. 161, p. 34, paragraph 87, and the Loizidou v. Turkey (Preliminary objections) judgment of 23 March 1995, Series A No. 310, p. 27, paragraph 72).

> It must also be borne in mind that, as a provision (art. 2) which not only safeguards the right to life but sets out the circumstances when the deprivation of life may be justified, Article 2 (art. 2) ranks as one of the most fundamental provisions in the Convention – indeed one which, in peacetime, admits of no derogation under Article 15 (art. 15). Together with Article 3 (art. 15 + 3) of the Convention, it also enshrines one of the basic values of the democratic societies making up the Council of Europe (see the above-mentioned Soering judgment, p. 34, paragraph 88). As such, its provisions must be strictly construed.

The scope of Article 2

The Tanribilir v. Turkey judgment of 16 November 2000 (Application No. 21422/93, available in French only – unofficial translation) concerned the suicide of a person in custody. The Court emphasised that in certain circumstances, Article 2 places a positive obligation on States to take practical measures:

> The Court also considers that Article 2 of the Convention may, in certain well-defined circumstances, place the authorities under a positive obligation to take practical preventive measures to protect the individual against others or, in certain special circumstances, against himself.

> However, it is necessary to interpret that obligation in a way that does not impose an impossible or disproportionate burden on the authorities and to bear in mind the difficulties which the security forces face in carrying out their duties

in modern societies, the unpredictability of human conduct and the operational choices which must be made in terms of priorities and resources.

That is in addition to the legislative measures which the States are required to implement, and to which we now turn.

2. Specific consequences derived from Article 2, paragraph 1

Material obligations flowing from Article 2, paragraph 1

Attempts on a person's life

The primary consequence of Article 2 (which must be read with Protocol No. 6, cited in Part II) is that the States must enact criminal laws to punish attempts on the lives of individuals.

Threatened persons

The Osman v. the United Kingdom case (28 October 1998) concerned the delicate question of persons who claim to have been threatened and demand police protection. In that case, a teacher showed an unhealthy interest in one of his pupils. Relations between the teacher and the pupil's family were strained. The story ended tragically when the teacher shot and fatally injured the pupil. On being arrested, he asked: "Why didn't you stop me before I did it, I gave you all the warning signs?" The judgment contains the following reasoning (the Osman v. the United Kingdom judgment of 28 October 1998, *Reports* 1998-VIII, paragraphs 115-122):

> The Court notes that the first sentence of Article 2, paragraph 1, enjoins the State not only to refrain from the intentional and unlawful taking of life, but also to take appropriate steps to safeguard the lives of those within its jurisdiction (see the L.C.B. v. the United Kingdom judgment of 9 June 1998, *Reports of Judgments and Decisions* 1998-III, p. 1403, paragraph 36). It is common ground that the State's obligation in this respect extends beyond its primary duty to secure the right to life by putting in place effective criminal-law provisions to deter the commission of offences against the person backed up by law-enforcement machinery for the prevention, suppression and sanctioning of breaches of such provisions. It is thus accepted by those appearing before the Court that Article 2 of the Convention may also imply in certain well-defined circumstances a positive obligation on the authorities to take preventive operational measures to protect an individual whose life is at risk from the criminal acts of another individual. The scope of this obligation is a matter of dispute between the parties.
>
> For the Court, and bearing in mind the difficulties involved in policing modern societies, the unpredictability of human conduct and the operational choices which must be made in terms of priorities and resources, such an obligation must be interpreted in a way which does not impose an impossible or disproportionate burden on the authorities. Accordingly, not every claimed risk to life can entail for the authorities a Convention requirement to take operational measures to prevent that risk from materialising. Another relevant consideration is the need to ensure that the police exercise their powers to control and prevent crime in a manner which fully respects the due process and other guarantees which legitimately place restraints on the scope of their action to investigate

crime and bring offenders to justice, including the guarantees contained in Articles 5 and 8 of the Convention.

In the opinion of the Court where there is an allegation that the authorities have violated their positive obligation to protect the right to life in the context of their above-mentioned duty to prevent and suppress offences against the person (see paragraph 115 above), it must be established to its satisfaction that the authorities knew or ought to have known at the time of the existence of a real and immediate risk to the life of an identified individual or individuals from the criminal acts of a third party and that they failed to take measures within the scope of their powers which, judged reasonably, might have been expected to avoid that risk. The Court does not accept the government's view that the failure to perceive the risk to life in the circumstances known at the time or to take preventive measures to avoid that risk must be tantamount to gross negligence or wilful disregard of the duty to protect life (see paragraph 107 above). Such a rigid standard must be considered to be incompatible with the requirements of Article 1 of the Convention and the obligations of Contracting States under that Article to secure the practical and effective protection of the rights and freedoms laid down therein, including Article 2 (see, *mutatis mutandis*, the above-mentioned McCann and Others judgment, p. 45, paragraph 146). For the Court, and having regard to the nature of the right protected by Article 2, a right fundamental in the scheme of the Convention, it is sufficient for an applicant to show that the authorities did not do all that could be reasonably expected of them to avoid a real and immediate risk to life of which they have or ought to have knowledge. This is a question which can only be answered in the light of all the circumstances of any particular case.

On the above understanding the Court will examine the particular circumstances of this case.

It may [...] be reasonably accepted that the police were informed of all relevant connected matters which had come to light by 4 May 1987 [...].

The Court for its part is not persuaded that the police's failure to do so at this stage can be impugned from the standpoint of Article 2 having regard to the state of their knowledge at that time. While Paget-Lewis' attachment to Ahmet Osman could be judged by the police officers who visited the school to be most reprehensible from a professional point of view, there was never any suggestion that Ahmet Osman was at risk sexually from him, less so that his life was in danger.

Accordingly, at that juncture, the police's appreciation of the situation and their decision to treat it as a matter internal to the school cannot be considered unreasonable.

On 7 August 1987 he was allowed to resume teaching, although not at Homerton House (see paragraph 35 above). It is most improbable that the decision to lift his suspension from teaching duties would have been made if it had been believed at the time that there was the slightest risk that he constituted a danger to the safety of young people in his charge. The applicants are especially critical of Dr Ferguson's psychiatric assessment of Paget-Lewis. However, that assessment was made on the basis of three separate interviews with Paget-Lewis and if it appeared to a professional psychiatrist that he did not at the time display any signs of mental illness or a propensity to violence it would be unreasonable to have expected the police to have construed the actions of Paget-Lewis as they were reported to them by the school as those of a mentally disturbed and highly dangerous individual.

In assessing the level of knowledge which can be imputed to the police at the relevant time, the Court has also had close regard to the series of acts of vandalism against the Osmans' home and property between May and November 1987 (see paragraphs 30, 36 and 37 above). It observes firstly that none of these incidents could be described as life-threatening and secondly that there was no evidence pointing to the involvement of Paget-Lewis. [...]

The Court has also examined carefully the strength of the applicants' arguments that Paget-Lewis on three occasions communicated to the police, either directly or indirectly, his murderous intentions (see paragraph 105 above). However, in its view these statements cannot be reasonably considered to imply that the Osman family were the target of his threats and to put the police on notice of such. [...]

In the view of the Court the applicants have failed to point to any decisive stage in the sequence of the events leading up to the tragic shooting when it could be said that the police knew or ought to have known that the lives of the Osman family were at real and immediate risk from Paget-Lewis. [...] As noted earlier (see paragraph 116 above), the police must discharge their duties in a manner which is compatible with the rights and freedoms of individuals. In the circumstances of the present case, they cannot be criticised for attaching weight to the presumption of innocence or failing to use powers of arrest, search and seizure having regard to their reasonably held view that they lacked at relevant times the required standard of suspicion to use those powers or that any action taken would in fact have produced concrete results.

For the above reasons, the Court concludes that there has been no violation of Article 2 of the Convention in this case.

In a case where the circumstances were different, the Court held that there had been a violation of Article 2 (the Akkok v. Turkey judgment of 10 October 2000, Applications Nos. 22947/93 and 22948/93).

Suicide in custody

In the Tanribilir v. Turkey judgment (16 November 2000, Application No. 21422/93, available in French only – unofficial translation), cited above, which concerned the suicide of a person in custody, the Court stated:

[...] not every presumed threat to life obliges the authorities, under the Convention, to take specific measures to prevent it from being carried out (see, *mutatis mutandis*, the Osman v. the United Kingdom judgment of 28 October 1998, *Reports* 1998-VIII, vol. 95, pp. 3159-3160, paragraphs 115-116).

The Court considers that, faced with the allegation that the authorities failed to fulfil their positive obligation to protect the life of a person being kept in custody in the context of their duty to supervise detainees and prevent suicides, it must be convinced that the authorities should have known at the time that the person concerned was at risk of committing such an act and that they did not take, within the framework of their powers, the measures which, from a reasonable point of view, would no doubt have dealt with that risk. For the Court, and regard being had to the nature of the right protected by Article 2, it is sufficient for an applicant to show that the authorities did not do all that could be reasonably expected of them to prevent a certain and immediate risk to life of which they were or should have been aware from becoming a reality. The answer to that question depends on all the circumstances of the case in point. The Court will therefore examine the particular circumstances of the case.

In the present case, the Court notes, first of all, that A.T. had been placed in custody at the gendarmerie station in Cizre [...].

The Court reiterates that any deprivation of physical freedom may by its nature entail mental distress on the part of detainees and, consequently, the risk of suicide. The systems of detention make provision for measures to avoid such risks to the life of those detained, such as removing any sharp objects, belts or shoelaces.

The Court observes that in this case the gendarmes took routine measures to prevent the suicide of the person being held: they searched A.T. on his arrival at the gendarmerie station and took his belt and shoelaces. According to their statements before the judicial authorities, they monitored the persons in custody, including A.T., every half hour (paragraph 26 above, statement of Kuzucu before Judge Turan; paragraph 29, depositions of Leyla Saglam and Behiye Bozkurt taken by the investigator, Tolgay).

Should the gendarmes have taken into account the need to monitor the detainee A.T. more closely than an ordinary detainee? The Court is not convinced that the measures taken by the gendarmes on this point can be called in question from the viewpoint of Article 2, regard being had to the evidence available to them at that precise time. A.T. was calm when he arrived at the gendarmerie station (paragraph 42 above). The means which he found of committing suicide, by making a rope from the sleeves cut from his shirt, was difficult to foresee. The preparations were made and the suicide carried out in complete silence (paragraph 41 above, statement of Dr Bayik).

The Court considers that the gendarmes are not to be criticised for not having taken special measures, such as placing a 24-hour guard outside the applicant's cell or confiscating his clothes [...].

[...] the Court observes that none of the evidence in the case-file indicates that the gendarmes should have reasonably foreseen that A.T. would commit suicide or that they should have placed a permanent guard outside his cell.

For the reasons set out above, the Court concludes that there has been no violation of Article 2 of the Convention under this head. (Available in French only – unofficial translation.)

See, to the same effect, the Keenan v. the United Kingdom case (judgment of 3 April 2001, Application No. 27229/95).

Persons who have died in custody

The Salman v. Turkey judgment of 27 June 2000 (Application No. 21986/93, paragraphs 99-103) concerned the death of a person while in custody. The respondent State claimed that he had suffered a heart attack. The Court stated:

> In the light of the importance of the protection afforded by Article 2, the Court must subject deprivations of life to the most careful scrutiny, taking into consideration not only the actions of State agents but also all the surrounding circumstances. Persons in custody are in a vulnerable position and the authorities are under a duty to protect them. Consequently, where an individual is taken into police custody in good health and is found to be injured on release, it is incumbent on the State to provide a plausible explanation of how those injuries were caused (see, among other authorities, Selmouni v. France [GC], No. 25803/94, paragraph 87, ECHR 1999-V). The obligation on the authorities to account for the treatment of an individual in custody is particularly stringent where that individual dies.

> In assessing evidence, the Court has generally applied the standard of proof "beyond reasonable doubt" (see the Ireland v. the United Kingdom judgment of 18 January 1978, Series A No. 25, pp. 64-65, paragraph 161). However, such proof may follow from the coexistence of sufficiently strong, clear and concordant inferences or of similar unrebutted presumptions of fact. Where the events in issue lie wholly, or in large part, within the exclusive knowledge of the authorities, as in the case of persons within their control in custody, strong presumptions of fact will arise in respect of injuries and death occurring during such detention. Indeed, the burden of proof may be regarded as resting on the authorities to provide a satisfactory and convincing explanation.

> The Court finds that the Commission's evaluation of the facts in this case accords with the above principles.

> Agit Salman was taken into custody in apparent good health and without any pre-existing injuries or active illness. No plausible explanation has been provided for the injuries to the left ankle, bruising and swelling of the left foot, the bruise to the chest and the broken sternum. The evidence does not support the government's contention that the injuries might have been caused during the arrest, or that the broken sternum was caused by cardiac massage. The opinion of Dr Kirangil that the chest bruise pre-dated the arrest and that Agit Salman died of a heart attack brought on by the stress of his detention alone and after a prolonged period of breathlessness was rebutted by the evidence of Professors Pounder and Cordner. In accepting their evidence as to the rapidity of death and the probability that the bruise and broken sternum were caused by the same event – a blow to the chest – the Commission did not fail to accord Dr Kirangil's evidence proper weight nor did it give undue preference to the evidence of Professors Cordner and Pounder. It may be observed that Dr Kirangil signed the Istanbul Forensic Medicine Institute report which was in issue before the Commission and on that basis could not claim to be either objective or independent. There is no substance, moreover, in the allegations of collusion between the two professors made by the Agent of the government at the hearing.

> The Court finds, therefore, that the government have not accounted for the death of Agit Salman by cardiac arrest during his detention at Adana Security Directorate and that the respondent State's responsibility for his death is engaged.

> It follows that there has been a violation of Article 2 in that respect.

Persons who have disappeared

In the Kurt v. Turkey case, the applicant claimed that there had been a violation of Article 2 on account of the disappearance of her son, who had been arrested. The Court looked at the evidence and stated (the Kurt v. Turkey judgment, *Reports* 1998-III, paragraphs 99 and 106-109):

> Having regard to the above considerations which are based on its own careful assessment of the evidence and the transcripts of the delegates' hearing, the Court is not persuaded that there exist any exceptional circumstances which would compel it to reach a conclusion different from that of the Commission. It considers that there is a sufficient factual and evidentiary basis on which the Commission could properly conclude, beyond reasonable doubt, that the applicant did see her son outside Hasan Kiliç's house on the morning of 25 November 1993, that he was surrounded by soldiers and village guards at the time and that he has not been seen since.
>
> [...]
>
> The Court recalls at the outset that it has accepted the Commission's findings of fact in respect of the detention of the applicant's son by soldiers and village guards on 25 November 1993. Almost four and a half years have passed without information as to his subsequent whereabouts or fate. In such circumstances the applicant's fears that her son may have died in unacknowledged custody at the hands of his captors cannot be said to be without foundation. She has contended that there are compelling grounds for drawing the conclusion that he has in fact been killed.
>
> However, like the Commission, the Court must carefully scrutinise whether there does in fact exist concrete evidence which would lead it to conclude that her son was, beyond reasonable doubt, killed by the authorities either while in detention in the village or at some subsequent stage. It also notes in this respect that in those cases where it has found that a Contracting State had a positive obligation under Article 2 to conduct an effective investigation into the circumstances surrounding an alleged unlawful killing by the agents of that State, there existed concrete evidence of a fatal shooting which could bring that obligation into play (see the above-mentioned McCann and Others judgment; and the Kaya v. Turkey judgment of 19 February 1998, *Reports* 1998-I).
>
> It is to be observed in this regard that the applicant's case rests entirely on presumptions deduced from the circumstances of her son's initial detention bolstered by more general analyses of an alleged officially tolerated practice of disappearances and associated ill-treatment and extra-judicial killing of detainees in the respondent State. The Court for its part considers that these arguments are not in themselves sufficient to compensate for the absence of more persuasive indications that her son did in fact meet his death in custody. As to the applicant's argument that there exists a practice of violation of, *inter alia*, Article 2, the Court considers that the evidence which she has adduced does not substantiate that claim.
>
> Having regard to the above considerations, the Court is of the opinion that the applicant's assertions that the respondent State failed in its obligation to protect her son's life in the circumstances described fall to be assessed from the standpoint of Article 5 of the Convention.

In the recent Çiçek v. Turkey case, on the other hand, the Court accepted that the circumstances gave rise to a presumption that the persons arrested must be dead, so that the responsibility of the respondent State was engaged (the Çiçek v. Turkey judgment of 27 February 2001, Application No. 25704/94, paragraphs 146-147) :

> The Court considers that there are a number of elements distinguishing the present case from other cases, such as Kurt v. Turkey (judgment of 25 May 1998, *Reports* 1998-III, p. 1182, paragraph 108), in which the Court held that there were insufficient persuasive indications that the applicant's son had met his death in custody. In the first place, six and a half years have now elapsed since Tahsin and Ali Ihsan Çiçek were apprehended and detained. Furthermore, it has been established that the two brothers were taken to a place of detention – the military area in Lice Regional Boarding School – by authorities for whom the State is responsible. Finally, the fact that the soldiers did not release Tahsin and Ali Ihsan Çiçek together with the other villagers within a few days, taken together with the other elements in the file, suggests that both were identified as persons under suspicion by the authorities (see above paragraph 78, especially Yarali's statement that if people were deemed clearly dangerous or required interrogation, they were handed over to the interrogation units at the end of a short period called "the observation period"). In the general context of the situation in south-east Turkey in 1994, it can by no means be excluded that the unacknowledged detention of such a person would be life-threatening (see the above cited Timurtas v. Turkey judgment, paragraph 85). It is to be recalled that the Court has held in earlier judgments that defects undermining the effectiveness of criminal law protection in the south-east during the period relevant also to this case, permitted or fostered a lack of accountability of members of the security forces for their actions (see Cemil Kiliç v. Turkey, No. 22492/93, paragraph 75, and Mahmut Kaya v. Turkey, No. 22535/93, paragraph 98, both to be published in ECHR 2000).

> For the above reasons, and taking into account that no information has come to light concerning the whereabouts of the applicant's sons for a period of six and a half years, the Court is satisfied that Tahsin and Ali Ihsan Çiçek must be presumed dead following an unacknowledged detention by the security forces. Consequently, the responsibility of the respondent State for their death is engaged. Noting that the authorities have not provided any explanation as to what occurred following Tahsin and Ali Ihsan's apprehension, and that they do not rely on any ground of justification in respect of any use of lethal force by their agents, it follows that liability for their death is attributable to the respondent Government (see Timurtas v. Turkey, cited above, paragraph 86). Accordingly, there has been a violation of Article 2 on that account.

(See also the Cyprus v. Turkey judgment of 10 May 2001, concerning the disappearance of Greek Cypriots who disappeared during the military operations carried out by Turkey in northern Cyprus in July and August 1974, paragraphs 110, 132 and 135-136.)

Physical torture without the death of the victim

The Court has already addressed the question of serious physical violence not involving death. It has agreed to consider a possible violation of Article 2 from that aspect. The Ihan v. Turkey judgment of 27 June 2000 serves to illustrate this point. In that case, the applicant had received a potentially lethal blow from a rifle butt inflicted by the gendarmes when he was being arrested. The Court stated (Application No. 22277/93, paragraphs 75-78):

> The Court recalls that in the present case the force used against Abdüllatif Ilhan was not in the event lethal. This does not exclude an examination of the applicant's complaints under Article 2. It may be observed that in three previous cases the Court has examined complaints under this provision where the alleged victim had not died as a result of the impugned conduct.

> In Osman v. the United Kingdom (judgment of 28 October 1998, *Reports* 1998-VIII, pp. 3159-3163, paragraphs 115-22), the applicant, Ahmet Osman, had been shot and seriously injured when a man fired a shotgun at close range at him and his father. His father had died. The Court concluded on the facts of that case that the United Kingdom authorities had not failed in any positive obligation under Article 2 to provide protection of their right to life within the meaning of the first sentence of Article 2. In the Yasa case (judgment cited above, pp. 2436-2441, paragraphs 92-108), the applicant was shot in the street by an unknown gunman, receiving eight bullet wounds but surviving. The Court, finding that the authorities had not failed to protect the applicant's life, held none the less that they had failed to comply with the procedural obligation under Article 2 to conduct an effective investigation into the attack. In L.C.B. v. the United Kingdom (judgment of 9 June 1998, *Reports* 1998-III, pp. 1403-1404, paragraphs 36-41), where the applicant, who suffered from leukaemia, was the daughter of a serviceman who had been on Christmas Island during the United Kingdom's nuclear tests, the Court noted that it was not suggested that the State had intentionally sought to deprive her of her life but examined under Article 2 whether the State had done all that could have been required of it to prevent the applicant's life from being avoidably put at risk. It found that the State had not failed in this regard.

> The Court observes that these three cases concerned the positive obligation on the State to protect the life of the individual from third parties or from the risk of illness under the first sentence of Article 2, paragraph 1. It considers, however, that it is only in exceptional circumstances that physical ill-treatment by State officials which does not result in death may disclose a breach of Article 2 of the Convention. It is correct that the criminal responsibility of those concerned in the use of force is not in issue in the proceedings under the Convention (see the McCann and Others judgment cited above, p. 51, paragraph 173). Nonetheless, the degree and type of force used and the unequivocal intention or aim behind the use of force may, among other factors, be relevant in assessing whether in a particular case the State agents' actions in inflicting injury short of death must be regarded as incompatible with the object and purpose of Article 2 of the Convention. In almost all cases where a person is assaulted or ill-treated by the police or soldiers, their complaints will fall to be examined rather under Article 3 of the Convention.

The Court recalls that Abdüllatif Ilhan suffered brain damage following at least one blow to the head with a rifle butt inflicted by gendarmes who had been ordered to apprehend him during an operation and who kicked and beat him when they found him hiding in some bushes. Two contemporaneous medical reports identified the head injury as being of a life-threatening character. This has left him with a long-term loss of function. The seriousness of his injury is therefore not in doubt.

However, the Court is not persuaded in the circumstances of this case that the use of force applied by the gendarmes when they apprehended Abdüllatif Ilhan was of such a nature or degree as to breach Article 2 of the Convention. Nor does any separate issue arise in this context concerning the alleged lack of prompt medical treatment for his injuries. It will, however, examine these aspects further under Article 3 of the Convention below.

It follows that there has been no violation of Article 2 of the Convention concerning the infliction of injuries on Abdüllatif Ilhan.

(See, to the same effect, the Berktay v. Turkey judgment of 1 March 2001, Application No. 22493/93.)

Abortion

The delicate matter of the protection of life before birth also arises.

In the Open Door and Dublin Well Woman v. Ireland judgment (29 October 1992, Series A No. 246-A, p. 28, paragraph 66), two companies had been prohibited from providing pregnant women with information on the possibility of obtaining abortions abroad. Abortion was prohibited in Ireland. The Court has declared:

> [...] that in the present case it is not called upon to examine whether a right to abortion is guaranteed under the Convention or whether the foetus is encompassed by the right to life as contained in Article 2 (art. 2). The applicants have not claimed that the Convention contains a right to abortion, as such, their complaint being limited to that part of the injunction which restricts their freedom to impart and receive information concerning abortion abroad (see paragraph 20 above).

The Court therefore did not adopt a position on the issue of abortion from the aspect of Article 2. However, the Commission had occasion to address the subject. In the X. v. the United Kingdom case (Application No. 8416/79, decision of 13 May 1980, *Decisions and Reports* 19, p. 248, paragraph 4, and p. 253, paragraph 23):

> The Commission, therefore, has to examine whether this application discloses any appearance of a violation of the provisions of the Convention invoked by the applicant, in particular Articles 2 and 8. It here recalls that the abortion law of High Contracting Parties to the Convention has so far been the subject of several applications under Article 25. The applicants either alleged that the legislation concerned violated the (unborn child's) right to life (Article 2) or they claimed that it constituted an unjustified interference with the (parents') right to respect

for private life (Article 8). Two applications invoking Article 2 were declared inadmissible by the Commission on the ground that the applicants – in the absence of any measure of abortion affecting them by reason of a close link with the foetus – could not claim to be "victims" of the abortion laws complained of (Application No. 867/60, X. v. Norway, *Collection of Decisions 6, Yearbook of the European Convention on Human Rights* 4, p. 270, and Application No. 7045/75, X. v. Austria, *Decisions and Reports* 7, p. 87). One application (No. 6959/75 – Brüggemann and Scheuten v. the Federal Republic of Germany), invoking Article 8, was declared admissible by the Commission, in so far as it had been brought by two women. The Commission, and subsequently the Committee of Ministers, concluded that there was no breach of Article 8 (*Decisions and Reports* 10, pp. 100-122). That conclusion was based on an interpretation of Article 8 which, *inter alia*, took into account the High Contracting Parties' law on abortion as applied at the time when the Convention entered into force (ibid., p. 117, paragraph 64 of the Commission's report).

After thus summarising the precedents, the Commission put forward a prudent answer, focusing on the necessary protection of the life of the mother, which abortion may ensure:

> The Commission considers that it is not in these circumstances called upon to decide whether Article 2 does not cover the foetus at all or whether it recognises a "right to life" of the foetus with implied limitations. It finds that the authorisation, by the United Kingdom authorities, of the abortion complained of is compatible with Article 2, paragraph 1, first sentence, because, if one assumes that this provision applies at the initial stage of the pregnancy, the abortion is covered by an implied limitation, protecting the life and health of the woman at that stage, of the "right to life" of the foetus.

Subsequently, however, in the H. v. Norway case (Application No. 17004/90, decision of 19 May 1992, *Decisions and Reports* 73, p. 155), the Commission accepted that the question of the protection of the foetus itself might be approached from the aspect of Article 2.

The Commission emphasised first of all that in the delicate area of abortion the Contracting States must retain a certain discretion. However, it did not preclude that in certain circumstances it might have to decide that the foetus may be afforded a certain amount of protection under Article 2, notwithstanding the fact that member states have widely differing opinions on the scope of the protection of the right to life of an unborn child.

In that case, however, the applicant's complaint concerning the lack of protection for the life of the unborn child under the Norwegian legislation was declared inadmissible. It must be noted that the application was submitted by the father of the unborn child, not the mother.

Expulsion of sick persons with impaired vital prognosis

In the D. v. the United Kingdom case (judgment of 2 May 1997), the complainant maintained that his expulsion to St Kitts engaged the responsibility of the United Kingdom under Article 2. He stated that he was in the terminal stage of his disease and that his life expectancy, which was already short, would be further reduced should he be suddenly deprived of the medical treatment he was receiving and returned to the country of destination. The applicant argued that there was a direct link of causation between his expulsion and the fact that his death would occur earlier, which meant that there was a violation of his right to life. He stated that Article 2 entailed a positive obligation to protect life, so that, in the circumstances of the case, the government were required not to take any measure likely to lead to a further reduction in his short life expectancy. The Court confined itself to examining the question under Article 3 of the Convention and did not resolve this point (the D. v. the United Kingdom judgment of 2 May 1997, *Reports* 1997-III, paragraph 59). The Court stated:

> The Court for its part shares the views of the Government and the Commission that the complaints raised by the applicant under Article 2 (art. 2) are indissociable from the substance of his complaint under Article 3 (art. 3) in respect of the consequences of the impugned decision for his life, health and welfare. It notes in this respect that the applicant stated before the Court that he was content to base his case under Article 3 (art. 3). Having regard to its finding that the removal of the applicant to St Kitts would give rise to a violation of Article 3 (art. 3) (see paragraph 54 above), the Court considers that it is not necessary to examine his complaint under Article 2 (art. 2).

Failure to inform the population of risks

The Guerra and Others v. Italy judgment of 19 February 1998 (*Reports* 1998-I) dealt with the question of the failure to inform the population of the risks associated with a chemical factory in the neighbourhood and also of the measures to be taken in the event of an accident in the factory. In that case, the Court held that there had been a violation of Article 8, on the ground that serious harm to the environment may affect the welfare of persons and deprive them of the enjoyment of their homes in such a way as to damage their private and family life (the applicants had remained until the production of fertilisers ceased, awaiting essential information which would have allowed them to evaluate the possible risks to them and their near relatives if they continued to reside on the territory of the municipality concerned, which was in danger in the event of an accident at the factory). The Court therefore considered that there was no need to examine the case under Article 2.

In a later case, the applicant also complained of a lack of information from the respondent State. In 1957 and 1958 the applicant's father had been on Christmas Island, where he served as a catering assistant in the Royal Air Force when four nuclear tests were being carried out. He also took part in the clean-up operations following the tests. The applicant was born in 1966. In about 1970 she was diagnosed as having leukaemia. Her records of admission to hospital state, under the heading "Summary of Possible Causative Factors", "Father – Radiation exposure". The applicant relied on Articles 2 and 3 of the Convention and complained that she had not been warned of the effects of her father's alleged exposure to radiation, which had prevented pre- and post-natal monitoring of her health that would have led to earlier diagnosis and treatment of her illness. She considered that her father's unmonitored exposure to radiation was the probable cause of the leukaemia from which she had suffered in her childhood. The Court held (the L.C.B. v. the United Kingdom case, judgment of 9 June 1998, *Reports* 1998-III, paragraphs 37-41):

> In a later case, [...] the State authorities [...] could reasonably have been confident that [the applicant's] father had not been dangerously irradiated.
>
> Nonetheless, in view of the lack of certainty on this point, the Court will also examine the question whether, in the event that there was information available to the authorities which should have given them cause to fear that the applicant's father had been exposed to radiation, they could reasonably have been expected, during the period in question, to provide advice to her parents and to monitor her health.
>
> The Court considers that the State could only have been required of its own motion to take these steps in relation to the applicant if it had appeared likely at that time that any such exposure of her father to radiation might have engendered a real risk to her health.
>
> Having examined the expert evidence submitted to it, the Court is not satisfied that it has been established that there is a causal link between the exposure of a father to radiation and leukaemia in a child subsequently conceived. As recently as 1993, the High Court judge sitting in the cases of Reay and Hope v. British Nuclear Fuels PLC, having examined a considerable amount of expert evidence, found that "the scales tilt[ed] decisively" in favour of a finding that there was no such causal link (see paragraph 19 above). The Court could not reasonably hold, therefore, that, in the late 1960s, the United Kingdom authorities could or should, on the basis of this unsubstantiated link, have taken action in respect of the applicant.
>
> Finally, in the light of the conflicting evidence of Dr Bross and Professor Eden (see paragraphs 29 and 33 above), and as the Commission also found (see paragraph 34 above), it is clearly uncertain whether monitoring of the applicant's health *in utero* and from birth would have led to earlier diagnosis and medical intervention such as to diminish the severity of her disease. It is perhaps arguable that, had there been reason to believe that she was in danger of contracting a life-threatening disease owing to her father's presence on Christmas Island, the State authorities would have been under a duty to have made this known to her parents whether or not they considered that the information would assist the applicant. However, this is not a matter which the Court is required to decide in view of its above findings (see paragraphs 38-39).
>
> In conclusion, the Court does not find it established that, given the information available to the State at the relevant time (see paragraph 37 above) concerning the likelihood of the applicant's father having been exposed to dangerous levels of radiation and of this having created a risk to her health, it could have been expected to act of its own motion to notify her parents of these matters or to take any other special action in relation to her.
>
> It follows that there has been no violation of Article 2.

Medical responsibility

For a case of responsibility in medical matters, reference should be made to the Calvelli and Ciglio v. Italy judgment of 17 January 2002, Application No. 32967/96, paragraphs 48-50.

Procedural obligations arising under Article 2, paragraph 1

In a recent judgment (the Cyprus v. Turkey case, 10 May 2001, Application No. 25781/94, paragraph 131, cited above), the Court continued to emphasise the positive obligation on States to investigate cases of death following the use of force. It stated:

> [...] the obligation to protect the right to life under Article 2 of the Convention, read in conjunction with the State's general duty under Article 1 to "secure to everyone within [its] jurisdiction the rights and freedoms defined in [the] Convention", requires by implication that there should be some form of effective official investigation when individuals have been killed as a result of the use of force by agents of the State (see, *mutatis mutandis*, the McCann and Others v. the United Kingdom judgment of 27 September 1995, Series A No. 324, p. 49, paragraph 161, and the Kaya v. Turkey judgment of 19 February 1998, *Reports* 1998-I, p. 329, paragraph 105) or by non-State agents (see, *mutatis mutandis*, the Ergi v. Turkey judgment of 28 July 1998, *Reports* 1998-IV, p. 1778, paragraph 82; the Yasa v. Turkey judgment of 2 September 1998, *Reports* 1998-VI, p. 2438, paragraph 100; and Tanrikulu v. Turkey [GC], No. 23763/94, paragraph 103, ECHR 1999-IV).

The Court has had occasion to state (the Tanrikulu v. Turkey judgment of 8 July 1999, *Reports* 1999-IV, paragraph 103):

> Nor is the issue of whether members of the deceased's family or others have lodged a formal complaint about the killing with the competent investigation authorities decisive. In the instant case the mere fact that the authorities were informed of the murder of the applicant's husband gave rise *ipso facto* to an obligation under Article 2 to carry out an effective investigation into the circumstances surrounding the death (see, *mutatis mutandis*, the Ergi v. Turkey judgment of 28 July 1998, *Reports* 1998-IV, p. 1778, paragraph 82, and the Yasa judgment cited above, p. 2438, paragraph 100).

The Hugh Jordan v. the United Kingdom judgment of 4 May 2001 (Application No. 24746/94, paragraph 105) sets out the reason for such an obligation:

> The essential purpose of such investigation is to secure the effective implementation of the domestic laws which protect the right to life and, in those cases involving State agents or bodies, to ensure their accountability for deaths occurring under their responsibility.

In the Kaya v. Turkey judgment, the Court stated that the large number of fatal incidents does not have the effect of relieving a State from its obligation to carry out investigations (the Kaya v. Turkey judgment of 19 February 1998, *Reports* 1998-I, paragraph 91):

> The Court notes that loss of life is a tragic and frequent occurrence in view of the security situation in south-east Turkey (see the above-mentioned Aydin

judgment, p. 1873, paragraph 14). However, neither the prevalence of violent armed clashes nor the high incidence of fatalities can displace the obligation under Article 2 to ensure that an effective, independent investigation is conducted into deaths arising out of clashes involving the security forces, more so in cases such as the present where the circumstances are in many respects unclear.

The Court regularly uses that formula, stating further that local difficulties in seeking evidence do not relieve the State of its obligation to carry out investigations (the Tanrikulu v. Turkey judgment of 8 July 1999, *Reports* 1999-IV, paragraph 103) :

> The Court is prepared to take into account, as indicated in previous judgments concerning Turkey (see, for instance, the Kaya, Ergi and Yasa judgments cited above, p. 326, paragraph 91, p. 1779, paragraph 85, and p. 2440, paragraph 104, respectively), the fact that loss of life is a tragic and frequent occurrence in the context of the security situation in south-east Turkey, which may have hampered the search for conclusive evidence. Nonetheless, such circumstances cannot have the effect of relieving the authorities of the obligation imposed by Article 2 to carry out an effective investigation.

The Güleç v. Turkey case concerned the death of a person at a demonstration during which the police had used their weapons. On that occasion, the Court stated that the investigations designed to shed light on the causes of death must be carried out by independent bodies (the Güleç v. Turkey judgment of 27 July 1998, *Reports* 1998-IV, paragraphs 80 and 82-83) :

> The Court further observes that Sirnak Provincial Administrative Council decided, on 18 October 1991, that there was no case to refer to the criminal courts, on the ground that it was "not possible on the basis of the evidence on the case file to identify who had killed and injured the victims" (see paragraph 28 above). Such a conclusion cannot be accepted, regard being had to the subjectivity shown by investigating officer Kurt and the nature of the administrative authority concerned, which was chaired by the Provincial Governor (who appointed the investigating officers and was in charge of the local gendarmerie) or his deputy, and composed of local representatives of the executive (the Director of Public Health and the Director of Agriculture, for example). Subsequently, on 13 November 1991, the Supreme Administrative Court noted that the Administrative Council had made a discontinuation order. Consequently, "[s]ince those responsible for the deaths and woundings [were] unknown", it was "impossible [for the court] to look into the case and give judgment" (see paragraph 29 above).

> [...] That being so, the Court, like the Commission, concludes that the investigation was not thorough nor was it conducted by independent authorities. What is more, it was conducted without the participation of the complainant, who did not receive notice of the order of 18 October 1991 or the decision of 13 November 1991.

> Consequently, there has been a breach of Article 2 of the Convention on account of the use of disproportionate force and the lack of a thorough investigation into the circumstances of the applicant's son's death.

In the Yasa v. Turkey case, the applicant claimed that his uncle had been the victim of armed assault because he was selling the newspaper *Özgür Gündem*. The assaults had taken place in the course of a series of attacks aimed, with the connivance, or indeed the direct participation, of State agents, against that pro-Kurdish publication and other publications. The Court held (the Yasa v. Turkey judgment of 2 September 1998, *Reports* 1998-VI, paragraph 107):

> In short, because the investigations carried out in the instant case did not allow of the possibility that given the circumstances of the case the security forces might have been implicated in the attacks and because, up till now, more than five years after the events, no concrete and credible progress has been made, the investigations cannot be considered to have been effective as required by Article 2.

The Hugh Jordan v. the United Kingdom judgment of 4 May 2001 (Application No. 24746/94, paragraphs 105-109 and 143) provides a summary of that line of decisions:

> The obligation to protect the right to life under Article 2 of the Convention, read in conjunction with the State's general duty under Article 1 of the Convention to "secure to everyone within [its] jurisdiction the rights and freedoms defined in [the] Convention", also requires by implication that there should be some form of effective official investigation when individuals have been killed as a result of the use of force (see, *mutatis mutandis*, the McCann judgment cited above, p. 49, paragraph 161, and the Kaya v. Turkey judgment of 19 February 1998, *Reports of Judgments and Decisions* 1998-I, p. 324, paragraph 86). The essential purpose of such investigation is to secure the effective implementation of the domestic laws which protect the right to life and, in those cases involving State agents or bodies, to ensure their accountability for deaths occurring under their responsibility. What form of investigation will achieve those purposes may vary in different circumstances. However, whatever mode is employed, the authorities must act of their own motion, once the matter has come to their attention. They cannot leave it to the initiative of the next of kin either to lodge a formal complaint or to take responsibility for the conduct of any investigative procedures (see, for example, *mutatis mutandis,* Ilhan v. Turkey [GC], No. 22277/93, ECHR 2000-VII, paragraph 63).

> For an investigation into alleged unlawful killing by State agents to be effective, it may generally be regarded as necessary for the persons responsible for and carrying out the investigation to be independent from those implicated in the events (see, for example, the Güleç v. Turkey judgment of 27 July 1998, *Reports* 1998-IV, paragraphs 81-82; Ögur v. Turkey [GC], No. 21954/93, ECHR 1999-III, paragraphs 91-92). This means not only a lack of hierarchical or institutional connection but also a practical independence (see for example the Ergi v. Turkey judgment of 28 July 1998, *Reports* 1998-IV, paragraphs 83-84, where the Public Prosecutor investigating the death of a girl during an alleged clash showed a lack of independence through his heavy reliance on the information provided by the gendarmes implicated in the incident).

> The investigation must also be effective in the sense that it is capable of leading to a determination of whether the force used in such cases was or was not justi-fied in the circumstances (for example, the Kaya v. Turkey judgment, cited above, p. 324, paragraph 87) and to the identification and punishment of those

responsible (Ögur v. Turkey, cited above, paragraph 88). This is not an obligation of result, but of means. The authorities must have taken the reasonable steps available to them to secure the evidence concerning the incident, including, *inter alia*, eyewitness testimony, forensic evidence and, where appropriate, an autopsy which provides a complete and accurate record of injury and an objective analysis of clinical findings, including the cause of death (see concerning autopsies, for example, Salman v. Turkey cited above, paragraph 106 ; concerning witnesses, for example, Tanrikulu v. Turkey [GC], No. 23763/94, ECHR 1999-IV, paragraph 109 ; concerning forensic evidence, for example, Gül v. Turkey [Section IV], No. 22676/93, paragraph 89). Any deficiency in the investigation which undermines its ability to establish the cause of death or the person or persons responsible will risk falling foul of this standard.

A requirement of promptness and reasonable expedition is implicit in this context (see the Yasa v. Turkey judgment of 2 September 1998, *Reports* 1998-IV, pp. 2439-2440, paragraphs 102-104 ; Çakici v. Turkey cited above, paragraphs 80, 87 and 106 ; Tanrikulu v. Turkey, cited above, paragraph 109 ; Mahmut Kaya v. Turkey [Section I], No. 22535/93, ECHR 2000-III, paragraphs 106-107). It must be accepted that there may be obstacles or difficulties which prevent progress in an investigation in a particular situation. However, a prompt response by the authorities in investigating a use of lethal force may generally be regarded as essential in maintaining public confidence in their adherence to the rule of law and in preventing any appearance of collusion in or tolerance of unlawful acts.

For the same reasons, there must be a sufficient element of public scrutiny of the investigation or its results to secure accountability in practice as well as in theory. The degree of public scrutiny required may well vary from case to case. In all cases, however, the next-of-kin of the victim must be involved in the procedure to the extent necessary to safeguard his or her legitimate interests (see Güleç v. Turkey, cited above, p. 1733, paragraph 82, where the father of the victim was not informed of the decisions not to prosecute ; Ögur v. Turkey, cited above, paragraph 92, where the family of the victim had no access to the investigation and court documents ; Gül v. Turkey judgment, cited above, paragraph 93).

[...]

It is not for this Court to specify in any detail which procedures the authorities should adopt in providing for the proper examination of the circumstances of a killing by State agents. While reference has been made for example to the Scottish model of enquiry conducted by a judge of criminal jurisdiction, there is no reason to assume that this may be the only method available. Nor can it be said that there should be one unified procedure providing for all requirements. If the aims of fact finding, criminal investigation and prosecution are carried out or shared between several authorities, as in Northern Ireland, the Court considers that the requirements of Article 2 may none the less be satisfied if, while seeking to take into account other legitimate interests such as national security or the protection of material relevant to other investigations, they provide for the necessary safeguards in an accessible and effective manner. In the present case, the available procedures have not struck the right balance.

Article 2, paragraph 2

Article 2, paragraph 2, is worded as follows:

> **2. Deprivation of life shall not be regarded as inflicted in contravention of this Article when it results from the use of force which is no more than absolutely necessary:**
>
> **a   in defence of any person from unlawful violence;**
>
> **b   in order to effect a lawful arrest or to prevent the escape of a person lawfully detained;**
>
> **c   in action lawfully taken for the purpose of quelling a riot or insurrection.**

1. The scope of Article 2, paragraph 2

In the McCann and Others v. the United Kingdom judgment (27 September 1995, Series A No. 324, paragraph 148), three members of the IRA (Irish Republican Army), suspected of preparing for a bomb attack, had been killed by members of the United Kingdom security forces. The Court provided valuable information on the scope of Article 2, paragraph 2 (and therefore on the situations in which the conditions of paragraph 2 of that Article must be observed).

> The Court considers that the exceptions delineated in paragraph 2 (art. 2-2) indicate that this provision (art. 2-2) extends to, but is not concerned exclusively with, intentional killing. As the Commission has pointed out, the text of Article 2 (art. 2), read as a whole, demonstrates that paragraph 2 (art. 2-2) does not primarily define instances where it is permitted intentionally to kill an individual, but describes the situations where it is permitted to "use force" which may result, as an unintended outcome, in the deprivation of life. The use of force, however, must be no more than "absolutely necessary" for the achievement of one of the purposes set out in sub-paragraphs *a, b* or *c* (art. 2-2-a, art. 2-2-b, art. 2-2-c) (see Application No. 10044/82, Stewart v. the United Kingdom, 10 July 1984, *Decisions and Reports* 39, pp. 169-171).

2. The concept of "absolute necessity" of the use of force "justifying" deprivation of life

In the same judgment, the Court defined the concept of the "absolute necessity" of the use of force (paragraph 149). It also defined the extent of its review of that concept (paragraph 150):

> In this respect the use of the term "absolutely necessary" in Article 2, paragraph 2 (art. 2-2), indicates that a stricter and more compelling test of necessity must be employed from that normally applicable when determining whether State action is "necessary in a democratic society" under paragraph 2 of Articles 8 to 11 (art. 8-2, art. 9-2, art. 10-2, art. 11-2) of the Convention. In particular, the force used must be strictly proportionate to the achievement of the aims set out in sub-paragraphs 2.*a, b* and *c* of Article 2 (art. 2-2-a-b-c).

In keeping with the importance of this provision (art. 2) in a democratic society, the Court must, in making its assessment, subject deprivations of life to the most careful scrutiny, particularly where deliberate lethal force is used, taking into consideration not only the actions of the agents of the State who actually administer the force but also all the surrounding circumstances including such matters as the planning and control of the actions under examination.

In the case in point, the Court, having regard to the circumstances, held that there had been a violation of Article 2 of the Convention.

3. Examples of the application of the Article

Rescue operations

In the Andronicou and Constantinou v. Cyprus case, the Court adjudicated on the death by shooting of an engaged couple in their home following police intervention occasioned by the threatening conduct of the young man towards his companion. In that case, one of the police officers had fired more than thirteen shots. The Court stated (the Andronicou and Constantinou v. Cyprus judgment of 9 October 1997, *Reports* 1997-VI, paragraphs 184-186) in respect of the preparation for the operation:

> It must be emphasised that one hour before midnight she was repeatedly heard screaming that Lefteris Andronicou was going to kill her (see paragraph 59 above) and that Lefteris Andronicou had already shown his capacity for violence by beating her (see paragraph 16 above). In these circumstances and in the knowledge that Lefteris Andronicou was armed, the authorities could reasonably consider that as midnight approached the negotiations had failed and that an attempt had to be made to get into the flat, disarm and arrest him and free Elsie Constantinou.

> In the Court's view the authorities' decision to use the MMAD officers in the circumstances as they were known at the time was justified. Recourse to the skills of a highly professionally trained unit like the MMAD would appear to be quite natural given the nature of the operation which was contemplated. The decision to use the MMAD officers was a considered one of last resort. It was discussed both at the highest possible level in the police chain of command and at ministerial level (see paragraph 55 above) and only implemented when the negotiations failed and, as noted above, in view of a reasonably held belief that the young woman's life was in imminent danger. While it is true that the officers deployed were trained to shoot to kill if fired at, it is to be noted that they were issued with clear instructions as to when to use their weapons. They were told to use only proportionate force and to fire only if Elsie Constantinou's life or their own lives were in danger (see paragraph 38 above).

> It is to be noted that no use of weapons was ever intended and in fact the authorities were deeply anxious to avoid any harm to the couple (see paragraphs 38 and 54 above). However, it was not unreasonable to alert the officers to the dangers which awaited them and to direct them carefully on firearms use. Furthermore, it must be stressed that the officers were not in fact informed that

Lefteris Andronicou was in possession of weapons in addition to the shotgun. They were told that this possibility could not be excluded (see paragraph 38 above). Seen in these terms the message could reasonably be considered to be a warning to the officers to use extreme caution when effecting the operation.

As to the decision to arm the officers with machine guns, it must be emphasised once again that the use of any firearm was never intended in the execution of the plan. However, given that Lefteris Andronicou was armed with a double-barrelled shotgun and it was not to be excluded that he had other weapons, the authorities had to anticipate all possible eventualities. It might be added that the machine guns had the advantage that they were fitted with flashlights which would enable the officers to overcome any difficulties encountered in identifying the precise location of the young woman in a dark room filled with tear gas and at the same time leave their hands free to control their weapons in the event of coming under fire. Furthermore, the use by the officers of their machine guns was subject to the same clear instructions as applied to the use of their pistols (see paragraph 38 above).

Having regard to the above considerations, the Court is of the view that it has not been shown that the rescue operation was not planned and organised in a way which minimised to the greatest extent possible any risk to the lives of the couple.

As regards the conduct of the agents themselves, the Court stated (the Andronicou and Constantinou v. Cyprus judgment of 9 October 1997, *Reports* 1997-VI, paragraphs 191-193):

The Court recalls its earlier finding that the rescue operation was mounted with the sole aims of freeing Elsie Constantinou and arresting Lefteris Andronicou and in a manner which minimised to the greatest extent possible any risk to life through recourse to lethal force (see paragraph 186 above). It is to be noted that the officers' use of lethal force in the circumstances was the direct result of Lefteris Andronicou's violent reaction to the storming of the flat. He sought to take the life of the first officer who entered the room.

The commission of inquiry concluded on the basis of the evidence before it that Lefteris Andronicou in fact fired the second shot at Elsie Constantinou (see paragraph 134 above). His reaction thus brought about a situation in which split-second decisions had to be taken to avert the real and immediate danger which he presented to Elsie Constantinou and to the members of the rescue team. Officer No. 2 believed that Lefteris Andronicou had shot dead one colleague and wounded another and that he still had not discharged the second cartridge in the shotgun. When he entered the room he saw Lefteris Andronicou holding Elsie Constantinou and appearing to make a threatening move. He also believed that Lefteris Andronicou might have other weapons. As it transpired, he did not have any other weapons and he was not holding the shotgun when Officer No. 2 entered.

The Court accepts, however, in line with the findings of the commission of inquiry, that Officers Nos. 2 and 4 honestly believed in the circumstances that it was necessary to kill him in order to save the life of Elsie Constantinou and their own lives and to fire at him repeatedly in order to remove any risk that he might reach for a weapon. It notes in this respect that the use of force by agents of the State in pursuit of one of the aims delineated in paragraph 2 of Article 2 of the Convention may be justified under this provision where it is based on an honest belief which is perceived, for good reasons, to be valid at the time but subsequently turns out to be mistaken. To hold otherwise would be to impose an unrealistic burden on the State and its law-enforcement personnel in the execution of their duty, perhaps to the detriment of their lives and the lives of others (see the McCann and Others judgment cited above, pp. 58-59, paragraph 200).

It is clearly regrettable that so much fire power was used in the circumstances to neutralise any risk presented by Lefteris Andronicou. However, the Court cannot with detached reflection substitute its own assessment of the situation for that of the officers who were required to react in the heat of the moment in what was for them a unique and unprecedented operation to save life. The officers were entitled to open fire for this purpose and to take all measures which they honestly and reasonably believed were necessary to eliminate any risk either to the young woman's life or to their own lives. It transpired at the commission of inquiry that only two of the officers' bullets actually struck her. While tragically they proved to be fatal, it must be acknowledged that the accuracy of the officers' fire was impaired through Lefteris Andronicou's action in clinging on to her thereby exposing her to risk.

The Court considers therefore that the use of lethal force in the circumstances, however regrettable it may have been, did not exceed what was "absolutely necessary" for the purposes of defending the lives of Elsie Constantinou and of the officers and did not amount to a breach by the respondent State of their obligations under Article 2, paragraph 2.*a*, of the Convention.

Contra: the Gül v. Turkey judgment of 14 December 2000 (Application No. 22676/93, paragraphs 78-82).

Peacekeeping operations

The Güleç v. Turkey case concerned the death of a person at a demonstration during which the law-enforcement agents had used their weapons. The Court stated (the Güleç v. Turkey judgment of 27 July 1998, *Reports* 1998-IV, paragraphs 70-83):

> [...] As the Commission rightly pointed out, the demonstration was far from peaceful, as was evidenced by the damage to moveable and immoveable property in the town and the injuries sustained by some gendarmes. Confronted with acts of violence which were, admittedly, serious, the security forces, who were not present in sufficient strength, called for reinforcements, and at least two armoured vehicles were deployed. Whereas the driver of the Condor, warrant-officer Nazim Ayhan, asserted that he had fired into the air, several witnesses, including some of the leading citizens of the town, said that shots had been fired at the crowd. Although this allegation was categorically denied by the Government, it is corroborated by the fact that nearly all the wounded demonstrators were hit in the legs; this would be perfectly consistent with ricochet wounds from bullets with a downward trajectory which could have been fired from the turret of an armoured vehicle.

The Court, like the Commission, accepts that the use of force may be justified in the present case under paragraph 2.*c* of Article 2, but it goes without saying that a balance must be struck between the aim pursued and the means employed to achieve it. The gendarmes used a very powerful weapon because they apparently did not have truncheons, riot shields, water cannons, rubber bullets or tear gas. The lack of such equipment is all the more incomprehensible and unacceptable because the province of Sirnak, as the Government pointed out, is in a region in which a state of emergency has been declared, where at the material time disorder could have been expected.

As to the question whether there were armed terrorists among the demonstrators, the Court notes that the Government produced no evidence to support that assertion. In the first place, no gendarme sustained a bullet wound either in the place where the applicant's son died or in other places passed by the demonstration. Secondly, no weapons or spent cartridges supposed to have belonged to PKK members were found on the spot. Moreover, prosecutions brought in the Diyarbakir National Security Court against the owners of thirteen rifles confiscated after the incidents, from which spent cartridges had been collected by the security forces, ended in acquittals, because the defendants had not taken part in the events in issue (see paragraph 8 above).

In conclusion, the Court considers that in the circumstances of the case the force used to disperse the demonstrators, which caused the death of Ahmet Güleç, was not absolutely necessary within the meaning of Article 2.

Military operations

The Ergi v. Turkey case (28 July 1998, *Reports* 1998-IV) concerned an ambush mounted by the security forces agencies against members of the PKK. The applicant claimed that his sister had been killed by blind shots fired by the security forces, who had repeatedly fired in a completely different direction from that of the alleged threat. The Court observed (the Ergi v. Turkey judgment of 28 July 1998, *Reports* 1998-IV, paragraphs 79-81 and 86):

[...] On the Government's own account, the security forces had carried out an ambush operation and had engaged in an armed clash with the PKK in the vicinity of the village (see paragraphs 16-17 above). As mentioned above, they disputed, and the Court has not found it established, that the bullet which killed Havva Ergi was fired by the security forces.

Furthermore, under Article 2 of the Convention, read in conjunction with Article 1, the State may be required to take certain measures in order to "secure" an effective enjoyment of the right to life.

In the light of the above considerations, the Court agrees with the Commission that the responsibility of the State is not confined to circumstances where there is significant evidence that misdirected fire from agents of the State has killed a civilian. It may also be engaged where they fail to take all feasible precautions in the choice of means and methods of a security operation mounted against an opposing group with a view to avoiding and, in any event, to minimising, incidental loss of civilian life.

Thus, even though it has not been established beyond reasonable doubt that the bullet which killed Havva Ergi had been fired by the security forces, the Court must consider whether the security forces' operation had been planned and conducted in such a way as to avoid or minimise, to the greatest extent possible, any risk to the lives of the villagers, including from the fire-power of the PKK members caught in the ambush.

[...] The gendarmerie officers' testimonies to the Commission had suggested that the ambush was organised in the north-west of the village without the distance between the village and the ambush being known. It was to be anticipated that PKK terrorists could have approached the village either following the path from the north or proceeding down the river bed to the north-east and in the latter event, they would have been able to penetrate to the edge of the village without being seen by the security forces to the north-west.

[...] The Court, having regard to the Commission's findings (see paragraphs 34-41 above) and to its own assessment, considers that it was probable that the bullet which killed Havva Ergi had been fired from the south or south-east, that the security forces had been present in the south and that there had been a real risk to the lives of the civilian population through being exposed to cross-fire between the security forces and the PKK. In the light of the failure of the authorities of the respondent State to adduce direct evidence on the planning and conduct of the ambush operation, the Court, in agreement with the Commission, finds that it can reasonably be inferred that insufficient precautions had been taken to protect the lives of the civilian population.

Accordingly, there has been a violation of Article 2 of the Convention.

Article 3 ECHR – Prohibition of torture

Article 3 is worded as follows:

> **No one shall be subjected to torture or to inhuman or degrading treatment or punishment.**

1. Scope and concepts

The scope of Article 3

The scope of this Article is absolute. That is what emerges from the Ireland v. the United Kingdom judgment (18 January 1978, Series A No. 25, p. 65, paragraph 163):

> The Convention prohibits in absolute terms torture and inhuman or degrading treatment or punishment, irrespective of the victim's conduct. Unlike most of the substantive clauses of the Convention and of Protocols Nos. 1 and 4 (P1, P4), Article 3 (art. 3) makes no provision for exceptions and, under Article 15, paragraph 2 (art. 15-2), there can be no derogation therefrom even in the event of a public emergency threatening the life of the nation.

As a consequence, the Ribitsch v. Austria judgment of 4 December 1995 provided the Court with the opportunity to state (the Ribitsch v. Austria judgment of 4 December 1995, Application No. 18896/91 Series A No. 336, paragraph 38) that:

> [...] In respect of a person deprived of his liberty, any recourse to physical force which has not been made strictly necessary by his own conduct diminishes human dignity and is in principle an infringement of the right set forth in Article 3 (art. 3) of the Convention. It reiterates that the requirements of an investigation and the undeniable difficulties inherent in the fight against crime cannot justify placing limits on the protection to be afforded in respect of the physical integrity of individuals (see the Tomasi v. France judgment of 27 August 1992, Series A No. 241-A, p. 42, paragraph 115).

It should be noted, in particular, that there is a presumption of a violation of Article 3 where a detained person displays injuries on being released whereas he was in good health when his deprivation of liberty commenced. On that point, reference may be made to the Selmouni v. France judgment of 28 July 1999, *Reports* 1999-V, paragraph 87:

> The Court considers that where an individual is taken into police custody in good health but is found to be injured at the time of release, it is incumbent on the State to provide a plausible explanation of how those injuries were caused, failing which a clear issue arises under Article 3 of the Convention (see the Tomasi v. France judgment of 27 August 1992, Series A No. 241-A, pp. 40-41, paragraphs 108-111, and the Ribitsch v. Austria judgment of 4 December 1995, Series A No. 336, pp. 25-26, paragraph 34).

That was the solution adopted in the Ribitsch v. Austria case, where the applicant presented bruises to the inside and the outside of his right arm (the Ribitsch v. Austria judgment of 4 December 1995, Application No. 18896/91, Series A No. 336, paragraphs 31 and 34):

> The Commission expressed the view that a State was morally responsible for any person in detention, since he was entirely in the hands of the police. In the event of injuries being sustained during police custody, it was for the Government to produce evidence establishing facts which cast doubt on the account of events given by the victim, particularly if this account was supported by medical certificates
>
> [...] On the basis of all the material placed before it, the Court concludes that the Government have not satisfactorily established that the applicant's injuries were caused otherwise than – entirely, mainly, or partly – by the treatment he underwent while in police custody.

(See, to the same effect, the Berktay v. Turkey judgment of 1 March 2001, Application No. 22493/93, paragraph 167.)

In that regard, it is important to emphasise that the Court does not consider itself to be bound by the findings of judicial proceedings internal to the States concerning the facts complained of by the applicants. In the Selmouni v. France judgment (the Selmouni v. France judgment of 28 July 1999, *Reports* 1999-V, paragraph 87), the Court stated:

> It also points out that in his criminal complaint and application to join the proceedings as a civil party, Mr Selmouni directed his allegations against the police officers in question (see paragraph 28 above) and that the issue of their guilt is a matter for the jurisdiction of the French courts, in particular the criminal courts, alone. Whatever the outcome of the domestic proceedings, the police officers' conviction or acquittal does not absolve the respondent State from its responsibility under the Convention (see the Ribitsch judgment cited above). It is accordingly under an obligation to provide a plausible explanation of how Mr Selmouni's injuries were caused.

Previously, in the Ribitsch case, cited above (4 December 1995, Series A No. 336, paragraphs 34-38), the Court had not been convinced by the government's explanation that the applicant's injuries had been caused by a fall against a vehicle door. The government had merely referred to the outcome of the domestic criminal proceedings to exclude their responsibility under Article 3.

In any event, Article 3 places the State under a procedural obligation to carry out an investigation, just like Article 2. The Labita v. Italy judgment states in that regard (the Labita v. Italy judgment of 6 April 2000, Application No. 26772/95, paragraph 131):

> The Court considers that where an individual makes a credible assertion that he has suffered treatment infringing Article 3 at the hands of the police or other similar agents of the State, that provision, read in conjunction with the State's general duty under Article 1 of the Convention to "secure to everyone within their jurisdiction the rights and freedoms defined in [...] [the] Convention",

requires by implication that there should be an effective official investigation. As with an investigation under Article 2, such investigation should be capable of leading to the identification and punishment of those responsible (see, in relation to Article 2 of the Convention, the McCann and Others v. the United Kingdom judgment of 27 September 1995, Series A No. 324, p. 49, paragraph 161 ; the Kaya v. Turkey judgment of 19 February 1998, *Reports* 1998-I, p. 324, paragraph 86 ; and the Yasa v. Turkey judgment of 2 September 1998, *Reports* 1998-VI, p. 2438, paragraph 98). Otherwise, the general legal prohibition of torture and inhuman and degrading treatment and punishment would, despite its fundamental importance (see paragraph 119 above), be ineffective in practice and it would be possible in some cases for agents of the State to abuse the rights of those within their control with virtual impunity (see the Assenov and Others judgment cited above, p. 3290, paragraph 102).

In that regard, the Akkoc v. Turkey judgment of 10 October 2000 sets out the basic conditions with which medical examinations of persons ill-treated during detention must comply (the Akkoc v. Turkey judgment of 10 October 2000, Applications Nos. 22947 and 22948/93, paragraph 118) :

The Court further endorses the comments expressed by the Commission concerning the importance of independent and thorough examinations of persons on release from detention. [...] Such examinations must be carried out by a properly qualified doctor, without any police officer being present and the report of the examination must include not only the detail of any injuries found but the explanations given by the patient as to how they occurred and the opinion of the doctor as to whether the injuries are consistent with those explanations. The practices of cursory and collective examinations illustrated by the present case undermines the effectiveness and reliability of this safeguard.

Clearly, all that applies only if there is a minimum amount of evidence of violence committed against the victim. Thus, in the Büyükdag v. Turkey [Section IV] judgment (21 December 2000, Application No. 28340/95, paragraph 46, available in French only – unofficial translation), the Court stated :

The allegations of ill-treatment must be supported before the Court by appropriate evidence (see, *mutatis mutandis,* the Klaas v. Germany judgment of 22 September 1993, Series A No. 269, p. 17, paragraph 30). For the purpose of establishing the facts alleged, the Court uses the standard of proof "beyond reasonable doubt"; such proof may follow from the coexistence of sufficiently strong, clear and concordant inferences or of similar unrebutted presumptions of fact (the Ireland v. the United Kingdom judgment of 18 January 1978, Series A No. 25, p. 65, paragraph 161, in fine).

With the stipulation that (same judgment, paragraph 53, available in French only – unofficial translation) :

As regards the other alleged violence, the Court recognises that, depending on circumstances, such conduct may fall within the scope of Article 3 of the Convention, even though it is not necessarily of such a kind as to leave physical or mental traces capable of being detected by medical examination.

In that case, the victim claimed, *inter alia*, to have been subjected to jets of water while undressed.

In the Kurt v. Turkey case, the applicant claimed that the respondent State had infringed Article 3 because her son had disappeared in circumstances in which the absence of the most basic judicial guarantees had not failed to expose intense physical torture. She further claimed to have seen with her own eyes the traces of blows inflicted by the security forces, which in itself gave reason to think that her son had suffered physical torture after being arrested. In that case, the Court had accepted that the applicant's son had been arrested by soldiers. However, the Court stated (the Kurt v. Turkey judgment of 25 May 1998, *Reports* 1998-III, paragraphs 116-117):

> In particular, the applicant has not presented any specific evidence that her son was indeed the victim of ill-treatment in breach of Article 3; nor has she adduced any evidence to substantiate her claim that an officially tolerated practice of disappearances and associated ill-treatment of detainees exists in the respondent State.

> The Court, like the Commission, considers that the applicant's complaints concerning the alleged violations by the respondent State of Article 3 in respect of her son should [...] be dealt with from the angle of Article 5 of the Convention.

Furthermore, Article 3 is applicable even when the degrading treatment is inflicted by persons other than agents of the State. On that point, see, in particular, the Mahmut Kaya v. Turkey [Section I] judgment (28 March 2000, Application No. 22535/93, paragraphs 115-116):

> The obligation imposed on High Contracting Parties under Article 1 of the Convention to secure to everyone within their jurisdiction the rights and freedoms defined in the Convention, taken together with Article 3, requires States to take measures designed to ensure that individuals within their jurisdiction are not subjected to torture or inhuman or degrading treatment, including such ill-treatment administered by private individuals (see the A. v. the United Kingdom judgment of 23 September 1998, *Reports* 1998-VI, p. 2699, paragraph 22). State responsibility may therefore be engaged where the framework of law fails to provide adequate protection (see, for example, the A. judgment cited above, p. 2700, paragraph 24) or where the authorities fail to take reasonable steps to avoid a risk of ill-treatment about which they knew or ought to have known (for example, *mutatis mutandis*, the Osman judgment cited above, pp. 3159-3160, paragraphs 115-116).

> The Court finds that the authorities knew or ought to have known that Hasan Kaya was at risk of being targeted as he was suspected of giving assistance to wounded members of the PKK. The failure to protect his life through specific measures and through the general failings in the criminal law framework placed him in danger not only of extra-judicial execution but also of ill-treatment from persons who were unaccountable for their actions. It follows that the State is responsible for the ill-treatment suffered by Hasan Kaya after his disappearance and prior to his death.

Last, in addition to the specific protective measures which States are required to take, they are also required to enact sufficient legislative provisions. An example may be seen in the A. v. the United Kingdom case of 23 September 1998, *Reports* 1998-VI, where the Court stated (paragraphs 22-24):

> The Court considers that the obligation on the High Contracting Parties under Article 1 of the Convention to secure to everyone within their jurisdiction the rights and freedoms defined in the Convention, taken together with Article 3, requires States to take measures designed to ensure that individuals within their jurisdiction are not subjected to torture or inhuman or degrading treatment or punishment, including such ill-treatment administered by private individuals (see, *mutatis mutandis,* the H.L.R. v. France judgment of 29 April 1997, *Reports* 1997-III, p. 758, paragraph 40). Children and other vulnerable individuals, in particular, are entitled to State protection, in the form of effective deterrence, against such serious breaches of personal integrity (see, *mutatis mutandis,* the X. and Y. v. the Netherlands judgment of 26 March 1985, Series A No. 91, pp. 11-13, paragraphs 21-27; the Stubbings and Others v. the United Kingdom judgment of 22 October 1996, *Reports* 1996-IV, p. 1505, paragraphs 62-64; and also the United Nations Convention on the Rights of the Child, Articles 19 and 37).

> The Court recalls that under English law it is a defence to a charge of assault on a child that the treatment in question amounted to "reasonable chastisement" (see paragraph 14 above). The burden of proof is on the prosecution to establish beyond reasonable doubt that the assault went beyond the limits of lawful punishment. In the present case, despite the fact that the applicant had been subjected to treatment of sufficient severity to fall within the scope of Article 3, the jury acquitted his stepfather, who had administered the treatment (see paragraphs 10-11 above).

> In the Court's view, the law did not provide adequate protection to the applicant against treatment or punishment contrary to Article 3. Indeed, the Government have accepted that this law currently fails to provide adequate protection to children and should be amended.

> In the circumstances of the present case, the failure to provide adequate protection constitutes a violation of Article 3 of the Convention.

Furthermore, Article 3 may be applicable where there is a mere threat of inhuman treatment, that is before that treatment becomes a reality.

Admittedly, in the Campbell and Cosans v. the United Kingdom case (25 February 1982, Series A No. 48, pp. 13-14, paragraph 30), the Court took the view that the threat of being subjected to corporal punishment at school did not give rise to a sufficient degree of humiliation or degradation to reach the threshold necessary for a violation of Article 3.

However, where there are serious and substantiated grounds to believe that a person will incur a real risk of being subjected to torture, or to degrading treatment or punishment, the Court applies Article 3. Thus, in the Soering v. the United Kingdom case (7 July 1989, Series A No. 161, pp. 35-36, paragraph 91), it considered that the threat hanging over the applicant was such that it could entail a violation of that Article. The case concerned extradition to a country (the United States, and in particular the State of Virginia) where the applicant might have had to await the death penalty in extremely harsh conditions, customarily described as "death row"; and the Commonwealth's

Attorney of the State of Virginia had decided to demand, and to continue to demand, the death penalty, because in his view the case called for it. The Court observed (p. 39, paragraphs 90 and 98-99):

> It is not normally for the Convention institutions to pronounce on the existence or otherwise of potential violations of the Convention. However, where an applicant claims that a decision to extradite him would, if implemented, be contrary to Article 3 (art. 3) by reason of its foreseeable consequences in the requesting country, a departure from this principle is necessary, in view of the serious and irreparable nature of the alleged suffering risked, in order to ensure the effectiveness of the safeguard provided by that Article (art. 3) (see paragraph 87 above).
>
> [...]
>
> If the national authority with responsibility for prosecuting the offence takes such a firm stance, it is hardly open to the Court to hold that there are no substantial grounds for believing that the applicant faces a real risk of being sentenced to death and hence experiencing the "death row phenomenon".

Accordingly, the prospect of the person concerned being exposed to that "syndrome" was such that Article 3 came into play.

This extended application of Article 3 must now be clarified by a precise analysis of the concepts which it entails.

The concepts found in Article 3

The concept of inhuman or degrading treatment

The concepts used in Article 3 are in essence relative. The B. v. France judgment (25 March 1992, Series A No. 232-C, p. 87, paragraph 83) is not the leading judgment on this point, but is a relatively recent decision which summarises the Court's definition of "inhuman or degrading treatment":

> In order to constitute a violation of Article 3 the treatment in question must attain a minimum degree of severity. Appraisal of this minimum degree is by its very essence relative; it depends on all the circumstances of the case, and in particular the nature and context, and the duration of the treatment, its physical or mental effects and, sometimes, the sex, age and state of health of the person concerned (the Ireland v. the United Kingdom judgment of 18 January 1978, Series A No. 25, p. 65, paragraph 162, and Tyrer v. the United Kingdom judgment of 25 April 1978, Series A No. 26, pp. 14-15, paragraphs 29-30).
>
> The Court in one case considered the treatment both "inhuman", because it had been applied with premeditation and for hours at a stretch, and had caused "if not actual bodily injury, at least intense physical and mental suffering", and "degrading" because it was such as to arouse in its victims feelings of fear, anguish and inferiority capable of humiliating and debasing them and possibly breaking their physical or moral resistance (the Ireland v. the United Kingdom judgment, loc. cit., p. 66, paragraph 167, and Soering v. the United Kingdom judgment of 7 July 1989, Series A No. 161, p. 39, paragraph 100).

In the light of that definition, the Court has very logically indicated that exclusion from an educational institution for two days does not attain a sufficient level of gravity to be capable of being classified as inhuman or degrading treatment (the Efstratiou v. Greece judgment of 18 December 1996, *Reports* 1996-VI, paragraph 41).

Nor is the public nature of the treatment necessarily a deciding factor. On that point, see the Raninen v. Finland judgment of 16 December 1997, *Reports* 1997-VIII, paragraph 55:

> [...] in considering whether a punishment or treatment is "degrading" within the meaning of Article 3, the Court will have regard to whether its object is to humiliate and debase the person concerned and whether, as far as the consequences are concerned, it adversely affected his or her personality in a manner incompatible with Article 3 (see the Albert and Le Compte v. Belgium judgment of 10 February 1983, Series A No. 58, p. 13, paragraph 22). In this connection, the public nature of the punishment or treatment may be a relevant factor. At the same time, it should be recalled, the absence of publicity will not necessarily prevent a given treatment from falling into that category: it may well suffice that the victim is humiliated in his or her own eyes, even if not in the eyes of others (see the Tyrer v. the United Kingdom judgment of 25 April 1978, Series A No. 26, p. 16, paragraph 32).

Furthermore, it is not essential that in order to constitute degrading treatment the treatment was intended to humiliate the person complaining about it. To that effect, see the V. v. the United Kingdom judgment of 16 December 1999, Application No. 24888/94, paragraph 71):

> In order for a punishment or treatment associated with it to be "inhuman" or "degrading", the suffering or humiliation involved must in any event go beyond that inevitable element of suffering or humiliation connected with a given form of legitimate treatment or punishment (ibid.). The question whether the purpose of the treatment was to humiliate or debase the victim is a further factor to be taken into account (see, for example, the Raninen v. Finland judgment of 16 December 1997, *Reports* 1997-VIII, pp. 2821-2822, paragraph 55), but the absence of any such purpose cannot conclusively rule out a finding of a violation of Article 3.

The concept of torture

To this definition of inhuman treatment and degrading treatment, it is necessary to add the definition of torture. Torture was initially defined in the Ireland v. the United Kingdom case (18 January 1978, Series A No. 25, p. 66, paragraph 167):

> The Court considers [...] that, whilst there exists on the one hand violence which [...] does not fall within Article 3 (art. 3) of the Convention, it appears on the other hand that it was the intention that the Convention, with its distinction between "torture" and "inhuman or degrading treatment", should by the first of these terms attach a special stigma to deliberate inhuman treatment causing very serious and cruel suffering.

As a general rule, the Court first considers whether the conduct in issue may be classified as "inhuman or degrading" and then determines whether it also reaches the degree of gravity necessary to be qualified as "torture". In the Adkoy v. Turkey judgment (18 December 1996, *Reports of Judgments and Decisions* 1996-VI, p. 2279, paragraph 64), it concluded for the first time that the applicant's treatment could only be classified as "torture".

> The Court recalls that the Commission found, *inter alia,* that the applicant was subjected to "Palestinian hanging", in other words, that he was stripped naked, with his arms tied together behind his back, and suspended by his arms (see paragraph 23 above).
>
> In the view of the Court this treatment could only have been deliberately inflicted ; indeed, a certain amount of preparation and exertion would have been required to carry it out. It would appear to have been administered with the aim of obtaining admissions or information from the applicant. In addition to the severe pain which it must have caused at the time, the medical evidence shows that it led to a paralysis of both arms which lasted for some time (see paragraph 23 above). The Court considers that this treatment was of such a serious and cruel nature that it can only be described as torture.

Particular notice should be given of the Selmouni v. France judgment, which marked a significant development in the case-law. In that case, the Court, sitting as a Grand Chamber, provided a new, wider definition of "torture", in the following passage (the Selmouni v. France judgment of 28 July 1999, *Reports* 1999-V, paragraphs 96-106) :

> In order to determine whether a particular form of ill-treatment should be qualified as torture, the Court must have regard to the distinction, embodied in Article 3, between this notion and that of inhuman or degrading treatment. As the European Court has previously found, it appears that it was the intention that the Convention should, by means of this distinction, attach a special stigma to deliberate inhuman treatment causing very serious and cruel suffering (see the Ireland v. the United Kingdom judgment cited above, pp. 66-67, paragraph 167).
>
> The United Nations Convention against Torture and Other Cruel, Inhuman or Degrading Treatment or Punishment, which came into force on 26 June 1987, also makes such a distinction, as can be seen from Articles 1 and 16 :

> #### Article 1
>
> "1. For the purposes of this Convention, the term 'torture' means any act by which severe pain or suffering, whether physical or mental, is intentionally inflicted on a person for such purposes as obtaining from him or a third person information or a confession, punishing him for an act he or a third person has committed or is suspected of having committed, or intimidating or coercing him or a third person, or for any reason based on discrimination of any kind, when such pain or suffering is inflicted by or at the instigation of or with the consent or acquiescence of a public official or other person acting in an official capacity. [...]"

> #### Article 16, paragraph 1
>
> "1. Each State Party shall undertake to prevent in any territory under its jurisdiction other acts of cruel, inhuman or degrading treatment or punishment which do not amount to torture as defined in Article 1, when such acts are committed

by or at the instigation of or with the consent or acquiescence of a public official or other person acting in an official capacity. In particular, the obligations contained in Articles 10, 11, 12 and 13 shall apply with the substitution for references to torture of references to other forms of cruel, inhuman or degrading treatment or punishment."

The Court finds that all the injuries recorded in the various medical certificates (see paragraphs 11-15 and 17-20 above) and the applicant's statements regarding the ill-treatment to which he had been subjected while in police custody (see paragraphs 18 and 24 above) establish the existence of physical and – undoubtedly (notwithstanding the regrettable failure to order a psychological report on Mr Selmouni after the events complained of) – mental pain or suffering. The course of the events also shows that the pain or suffering was inflicted on the applicant intentionally for the purpose of, *inter alia*, making him confess to the offence which he was suspected of having committed. Lastly, the medical certificates annexed to the case file show clearly that the numerous acts of violence were directly inflicted by police officers in the performance of their duties.

The acts complained of were such as to arouse in the applicant feelings of fear, anguish and inferiority capable of humiliating and debasing him and possibly breaking his physical and moral resistance. The Court therefore finds elements which are sufficiently serious to render such treatment inhuman and degrading (see the Ireland v. the United Kingdom judgment cited above, pp. 66-67, paragraph 167, and the Tomasi judgment cited above, p. 42, paragraph 115). In any event, the Court reiterates that, in respect of a person deprived of his liberty, recourse to physical force which has not been made strictly necessary by his own conduct diminishes human dignity and is in principle an infringement of the right set forth in Article 3 (see the Ribitsch judgment cited above, p. 26, paragraph 38, and the Tekin v. Turkey judgment of 9 June 1998, *Reports* 1998-IV, pp.1517-1518, paragraph 53).

In other words, it remains to be established in the instant case whether the "pain or suffering" inflicted on Mr Selmouni can be defined as "severe" within the meaning of Article 1 of the United Nations Convention. The Court considers that this "severity" is, like the "minimum severity" required for the application of Article 3, in the nature of things, relative; it depends on all the circumstances of the case, such as the duration of the treatment, its physical or mental effects and, in some cases, the sex, age and state of health of the victim, etc.

The Court has previously examined cases in which it concluded that there had been treatment which could only be described as torture (see the Aksoy judgment cited above, p. 2279, paragraph 64, and the Aydin judgment cited above, pp. 1891-1892, paragraphs 83-84 and 86). However, having regard to the fact that the Convention is a "living instrument which must be interpreted in the light of present-day conditions" (see, among other authorities, the following judgments: Tyrer v. the United Kingdom, 25 April 1978, Series A No. 26, pp. 15-16, paragraph 31; Soering cited above, p. 40, paragraph 102; and Loizidou v. Turkey, 23 March 1995, Series A No. 310, pp. 26-27, paragraph 71), the Court considers that certain acts which were classified in the past as "inhuman and degrading treatment" as opposed to "torture" could be classified differently in future. It takes the view that the increasingly high standard being required in the area of the protection of human rights and fundamental liberties correspondingly and inevitably requires greater firmness in assessing breaches of the fundamental values of democratic societies.

The Court is satisfied that a large number of blows were inflicted on Mr Selmouni. Whatever a person's state of health, it can be presumed that such intensity of blows will cause substantial pain. Moreover, a blow does not automatically leave a visible mark on the body. However, it can be seen from Dr Garnier's medical report of 7 December 1991 (see paragraphs 18-20 above) that the marks of the violence Mr Selmouni had endured covered almost all of his body.

The Court also notes that the applicant was dragged along by his hair; that he was made to run along a corridor with police officers positioned on either side to trip him up; that he was made to kneel down in front of a young woman to whom someone said "Look, you're going to hear somebody sing"; that one police officer then showed him his penis, saying "Here, suck this", before urinating over him; and that he was threatened with a blowlamp and then a syringe (see paragraph 24 above). Besides the violent nature of the above acts, the Court is bound to observe that they would be heinous and humiliating for anyone, irrespective of their condition.

The Court notes, lastly, that the above events were not confined to any one period of police custody during which – without this in any way justifying them – heightened tension and emotions might have led to such excesses. It has been clearly established that Mr Selmouni endured repeated and sustained assaults over a number of days of questioning (see paragraphs 11-14 above).

Under these circumstances, the Court is satisfied that the physical and mental violence, considered as a whole, committed against the applicant's person caused "severe" pain and suffering and was particularly serious and cruel. Such conduct must be regarded as acts of torture for the purposes of Article 3 of the Convention.

[...]

There has therefore been a violation of Article 3.

The Court was to use that definition again, making a number of detailed points. See, for example, the Salman v. Turkey judgment (27 June 2000, Application No. 21986/93, paragraphs 114-115):

In addition to the severity of the treatment, there is a purposive element, as recognised in the United Nations Convention against Torture and Other Cruel, Inhuman or Degrading Treatment or Punishment, which came into force on 26 June 1987, which defines torture in terms of the intentional infliction of severe pain or suffering with the aim, *inter alia,* of obtaining information, inflicting punishment or intimidating (Article 1 of the United Nations convention).

Having regard to the nature and degree of the ill-treatment (*falaka* and a blow to the chest) and to the strong inferences that can be drawn from the evidence that it occurred during interrogation about Agit Salman's suspected participation in PKK activities, the Court finds that it involved very serious and cruel suffering that may be characterised as torture (see also Selmouni cited above, paragraphs 96-105).

It should be noted that the Court has taken care to state that the concept of severe suffering is relative. Thus in the Dikme v. Turkey [Section I] judgment of 11 July 2000 (Application No. 20869/92, paragraphs 94-96) :

> As the Court has previously found, the criterion of "severity" referred to in the Article cited above is, in the nature of things, relative, like the "minimum severity" required for the application of Article 3 (ibid., paragraph 100) ; it depends on all the circumstances of the case, such as the duration of the treatment, its physical and/or mental effects and, in some cases, the victim's sex, age and state of health (see, among other authorities, Labita cited above, paragraph 120).
>
> In the instant case the first applicant undeniably lived in a permanent state of physical pain and anxiety owing to his uncertainty about his fate and to the blows repeatedly inflicted on him during the lengthy interrogation sessions to which he was subjected throughout his time in police custody.
>
> The Court considers that such treatment was intentionally meted out to the first applicant by agents of the State in the performance of their duties, with the aim of extracting a confession or information about the offences of which he was suspected.
>
> In those circumstances the Court finds that the violence inflicted on the first applicant, taken as a whole and having regard to its purpose and duration, was particularly serious and cruel and was capable of causing "severe" pain and suffering. It therefore amounted to torture within the meaning of Article 3 of the Convention.

That must inevitably have consequences on the classification of inhuman or degrading treatment.

2. Examples of the application of Article 3

Article 3 applies to many situations. The following are a number of examples.

Inhuman treatment, ill-treatment and police procedures

On arrest

The question has arisen whether arrest and detention without any procedural guarantees may in itself fall within the scope of Article 3. In the Ciçek v. Turkey case, the applicant had had no further news of her sons, who had disappeared after being arrested. The Court had reached the conclusion that they must be presumed dead and had found that there had been a violation of Article 2. The applicant also claimed that there had been a violation of Article 3. The Court held (the Ciçek v. Turkey judgment of 27 February 2001, Application No. 25704/94, paragraphs 152, 154-156 and 158) :

> Relying, *mutatis mutandis*, on the arguments used to support her complaints under Article 2, the applicant maintains that the respondent State is in breach of Article 3 of the Convention since the very fact of her sons' disappearance in a context devoid of the most basic judicial safeguards must have exposed them to acute psychological torture. In addition, she was told that her sons had been ill-treated in the regional boarding school. The applicant submits that this presumption must be considered even more compelling in view of the existence of a high incidence of torture of detainees in the respondent State [...].

Having regard to the strict standards applied in the interpretation of Article 3 of the Convention, according to which ill-treatment must attain a minimum level of severity to fall within the provision's scope and the practice of the Convention organs that requires compliance with a standard of proof "beyond reasonable doubt" that ill-treatment of such severity occurred, the Court is not satisfied that the disappearance of the applicant's sons in the circumstances of the instant case can be categorised in terms of this provision (see the Ireland v. the United Kingdom judgment of 18 January 1978, Series A No. 25, p. 65, paragraphs 161-62, the Kurt v. Turkey judgment, cited above, the report of the Commission, p. 1216, paragraph 195).

Where an apparent forced disappearance is characterised by a total lack of information, whether the person is alive or dead or the treatment which he or she may have suffered can only be a matter of speculation. In this respect, the Court first recalls its establishment of the facts that following their arrest on 10 May 1994 the detainees were not subjected to ill-treatment in the regional boarding school (see above paragraph 141). Moreover, the applicant has not presented any specific evidence that her sons were indeed the victims of ill-treatment in breach of Article 3 ; nor can the allegation that her sons were the victims of an officially tolerated practice of disappearances and associated ill-treatment of detainees be said to have been substantiated.

The Court recalls that the acute concern which must arise in relation to the treatment of persons apparently held without official record and excluded from the requisite judicial guarantees is an added and aggravated aspect of the issues arising under Article 5 (see the above cited Kurt v. Turkey judgment, p. 1183, paragraph 115) [...].

The Court concludes therefore that there has been no violation of Article 3 of the Convention in respect of Tahsin Çiçek and Ali Ihsan Çiçek.

During custody

There is clearly a violation of Article 3 where a person is physically assaulted while in custody.

The Court so observed in the Tomasi v. France case, where it stated that "no one has claimed that the marks noted on the applicant's body could have dated from a period prior to his having been taken into custody or could have originated in an act carried out by the applicant against himself or again as a result of an escape attempt" (Tomasi v. France, 27 August 1992, Series A No. 241-A, pp. 40-42, paragraphs 110 and 115). Generally, that judgment (which preceded the Selmouni v. France judgment) sums up the Court's approach as regards persons subjected to police investigations. The Court notes that :

> It does not consider that it has to examine the system of police custody in France and the rules pertaining thereto, or, in this case, the length and the timing of the applicant's interrogations. It finds it sufficient to observe that the medical certificates and reports, drawn up in total independence by medical practitioners, attest to the large number of blows inflicted on Mr Tomasi and their intensity; these are two elements which are sufficiently serious to render such treatment inhuman and degrading. The requirements of the investigation and the undeniable difficulties inherent in the fight against crime, particularly with regard

to terrorism, cannot result in limits being placed on the protection to be afforded in respect of the physical integrity of individuals.

In the Berktay v. Turkey [Section IV] case (1 March 2001, Application No. 22493/93, paragraphs 168-170), the applicant had fallen from a balcony during a search carried out by six police officers in the applicant's presence:

> The Court emphasises that the fact that the police officers were acquitted in the criminal proceedings does not relieve the respondent State of its responsibility under the Convention. It was therefore for the Government to provide a plausible explanation for the origin of the second applicant's injuries. However, the Government merely refer to the outcome of the domestic criminal proceedings, where decisive weight was attached to the police officers' explanation that the second applicant had thrown himself from the balcony. The Court finds that explanation unconvincing and refers in that regard to its findings above (paragraphs 130-136).

> Recalling the obligation for the authorities to account for individuals placed under their control, and on the basis of all the evidence before it, the Court therefore considers that in the circumstances of the case the respondent State is responsible for the injuries caused by the second applicant's fall while he was under the control of six police officers [...].

> The Court therefore concludes that there has been a violation of Article 3 of the Convention.

However, the Court does not find a violation of Article 3 in all situations in which physical injuries are found. In the Klaas v. Germany case (judgment of 22 September 1993, Series A No. 269, pp. 17-18, paragraph 30), the Court considered that "[t]he admitted injuries sustained by the [...] applicant were consistent with [...] the police officers' version of events". Since it found no reprehensible conduct on the part of the police, the Court, like the national courts, did not find that there had been a breach of Article 3:

> No material has been adduced in the course of the Strasbourg proceedings which could call into question the findings of the national courts and add weight to the applicant's allegations either before the Commission or the Court.

As already stated, it is all a question of proof. Above all, it is necessary to determine the origin of the injuries. Still in the Klaas case, the Court observed that:

> The Court would distinguish the present case from that of Tomasi v. France (see the judgment of 27 August 1992, Series A No. 241-A, pp. 40-42, paragraphs 108-115) where certain inferences could be made from the fact that Mr Tomasi had sustained unexplained injuries during forty-eight hours spent in police custody.

> No cogent elements have been provided which could lead the Court to depart from the findings of fact of the national courts.

On the wearing of handcuffs, see the Raninen v. Finland judgment of 16 December 1997, *Reports* 1997-VIII, paragraphs 52-59 (no violation in that case).

During attempted flight or escape

The Caloc v. France case of 20 July 2000 concerned the use of force by gendarmes during an attempted flight from custody. The Court stated (the Caloc v. France judgment of 20 July 2000, Application No. 33951/96, paragraphs 97-101):

> [...] the Court cannot discern any facts capable of casting doubt on the domestic courts' findings as regards the cause of the physical pain and after-effects described above; it may therefore be considered that those phenomena resulted from the violence used during the applicant's attempted escape (see the Klaas judgment cited above, p. 17, paragraph 30, and, by way of contrast, the Ribitsch judgment cited above, pp. 25-26, paragraph 34).

> It is therefore the Court's task to determine whether the force used in the instant case was proportionate. In this connection, the Court attaches particular weight to the injuries sustained. In the incident case, the Court [...] notes that [...] in his expert report of 29 September 1989 Dr Cayol concluded that the problems experienced as a result of the police officers' intervention had caused "total physical incapacity for three days [and] temporary total unfitness for work for nineteen days".

> The Court is of the opinion that, in view of the applicant's injuries, which mainly affected his right shoulder, it can be assumed that the decision to certify him unfit for work for a period of twenty days was necessitated by the specific nature of his occupation as a heavy-plant driver.

> The Court points out that in the instant case the applicant did not deny having attempted to escape. In addition, it is apparent from the records of the interviews on 29 and 30 September 1988 that the applicant acknowledged that he had "resisted" and "jostled" the police officers while attempting to run away. It is also clear from the record of the applicant's interview on 28 February 1989 that he acknowledged "having put up some resistance" to the policemen who were attempting to restrain him. Furthermore, it is not apparent from the evidence given on 1 March 1989 by Dr Thomas, who examined him while he was in police custody, that the applicant had been beaten. Nor does the medical certificate drawn up by Dr Kéclard indicate that he observed any signs of blows to the applicant's body.

> The Court consequently considers, like the Commission, that it has not been established that the force used during the incident was excessive or disproportionate.

> There has accordingly been no violation of Article 3 of the Convention as regards the force used against the applicant during his attempted escape.

Inhuman treatment, penalties, sanctions and punishment

Disciplinary sanctions and corporal punishment

The Court reached the conclusion that corporal punishment inflicted on a juvenile delinquent – three strokes of the birch – was to be analysed as a degrading sanction for the purposes of Article 3 (the Tyrer v. the United Kingdom judgment of 25 April 1978, Series A No. 26).

Nonetheless, the threat of the use of corporal punishment as a disciplinary measure in schools is not sufficient to constitute degrading treatment (the Campbell and Cosans v. the United Kingdom judgment of 25 February 1982, Series A No. 48).

The Court has also concluded that the "disciplinary sanction" imposed by a headmaster on a pupil aged seven years (three "whacks" on the bottom through his shorts with a rubber-soled gym shoe) did not attain the minimum level of severity required to fall within the scope of Article 3 (the Costello-Roberts v. the United Kingdom judgment of 25 March 1993, Series A No. 247-C).

Judicial procedures and criminal penalties

In the V. v. the United Kingdom case, the applicant, who when a minor had been convicted of a criminal offence before an adult court, alleged that the cumulative effect of a number of factors – the age of criminal responsibility, the accusatory and public procedure before a court for adults, the length of the proceedings, the composition of the jury, formed of twelve unknown adults, the layout of the courtroom, the striking presence of the media and the public, the public attacks on the vehicle which took him to the court and the disclosure of his identity, combined with a number of other factors connected with the penalty – had amounted to a violation of Article 3. The Court held (the V. v. the United Kingdom judgment of 16 December 1999, Application No. 24888/94, paragraphs 71-75 and 77-80) :

> Treatment has been held by the Court to be "inhuman" because, *inter alia*, it was premeditated, was applied for hours at a stretch and caused either actual bodily injury or intense physical and mental suffering, and also "degrading" because it was such as to arouse in its victims feelings of fear, anguish and inferiority capable of humiliating and debasing them. In order for a punishment or treatment associated with it to be "inhuman" or "degrading", the suffering or humiliation involved must in any event go beyond that inevitable element of suffering or humiliation connected with a given form of legitimate treatment or punishment (ibid.). The question whether the purpose of the treatment was to humiliate or debase the victim is a further factor to be taken into account (see, for example, the Raninen v. Finland judgment of 16 December 1997, *Reports* 1997-VIII, pp. 2821-2822, paragraph 55), but the absence of any such purpose cannot conclusively rule out a finding of a violation of Article 3.

> The Court has considered first whether the attribution to the applicant of criminal responsibility in respect of acts committed when he was ten years old could, in itself, give rise to a violation of Article 3. In doing so, it has regard to the principle, well established in its case-law, that since the Convention is a living instrument, it is legitimate when deciding whether a certain measure is acceptable under one of its provisions to take account of the standards prevailing amongst the member States of the Council of Europe (see the Soering judgment cited above, p. 40, paragraph 102 ; and also the Dudgeon v. the United Kingdom judgment of 22 October 1981, Series A No. 45, and the X., Y. and Z. v. the United Kingdom judgment of 22 April 1997, *Reports* 1997-II).

In this connection, the Court observes that, at the present time, there is not yet a commonly accepted minimum age for the attribution of criminal responsibility in Europe.

The Court concludes that the attribution of criminal responsibility to the applicant does not in itself give rise to a breach of Article 3 of the Convention.

The second part of the applicant's complaint under Article 3 concerning the trial relates to the fact that the criminal proceedings took place over three weeks in public in an adult Crown Court with attendant formality, and that, after his conviction, his name was permitted to be published.

[ ]

The Court considers [that there is] an international tendency in favour of the protection of the privacy of juvenile defendants [...]. However, whilst the existence of such a trend is one factor to be taken into account when assessing whether the treatment of the applicant can be regarded as acceptable under the other Articles of the Convention, it cannot be determinative of the question whether the trial in public amounted to ill-treatment attaining the minimum level of severity necessary to bring it within the scope of Article 3 (see paragraph 70 above).

The Court recognises that the criminal proceedings against the applicant were not motivated by any intention on the part of the State authorities to humiliate him or cause him suffering. [...]

Even if there is evidence that proceedings such as those applied to the applicant could be expected to have a harmful effect on an eleven-year-old child (see paragraphs 17-19 above), the Court considers that any proceedings or inquiry to determine the circumstances of the acts committed by T. and the applicant, whether such inquiry had been carried out in public or in private, attended by the formality of the Crown Court or informally in the youth court, would have provoked in the applicant feelings of guilt, distress, anguish and fear. The psychiatric evidence shows that before the trial commenced he was suffering from the post-traumatic effects of the offence; that he cried inconsolably and found it difficult and distressing when asked to talk about what he and T. had done to the two-year-old, and that he suffered fears of punishment and terrible retribution (see paragraphs 11-12 above). Whilst the public nature of the proceedings may have exacerbated to a certain extent these feelings in the applicant, the Court is not convinced that the particular features of the trial process as applied to him caused, to a significant degree, suffering going beyond that which would inevitably have been engendered by any attempt by the authorities to deal with the applicant following the commission by him of the offence in question (see paragraph 71 above).

In conclusion, therefore, the Court does not consider that the applicant's trial gave rise to a violation of Article 3 of the Convention.

In that case the applicant had been sentenced to be detained during Her Majesty's pleasure. Accordingly, the minister had informed the applicant in writing that he would have to serve a period of fifteen years in order to satisfy the requirements of punishment and deterrence. The applicant then applied for leave to seek a judicial review of that decision, arguing in particular that the length of the period of punishment set by the minister was disproportionate and had been determined without taking account of the requirements of readjustment. Leave was granted. The Divisional Court upheld the applicant's complaints in part. The Court of Appeal dismissed the minister's appeal. The House of Lords dismissed the minister's appeal and allowed the applicant's cross-appeal. The House of Lords held that the adoption by the minister, in the context of the implementation of the procedure for setting the term, of a policy which, even in exceptional circumstances, did not take account of the progress and development of a child detained during Her Majesty's pleasure was arbitrary. The majority of the House of Lords further held that in determining the length of sentence, the minister was exercising a power comparable to that of the sentencing judge and, like the latter, must disregard the pressure of public opinion. The minister had been mistaken to give weight to public protests concerning length of the punitive part to be served by the applicant and had not shown fairness from the procedural aspect, which had rendered his decision arbitrary. His decision was therefore annulled. The minister then informed Parliament that in the light of the judgment of the House of Lords, he had adopted a new policy concerning young persons sentenced for murder to be detained during Her Majesty's pleasure, namely that the punitive period initially set would be reconsidered by the minister in the light of the progress and development of the person concerned. The minister invited the applicant's representatives to submit observations with a view to setting a different term. At the time when the European Court of Human Rights adopted its judgment, no decision had been taken regarding the applicant's sentence. The Court held (the V. v. the United Kingdom judgment of 16 December 1999, Application No. 24888/94, paragraphs 95-101) :

> The Commission agreed with the Government. It referred to the Hussain v. the United Kingdom judgment of 21 February 1996 (*Reports* 1996-I), where the Court held that the sentence of detention during Her Majesty's pleasure was primarily preventative, attracting the guarantees of Article 5, paragraph 4 (see paragraphs 115 and 119 below). It could not, therefore, be said that the applicant had forfeited his liberty for life or that his detention gave rise to a violation of Article 3.

> The Court recalls that following the applicant's conviction for murder in November 1993 he automatically became subject to the sentence of detention during Her Majesty's pleasure. According to English law and practice, juveniles sentenced to detention during Her Majesty's pleasure must initially serve a period of detention, "the tariff", to satisfy the requirements of retribution and deterrence. Thereafter it is legitimate to continue to detain the offender only if this appears to be necessary for the protection of the public (see paragraphs 40-42 above and the Hussain judgment cited above, pp. 269-270, paragraph 54). The applicant's tariff was initially fixed at fifteen years by the Home Secretary on 22 July 1994. However, this decision was quashed by the House of Lords on 12 June 1997 and at the date of adoption of the present judgment no new tariff has been set. The applicant makes no complaint about his current conditions of detention, although he does contend that his transfer at the age of eighteen to a Young Offenders' Institution and thereafter to an adult prison might raise issues under Article 3.

> In assessing whether the above facts constitute ill-treatment of sufficient severity to violate Article 3 (see paragraph 70 above), the Court has regard to the fact that

Article 37 of the UN convention prohibits life imprisonment without the possibility of release in respect of offences committed by persons below the age of eighteen and provides that the detention of a child "shall be used only as a measure of last resort and for the shortest appropriate period of time", and that Rule 17.1.*b* of the Beijing Rules recommends that "[r]estrictions on the personal liberty of the juvenile shall [...] be limited to the possible minimum" (see paragraphs 45-46 above).

The Court recalls that States have a duty under the Convention to take measures for the protection of the public from violent crime (see, for example, the A. v. the United Kingdom judgment of 23 September 1998, *Reports* 1998-VI, p. 2699, paragraph 22, and the Osman v. the United Kingdom judgment of 28 October 1998, *Reports* 1998-VIII, p. 3159, paragraph 115). It does not consider that the punitive element inherent in the tariff approach itself gives rise to a breach of Article 3, or that the Convention prohibits States from subjecting a child or young person convicted of a serious crime to an indeterminate sentence allowing for the offender's continued detention or recall to detention following release where necessary for the protection of the public (see the Hussain judgment cited above, p. 269, paragraph 53).

The applicant has not yet reached the stage in his sentence where he is able to have the continued lawfulness of his detention reviewed with regard to the question of dangerousness and, although he has not yet been notified of any new tariff, it can be assumed that he is currently detained for the purposes of retribution and deterrence. Until a new tariff has been set, it is not possible to draw any conclusions regarding the length of punitive detention to be served by the applicant. At the time of adoption of the present judgment he has been detained for six years since his conviction in November 1993. The Court does not consider that, in all the circumstances of the case including the applicant's age and his conditions of detention, a period of punitive detention of this length can be said to amount to inhuman or degrading treatment.

Finally, the Court observes that it cannot be excluded, particularly in relation to a child as young as the applicant at the time of his conviction, that an unjustifiable and persistent failure to fix a tariff, leaving the detainee in uncertainty over many years as to his future, might also give rise to an issue under Article 3. In the present case, however, in view of the relatively short period of time during which no tariff has been in force and the need to seek the views, *inter alia,* of both the applicant and T. (see paragraph 28 above), no such issue arises.

It follows that there has been no violation of Article 3 in respect of the applicant's sentence.

Inhuman or degrading treatment and conditions of detention

General aspects

Generally, it should be observed that in the Kudla v. Poland judgment (26 October 2000, Application No. 30210/96, paragraphs 92-94) the Court stated that:

On the other hand, the Court has consistently stressed that the suffering and humiliation involved must in any event go beyond that inevitable element of suffering or humiliation connected with a given form of legitimate treatment or punishment (see, *mutatis mutandis*, the Tyrer v. the United Kingdom judgment of 25 April 1978, Series A No. 26, p. 15, paragraph 30; the Soering v. the United Kingdom judgment of 7 July 1989, Series A No. 161, p. 39, paragraph 100; and V. v. the United Kingdom, cited above).

Measures depriving a person of his liberty may often involve such an element. Yet it cannot be said that the execution of detention on remand in itself raises an issue under Article 3 of the Convention. Nor can that Article be interpreted as laying down a general obligation to release a detainee on health grounds or to place him in a civil hospital to enable him to obtain a particular kind of medical treatment.

Nevertheless, under this provision the State must ensure that a person is detained in conditions which are compatible with respect for his human dignity, that the manner and method of the execution of the measure do not subject him to distress or hardship of an intensity exceeding the unavoidable level of suffering inherent in detention and that, given the practical demands of imprisonment, his health and well-being are adequately secured by, among other things, providing him with the requisite medical assistance (see, *mutatis mutandis*, the Aerts v. Belgium judgment of 30 July 1998, *Reports* 1998-V, p. 1966, paragraphs 64 *et seq.*).

In the Dougoz v. Greece case, the applicant had been convicted of drugs offences, released from prison and placed in detention pending expulsion. He complained of the conditions of his detention (the Dougoz v. Greece [Section III] judgment of 6 March 2001, Application No. 40907/98, paragraphs 45-46 and 48):

In the present case the Court notes that the applicant was first held for several months at the Drapetsona Police Station, which is a detention centre for persons held under Aliens legislation. He alleges, *inter alia*, that he was confined in an overcrowded and dirty cell with insufficient sanitary and sleeping facilities, scarce hot water, no fresh air or natural daylight and no yard in which to exercise. It was even impossible for him to read a book because his cell was so overcrowded. In April 1998 he was transferred to the Police Headquarters in Alexandras Avenue, where conditions were similar to those in Drapetsona and where he was detained until 3 December 1998, the date of his expulsion to Syria.

[...]

The Court considers that conditions of detention may sometimes amount to inhuman or degrading treatment. In the Greek case (*Yearbook of the European Convention on Human Rights* 12, 1969), the Commission reached this conclusion regarding overcrowding and inadequate facilities for heating, sanitation, sleeping arrangements, food, recreation and contacts with the outside world. When assessing conditions of detention, account has to be taken of the cumulative effects of these conditions, as well as of specific allegations made by the applicant. In the present case, although the Court has not conducted an on-site visit, it notes that the applicant's allegations are corroborated by the conclusions of the CPT report of 29 November 1994 regarding the Police Headquarters in Alexandras Avenue. In its report the CPT stressed that the cellular accommodation and detention regime in that place were quite unsuitable for a period in excess of a few days, the occupancy levels being grossly excessive and the sanitary facilities appalling. Although the CPT had not visited the Drapetsona detention centre at that time, the Court notes that the Government had described the conditions in Alexandras as being the same as in Drapetsona, and the applicant himself conceded that the former were slightly better with natural light, air in the cells and adequate hot water.

In the light of the above, the Court considers that the conditions of detention of the applicant in the Alexandras Police Headquarters and the Drapetsona detention centre, in particular the serious overcrowding and absence of sleeping facilities, combined with the inordinate length of the period during which he was detained in such conditions, amounted to degrading treatment contrary to Article 3.

See, to the same effect, the Peers v. Greece [Section II] judgment of 19 April 2001 (Application No. 28524/95, paragraph 75):

> The Court takes particularly into account that, for at least two months, the applicant had to spend a considerable part of each 24-hour period practically confined to his bed in a cell with no ventilation and no window which would at times become unbearably hot. He also had to use the toilet in the presence of another inmate and be present while the toilet was being used by his cellmate. The Court is not convinced by the Government's allegation that these conditions have not affected the applicant in a manner incompatible with Article 3. On the contrary, the Court is of the opinion that the prison conditions complained of diminished the applicant's human dignity and arose in him feelings of anguish and inferiority capable of humiliating and debasing him and possibly breaking his physical or moral resistance. In sum, the Court considers that the conditions of the applicant's detention in the segregation unit of the Delta wing of the Koridallos prison amounted to degrading treatment within the meaning of Article 3 of the Convention.

See also the Akdeniz and Others v. Turkey [Section II] judgment of 31 May 2001 (Application No. 23954/94, paragraph 98) concerning persons detained outside.

Persons with mental problems

The Court has had the opportunity to adopt a position on the conditions of detention and disciplinary measures in the case of a person suffering from mental problems. In the Keenan v. the United Kingdom case, which concerned a person in detention who died by suffocation after hanging himself while serving a four-month prison sentence (judgment of 3 April 2001, [Section III], Application No. 27229/95, paragraphs 110-113 and 115), the Court held:

> It is relevant in the context of the present application to recall also that the authorities are under an obligation to protect the health of persons deprived of liberty (Hurtado v. Switzerland, Commission Report 8 July 1993, Series A No. 280, p. 16, paragraph 79). The lack of appropriate medical treatment may amount to treatment contrary to Article 3 (see Ilhan v. Turkey [GC], No. 22277/93, ECHR 2000-VII, paragraph 87). In particular, the assessment of whether the treatment or punishment concerned is incompatible with the standards of Article 3 has, in

71

the case of mentally-ill persons, to take into consideration their vulnerability and their inability, in some cases, to complain coherently or at all about how they are being affected by any particular treatment (see for example the Herczegfalvy v. Austria judgment of 24 September 1992, Series A No. 244, paragraph 82; and the Aerts v. Belgium judgment of 30 July 1998, *Reports* 1998-V, p. 1966, paragraph 66).

The Court recalls that Mark Keenan was suffering from a chronic mental disorder, which involved psychotic episodes and feelings of paranoia. He was also diagnosed as suffering from a personality disorder. The history of his detention in Exeter prison from 14 April 1993 disclosed episodes of disturbed behaviour when he was removed from the hospital wing to normal location. This involved the demonstration of suicidal tendencies, possible paranoid-type fears and aggressive and violent outbursts. That he was suffering anguish and distress during this period and up until his death cannot be disputed. [...] His letter to his doctor, received after his death, shows a high level of desperation (paragraph 44 above). However, as the Commission stated in its majority opinion, it is not possible to distinguish with any certainty to what extent his symptoms during this time, or indeed his death, resulted from the conditions of his detention imposed by the authorities.

The Court considers, however, that this difficulty is not determinative of the issue as to whether the authorities fulfilled their obligation under Article 3 to protect Mark Keenan from treatment or punishment contrary to this provision. While it is true that the severity of suffering, physical or mental, attributable to a particular measure has been a significant consideration in many of the cases decided by the Court under Article 3, there are circumstances where proof of the actual effect on the person may not be a major factor. For example, in respect of a person deprived of his liberty, recourse to physical force which has not been made strictly necessary by his own conduct diminishes human dignity and is in principle an infringement of the right set forth in Article 3 (see the Ribitsch v. Austria judgment of 4 December 1995, Series A No. 336, p. 26, paragraph 38, and the Tekin v. Turkey judgment, cited above, pp. 1517-1518, paragraph 53). Similarly, treatment of a mentally-ill person may be incompatible with the standards imposed by Article 3 in the protection of fundamental human dignity, even though that person may not be able, or capable of, pointing to any specific ill-effects.

In this case, the Court is struck by the lack of medical notes concerning Mark Keenan, who was an identifiable suicide risk and undergoing the additional stresses that could be foreseen from segregation and, later, disciplinary punishment. From 5 May to 15 May 1993, when he died, there were no entries in his medical notes. Given that there were a number of prison doctors who were involved in caring for Mark Keenan, this shows an inadequate concern to maintain full and detailed records of his mental state and undermines the effectiveness of any monitoring or supervision process [...].

The lack of effective monitoring of Mark Keenan's condition and the lack of informed psychiatric input into his assessment and treatment disclose significant defects in the medical care provided to a mentally-ill person known to be a suicide risk. The belated imposition on him in those circumstances of a serious disciplinary punishment – seven days' segregation in the punishment block and an additional twenty-eight days to his sentence imposed two weeks after the event and only nine days before his expected date of release – which may well have threatened his physical and moral resistance, is not compatible with the standard of treatment required in respect of a mentally-ill person. It must be regarded as constituting inhuman and degrading treatment and punishment within the meaning of Article 3 of the Convention.

Handicapped persons

Concerning a handicapped detainee, see the Price v. the United Kingdom [Section III] judgment of 10 July 2001, paragraphs 21-30.

Inhuman or degrading treatment and patients confined in psychiatric hospitals

As regards treatment given to a person confined in a psychiatric hospital, the Court has stated a number of principles of great interest in the Herczegfalvy v. Austria judgment of 24 September 1992, Series A No. 244, pp. 25-26, paragraph 82):

> The Court considers that the position of inferiority and powerlessness which is typical of patients confined in psychiatric hospitals calls for increased vigilance in reviewing whether the Convention has been complied with. While it is for the medical authorities to decide, on the basis of the recognised rules of medical science, on the therapeutic methods to be used, if necessary by force, to preserve the physical and mental health of patients who are entirely incapable of deciding for themselves and for whom they are therefore responsible, such patients nevertheless remain under the protection of Article 3 (art. 3), whose requirements permit of no derogation.

> The established principles of medicine are admittedly in principle decisive in such cases; as a general rule, a measure which is a therapeutic necessity cannot be regarded as inhuman or degrading.

The Court was careful to add:

> The Court must nevertheless satisfy itself that the medical necessity has been convincingly shown to exist.

In the same area, note should be taken of the Aerts v. Belgium judgment of 30 July 1998, *Reports* 1998-V, paragraphs 65-66, where the Court did not find a violation of Article 3 in spite of conditions which were unsatisfactory and not conducive to the effective treatment of the inmates, and pointed out that there was no proof that a deterioration in the applicant's mental health had been observed.

Degrading treatment and lack of respect for personality

Where a difference in treatment indicates contempt or lack of respect for the personality of the person concerned and tends to humiliate or disparage him, there may be a violation of Article 3 (the Abdulaziz, Cabales and Balkandali v. the United Kingdom judgment of 28 May 1985, Series A No. 94). Contra: the Smith and Grady v. the United Kingdom judgment of 27 September 1999, Applications Nos. 33985/96 and 33986/96, paragraph 122.

Inhuman or degrading treatment, extradition and expulsion, political refugees

Extradition

Once again we return to the Soering case, cited above, and the "death row" issue, not this time in order to mention the implementation of Article 3 in the event of a "threat" of inhuman treatment, but in order to illustrate the application of that Article in relation to extradition, even though the country applying for extradition is not a Party to the Convention (see also Article 1, above). The Court applies Article 3 provided that there is a risk of inhuman treatment in the applicant State, in this case the United States. The Court considered (judgment of 7 July 1989, Series A No. 161, pp. 35 and 44-45, paragraphs 90-91 and 111) that:

> It is not normally for the Convention institutions to pronounce on the existence or otherwise of potential violations of the Convention. However, where an applicant claims that a decision to extradite him would, if implemented, be contrary to Article 3 (art. 3) by reason of its foreseeable consequences in the requesting country, a departure from this principle is necessary, in view of the serious and irreparable nature of the alleged suffering risked, in order to ensure the effectiveness of the safeguard provided by that Article (art. 3) (see paragraph 87 above).

> [...] the decision by a Contracting State to extradite a fugitive may give rise to an issue under Article 3 (art. 3), and hence engage the responsibility of that State under the Convention, where substantial grounds have been shown for believing that the person concerned, if extradited, faces a real risk of being subjected to torture or to inhuman or degrading treatment or punishment in the requesting country. The establishment of such responsibility inevitably involves an assessment of conditions in the requesting country against the standards of Article 3 (art. 3) of the Convention. Nonetheless, there is no question of adjudicating on or establishing the responsibility of the receiving country, whether under general international law, under the Convention or otherwise. In so far as any liability under the Convention is or may be incurred, it is liability incurred by the extraditing Contracting State by reason of its having taken action which has as a direct consequence the exposure of an individual to proscribed ill-treatment.

> [...]

> [...] having regard to the very long period of time spent on death row in such extreme conditions, with the ever present and mounting anguish of awaiting execution of the death penalty, and to the personal circumstances of the applicant, especially his age and mental state at the time of the offence, the applicant's extradition to the United States would expose him to a real risk of treatment going beyond the threshold set by Article 3 (art. 3).

> [...]

> Accordingly, the Secretary of State's decision to extradite the applicant to the United States would, if implemented, give rise to a breach of Article 3 (art. 3).

Expulsion

In the Cruz Varas and Others v. Sweden judgment (20 March 1991, Series A No. 201, p. 28, paragraph 70), the Court decided that these principles also apply to expulsion decisions. Another example may be found in the Ahmed v. Austria judgment of 17 December 1996. In that case, the applicant, originally from Somalia and residing in Austria, had lost his right as a political refugee after committing an offence. Before finding that his expulsion would expose him to inhuman treatment, the Court recalled to mind a number of fundamental points (the Ahmed v. Austria judgment of 17 December 1996, *Reports* 1996-VI, paragraphs 38-41) :

> The Court reiterates in the first place that Contracting States have the right, as a matter of well-established international law and subject to their treaty obligations including the Convention, to control the entry, residence and expulsion of aliens. It also notes that the right to political asylum is not contained in either the Convention or its Protocols (see the Vilvarajah and Others v. the United Kingdom judgment of 30 October 1991, Series A No. 215, p. 34, paragraph 102).
>
> However, the expulsion of an alien by a Contracting State may give rise to an issue under Article 3 (art. 3), and hence engage the responsibility of that State under the Convention, where substantial grounds have been shown for believing that the person in question, if expelled, would face a real risk of being subjected to treatment contrary to Article 3 (art. 3) in the receiving country. In these circumstances, Article 3 (art. 3) implies the obligation not to expel the person in question to that country (see the Soering v. the United Kingdom judgment of 7 July 1989, Series A No. 161, p. 35, paragraphs 90 91 ; the Cruz Varas and Others v. Sweden judgment of 20 March 1991, Series A No. 201, p. 28, paragraphs 69-70 ; the above-mentioned Vilvarajah and Others judgment, p. 34, paragraph 103 ; and the Chahal v. the United Kingdom judgment of 15 November 1996, *Reports of Judgments and Decisions* 1996-V, p. 1853, paragraphs 73-74).
>
> The Court further reiterates that Article 3 (art. 3), which enshrines one of the fundamental values of democratic societies (see the above-mentioned Soering judgment, p. 34, paragraph 88), prohibits in absolute terms torture or inhuman or degrading treatment or punishment, irrespective of the victim's conduct. Unlike most of the substantive clauses of the Convention and of Protocols Nos. 1 and 4 (P1, P4), Article 3 (art. 3) makes no provision for exceptions and no derogation from it is permissible under Article 15 (art. 15) even in the event of a public emergency threatening the life of the nation (see the Ireland v. the United Kingdom judgment of 18 January 1978, Series A No. 25, p. 65, paragraph 163 ; the Tomasi v. France judgment of 27 August 1992, Series A No. 241-A, p. 42, paragraph 115 ; and the above-mentioned Chahal judgment, p. 1855, paragraph 79).
>
> The above principle is equally valid when issues under Article 3 (art. 3) arise in expulsion cases. Accordingly, the activities of the individual in question, however undesirable or dangerous, cannot be a material consideration. The protection afforded by Article 3 (art. 3) is thus wider than that provided by Article 33 of the 1951 Convention relating to the Status of Refugees (see paragraph 24 above and the above-mentioned Chahal judgment, p. 1855, paragraph 80).

The Court clearly stated in the D. v. the United Kingdom judgment (2 May 1997, *Reports of Judgments and Decisions* 1997-III, p. 791, paragraphs 46 and 48-50) that the responsibility of the contracting States is engaged whether the alleged ill-treatment emanates directly or indirectly from the public authorities of the country of destination.

[...] in exercising their right to expel such aliens Contracting States must have regard to Article 3 of the Convention (art. 3), which enshrines one of the fundamental values of democratic societies. It is precisely for this reason that the Court has repeatedly stressed in its line of authorities involving extradition, expulsion or deportation of individuals to third countries that Article 3 (art. 3) prohibits in absolute terms torture or inhuman or degrading treatment or punishment and that its guarantees apply irrespective of the reprehensible nature of the conduct of the person in question [...].

[...]

It is true that this principle has so far been applied by the Court in contexts in which the risk to the individual of being subjected to any of the proscribed forms of treatment emanates from intentionally inflicted acts of the public authorities in the receiving country or from those of non-State bodies in that country when the authorities there are unable to afford him appropriate protection (see, for example, the Ahmed judgment, loc. cit., p. 2207, paragraph 44).

Aside from these situations and given the fundamental importance of Article 3 (art. 3) in the Convention system, the Court must reserve to itself sufficient flexibility to address the application of that Article (art. 3) in other contexts which might arise. It is not therefore prevented from scrutinising an applicant's claim under Article 3 (art. 3) where the source of the risk of proscribed treatment in the receiving country stems from factors which cannot engage either directly or indirectly the responsibility of the public authorities of that country, or which, taken alone, do not in themselves infringe the standards of that Article (art. 3). To limit the application of Article 3 (art. 3) in this manner would be to undermine the absolute character of its protection. In any such contexts, however, the Court must subject all the circumstances surrounding the case to a rigorous scrutiny, especially the applicant's personal situation in the expelling State.

Against this background the Court will determine whether there is a real risk that the applicant's removal would be contrary to the standards of Article 3 (art. 3) in view of his present medical condition. In so doing the Court will assess the risk in the light of the material before it at the time of its consideration of the case, including the most recent information on his state of health (see the Ahmed judgment, loc. cit., p. 2207, paragraph 43).

In that case, the applicant was diagnosed as HIV positive and suffered from Aids. The government wished to expel him to St Kitts after he had been sentenced to a term of imprisonment for drug trafficking. In the judgment, the Court observed that "the applicant [was] in the advanced stages of a terminal and incurable illness" and that "it [was] not disputed that his removal [would] hasten his death. There [was] a serious risk that the conditions of adversity which await[ed] him in St Kitts [would] further reduce his already limited life expectancy and subject him to acute mental and physical suffering" (paragraphs 51 and 52-54).

In view of these exceptional circumstances and bearing in mind the critical stage now reached in the applicant's fatal illness, the implementation of the decision to remove him to St Kitts would amount to inhuman treatment by the respondent State in violation of Article 3 (art. 3).

The Court also notes in this respect that the respondent State has assumed responsibility for treating the applicant's condition since August 1994. He has become reliant on the medical and palliative care which he is at present receiving and is no doubt psychologically prepared for death in an environment which is both familiar and compassionate. Although it cannot be said that the conditions which would confront him in the receiving country are themselves a breach of the standards of Article 3 (art. 3), his removal would expose him to a real risk of dying under most distressing circumstances and would thus amount to inhuman treatment.

[...]

Against this background the Court emphasises that aliens who have served their prison sentences and are subject to expulsion cannot in principle claim any entitlement to remain in the territory of a Contracting State in order to continue to benefit from medical, social or other forms of assistance provided by the expelling State during their stay in prison.

However, in the very exceptional circumstances of this case and given the compelling humanitarian considerations at stake, it must be concluded that the implementation of the decision to remove the applicant would be a violation of Article 3 (art. 3).

The Court [Section III] held otherwise in the case of Bensaid v the United Kingdom (judgment of 6 February 2001). In that case, the applicant was to be expelled from the United Kingdom, since the authorities considered that his marriage was a marriage of convenience. The applicant had pleaded his mental health (schizophrenia), the difficulty in obtaining in Algeria the treatment which he was receiving other than as an inpatient, the consequences for his health and the political situation in that country. The Court held (the Bensaid v. the United Kingdom judgment of 6 February 2001, Application No. 44599/98, paragraphs 34 and 36-41):

While it is true that Article 3 has been more commonly applied by the Court in contexts in which the risk to the individual of being subjected to any of the proscribed forms of treatment emanates from intentionally inflicted acts of the public authorities or non-State bodies in the receiving country (for example, the Ahmed v. Austria judgment, loc. cit., paragraph 44), the Court has, in light of the fundamental importance of Article 3, reserved to itself sufficient flexibility to address the application of that Article in other contexts which might arise. It is not therefore prevented from scrutinising an applicant's claim under Article 3 where the source of the risk of proscribed treatment in the receiving country stems from factors which cannot engage either directly or indirectly the responsibility of the public authorities of that country, or which, taken alone, do not in themselves infringe the standards of that Article. To limit the application of Article 3 in this manner would be to undermine the absolute character of its protection. In any such contexts, however, the Court must subject all the circumstances surrounding the case to rigorous scrutiny, especially the applicant's personal situation in the expelling State (see the D. v. the United Kingdom judgment of 2 May 1997, *Reports* 1997-III, paragraph 49).

[...]

In the present case, the applicant is suffering from a long-term mental illness, schizophrenia. He is currently receiving medication, olanzapine, which assists him in managing his symptoms. If he returns to Algeria, this drug will no longer be available to him free as an outpatient. He is not enrolled in any social insurance fund and cannot claim any reimbursement. It is, however, the case that the drug would be available to him if he was admitted as an inpatient and that it would be potentially available on payment as an outpatient. It is also the case that other medication, used in the management of mental illness, is likely to be available. The nearest hospital for providing treatment is at Blida, some 75-80 km from the village where his family live.

The difficulties in obtaining medication and the stresses inherent in returning to this part of Algeria, where there is violence and active terrorism, are alleged to endanger seriously his health. Deterioration in the applicant's already existing mental illness could involve relapse into hallucinations and psychotic delusions involving self-harm and harm to others, as well as restrictions in social function- ing [...]. The Court considers that the suffering associated with such a relapse could, in principle, fall within the scope of Article 3.

The Court observes, however, that the applicant faces the risk of relapse even if he stays in the United Kingdom as his illness is long term and requires constant management. Removal will arguably increase the risk, as will the differences in available personal support and accessibility of treatment. The applicant has argued, in particular, that other drugs are less likely to be of benefit to his con- dition, and also that the option of becoming an inpatient should be a last resort. Nonetheless medical treatment is available to the applicant in Algeria. The fact that the applicant's circumstances in Algeria would be less favourable than those enjoyed by him in the United Kingdom is not decisive from the point of view of Article 3 of the Convention.

The Court finds that the risk that the applicant will suffer a deterioration in his condition if he is returned to Algeria and that, if he did, he would not receive adequate support or care is to a large extent speculative. [...] The applicant is not himself a likely target of terrorist activity. Even if his family does not have a car, this does not exclude the possibility of other arrangements being made.

The Court accepts the seriousness of the applicant's medical condition. Having regard, however, to the high threshold set by Article 3, particularly where the case does not concern the direct responsibility of the Contracting State for the infliction of harm, the Court does not find that there is a sufficiently real risk that the applicant's removal in these circumstances would be contrary to the standards of Article 3. It does not disclose the exceptional circumstances of the D. case (cited above) where the applicant was in the final stages of a terminal illness, Aids, and had no prospect of medical care or family support on expulsion to St Kitts.

The Court finds, therefore, that the implementation of the decision to remove the applicant to Algeria would not violate Article 3 of the Convention.

It should be noted that in order to ascertain the existence of a risk of inhuman or degrading treatment, it is therefore necessary to refer as a matter of priority to the circumstances of which the State in question was or should have been aware at the time of the expulsion (or removal) but that does not prevent the Court from taking subsequent information into account; this may serve to confirm or to invalidate the manner in which the Contracting Party concerned determined whether the applicants' fears were well founded (see, *mutatis mutandis*, the Cruz Varas and Others v. Sweden judgment of 20 March 1991, Series A No. 201, p. 30, paragraph 76).

Removal

On the removal of a nine-year-old girl to her country of origin, see the Nsona v. the Netherlands judgment of 28 November 1996, Application No. 23366/94, *Reports* 1996-V, paragraphs 103-104): no violation.

Inaction on the part of the social services or inadequacy of the legislation

The Z. and Others v. the United Kingdom judgment concerns the failure of the social services to protect minors. The Court stated (judgment of 10 May 2001, Application No. 29392/95, paragraphs 73-74):

> [...] These measures [Articles 1 and 3] should provide effective protection, in particular, of children and other vulnerable persons and include reasonable steps to prevent ill-treatment of which the authorities had or ought to have had knowledge (*mutatis mutandis*, the Osman v. the United Kingdom judgment of 28 October 1998, *Reports* 1998-VIII, paragraph 116).

> There is no dispute in the present case that the neglect and abuse suffered by the four child applicants reached the threshold of inhuman and degrading treatment (as recounted in paragraphs 11 to 36 above). This treatment was brought to the local authority's attention, at the earliest in October 1987. It was under a statutory duty to protect the children and had a range of powers available to them, including removal from their home. The children were, however, only taken into emergency care, at the insistence of the mother, on 30 April 1992. Over the intervening period of four and a half years, they had been subject in their home to what the child consultant psychiatrist who examined them referred to as horrific experiences (see paragraph 40 above). The Criminal Injuries Compensation Board had also found that the children had been subject to appalling neglect over an extended period and suffered physical and psychological injury directly attributable to a crime of violence (see paragraph 49 above). The Court acknowledges the difficult and sensitive decisions facing social services and the important countervailing principle of respecting and preserving family life. The present case, however, leaves no doubt as to the failure of the system to protect these child applicants from serious, long-term neglect and abuse.

That judgment is similar to the A. v. the United Kingdom judgment of 23 September 1998, *Reports* 1998-VI, cited above.

Destruction of material assets

A number of cases have raised the question whether the destruction of material assets may constitute a violation of Article 3.

In the Mentes and Others v. Turkey judgment, the Court had not considered that aspect, on the ground that it had already considered the destruction of the applicants' houses under Article 8. In that case, the Commission had concluded that there had been a violation of Article 3 (the Mentes and Others v. Turkey judgment of 28 November 1997, *Reports* 1997-VIII, paragraphs 74-77).

In the Selçuk and Asker v. Turkey judgment, on the other hand, the Court agreed that there had been a violation of Article 3 because the security forces had burnt down the applicants' homes (the Selçuk and Asker judgment of 24 April 1998, *Reports* 1998-II, paragraphs 77-80) :

> The Court refers to the facts which it finds to be established in the present case (see paragraphs 27, 28, 30 and 57 above). It recalls that Mrs Selçuk and Mr Asker were aged respectively 54 and 60 at the time and had lived in the village of Islamköy all their lives (see paragraph 8 above). Their homes and most of their property were destroyed by the security forces, depriving the applicants of their livelihoods and forcing them to leave their village. It would appear that the exercise was premeditated and carried out contemptuously and without respect for the feelings of the applicants. They were taken unprepared ; they had to stand by and watch the burning of their homes ; inadequate precautions were taken to secure the safety of Mr and Mrs Asker ; Mrs Selçuk's protests were ignored, and no assistance was provided to them afterwards.
>
> Bearing in mind in particular the manner in which the applicants' homes were destroyed (see the above-mentioned Akdivar and Others judgment, p. 1216, paragraph 91) and their personal circumstances, it is clear that they must have been caused suffering of sufficient severity for the acts of the security forces to be categorised as inhuman treatment within the meaning of Article 3.
>
> [...] However, even if it were the case that the acts in question were carried out without any intention of punishing the applicants, but instead to prevent their homes being used by terrorists or as a discouragement to others, this would not provide a justification for the ill-treatment.
>
> In conclusion, the Court finds that the particular circumstances of this case disclose a violation of Article 3.

See, to the same effect, the Bilgin v. Turkey judgment of 16 November 2000, Application No. 23819/94, paragraph 103.

The fate of the close relatives of victims of a violation of Article 3

The Court has ruled on the implementation of Article 3 as regards the close relatives of persons alleged to have been victims of a violation of Article 2 or Article 3. Thus, in the Çakici v. Turkey case (8 July 1999, Application No. 23657/94, paragraphs 98-99), it held :

The Court observes that in the Kurt case (Kurt judgment cited above, pp. 1187-1188, paragraphs 130-134), which concerned the disappearance of the applicant's son during an unacknowledged detention, it found that the applicant had suffered a breach of Article 3 having regard to the particular circumstances of the case. It referred particularly to the fact that she was the mother of a victim of a serious human rights violation and herself the victim of the authorities' complacency in the face of her anguish and distress. The Kurt case does not, however, establish any general principle that a family member of a "disappeared person" is thereby a victim of treatment contrary to Article 3.

Whether a family member is such a victim will depend on the existence of special factors which gives the suffering of the applicant a dimension and character distinct from the emotional distress which may be regarded as inevitably caused to relatives of a victim of a serious human rights violation. Relevant elements will include the proximity of the family tie – in that context, a certain weight will attach to the parent-child bond – the particular circumstances of the relationship, the extent to which the family member witnessed the events in question, the involvement of the family member in the attempts to obtain information about the disappeared person and the way in which the authorities responded to those enquiries. The Court would further emphasise that the essence of such a violation does not so much lie in the fact of the "disappearance" of the family member but rather concerns the authorities' reactions and attitudes to the situation when it is brought to their attention. It is especially in respect of the latter that a relative may claim directly to be a victim of the authorities' conduct.

In the present case, the applicant was the brother of the disappeared person. Unlike the applicant in the Kurt case, he was not present when the security forces took his brother, as he lived with his own family in another town. It appears also that, while the applicant was involved in making various petitions and enquiries to the authorities, he did not bear the brunt of this task, his father Tevfik Çakici taking the initiative in presenting the petition of 22 December 1993 to the Diyarbakir National Security Court. Nor have any aggravating features arising from the response of the authorities been brought to the attention of the Court in this case. Consequently, the Court perceives no special features existing in this case which would justify finding an additional violation of Article 3 of the Convention in relation to the applicant himself. Accordingly, there has been no breach of Article 3 as concerns the applicant in this case.

Article 4 ECHR – Prohibition of slavery and forced labour

Article 4, paragraph 1

Article 4, paragraph 1, is worded as follows:

> **1. No one shall be held in slavery or servitude.**

1. The concept of servitude

The Van Droogenbroeck v. Belgium case provides an indication of the concept of "servitude". In that case, the applicant had been convicted of theft and been sentenced to two years' imprisonment and been placed at the disposal of the government for ten years. In Belgian law, this "placing at the disposal of the government" must be analysed as a penalty and not as a security measure; it is imposed in addition to a principal custodial penalty and at the same time as that penalty and it begins to take effect upon expiry of the custodial penalty. It is valid for a period determined by law. Under the Belgian legislation, "recidivists and habitual offenders who are at the disposal of the Minister of Justice shall, if necessary, be detained in an establishment". The phrase "if necessary" shows that the law leaves a wide discretion as to the choice of the implementing measures: internment, semi-freedom, supervised freedom, etc. The minister may grant the person concerned conditional release either upon expiry of the principal penalty, failing which the latter is interned, or in the course of internment; he may also revoke such a measure at a later date.

Before the Court, the applicant referred to Article 5 (see below) of the Convention on cases of deprivation of freedom and claimed that the internments to which he had been subjected originated not in the sentence of a "competent court" but in decisions of the Minister of Justice. He therefore complained of the fact that his being placed at the disposal of the government, and subjected to the goodwill of the authorities, had placed him in a state of servitude contrary to Article 4, paragraph 1. The Court proceeded from the principle that respect for Article 5, paragraph 1, precludes at the outset the state of servitude, apart from in the circumstances which it defined (the Van Droogenbroeck v. Belgium judgment of 24 June 1982, Series A No. 50, p. 32, paragraph 58):

> The situation complained of did not violate Article 5, paragraph 1 (art. 5-1) (see paragraph 42 above). Accordingly, it could have been regarded as servitude only if it involved a "particularly serious" form of "denial of freedom" (see paragraphs 79-80 of the Commission's report), which was not so in the present case.

In the Cyprus v. Turkey case (judgment of 10 May 2001), the Grand Chamber of the Court had the opportunity to examine a complaint based on Article 4. However, it confined itself to examining the question from the aspect of proof. The facts set out in the application related to the military operations carried out by Turkey in northern Cyprus in July and August 1974 and to the still existing division of the territory of Cyprus. The applicant government maintained, in essence, that approximately 1 491 Greek Cypriots were still missing 20 years after the end of the hostilities. These persons had last been seen alive when they were detained under the authority of Turkey and the respondent State had never given any explanation of their fate. The applicant government claimed that, in the absence of an irrefutable conclusion that the missing persons were now dead, it must be presumed that they were still detained in conditions which, given the time which had elapsed since the events of 1974, must be qualified as servitude. The Court held (the Cyprus v. Turkey judgment of 10 May 2001, Application No. 25781/94, paragraphs 139-141) :

> The Commission found that there had been no breach of Article 4, being of the view that there was nothing in the evidence which could support the assumption that during the relevant period any of the missing persons were still in Turkish custody and were being held in conditions which violated Article 4.

> The Court agrees with the Commission's finding. It notes in this respect that, like the Commission, it has refused to speculate on the fate or whereabouts of the missing persons. Furthermore, it has accepted the facts as established by the Commission.

> It follows that no breach of Article 4 of the Convention has been established.

2. Consent and a state of servitude

The Commission has addressed the case of young English boys who had while minors undertaken to serve for nine years in the British marines. The army refused to release them from their obligations. They then brought an action on the ground that that constituted a case of servitude, given their youth when they gave the undertaking. Although Article 4, paragraph 3, expressly provides that military service is not to be regarded as forced labour, the Commission agreed to examine whether in that case military service constituted a state of "servitude" and eventually found that it did not (the W., X., Y. and Z. v. the United Kingdom case, Applications Nos. 3435-3438/67, *Collection of Decisions* 1968-IV, pp. 20-21) :

> The Commission is of the opinion that "servitude" and "forced or compulsory labour" are distinguished in Article 4 and, although they must in fact often overlap, they cannot be treated as equivalent, and that the clause excluding military service expressly from the scope of the term "forced or compulsory labour" does not forcibly exclude such service in all circumstances from an examination in the light of the prohibition directed against "slavery or servitude";

> [...]

> [...] whereas consequently the terms of service if not amounting to a state of servitude for adult servicemen, can neither have that character for boys who enter the services with their parents' consent.

Article 4, paragraph 2 – Prohibition of forced labour

Article 4, paragraph 2, is worded as follows:

> **2. No one shall be required to perform forced or compulsory labour.**

The Court has had the opportunity to interpret the concept of "compulsory labour". In the Van der Mussele v. Belgium judgment, the applicant, a Belgian national born in 1952, lived in Antwerp, where he practised as an avocat. He was admitted to the roll of pupils on 27 September 1976, completed his pupillage on 1 October 1979 and had since been on the roll of the Bar. While he was a pupil, he was appointed by the court to assist a defendant. *Avocats* appointed by the court were not entitled either to any remuneration or to reimbursement of their costs. The applicant complained of the appointment by the court not as such but in so far as a refusal would have entailed sanctions and in so far as he was not entitled to payment or to costs. He saw this as "forced or compulsory labour", incompatible with Article 4, paragraph 2. The Court held (judgment of 23 November 1983, Series A No. 70, p. 16, paragraphs 32-36 and 38):

> Article 4 (art. 4) does not define what is meant by "forced or compulsory labour" and no guidance on this point is to be found in the various Council of Europe documents relating to the preparatory work of the European Convention.
>
> As the Commission and the Government pointed out, it is evident that the authors of the European Convention – following the example of the authors of Article 8 of the draft International Covenant on Civil and Political Rights – based themselves, to a large extent, on an earlier treaty of the International Labour Organisation, namely Convention No. 29 concerning Forced or Compulsory Labour.
>
> [...]
>
> The Court will [...] take into account the above-mentioned ILO Conventions – which are binding on nearly all the member States of the Council of Europe, including Belgium – and especially Convention No. 29. There is in fact a striking similarity, which is not accidental, between paragraph 3 of Article 4 (art. 4-3) of the European Convention and paragraph 2 of Article 2 of Convention No. 29. Paragraph 1 of the last-mentioned Article provides that "for the purposes" of the latter Convention, the term "forced or compulsory labour" shall mean "all work or service which is exacted from any person under the menace of any penalty and for which the said person has not offered himself voluntarily". This definition can provide a starting-point for interpretation of Article 4 (art. 4) of the European Convention. However, sight should not be lost of that Convention's special features or of the fact that it is a living instrument to be read "in the light of the notions currently prevailing in democratic States" (see, *inter alia*, the Guzzardi judgment of 6 November 1980, Series A No. 39, p. 34, paragraph 95).

It was common ground between those appearing before the Court that the services rendered by Mr Van der Mussele to Mr Ebrima amounted to "labour" for the purposes of Article 4, paragraph 2 (art. 4-2). It is true that the English word "labour" is often used in the narrow sense of manual work, but it also bears the broad meaning of the French word *"travail"* and it is the latter that should be adopted in the present context. [...]

It remains to be ascertained whether there was "forced or compulsory" labour. The first of these adjectives brings to mind the idea of physical or mental constraint, a factor that was certainly absent in the present case. As regards the second adjective, it cannot refer just to any form of legal compulsion or obligation. For example, work to be carried out in pursuance of a freely negotiated contract cannot be regarded as falling within the scope of Article 4 (art. 4) on the sole ground that one of the parties has undertaken with the other to do that work and will be subject to sanctions if he does not honour his promise. On this point, the minority of the Commission agreed with the majority. What there has to be is work "exacted [...]. under the menace of any penalty" and also performed against the will of the person concerned, that is work for which he "has not offered himself voluntarily".

[...]

Had Mr Van der Mussele refused without good reason to defend Mr Ebrima, his refusal would not have been punishable with any sanction of a criminal character. On the other hand, he would have run the risk of having the Council of the Ordre strike his name off the roll of pupils or reject his application for entry on the register of *avocats* (see paragraph 19 above); these prospects are sufficiently daunting to be capable of constituting "the menace of [a] penalty", having regard both to the use of the adjective "any" in the definition and to the standards adopted by the ILO on this point ("Abolition of Forced Labour": General Survey by the Committee of Experts on Application of Conventions and Recommendations, 1979, paragraph 21).

It must next be determined whether the applicant "offered himself voluntarily" for the work in question.

According to the majority of the Commission, the applicant had consented in advance to the situation he complained of, so that it ill became him to object to it subsequently.

[...]

This argument, which was supported by the Government, correctly reflects one aspect of the situation; nevertheless, the Court cannot attach decisive weight thereto. Mr Van der Mussele undoubtedly chose to enter the profession of *avocat,* which is a liberal profession in Belgium, appreciating that under its rules he would, in accordance with a long-standing tradition, be bound on occasions to render his services free of charge and without reimbursement of his expenses. However, he had to accept this requirement, whether he wanted to or not, [...].

[…] the Court prefers to adopt a[n] […] approach. Having held that there existed a risk comparable to "the menace of [a] penalty" (see paragraph 35 above) and then that relative weight is to be attached to the argument regarding the applicant's "prior consent" (see paragraph 36 above), the Court will have regard to all the circumstances of the case in the light of the underlying objectives of Article 4 (art. 4) of the European Convention in order to determine whether the service required of Mr Van der Mussele falls within the prohibition of compulsory labour. This could be so in the case of a service required in order to gain access to a given profession, if the service imposed a burden which was so excessive or disproportionate to the advantages attached to the future exercise of that profession, that the service could not be treated as having been voluntarily accepted beforehand; this could apply, for example, in the case of a service unconnected with the profession in question.

The structure of Article 4 (art. 4) is informative on this point. Paragraph 3 (art. 4-3) is not intended to "limit" the exercise of the right guaranteed by paragraph 2 (art. 4-2), but to "delimit" the very content of this right, for it forms a whole with paragraph 2 (art. 4-2) and indicates what "the term 'forced or compulsory labour' shall not include" *(ce qui "n'est pas considéré comme 'travail forcé ou obligatoire'")*. This being so, paragraph 3 (art. 4-3) serves as an aid to the interpretation of paragraph 2 (art. 4-2).

The four sub-paragraphs of paragraph 3 (art. 4-3-a, art. 4-3-b, art. 4-3-c, art. 4-3-d), notwithstanding their diversity, are grounded on the governing ideas of the general interest, social solidarity and what is in the normal or ordinary course of affairs. The final sub-paragraph, namely sub-paragraph *d* (art. 4-3-d) which excludes "any work or service which forms part of normal civil obligations" from the scope of forced or compulsory labour, is of especial significance in the context of the present case.

Following those reasons, and given the applicant's situation, the Court decided that the task of providing free assistance imposed in the context of a freely chosen profession did not necessarily constitute forced labour. The judgment continues as follows (p. 21, paragraph 40):

The Court would recall that Mr Van der Mussele had voluntarily entered the profession of *avocat* with knowledge of the practice complained of. This being so, a considerable and unreasonable imbalance between the aim pursued – to qualify as an *avocat* – and the obligations undertaken in order to achieve that aim would alone be capable of warranting the conclusion that the services exacted of Mr Van der Mussele in relation to legal aid were compulsory despite his consent. No such imbalance is disclosed by the evidence before the Court, notwithstanding the lack of remuneration and of reimbursement of expenses – which in itself is far from satisfactory.

Having regard, furthermore, to the standards still generally obtaining in Belgium and in other democratic societies, there was thus no compulsory labour for the purposes of Article 4, paragraph 2 (art. 4-2), of the Convention.

Article 4, paragraph 3 – Derogatory clause

Article 4, paragraph 3, is worded as follows:

> **3. For the purpose of this Article the term "forced or compulsory labour" shall not include:**
>
> a any work required to be done in the ordinary course of detention imposed according to the provisions of Article 5 of this Convention or during conditional release from such detention;
>
> b any service of a military character or, in case of conscientious objectors in countries where they are recognised, service exacted instead of compulsory military service;
>
> c any service exacted in case of an emergency or calamity threatening the life or well-being of the community;
>
> d any work or service which forms part of normal civic obligations.

1. Work imposed on persons detained under Article 5

As regards work by persons given custodial sentences (the Van Droogenbroeck v. Belgium case, 24 June 1982, Series A No. 50, p. 33, paragraphs 59-60, where an imprisoned person had been induced to work in order to acquire the sum set as a condition of his release), the Court notes that:

> In practice, once release is conditional on the possession of savings from pay for work done in prison (see paragraphs 13, 16 and 17 above), one is not far away from an obligation in the strict sense of the term.
>
> However, it does not follow that the complaint is well founded, for failure to observe Article 5, paragraph 4 (art. 5-4) (see paragraph 56 above), does not automatically mean that there has been failure to observe Article 4 (art. 4): the latter Article authorises, in paragraph 3.*a* (art. 4-3-a), work required to be done in the ordinary course of detention which has been imposed, as was here the case, in a manner that does not infringe paragraph 1 of Article 5 (art. 5-1). Moreover, the work which M. Van Droogenbroeck was asked to do did not go beyond what is "ordinary" in this context since it was calculated to assist him in reintegrating himself into society and had as its legal basis provisions which find an equivalent in certain other member States of the Council of Europe (see paragraph 25 above and, *mutatis mutandis*, the above-mentioned De Wilde, Ooms and Versyp judgment, Series A No. 12, pp. 44-45, paragraphs 89-90).
>
> Accordingly, the Belgian authorities did not fail to observe the requirements of Article 4 (art. 4).

It will be noted that in passing the Court examined the effect of compliance with Article 5 on the lawfulness of forced labour. It had already done so in the De Wilde, Ooms and Versyp v. Belgium case, where the applicants had been detained and forced to work for pay. Although in that case the Court held (judgment of 18 June 1971, Series A No. 12, p. 44, paragraphs 89-90) that there had been a violation of Article 5, paragraph 4, it did not draw the conclusion that that entailed a violation of Article 4. Article 5, paragraph 1, had been observed. The Court observed:

> The Court too has, in these cases, found a violation of the rights guaranteed by Article 5, paragraph 4 (art. 5-4) (see paragraphs 74 to 80 above), but it does not think that it must deduce there from a violation of Article 4 (art. 4). It in fact considers that paragraph 3.*a* of Article 4 (art. 4-3-a) authorises work ordinarily required of individuals deprived of their liberty under Article 5, paragraph 1.*e* (art. 5-1-e). The Court has found moreover, on the basis of information before it, that no violation of Article 5, paragraph 1.*e* (art. 5-1-e), has been established in respect of De Wilde, Ooms and Versyp (see paragraphs 67 to 70 above).

> Furthermore, the duty to work imposed on the three applicants has not exceeded the "ordinary" limits, within the meaning of Article 4, paragraph 3.*a* (art. 4-3-a), of the Convention, because it aimed at their rehabilitation and was based on a general standard, Section 6 of the 1891 Act, which finds its equivalent in several member States of the Council of Europe (see paragraph 38 above and Appendices IV and V to the Commission's report).

> The Belgian authorities did not therefore fail to comply with the requirements of Article 4 (art. 4).

2. Civic work, civic obligations and the obligation to pay

In the Karlheinz-Schmidt v. Germany case (judgment of 18 July 1994, Series A No. 291-B, p. 32, paragraph 23), the application concerned the obligation imposed on men only to serve in the fire brigade or to pay a financial contribution.

> [...] the Court considers that compulsory fire service such as exists in Baden-Württemberg is one of the "normal civic obligations" envisaged in Article 4, paragraph 3.*d* (art. 4-3-d). It observes further that the financial contribution which is payable – in lieu of service – is, according to the Federal Constitutional Court (see paragraph 15 above), a "compensatory charge". The Court therefore concludes that, on account of its close links with the obligation to serve, the obligation to pay also falls within the scope of Article 4, paragraph 3.*d* [...].

(As regards compliance with the obligation to serve in the fire brigade or to pay a financial contribution in conjunction with Article 14 of the Convention, see, under Article 14, Discriminatory differences in treatment.)

Article 5 ECHR – Right to liberty and security

Article 5, paragraph 1

Article 5, paragraph 1, of the Convention is worded as follows:

---

1. Everyone has the right to liberty and security of person. No one shall be deprived of his liberty save in the following cases and in accordance with a procedure prescribed by law:

   a the lawful detention of a person after conviction by a competent court;

   b the lawful arrest or detention of a person for non-compliance with the lawful order of a court or in order to secure the fulfilment of any obligation prescribed by law;

   c the lawful arrest or detention of a person effected for the purpose of bringing him before the competent legal authority on reasonable suspicion of having committed an offence or when it is reasonably considered necessary to prevent his committing an offence or fleeing after having done so;

   d the detention of a minor by lawful order for the purpose of educational supervision or his lawful detention for the purpose of bringing him before the competent legal authority;

   e the lawful detention of persons for the prevention of the spreading of infectious diseases, of persons of unsound mind, alcoholics or drug addicts or vagrants;

   f the lawful arrest or detention of a person to prevent his effecting an unauthorised entry into the country or of a person against whom action is being taken with a view to deportation or extradition.

---

1. The concept of deprivation of liberty

Article 5, paragraph 1, refers specifically to cases of deprivation of liberty. The concept of "deprivation of liberty" should be clearly defined.

Deprivation of liberty and restriction of liberty

Compulsory residence order

In the Guzzardi v. Italy judgment (6 November 1980, Series A No. 39, pp. 33-35, paragraphs 92-93 and 95), the Court addressed the distinction between restriction and deprivation of liberty, which alone falls within the scope of Article 5, paragraph 1. In that case, Mr Guzzardi had been ordered to reside on a small Italian island in circumstances which, taken in combination with others, "raise[d] an issue of categorisation from the viewpoint of Article 5". And the question arose whether, in spite of the fact that he was not detained in custody, that compulsory residence order might be assimilated to an actual deprivation of liberty. The judgment states:

> The Court recalls that in proclaiming the "right to liberty", paragraph 1 of Article 5 (art. 5-1) is contemplating the physical liberty of the person; its aim is to ensure that no one should be dispossessed of this liberty in an arbitrary fashion. As was pointed out by those appearing before the Court, the paragraph is not concerned with mere restrictions on liberty of movement; such restrictions are governed by Article 2 of Protocol No. 4 (P4-2) which has not been ratified by Italy. In order to determine whether someone has been "deprived of his liberty" within the meaning of Article 5 (art. 5), the starting point must be his concrete situation and account must be taken of a whole range of criteria such as the type, duration, effects and manner of implementation of the measure in question (see the Engel and Others judgment of 8 June 1976, Series A No. 22, p. 24, paragraphs 58-59).

> The difference between deprivation of and restriction upon liberty is none the less merely one of degree or intensity, and not one of nature or substance. Although the process of classification into one or other of these categories some-times proves to be no easy task in that some borderline cases are a matter of pure opinion, the Court cannot avoid making the selection upon which the applica-bility or inapplicability of Article 5 (art. 5) depends.

> [...]

> Whilst the area around which the applicant could move far exceeded the dimen-sions of a cell and was not bounded by any physical barrier, it covered no more than a tiny fraction of an island to which access was difficult and about nine-tenths of which was occupied by a prison. Mr Guzzardi was housed in part of the hamlet of Cala Reale which consisted mainly of the buildings of a former medical establishment which were in a state of disrepair or even dilapidation, a carabi-nieri station, a school and a chapel. He lived there principally in the company of other persons subjected to the same measure and of policemen.

> [...]

> The Court considers on balance that the present case is to be regarded as one involving deprivation of liberty.

The Court therefore undertakes an assessment of the case in point.

Holding aliens in an international zone

In relation to holding asylum seekers in a transit zone or international zone of an airport (in this case at Paris-Orly), the Court considered (the Amuur v. France judgment of 25 June 1996, *Reports of Judgments and Decisions* 1996-III, No. 11, pp. 847-848, paragraphs 41 and 43):

> The Court notes in the first place that in the fourth paragraph of the Preamble to its Constitution of 27 October 1946 (incorporated into that of 4 October 1958), France enunciated the right to asylum in "the territories of the Republic" for "everyone persecuted on account of his action in the cause of freedom". France is also party to the 1951 Geneva Convention Relating to the Status of Refugees, Article 1 of which defines the term "refugee" as "any person who [has a] well-founded fear of being persecuted for reasons of race, religion, nationality, membership of a particular social group or political opinion".

The Court also notes that many member States of the Council of Europe have been confronted for a number of years now with an increasing flow of asylum seekers. It is aware of the difficulties involved in the reception of asylum seekers at most large European airports and in the processing of their applications. The report of the Parliamentary Assembly of the Council of Europe, of 12 September 1991, is revealing on this point (see paragraph 26 above).

Contracting States have the undeniable sovereign right to control aliens' entry into and residence in their territory. The Court emphasises, however, that this right must be exercised in accordance with the provisions of the Convention, including Article 5 (art. 5).

[...] (See the Guzzardi v. Italy judgment of 6 November 1980, Series A No.39, p. 33, paragraph 92.)

Holding aliens in the international zone does indeed involve a restriction upon liberty, but one which is not in every respect comparable to that which obtains in centres for the detention of aliens pending deportation. Such confinement, accompanied by suitable safeguards for the persons concerned, is acceptable only in order to enable States to prevent unlawful immigration while complying with their international obligations, particularly under the 1951 Geneva Convention Relating to the Status of Refugees and the European Convention on Human Rights. States' legitimate concern to foil the increasingly frequent attempts to circumvent immigration restrictions must not deprive asylum seekers of the protection afforded by these conventions.

Such holding should not be prolonged excessively, otherwise there would be a risk of it turning a mere restriction on liberty – inevitable with a view to organising the practical details of the alien's repatriation or, where he has requested asylum, while his application for leave to enter the territory for that purpose is considered – into a deprivation of liberty. In that connection account should be taken of the fact that the measure is applicable not to those who have committed criminal offences but to aliens who, often fearing for their lives, have fled from their own country.

Although by the force of circumstances the decision to order holding must necessarily be taken by the administrative or police authorities, its prolongation requires speedy review by the courts, the traditional guardians of personal liberties. Above all, such confinement must not deprive the asylum seeker of the right to gain effective access to the procedure for determining refugee status.

In that case, the French Government and the Commission shared the view that there had been no deprivation of liberty and attached "particular weight to the fact that the applicants could at any time have removed themselves from the sphere of application of the measure in issue". However, the Court stated:

The mere fact that it is possible for asylum seekers to leave voluntarily the country where they wish to take refuge cannot exclude a restriction on liberty, the right to leave any country, including one's own, being guaranteed, moreover, by Protocol No. 4 to the Convention (P4). Furthermore, this possibility becomes theoretical if no other country offering protection comparable to the protection they expect to find in the country where they are seeking asylum is inclined or prepared to take them in.

The Court concluded that "holding the applicants in the transit zone of Paris-Orly airport was equivalent in practice, in view of the restrictions suffered, to a deprivation of liberty". The applicants, who had arrived on 9 March 1992, were kept in the transit zone of the airport for twenty days, were left to their own devices, placed under strict and constant police surveillance and had no legal and social assistance. The Court also noted that "until 26 March neither the length nor the necessity of that confinement were reviewed by a court".

Disciplinary judgments

The Court has held that the fact of confining soldiers to their dwellings or to military buildings or premises does not constitute a deprivation of liberty (the Engel and Others v. the Netherlands judgment, 8 June 1976, Series A No. 22).

That is not the case for all disciplinary measures.

Hospitalisation

In the Nielsen v. Denmark case (judgment of 28 November 1988, Series A No. 144), the Court held that the hospitalisation of a minor in a child psychiatric ward, at the request of his mother, did not constitute a deprivation of liberty within the meaning of Article 5, but represented the exercise by a mother aware of her responsibilities of her parental rights in the interest of the child.

Consent and deprivation of liberty

The fact that there is consent to incarceration does not inevitably mean that there is no deprivation of liberty: the fact that an individual freely surrenders to the authorities and agrees to be detained does not relieve those authorities of the obligation to comply with Article 5 (the De Wilde, Ooms and Versyp v. Belgium judgment of 28 May 1970, Series A No. 12).

2. Cases of deprivation of liberty authorised by the Convention

General aspects

Article 5, paragraph 1, provides that no one is to be deprived of his liberty save in the "following cases" and in accordance with a "procedure prescribed by law".

Observation of the procedures prescribed by law

As regards observation of the "procedures prescribed by law", the Court refers principally to compliance with national law. In the Wassink v. the Netherlands case (judgment of 27 September 1990, Application No. 12535/86, paragraph 24), it stated:

> On the question whether detention is "lawful", including whether it complies with "a procedure prescribed by law", the Convention refers back essentially to

national law and lays down the obligation to conform to the substantive and procedural rules thereof. However, it requires in addition that any deprivation of liberty should be consistent with the purpose of Article 5 (art. 5), namely to protect individuals from arbitrariness (see, as the most recent authority, the Van der Leer judgment of 21 February 1990, Series A No. 170, p. 12, paragraph 22).

The same formula was used in the Benham v. the United Kingdom judgment (10 June 1996, *Reports of Judgments and Decisions* 1996-III, p. 765, paragraph 40):

> The main issue to be determined in the present case is whether the disputed detention was "lawful", including whether it complied with "a procedure prescribed by law". The Convention here essentially refers back to national law and states the obligation to conform to the substantive and procedural rules thereof, but it requires in addition that any deprivation of liberty should be consistent with the purpose of Article 5 (art. 5), namely to protect individuals from arbitrariness (see the Quinn v. France judgment of 22 March 1995, Series A No. 311, p. 18, paragraph 47).

In the following paragraph (paragraph 41), however, the Court also states that failure to comply with domestic law entails a violation of Article 5 and that it must therefore ascertain whether domestic law was correctly applied:

> It is in the first place for the national authorities, notably the courts, to interpret and apply domestic law. However, since under Article 5, paragraph 1 (art. 5-1), failure to comply with domestic law entails a breach of the Convention, it follows that the Court can and should exercise a certain power to review whether this law has been complied with (see the Bouamar v. Belgium judgment of 29 February 1988, Series A No. 129, p. 21, paragraph 49). [For a slightly different wording: see the Wloch v. Poland judgment of 19 October 2000, Application No. 27785/95, paragraph 110.]

In the Wassink v. the Netherlands case, the State Prosecutor had requested the President of a court to extend the applicant's psychiatric confinement. The President extended the applicant's detention, but without the attendance of a registrar, as required by law. The President explained that circumstances connected with the organisation of the court prevented a registrar from being present in all cases of emergency internment: there were three large psychiatric hospitals within the area for which the court was responsible and the court was understaffed. The applicant had brought actions against that decision, notably on that ground. In his submissions, the Attorney General attached to the Court of Cassation considered that the second of the applicant's pleas (absence of a registrar) was well founded, but the Court of Cassation declared the appeal inadmissible on the ground that the applicant no longer had an interest in having the contested decision annulled, since the maximum period of emergency internment had already expired. The Court held:

> [...] the fact that no registrar was present at the hearing infringed Article 72 of Regulation I made in pursuance of the Judiciary (Organisation) Act (see paragraph 18 above) and this was also the opinion of the Attorney General.

> Consequently, there was in this respect a failure to comply with a "procedure prescribed by law", which amounted to a breach of Article 5, paragraph 1 (art. 5-1), of the Convention. Indeed the Government conceded this.

It remains to distinguish cases of error from those of intentional breach of procedures prescribed by law. In the Bozano v. France judgment, the Court stated (the Bozano v. France judgment of 18 December 1986, Series A No. 111, p. 23, paragraph 55):

> The applicant contended that the police action of 26 to 27 October 1979 was automatically deprived of any legal basis when the deportation order was retroactively quashed by the Limoges Administrative Court.
>
> The Commission's Delegate disagreed with this contention. The Government argued that it was inconsistent with the Commission's case-law (report of 17 July 1980 on Application No. 6871/75, Caprino v. the United Kingdom, p. 23, paragraph 65), but they did not state this as their firm opinion; in their view it was a complex point and one which the applicant had not given the French courts an opportunity to consider.
>
> The argument adduced on Mr Bozano's behalf does not entirely convince the Court either, despite its undeniable logic. It may happen that a Contracting State's agents conduct themselves unlawfully in good faith. In such cases, a subsequent finding by the courts that there has been a failure to comply with domestic law may not necessarily retrospectively affect the validity, under domestic law, of any implementing measures taken in the meantime.
>
> On the other hand, it is conceivable that matters would be different if the authorities at the outset knowingly contravened the legislation in force and, in particular, if their original decision was an abuse of powers.

Thus, in the Benham v. the United Kingdom judgment (10 June 1996, *Reports of Judgments and Decisions* 1996-III, p. 765, paragraph 42), the Court stated:

> A period of detention will in principle be lawful if it is carried out pursuant to a court order. A subsequent finding that the court erred under domestic law in making the order will not necessarily retrospectively affect the validity of the intervening period of detention. For this reason, the Strasbourg organs have consistently refused to uphold applications from persons convicted of criminal offences who complain that their convictions or sentences were found by the appellate courts to have been based on errors of fact or law (see the Bozano v. France judgment of 18 December 1986, Series A No. 111, p. 23, paragraph 55, and the report of the Commission of 9 March 1978 on Application No. 7629/76, Krzycki v. Germany, *Decisions and Reports* 13, pp. 60-61).

In cases in which compliance with and the interpretation of the law present no difficulties, such as the observance of certain time-limits, a breach of the legal requirements will entail a violation of Article 5. In that regard, one case is of particular interest to practitioners: exceeding the prescribed period of detention in custody entails in itself a violation of Article 5, paragraph 1.*c* (the K.-F. v. Germany judgment of 27 November 1997, Application No. 25629/94, *Reports* 1997-VII, paragraphs 70-73):

> The Court reiterates in this connection that the list of exceptions to the right to liberty secured in Article 5, paragraph 1, is an exhaustive one and only a narrow

interpretation of those exceptions is consistent with the aim of that provision, namely to ensure that no one is arbitrarily deprived of his or her liberty (see, as the most recent authority, the Giulia Manzoni judgment cited above, p. 1191, paragraph 25).

It is true that the Court has accepted that, in certain circumstances, there may be some limited delay before a detained person is released. However, this has been in cases where the period of detention was not laid down in advance by statute and ended as a result of a court order. Practical considerations relating to the running of the courts and the completion of special formalities mean that the execution of such a court order may take time (see the Quinn v. France judgment of 22 March 1995, Series A No. 311, p. 17, paragraph 42, and the Giulia Manzoni judgment cited above, p. 1191, paragraph 25).

However, in the instant case, the maximum period of twelve hours' detention for the purposes of checking identity was laid down by law and was absolute. Since the maximum period of detention was known in advance, the authorities responsible for the detention were under a duty to take all necessary precautions to ensure that the permitted duration was not exceeded. That applies also to the recording of Mr K.-F.'s personal details, which – being included among the measures for checking identity – should have been carried out during the period of detention allotted for that purpose.

Having regard to those factors, the Court holds that, because the maximum period laid down by law for detaining the applicant was exceeded, there has been a breach of Article 5, paragraph 1.*c.*

Last, in the Kawka v. Poland judgment (9 January 2001, Application No. 25874/94, paragraph 48), the Court observed, as is its wont:

However, the "lawfulness" of detention under domestic law is the primary, but not always a decisive element. The Court must, in addition, be satisfied that detention during the period under consideration, was compatible with the purpose of Article 5, paragraph 1, of the Convention, which is to prevent persons from being deprived of their liberty in an arbitrary manner.

However, it also pointed out in regard to compliance with the procedures prescribed by law (paragraphs 48, in fine, and 49):

Moreover, the Court must ascertain whether domestic law itself is in conformity with the Convention, including the general principles expressed or implied therein (see, among many other authorities, the Winterwerp v. the Netherlands judgment of 24 October 1979, Series A No. 33, pp. 19-20, paragraph 45; and the Erkalo v. the Netherlands judgment of 2 September 1998, *Reports of Judgments and Decisions* 1998-VI, p. 2477, paragraph 52).

The Court stresses in this connection that where deprivation of liberty is concerned, it is particularly important that the general principle of legal certainty is satisfied. It is therefore essential that the conditions for deprivation of liberty under domestic law should be clearly defined, and that the law itself be foreseeable in its application, so that it meets the standard of "lawfulness" set by the Convention, a standard which requires that all law should be sufficiently precise to allow the person – if needed, to obtain the appropriate advice – to foresee, to a degree that is reasonable in the circumstances, the consequences which a given action may entail (see the S.W. v. the United Kingdom judgment of 22 November 1995, Series A No. 335-B, pp. 41-42, paragraphs 35-36, and, *mutatis mutandis*, the *Sunday Times* v. the United Kingdom (No. 1) judgment of 26 April 1979, Series A No. 30, p. 31, paragraph 49; the Halford v. the United Kingdom judgment of 25 June 1997, *Reports* 1997-III, p. 1017, paragraph 49; and the Steel and Others v. the United Kingdom judgment of 23 September 1998, *Reports* 1998-VII, p. 2735, paragraph 54).

The wording of the Dougoz v. Greece judgment of 6 March 2001, Application No. 40907/98, perfectly summarises the situation (paragraph 55):

> [...] the Court recalls that in laying down that any deprivation of liberty must be effected "in accordance with a procedure prescribed by law", Article 5, paragraph 1, primarily requires that any arrest or detention have a legal basis in domestic law. However, these words do not merely refer back to domestic law; they also relate to the quality of the law, requiring it to be compatible with the rule of law, a concept inherent in all Articles of the Convention. Quality in this sense implies that where a national law authorises deprivation of liberty, it must be sufficiently accessible and precise, in order to avoid all risk of arbitrariness (see the Amuur v. France judgment of 25 June 1996, *Reports of Judgments and Decisions* 1996-III, paragraph 50).

General observations on the cases set out in Article 5, paragraph 1

The cases of deprivation of liberty provided for in Article 5, paragraph 1, call for the following general remarks.

These cases of deprivation are listed exhaustively. The Court therefore considers that they must be given a strict interpretation. In the Ciulla v. Italy judgment (22 February 1989, Series A No. 148, p. 18, paragraph 41), the Court stated:

> Certainly the Court does not underestimate the importance of Italy's struggle against organised crime, but it observes that the exhaustive list of permissible exceptions in paragraph 1 of Article 5 (art. 5-1) of the Convention must be interpreted strictly (see, as the most recent authority, the Bouamar judgment of 29 February 1988, Series A No. 129, p. 19, paragraph 43).

Clearly, that does not preclude a number of grounds of detention based on Article 5 from being applicable. The Court has frequently had occasion to state (see, for example, the Eriksen v. Norway judgment of 27 May 1997, Application No. 17391/90, *Reports* 1997-III, paragraphs 76 and 85-86):

> The Court reiterates that Article 5, paragraph 1, of the Convention (art. 5-1) contains a list of permissible grounds of deprivation of liberty which is exhaustive. However, the applicability of one ground does not necessarily preclude that of another; a detention may, depending on the circumstances, be justified under more than one sub-paragraph (see, for instance, the X. v. the United Kingdom judgment of 5 November 1981, Series A No. 46, pp. 17-18, paragraphs 36-39).
>
> [...]
>
> In the light of the foregoing, the Court is satisfied that the detention in issue was directly linked to the applicant's initial conviction in 1984 and can thus be

regarded as "lawful detention [...] after conviction by a competent court" for the purposes of Article 5, paragraph 1.*a*, of the Convention (art. 5-1-a).

The Court has come to the conclusion that, in the exceptional circumstances of the present case, the applicant's detention on remand could also be justified on the basis of paragraph 1.*c* of Article 5 (art. 5-1-c), as detention of a person "when it is reasonably considered necessary to prevent his committing an offence".

However, the Court does not systematically carry out a close examination of all the sub-paragraphs of Article 5, paragraph 1. In the same case, it stated (paragraphs 87-88):

The Court accordingly concludes that the deprivation of the applicant's liberty from 25 February to 15 May 1990 was justified under both sub-paragraphs *a* and *c* of Article 5, paragraph 1, of the Convention (art. 5-1-a, art. 5-1-c).

Having reached that conclusion, the Court does not find it necessary to examine whether sub-paragraph *e* (art. 5-1-e) also applied in the instant case.

It is still the case that detention is not lawful under Article 5 unless it genuinely pursues one of the aims set out in that provision. The conduct of the detention must indicate that it is actually justified by the aim(s) referred to in Article 5, paragraph 1, on which the respondent State relies. From that aspect, the Court ascertains in particular that there has not been an abuse of procedure. That approach is quite clear in the Quinn v France judgment on the case of deprivation of liberty provided for in sub-paragraph *f*. The Court stated (judgment of 22 March 1995, Series A No. 311, p. 19, paragraph 47):

[...] the Court does not discern in the present case any evidence to suggest that the detention pending extradition pursued an aim other than that for which it was ordered and that it was pre-trial detention in disguise. In particular the circumstances of Mr Quinn's arrest and the fact that proceedings were conducted concurrently cannot in themselves warrant the conclusion that there was abuse, for purposes relating to national law, of the extradition procedure and accordingly that the detention ordered in response to the request of the Geneva investigating judge was unlawful.

Thus, the Court requires not only compliance with the procedures prescribed by law in the sense indicated above, but also that any deprivation of liberty complies with the aim pursued by Article 5: to protect the individual against arbitrariness. The Court ascertains whether the authorities showed bad faith in using the possibilities of detention provided for in Article 5. In the Kemmache v. France (No. 3) judgment, Series A No. 296-C, p. 89, paragraph 45), the Court, after examining the decisions ordering provisional detention, observed that:

[Such decisions] disclose neither abuse of authority nor bad faith nor arbitrariness.

In certain cases, the Court has held that the detention had not been lawful for the purposes of Article 5 precisely because of arbitrariness on the part of the State. The Bozano v. France judgment (18 December 1986, Series A No. 111, p. 23, paragraph 54, and p. 26, paragraph 60) provides an example. That case concerned a person who had been convicted in Italy and who resided in France; an attempt to extradite him had been unsuccessful because the French courts refused to order his extradition; the French authorities had then arrested him in order to expel him to Switzerland; and he ended up in Italy, where he served his sentence. The proceedings related to his brief detention by France.

In that case, the Court first recalled that the requirement of lawfulness laid down in Article 5 as regards detention is essentially satisfied by compliance at national level with the procedural and substantive rules governing the various forms of deprivation of liberty provided for in Article 5 of the Convention.

However, the Court also stated in that judgment that that lawfulness cannot depart from the existence of good faith as regards the aim relied on and authorised by Article 5. Where there is arbitrariness there is unlawfulness. In that case, the Court observed (ibid.):

> The main issue to be determined is whether the disputed detention was "lawful", including whether it was in accordance with "a procedure prescribed by law". The Convention here refers essentially to national law and establishes the need to apply its rules, but it also requires that any measure depriving the individual of his liberty must be compatible with the purpose of Article 5 (art. 5), namely to protect the individual from arbitrariness (see, as the most recent authority, the Ashingdane judgment of 28 May 1985, Series A No. 93, p. 21, paragraph 44). What is at stake here is not only the "right to liberty" but also the "right to security of person".

> Viewing the circumstances of the case as a whole and having regard to the volume of material pointing in the same direction, the Court consequently concludes that the applicant's deprivation of liberty in the night of 26 to 27 October 1975 was neither "lawful", within the meaning of Article 5, paragraph 1.*f* (art. 5-1-f), nor compatible with the "right to security of person". Depriving Mr Bozano of his liberty in this way amounted in fact to a disguised form of extradition designed to circumvent the negative ruling of 15 May 1979 by the Indictment Division of the Limoges Court of Appeal, and not to "detention" necessary in the ordinary course of "action [...] taken with a view to deportation".

Detailed presentation of the different cases of deprivation of liberty

Article 5, paragraph 1.a – Detention possible after conviction by a court

Link of causation between detention and the conviction to which it is attributed

The above-mentioned Bozano v. France judgment (18 December 1986, Series A No. 111, pp. 22-23, paragraph 53) provides an interpretation of the expression "detained after" conviction and the link of causation which it implies. After condemning the deprivation of liberty imposed on Mr Bozano in the context of an alleged expulsion (Article 5, paragraph 1.*f,* see above), the

Court went on to state that France could not rely on Article 5, paragraph 1.*a*, to justify detention which it had decided upon in order to remove Mr Bozano to Switzerland:

> The impugned forcible removal was effected "after" the aforementioned conviction only in a chronological sense. In the context of Article 5, paragraph 1.*a* (art. 5-1-a), however, the preposition "after" denotes a causal link in addition to a succession of events in time; it serves to designate detention "consequent upon" and not merely "subsequent to" the criminal court's decision (see, as the most recent authority, the Van Droogenbroeck judgment of 24 June 1982, Series A No. 50, p. 19, paragraph 35). This was not so in the instant case, since it was not incumbent on the French authorities themselves to execute the judgment delivered by the Genoa Assize Court of Appeal on 22 May 1975.

In the Eriksen v. Norway case, the Court had a further opportunity to adjudicate on the link of causation between detention and a previous conviction. On 20 September 1984, the Kragerø regional court had found the applicant guilty of the offences charged and had sentenced him to twenty days' imprisonment. The court also authorised the prosecution to use any of the security measures referred to in Article 39, paragraph 1, of the Criminal Code during a maximum period of five years. The court considered that it could not prevent the competent authorities from having recourse, if necessary, to internment on grounds of security in a prison or a security ward, in accordance with Article 39, paragraph 1.*e* and *f,* having regard to Mr Eriksen's physical strength and to his virtually complete lack of self-control in certain circumstances. The authorities needed to do so. The applicant then challenged the decision on security internment before the Supreme Court.

In a decision of 12 January 1985, that decision was upheld. On 26 October 1989, the institution in which the applicant was interned considered the question of the prolongation of the security measures, since the court authorisation was due to expire on 25 February 1990, and decided to recommend that the prosecution extend that authorisation. On 7 February 1990, the chief of police requested the regional court to place the applicant in provisional detention for four weeks, pursuant to Article 171 of the Code of Criminal Procedure, 1981, in order to obtain a medical opinion for the hearing of the application for prolongation of the authorisation to apply security measures. It was made clear that the previous authorisation would expire on 25 February 1990. On 12 February 1990, the regional court examined the question of provisional detention. The applicant claimed that such detention after 25 February 1990 would amount to punishing him twice for the same offences. He further alleged that the authorities were requesting provisional detention on the sole ground that they had failed to take the necessary procedural measures, although they had been aware for five years of the date of expiry of the authorisation in question. On 12 February 1990, the Kragerø regional court decided to place the applicant in detention for four weeks after 25 February 1990. On 14 May 1990, the Attorney General (Riksadvokaten) withdrew his request for prolongation of the authorisation to subject Mr Eriksen to security measures. The applicant was released. He subsequently committed further offences. The Court held (the Eriksen v. Norway judgment of 27 May 1997, *Reports* 1997-III, paragraph 68) :

> In the Commission's view the detention could not be justified under sub-paragraph *a* (art. 5-1-a). The Delegate stated that it could not be decisive under that provision (art. 5-1-a) that there was a formal and causal link between the detention and the initial conviction warranting the Article 39 authorisation in 1985. Otherwise, it would have the unfortunate consequence that national authorities would be allowed to detain a person on remand for a long time, in this case almost three months, after the expiry of a maximum period and even if it had not been established that the conditions under any of the sub-paragraphs of Article 5, paragraph 1 (art. 5-1), had been fulfilled. The criteria of causal link had been applied by the Court in cases of quite different nature, namely in relation to orders for re-detention imposed during the period of a judicial authorisation given on the basis of an initial conviction (see the Van Droogenbroeck v. Belgium judgment of 24 June 1982, Series A No. 50, pp. 21-22, paragraph 40, and the Weeks v. the United Kingdom judgment of 2 March 1987, Series A No. 114, p. 26, paragraph 49). However, the present case concerned detention after the expiry of such an authorisation.

The applicant maintained that in the absence of a new offence, the decision to extend the authorisation to use security measures did not embody an assessment of culpability or constitute a "conviction" within the meaning of sub-paragraph *a* (art. 5-1-a). A deprivation of liberty consequent upon such a decision could not therefore be detention "after conviction" for the purposes of that provision (art. 5-1-a). The Court went on (same judgment, paragraphs 78-85) :

> There can be no doubt that if a court decides to extend preventive detention imposed by way of a security measure prior to the expiry of the authorised period, such a prolongation in principle falls within Article 5, paragraph 1.*a* (art. 5-1-a), as "detention of a person after conviction by a competent court". Admittedly, with the passage of time, the link between the initial conviction and a prolongation may become less strong and may eventually be broken, where the prolongation no longer has any connection with the objectives of the initial decision or was based on an assessment that was unreasonable in terms of those objectives (see, *mutatis mutandis*, the above-mentioned Van Droogenbroeck judgment, pp. 21-22, paragraph 40).
>
> It may not always be possible to obtain the court's decision on a request for an extension prior to expiry of the original period, either because that period is rather short – as is normally the case – or because it may be necessary to obtain further updated medical reports which may not be available by the expiry date. For this reason the second paragraph of Article 171 of the Code of Criminal Procedure provides that the person concerned may be detained on remand when it is proposed to extend the maximum period for using security measures [...].
>
> The Commission found no reason to doubt that the procedural requirements of Norwegian law had been observed [...].
>
> The Commission further expressed the view that the facts of the case disclosed that the authorities' fear that the applicant, if released, might commit criminal acts had been well-founded. On the other hand, it found that the applicant's

detention after 25 February 1990 pursuant to Article 171 of the Code of Criminal Procedure had not been based on, or related to, any criminal act he had committed and that the detention orders had had no connection in law with any investigation which had been conducted in this respect.

However, the Court observes that, in a decision of 26 January 1996 in a similar case, the Norwegian Supreme Court stressed the importance of the connection between the initial offence grounding an authorisation to use security measures and any prolongation of such measures. The Supreme Court emphasised that one could not read into the second paragraph of Article 171 of the Code of Criminal Procedure a requirement of reasonable suspicion of a new criminal offence having been committed. Since the initial criminal offence could justify prolongation of an authorisation to use security measures, that offence could also furnish the basis for remand in custody under that provision provided that the other conditions, such as the risk of reoffending, were met. Where a decision to remand an offender in custody was made as a step in the proceedings concerning prolongation of security measures, the Supreme Court considered that the remand in custody had the necessary connection with the criminal acts committed (and their lawful prosecution). This interpretation of Article 171 would not in the Supreme Court's view contravene the Convention; in this respect it referred to Article 5, paragraph 1.*a* and *c* (art. 5-1-a, art. 5-1-c) (see paragraph 57 above).

The Court has considered whether this approach of the Norwegian Supreme Court to the interpretation and application of Article 5, paragraph 1.*a* and *c* (art. 5-1-a, art. 5-1-c), in relation to detention under the provisions in issue may also be followed in the particular circumstances of the present case.

The applicant's detention from 25 February to 15 May 1990 was ordered pending examination of the appropriateness of prolonging the authorisation to use security measures. Had a prolongation been granted, it would, as transpires from the relevant court decisions (see paragraphs 37-39 and 41 above), have been based on the offences which had grounded the applicant's initial conviction [...].

Furthermore, the detention was consistent with the objectives of that authorisation (see paragraph 20 above). [...]

It was essentially because of the persistence of the above-mentioned circumstances, and the likelihood of the Article 39 authorisation being prolonged, that the District Court ordered the applicant's detention under Article 171 of the Code of Criminal Procedure and that the appellate courts upheld those orders (see paragraphs 37-39, 41 and 46 above).

In the light of the foregoing, the Court is satisfied that the detention in issue was directly linked to the applicant's initial conviction in 1984 and can thus be regarded as "lawful detention [...] after conviction by a competent court" for the purposes of Article 5, paragraph 1.*a*, of the Convention (art. 5-1-a).

The nature of a conviction which justifies detention under Article 5, paragraph 1.a

In the V. v. the United Kingdom judgment, the Court considered the case of a minor found guilty of murder whom the judge had sentenced, in accordance with the law, to be detained during Her Majesty's pleasure. The applicant claimed that such a decision was arbitrary and that there had been a violation of Article 5, paragraph 1. In his submission, it was arbitrary to impose the same penalty – detention during Her Majesty's pleasure – on all young persons found guilty of murder without taking their history and personal needs into account. In that regard, he relied on Article 37, paragraph *b*, of the United Nations Convention on the Rights of the Child and on Rules 16 and 17, paragraph 1.*a* and *b*, of the Beijing Rules, which, *inter alia*, require that sentences of detention imposed on children be as short as possible and that sentencers have regard, as the guiding factor, to the well-being of the child. The Court rejected that argument and referred to Article 3 of the Convention (the V. v. the United Kingdom judgment of 16 December 1999, Application No. 24888/94, paragraphs 103-104):

> The Government, with whom the Commission agreed, denied that the sentence of detention during Her Majesty's pleasure was unlawful or arbitrary, and pointed out that its purpose was to enable consideration to be given to the specific circumstances of the applicant's case, so that he would be detained only for so long as was necessary with regard to the need for punishment, rehabilitation and the protection of the community.

> The Court observes that the applicant was detained following conviction by a competent court; in other words, his detention falls within the scope of Article 5, paragraph 1.*a*, of the Convention. There can be no question but that the sentence of detention during Her Majesty's pleasure is lawful under English law and was imposed in accordance with a procedure prescribed by law. Moreover, it cannot be said that the applicant's detention is not in conformity with the purposes of the deprivation of liberty permitted by Article 5, paragraph 1.*a*, so as to be arbitrary (see the Weeks v. the United Kingdom judgment of 2 March 1987, Series A No. 114, p. 23, paragraph 42; and the Hussain judgment cited above, p. 269, paragraph 53, where the Court referred to the question of the lifelong detention of a juvenile as possibly raising an issue under Article 3, but not Article 5, paragraph 1).

> It follows that there has been no violation of Article 5, paragraph 1, of the Convention in the present case.

The application of penalties and Article 5, paragraph 1.a

The Court has had the opportunity to consider the compatibility of measures for the application of penalties with Article 5, paragraph 1, in conjunction with Article 14. In the case of Gerger v. Turkey, the applicant claimed that because he had been given a custodial sentence under the provisions of Law No. 3713, the Anti-Terrorism Act, he was unable to obtain conditional release until he had served three quarters of his sentence, whereas those sentenced under the general law were able to take advantage of that provision once they had completed one half of their sentence. He regarded this as discrimination. The Court observed (the Gerger v. Turkey judgment of 8 July 1999, Application No. 24919/94, paragraphs 67-69):

> The Court considers that this question relates to "the lawful detention of a person after conviction by a competent court" and should therefore be examined under Article 14 taken together with Article 5, paragraph 1.*a*, of the Convention. [...]

The Government submitted that Article 5, paragraph 1.*a*, did not secure convicted prisoners a right to automatic parole. They added that in any event the restrictions on entitlement to parole imposed on persons convicted of an offence under the Prevention of Terrorism Act were warranted by the intrinsic seriousness of such offences.

The Court considers, firstly, that, although Article 5, paragraph 1.*a*, of the Convention does not guarantee a right to automatic parole, an issue may arise under that provision taken together with Article 14 of the Convention if a settled sentencing policy affects individuals in a discriminatory manner.

The Court notes that in principle the aim of Law No. 3713 is to penalise people who commit terrorist offences and that anyone convicted under that law will be treated less favourably with regard to automatic parole than persons convicted under the ordinary law. It deduces from that fact that the distinction is made not between different groups of people, but between different types of offence, according to the legislature's view of their gravity. The Court sees no ground for concluding that that practice amounts to a form of "discrimination" that is contrary to the Convention. Consequently, there has been no violation of Article 14 taken together with Article 5, paragraph 1.*a*, of the Convention.

Article 5, paragraph 1.b – Detention to secure the fulfilment of an obligation prescribed by law

The Lawless judgment (1 July 1961, Series A No. 3, p. 47, paragraph 9) sets out the conditions for the application of sub-paragraph *b*. The Court held in that judgment that "obligations prescribed by law", which render detention possible, are specific obligations and not obligations of a general nature (such as the obligation to respect the existing legal order) In that case, Mr Lawless had been arrested because he was a member of the IRA. The Court observed:

> [...] with regard to Article 5, paragraph 1.*b* (art. 5-1-b), in fine, the detention of Lawless by order of a Minister of State on suspicion of being engaged in activities prejudicial to the preservation of public peace and order or to the security of the State cannot be deemed to be a measure taken "in order to secure the fulfilment of any obligation prescribed by law", since that clause does not contemplate arrest or detention for the prevention of offences against public peace and public order or against the security of the State but for securing the execution of specific obligations imposed by law.

The Court has also specified, if necessary, that the obligation must exist prior to the incarceration which is supposed to sanction the violation of the obligation. In the Ciulla v. Italy case, the applicant had been incarcerated until the decision requiring him to reside in a certain place became enforceable, in order to ensure that he did not avoid doing so. The Court stated (judgment of 22 February 1989, Series A No. 148, paragraph 36):

> The Government did not claim that there had been "non-compliance with the [...] order of a court" but submitted that Mr Ciulla's arrest and detention were intended to "secure the fulfilment of [an] obligation prescribed by law".

> These latter words denote an obligation, of a specific and concrete nature (see the Guzzardi judgment of 6 November 1980, Series A No. 39, paragraph 101), already incumbent on the person concerned. But the obligation – in itself a specific and

103

concrete one – to go and live in the designated locality arose only on 24 May 1984 (see paragraph 17 above) and not as early as 8 May 1984, when the impugned decision was given.

For cases of incarceration for non-payment of taxes, see the Benham v. the United Kingdom judgment (10 June 1996, *Reports of Judgments and Decisions* 1996-III, p. 765, paragraphs 35-47) or the Peerks and Others v. the United Kingdom judgment (12 October 1999, Applications Nos. 25277/94 and 25279/94) (no violation of Article 5, paragraph 1).

Article 5, paragraph 1.c – Detention for the purpose of bringing a person before the competent legal authority when he has or on reasonable suspicion of his having committed an offence

The detention must form part of a criminal context

In the Ciulla v. Italy case (judgment of 22 February 1989, Series A No. 148, paragraph 38), the Court held that:

> [...] sub-paragraph *c* (art. 5-1-c), permits deprivation of liberty only in connection with criminal proceedings. This is apparent from its wording, which must be read in conjunction both with sub-paragraph *a* and with paragraph 3 (art. 5-1-c + 5-1-a, art. 5-1-c + 5-3), which forms a whole with it (on the latter point see, *inter alia*, the de Jong, Baljet and Van den Brink judgment previously cited, Series A No. 77, p. 22, paragraph 44).

In the Wloch v. Poland case, the Court held (judgment of 19 October 2000, Application No. 27785/95, paragraph 109):

> [...] Article 5, paragraph 1.*c*, requires that the facts invoked can be reasonably considered as falling under one of the sections describing criminal behaviour in the Criminal Code. Thus, there could clearly not be a "reasonable suspicion" if the acts or facts invoked against a detained person did not constitute a crime at the time when they occurred.

In that case, the applicant had been placed in provisional detention on suspicion of being involved in trafficking in children, contrary to Article IX of the transitional provisions of the 1969 Code, and of having incited certain persons to give false evidence during the judicial proceedings. Up to the material time, the Polish courts had never applied that provision and, accordingly, it had given rise to significant problems of interpretation, concerning as it did constituent elements of the offence. The Court considered that, overall, there was no evidence that the interpretation of the legal provisions on which the domestic authorities relied was so arbitrary or unreasonable as to render the applicant's detention unlawful.

The arrest or detention must be justified by "reasonable suspicions" that the person concerned has committed an offence or by reasonable grounds to believe that it is "necessary" to prevent him from committing an offence

In the Fox, Campbell and Hartley v. the United Kingdom judgment (30 August 1990, Series A No. 182, p. 16, paragraphs 32 and 34), which concerned arrests carried out by the Northern Ireland police on the basis of statutory provisions, the Court defined a "plausible suspicion" justifying arrest:

> The "reasonableness" of the suspicion on which an arrest must be based forms an essential part of the safeguard against arbitrary arrest and detention which is laid down in Article 5, paragraph 1.*c* (art. 5-1-c). The Court agrees with the Commission and the Government that having a "reasonable suspicion" presupposes the existence of facts or information which would satisfy an objective observer that the person concerned may have committed the offence. What may be regarded as "reasonable" will however depend upon all the circumstances.

> In this respect, terrorist crime falls into a special category. Because of the attendant risk of loss of life and human suffering, the police are obliged to act with utmost urgency in following up all information, including information from secret sources. Further, the police may frequently have to arrest a suspected terrorist on the basis of information which is reliable but which cannot, without putting in jeopardy the source of the information, be revealed to the suspect or produced in court to support a charge.

> As the Government pointed out, in view of the difficulties inherent in the investigation and prosecution of terrorist-type offences in Northern Ireland, the "reasonableness" of the suspicion justifying such arrests cannot always be judged according to the same standards as are applied in dealing with conventional crime. Nevertheless, the exigencies of dealing with terrorist crime cannot justify stretching the notion of "reasonableness" to the point where the essence of the safeguard secured by Article 5, paragraph 1.*c* (art. 5-1-c), is impaired (see, *mutatis mutandis*, the Brogan and Others judgment previously cited, Series A No. 145-B, pp. 32-33, paragraph 59).

> The majority of the Commission, with whom the applicants agreed, were of the opinion that "the Government [had] not provided any information which would allow the Commission to conclude that the suspicions against the applicants at the time of their arrest were 'reasonable' within the meaning of Article 5 paragraph 1.*c* (art. 5-1-c), of the Convention or that their arrest was based on anything more than the 'honestly held suspicion' which was required under Northern Ireland law" (see paragraph 61 of the Commission's report).

> The Government argued that they were unable to disclose the acutely sensitive material on which the suspicion against the three applicants was based because of the risk of disclosing the source of the material and thereby placing in danger the lives and safety of others. In support of their contention that there was nevertheless reasonable suspicion, they pointed to the facts that the first two applicants had previous convictions for serious acts of terrorism connected with the Provisional IRA (see paragraph 12 above) and that all three applicants were questioned during their detention about specific terrorist acts of which they were suspected (see paragraphs 10 and 14 above). In the Government's submission these facts were sufficient to confirm that the arresting officer had a bona fide or genuine suspicion and they maintained that there was no difference in substance between a bona fide or genuine suspicion and a reasonable suspicion. The Government observed moreover that the applicants themselves did not contest that they were arrested and detained in connection with acts of terrorism (see paragraph 55 of the Commission's report).

The Government also stated that, although they could not disclose the information or identify the source of the information which led to the arrest of the applicants, there did exist in the case of the first and second applicants strong grounds for suggesting that at the time of their arrest the applicants were engaged in intelligence gathering and courier work for the Provisional IRA and that in the case of the third applicant there was available to the police material connecting him with the kidnapping attempt about which he was questioned.

Certainly Article 5, paragraph 1.*c* (art. 5-1-c), of the Convention should not be applied in such a manner as to put disproportionate difficulties in the way of the police authorities of the Contracting States in taking effective measures to counter organised terrorism (see, *mutatis mutandis*, the Klass and Others judgment of 6 September 1978, Series A No. 28, pp. 27 and 30-31, paragraphs 58 and 68). It follows that the Contracting States cannot be asked to establish the reasonableness of the suspicion grounding the arrest of a suspected terrorist by disclosing the confidential sources of supporting information or even facts which would be susceptible of indicating such sources or their identity.

Nevertheless, the Court must be enabled to ascertain whether the essence of the safeguard afforded by Article 5, paragraph 1.*c* (art. 5-1-c), has been secured. Consequently the respondent Government have to furnish at least some facts or information capable of satisfying the Court that the arrested person was reasonably suspected of having committed the alleged offence. This is all the more necessary where, as in the present case, the domestic law does not require reasonable suspicion, but sets a lower threshold by merely requiring honest suspicion.

The Court accepts that the arrest and detention of each of the present applicants was based on a bona fide suspicion that he or she was a terrorist, and that each of them, including Mr Hartley, was questioned during his or her detention about specific terrorist acts of which he or she was suspected.

The fact that Mr Fox and Ms Campbell both have previous convictions for acts of terrorism connected with the IRA (see paragraph 12 above), although it could reinforce a suspicion linking them to the commission of terrorist-type offences, cannot form the sole basis of a suspicion justifying their arrest in 1986, some seven years later.

The fact that all the applicants, during their detention, were questioned about specific terrorist acts, does no more than confirm that the arresting officers had a genuine suspicion that they had been involved in those acts, but it cannot satisfy an objective observer that the applicants may have committed these acts.

The aforementioned elements on their own are insufficient to support the conclusion that there was "reasonable suspicion".

The Court applied those principles in another recent case involving terrorism (the O'Hara v. the United Kingdom judgment of 16 October 2001, Application No. 37555/97, paragraphs 37-44):

In the present case, the Court recalls that the applicant was arrested by Detective Constable S. on suspicion of having committed a terrorist offence, namely the murder of Mr Konig. After six days and thirteen hours in detention, during which time he was questioned by police officers without making any reply, the applicant was released. The lawfulness of the arrest was challenged by the applicant in domestic proceedings, where the courts rejected his complaints.

The Court notes, first of all, that the standard of suspicion set by domestic law for arrest is that of honest suspicion on reasonable grounds (Section 12, paragraph 1.*b*, of the 1984 Act, see paragraphs 23-24 above). The present application is therefore to be distinguished from the previous cases of Fox, Campbell and Hartley and Murray v. the United Kingdom (cited above) in which the Court examined complaints about arrest effected under provisions requiring only an honest suspicion. In the applicant's case, his claims that his arrest was not justified by a suspicion, held on reasonable grounds, that he had committed an offence, was examined by three levels of domestic courts. In those proceedings, evidence was given by the arresting officer, Detective Constable S., concerning the circumstances of the arrest and the applicant was given the opportunity to cross examine. This must be regarded *per se* as providing a significant safeguard against arbitrary arrest.

As regards the basis for the applicant's arrest, the arresting officer Detective Constable S. gave evidence that he had been given information by a superior officer, at a briefing prior to the arrest, that the applicant was suspected of involvement in the murder of Kurt Konig. [...] To the extent therefore that the applicant complains before this Court that no information was elicited during the domestic proceedings concerning the briefing, the Court considers that this was the consequence of the way in which the applicant pursued his claims.

In the proceedings before the Court, the Government have explained that the information which led the police to arrest the applicant was obtained independently from four separate informers, who had proved previously reliable and whose information concerning the murder was consistent. It was this information which was the basis of the decision to arrest the applicant and in respect of which instructions were given by the briefing officer to the arresting officer Detective Constable S. The applicant has disputed that this information was in fact received or that it could be regarded as reliable, since he was not involved in the incident. He argued that he was arrested as part of an arbitrary police policy which targeted him as a prominent member of Sinn Fein. The Court recalls, however, that no challenge was made in the domestic proceedings by the applicant to the good faith of any of the officers involved in the arrest or detention. [...] It had not been disputed by the applicant that a briefing had occurred, attended by police officers, at which information was passed on concerning the identity of persons involved in the murder of Kurt Konig and steps taken to plan a number of arrests.

The Court recalls that in the case of Fox, Campbell and Hartley (judgment cited above, pp. 8-9, paragraphs 8-14), two of the applicants had been arrested when their car had been stopped and searched. There had allegedly been information known to the police prior to this incident that they were suspected of being members of the IRA and involved in intelligence gathering. The third applicant had been arrested on suspicion of involvement in a kidnapping, without any indication given as to the basis for the suspicion beyond reference to sensitive material available to the police connecting him with the incident. This was found by the Court in respect of all three applicants not to meet the minimum standard set by Article 5, paragraph 1, for judging the reasonableness of an arrest of an individual. On the other hand, in the Murray case (judgment cited above, p. 28, paragraphs 61-62) the standard was satisfied when the arrest of the applicant, on suspicion of involvement in the collection of funds for the purchase of arms, was based on information provided to the arresting officer that the applicant's brothers had been convicted in the United States of similar offences which implied collaboration with "trustworthy" persons in Northern Ireland and the applicant was known to have visited the United States and maintained contacts with her brothers, elements which were not necessarily incriminating of the applicant. There may thus be a fine line between those cases where the suspicion grounding the arrest is not sufficiently founded on objective facts and those which are. Whether the requisite standard is satisfied and whether the guarantee against arbitrary arrest laid down by Article 5, paragraph 1.*c*, is thereby satisfied depends on the particular circumstances of the each case.

The suspicion in the present case was based on information passed on at a police briefing from informers which identified the applicant as one of a number of persons suspected of involvement in a specific terrorist event, the murder of Mr Konig. There is no basis in the material provided for the Court to reject the Government's submissions on this point. The arrest was therefore a pre-planned operation, more akin to the arrest in the Murray case, and was based on slightly more specific detail than in the Fox, Campbell and Hartley case. In these circumstances, and having regard to additional distinguishing elements referred to above (see paragraphs 38-40), the Court considers that the domestic courts' approach – that the judge was entitled on the sparse materials before him to infer the existence of reasonable grounds of suspicion – was not incompatible with the standard imposed by Article 5, paragraph 1.*c*, of the Convention.

The applicant argued, with some force, that police officers should not be able to hide behind references to anonymous informants by way of justifying abuse of their power of arrest. The Court re-iterates, however, that the applicant did not attempt to raise in the domestic proceedings any complaints concerning bad faith or oppression. [...]

The Court does not find therefore that the approach of the domestic courts to the standard of suspicion in this case removed the accountability of the police for arbitrary arrest or conferred on the police any impunity with regard to arrests conducted on the basis of confidential information. In the circumstances, the suspicion against the applicant reached the required level as it was based on specific information that he was involved in the murder of Kurt Konig and the purpose of the deprivation of liberty was to confirm or dispel that suspicion. The applicant can accordingly be said to have been arrested and detained on "reasonable suspicion" of a criminal offence, within the meaning of sub-paragraph *c* of Article 5, paragraph 1.

The Berktay v. Turkey case provides another example of the application of those principles (judgment of 1 March 2001, Application No. 22493/93, paragraphs 197-201, available in French only – unofficial translation):

The Court now turns to the particular circumstances of the case: the second applicant, who was seventeen years old at the material time, was being supervised by five police officers and deprived of his liberty while his home was being searched (paragraphs 128-129 above). However, the reasons for his arrest are not evident from the documents in the case-file. The record of the arrest of 3 February 1993 mentioned that the second applicant had been arrested on the ground of separatist propaganda; the applicants and Esma Berktay stated that Devrim had been arrested and placed in custody because he did not have his identity card with him.

Article 13, paragraph *g*, of the law on the duties and powers of the police, to which the Government refer, authorises any police officer to arrest, without a warrant, any person in respect of whom there is serious indication or evidence that he has committed or attempted to commit an offence (paragraph 117 above).

In that regard, the Court emphasises that the "plausibility" of the suspicion on which an arrest must be based constitutes an essential element of the protection afforded by Article 5, paragraph 1.*c*, against arbitrary deprivation of liberty. The fact that there are plausible suspicions presupposes the existence of facts or information which would satisfy an objective observer that the individual in question may have committed the offence. The Court reiterates that it is for the respondent Government to provide it with at least some facts or information capable of convincing it that there are plausible grounds for suspecting that the person arrested committed the alleged offence (see, among other authorities, the Fox, Campbell and Hartley v. the United Kingdom judgment of 30 August 1990, Series A No. 182, p. 16, paragraph 32).

Referring to its considerations on the evaluation of evidence concerning the arrest and detention of the second applicant (paragraphs 125-129 above), the Court observes that the evidence in the case-file does not support the conclusion that there were any plausible suspicions. Furthermore, since, apart from the record of the arrest, the Government have not provided any other indications in support of the suspicions against the second applicant, the Government's explanations do not satisfy the minimum conditions of Article 5, paragraph 1.*c*.

In those circumstances, the Court does not consider that the deprivation of liberty imposed on Devrim Berktay while his home was being searched was a "lawful detention" implemented because there were "plausible reasons to suspect that [the person concerned had] committed an offence".

The Eriksen v. Norway judgment, cited above (for an account of the facts, reference should be made to Article 5, paragraph 1.*a*) illustrates the situation in which it is necessary to prevent someone from committing an offence (the Eriksen v. Norway judgment of 27 May 1997, *Reports* 1997-III, paragraphs 70-71 and 86-87):

> The Government argued that the applicant's detention from 25 February to 15 May 1990 could also be justified on the basis of sub-paragraph *c* (art. 5-1-c), in that it had been imposed in connection with criminal proceedings against the applicant and could "reasonably [be] considered necessary to prevent his committing an offence".

> The Commission took the opposite view. The deprivation of liberty had not been based on or related to any criminal act committed by the applicant or any investigation pursued in this respect. Nor had it been ordered in the context of criminal proceedings instituted against the applicant. It had been designed rather to keep him detained while the authorities obtained the necessary evidence for the forthcoming hearing on the question of prolonging the authorisation to use

security measures under Article 39 of the Penal Code. The chief of police's request of 7 February 1990 had relied merely on the need to obtain a medical opinion pending the hearing on the Article 39 issue (see paragraph 35 above). The Delegate, in any event, pointed out that, to the extent that the detention was linked to the applicant's conviction in 1984, which the Commission disputed, it was sub-paragraph *a* (art. 5-1-a), not *c* (art. 5-1-c), which would be relevant. In this connection, he referred to the Court's Wemhoff v. Germany judgment (27 June 1968, Series A No. 7, p. 23, paragraph 9).

Furthermore, the Commission observed that the relevant court decisions had failed to mention any concrete and specific offence which it was necessary to prevent the applicant from committing. Rather, they had referred to a general risk of the applicant's threatening and violent behaviour because of his mental disorder. Whether his mental condition was such as to warrant the imposition of security measures remained to be determined at a later stage (see paragraphs 37-39, 41 and 44 above). In these circumstances, the applicant's detention on remand could not be based on Article 5, paragraph 1.*c* (art. 5-1-c), which should be given a narrow interpretation (see the Guzzardi v. Italy judgment of 6 November 1980, Series A No. 39, pp. 38-39, paragraph 102).

[...]

The Court has come to the conclusion that, in the exceptional circumstances of the present case, the applicant's detention on remand could also be justified on the basis of paragraph 1.*c* of Article 5 (art. 5-1-c), as detention of a person "when it is reasonably considered necessary to prevent his committing an offence".

In view of the nature and extent of the applicant's previous convictions for threatening behaviour and physical assault and his mental state at the relevant time (see paragraphs 6-19, 22, 26, 28, 30, 32 and 37 above), there were substantial grounds for believing that he would commit further similar offences. He had in fact done so after his release on 15 May 1990 (see paragraphs 50-51 above). The offences apprehended were thus sufficiently concrete and specific to meet the standard enunciated by the Court in the above-mentioned Guzzardi judgment (pp. 38-39, paragraph 102).

As a rule, Article 5, paragraph 1.*c* (art. 5-1-c), would not provide a justification for the re-detention or continued detention of a person who has served a sentence after conviction of a specific criminal offence where there is a suspicion that he might commit a further similar offence.

However, in the Court's opinion the position is different when a person is detained with a view to determining whether he should be subjected, after expiry of the maximum period prescribed by a court, to a further period of security detention imposed following conviction for a criminal offence. In a situation such as that in the present case, the authorities were entitled, having regard to the applicant's impaired mental state and history as well as to his established and foreseeable propensity for violence, to detain the applicant pending the determination by a court of the Prosecutor's request for a prolongation of the Article 39 authorisation.

Such a "bridging" detention was of a short duration, was imposed in order to bring the applicant before a judicial authority and was made necessary by the need to obtain updated medical reports on the applicant's mental health as well as by the serious difficulties facing the authorities in arranging preventive supervision outside prison due to the applicant's aggressive conduct and his objection to close supervision (see paragraphs 17, 19, 24, 26, 28, 33 and 49 above).

Against this background, the period of detention in question can be seen as closely linked to the original criminal proceedings in 1984 and the resulting conviction and security measures (see, *mutatis mutandis*, the Ciulla v. Italy judgment of 22 February 1989, Series A No. 148, p. 16, paragraph 38).

The Court accordingly concludes that the deprivation of the applicant's liberty from 25 February to 15 May 1990 was justified under both sub-paragraphs *a* and *c* of Article 5, paragraph 1, of the Convention (art. 5-1-a, art. 5-1-c).

An earlier judgment had already dealt with the compatibility between detention and the requirements of Article 5, paragraph 1.*c*, concerning the need to prevent offences (see the Ciulla v. Italy judgment of 22 February 1989, Series A No. 148, paragraph 40).

The purpose of the arrest must be to bring the person concerned before the competent judicial authority

The K.-F. v. Germany judgment (judgment of 27 November 1997, Application No. 25629/94, *Reports* 1997-VII, paragraphs 59-60), states:

> [...] Article 5, paragraph 1.*c*, [...] [requires] [...] that the arrest and detention be effected for the purpose of bringing the person concerned before the competent legal authority.

The older Lawless judgment stated that that requirement concerns all persons arrested or detained pursuant to that sub-paragraph. The Court states (judgment of 1 July 1961, Series A No. 3, p. 47, paragraph 14):

> [...] the wording of Article 5, paragraph 1.*c* (art. 5-1-c), is sufficiently clear [...] it is evident that the expression "effected for purpose of bringing him before the competent legal authority" qualifies every category of cases of arrest or detention referred to in that sub-paragraph (art. 5-1-c); whereas it follows that the said clause permits deprivation of liberty only when such deprivation is effected for the purpose of bringing the person arrested or detained before the competent judicial authority, irrespective of whether such person is a person who is reasonably suspected of having committed an offence, or a person whom it is reasonably considered necessary to restrain from committing an offence, or a person whom it reasonably considered necessary to restrain from absconding after having committed an offence;
>
> Whereas, further, paragraph 1.*c* of Article 5 (art. 5-1-c) can be construed only if read in conjunction with paragraph 3 of the same Article (art. 5-3), with which it forms a whole; whereas paragraph 3 (art. 5-3) stipulates categorically that "everyone arrested or detained in accordance with the provisions of paragraph 1.*c* of this Article (art. 5-1-c) shall be brought promptly before a judge [...]" and "shall be entitled to trial within a reasonable time"; whereas it plainly entails the obligation to bring everyone arrested or detained in any of the circumstances contemplated by the provisions of paragraph 1.*c* (art. 5-1-c) before a judge for the purpose of examining the question of deprivation of liberty or for the purpose of

111

deciding on the merits; whereas such is the plain and natural meaning of the wording of both paragraph 1.*c*, and paragraph 3 of Article 5 (art. 5-1-c, art. 5-3).

It must be pointed out that an arrest followed by custody, and then by release without charge or without being brought before the competent legal authority, in the absence of sufficient grounds, does not in itself entail a violation of Article 5. In the Brogan and Others v. the United Kingdom judgment of 29 November 1998, Applications Nos. 11209/84, 11234/84, 11266/84 and 11386/85, Series A No. 145-B, paragraph 53), the Court observed:

> The fact that the applicants were neither charged nor brought before a court does not necessarily mean that the purpose of their detention was not in accordance with Article 5, paragraph 1.*c* (art. 5-1-c). As the Government and the Commission have stated, the existence of such a purpose must be considered independently of its achievement and sub-paragraph *c* of Article 5, paragraph 1 (art. 5-1-c), does not presuppose that the police should have obtained sufficient evidence to bring charges, either at the point of arrest or while the applicants were in custody.
>
> Such evidence may have been unobtainable or, in view of the nature of the suspected offences, impossible to produce in court without endangering the lives of others. There is no reason to believe that the police investigation in this case was not in good faith or that the detention of the applicants was not intended to further that investigation by way of confirming or dispelling the concrete suspicions which, as the Court has found, grounded their arrest (see paragraph 51 above). Had it been possible, the police would, it can be assumed, have laid charges and the applicants would have been brought before the competent legal authority.
>
> Their arrest and detention must therefore be taken to have been effected for the purpose specified in paragraph 1.*c* (art. 5-1-c).

Domestic law on arrest and detention must satisfy certain criteria

As regards the requirement that the domestic law relied on as the basis for arrest and detention must be sufficiently clear, the Court held in the Jecius v. Lithuania case (judgment of 31 July 2000, Application No. 34578/97, paragraph 59):

> The Court notes that the prosecutor's letter of 13 June 1996 (paragraph 16 above), the Ombudsman's decision of 21 November 1996 (paragraph 23 above), the letter of the President of the Criminal Division of the Supreme Court dated 30 December 1996 (paragraph 27 above) and the respondent Government's submissions to the Court (paragraph 54 above) present three different answers to the question which part of the applicant's detention was covered by former Article 226, paragraph 6, of the Code of Criminal Procedure, with the result that the applicant's detention could purportedly be justified by that provision until 4, 14 or 21 June 1996. The Court does not deem it necessary to resolve this discrepancy as to the practical effects of former Article 226, paragraph 6, of the Code of Criminal Procedure, because it has been shown to have been vague enough to cause confusion even amongst the competent State authorities. It was

therefore incompatible with the requirements of "lawfulness" under Article 5, paragraph 1, of the Convention. Furthermore, the above provision permitted detention by reference to matters wholly extraneous to Article 5, paragraph 1.

It follows that the applicant's deprivation of liberty by reference to former Article 226, paragraph 6, of the Code of the Criminal Procedure was not prescribed by law, within the meaning of Article 5, paragraph 1, of the Convention.

The Court has also considered the case of a person who has been charged, who is detained before being brought before a court but where the detention order had expired and where the law made no provision for that situation (the Baranowski v. Poland case, judgment of 28 March 2000, Application No. 28358/95, paragraphs 53-58):

> Turning to the circumstances of the present case, the Court notes that the parties agree that between the date of expiry of the detention order of 30 December 1993 – namely 31 January 1994 – and the Lódz Regional Court's subsequent decision of 24 May 1994 on the applicant's liberty, there had been no judicial decision authorising the applicant's detention. It is also common ground that during this time the applicant was kept in detention solely on the basis of the fact that a bill of indictment had in the meantime been lodged with the court competent to deal with his case.
>
> The Court observes that the domestic practice of keeping a person in detention under a bill of indictment was not based on any specific legislative provision or case-law but, as the Commission had found and the parties acknowledged before the Court, stemmed from the fact that Polish criminal legislation at the material time lacked clear rules governing the situation of a detainee in court proceedings, after the expiry of the term of his detention fixed in the last detention order made at the investigation stage.
>
> Against this background, the Court considers, first, that the relevant Polish criminal legislation, by reason of the absence of any precise provisions laying down whether – and if so, under what conditions – detention ordered for a limited period at the investigation stage could properly be prolonged at the stage of the court proceedings, does not satisfy the test of "foreseeability" of a "law" for the purposes of Article 5, paragraph 1, of the Convention.
>
> Secondly, the Court considers that the practice which developed in response to the statutory lacuna, whereby a person is detained for an unlimited and unpredictable time and without his detention being based on a concrete legal provision or on any judicial decision is in itself contrary to the principle of legal certainty, a principle which is implied in the Convention and which constitutes one of the basic elements of the rule of law.
>
> In that context, the Court also stresses that, for the purposes of Article 5, paragraph 1, of the Convention, detention which extends over a period of several months and which has not been ordered by a court or by a judge or any other person "authorised [...] to exercise judicial power" cannot be considered "lawful" in the sense of that provision. While this requirement is not explicitly stipulated in Article 5, paragraph 1, it can be inferred from Article 5 read as a whole, in particular the wording in paragraph 1.*c* ("for the purpose of bringing him before the competent legal authority") and paragraph 3 ("shall be brought promptly before a judge or other officer authorised by law to exercise judicial power"). In

addition, the habeas corpus guarantee contained in Article 5, paragraph 4, further supports the view that detention which is prolonged beyond the initial period foreseen in paragraph 3 necessitates "judicial" intervention as a safeguard against arbitrariness. In the Court's opinion, the protection afforded by Article 5, paragraph 1, against arbitrary deprivations of liberty would be seriously under-mined if a person could be detained by executive order alone following a mere appearance before the judicial authorities referred to in paragraph 3 of Article 5.

In conclusion and on the facts of the present case, the Court considers that the applicant's detention was not "lawful" within the meaning of Article 5, paragraph 1, of the Convention. Consequently, there has been a breach of that provision.

(See the Grauslys v. Lithuania judgment of 10 October 2000, Application No. 36743/97, paragraphs 37-41.)

The particular case of actual release after it has been ordered

In the Labita v. Italy case, the applicant's release had been ordered. The judgment was delivered in the evening, at approximately 10 p.m. The applicant, who had been in court when judgment was pronounced, was returned to prison without having his handcuffs removed and arrived there at 12.25 a.m. In the absence of the officer of the registry, whose presence was required in the case of a person subject to a special detention arrangement, the applicant was not to be released until 8.30 a.m. The Court held (the Labita v. Italy judgment of 6 April 2000, Application No. 26772/95, para-graphs 171-173):

> The Court reiterates that the list of exceptions to the right to liberty secured in Article 5, paragraph 1, is an exhaustive one and only a narrow interpretation of those exceptions is consistent with the aim of that provision, namely to ensure that no one is arbitrarily deprived of his or her liberty (see, among other auth-orities, the Giulia Manzoni v. Italy judgment of 1 July 1997, *Reports* 1997-IV, p. 1191, paragraph 25, and the Quinn v. France judgment of 22 March 1995, Series A No. 311, pp. 17-18, paragraph 42).
>
> While it is true that for the purposes of Article 5, paragraph 1.*c*, detention ceases to be justified "on the day on which the charge is determined" (see paragraph 147 above) and that, consequently, detention after acquittal is no longer covered by that provision, "some delay in carrying out a decision to release a detainee is often inevitable, although it must be kept to a minimum" (see the Giulia Manzoni judgment cited above, p. 1191, paragraph 25, in fine).
>
> The Court observes, however, that in the instant case the delay in the applicant's release was only partly attributable to the need for the relevant administrative formalities to be carried out. The additional delay in releasing the applicant between 12.25 a.m. and the morning of 13 November 1993 was caused by the registration officer's absence. It was only on the latter's return that it was possible to verify whether any other reasons existed for keeping the applicant in deten-tion and to put in hand the other administrative formalities required on release (see paragraph 24 above).
>
> In these circumstances, the applicant's continued detention after his return to Termini Imerese Prison did not amount to a first step in the execution of the

order for his release and therefore did not come within sub-paragraph 1.*c*, or any other sub-paragraph, of Article 5.

Article 5, paragraph 1.d – Detention of a minor in the context of supervised education or for the purpose of being brought before a court

On supervised education, the Bouamar judgment (29 February 1988, Series A No. 129, paragraph 11, p. 21, paragraphs 50-51, and p. 22, paragraph 53) illustrates sub-paragraph *d*. In that case the applicant, a minor who had committed serious offences, was placed in a remand prison on nine occasions for periods of not more than two weeks. Detention in a remand prison is a possibility available under Belgian law where it is not possible to find a person or an institution capable of receiving the minor immediately. The Court held that:

> The third placement in Lantin Prison was ordered by the Juvenile Court on 4 March 1980, after "fresh offences" had been committed by the applicant between 1 January and 27 February.

> The order recorded that the applicant was "stubbornly unresponsive to any custodial, protective or educative measure". By way of justifying the material impossibility of finding "an institution appropriate to [his] behaviour", it cited the fact that "the State reformatories were open institutions".

> [...]

> [...] the confinement of a juvenile in a remand prison does not necessarily contravene sub-paragraph *d* (art. 5-1-d), even if it is not in itself such as to provide for the person's "educational supervision". As is apparent from the words "for the purpose of" (*"pour"*), the "detention" referred to in the text is a means of ensuring that the person concerned is placed under "educational supervision", but the placement does not necessarily have to be an immediate one. Just as Article 5, paragraph 1, recognises – in sub-paragraphs *c* and *a* (art. 5-1-c, art. 5-1-a) – the distinction between pre-trial detention and detention after conviction, so sub-paragraph *d* (art. 5-1-d) does not preclude an interim custody measure being used as a preliminary to a regime of supervised education, without itself involving any supervised education. In such circumstances, however, the imprisonment must be speedily followed by actual application of such a regime in a setting (open or closed) designed and with sufficient resources for the purpose.

> In the instant case, the applicant was, as it were, shuttled to and fro between the remand prison at Lantin and his family. In 1980 alone, the juvenile courts ordered his detention nine times and then released him on or before the expiry of the statutory limit of fifteen days; in all, he was thus deprived of his liberty for 119 days during the period of 291 days from 18 January to 4 November 1980 (see paragraph 8 above).

> In the Government's submission, the placements complained of were part of an educative programme initiated by the courts, and Mr Bouamar's behaviour during the relevant time enabled them to gain a clearer picture of his personality.

> The Court does not share this view. The Belgian State chose the system of educational supervision with a view to carrying out its policy on juvenile

115

delinquency. Consequently it was under an obligation to put in place appropriate institutional facilities which met the demands of security and the educational objectives of the 1965 Act, in order to be able to satisfy the requirements of Article 5, paragraph 1.*d* (art. 5-1-d), of the Convention (see, among other authorities and, *mutatis mutandis,* the Guincho judgment of 10 July 1984, Series A No. 81, p. 16, paragraph 38, and the De Cubber judgment of 26 October 1984, Series A No. 86, p. 20, paragraph 35).

Nothing in the evidence, however, shows that this was the case. At the time of the events in issue, Belgium did not have – at least in the French-speaking region in which the applicant lived – any closed institution able to accommodate highly disturbed juveniles (see paragraph 28 above). The detention of a young man in a remand prison in conditions of virtual isolation and without the assistance of staff with educational training cannot be regarded as furthering any educational aim.

The improvement observed in Mr Bouamar's behaviour is certainly not accounted for by the successive periods of imprisonment complained of but by the care he received in quite different surroundings after his release from Lantin Prison (see paragraph 18 above).

The Court accordingly concludes that the nine placement orders, taken together, were not compatible with sub-paragraph *d* (art. 5-1-d). Their fruitless repetition had the effect of making them less and less "lawful" under sub-paragraph *d* (art. 5-1-d), especially as Crown Counsel never instituted criminal proceedings against the applicant in respect of the offences alleged against him.

There was therefore a breach of Article 5, paragraph 1 (art. 5-1), of the Convention.

Article 5, paragraph 1.e – Detention of persons of unsound mind, alcoholics, persons suffering from infectious diseases or vagrants

Detention of persons of unsound mind

The Winterwerp v. the Netherlands judgment of 24 October 1979, Series A No. 33, p. 16, paragraph 37, illustrates the scope of sub-paragraph *e* as regards the concept of "persons of unsound mind":

> The Convention does not state what is to be understood by the words "persons of unsound mind". This term is not one that can be given a definitive interpretation: as was pointed out by the Commission, the Government and the applicant, it is a term whose meaning is continually evolving as research in psychiatry progresses, an increasing flexibility in treatment is developing and society's attitude to mental illness changes, in particular so that a greater understanding of the problems of mental patients is becoming more wide-spread.

> In any event, sub-paragraph *e* of Article 5, paragraph 1 (art. 5-1-e), obviously cannot be taken as permitting the detention of a person simply because his views or behaviour deviate from the norms prevailing in a particular society.

In that judgment, the Court also defined the three minimum conditions that must be satisfied in order for there to be a "lawful detention of a person of unsound mind" (paragraph 39):

In the Court's opinion, except in emergency cases, the individual concerned should not be deprived of his liberty unless he has been reliably shown to be of "unsound mind". The very nature of what has to be established before the competent national authority – that is, a true mental disorder – calls for objective medical expertise. Further, the mental disorder must be of a kind or degree warranting compulsory confinement. What is more, the validity of continued confinement depends upon the persistence of such a disorder (see, *mutatis mutandis*, the Stögmüller judgment of 10 November 1969, Series A No. 9, pp. 39-40, paragraph 4, and the above-mentioned De Wilde, Ooms and Versyp judgment, p. 43, paragraph 82).

With specific regard to the "medical expertise", the Court further stated in the X. v. the United Kingdom judgment of 5 November 1981, Series A No. 46, p. 19, paragraph 41:

> [...] neither can it be inferred from the Winterwerp judgment that the "objective medical expertise" must in all conceivable cases be obtained before rather than after confinement of a person on the ground of unsoundness of mind. Clearly, where a provision of domestic law is designed, amongst other things, to authorise emergency confinement of persons capable of presenting a danger to others, it would be impracticable to require thorough medical examination prior to any arrest or detention. A wide discretion must in the nature of things be enjoyed by the national authority empowered to order such emergency confinements.

For a case where detention without a prior medical expertise was not held to be justified by an emergency, see the Varbanov v. Bulgaria judgment of 5 October 2000, Application No. 31365/96, paragraph 48.

In the Johnson v. the United Kingdom case, the applicant had been confined in a maximum security psychiatric hospital. Some time later, a committee ordered that the applicant be released on condition that he underwent psychiatric supervision by Dr ... and by a psychiatric social worker and that he resided in supervised accommodation approved by those two persons. The applicant was not to be released until suitable accommodation had been found. The court held (judgment of 24 October 1997, *Reports* 1997-VII, paragraphs 62-67):

> It is to be recalled [...] that the Court in its Luberti judgment (cited above, pp. 13-15, paragraph 29) accepted that the termination of the confinement of an individual who has previously been found by a court to be of unsound mind and to present a danger to society is a matter that concerns, as well as that individual, the community in which he will live if released. Having regard to the pressing nature of the interests at stake, and in particular the very serious nature of the offence committed by Mr Luberti when mentally ill, it was accepted in that case that the responsible authority was entitled to proceed with caution and needed some time to consider whether to terminate his confinement, even if the medical evidence pointed to his recovery.
>
> In the view of the Court it must also be acknowledged that a responsible authority is entitled to exercise a similar measure of discretion in deciding whether in the light of all the relevant circumstances and the interests at stake it would in fact be appropriate to order the immediate and absolute discharge of a person who is no longer suffering from the mental disorder which led to his confinement.

That authority should be able to retain some measure of supervision over the progress of the person once he is released into the community and to that end make his discharge subject to conditions. It cannot be excluded either that the imposition of a particular condition may in certain circumstances justify a deferral of discharge from detention, having regard to the nature of the condition and to the reasons for imposing it. It is, however, of paramount importance that appropriate safeguards are in place so as to ensure that any deferral of discharge is consonant with the purpose of Article 5, paragraph 1, and with the aim of the restriction in sub-paragraph *e* (see paragraph 60 above) and, in particular, that discharge is not unreasonably delayed.

Having regard to the above considerations, the Court is of the opinion that the 1989 Tribunal could in the exercise of its judgment properly conclude that it was premature to order Mr Johnson's absolute and immediate discharge from Rampton Hospital. While it is true that the Tribunal was satisfied on the basis of its own assessment and the medical evidence before it (see paragraphs 17 and 18 above) that the applicant was no longer suffering from mental illness, it nevertheless considered that a phased conditional discharge was appropriate in the circumstances. [...] It was not therefore unreasonable for the Tribunal to consider, having regard to the views of Dr Wilson and Dr Cameron, that the applicant should be placed under psychiatric and social-worker supervision and required to undergo a period of rehabilitation in a hostel on account of the fact that "the recurrence of mental illness requiring recall to hospital cannot be excluded" (see paragraph 18 above). The Tribunal was also in principle justified in deferring the applicant's release in order to enable the authorities to locate a hostel which best suited his needs and provided him with the most appropriate conditions for his successful rehabilitation.

As to the conditions imposed on Mr Johnson's discharge, it is to be noted that the requirement to remain under the psychiatric supervision of Dr Cameron and the social-worker supervision of Mr Patterson (see paragraph 19 above) would not have hindered his immediate release from Rampton Hospital into the community and cannot be said to raise an issue under Article 5, paragraph 1, of the Convention.

However, while imposing the hostel residence requirement on the applicant and deferring his release until the arrangements had been made to its satisfaction, the Tribunal lacked the power to guarantee that the applicant would be relocated to a suitable post-discharge hostel within a reasonable period of time. The onus was on the authorities to secure a hostel willing to admit the applicant. It is to be observed that they were expected to proceed with all reasonable expedition in finalising the arrangements for a placement (see paragraph 44 above). While the authorities made considerable efforts to this end, these efforts were frustrated by the reluctance of certain hostels to accept the applicant as well as by the latter's negative attitude with respect to the options available (see paragraphs 20 and 21 above). They were also constrained by the limited number of available placements. Admittedly, a suitable hostel may have been located within a reasonable period of time had the applicant adopted a more positive approach to his rehabilitation. However, this cannot refute the conclusion that neither the Tribunal nor the authorities possessed the necessary powers to ensure that the condition could be implemented within a reasonable time. Furthermore, the earliest date on which the applicant could have had his continued detention reviewed was twelve months after the review conducted by the June 1989 Tribunal (see paragraph 44 above).

[...]

In these circumstances, it must be concluded that the imposition of the hostel residence condition by the June 1989 Tribunal led to the indefinite deferral of the applicant's release from Rampton Hospital, especially since the applicant was unwilling after October 1990 to co-operate further with the authorities in their efforts to secure a hostel, thereby excluding any possibility that the condition could be satisfied. [...]

Having regard to the situation which resulted from the decision taken by the latter Tribunal and to the lack of adequate safeguards, including provision for judicial review to ensure that the applicant's release from detention would not be unreasonably delayed, it must be considered that his continued confinement after 15 June 1989 cannot be justified on the basis of Article 5, paragraph 1.*e*, of the Convention (see paragraph 63 above).

Detention of alcoholics

In the Witold Litwa v. Poland case, the applicant had been detained for several hours in a sobering-up centre after an employee of the post office in which he was called the police and reported that he was drunk and offensive. In fact the post office was full and the applicant, who was half blind, had complained (judgment of 4 April 2000, Application No. 26629/95, paragraphs 60-80). The Court first dealt with the concept of "alcoholic":

> The Court observes that the word "alcoholics", in its common usage, denotes persons who are addicted to alcohol. On the other hand, in Article 5, paragraph 1, of the Convention this term is found in a context that includes a reference to several other categories of individuals, that is, persons spreading infectious diseases, persons of unsound mind, drug addicts and vagrants. There is a link between all those persons in that they may be deprived of their liberty either in order to be given medical treatment or because of considerations dictated by social policy, or on both medical and social grounds. It is therefore legitimate to conclude from this context that a predominant reason why the Convention allows the persons mentioned in paragraph 1.*e* of Article 5 to be deprived of their liberty is not only that they are dangerous for public safety but also that their own interests may necessitate their detention (see the Guzzardi v. Italy judgment of 6 November 1980, Series A No. 39, p. 37, paragraph 98, in fine).

> This *ratio legis* indicates how the expression "alcoholics" should be understood in the light of the object and purpose of Article 5, paragraph 1.*e*, of the Convention. It indicates that the object and purpose of this provision cannot be interpreted as only allowing the detention of "alcoholics" in the limited sense of persons in a clinical state of "alcoholism". The Court considers that, under Article 5, paragraph 1.*e*, of the Convention, persons who are not medically diagnosed as "alcoholics", but whose conduct and behaviour under the influence of alcohol pose a threat to public order or themselves, can be taken into custody for the protection of the public or their own interests, such as their health or personal safety.

> That does not mean that Article 5, paragraph 1.*e*, of the Convention can be interpreted as permitting the detention of an individual merely because of his alcohol

119

intake. However, the Court considers that in the text of Article 5 there is nothing to suggest that this provision prevents that measure from being applied by the State to an individual abusing alcohol, in order to limit the harm caused by alcohol to himself and the public, or to prevent dangerous behaviour after drinking. On this point, the Court observes that there can be no doubt that the harmful use of alcohol poses a danger to society and that a person who is in a state of intoxication may pose a danger to himself and others, regardless of whether or not he is addicted to alcohol.

The Court further finds that this meaning of the term "alcoholics" is confirmed by the preparatory work of the Convention (see paragraphs 33 to 39 above). In that regard, the Court observes that in the commentary on the preliminary draft Convention it is recorded that the text of the relevant Article covered the right of the signatory States to take measures to combat vagrancy and "drunkenness" (*"l'alcoolisme"* in French). It is further recorded that the Committee of Experts had no doubt that this could be agreed "since such restrictions were justified by the requirements of public morality and order".

In this respect, the Court entertains serious doubts as to whether it can be said that the applicant behaved in such a way, influenced by alcohol, that he posed a threat to the public or himself, or that his own health, well-being or personal safety were endangered. The Court's doubts are reinforced by the rather trivial factual basis for the detention and the fact that the applicant is almost blind.

The Court reiterates that a necessary element of the "lawfulness" of the detention within the meaning of Article 5, paragraph 1.*e*, is the absence of arbitrariness. The detention of an individual is such a serious measure that it is only justified where other, less severe measures have been considered and found to be insufficient to safeguard the individual or public interest which might require that the person concerned be detained. That means that it does not suffice that the deprivation of liberty is executed in conformity with national law but it must also be necessary in the circumstances.

However, in the applicant's case no consideration appears to have been given to the fact that Section 40 of the Law of 26 October 1982 provides for several different measures which may be applied to an intoxicated person, among which detention in a sobering-up centre is the most extreme one. Indeed, under that section, an intoxicated person does not necessarily have to be deprived of his liberty since he may well be taken by the police to a public-care establishment or to his place of residence (see paragraph 26).

The absence of any such considerations in the present case, although expressly foreseen by the domestic law, has finally persuaded the Court that the applicant's detention cannot be considered "lawful" under Article 5, paragraph 1.*e*. There has therefore been a breach of that provision.

Detention of vagrants

The De Wilde, Ooms and Versyp judgment of 18 June 1971 (Applications Nos. 2832/66, 2835/66 and 2899/66, Series A No. 12, paragraphs 68-69) concerned a case of vagrancy and provides the definition of that term:

> The Convention does not contain a definition of the term "vagrant". The definition of Article 347 of the Belgian Criminal Code reads: "vagrants are persons who have

no fixed abode, no means of subsistence and no regular trade or profession". Where these three conditions are fulfilled, they may lead the competent authorities to order that the persons concerned be placed at the disposal of the Government as vagrants. The definition quoted does not appear to be in any way irreconcilable with the usual meaning of the term "vagrant", and the Court considers that a person who is a vagrant under the terms of Article 347 in principle falls within the exception provided for in Article 5, paragraph 1.*e* (art. 5-1-e), of the Convention.

In the present cases the want of a fixed abode and of means of subsistence resulted not merely from the action of the persons concerned in reporting voluntarily to the police but from their own declarations made at the time: all three stated that they were without any employment (see paragraphs 16, 23 and 28 above). As to the habitual character of this lack of employment the magistrates at Charleroi, Namur and Brussels were in a position to deduce this from the information available to them concerning the respective applicants. This would, moreover, also be indicated by the fact that, although they purported to be workers, the three applicants were apparently not in a position to claim the minimum number of working days required to be effected within a given period which, in accordance with the Royal Decree of 20 December 1963 (Articles 118 *et seq.*), would have qualified them for unemployment benefits.

Having thus the character of a "vagrant", the applicants could, under Article 5, paragraph 1.*e* (art. 5-1-e), of the Convention, be made the subject of a detention provided that it was ordered by the competent authorities and in accordance with the procedure prescribed by Belgian law.

Article 5, paragraph1.f – Arrest and detention of a person in order to prevent him from unlawfully entering the territory, or against whom expulsion or extradition proceedings are pending

Extradition

In the Quinn v. France judgment, concerning extradition, the Court stated (22 March 1995, Series A No. 311, p. 19, paragraph 48):

> It is clear from the wording of both the French and the English versions of Article 5, paragraph 1.*f* (art. 5-1-f), that deprivation of liberty under this sub-paragraph will be justified only for as long as extradition proceedings are being conducted. It follows that if such proceedings are not being prosecuted with due diligence, the detention will cease to be justified under Article 5, paragraph 1.*f.*

It should be noted, however, that the conduct of the person facing the extradition proceedings may cause delays for which the State concerned is not responsible (the Kolompar v. Belgium judgment of 24 September 1992, Series A No. 235-C, paragraphs 40-43):

> The Court notes that the period spent in detention pending extradition was unusually long (see paragraph 36, in fine, above). However, the extradition proceedings properly so-called were completed by 2 May 1984 (see paragraph 14 above), less than one month after the decision to revoke the order remanding the applicant in custody in respect of his alleged offences in Belgium, at a time when he had not yet been tried in the Antwerp Criminal Court (see paragraph 13

above). The detention was continued as a result of the successive applications for a stay of execution or for release which Mr Kolompar lodged on 29 October 1984, 2 January 1985, 15 June 1985, 21 June 1985 and 17 September 1985 (see paragraphs 15-25 above), as well as the time which the Belgian authorities required to verify the applicant's alibi in Denmark (see paragraphs 17 and 20 above).

The authorities and courts before which the case came prior to the beginning, on 17 September 1985, of the urgent application proceedings gave their decisions within a normal time (see paragraphs 15-23 above). To that extent it appears beyond doubt that the requirements of Article 5, paragraph 1.f (art. 5-1-f), were complied with.

For the subsequent period (see paragraphs 24-26 above), the Court recognises the force of the Government's arguments based on Articles 751 and 748, last sub-paragraph, of the Belgian Judicial Code (see paragraph 38 above). It notes in addition that, at first instance, Mr Kolompar waited nearly three months before replying to the submissions of the Belgian State (24 December 1985-19 March 1986); then, on appeal, he requested that the hearing of the case be postponed and failed to notify the authorities that he was unable to pay a lawyer.

His Netherlands lawyer, when questioned by the Court on these last two points at the hearing on 23 March 1992, stated merely that the request for a postponement had been made on the initiative of a Belgian colleague, who had represented the applicant at the time and that it had not been possible under the Judicial Code in this case to appoint a lawyer to act for him free of charge, although this last affirmation was denied by the Government (see paragraph 38 above).

Whatever the case may be, the Belgian State cannot be held responsible for the delays to which the applicant's conduct gave rise. The latter cannot validly complain of a situation which he largely created.

The Court accordingly concludes that there has been no violation of Article 5, paragraph 1 (art. 5-1).

Expulsion

The Chahal v. the United Kingdom judgment dealt with a case of expulsion (judgment of 15 November 1996, Application No. 22414/93, *Reports* 1996-V, paragraphs 112 and 117-123):

The Court recalls that it is not in dispute that Mr Chahal has been detained "with a view to deportation" within the meaning of Article 5, paragraph 1.f (art. 5-1-f) (see paragraph 109 above). Article 5, paragraph 1.f (art. 5-1-f), does not demand that the detention of a person against whom action is being taken with a view to deportation be reasonably considered necessary, for example to prevent his committing an offence or fleeing; in this respect Article 5, paragraph 1.f (art. 5-1-f), provides a different level of protection from Article 5, paragraph 1.c (art. 5-1-c).

Indeed, all that is required under this provision (art. 5-1-f) is that "action is being taken with a view to deportation". It is therefore immaterial, for the purposes of Article 5, paragraph 1.f (art. 5-1-f), whether the underlying decision to expel can be justified under national or Convention law.

The Court recalls, however, that any deprivation of liberty under Article 5, paragraph 1.f (art. 5-1-f), will be justified only for as long as deportation proceedings are in progress. If such proceedings are not prosecuted with due diligence, the detention will cease to be permissible under Article 5, paragraph 1.*f* (art. 5-1-f) (see the Quinn v. France judgment of 22 March 1995, Series A No. 311, p. 19, paragraph 48, and also the Kolompar v. Belgium judgment of 24 September 1992, Series A No. 235-C, p. 55, paragraph 36).

It is thus necessary to determine whether the duration of the deportation proceedings was excessive.

[...]

Against this background, and bearing in mind what was at stake for the applicant and the interest that he had in his claims being thoroughly examined by the courts, none of the periods complained of can be regarded as excessive, taken either individually or in combination. Accordingly, there has been no violation of Article 5, paragraph 1.*f,* of the Convention (art. 5-1-f) on account of the diligence, or lack of it, with which the domestic procedures were conducted.

It also falls to the Court to examine whether Mr Chahal's detention was "lawful" for the purposes of Article 5, paragraph 1.*f* (art. 5-1-f), with particular reference to the safeguards provided by the national system.

Where the "lawfulness" of detention is in issue, including the question whether "a procedure prescribed by law" has been followed, the Convention refers essentially to the obligation to conform to the substantive and procedural rules of national law, but it requires in addition that any deprivation of liberty should be in keeping with the purpose of Article 5 (art. 5), namely to protect the individual from arbitrariness.

There is no doubt that Mr Chahal's detention was lawful under national law and was effected "in accordance with a procedure prescribed by law" (see paragraphs 43 and 64 above). However, in view of the extremely long period during which Mr Chahal has been detained, it is also necessary to consider whether there existed sufficient guarantees against arbitrariness.

In this context, the Court observes that the applicant has been detained since 16 August 1990 on the ground, essentially, that successive Secretaries of State have maintained that, in view of the threat to national security represented by him, he could not safely be released (see paragraph 43 above). [...]

However, in the context of Article 5, paragraph 1, of the Convention (art. 5-1), the advisory panel procedure (see paragraphs 29-32 and 60 above) provided an important safeguard against arbitrariness. This panel, which included experienced judicial figures (see paragraph 29 above) was able fully to review the evidence relating to the national security threat represented by the applicant.

In conclusion, the Court recalls that Mr Chahal has undoubtedly been detained for a length of time which is bound to give rise to serious concern. However, in view of the exceptional circumstances of the case and the facts that the national authorities have acted with due diligence throughout the deportation proceedings against him and that there were sufficient guarantees against the arbitrary deprivation of his liberty, this detention complied with the requirements of Article 5, paragraph 1.*f* (art. 5-1-f).

123

Article 5, paragraph 2 – The right to be informed of the charges

Article 5, paragraph 2, is worded as follows:

> **2. Everyone who is arrested shall be informed promptly, in a language which he understands, of the reasons for his arrest and of any charge against him.**

1. The scope of paragraph 2

In the Van der Leer v. the Netherlands case, the Mayor had ordered that the applicant be confined in a local psychiatric hospital. Before the Court, the applicant had claimed that she had not been immediately informed of the confinement order. The government had replied that "paragraph 2 [...] did not apply in the case in question because the words 'arrest' and 'charge' showed that it was only relevant to cases arising under criminal law". The Court held otherwise (the Van der Leer v. the Netherlands judgment of 21 February 1990, Series A No. 170-A, p. 13, paragraphs 27 and 28):

> The Court is not unmindful of the criminal-law connotation of the words used in Article 5, paragraph 2 (art. 5-2). However, it agrees with the Commission that they should be interpreted "autonomously", in particular in accordance with the aim and purpose of Article 5 (art. 5), which are to protect everyone from arbitrary deprivations of liberty. Thus the "arrest" referred to in paragraph 2 of Article 5 (art. 5-2) extends beyond the realm of criminal-law measures. Similarly, in using the words "any charge" *("toute accusation")* in this provision, the intention of the drafters was not to lay down a condition for its applicability, but to indicate an eventuality of which it takes account.

> The close link between paragraphs 2 and 4 of Article 5 (art. 5-2, art. 5-4) supports this interpretation. Any person who is entitled to take proceedings to have the lawfulness of his detention decided speedily cannot make effective use of that right unless he is promptly and adequately informed of the reasons why he has been deprived of his liberty (see, *mutatis mutandis*, the X. v. the United Kingdom judgment of 5 November 1981, Series A No. 46, p. 28, paragraph 66).

2. The application of paragraph 2

Content and form of the information

In the Murray v. the United Kingdom judgment (28 October 1994, Application No. 14310/88, Series A No. 300-A, paragraph 76), the Court pointed out that the mere reference, without more, to the legal basis for an arrest is ineffective:

> It is common ground that [...] arresting officer, Corporal D., also told Mrs Murray the section of the 1978 Act under which the arrest was being carried out (see paragraphs 12 and 36 above). This bare indication of the legal basis for the arrest,

taken on its own, is insufficient for the purposes of Article 5, paragraph 2 (art. 5-2) (see the above-mentioned Fox, Campbell and Hartley judgment, p. 19, paragraph 41).

In the Fox, Campbell and Hartley v. the United Kingdom case (judgment of 30 August 1990, Series A No. 182, p. 19, paragraph 40), the Court had held that the information given to persons who have been arrested must relate to both factual and legal matters:

> Paragraph 2 of Article 5 (art. 5-2) contains the elementary safeguard that any person arrested should know why he is being deprived of his liberty. This provision is an integral part of the scheme of protection afforded by Article 5 (art. 5): by virtue of paragraph 2 (art. 5-2), any person arrested must be told, in simple, non-technical language that he can understand, the essential legal and factual grounds for his arrest, so as to be able, if he sees fit, to apply to a court to challenge its lawfulness in accordance with paragraph 4 (art. 5-4) (see the Van der Leer judgment of 21 February 1990, Series A No. 170, p. 13, paragraph 28).

On the other hand, the information given to a person who has been arrested does not need to be in any particular form. The specific questions asked for the purposes of the investigation may serve to inform the person concerned of the grounds for his deprivation of liberty; and the fact that a person is arrested red-handed is a factor which, when taken with others, indicate that the person concerned is sufficiently informed of the offence of which he is accused. The Dikme judgment (11 July 2000, Application No. 20869/92, paragraphs 54-57) illustrates that hypothesis:

> In the instant case the Court notes that the reason for the first applicant's arrest was that he produced false papers during an identity check by the police. It considers that, having regard to the criminal and intentional nature of that act, the first applicant cannot maintain that he did not understand why he was arrested and taken to the local police station at 7.30 a.m. on 10 February 1992 (see paragraph 12 above).
>
> The same applies to the reasons why the first applicant had to wait at the police station and was taken into police custody at the branch, where he was allegedly interrogated by officers intent on making him disclose his true identity (see paragraph 12 above).
>
> For the rest, the first applicant stated that he had been interrogated throughout his sixteen days in police custody. He alleged that the officers who had started the interrogation were members of the "anti-Dev-Sol" squad (see paragraph 12 above) and that after the first interrogation session, at about 7 p.m., a member of the secret service had threatened him, saying: "You belong to Devrimci Sol, and if you don't give us the information we need, you'll be leaving here feet first!" (see paragraph 13 above).
>
> In the Court's opinion, that statement gave a fairly precise indication of the suspicions concerning the first applicant. Accordingly, and having regard to the illegal nature of the organisation in question and to the reasons he may have had for concealing his identity and fearing the police (his sister had been killed in a clash with the police – see paragraph 23 above), the Court considers that Mr Dikme should or could already have realised at that stage that he was suspected of being involved in prohibited activities such as those of Dev-Sol.

Point at which the information must be provided

In the Fox, Campbell and Hartley v. the United Kingdom case, the applicants complained that "they were not given at the time of their arrest adequate and understandable information of the substantive grounds for their arrest". In its judgment (30 August 1990, Series A No. 182, p. 19, paragraph 40), the Court interpreted Article 5, paragraph 2, as follows:

> Paragraph 2 of Article 5 (art. 5-2) contains the elementary safeguard that any person arrested should know why [...]. Whilst this information must be conveyed "promptly" (in French: *"dans le plus court délai"*), it need not be related in its entirety by the arresting officer at the very moment of the arrest. Whether the content and promptness of the information conveyed were sufficient is to be assessed in each case according to its special features.

In that case, the Court had taken the view that, on the facts, the applicants had been informed while being interviewed, a few hours after their arrest, why they had been arrested. It therefore held that the requirements of Article 5, paragraph 2, had been satisfied (ibid., pp. 19-20, paragraphs 41-43):

> On being taken into custody, Mr Fox, Ms Campbell and Mr Hartley were simply told by the arresting officer that they were being arrested under Section 11, paragraph 1, of the 1978 Act on suspicion of being terrorists (see paragraphs 9 and 13 above). This bare indication of the legal basis for the arrest, taken on its own, is insufficient for the purposes of Article 5, paragraph 2 (art. 5-2), as the Government conceded.

> However, following their arrest all of the applicants were interrogated by the police about their suspected involvement in specific criminal acts and their suspected membership of proscribed organisations (see paragraphs 9, 10 and 14 above). There is no ground to suppose that these interrogations were not such as to enable the applicants to understand why they had been arrested. The reasons why they were suspected of being terrorists were thereby brought to their attention during their interrogation.

> Mr Fox and Ms Campbell were arrested at 3.40 p.m. on 5 February 1986 at Woodbourne RUC station and then separately questioned the same day between 8.15 p.m. and 10.00 p.m. at Castlereagh Police Office (see paragraph 9 above). Mr Hartley, for his part, was arrested at his home at 7.55 a.m. on 18 August 1986 and taken to Antrim Police Station where he was questioned between 11.05 a.m. and 12.15 p.m. (see paragraph 13 above). In the context of the present case these intervals of a few hours cannot be regarded as falling outside the constraints of time imposed by the notion of promptness in Article 5, paragraph 2 (art. 5-2).

> In conclusion there was therefore no breach of Article 5, paragraph 2 (art. 5-2), in relation to any of the applicants.

It should be noted, incidentally, that in an earlier judgment, the X. v. the United Kingdom judgment of 16 July 1980, the Court had required that a sick person be given immediate information on arriving at a hospital. For a more recent application, see the H.B. v. Switzerland judgment of 5 April 2001, Application No. 26899/95, paragraphs 44-49.

Article 5, paragraph 3 – The right of persons who have been arrested to be brought before a judge and tried within a reasonable time or released

Article 5, paragraph 3, is worded as follows:

> 3. Everyone arrested or detained in accordance with the provisions of paragraph 1.*c* of this Article shall be brought promptly before a judge or other officer authorised by law to exercise judicial power and shall be entitled to trial within a reasonable time or to release pending trial. Release may be conditioned by guarantees to appear for trial.

1. Importance, purpose and content of the right provided for in Article 5, paragraph 3

The Court has on several occasions emphasised the fundamental nature of the right of a person who has been arrested to be "brought promptly before a judge" and to be "tri[ed] within a reasonable time or [...] release[d] pending trial". In the Brogan and Others v. the United Kingdom case, which concerned the detention of persons suspected of terrorism, the Court stated (judgment of 29 November 1988, Series A No. 145-B, p. 32, paragraph 58, in fine):

> [Article 5 (art. 5)] enshrines a fundamental human right, namely the protection of the individual against arbitrary interferences by the State with his right to liberty (see the Bozano judgment of 18 December 1986, Series A No. 111, p. 23, paragraph 54). Judicial control of interferences by the executive with the individual's right to liberty is an essential feature of the guarantee embodied in Article 5, paragraph 3 (art. 5-3), which is intended to minimise the risk of arbitrariness. Judicial control is implied by the rule of law, "one of the fundamental principles of a democratic society [...], which is expressly referred to in the Preamble to the Convention" (see, *mutatis mutandis,* the above-mentioned Klass and Others judgment, Series A No. 28, pp. 25-26, paragraph 55) and "from which the whole Convention draws its inspiration" (see, *mutatis mutandis,* the Engel and Others judgment of 8 June 1976, Series A No. 22, p. 28, paragraph 69).

The Court developed and propounded its point of view in the Aquilina v. Malta judgment (29 April 1999, Application No. 25642/94, *Reports* 1999-III, paragraph 47):

> [...] It is essentially the object of Article 5, paragraph 3, which forms a whole with paragraph 1.*c,* to require provisional release once detention ceases to be reasonable. The fact that an arrested person had access to a judicial authority is not sufficient to constitute compliance with the opening part of Article 5, paragraph 3. This provision enjoins the judicial officer before whom the arrested person appears to review the circumstances militating for or against detention, to decide by reference to legal criteria whether there are reasons to justify detention, and to order release if there are no such reasons (see the de Jong, Baljet and

Van den Brink v. the Netherlands judgment of 22 May 1984, Series A No. 77, pp. 21-24, paragraphs 44, 47 and 51). In other words, Article 5, paragraph 3, requires the judicial officer to consider the merits of the detention.

This pre-eminence of the right to be brought "promptly before a judge" and to be "tried within a reasonable time or [...] released pending trial" shows, for example, that domestic legislation cannot absolutely preclude the principle of liberation on bail for a particular offence. That was held in two cases, S.B.C. v. the United Kingdom (judgment of 19 June 2001, Application No. 39360/98) and Caballero v. the United Kingdom (judgment of 8 February 2000, Application No. 32819/96, paragraph 18). The applicants complained of a violation of Article 5, paragraph 3, in the light of a law which provided that "[a]ny person who in any proceedings has been charged with or convicted of an offence to which this section applies [murder, attempted murder ...] shall not be granted bail in those proceedings". The applicants stated that "the automatic denial of bail pending trial pursuant to Section 25 of the Criminal Justice and Public Order Act 1994 ("the 1994 Act") consti-tuted a violation of Article 5, paragraph 3, of the Convention". The Court upheld their plea.

It should be further specified that the guarantees set out in Article 5, para-graph 3, apply only where detention is lawful for the purposes of Article 5, paragraph 1.*c.* Where there is a violation of Article 5, paragraph 1.*c*, a complainant cannot at the same time rely on a violation of Article 5, para-graph 3 (see the Jecius v. Lithuania judgment of 31 July 2000, Application No. 34578/97, paragraph 75):

> The Court first notes that, from the moment of his arrest on 8 February until 14 March 1996, the applicant was held in preventive detention, to which Article 5, paragraph 1.*c*, of the Convention did not apply (see paragraphs 51-52 above). Consequently, the guarantee for the applicant to be brought promptly before an appropriate officer under Article 5, paragraph 3, was not applicable to his period in preventive detention.

Apart from the fundamental nature of Article 5, paragraph 3, the two provi-sions contained therein must be addressed separately:

– the right to be brought "promptly" before a judge; and

– the right to trial within a reasonable time or to be released pending trial.

2. The right of a person who has been arrested to be brought "promptly" before a judge

The first right referred to in Article 5, paragraph 3, is the right of any person who has been arrested to be brought "promptly" before a judge.

The scope of the right to be brought before a judge without delay

In the Brogan case (cited above, p. 31, the beginning of paragraph 58), the Court defined the scope *ratione temporis* of the right laid down in Article 5, paragraph 3. A detained person may rely on that right provided that his detention is continuing and he is not released promptly:

> The fact that a detained person is not charged or brought before a court does not in itself amount to a violation of the first part of Article 5, paragraph 3 (art. 5-3). No violation of Article 5, paragraph 3 (art. 5-3), can arise if the arrested person is released "promptly" before any judicial control of his detention would have been feasible (see the de Jong, Baljet and Van den Brink judgment of 22 May 1984, Series A No. 77, p. 25, paragraph 52). If the arrested person is not released promptly, he is entitled to a prompt appearance before a judge or judicial officer.

Characteristics of the appearance before a judge

Promptness

If a person who has been arrested is not released immediately, he must be brought promptly before a judge. It remains to consider the meaning of the word "promptly" (*"aussitôt"* in French). In the Brogan judgment, cited above, the Court held that a period of detention of four days and six hours by the police without being brought before a judge exceeds the limits permissible under Article 5, paragraph 3, even where the delicate definition of terrorism arose. The Court held (p. 33, paragraphs 59 and 62):

> The obligation expressed in English by the word "promptly" and in French by the word *"aussitôt"* is clearly distinguishable from the less strict requirement in the second part of paragraph 3 (art. 5-3) ("reasonable time"/*"délai raisonnable"*) and even from that in paragraph 4 of Article 5 (art. 5-4) ("speedily"/*"à bref délai"*). The term "promptly" also occurs in the English text of paragraph 2 (art. 5-2), where the French text uses the words *"dans le plus court délai"*. As indicated in the Ireland v. the United Kingdom judgment (18 January 1978, Series A No. 25, p. 76, paragraph 199), "promptly" in paragraph 3 (art. 5-3) may be understood as having a broader significance than *"aussitôt"*, which literally means immediately. Thus confronted with versions of a law-making treaty which are equally authentic but not exactly the same, the Court must interpret them in a way that reconciles them as far as possible and is most appropriate in order to realise the aim and achieve the object of the treaty (see, *inter alia*, the *Sunday Times* judgment of 26 April 1979, Series A No. 30, p. 30, paragraph 48, and Article 33, paragraph 4 of the Vienna Convention of 23 May 1969 on the Law of Treaties).
>
> The use in the French text of the word *"aussitôt"*, with its constraining connotation of immediacy, confirms that the degree of flexibility attaching to the notion of "promptness" is limited, even if the attendant circumstances can never be ignored for the purposes of the assessment under paragraph 3 (art. 5-3). Whereas promptness is to be assessed in each case according to its special features (see the above-mentioned de Jong, Baljet and Van den Brink judgment, Series A No. 77, p. 25, paragraph 52), the significance to be attached to those features can never be taken to the point of impairing the very essence of the right guaranteed by Article 5, paragraph 3 (art. 5-3), that is to the point of effectively negativing the State's obligation to ensure a prompt release or a prompt appearance before a judicial authority.

[...] the scope for flexibility in interpreting and applying the notion of "promptness" is very limited. In the Court's view, even the shortest of the four periods of detention, namely the four days and six hours spent in police custody by Mr McFadden (see paragraph 18 above), falls outside the strict constraints as to time permitted by the first part of Article 5, paragraph 3 (art. 5-3). To attach such importance to the special features of this case as to justify so lengthy a period of detention without appearance before a judge or other judicial officer would be an unacceptably wide interpretation of the plain meaning of the word "promptly". An interpretation to this effect would import into Article 5, paragraph 3 (art. 5-3), a serious weakening of a procedural guarantee to the detriment of the individual and would entail consequences impairing the very essence of the right protected by this provision. The Court thus has to conclude that none of the applicants was either brought "promptly" before a judicial authority or released "promptly" following his arrest. The undoubted fact that the arrest and detention of the applicants were inspired by the legitimate aim of protecting the community as a whole from terrorism is not on its own sufficient to ensure compliance with the specific requirements of Article 5, paragraph 3 (art. 5-3).

Likewise, the mere fact that detention is legal from the viewpoint of domestic law does not provide grounds for derogating from Article 5, paragraph 3. In the Demir and Others v. Turkey case, the government claimed that the applicants (who had been held for at least twenty-three days and at least sixteen days respectively) had been detained in the context of an investigation involving thirty-five suspects and carried out in accordance with the relevant legislation. They were brought before a judge immediately the investigation was completed. The government argued that "it [had been] necessary to carry out a more thorough and careful police inquiry in order to gather all the evidence and assess it with a view to establishing the facts and identifying the persons who participated"; it was "natural that there should be longer periods of police custody to allow the Turkish authorities to complete the investigation of the offences concerned and thus be sure that they [could] bring those responsible for terrorist acts before the courts". Furthermore, in the government's submission, not only had the investigation been difficult, but the applicants had ultimately been found guilty. The Court stated (judgment of 23 September 1998, Applications Nos. 21380/93, 21381/93 and 21383/93, paragraphs 52-53):

> In the Court's opinion, the mere fact that the detention concerned was in accordance with domestic law – a fact that has not been disputed (see paragraph 22 above) – cannot justify under Article 15 measures derogating from Article 5, paragraph 3.
>
> As to the Government's assertions about the "thorough" and "careful" nature of the police investigation that had to be conducted, they do not provide an answer to the central question at issue, namely for what precise reasons relating to the actual facts of the present case would judicial scrutiny of the applicants' detention have prejudiced the progress of the investigation. In respect of such lengthy periods of detention in police custody it is not sufficient to refer in a general way to the difficulties caused by terrorism and the number of people involved in the inquiries.
>
> The Government further argued that in the present case the suspicions which had prompted the applicants' arrest had been confirmed, as they had been found

guilty as charged and had been convicted of a "terrorist" offence (see paragraphs 16, 20 and 47 above).

In that connection the Court reiterates that the eventual conviction of a suspect can at the most serve to confirm that the suspicions which led to his arrest (Article 5, paragraph 1.*c*) were well-founded, but is not indispensable (see, for example, the previously cited Murray judgment, p. 30, paragraph 67). On the other hand, it has no bearing on the question whether there was a situation which necessitated the detention of suspects incommunicado for such lengthy periods, as their conviction does not, as such, give any indication of the circumstances surrounding both the deprivation of liberty and the investigation in issue, any more than it can remove after the event the risks of arbitrary treatment which Article 5, paragraph 3, is intended to prevent.

(*Idem* the Dikme v. Turkey judgment of 11 July 2000, Application No. 20869/92.)

In the recent Altay v. Turkey judgment (22 May 2001, Application No. 22279/93, paragraphs 64-65, available in French only – unofficial translation), the Court referred to one of the objectives implicit in the right to be brought "promptly" before a judge, which, *inter alia*, makes it possible to prevent ill-treatment:

> The Court has accepted on a number of occasions in the past that the investigation of terrorist offences undoubtedly presents the authorities with special problems (see, among other authorities, the Brogan and Others judgment, cited above, p. 33, paragraph 61, the Murray v. the United Kingdom judgment of 28 October 1994, Series A No. 300-A, p. 27, paragraph 55, and the Dikme v. Turkey judgment, Application No. 208962/92, paragraph 64, ECHR 2000). That does not mean, however, that the authorities have *carte blanche* under Article 5 to arrest suspects and detain them in police custody, free from effective control by the domestic courts and, in the final instance, by the Convention's supervisory institutions, whenever they consider that there has been a terrorist offence (see, *mutatis mutandis*, the Murray judgment, cited above, p. 27, paragraph 58).

> The Court also recalls the importance of Article 5 in the Convention system: it enshrines a fundamental human right, namely the protection of the individual against arbitrary interferences by the State with his right to liberty. Judicial control of interferences by the executive is an essential feature of the guarantee embodied in Article 5, paragraph 3, which is intended to minimise the risk or arbitrariness and to secure the rule of law, "one of the fundamental principles of a democratic society [...], which is expressly referred to in the Preamble to the Convention" (see, for example, the Sakik and Others judgment of 26 November 1997, *Reports* 1997-VII, pp. 2623-2624, paragraph 44). Furthermore, only prompt judicial intervention can lead to the detection and prevention of serious forms of ill-treatment – such as those alleged by Mr Altay (see paragraph 48 above) – to which detainees are in danger of being subjected, particularly as a means of extracting confessions from them (see the Dikme judgment, cited above, paragraph 66).

In that case, the Court held that there had been a violation of Article 5, paragraph 3, since the detention had lasted for fifteen days without the applicant being brought before a judge (*idem* paragraph 66). The Court reached the same conclusion in the recent O'Hara v. the United Kingdom judgment (16 October 2001, Application No. 37555/97, paragraphs 13-15 and 45-46), where the applicant, who was suspected of terrorist offences, had been detained by the police for six days and thirteen hours and then released without charge. On the other hand, arrest followed by production of the person concerned before a judge on the following day is consistent with the criteria laid down in Article 5, paragraph 3 (the Egmez v. Cyprus judgment of 21 December 2000, Application No. 30873/96, paragraphs 17-20 and 90); and bringing the detained person before a judge within forty-eight hours has been deemed sufficient (the Aquilina v. Malta judgment of 29 April 1999, Application No. 25642/94, paragraph 51):

> The Court shares the parties' view that the applicant's appearance before a magistrate two days after his arrest (see paragraph 9 above) could be regarded as "prompt" for the purposes of Article 5, paragraph 3.

(*Idem* the Grauzinis v. Lithuania judgment of 10 October 2000, Application No. 37975/97, paragraph 25.)

The person arrested must be brought "automatically" before a judge

It is not enough that the person is brought before a judge promptly; that procedure must take place automatically. The Court so held in the Aquilina v. Malta judgment (29 April 1999, Application No. 25642/94, *Reports* 1999-III, paragraph 49):

> In addition to being prompt, the judicial control of the detention must be automatic (see the de Jong, Baljet and Van den Brink judgment cited above, p. 24, paragraph 51). It cannot be made to depend on a previous application by the detained person. Such a requirement would not only change the nature of the safeguard provided for under Article 5, paragraph 3, a safeguard distinct from that in Article 5, paragraph 4, which guarantees the right to institute proceedings to have the lawfulness of detention reviewed by a court (see the de Jong, Baljet and Van den Brink judgment cited above, pp. 25-26, paragraph 57). It might even defeat the purpose of the safeguard under Article 5, paragraph 3, which is to protect the individual from arbitrary detention by ensuring that the act of deprivation of liberty is subject to independent judicial scrutiny (see, *mutatis mutandis*, the Kurt v. Turkey judgment of 25 May 1998, *Reports* 1998-III, p. 1185, paragraph 123). Prompt judicial review of detention is also an important safeguard against ill-treatment of the individual taken into custody (see the Aksoy v. Turkey judgment of 18 December 1996, *Reports* 1996-VI, p. 2282, paragraph 76). Furthermore, arrested persons who have been subjected to such treatment might be incapable of lodging an application asking the judge to review their detention. The same could hold true for other vulnerable categories of arrested persons, such as the mentally weak or those who do not speak the language of the judicial officer.

(*Idem* the Niedbala v. Poland judgment of 4 July 2000, Application No. 27915/95, paragraph 50.)

A person who had been arrested need only be brought before a judge once

Last, it should be noted that Article 5, paragraph 3, does not require that a person who has been arrested be brought before a judge more than once. Thus, in the Jecius v. Lithuania judgment, the Court held (judgment of 31 July 2000, Application 34578/97, paragraph 84):

> The Court considers that the reading of the words "brought promptly" in Article 5, paragraph 3, implies that the right to be brought before an appropriate officer relates to the time when a person is first deprived of his liberty under Article 5, paragraph 1.*c*. The obligation on Contracting States under Article 5, paragraph 3, is therefore limited to bringing the detainee promptly before an appropriate officer at that initial stage, although Article 5, paragraph 4, of the Convention may in certain cases require that the person be subsequently brought before a judge for the purpose of effectively contesting the lawfulness of his detention when it lasts for a long time (see, *mutatis mutandis*, European Commission of Human Rights, Trzaska v. Poland, No. 25792/94, Report of 19 May 1998, paragraphs 71-81).

The qualities of the "officer" or "judge" before whom a person who has been arrested must be brought

Principles

The concept of "officer" is essential to the application of Article 5. The principle was established in the Schiesser v. Switzerland judgment (4 December 1979, Series A No. 34, pp. 11-12, paragraphs 25-26; pp. 13-14, paragraph 31; p. 16, paragraph 38). There is no need to describe the facts, except to mention that Mr Schiesser had been brought before a member of the Attorney General's office. Could the Attorney in question be regarded as an "officer authorised by law to exercise judicial power"? The Court examined the concepts of "officer" and "judge" and then set out the following criteria before announcing its decision:

> [...] the Court has to ascertain only whether the said Attorney possessed the attributes of an "officer authorised by law to exercise judicial power".

> This last phrase has three components.

> The second component ("authorised by law to exercise") does not give rise to any difficulty: the Winterthur District Attorney exercised in the instant case powers conferred on him by cantonal law (see paragraphs 7, 12 and 15-17 above); this is contested neither by the Commission, nor by the Government, nor by the applicant.

> The first and third components ("officer", "judicial power") have to be considered together.

> [...]

> [...] the "officer" is not identical with the "judge" but must nevertheless have some of the latter's attributes, that is to say he must satisfy certain conditions each of which constitutes a guarantee for the person arrested.

133

The first of such conditions is independence of the executive and of the parties (see, *mutatis mutandis,* the above-mentioned Neumeister judgment, p. 44). This does not mean that the "officer" may not be to some extent subordinate to other judges or officers provided that they themselves enjoy similar independence.

In addition, under Article 5, paragraph 3 (art. 5-3), there is both a procedural and a substantive requirement. The procedural requirement places the "officer" under the obligation of hearing himself the individual brought before him (see, *mutatis mutandis,* the above-mentioned Winterwerp judgment, p. 24, paragraph 60); the substantive requirement imposes on him the obligations of reviewing the circumstances militating for or against detention, of deciding, by reference to legal criteria, whether there are reasons to justify detention and of ordering release if there are no such reasons (the above-mentioned Ireland v. the United Kingdom judgment, p. 76, paragraph 199).

In verifying whether these various conditions are satisfied, the Court does not have to deal with questions that do not arise in the instant case, for example whether an officer is fitted, by reason of his training or experience, to exercise judicial power.

[...]

The Court is therefore of the opinion that the Winterthur District Attorney offered in the present case the guarantees of independence and the procedural and substantive guarantees inherent in the notion of "officer authorised by law to exercise judicial power". There has accordingly been no breach of Article 5, paragraph 3 (art. 5-3).

It must be emphasised that the Court accords the greatest importance to objective appearances at the time when the decision on detention is taken. It expressly said so in the Nikolova v. Bulgaria judgment (25 March 1999, Application No. 31195/96, *Reports* 1999-II, paragraphs 49, 51 and 53):

[...] objective appearances at the time of the decision on detention are material: if it appears at that time that the "officer" may later intervene in subsequent criminal proceedings on behalf of the prosecuting authority, his independence and impartiality are capable of appearing open to doubt (see the Huber v. Switzerland judgment of 23 October 1990, Series A No. 188, p. 18, paragraph 43, and the Brincat v. Italy judgment of 26 November 1992, Series A No. 249-A, p. 12, paragraph 21) [...].

Applications

The Court took that approach in, among other cases, the Assenov and Others v. Bulgaria judgment (judgment of 28 October 1998, Application No. 24760/94, *Reports* 1998-VIII, paragraphs 148-150):

The Court recalls that on 28 July 1995 Mr Assenov was brought before an investigator who questioned him, formally charged him, and took the decision to detain him on remand (see paragraph 33 above). It notes that, under Bulgarian law, investigators do not have the power to make legally binding decisions as to the detention or release of a suspect. Instead, any decision made by an investigator is capable of being overturned by the prosecutor, who may also withdraw a case from an investigator if dissatisfied with the latter's approach (see paragraphs 66-69 above). It follows that the investigator was not sufficiently independent properly to be described as an "officer authorised by law to exercise judicial power" within the meaning of Article 5, paragraph 3.

Mr Assenov was not heard in person by prosecutor A., who approved the investigator's decision (see paragraph 33 above), or by any of the other prosecutors who later decided that he should continue to be detained. In any case, since any one of these prosecutors could subsequently have acted against the applicant in criminal proceedings (see paragraph 66 above), they were not sufficiently independent or impartial for the purposes of Article 5, paragraph 3.

The Court considers, therefore, that there has been a violation of Article 5, paragraph 3, on the ground that the applicant was not brought before an "officer authorised by law to exercise judicial power".

The Court has had occasion to consider the special procedures applicable to members of the armed forces. The de Jong, Baljet and Van den Brink v. the Netherlands judgment provides an illustration (22 May 1984, Series A No. 77, p. 24, paragraphs 48-49). In that case, the question for the Court was whether an *auditeur militaire* could be considered an officer authorised to adopt a decision on detention. The Court considered that he could not, and made two points:

> In addition, the *auditeur militaire* did not enjoy the kind of independence demanded by Article 5, paragraph 3 (art. 5-3). Although independent of the military authorities, the same *auditeur militaire* could be called upon to perform the function of prosecuting authority after referral of the case to the Military Court (Article 126, first paragraph, of the Military Code – see paragraph 19, first subparagraph, above). He would thereby become a committed party to any criminal proceedings subsequently brought against the serviceman on whose detention he was advising prior to referral for trial. In sum, the *auditeur militaire* could not be "independent of the parties" (see the extract from the Schiesser judgment quoted above at paragraph 47) at this preliminary stage precisely because he was liable to become one of the parties at the next stage of the procedure (see the judgment of today's date in the case of Duinhof and Duijf, Series A No. 79, paragraph 38).

(*Idem* the Hood v. the United Kingdom judgment of 18 February 1999, Application No. 27267/95, *Reports* 1999-I, paragraphs 56-57, where the applicant had been placed under arrest by his commanding officer before facing a court martial and the unit adjutant (the commanding officer's deputy) had acted as assistant prosecuting officer in the proceedings; see also the Stephen Jordan v. the United Kingdom judgment of 14 March 2000, Application No. 30280/96, paragraph 27.)

In a recent case of H.B. v. Switzerland (judgment of 5 April 2001, Application No. 26899/95, paragraphs 55-64), the Court considered the particular case of a person who had been brought before an investigating judge. On completion of the judicial investigation, a case can be referred for trial before the District Court or before the President of the District Court, or before the Court of Appeal or again before the Criminal Court of the Canton of Solothurn. If the case is referred to the District Court or the President of the

District Court, the investigating judge who decided to refer it must set out in his decision a summary of the facts, the legal classification of the offence and the criminal provisions applicable. No member of the prosecution is then present at the trial. The Court noted:

> [...] Before an "officer" can be said to exercise "judicial power" within the meaning of [Article 5, paragraph 3], he or she must satisfy certain conditions providing a guarantee to the person detained against any arbitrary or unjustified deprivation of liberty. Thus, the "officer" must be independent of the executive and the parties. In this respect, objective appearances at the time of the decision on detention are material: if it appears at that time that the "officer" may later intervene in subsequent criminal proceedings on behalf of the prosecuting authority, his independence and impartiality may be open to doubt. The "officer" must hear the individual brought before him in person and review, by reference to legal criteria, whether or not the detention is justified. If it is not so justified, the "officer" must have the power to make a binding order for the detainee's release (see the Assenov and Others v. Bulgaria judgment of 28 October 1998, *Reports of Judgments and Decisions* 1998-VIII, p. 3298, paragraph 146, and the Huber v. Switzerland judgment of 23 October 1990, Series A No. 188, p. 18, paragraph 43).

In the present case, the Court notes that upon his arrest the applicant was heard in person by the investigating judge. Moreover, it has not been contested by the applicant that he could at any time have been released from detention, as provided for by Section 50 of the Code of Criminal Procedure of the Canton of Solothurn.

An issue arises, however, as to the independence and impartiality of the investigating judge, in particular whether he met the conditions of an "officer authorised by law to exercise judicial power" as required by Article 5, paragraph 3, of the Convention. In examining this issue the Court is called upon to consider whether the investigating judge would, at a later stage, have been entitled to intervene on behalf of the prosecuting authority.

It is not in disagreement between the parties that upon the applicant's arrest and detention it was open which of the criminal jurisdictions of the Canton of Solothurn would eventually try the applicant if his case was referred to trial, in particular the District Court, the District Court President, the Court of Appeal or the Criminal Court of the Canton of Solothurn.

The Court has first examined the situation if the subsequent trial had been conducted before the District Court. The parties disagreed as to the position of the investigating judge in such proceedings.

The Court notes that in such a case the investigating judge, when closing the preliminary investigations, prepares a final order containing a summary description of the facts, the legal description of the offence and the applicable criminal provisions. It is true that both the Federal Court in its judgment of 13 April 1999 and the Government before the Court have referred to the merely declaratory and orienting character of this order.

Nevertheless, in the ensuing trial before the District Court there is no formal bill of indictment, nor will a member of the Public Prosecutor's office be present at the trial. Rather, it is the investigating judge who in his final order will provide the framework for the facts and their legal qualification within which the District Court then conducts its trial. As such, the order contains substantial elements, and indeed will exercise important functions, of a bill of indictment.

In these circumstances, the Court considers that, when the investigating judge decided on the applicant's arrest and detention, it appeared that, had his case been referred to trial before the District Court, the investigating judge ordering his detention on remand would have been "entitled to intervene in the subsequent criminal proceedings as a representative of the prosecuting authority" (see the Huber judgment cited above, p. 18, paragraph 43).

In view thereof, it is unnecessary to examine, in addition, the situation if the case had been referred for trial to other jurisdictions, in particular the Criminal Court or the Court of Appeal of the Canton of Solothurn, or whether the investigating judge was in fact independent of the Public Prosecutor's office.

The Court considers, therefore, that there has been a violation of Article 5, paragraph 3, of the Convention on the ground that the applicant was not brought before an "officer authorised by law to exercise judicial power".

3. Provisional detention and the right to trial within a reasonable time or to release pending trial

Article 5, paragraph 3, establishes a second right: the right to "trial within a reasonable time or to release pending trial".

The meaning of the right to trial within a reasonable time "or" to release

In the Neumeister v. Austria case (judgment of 27 June 1968, Series A No. 8, p. 37, paragraphs 4-5; p. 38, paragraph 8; p. 40, paragraph 12; and p. 41, paragraph 15), the Court explained the scope of that provision. It ruled out any possibility of an alternative between the right of a detained person to trial within a reasonable time and the right to release that might be suggested by the use of the word "or":

> The Court is of the opinion that this provision cannot be understood as giving the judicial authorities a choice between either bringing the accused to trial within a reasonable time or granting him provisional release even subject to guarantees. The reasonableness of the time spent by an accused person in detention up to the beginning of the trial must be assessed in relation to the very fact of his detention. Until conviction, he must be presumed innocent, and the purpose of the provision under consideration is essentially to require his provisional release once his continuing detention ceases to be reasonable. [...]

(*Idem* the Jablonski v. Poland judgment of 21 December 2000, Application No. 33492/96, paragraphs 83-84.)

Determination of the period to be taken into account as "provisional detention" within the meaning of the Convention

In the Muller v. France judgment, the Court stated that the period to be taken into consideration begins as soon as the person concerned is deprived of his liberty. The relevant date is the date on which the person concerned is taken into custody and not the later date on which a detention order is made by a judge (judgment of 17 March 1997, Application No. 21802/92, *Reports* 1997-II, paragraph 34):

> The period to be taken into consideration started on 13 December 1988, when the applicant was taken into police custody [...].

In the Labita v. Italy judgment, the Court stated that the period of detention ends when a decision on guilt is reached, even if only at first instance (the Labita v. Italy judgment of 6 April 2000, Application No. 26772/95, paragraphs 171-173):

> The Court reiterates that the end of the period referred to in Article 5, paragraph 3, is "the day on which the charge is determined, even if only by a court of first instance" (see the Wemhoff v. Germany judgment of 27 June 1968, Series A No. 7, p. 23, paragraph 9).

(*Idem* in the Olstowski v. Poland judgment of 15 November 2001, Application No. 34052/96, paragraph 67.)

What about the period of detention in the event of an appeal? The period between the date of conviction and the date on which that conviction is set aside on appeal and the case remitted for a fresh consideration must be excluded from the period to be taken into consideration. That situation was considered in the Kudla case, where the applicant had been arrested and incarcerated on 4 October 1993, had appeared before the court and been convicted on 1 June 1995, had appealed against the judgment, which was set aside on 22 February 1996, and had eventually been released on bail on 29 October 1996 before his case was re-heard (the Kudla v. Poland judgment of 26 October 2000, Application No. 30210/96, paragraph 104):

> [...] the Court reiterates that, in view of the essential link between Article 5, paragraph 3, of the Convention and paragraph 1.*c* of that Article, a person convicted at first instance cannot be regarded as being detained "for the purpose of bringing him before the competent legal authority on reasonable suspicion of having committed an offence", as specified in the latter provision, but is in the position provided for by Article 5, paragraph 1.*a*, which authorises deprivation of liberty "after conviction by a competent court" (see, for example, the B. v. Austria judgment of 28 March 1990, Series A No. 175, pp. 14-16, paragraphs 36-39). Accordingly, the applicant's detention from 1 June 1995, the date of his original first-instance conviction, to 22 February 1996, the date on which that conviction was quashed and his case remitted, cannot be taken into account for the purposes of Article 5, paragraph 3.

In those circumstances, the period of detention may consist of a number of distinct terms. In the same judgment, the Court stated (paragraph 105):

> The Court consequently finds that the period to be taken into consideration consisted of two separate terms, the first lasting from 4 October 1993 to 1 June 1995 and the second from 22 February to 29 October 1996, and amounted to two years, four months and three days.

For an identical solution, see the Vaccaro v. Italy judgment of 16 November 2000, Application No. 41852/98, paragraphs 31-33. Similarly, where there are a number of periods of detention separated by release, they must be aggregated (the Bouchet v. France judgment of 20 March 2001, Application No. 33591/96, paragraph 33, available in French only – unofficial translation):

> The periods to be taken into consideration ran from 8 January 1996, the date on which a detention order was made in respect of the applicant, until 18 March 1996, the date on which he was released under judicial supervision, and from 26 March 1996, when he was again placed in custody, until 3 July 1997, the date of the judgment of the Assize Court whereby he was convicted and sentenced to one year's imprisonment. The total period of incarceration was therefore seventeen months and seventeen days.

The Court's general approach in assessing the reasonableness of the duration of detention

In the W. v. Switzerland case (judgment of 26 January 1993, Series A No. 254, p. 15, paragraph 30), the applicant, who was prosecuted for a series of economic offences, complained of the length of his provisional detention, which had lasted four years and three days. The Court precluded the idea of a maximum length of detention imposed by Article 5, paragraph 3.

> The Commission's opinion was based on the idea that Article 5, paragraph 3 (art. 5-3), implies a maximum length of pre-trial detention. The Court cannot subscribe to this opinion, which moreover finds no support in its case-law. That case-law in fact states that the reasonable time cannot be assessed *in abstracto* (see, *mutatis mutandis*, the Stögmüller v. Austria judgment of 10 November 1969, Series A No. 9, p. 40, paragraph 4). As the Court has already found in the Wemhoff v. Germany judgment of 27 June 1968, the reasonableness of an accused person's continued detention must be assessed in each case according to its special features (Series A No. 7, p. 24, paragraph 10).

The Erdem v. Germany judgment (5 July 2001, Application No. 38321/97, paragraph 39, available in French only – unofficial translation) begins with a reference to that principle and summarises the Court's approach in examining the reasonableness of a period of detention:

> The Court recalls that the reasonableness of a period of detention does not lend itself to abstract evaluation. The lawfulness of the continuing detention of an accused must be assessed in each case according to the specific characteristics of the case. Continuing incarceration is justified in a given case only if specific indications show a genuine requirement in the public interest that, notwithstanding the presumption of innocence, prevails over the rule requiring respect for individual liberty laid down in Article 5 of the Convention (see, among other authorities, the Labita v. Italy [GC] judgment, No. 26772/95, paragraphs 152 *et seq.*, ECHR 2000-IV, and the Kudla v. Poland [GC] judgment, No. 30210/96, paragraph 110, ECHR 2000-XI).

> It is primarily for the national judicial authorities to ensure that in a given case the duration of the provisional detention of an accused does not exceed what is reasonable. To that end, they must examine all the circumstances susceptible of disclosing or precluding the existence of a genuine requirement in the public

interest which, regard being had to the presumption of innocence, justifies an exception to the rule requiring respect for individual liberty and to refer thereto in their decisions on applications for release. It is essentially on the basis of the grounds set out in those decisions, and of the true facts stated by the accused in his petitions, that the Court must determine whether or not there has been a violation of Article 5, paragraph 3, of the Convention.

The persistence of plausible reasons to suspect that the person arrested has committed an offence is a condition *sine qua non* of the lawfulness of continuing detention, but at the end of a certain time it is not enough: the Court must then establish whether the other grounds adopted by the judicial authorities continue to render the deprivation of liberty lawful. When they prove to be "relevant" and "sufficient", the Court goes on to ascertain whether the competent national authorities employed "special diligence" in the conduct of the proceedings (see, in particular, the Tomasi v. France judgment of 27 August 1992, Series A No. 241-A, p. 35, paragraph 84, the I.A. v. France judgment of 23 September 1998, *Reports of Judgments and Decisions* 1998-VII, pp. 2978-2979, paragraph 102, and the Amiram Bar v. France decision, No. 37863/97, 7 September 1999).

The Court has had occasion to specify the approach which the national courts must take in examining the matters which do or do not justify continuing detention. They must appraise the factors (sureties, police supervision) which may permit release. In the Jablonski v. Poland judgment (21 December 2000, Application No. 33492/96, paragraphs 83-84):

> [...] the Court observes that under Article 5, paragraph 3, the authorities, when deciding whether a person should be released or detained, are obliged to consider alternative measures of ensuring his appearance at trial. Indeed, that Article lays down not only the right to "trial within a reasonable time or release pending trial" but also provides that "release may be conditioned by guarantees to appear for trial" (see, *mutatis mutandis*, the Neumeister v. Austria judgment of 27 June 1968, Series A No. 8, p. 3, paragraph 3).

> That provision does not give the judicial authorities a choice between either bringing the accused to trial within a reasonable time or granting him provisional release – even subject to guarantees. Until conviction he must be presumed innocent, and the purpose of Article 5, paragraph 3, is essentially to require his provisional release once his continuing detention ceases to be reasonable (see the Neumeister judgment cited above, paragraph 4).

> Turning to the circumstances of the present case, the Court notes that over the period of those several years which the applicant spent in pre-trial detention no consideration appears to have been given to the possibility of imposing on him other "preventive measures" – such as bail or police supervision – expressly foreseen by Polish law to secure the proper conduct of the criminal proceedings (see paragraph 60 above).

Examples of the application of the rule

The Court always adopts a global approach when determining the reasonableness of a period of detention. Extracts do not always do justice to its reasoning in its entirety. Subject to that reservation, they do provide certain indications.

Examples of the duration of detention

The Court has had many opportunities to state that a period of detention of more than four years must be in response to special circumstances: see, for example, the Richet v. France judgment of 13 February 2001, Application No. 34947/97, paragraph 60, available in French only – unofficial translation:

> [...] a period of provisional detention of more than four years and eight months must be accompanied by particularly compelling justification.

As regards the detention of a minor for approximately two years, the Assenov and Others v. Bulgaria judgment contains the following passage (judgment of 28 October 1998, Application No. 24760/94, paragraphs 156-158):

> The Court notes that on 28 July 1995 Mr Assenov was charged with sixteen or more burglaries and robberies, the latter involving some violence (see paragraph 33 above). Although he had first been questioned in connection with the investigation into this series of thefts in January 1995 (see paragraph 32 above), a number of the offences with which he was charged were committed subsequently; the last robbery having taken place on 24 July, three days before his arrest.

> In these circumstances, the Court considers that the national authorities were not unreasonable in fearing that the applicant might reoffend if released.

> However, the Court recalls that the applicant was a minor and thus, according to Bulgarian law, should have been detained on remand only in exceptional circumstances (see paragraph 69 above). It was, therefore, more than usually important that the authorities displayed special diligence in ensuring that he was brought to trial within a reasonable time.

> The Government have submitted that it took two years for the case to come to trial because it was particularly complex, requiring a lengthy investigation. However, it would appear from the information available to the Court that during one of those years, September 1995 to September 1996, virtually no action was taken in connection with the investigation: no new evidence was collected and Mr Assenov was questioned only once, on 21 March 1996 (see paragraphs 34 and 42 above). Moreover, given the importance of the right to liberty, and the possibility, for example, of copying the relevant documents rather than sending the original file to the authority concerned on each occasion, the applicant's many appeals for release should not have been allowed to have the effect of suspending the investigation and thus delaying his trial (see the above-mentioned Toth judgment, p. 21, paragraph 77).

> Against this background, the Court finds that Mr Assenov was denied a "trial within a reasonable time", in violation of Article 5, paragraph 3.

Grounds for continuing detention

We shall confine ourselves to examining two types of grounds.

First, we shall look at the persistence of plausible reasons for suspecting the detained person, a condition *sine qua non* of the lawfulness of continuing detention. In the Labita v. Italy judgment (6 April 2000, Application

No. 26772/95, paragraphs 156-161), which concerned the implication of a person by a *pentito* offender, the Court held:

> However, for there to be reasonable suspicion there must be facts or information which would satisfy an objective observer that the person concerned may have committed an offence (see the Erdagöz judgment cited above, p. 2314, paragraph 51, in fine, and the Fox, Campbell and Hartley v. the United Kingdom judgment of 30 August 1990, Series A No. 182, pp. 16-17, paragraph 32).

> In the instant case, the allegations against the applicant came from a single source, a *pentito* who had stated in 1992 that he had learned indirectly that the applicant was the treasurer of a Mafia-type organisation (see paragraph 10 above). According to the authorities in question, in May 1992 those statements constituted sufficient evidence to justify keeping the applicant in detention [...].

> The Court is conscious of the fact that the co-operation of *pentiti* is a very important weapon in the Italian authorities' fight against the Mafia. However, the use of statements by *pentiti* does give rise to difficult problems as, by their very nature, such statements are open to manipulation and may be made purely in order to obtain the advantages which Italian law affords to *pentiti*, or for personal revenge. The sometimes ambiguous nature of such statements and the risk that a person might be accused and arrested on the basis of unverified allegations that are not necessarily disinterested must not, therefore, be underestimated (see Contrada v. Italy, Application No. 27143/95, Commission decision of 14 January 1997, *Decisions and Reports* 88-B, p. 112).

> For these reasons, as the domestic courts recognise, statements of *pentiti* must be corroborated by other evidence. Furthermore, hearsay must be supported by objective evidence.

> That, in the Court's view, is especially true when a decision is being made whether to prolong detention pending trial. While a suspect may validly be detained at the beginning of proceedings on the basis of statements by *pentiti*, such statements necessarily become less relevant with the passage of time, especially where no further evidence is uncovered during the course of the investigation.

> In the instant case, the Court notes that, as the Trapani District Court and Palermo Court of Appeal confirmed in their decisions acquitting the applicant, there was no evidence to corroborate the hearsay evidence of B.F. On the contrary, B.F.'s main, if indirect, source of information had died in 1989 and had, in turn, obtained it on hearsay from another person who had also been killed before he could be questioned. Furthermore, B.F.'s statements had already been contradicted during the course of the investigation by other *pentiti* who had said that they did not recognise the applicant (see paragraph 18 above).

> In these circumstances, very compelling reasons would be required for the applicant's lengthy detention (two years and seven months) to have been justified under Article 5, paragraph 3.

We shall not look at the risk of flight. In the Bebboub alias Hussein Ali v. France judgment (9 November 1999, Application No. 37786/97, paragraphs 41-42, available in French only – unofficial translation), the Court held that there had been a violation of Article 5, paragraph 3. It observed:

> In their decisions on the applicant's provisional detention, the competent courts considered that there was a danger that the applicant would abscond should he

be released. They relied essentially on the fact that the applicant had no fixed abode in France, had no recognisable resources and was in an irregular position, with false papers. That is the case of the judgments of the Indictments Division of the Paris Court of Appeal of 23 July 1996, 15 November 1996 and 25 July 1997. Without doubt, those are circumstances likely to characterise a danger of flight. However, the Court considers that when such a danger necessarily decreases with time (the Neumeister v. Austria judgment of 27 June 1968, Series A No. 8, p. 39, paragraph 10), the judicial authorities failed to state why there was reason to consider in this case that the danger persisted after more than three years of detention.

The Court further finds that the judgment of 25 July 1997 refers to the inadequacy of court supervision and therefore recognises that the question as to whether the applicant was capable of providing adequate guarantees that he would appear in court should he be released was considered. There, too, however, the Court can only note the absence of reasoning in that decision. Nor was there any further reference to that possibility in the later decisions.

(For a case of detention of three years and three months where the Court accepted that sufficient reasons had been stated for the danger of flight, even though the various steps in the proceedings had lasted too long, see the Cesky v. the Czech Republic judgment of 6 June 2000, paragraph 79.)

A final point is that Article 5, paragraph 3, does not require as such that a detained person must be released on grounds of health (the Jablonski v. Poland judgment of 21 December 2000, Application No. 33492/96, paragraph 82):

> The applicant suggested that the courts should have released him because his health was very bad and had constantly been aggravated by his detention. The Court would however point out that Article 5, paragraph 3, cannot be read as obliging the national authorities to release a detainee on account of his state of health. The question of whether or not the condition of the person in custody is compatible with his continued detention should primarily be determined by the national courts and, as the Court has held in the context of Article 3 of the Convention, those courts are in general not obliged to release him on health grounds or to place him in a civil hospital to enable him to receive a particular kind of medical treatment (see Kudla v. Poland cited above, paragraph 93).

In the context of the citation of extracts, it is interesting to look at the way in which the Court evaluates the reasons provided by the national courts as justification for the detention.

The Court's assessment of the drafting of national decisions

As regards the imprecision of the reasons stated by the national courts, reference may be made to the Labita v. Italy judgment (judgment of 6 April 2000, Application No. 26772/95, paragraphs 162-164):

> The national courts referred to the risk of pressure being brought to bear on witnesses and of evidence being tampered with, the fact that the accused were dangerous, the complexity of the case and the requirements of the investigation. [...]

143

The Court observes that the grounds stated in the relevant decisions were reasonable, at least initially, though very general, too. The judicial authorities referred to the prisoners as a whole and made no more than an abstract mention of the nature of the offence. They did not point to any factor capable of showing that the risks relied on actually existed and failed to establish that the applicant, who had no record and whose role in the Mafia-type organisation concerned was said to be minor (the prosecutor called for a three-year sentence in his case), posed a danger. No account was taken of the fact that the accusations against the applicant were based on evidence which, with time, had become weaker rather than stronger.

The Court accordingly considers that the grounds stated in the impugned decisions were not sufficient to justify the applicant's being kept in detention for two years and seven months.

In the I.A. v. France judgment (23 September 1998, Application No. 28213/95, paragraph 108), the Court pointed to the lack of consistency in providing a reason for continuing detention during the investigation:

The Court accepts that in some cases the safety of a person under investigation requires his continued detention, for a time at least. However, this can only be so in exceptional circumstances having to do with the nature of the offences concerned, the conditions in which they were committed and the context in which they took place.

In the present case this ground appears in the order of 9 December 1991, but not in that of 16 June 1992; it is repeated in the orders of 14 September, 17 November and 4 December 1992, but is missing from that of 13 January 1993; it reappears in the orders of 5 March and 2 April 1993 but is no longer found in the decisions of 21 April, 10 May and 4, 18 and 25 June 1993; it is cited again in that of 9 July 1993, but not in that of 23 July 1993, and then reappears in the seven orders made between 13 August and 5 November 1993; it is not mentioned in the decisions of 22 and 23 November and 10 December 1993, but is mentioned in that of 17 December 1993; it is missing from the decision of 7 January 1994, but is found again in those of 21 January and 4, 14 and 22 February 1994; the decisions of 4 and 11 March no longer refer to it, but it reappears in that of 18 March 1994.

This ground was therefore cited intermittently by the judicial authorities, as if the dangers threatening the applicant regularly disappeared and reappeared.

Moreover, the few decisions which refer to factors that might explain why there was a need to protect the applicant mention the risk of "revenge attacks by the victim's family" or "reprisals" (orders of 9 December 1991 and 4 December 1992), or the "fear" expressed by the applicant on account of the "frequently barbaric and unjust [Lebanese] customs" (orders of 14 September and 17 November 1992). In particular, they omit to specify why there was such a need when almost all the victim's family lived in Lebanon.

In the Erdem v. Germany judgment, the Court highlighted a blatant repetitiveness in the reasons for continuing detention (judgment of 5 July 2001, Application No. 38321/97, paragraphs 43-45, available in French only – unofficial translation):

As regards the gravity of the offences attributed to the applicant and the persistence of the suspicions in relation to him, the Court notes that only the persistence of suspicion that he belonged to a terrorist organisation, which attracted a maximum prison sentence of ten years, and not suspicion of murder, was set out in the decisions ordering extension of the applicant's provisional detention; furthermore, the applicant was eventually convicted of belonging to a terrorist organisation and sentenced to six years' imprisonment. The duration of his provisional detention therefore virtually coincided with that of his prison sentence.

As regards the risk of flight, the Court considers that the competent courts could legitimately believe in the persistence of such risk, based on the applicant's foreign nationality, the fact that he had no personal ties and no residence in Germany, and his frequent travels in the Middle East and France (see paragraph 17 above). However, the Court considers that although these grounds were relevant, at least at the beginning of the period of detention, they were not in themselves sufficient to justify such a long deprivation of liberty.

Furthermore, the courts reproduced the earlier reasons almost to the letter without specifying whether there were any new factors to justify continuing to detain the applicant.

Last, as regards the need to state the grounds on which measures other than incarceration would be insufficient, mention should be made of the Kreps v. Poland judgment of (26 July 2001, Application No. 34097/96, paragraph 43):

> The Court observes that in the present case the relevant judicial authorities advanced two principal reasons for the applicant's continued detention, namely the serious nature of the offences with which he had been charged and the need to ensure the proper conduct of his trial (see paragraphs 17-18 and 22 above).

> The Court accepts that the suspicion against the applicant of having committed the serious offences with which he had been charged may initially have justified his detention. However, it cannot accept that it could be a "relevant and sufficient" ground for his being held in custody for nearly four years.

> As regards the need to secure the conduct of the proceedings, the Court notes that the authorities, while repeating that argument, did not indicate a single circumstance suggesting that, if released, the applicant would abscond or evade justice, or any sentence that might be imposed on him, or that he would otherwise upset the course of the trial (see paragraphs 17-18, 22 and 25 above).

> In that context, the Court further observes that the Regional Court and the Court of Appeal did not take into account any other possible guarantees that the applicant would appear for trial – such as bail or release under police supervision – explicitly provided for by Polish law to secure the proper conduct of criminal proceedings (see paragraph 33 above). Nor did the courts mention whether, and if so, why those alternative measures would not have ensured the applicant's presence before them or why, had he been released, his trial would not have followed its proper course.

> The Court is, therefore, not satisfied that the reasons given to justify the applicant's detention were "sufficient" and "relevant", as required under Article 5, paragraph 3.

Assessment by the Court of the diligence of the national authorities

As regards the diligence which must be shown in conducting proceedings, the Court has indicated on a number of occasions (the Erdem v. Germany judgment of 5 July 2001, Application No. 38321/97, paragraph 46, available in French only – unofficial translation) :

> As regards the conduct of the proceedings, the Court is not unaware that the particular speed with which a detained accused is entitled to have his case examined must not harm the judicial officers' efforts to carry out their tasks with the desired care (the Tomasi judgment, cited above, paragraph 102).

Thus, the Court considered that the investigations carried out in a case concerning the Mafia, which had led to the applicant's being detained for two years and seven months, had been conducted with sufficient diligence (the Contrada v. Italy judgment of 24 August 1998, Application No. 27143/95, *Reports* 1998-V, paragraphs 66-68) :

> The Court observes that Mr Contrada was detained pending trial for two years, seven months and seven days, approximately fourteen months during the investigation and the remainder during the trial before the court (see paragraph 53 above). It notes that the Public Prosecutor's office had to take a number of highly complex steps in the investigation, including checking the statements of the *pentiti* in minute detail, obtaining many items of evidence, hearing witnesses – in particular, police officers and judges engaged in the fight against the Mafia – and obtaining international judicial assistance. During that same stage of the proceedings the applicant was implicated by other *pentiti*, which entailed additional investigative measures being taken. Subsequently, the trial court heard evidence from no less than 250 witnesses or people being tried for offences connected with those of which the applicant was accused. Seven *pentiti* were, for security reasons, questioned in the Rome and Padua prisons in which they were detained. Three confrontations were organised. Between 4 November and 29 December 1994 all thirteen hearings were devoted to hearing evidence from the applicant (see paragraph 32 above).

> The right of an accused in detention to have his case examined with particular expedition must not hinder the efforts of the courts to carry out their tasks with proper care (see the W. v. Switzerland judgment cited above, p. 19, paragraph 42). In the instant case, with the exception of the analysis of the data relating to Mr Contrada's mobile telephones, which could and should have been carried out earlier, and the excessive workload referred to by the trial court on 31 March 1995 (see paragraphs 23 and 26 above), the Court sees no particular reason to criticise the relevant national authorities' conduct of the case, especially as, when the maximum periods of detention pending trial were extended, the trial court offered to increase the rate of the hearings, but the defence declined (see paragraph 32 above).

> Furthermore, although investigative measures such as the hearing of witnesses and confrontations are quite unexceptional in criminal cases, it should not be forgotten that trials of presumed members of the Mafia, or, as in the present case, of persons suspected of supporting that organisation from within State institutions, are particularly sensitive and complicated. With its rigid hierarchical structure and very strict rules and its substantial power of intimidation based on the

rule of silence and the difficulty in identifying its followers, the Mafia represents a sort of criminal opposition force capable of influencing public life directly or indirectly and of infiltrating the institutions. It is for that reason – to enable the "organisation" to be undermined through information supplied by former "members" – that detailed inquiries are necessary.

[...] In the light of the foregoing, the Court considers that the authorities who dealt with the case could reasonably base the detention in issue on relevant and sufficient grounds and that they conducted the proceedings without delay.

There has therefore been no violation of Article 5, paragraph 3.

The Court has also had many occasions to condemn the lack of speed in proceedings. It has held that a period of ten months between a judgment being set aside and the case being re-examined exceeded the requirement for speed laid down in Article 5, paragraph 3 (the Punzelt v. the Czech Republic judgment of 25 April 2000, Application No. 31315/96, paragraphs 81-83):

> As regards the conduct of the proceedings by the national authorities, the Court notes, in particular, that more than eight months elapsed between the filing of the indictment and the hearing before the City Court on 28 June 1994. This period does not appear, as such, to be excessive as during this time the City Court had to deal with several requests for further evidence to be taken which the applicant made, notwithstanding that at the end of the investigation he had expressly stated that he had no other proposals in this respect.

> However, the City Court subsequently adjourned three other hearings to enable further evidence to be taken. As a result, it delivered its first judgment after a delay of another six months.

> Subsequently the Court of Cassation quashed the judgment of 10 January 1995 on the ground that the City Court had not established or considered all the relevant facts of the case, that it had applied the law erroneously and that its judgment was unclear. Despite the Supreme Court's intervention to accelerate the proceedings, the City Court did not deliver its second judgment until 16 January 1996, that is to say ten months after its first judgment had been quashed.

> In these circumstances, the Court finds that "special diligence" was not displayed in the conduct of the proceedings.

> Accordingly, there has been a violation of Article 5, paragraph 3, of the Convention as a result of the length of the applicant's detention on remand.

4. Considerations relating to the guarantees accompanying release and in particular the setting of bail

The Iwanczuk v. Poland judgment (15 November 2001, Application No. 25196/94, paragraphs 66-70) concerns the principles governing the setting of and the procedures for providing the necessary securities:

> The Court recalls that according to its case-law, the amount of the bail must be "assessed principally in relation to the person concerned, his assets [...] in other words to the degree of confidence that is possible that the prospect of loss of security in the event of his non-appearance at a trial will act as a sufficient deterrent to dispel any wish on his part to abscond" (see the Neumeister v. Austria

judgment of 27 June 1968, Series A, p. 40, paragraph 14). The accused whom the judicial authorities declare themselves prepared to release on bail must faithfully furnish sufficient information, that can be checked if need be, about the amount of bail to be fixed. As the fundamental right to liberty as guaranteed by Article 5 of the Convention is at stake, the authorities must take as much care in fixing appropriate bail as in deciding whether or not the accused's continued detention is indispensable (European Commission of Human Rights, No. 8339/78, report of 11 December 1980, *Decisions and Reports* 23, p. 137).

In the present case, the Court observes that the Wroclaw Regional Court decided to release the applicant on bail on 21 December 1993. The amount of bail thus fixed was 2 000 000 000 (old) zlotys. The Court of Appeal subsequently upheld the amount of bail, finding that there was no impediment to the bail being deposited in bonds or as a mortgage on the applicant's real estate. On 18 January 1994 the Regional Court reduced the bail to 1 500 000 000 (old) zlotys. The applicant further requested that the bail be accepted in the form of mortgage, and enclosed an expert estimate of his property. Several other decisions ensued, in which the sum of bail and its form were changed. Finally in April the bail of 100 000 000 (old) zlotys to be paid in cash and 750 million in mortgage was accepted. The applicant was released on 5 May 1994, after the bail was duly deposited, that is four months and fourteen days after the decision to release him was taken.

The Court observes that the authorities found already in December 1993, as shown by the decision of the Wroclaw Regional Court of 21 December 1993, that the applicant's release as such would not jeopardise the further course of the proceedings. However, the applicant was released only in May 1994 as during that period the decisions as to the sum and form of the bail were changed several times.

The Court notes that the applicant promptly complied with his obligation to provide relevant information as to his assets. It was only the assessment of the actual sum of the bail to be deposited, that the courts kept changing. The main difficulty, however, consisted in determining the form of the bail, that is whether it should be deposited in cash, in State bonds or by way of mortgage on the applicant's real property. Regard must be had to the fact that the authorities at a certain point refused that the bail be deposited in the form of mortgage, without questioning the applicant's title to the property concerned. This, in the Court's view, implies that the authorities were reticent to accept the bail, which, in case of the applicant's non-appearance for the trial, would require undertaking certain formalities in order to seize the assets. This in itself, in the Court's opinion, cannot be regarded as sufficient ground on which to maintain for four months the detention on remand which had already been deemed unnecessary by the decision of the competent judicial authority.

In view of the fact that the proceedings relating to the amount and the modalities of payment of the bail lasted as long as four months and fourteen days, whereas the applicant remained in detention throughout this period, after the decision was taken that his further detention was unnecessary, and that no adequate reasons were forwarded by the authorities to justify successive changes of decisions concerning the form in which bail was to be deposited, the Court finds that there has been a violation of Article 5, paragraph 3, of the Convention.

Article 5, paragraph 4 – The right to take proceedings in respect of detention

Article 5, paragraph 4, is worded as follows:

> 4. **Everyone who is deprived of his liberty by arrest or detention shall be entitled to take proceedings by which the lawfulness of his detention shall be decided speedily by a court and his release ordered if the detention is not lawful.**

1. The place of Article 5, paragraph 4, and its interaction with paragraphs 1 and 3

Paragraph 4 of Article 5 has an autonomous place and role within Article 5. It applies to many situations, in particular cumulatively with paragraphs 1 and 3.

Article 5, paragraph 4, and its interaction with paragraph 1 of Article 5

In the Kolompar v. Belgium judgment (24 September 1992, Application No. 11613/85, Series A No. 235-C, paragraph 45), in an extradition case, the Court held:

> The mere fact that the Court has found no breach of the requirements of paragraph 1 of Article 5 (art. 5-1) does not mean that it is dispensed from carrying out a review of compliance with paragraph 4 (art. 5-4); the two paragraphs are separate provisions and observance of the former does not necessarily entail observance of the latter (see for example the De Wilde, Ooms and Versyp v. Belgium judgment of 18 June 1971, Series A No. 12, pp. 39-40, paragraph 73). Moreover, the Court has consistently stressed the importance of Article 5, paragraph 4 (art. 5-4), in particular in extradition cases (see the Sanchez-Reisse v. Switzerland judgment of 21 October 1986, Series A No. 107, pp. 16-22, paragraphs 42-61).

In those circumstances, the following question arises: does Article 5, paragraph 4, require that every person detained for whatever reason be entitled to have the legality of his detention reviewed? Or is it enough that the initial decision on detention should be taken by a body which combines all the factors inherent in the concept of "court" within the meaning of Article 5, paragraph 4 (art. 5-4)? Are proceedings in the context of Article 5, paragraph 4, then limited to detention decisions taken by bodies not having those characteristics? That question was answered in the De Wilde, Ooms and Versyp v. Belgium judgment of 18 June 1971, Applications Nos. 2832/66, 2835/66 and 2899/66, Series A No. 12, paragraph 76), where the Court stated:

> At first sight, the wording of Article 5, paragraph 4 (art. 5-4), might make one think that it guarantees the right of the detainee always to have supervised by a court the lawfulness of a previous decision which has deprived him of his liberty. The two official texts do not however use the same terms, since the English text speaks of "proceedings" and not of "appeal", "recourse" or "remedy" (compare Articles 13 and 26 (art. 13, art. 26)). Besides, it is clear that the purpose of Article 5,

paragraph 4 (art. 5-4), is to assure to persons who are arrested and detained the right to a judicial supervision of the lawfulness of the measure to which they are thereby subjected; the word "court" ("tribunal") is there found in the singular and not in the plural. Where the decision depriving a person of his liberty is one taken by an administrative body, there is no doubt that Article 5, paragraph 4 (art. 5-4), obliges the Contracting States to make available to the person detained a right of recourse to a court; but there is nothing to indicate that the same applies when the decision is made by a court at the close of judicial proceedings. In the latter case the supervision required by Article 5, paragraph 4 (art. 5-4), is incorporated in the decision; this is so, for example, where a sentence of imprisonment is pronounced after "conviction by a competent court" (Article 5, paragraph 1.*a*, of the Convention) (art. 5-1-a). It may therefore be concluded that Article 5, paragraph 4 (art. 5-4), is observed if the arrest or detention of a vagrant, provided for in paragraph 1.*e* (art. 5-1-e), is ordered by a "court" within the meaning of paragraph 4 (art. 5-4).

It results, however, from the purpose and object of Article 5 (art. 5), as well as from the very terms of paragraph 4 (art. 5-4) ("proceedings", *"recours"*), that in order to constitute such a "court" an authority must provide the fundamental guarantees of procedure applied in matters of deprivation of liberty. If the procedure of the competent authority does not provide them, the State could not be dispensed from making available to the person concerned a second authority which does provide all the guarantees of judicial procedure.

The Court thus brings out the theory that the control required by Article 5, paragraph 4, is incorporated in the control under Article 5, paragraph 1, particulary in connection with criminal convictions.

However, the fact that the initial detention decision issues from a court within the meaning of Article 5, paragraph 4, does not necessarily deprive the detained person of the right subsequently to bring proceedings on the basis of that provision. Thus, in the Van Droogenbroeck v. Belgium judgment (24 June 1982, Application No. 7906/77, Series A No. 50, paragraph 45), the Court held:

> [...] it would be contrary to the object and purpose of Article 5 (art. 5) [...] to interpret paragraph 4 [...] as making this category of confinement immune from subsequent review of lawfulness merely provided that the initial decision issued from a court.

It may be the case, in particular, that the grounds justifying detention for the purposes of Article 5, paragraph 1, may cease to exist, when it will be necessary to carry out a subsequent review under Article 5, paragraph 4. That is so in the case of detention justified by paragraph 1.*e*, concerning the confinement of persons of unsound mind. Even though they were confined by a court, they must be able to bring proceedings because their mental state may change, as in the Winterwerp v. the Netherlands case (judgment of 24 October 1979, Series A No. 33, pp. 22-23, paragraph 55):

> The very nature of the deprivation of liberty under consideration would appear to require a review of lawfulness to be available at reasonable intervals.

(*Idem* X. v. the United Kingdom, cited above, Series A No. 33, p. 23, paragraph 55, and No. 46, pp. 22-23, paragraph 52.)

Furthermore, that may apply when the initial decision is a conviction within the meaning of Article 5, paragraph 1.*a*. In fact, following conviction a person may be released, subject to possible reincarceration, or may be detained for an indefinite period. The Van Droogenbroeck v. Belgium judgment (24 June 1982, Series A No. 50, p. 26, paragraph 48) dealt with that situation. In that case, the criminal court had sentenced the applicant, primarily, to a term of imprisonment, and had also ordered that he be placed at the disposal of the government. This "placing at the Government's disposal" included the possibility that the Minister of Justice could detain him should he represent a "danger to society" once the main sentence had been served. There was without doubt an initial decision of a court; but the Court considered that there was an arbitrary risk when the minister took a decision assessing the "danger" which would justify reincarceration. That made it necessary to apply Article 5, paragraph 4. The Court observed, generally:

> Quite apart from conformity with domestic law, "no detention that is arbitrary can ever be regarded as 'lawful'" for the purposes of paragraph 1 (art. 5-1) (see, amongst others, the above-mentioned X. v. the United Kingdom judgment, Series A No. 46, p. 19, paragraph 43). This is the limit which the Minister of Justice must not exceed in the exercise of the wide discretion he enjoys in executing, or implementing, the initial court decision. This requirement is rendered all the more compelling by the seriousness of what is at stake, namely the possibility that the individual may be deprived of his liberty for up to ten years (Section 23 of the Act) or even longer (Section 22). This type of detention would no longer be in conformity with the Convention if it ceased to be based on reasons that are plausible and consistent with the objectives of the Social Protection Act; for the purposes of Article 5 (art. 5), it would become "unlawful". It follows that the individual concerned must be entitled to apply to a "court" having jurisdiction to determine whether or not there has been a violation of that kind; this possibility must be open to him during the course of his detention – once a certain period has elapsed since the detention began and thereafter at reasonable intervals (see, *mutatis mutandis*, the above-mentioned X. v. the United Kingdom judgment, Series A No. 46, pp. 22-23, paragraph 52) – and also at the moment of any return to detention after being at liberty.

(*Idem* the Silva Rocha v. Portugal judgment of 15 November 1996, *Reports* 1996-V, paragraphs 27-30; the Iribarne Pérez v. France judgment of 24 October 1995, Series A No. 325-C, paragraphs 29-30; or the Winne v. the United Kingdom judgment of 18 July 1994, Application No. 15484/89, Series A No. 294-A, paragraph 33, concerning discretionary life sentences which, unlike mandatory life sentences, apply not because of the inherent gravity of the offence but owing to the presence of factors liable to change with time, namely mental instability and danger; and the Hussain v. the United Kingdom judgment of 21 February 1996, *Reports* 1996-I.)

There are even cases where the procedure followed by the court which convicted the person concerned did not provide the "guarantees appropriate to the kind of deprivation of liberty in question", as required by

Article 5, paragraph 4 (the above-mentioned Winterwerp judgment, paragraph 57). The incorporation theory does not then apply and the meaning of the control provided for in Article 5, paragraph 4, becomes fully apparent. The Court has been faced with such situations. In the recent case of V. v. the United Kingdom (16 December 1999, Application No. 24888/94, paragraphs 119-120), the applicant had been found guilty of murder and the court, acting in accordance with the law, had sentenced him to be detained during Her Majesty's pleasure. The Court stated:

> The Court recalls that where a national court, after convicting a person of a criminal offence, imposes a fixed sentence of imprisonment for the purposes of punishment, the supervision required by Article 5, paragraph 4, is incorporated in that court decision (see the De Wilde, Ooms and Versyp v. Belgium judgment of 18 June 1971, Series A No. 12, pp. 40-41, paragraph 76, and the Wynne judgment cited above, p. 15, paragraph 36). This is not the case, however, in respect of any ensuing period of detention in which new issues affecting the lawfulness of the detention may arise (see the Weeks judgment cited above, p. 28, paragraph 56, and the Thynne, Wilson and Gunnell v. the United Kingdom judgment of 25 October 1990, Series A No. 190-A, pp. 26-27, paragraph 68). Thus, in the Hussain judgment (op. cit., pp. 269-270, paragraph 54), the Court decided in respect of a young offender detained during Her Majesty's pleasure that, after the expiry of the tariff period, Article 5, paragraph 4, required that he should be able periodically to challenge the continuing legality of his detention since its only justification could be dangerousness, a characteristic subject to change. In the Hussain case the Court was not called upon to consider the position under Article 5, paragraph 4, prior to the expiry of the tariff (op. cit., p. 266, paragraph 44).
>
> The Court has already determined that the failure to have the applicant's tariff set by an independent tribunal within the meaning of Article 6, paragraph 1, gives rise to a violation of that provision (see paragraph 114 above). Accordingly, given that the sentence of detention during Her Majesty's pleasure is indeterminate and that the tariff was initially set by the Home Secretary rather than the sentencing judge, it cannot be said that the supervision required by Article 5, paragraph 4, was incorporated in the trial court's sentence (see the De Wilde, Ooms and Versyp judgment and the Wynne judgment cited in paragraph 119 above).

Therefore it all depends on the circumstances. The Court stated that the control required by paragraph 4 is not necessarily the same for all cases of detention authorised by Article 5, paragraph 1. In the Van Droogenbroeck v. Belgium case (judgment of 24 June 1982, Series A No. 50, p. 24, paragraph 47), it noted in particular that:

> The Court recalls that the scope of the obligation undertaken by the Contracting States under paragraph 4 of Article 5 (art. 5-4) "will not necessarily be the same in all circumstances and as regards every category of deprivation of liberty" (see the above-mentioned X. v. the United Kingdom judgment, Series A No. 46, p. 22, paragraph 52). It has not overlooked the fact that in the present case the detention at issue was covered only by sub-paragraph *a* of paragraph 1 (art. 5-1-a) and not by sub-paragraph *e* (art. 5-1-e), as in the Winterwerp and the De Wilde, Ooms and Versyp cases, or by both of those sub-paragraphs taken together, as in the case of X. v. the United Kingdom (ibid., pp. 17-18, paragraph 39).

Article 5, paragraph 4, and its interaction with paragraph 3 of Article 5

As regards, last, the consequences of compliance with Article 5, paragraph 3, for Article 5, paragraph 4, reference should be made to the de Jong, Baljet and Van den Brink v. the Netherlands case (judgment of 22 May 1984, Series A No. 77, pp. 25-26, paragraph 57). In that judgment the Court referred to the cumulative application of paragraphs 3 and 4. In that case, the persons arrested were not only entitled to be "brought promptly before a judge" but also entitled to "take proceedings by which the lawfulness of [their] detention [should] be decided speedily by a court":

> [...] the guarantee assured by paragraph 4 (art. 5-4) is of a different order from, and additional to, that provided by paragraph 3 (art. 5-3). The Court itself has on several previous occasions examined whether the same set of facts gave rise to a breach of both paragraphs 3 and 4 of Article 5 (art. 5-3, art. 5-4), without ever suggesting that the safeguards provided might not apply concurrently (see the Neumeister judgment of 27 June 1968, Series A No. 8, pp. 36-41 and 43-44, paragraphs 3-15 and 22-25; the Matznetter judgment of 10 November 1969, Series A No. 9, pp. 31-35, paragraphs 2-13; the above-mentioned Ireland v. the United Kingdom judgment, Series A No. 25, pp. 75-77, paragraphs 199-200). The Court sees no reason in the present case not to apply these two paragraphs concurrently.

The Court also noted (ibid.) :

> The procedure followed for bringing a person before the "competent legal authority" in accordance with paragraph 3 taken in conjunction with paragraph 1.c (art. 5-3 + 5-1-c) may admittedly have a certain incidence on compliance with paragraph 4. For example, where that procedure culminates in a decision by a "court" ordering or confirming deprivation of the person's liberty, the judicial control of lawfulness required by paragraph 4 is incorporated in this initial decision (see the De Wilde, Ooms and Versyp judgment of 18 June 1971, Series A No. 12, p. 40, paragraph 76, and the above-mentioned Van Droogenbroeck judgment, Series A No. 50, p. 23, paragraphs 44-45). [...]

2. The content of the right of a detained person to bring proceedings in respect of his continuing detention

The right to an effective remedy

The Soumare v. France judgment deals with the lack of sufficient certainty of the remedies. In that case, Mr Soumare had been sentenced by a judgment of 10 June 1991 of the Paris Court of Appeal to ten years' imprisonment and had also been ordered to pay a fine to the customs officers, with imprisonment in default (a detention measure intended to guarantee payment of the fine). After serving his general sentence, he was further detained for almost six months under the "default" provision for failing to pay the fine to the customs authorities. Mr Soumare claimed that the various proceedings which he brought (before the urgent applications judge and then before the Paris Court of Appeal) could not be regarded as effective remedies for the purposes of Article 5, paragraph 4, particularly in the light of the reasons stated by the Paris Court of Appeal stating that it had no jurisdiction in matters of imprisonment in default, thereby referring to a judgment of the Civil Division of the Court of Cassation, which was itself at odds with the case-law of the Commercial Division of the Court of Cassation. Such reasoning, in Mr Soumare's submission, rendered any appeal on a point of law illusory. The Court stated (judgment of 24 August 1998, Application No. 23824/94, *Reports* 1998-V, paragraphs 38-44) :

> [...] the Court points out that for the purposes of Article 7 of the Convention it has held that imprisonment in default constitutes a penalty (see the Jamil judgment referred to above) and that such imprisonment subsequent to the serving of the main sentence may consequently be considered to be separate detention for the purposes of Article 5, paragraph 4, of the Convention.
>
> In the instant case the applicant applied on 11 August 1994 to the President of the Nancy Tribunal de Grande Instance under Article 752 of the Code of Criminal Procedure (see paragraph 20 above) to have the order for his imprisonment in default discharged on the basis that he was insolvent. He relied on a certificate attesting that he had no income-tax liability. The President considered that that document did not provide sufficient proof that he was insolvent and referred the case to the court – the Paris Court of Appeal – that had sentenced him, which dismissed the application on the ground that it had no jurisdiction.
>
> The Government maintained that the Paris Court of Appeal had erred in its construction of the provisions of the Code of Criminal Procedure as it had not followed an earlier decision in which it had been held that, *inter alia*, the Court of Cassation had jurisdiction to rule on cases of imprisonment in default. The Court does not, however, consider that it must determine that question of French law (see, among other authorities, and *mutatis mutandis*, the Vasilescu v. Romania judgment of 22 May 1998, *Reports of Judgments and Decisions* 1998-III, p. 1075, paragraph 39), or express a view on the appropriateness of the domestic courts' choice of policy as regards case-law. Its task is confined to determining whether the consequences of that choice are in conformity with the Convention (see, *mutatis mutandis*, the Brualla Gómez de la Torre v. Spain judgment of 19 December 1997, *Reports* 1997-VIII, p. 2955, paragraph 32). [...]
>
> The change in the Court of Cassation's case-law began in 1994 and has subsequently been confirmed. In these circumstances, that issue of domestic law may be considered to have been uncertain at the material time and the case-law on the subject recent and in the formative stage. [...]
>
> In addition, the fact that the Paris Court of Appeal expressly relied on a decision of the Court of Cassation in dismissing as unfounded in law the application to have the order discharged was a decisive factor in instilling in the applicant the belief that it would be pointless to seek satisfaction through an appeal to the Court of Cassation. Since, in the Government's submission, the specialised judges of the Paris Court of Appeal had not correctly applied the law and had not followed the decisions of the Commercial Division of the Court of Cassation, it would be inappropriate to require the applicant and his officially assigned lawyer to regard an appeal to the Court of Cassation as an effective remedy.
>
> In that respect, the Court reiterates that the existence of a remedy must be sufficiently certain, failing which it will lack the accessibility and effectiveness required for the purposes of Article 5, paragraph 4 (see among other authorities,

and *mutatis mutandis*, the Van Droogenbroeck judgment cited above, p. 30, paragraph 54, and the Sakik and Others v. Turkey judgment of 26 November 1997, *Reports* 1997-VII, p. 2625, paragraph 53).

Further, the Court observes that if the applicant had appealed to the Court of Cassation, his appeal, being a criminal appeal, would have been considered by the Criminal Division, which, at the material time, had not yet aligned its case-law with that of the Commercial Division.

As regards the exercise and effectiveness of the application to the urgent applications judge to determine whether Mr Soumare was solvent, the Court observes that in the instant case the judge considered only the prima-facie validity of the detention. It is true that the judge's decision to refer the case to the court that had passed sentence (see paragraph 16 above) complied with Article 710, first paragraph, of the Code of Criminal Procedure (see paragraph 20 above). The decision must, however, be analysed in the light of the case-law at that time, the characteristic feature of which was great uncertainty over whether the urgent applications judge had power to consider whether the debtor was insolvent (see paragraph 25 above). In those circumstances, the judge's decision could in any event have been effective for the purposes of Article 5, paragraph 4, only if the Paris Court of Appeal had accepted that it had jurisdiction.

[...]

Consequently, the Court [...] holds that there has been a violation of Article 5, paragraph 4.

(*Idem* the Sakik and Others v. Turkey judgment of 26 November 1997, Applications Nos. 23878/94, 23879/94, 23880/94, 23881/94, 23882/94 and 23883/94, *Reports* 1997-VII, paragraphs 49-53).

For a case in which no proceedings were possible, see the Varbanov v. Bulgaria judgment (5 October 2000, Application No. 31365/96, paragraph 61).

The R.M.D. v. Switzerland judgment (26 September 1997, Application No. 19800/92, *Reports* 1997-VI, paragraphs 48-49, 51-52 and 54-55) concerned the difficulties encountered by an applicant in having his action considered. He was transferred from one canton to another before his applications were examined. The Court observed:

Under the settled case-law of the Swiss courts, [...] an application for release must be struck out where the person detained is no longer within the jurisdiction of the canton concerned. That was what both the Lucerne Court of Appeal (see paragraph 25 above) and the investigating judge in the Canton of Zürich (see paragraph 8 above) did in this case.

Admittedly, the applicant could have applied for release in the cantons of Glarus, St Gall and Aargau, where he was detained for eleven, eighteen and ten days respectively (see paragraphs 13, 14 and 20-21 above). However, he was at that time still waiting for the judgment of the Lucerne Court of Appeal and indeed of the Federal Court, and as the Court has already noted above, he was expecting to be transferred to another canton at any moment. Regard being had to the time that such applications take, to the practical difficulties that persons held in custody may encounter in arranging effective representation and to the resulting feeling

155

of helplessness, the applicant cannot be blamed for failing to avail himself of those remedies.

[...]

In that connection, the Court reiterates that the Convention is intended to guarantee not rights that are theoretical or illusory but rights that are practical and effective (see the Artico v. Italy judgment of 13 May 1980, Series A No. 37, p. 16, paragraph 33).

In the present case it was not disputed that Mr R.M.D. could have made an application for release in each canton. Had he been detained in one canton only, the procedure would undoubtedly have satisfied the requirements of Article 5, paragraph 4, of the Convention. The problem was not that remedies were unavailable in each of the cantons, but that they were ineffective in the applicant's particular situation. Having been successively transferred from one canton to another, he was unable, owing to the limits of the cantonal courts' jurisdiction, to obtain a decision on his detention from a court, as he was entitled to do under Article 5, paragraph 4.

[...]

[...] however, the Court considers that those circumstances cannot justify the applicant's being deprived of his rights under Article 5, paragraph 4. Where, as in this instance, a detained person is continually transferred from one canton to another, it is for the State to organise its judicial system in such a way as to enable its courts to comply with the requirements of that Article.

Consequently, the Court dismisses the Government's preliminary objection and holds on the merits that there has been a violation of Article 5, paragraph 4.

It is now necessary to deal with three concepts referred to in paragraph 4 of Article 5: the concepts of "speedily", "lawful" and "court".

The detention must be examined "speedily"

"Speedily" refers to the period during which the detained person must bring an action to have the lawfulness of his detention examined. It also refers to the period during which the action must be examined. One example is given for each of these two aspects. There is a third aspect: the Court requires that a number of applications must be possible.

The period within which an application must be lodged

The above-mentioned de Jong, Baljet and Van den Brink judgment (22 May 1984, Series A No. 77, p. 26, paragraph 58) deals with the first aspect. In that case, the possibility of bringing an action in respect of the detention was conditional on the persons concerned being referred to the trial court. The Court observed:

> In addition, Article 34 of the Military Code is capable in practice of leading to a "speedy" decision, depending upon how rapidly the referral for trial occurs in the particular circumstances. Mr de Jong was seven days, Mr Baljet eleven days and Mr Van den Brink six days in custody before being referred for trial (see paragraphs 23 and 27 above) and hence without a remedy. In the Court's view, even

having regard to the exigencies of military life and military justice, the length of absence of access to a court was in each case such as to deprive the applicant of his entitlement to bring proceedings to obtain a "speedy" review of the lawfulness of his detention.

The period within which a response to an application is required

The Sabeur Ben Ali v. Malta judgment (29 June 2000, Application No. 35892/97, paragraph 38) concerns the second aspect: the short period within which the action must be examined. In that judgment the Court said that a period of eight weeks would in itself appear to be too long:

> The Court has considered, for example, that a period of approximately eight weeks from the lodging of an application to judgment appears prima facie difficult to reconcile with the notion of "speedily" (the E. v. Norway judgment of 29 August 1990, Series A No. 181-A, p. 27, paragraph 64).

Furthermore, in the G.B. v. Switzerland judgment, concerning a person who had been arrested on suspicion of having taken part in terrorist attacks (30 November 2000, Application No. 27426/95, paragraphs 28-39), the Court held that a period of one month did not satisfy the requirement for brevity in Article 5, paragraph 4; and in the Rehbock v. Slovenia judgment (28 November 2000, Application No. 29462/95, paragraphs 84-88), the Court considered that a period of twenty-three days was too long.

In the Letellier v. France judgment (26 June 1991, Series A No. 207, p. 22, paragraph 56), the Court held that examination of an application lodged under paragraph 4 is sometimes relatively long because the application is the subject of an appeal and an appeal on a point of law. That does not necessarily entail a breach of the requirement that the application be examined "speedily", provided that the person concerned has been able to submit fresh applications at any time and these have been dealt with speedily. In that case, a number of applications had been submitted. The judgment contains a passage which makes clear what periods for examination of actions are to be regarded as reasonable:

> The Court has certain doubts about the overall length of the examination of the second application for release, in particular before the indictments divisions called upon to rule after a previous decision had been quashed in the Court of Cassation; it should however be borne in mind that the applicant retained the right to submit a further application at any time. Indeed from 14 February 1986 to 5 August 1987 she lodged six other applications, which were all dealt with in periods of from eight to twenty days (see paragraph 23 above).

In an action concerning committal to a psychiatric institution, the Court had occasion to make a finding of violation where it had taken twenty months to examine an applicant owing to the rather long time taken to prepare expert reports. This was the Musial v. Poland case (judgment of 25 March 1999, Application No. 24557/94, *Reports* 1999-II, paragraph 43):

> Such a lapse of time, namely one year, eight months and eight days, will be incompatible with the notion of speediness within the meaning of Article 5, paragraph 4, of the Convention unless there are exceptional grounds to justify it. The

Court will accordingly consider whether any such grounds existed in the present case in the light of the arguments adduced by the Government.

[...]

Similarly, the fact that the Katowice Regional Court appointed experts at the applicant's specific request did not in itself discharge that court from its obligation to rule speedily on his request for release. The Court sees no cause in the circumstances of the present case for departing from the usual principle that the primary responsibility for delays resulting from the provision of expert opinions rests ultimately with the State (see, *mutatis mutandis*, the Capuano v. Italy judgment of 25 June 1987, Series A No. 119, p. 14, paragraph 32).

[...] the Court acknowledges that, in proceedings concerning a review of a psychiatric detention, the complexity of the medical issues involved in a case is a factor which may be taken into account when assessing compliance with the requirements of Article 5, paragraph 4, of the Convention. Nevertheless, the complexity of a medical dossier, however exceptional, cannot absolve national authorities from their essential obligations under this provision. Moreover, it has not in any event been shown that in the present case there was a causal link between the complexity of the medical issues which might arguably have been involved in the assessment of the applicant's condition and the delay in the preparation of the expert opinion.

The Government have therefore failed to show that there were in this case such exceptional grounds as could justify the period in question.

(*Idem* the Baranowski v. Poland judgment of 28 March 2000, Application No. 28358/95, paragraphs 70-77.)

The requirement that proceedings must be capable of being brought regularly

It remains, specifically, that the Court requires that regular actions can be brought for the purposes of having the lawfulness of detention examined. Thus, in the Assenov and Others v. Bulgaria judgment (28 October 1998, Application No. 24760/94, *Reports* 1998-VIII, paragraphs 162 and 164-165), the Court held that a provision limiting a detained person's right to bring proceedings to a single application was incompatible with Article 5, paragraph 4:

[...] Article 5, paragraph 4, requires that a person detained on remand must be able to take proceedings at reasonable intervals to challenge the lawfulness of his detention (see the Bezicheri v. Italy judgment of 25 October 1989, Series A No. 164, pp. 10-11, paragraphs 20-21). In view of the assumption under the Convention that such detention is to be of strictly limited duration (see paragraph 154 above), periodic review at short intervals is called for (see the above-mentioned Bezicheri case, loc. cit.).

[...] the Court notes that under Bulgarian law a person detained on remand is only entitled to apply to have the lawfulness of this detention reviewed by a court on one single occasion (see paragraph 75 above). Thus a second such request on the part of the applicant was rejected on this ground by the Shoumen District Court on 19 September 1995 (see paragraph 41 above).

In conclusion, in view in particular of the impossibility for the applicant, during his two years of pre-trial detention, to have the continuing lawfulness of this detention determined by a court on more than one occasion, and the failure of the court to hold an oral hearing on that occasion, the Court finds that there has been a violation of Article 5, paragraph 4, of the Convention.

(*Idem* the Oldham v. the United Kingdom judgment of 26 September 2000, Application No. 36273/97, paragraph 30, concerning the recall, at the government's discretion, of persons sentenced to life imprisonment who have been released on licence after serving the tariff.)

As regards committal to a psychiatric institution, the Megyeri v. Germany judgment contains the following passage (judgment of 12 May 1992, Application No. 13770/88, Series A No. 237-A, paragraph 22):

> [...] A person of unsound mind who is compulsorily confined in a psychiatric institution for an indefinite or lengthy period is in principle entitled, at any rate where there is no automatic periodic review of a judicial character, to take proceedings "at reasonable intervals" before a court to put in issue the "lawfulness" – within the meaning of the Convention – of his detention (see, *inter alia*, the X. v. the United Kingdom judgment of 5 November 1981, Series A No. 46, p. 23, paragraph 52).

(*Idem* the Musial v. Poland judgment of 25 March 1999, Application No. 24557/94, *Reports* 1999-II, paragraph 43; and the Egmez v. Cyprus judgment of 21 December 2000, paragraph 94.)

Examination of the action must concern the "lawfulness" of the detention

The second important concept is that of "lawfulness". In the Brogan and Others v. the United Kingdom judgment (29 November 1988, Series A No. 145-B, pp. 34-35, paragraph 65), some indication of the concept of lawfulness is given:

> According to the Court's established case-law, the notion of "lawfulness" under paragraph 4 (art. 5-4) has the same meaning as in paragraph 1 (art. 5-1) (see notably the Ashingdane judgment of 28 May 1985, Series A No. 93, p. 23, paragraph 52); and whether an "arrest" or "detention" can be regarded as "lawful" has to be determined in the light not only of domestic law, but also of the text of the Convention, the general principles embodied therein and the aim of the restrictions permitted by Article 5, paragraph 1 (art. 5-1) (see notably the above-mentioned Weeks judgment, Series A No. 114, p. 28, paragraph 57). By virtue of paragraph 4 of Article 5 (art. 5-4), arrested or detained persons are entitled to a review bearing upon the procedural and substantive conditions which are essential for the "lawfulness", in the sense of the Convention, of their deprivation of liberty. This means that, in the instant case, the applicants should have had available to them a remedy allowing the competent court to examine not only compliance with the procedural requirements set out in Section 12 of the 1984 Act but also the reasonableness of the suspicion grounding the arrest and the legitimacy of the purpose pursued by the arrest and the ensuing detention.

This case-law is often cited in later judgments, as in the Assenov and Others v. Bulgaria judgment (28 October 1998, Application No. 24760/94, *Reports* 1998-VIII, paragraph 162):

> The Court recalls that by virtue of Article 5, paragraph 4, an arrested or detained person is entitled to bring proceedings for the review by a court of the procedural and substantive conditions which are essential for the "lawfulness", in the sense of Article 5, paragraph 1 (see paragraph 139 above), of his or her deprivation of liberty (see the above-mentioned Brogan and Others judgment, p. 34, paragraph 65).

Nor does it come as a surprise to find the following passage in the Nikolova v. Bulgaria judgment (25 March 1999, Application No. 31195/96, *Reports* 1999-II, paragraph 61):

> The Plovdiv Regional Court when examining the applicant's appeal against her detention on remand apparently followed the case-law of the Supreme Court at that time and thus limited its consideration of the case to a verification of whether the investigator and the prosecutor had charged the applicant with a "serious wilful crime" within the meaning of the Criminal Code and whether her medical condition required release (see paragraphs 19 and 30-31 above).
>
> In her appeal of 14 November 1995, however, the applicant had advanced substantial arguments questioning the soundness of the charges against her and the grounds for her detention. She had referred to concrete facts, such as that she had not attempted to abscond or obstruct the investigation during the months since she had become aware of the criminal proceedings against her, and that she had a family and a stable way of life. The applicant had also asserted that the evidence against her was weak as the charges were based only on the auditors' report. In her submission there was nothing to support the accusation that she, and not any of the other six persons in possession of keys to the cashier's office, had actually misappropriated the missing funds. In its decision of 11 December 1995 the Regional Court devoted no consideration to any of these arguments, apparently treating them as irrelevant to the question of the lawfulness of the applicant's detention on remand (see paragraphs 16 and 19 above).
>
> While Article 5, paragraph 4, of the Convention does not impose an obligation on a judge examining an appeal against detention to address every argument contained in the appellant's submissions, its guarantees would be deprived of their substance if the judge, relying on domestic law and practice, could treat as irrelevant, or disregard, concrete facts invoked by the detainee and capable of putting in doubt the existence of the conditions essential for the "lawfulness", in the sense of the Convention, of the deprivation of liberty. The submissions of the applicant in her appeal of 14 November 1995 contained such concrete facts and did not appear implausible or frivolous. By not taking these submissions into account the Regional Court failed to provide the judicial review of the scope and nature required by Article 5, paragraph 4, of the Convention.

The action must be examined by a "court"

In the De Wilde, Ooms and Versyp v. Belgium judgment of 18 June 1971, Applications Nos. 2832/66, 2835/66 and 2899/66, Series A No. 12, paragraph 78, the Court stated that "courts" within the meaning of Article 5, paragraph 4, must be taken to mean:

> [...] [the] bodies which exhibit not only common fundamental features, of which the most important is independence of the executive and of the parties to the case (see Neumeister judgment of 27 June 1968, Series A, p. 44, paragraph 24), but also the guarantees of judicial procedure.

In the same judgment, the Court also stated (paragraph 76) that:

> [...] in order to constitute [...] a "court" [in the meaning of Article 5, paragraph 4], an authority must provide the fundamental guarantees of procedure applied in matters of deprivation of liberty.

In the D.N. v. Switzerland judgment, the Court examined the conditions of impartiality peculiar to a "court" within the meaning of Article 5, paragraph 4 (judgment of 29 March 2001, Application No. 27154/95, paragraphs 41-46 and 48-57):

> According to the Court's case-law, although it is not always necessary for proceedings under Article 5, paragraph 4, to be attended by the same guarantees as those required under Article 6, paragraph 1, for criminal or civil litigation, they must have a judicial character and provide guarantees appropriate to the kind of deprivation of liberty in question (see Niedbala v. Poland, Application No. 27915/95, paragraph 66, 4 July 2000, unreported).

> It is true that Article 5, paragraph 4, of the Convention, which enshrines the right "to take proceedings [...]] by a court", does not stipulate the requirement of that court's independence and impartiality and thus differs from Article 6, paragraph 1, which refers, *inter alia*, to an "independent and impartial tribunal". However, the Court has held that independence is one of the most important constitutive elements of the notion of a "court", as referred to in several Articles of the Convention (see the De Wilde, Ooms and Versyp v. Belgium judgment of 18 June 1970, Series A No. 12, pp. 41-42, paragraph 78). In the Court's opinion, it would be inconceivable that Article 5, paragraph 4, of the Convention, relating, *inter alia*, to such a sensitive issue as the deprivation of liberty of "persons of unsound mind" within the meaning of Article 5, paragraph 1.*e*, should not equally envisage, as a fundamental requisite, the impartiality of that court.

> In the present case, the applicant contended that R.W. had had a preconceived opinion when deciding as one of five members of the Administrative Appeals Commission on her request for release from psychiatric detention. The applicant pointed out in particular that R.W. had interviewed her and expressed himself before the hearing on her state of health and on his proposal to the Commission about her release.

> In examining the impartiality of R.W. in exercising his functions as judge rapporteur, the Court recalls that impartiality must be determined by a subjective test, that is on the basis of the personal conviction of a particular judge in a given case, and also by an objective test, that is ascertaining whether the judge offered guarantees sufficient to exclude any legitimate doubt in this respect (see, among other authorities, the Castillo Algar v. Spain judgment of 28 October 1998, *Reports of Judgments and Decisions* 1998-VIII, p. 3116, paragraphs 43 *et seq.*).

The personal impartiality of a judge must be presumed until there is proof to the contrary, and in the present case no such proof has been put forward (see the Hauschildt v. Denmark judgment of 24 May 1989, Series A No. 154, p. 21, paragraph 47).

Under the objective test, it must be determined whether, irrespective of the judge's personal conduct, there are ascertainable facts which may raise doubts as to his impartiality. Account must be taken in particular of internal organisation, though the mere fact that civil servants sit on account of their experience cannot give rise to doubts as to the independence and impartiality of the court (see the Piersack v. Belgium judgment of 1 October 1982, Series A No. 53, p. 15, paragraph 30.*d*, and the Stallinger and Kuso v. Austria judgment of 23 April 1997, *Reports* 1997-II, p. 677, paragraph 37). In this respect even appearances may be of a certain importance. What is at stake is the confidence which the courts in a democratic society must inspire in the public, including the parties to the proceedings. Accordingly, any judge in respect of whom there is a legitimate reason to fear a lack of impartiality must withdraw. In deciding whether in a given case there is a legitimate reason to fear that a particular judge lacks impartiality, the standpoint of the parties concerned is important but not decisive. What is decisive is whether this fear can be held to be objectively justified (see, *mutatis mutandis*, the Hauschildt judgment cited above, p. 21, paragraph 48).

The Court has had regard to the extent and nature of R.W.'s activities. As it has been emphasised by the Government, R.W. exercised one and the same function throughout the proceedings. He was acting as judge rapporteur who was called upon fully to examine, to assess, and to comment upon the applicant's state of health and thereby to decide whether or not she should be released from psychiatric detention.

Both the Government and the dissenting opinion contained in the Commission's report pointed out, in addition, that R.W.'s activities constituted typical functions of a judge rapporteur who with his specialised knowledge was logically called upon to hear evidence. Moreover, his activities could be compared to those of delegates of the former Commission who would make a proposal after having taken evidence in application of former Article 28, paragraph *a*, of the Convention.

The Court has distinguished the following activities of R.W. as judge rapporteur. First, on 15 December 1994 he conducted an interview with the applicant as a result of which he concluded that "[he would] propose to the court to dismiss the action". Next, on 23 December 1994 he submitted his expert opinion on the applicant's state of health in which he stated that "if the applicant's situation [did] not clearly improve until the date of the hearing, [he would] recommend dismissal of the action". Five days later, on 28 December 1994, the Administrative Appeals Commission conducted a hearing at which the applicant and other persons were heard; all judges were present, including R.W. Finally, still on 28 December, the Administrative Appeals Commission issued its decision which was prepared by all judges, including R.W.

In view of these various activities, the present case differs, in the Court's opinion, from proceedings where a judge rapporteur is in a position, after the hearing and during the court's deliberations, to examine and comment upon specialised evidence, for instance expert opinions, submitted to the court by an external specialist. The situation also differs from that of the delegates of the former Commission who, when taking evidence, were not in a position to inform the parties as to any proposals they might later make before the Commission, since the Commission's proceedings were conducted in camera (see former Article 33 of the Convention).

Indeed, while it is to be expected that a court-appointed expert will duly transmit the expert opinion, with its conclusions, both to the court and to the parties to the proceedings, it is unusual for an expert judge, as in the present case, to have formed his or her opinion and disclosed it to the parties before the hearing.

It is true that, according to the Federal Court's case-law, the position of an expert within the framework of psychiatric detention differs substantially from that of an expert consulted in proceedings in which evidence is taken (see paragraph 26 above). However, in the Court's opinion, in either proceedings experts are only called upon to assist a court with pertinent advice derived from their specialised knowledge without having adjudicative functions. It is up to the particular court and its judges to assess such expert advice together with all other relevant information and evidence. An issue will arise as to the impartiality of the court under the objective test if it is called upon to assess evidence which had previously been given by one of its judges in the form of expert advice. The Court must accordingly examine the apprehensions which arose for the applicant in the course of these proceedings.

When the applicant attended the hearing before the Administrative Appeals Commission on 28 December 1994, R.W. had already twice formulated his conclusion – orally during the interview on 15 December, and in writing in his report of 23 December – that, as a result of the psychiatric examination, he would propose to the Administrative Appeals Commission to dismiss her request for release from detention. In the Court's opinion, this situation raised legitimate fears in the applicant that, as a result of R.W.'s position in these proceedings, he had a preconceived opinion as to her request for release from detention and that he was not, therefore, approaching her case with due impartiality (see, *mutatis mutandis*, the de Haan v. the Netherlands judgment of 26 August 1997, *Reports* 1997-IV, pp. 1392-1393, paragraph 51).

The applicant's fears would have been reinforced by R.W.'s position on the bench of the Administrative Appeals Commission where he was the sole psychiatric expert among the judges as well as the only person who had interviewed her. The applicant could legitimately fear that R.W.'s opinion carried particular weight in taking the decision.

In the Court's view, these circumstances taken as a whole serve objectively to justify the applicant's apprehension that R.W., sitting as a judge in the Administrative Appeals Commission, lacked the necessary impartiality.

Consequently, there has been a violation of Article 5, paragraph 4, of the Convention in the present case.

3. Procedural guarantees

In the Megyeri v. Germany judgment, the Court stated (judgment of 12 May 1992, Application No. 13770/88, Series A No. 237-A, paragraph 22):

> The principles which emerge from the Court's case-law on Article 5, paragraph 4 (art. 5-4), include the following:
>
> [...]
>
> (b) Article 5, paragraph 4 (art. 5-4), requires that the procedure followed have a judicial character and give to the individual concerned guarantees appropriate to the kind of deprivation of liberty in question; in order to determine whether a proceeding provides adequate guarantees, regard must be had to the particular nature of the circumstances in which such proceeding takes place (see, as the most recent authority, the Wassink v. the Netherlands judgment of 27 September 1990, Series A No. 185-A, p. 13, paragraph 30).
>
> (c) The judicial proceedings referred to in Article 5, paragraph 4 (art. 5-4), need not always be attended by the same guarantees as those required under Article 6, paragraph 1 (art. 6-1), for civil or criminal litigation. Nonetheless, it is essential that the person concerned should have access to a court and the opportunity to be heard either in person or, where necessary, through some form of representation. Special procedural safeguards may prove called for in order to protect the interests of persons who, on account of their mental disabilities, are not fully capable of acting for themselves (see the Winterwerp v. the Netherlands judgment of 24 October 1979, Series A No. 33, p. 24, paragraph 60).

With specific regard to persons committed to psychiatric institutions, the Winterwerp v. the Netherlands judgment (judgment of 24 October 1979, Series A No. 33, p. 24, paragraph 60) already contained the following passage:

> [...] Mental illness may entail restricting or modifying the manner of exercise of such a right (see, as regards Article 6, paragraph 1 (art. 6-1), the above-mentioned Golder judgment, p. 19, paragraph 39), but it cannot justify impairing the very essence of the right. [...]

The Court had gone on to say (paragraphs 66, 61 and 67):

> [...] Article 5, paragraph 4 (art. 5-4), does not require that persons committed to care under the head of "unsound mind" should themselves take the initiative in obtaining legal representation before having recourse to a court.
>
> [...]
>
> As to the particular facts, the applicant was never associated, either personally or through a representative, in the proceedings leading to the various detention orders made against him: he was never notified of the proceedings or of their outcome; neither was he heard by the courts or given the opportunity to argue his case.
>
> [...]
>
> Mr Winterwerp was accordingly the victim of a breach of Article 5, paragraph 4 (art. 5-4).

Concerning proceedings brought by persons detained in accordance with Article 5, paragraph 1.*c*, the Court stated in the Assenov and Others v. Bulgaria judgment (28 October 1998, Application No. 24760/94, *Reports* 1998-VIII, paragraphs 162 and 165) that under Article 5, paragraph 4, there must be a hearing:

> In the case of a person whose detention falls within the ambit of Article 5, paragraph 1.*c*, a hearing is required (see the above-mentioned Schiesser judgment, p. 13, paragraphs 30-31, the Sanchez-Reisse v. Switzerland judgment of 21 October 1986, Series A No. 107, p. 19, paragraph 51, and the Kampanis v. Greece judgment of 13 July 1995, Series A No. 318-B, p. 45, paragraph 47).
>
> [...] [in view of] [...] the failure of the court to hold an oral hearing on that occasion, the Court finds that there has been a violation of Article 5, paragraph 4, of the Convention.

In the Lamy v. Belgium judgment, concerning provisional detention (judgment of 30 March 1989, Series A No. 151, p. 17, paragraph 29), the Court considered the right of access to the documents in the case-file and observance of the adversarial principle. It observed:

> The appraisal of the need for a remand in custody and the subsequent assessment of guilt are too closely linked for access to documents to be refused in the former case when the law requires it in the latter case.
>
> Whereas Crown Counsel was familiar with the whole file, the procedure did not afford the applicant an opportunity of challenging appropriately the reasons relied upon to justify a remand in custody. Since it failed to ensure equality of arms, the procedure was not truly adversarial (see, *mutatis mutandis*, the Sanchez-Reisse judgment previously cited, Series A No. 107, p. 19, paragraph 51).
>
> There was therefore a breach of Article 5, paragraph 4 (art. 5-4).

(*Idem* the Nikolova v. Bulgaria judgment of 25 March 1999, Application No. 31195/96, *Reports* 1999-II, paragraph 61; the Sanchez-Reisse v. Switzerland judgment of 21 October 1986, Series A No. 107, p. 19, paragraph 51, the Toth v. Austria judgment of 12 December 1991, Series A No. 224, p. 23, paragraph 84, and the Kampanis v. Greece judgment of 13 July 1995, Series A No. 318-B, p. 45, paragraph 47; and the Wloch v. Poland judgment of 19 October 2000, paragraph 127.)

In the Lietzow v. Germany judgment, the Court held that Article 5, paragraph 4, prevented a detained suspect from being denied access to certain documents on the ground that that would entail a danger that the investigation would become too onerous (judgment of 13 February 2001, Application No. 24479/94, paragraphs 47-48):

> The Court is aware that the Public Prosecutor denied the requested access to the file documents on the basis of Article 147, paragraph 2, of the Code of Criminal Procedure, arguing that to act otherwise would entail the risk of compromising the success of the on-going investigations, which were said to be very complex and to involve a large number of other suspects. This view was endorsed by the Frankfurt Court of Appeal in its decision of 24 April 1992 (see paragraph 19 above).

The Court acknowledges the need for criminal investigations to be conducted efficiently, which may imply that part of the information collected during them is to be kept secret in order to prevent suspects from tampering with evidence and undermining the course of justice. However, this legitimate goal cannot be pursued at the expense of substantial restrictions on the rights of the defence. Therefore, information which is essential for the assessment of the lawfulness of a person's detention should be made available in an appropriate manner to the suspect's lawyer.

In these circumstances, and given the importance in the District Court's reasoning of the statements made by Mr W. and Mr N., which could not be adequately challenged by the applicant, as they had not been communicated to him, the procedure before the Frankfurt District Court, which reviewed the lawfulness of the applicant's detention on remand, did not comply with the guarantees afforded by Article 5, paragraph 4. This provision has therefore been violated.

It should be noted, last, that Article 5, paragraph 4, does not require an appeal, provided that the detention is considered by a "court" within the meaning of that Article. In that regard, reference should by made to the Grauzinis v. Lithuania judgment of 10 October 2000 (Application No. 37975/97, paragraph 32):

> Article 5, paragraph 4, guarantees no right, as such, to appeal against decisions ordering or extending detention as the above provision speaks of "proceedings" and not of "appeal". The intervention of one organ satisfies Article 5, paragraph 4, on condition that the procedure followed has a judicial character and gives to the individual concerned guarantees appropriate to the kind of deprivation of liberty in question (see the Jecius judgment cited above, paragraph 100). However, where domestic law provides for a system of appeal, the appellate body must also comply with Article 5, paragraph 4 (see the Toth v. Austria judgment of 12 December 1991, Series A No. 224, paragraph 84).

Article 5, paragraph 5 – The right to compensation

Article 5, paragraph 5, is worded as follows:

> 5. **Everyone who has been the victim of arrest or detention in contravention of the provisions of this Article shall have an enforceable right to compensation.**

1. The scope of paragraph 5

In the Brogan and Others v. the United Kingdom judgment (29 November 1988, Series A No. 145-B, p. 35, paragraphs 66- 67), the Court observed:

> The Government argued, *inter alia,* that the aim of paragraph 5 (art. 5-5) is to ensure that the victim of an "unlawful" arrest or detention should have an enforceable right to compensation. In this regard, they have also contended that "lawful" for the purposes of the various paragraphs of Article 5 (art. 5) is to be construed as essentially referring back to domestic law and in addition as excluding any element of arbitrariness. They concluded that even in the event of a violation being found of any of the first four paragraphs, there has been no violation of paragraph 5 because the applicants' deprivation of liberty was lawful under Northern Ireland law and was not arbitrary.
>
> The Court, like the Commission, considers that such a restrictive interpretation is incompatible with the terms of paragraph 5 (art. 5-5) which refers to arrest or detention "in contravention of the provisions of this Article".
>
> In the instant case, the applicants were arrested and detained lawfully under domestic law but in breach of paragraph 3 of Article 5 (art. 5-3). This violation could not give rise, either before or after the findings made by the European Court in the present judgment, to an enforceable claim for compensation by the victims before the domestic courts; this was not disputed by the Government.
>
> Accordingly, there has also been a breach of paragraph 5 (art. 5-5) in this case in respect of all four applicants.

2. The concept of "compensation"

In the Wassink v. the Netherlands case, the applicant had been committed to a psychiatric hospital in circumstances that did not satisfy the requirement of a "procedure prescribed by law" in Article 5, paragraph 1. He claimed that he could secure compensation for that violation of Article 5, paragraph 1, only under the article of the Netherlands Civil Code on civil responsibility. That provision applies only if actual damage can be shown. The applicant claimed that "[I]n this case, the existence of damage would have been almost impossible to prove because it could not be affirmed with absolute certainty that proceedings conducted in conformity with Article 5 of the Convention would have led to the desired result".

The Court observed (the Wassink v. the Netherlands judgment of 27 September 1990, Series A No. 185-A, p. 14, paragraph 38) :

> In the Court's view, paragraph 5 of Article 5 (art. 5-5) is complied with where it is possible to apply for compensation in respect of a deprivation of liberty effected in conditions contrary to paragraphs 1, 2, 3 or 4 (art. 5-1, art. 5-2, art. 5-3 or art. 5-4). It does not prohibit the Contracting States from making the award of compensation dependent upon the ability of the person concerned to show damage resulting from the breach. In the context of Article 5, paragraph 5 (art. 5-5), as for that of Article 25 (art. 25) (see, *inter alia,* the Huvig judgment of 24 April 1990, Series A No. 176-B, pp. 56-57, paragraph 35), the status of "victim" may exist even where there is no damage, but there can be no question of "compensation" where there is no pecuniary or non-pecuniary damage to compensate.

Article 6 ECHR – The right to a fair trial

Article 6, paragraph 1

Article 6, paragraph 1, lays down general provisions on the administration of justice. It is worded as follows:

> 1. In the determination of his civil rights and obligations or of any criminal charge against him, everyone is entitled to a fair and public hearing within a reasonable time by an independent and impartial tribunal established by law. Judgment shall be pronounced publicly but the press and public may be excluded from all or part of the trial in the interests of morals, public order or national security in a democratic society, where the interests of juveniles or the protection of the private life of the parties so require, or to the extent strictly necessary in the opinion of the court in special circumstances where publicity would prejudice the interests of justice.

1. The sphere of application of the "right to a tribunal"

The "right to a tribunal" defined in Article 6 can be relied on in connection with the "determination of [a person's] civil rights and obligations" (in French: *"contestations sur ses droits et obligations de caractère civil"*) or of "any criminal charge" against the person claiming the right (in French: *"accusation en matière pénale"*). The notions of "disputes (contestations) over civil rights and obligations" and "criminal charge" will now be explained in turn.

The right to a tribunal for the "determination of civil rights and obligations"

The expression "dispute" (contestation) over "civil rights and obligations" calls for a thorough approach to each of those terms.

The concept of "dispute" (contestation)

In the Benthem v. the Netherlands judgment (23 October 1985, Series A No. 97, p. 15, paragraph 32), the Court summarised its case-law on the notion of "dispute":

> The principles that emerge from the Court's case-law include the following:
>
> (a) Conformity with the spirit of the Convention requires that the word "contestation" (dispute) should not be "construed too technically" and should be "given a substantive rather than a formal meaning" (see the Le Compte, Van Leuven and De Meyere judgment of 23 June 1981, Series A No. 43, p. 20, paragraph 45).
>
> (b) The "contestation" (dispute) may relate not only to "the actual existence of a [...] right" but also to its scope or the manner in which it may be exercised

169

(see the same judgment, loc. cit., p. 22, paragraph 49). It may concern both "questions of fact" and "questions of law" (see the same judgment, loc. cit., p. 23, paragraph 51, in fine, and the Albert and Le Compte judgment of 10 February 1983, Series A No. 58, p. 16, paragraph 29, in fine, and p. 19, paragraph 36).

(c) The "contestation" (dispute) must be genuine and of a serious nature (see the Sporrong and Lönnroth judgment of 23 September 1982, Series A No. 52, p. 30, paragraph 81).

(d) According to the Ringeisen judgment of 16 July 1971, "the [...] expression *'contestations sur (des) droits et obligations de caractère civil'* [disputes over civil rights and obligations] covers all proceedings the result of which is decisive for [such] rights and obligations" (Series A No. 13, p. 39, paragraph 94). However, "a tenuous connection or remote consequences do not suffice for Article 6, paragraph 1 (art. 6-1) [...] : civil rights and obligations must be the object – or one of the objects – of the 'contestation' (dispute) ; the result of the proceedings must be directly decisive for such a right" (see the above-mentioned Le Compte, Van Leuven and De Meyere judgment, Series A No. 43, p. 21, paragraph 47).

In that case a dispute between an individual and the State over the issue of a licence to exploit a petrol distribution installation constituted a dispute (contestation) within the meaning of the Convention. The State maintained that no right had yet been created and, consequently, that no dispute had arisen. The Court pointed out that the applicant had had a municipal permit to begin to use the installation.

It will have been noted that the "dispute" must be "determinant" for the right relied on. For the "determinant" nature (in contrast to a tenuous link or remote effects) of proceedings as a necessary precondition of the existence of a "dispute" for the purposes of Article 6, paragraph 1, see the Balmer-Schafroth and Others v. Switzerland judgment (26 August 1997, *Reports* 1997-IV, paragraph 40), where the Court noted :

> It will be recalled that the applicants asked the Federal Council to refuse to extend the operating licence on the ground that, in their submission, Mühleberg power station had serious and irremediable construction defects, it did not satisfy current safety standards and its condition entailed a greater than usual risk of accident (see paragraph 9 above). They endeavoured to prove the existence of the alleged technical deficiencies and the need to lessen the resulting danger to the population and the environment in general by every available means. However, they did not for all that establish a direct link between the operating conditions of the power station which were contested by them and their right to protection of their physical integrity, as they failed to show that the operation of Mühleberg power station exposed them personally to a danger that was not only serious but also specific and, above all, imminent. In the absence of such a finding, the effects on the population of the measures which the Federal Council could have ordered to be taken in the instant case therefore remained hypothetical. Consequently, neither the dangers nor the remedies were established with a degree of probability that made the outcome of the proceedings directly decisive within the meaning of the Court's case-law for the right relied on by the

applicants. In the Court's view, the connection between the Federal Council's decision and the right invoked by the applicants was too tenuous and remote.

Article 6, paragraph 1, is accordingly not applicable in the instant case.

(See the Athanassoglou and Others v. Switzerland judgment of 6 April 2000, Application No. 27644/95.)

To summarise, we shall refer to the Acquaviva v. France judgment (21 November 1995, Application No. 19248/91, Series A No. 333-A, paragraph 46), where the Court stated:

> According to the principles laid down in its case-law (see the judgments of Zander v. Sweden, 25 November 1993, Series A No. 279-B, p. 38, paragraph 22, and Kerojärvi v. Finland, 19 July 1995, Series A No. 322, p. 12, paragraph 32), the Court must ascertain whether there was a dispute ("contestation") over a "right" which can be said, at least on arguable grounds, to be recognised under domestic law. The dispute must be genuine and serious; it may relate not only to the existence of a right but also to its scope and the manner of its exercise; and, finally, the outcome of the proceedings must be directly decisive for the right in question.

(See also the Le Compte, Van Leuven and De Meyere v. Belgium judgment of 23 June 1981, Series A No. 43, p. 21, paragraph 47; the Fayed v. the United Kingdom judgment of 21 September 1994, Series A No. 294-B, p. 46, paragraph 56; and the Masson and Van Zon v. the Netherlands judgment of 28 September 1995, Series A No. 327-A, p. 17, paragraph 44.)

The notion of "civil rights and obligations"

The dispute must be over "civil rights and obligations". In order to define "civil rights and obligations", we shall first define the concept of "right/ obligation" and then explain the concept of "civil".

The notion of right and obligation

The Court has pointed out on a number of occasions (see, for example, the Al-Adsani v. the United Kingdom judgment of 21 November 2001, Application No. 35763/97, paragraph 46) that:

> Article 6, paragraph 1, does not itself guarantee any particular content for "civil rights and obligations" in the substantive law of the Contracting States. It extends only to contestations (disputes) over "civil rights and obligations" which can be said, at least on arguable grounds, to be recognised under domestic law (see Z. and Others v. the United Kingdom [GC], No. 29392/95, paragraph 87, ECHR 2001, and the authorities cited therein).

That formula is quite similar to the one used in the James and Others v. the United Kingdom judgment (21 February 1986, Series A No. 98, p. 46, paragraph 81), according to which, in order to fall within the scope of Article 6, the civil "rights and obligations" must, in addition to their own particular content, be at least recognised as rights under national law.

> Article 6, paragraph 1 (art. 6-1), extends only to "contestations" (disputes) over (civil) "rights and obligations" which can be said, at least on arguable grounds,

to be recognised under domestic law; it does not in itself guarantee any particular content for (civil) "rights and obligations" in the substantive law of the Contracting States.

It is therefore necessary to refer to the legal order of the respondent State in order to determine whether one is dealing with "rights and obligations".

That principle includes a number of subtle distinctions, however.

Take, first of all, the result of the Al-Adsani v. the United Kingdom judgment, where the Court referred to the government's argument that the principle of immunity based in this case on international law precluded the application of Article 6, paragraph 1 (paragraphs 47-49):

> Whether a person has an actionable domestic claim may depend not only on the substantive content, properly speaking, of the relevant civil right as defined under national law but also on the existence of procedural bars preventing or limiting the possibilities of bringing potential claims to court. In the latter kind of case Article 6, paragraph 1, may be applicable. Certainly the Convention enforcement bodies may not create by way of interpretation of Article 6, paragraph 1, a substantive civil right which has no legal basis in the State concerned. However, it would not be consistent with the rule of law in a democratic society or with the basic principle underlying Article 6, paragraph 1 – namely that civil claims must be capable of being submitted to a judge for adjudication – if, for example, a State could, without restraint or control by the Convention enforcement bodies, remove from the jurisdiction of the courts a whole range of civil claims or confer immunities from civil liability on large groups or categories of persons (see the Fayed v. the United Kingdom judgment of 21 September 1994, Series A No. 294-B, paragraph 65).
>
> The proceedings which the applicant intended to pursue were for damages for personal injury, a cause of action well known to English law. The Court does not accept the Government's submission that the applicant's claim had no legal basis in domestic law since any substantive right which might have existed was extinguished by operation of the doctrine of State immunity. It notes that an action against a State is not barred *in limine*: if the defendant State waives immunity, the action will proceed to a hearing and judgment. The grant of immunity is to be seen not as qualifying a substantive right but as a procedural bar on the national courts' power to determine the right.
>
> The Court is accordingly satisfied that there existed a serious and genuine dispute over civil rights. It follows that Article 6, paragraph 1, was applicable to the proceedings in question.

(See the McElhinney v. Ireland judgment of 21 November 2001, Application No. 31253/96, paragraphs 23-26.)

That summarises the position as regards the influence of procedural rules on the existence of civil "rights and obligations.

At this point, it is appropriate also to describe the case-law that emerges from the Pudas v. Sweden judgment (judgment of 21 October 1987, Application No. 10426/83, Series A No. 125-A, paragraph 34). In that case, the applicant had obtained a licence to operate a taxi on certain routes. The licence was valid until further notice. Subsequently, a company was granted a licence covering the same route and the licence granted to the applicant was revoked. The respondent government maintained that national law conferred no right to a licence of the kind in question, to be issued to anyone who fulfilled certain conditions. Nor did the licence give rise to a "right" for the benefit of the applicant, since it was issued not for a fixed period but merely "until further notice". Last, its revocation was essentially the consequence of an assessment of policy issues not capable of or suited to judicial review. The Court stated:

> The Court agrees with the Commission that, on being granted a licence, the applicant acquired certain consequential rights.
>
> To begin with, subject to the possibility of its being revoked, the licence conferred a "right" on the applicant in the form of an authorisation to carry out a transport service in accordance with the conditions prescribed in it and laid down by domestic law (see paragraphs 9, 16 and 17 above). It is true that the licence did not specify the conditions on which it could be revoked and that the law allows a certain discretion as regards revocation, but it follows from generally recognised legal and administrative principles that the authorities did not have an unfettered discretion in this respect.
>
> The applicant could plausibly and arguably maintain that according to Swedish law he was entitled to continue his business under the licence.

In the absence of an expressly recognised right, it is therefore sufficient to make out a plausible and arguable case for the existence of a right under domestic law (see also the Editions Périscope v. France judgment of 26 March 1992, Series A No. 234-B, p. 64, paragraph 35).

The Anne-Marie Andersson v. Sweden judgment (27 August 1997, Application No. 20022/92, *Reports* 1997-IV, paragraphs 35-37) illustrates a situation where the Court accepted that the applicant did not have a civil "right or obligation". In that case, a psychiatrist had provided the social services with information about a patient whose health could have a detrimental effect on her child. Under Swedish law he was obliged to do so. The applicant complained that she had been unable to challenge the psychiatrist's report before a court before it was communicated to the Social Council. The Court declared:

> In the case under consideration, if the chief psychiatrist possessed information about the applicant patient to the effect that intervention by the Social Council was necessary for the protection of her under-age son, the psychiatrist was under a duty to report immediately to the Social Council. That duty extended to all data in her possession which were potentially relevant to the Social Council's investigation into the need to take protective measures with respect to the son (see paragraphs 17-19 above) and depended exclusively on the relevance of those data (Section 71, sub-sections 2 and 4, of the Social Services Act).
>
> In addition to the scope of this obligation, as described above, the Court notes that the psychiatrist enjoyed a very wide discretion in assessing what data would be of importance to the Social Council's investigation (ibid.). In this regard, she

had no duty to hear the applicant's views before transmitting the information to the Social Council (see paragraph 21 above).

Accordingly, it transpires from the terms of the legislation in issue that a "right" to prevent communication of such data could not, on arguable grounds, be said to be recognised under national law (see the Masson and Van Zon v. the Netherlands judgment of 28 September 1995, Series A No. 327-A, pp. 19-20, paragraphs 49-52). No evidence suggesting the contrary has been adduced before the Court.

Having regard to the foregoing, the Court reaches the conclusion that Article 6, paragraph 1, was not applicable to the proceedings under consideration and has therefore not been violated in the present case.

In the Kervoêlen v. France case (judgment of 27 March 2001, Application No. 35585/97, paragraphs 23-30), the Court held that where a licence to operate a bar had expired it could not be argued that there had been a decision on a right entailing the application of Article 6, paragraph 1 (the Tre Traktörer AB v. Sweden judgment of 7 July 1989, Series A No. 159, paragraph 43).

A "civil" right or obligation

The rights and obligations must also be "civil" in nature. The concept is one which is quite difficult to define and which develops with time.

First of all, it should be noted that the Court has emphasised the autonomy of this notion in relation to domestic law, and recognised that national law has played a certain role in defining the concept. In the König v. Germany case (28 June 1978, Series A No. 27, pp. 29-30, paragraphs 88-89), it declared, in particular, that:

> [...] the concept of "civil rights and obligations" cannot be interpreted solely by reference to the domestic law of the respondent State. [...]

> Whilst the Court thus concludes that the concept of "civil rights and obligations" is autonomous, it nevertheless does not consider that, in this context, the legislation of the State concerned is without importance. Whether or not a right is to be regarded as civil within the meaning of this expression in the Convention must be determined by reference to the substantive content and effects of the right – and not its legal classification – under the domestic law of the State concerned.

However, the Court has expressly refused to provide a general definition of the "civil" nature of the rights and obligations referred to in Article 6. In the above-mentioned Benthem judgment (ibid., p. 16, paragraph 35), it stated:

> The Court does not consider that it has to give on this occasion an abstract definition of the concept of "civil rights and obligations".

The Court merely deemed it appropriate to state that the expression "civil" rights and obligations must not be taken to reflect the distinction between matters governed by private law and those governed by public law as maybe found in domestic law, or as limiting the application of Article 6, paragraph 1, solely to disputes between individuals. Apart from national labels and the quality of the parties, all that counts is the nature of the right in issue. In the above-mentioned König judgment (p. 30, paragraph 90), the Court held:

> Article 6, paragraph 1 (art. 6-1), covers private-law disputes in the traditional sense, that is disputes between individuals or between an individual and the State to the extent that the latter had been acting as a private person, subject to private law; [and not] disputes between an individual and the State acting in its sovereign capacity.
>
> [...]
>
> Only the character of the right (at issue) is relevant.

There the Court was making reference to its case-law deriving from the Ringelsen v. Austria judgment (16 July 1971, Series A No. 13, p. 39, paragraph 94), where it had already noted:

> The character of the legislation which governs how the matter is to be determined (civil, commercial, administrative law [...]) and that of the authority which is invested with jurisdiction in the matter (ordinary court, administrative body, [...]) are [...] of little consequence.

What matters to the Court is therefore the intrinsic nature of the right or obligation in issue, which must be "private". The wording of the Pudas v. Sweden judgment (judgment of 21 October 1987, Application No. 10426/83, Series A No. 125-A, paragraph 35) is wholly in keeping with that line of decisions (paragraph 35). In that judgment the Court noted:

> Article 6, paragraph 1 (art. 6-1), applies irrespective of the status of parties, as of the character of the legislation which governs how the dispute is to be determined and the character of the authority which is invested with jurisdiction in the matter; it is enough that the outcome of the proceedings should be decisive for private rights and obligations (see notably the Deumeland judgment of 29 May 1986, Series A No. 100, p. 22, paragraph 60, and the Baraona judgment of 8 July 1987, Series A No. 122, pp. 17-18, paragraph 42).

In reality, the Court will find that the right in question is "civil" or "private" provided that the interests involved are economic in nature.

That naturally applies to the procedures governing the exercise of the right of property (see the Mahieu v. France judgment of 19 June 2001, Application No. 43288/98, on the prior authorisation to operate a farm).

However, it also applies in matters of social legislation. Thus, in the Francesco Lombardo v. Italy case (judgment of 26 November 1992, Series A No. 249-B), a police officer *(carabiniere)* who had been invalided out of the service maintained that his invalidity was the consequence of sickness "due to his service" and therefore claimed an "enhanced ordinary pension". The Court considered that the applicant's complaints were not connected with either the "recruitment" or the "employment", and only indirectly concerned with the "termination of service", of an official, since they related to a claim of a purely pecuniary right which had arisen after he had left the service. In those circumstances, and since in discharging its obligation to pay the pensions in issue the Italian State was not using "discretionary powers" and could be compared to an employer who is a party to a contract of employment governed by private law, the Court concluded that the applicant's claims had a "civil" character for the purposes of Article 6, paragraph 1 (see the above-mentioned Neigel judgment, pp. 410-411, paragraph 43).

Likewise, in the Schuler-Zgraggen v. Switzerland judgment (24 June 1993, Series A No. 263, p. 17, paragraph 46), the Court noted in relation to questions concerning an invalidity pension and social security benefits:

> The most important [consideration] lies in the fact that despite the public-law features pointed out by the Government, the applicant was not only affected in her relations with the administrative authorities as such but also suffered an interference with her means of subsistence; she was claiming an individual, economic right flowing from specific rules laid down in a federal statute (see paragraph 35 above).

(See also the Feldbrugge v. the Netherlands judgment of 29 May 1986, Series A No. 99, pp. 12-16, paragraphs 26-40; and the Salesi v. Italy judgment of 26 February 1993, Series A No. 257-E, pp. 59-60, paragraph 19.)

To summarise:

> Article 6, paragraph 1 (art. 6-1), is applicable where an action is "pecuniary" in nature and is founded on an alleged infringement of rights which are likewise pecuniary rights, notwithstanding the origin of the dispute and the fact that the administrative courts have jurisdiction (see, among other authorities, the Editions Périscope judgment, previously cited, p. 66, paragraph 40, and the Beaumartin v. France judgment of 24 November 1994, Series A No. 296-B, pp. 60-61, paragraph 28).

(The Procola v. Luxembourg judgment of 28 September 1995, Series A No. 326, paragraph 38; the Editions Périscope v. France judgment of 26 March 1992, Series A No. 249-B; the De Sanra v. Italy judgment of 2 September 1997, *Reports* 1997-V, paragraphs 16-18; the Beaumartin judgment, pp. 60-61, paragraph 28; the Ortenberg v. Austria judgment of 25 November 1994, Series A No. 295-B, pp. 48-49, paragraph 28, and also, by implication, the Van de Hurk v. the Netherlands judgment of 19 April 1994, Series A No. 288, p. 16, paragraph 43; and the Znatta v. France judgment of 28 March 2000, Application No. 38042/97, concerning proceedings for the annulment of a prefectorial decree ordering an expropriation in the public interest.)

That does not mean, however, that the Court disregards fundamental distinctions drawn by national law which touch on the very core of the functioning of the States and of their discretionary power. Thus, in the Atgento v. Italy judgment (2 September 1997, *Reports* 1997-V, paragraph 18), the Court stated:

> The Court observes that in the law of many member States of the Council of Europe there is a basic distinction between civil servants and employees governed by private law. This has led it to hold that "disputes relating to the recruitment, careers and termination of service of civil servants are as a general rule outside the scope of Article 6, paragraph 1" (see the Massa v. Italy judgment

of 24 August 1993, Series A No. 265-B, p. 20, paragraph 26, and the Neigel v. France judgment of 17 March 1997, *Reports of Judgments and Decisions* 1997-II, pp. 410-411, paragraph 43).

In fact, the Court also applies a different test from the one deriving from the pecuniary aspect. It endeavours to ascertain whether, in the case before it, the State is involved as the holder of public authority responsible for protecting the general interests (see the Fogarty v. the United Kingdom judgment of 21 November 2001, Application No. 37112/97, paragraph 28):

> The Court recalls that in the above-mentioned Pellegrin judgment, it adopted a functional test for the purposes of determining the applicability of Article 6, paragraph 1, to employment disputes involving public servants, based on the nature of the employee's duties and responsibilities. An employment dispute is excluded from the scope of Article 6, paragraph 1, if it concerns a public servant whose duties typify the specific activities of the public service in so far as he or she acts as the depository of public authority responsible for protecting the general interests of the State.

An obvious example of such activities is provided by the armed forces and the police. In the R. v. Belgium case (judgment of 27 February 2001, Application No. 33919/96, paragraphs 44-45, available in French only – unofficial translation), the Court stated:

> In the light of that case-law, the Court considers that the applicant's claim for payment of a pension by way of compensation for the injuries received in discharging military obligations as a reserve officer does not concern a civil right within the meaning of Article 6, paragraph 1, of the Convention. The Court finds that where a member of the reserve service is required to complete periods of active service, he has military status during those periods. Regard being had to the principles laid down in the above-mentioned Pellegrin judgment, his situation cannot be distinguished from that of a serving member of the armed forces and therefore characteristically comes within the specific activities of the public administration, in so far as the latter acts as the depository of public authority responsible for protecting the general interests of the State. Such a conclusion is all the more compelling in the present case, given the applicant's description of the tasks carried out in the course of his activities as a reserve officer. It therefore considers that the present dispute does not concern a civil right or obligation.

> Accordingly, Article 6, paragraph 1, does not apply in the present case.

(See also the Devlin v. the United Kingdom judgment of 30 October 2001, Application No. 29545/95, paragraphs 23-26; for the application of Article 6 to a caretaker in a municipal public school, see the Procaccini v. Italy judgment of 30 March 2000, Application No. 31631/96.)

In the light of all those factors, and in order to return to the "pecuniary" test, it is appropriate to cite a long passage from the recent and very interesting Ferrazzini v. Italy judgment (12 July 2001, Application No. 44759/98, paragraphs 24-31) concerning a tax dispute, where the Court, sitting as a Grand Chamber, declared:

> According to the Court's case-law, the concept of "civil rights and obligations" cannot be interpreted solely by reference to the domestic law of the respondent

State. The Court has on several occasions affirmed the principle that this concept is "autonomous", within the meaning of Article 6, paragraph 1, of the Convention (see, among other authorities, the König v. the Federal Republic of Germany judgment of 28 June 1978, Series A No. 27, pp. 29-30, paragraphs 88-89, and the Baraona v. Portugal judgment of 8 July 1987, Series A No. 122, pp. 17-18, paragraph 42). The Court confirms this case-law in the instant case. It considers that any other solution is liable to lead to results that are incompatible with the object and purpose of the Convention (see, *mutatis mutandis*, the König judgment cited above, paragraph 88, and Maaouia v. France [GC], No. 39652/98, paragraph 34, ECHR 2000-X).

Pecuniary interests are clearly at stake in tax proceedings, but merely showing that a dispute is "pecuniary" in nature is not in itself sufficient to attract the applicability of Article 6, paragraph 1, under its "civil" head (see the Pierre-Bloch v. France judgment of 21 October 1997, *Reports of Judgments and Decisions* 1997-VI, p. 2223, paragraph 51, and Pellegrin v. France [GC], No. 28541/95, paragraph 60, ECHR 1999-VIII, see the Editions Périscope v. France judgment of 26 March 1992, Series A No. 234-B, p. 66, paragraph 40). In particular, according to the traditional case-law of the Convention institutions,

> "There may exist 'pecuniary' obligations vis-à-vis the State or its subordinate authorities which, for the purpose of Article 6, paragraph 1, are to be considered as belonging exclusively to the realm of public law and are accordingly not covered by the notion of 'civil rights and obligations'. Apart from fines imposed by way of 'criminal sanction', this will be the case, in particular, where an obligation which is pecuniary in nature derives from tax legislation or is otherwise part of normal civic duties in a democratic society" (see, among other authorities, the Schouten and Meldrum v. the Netherlands judgment of 9 December 1994, Series A No. 304, p. 21, paragraph 50; Application No. 11189/84, Commission decision of 11 December 1986, *Decisions and Reports* 50, pp. 121 and 140; and Application No. 20471/92, Commission decision of 15 April 1996, *Decisions and Reports* 85, pp. 29 and 46).

The Convention is, however, a living instrument to be interpreted in the light of present-day conditions (see, among other authorities, the Johnston and Others v. Ireland judgment, Series A No. 112, p. 25, paragraph 53), and it is incumbent on the Court to review whether, in the light of changed attitudes in society as to the legal protection that falls to be accorded to individuals in their relations with the State, the scope of Article 6, paragraph 1, should not be extended to cover disputes between citizens and public authorities as to the lawfulness under domestic law of the tax authorities' decisions.

Relations between the individual and the State have clearly developed in many spheres during the fifty years which have elapsed since the Convention was adopted, with State regulation increasingly intervening in private-law relations. This has led the Court to find that procedures classified under national law as being part of "public law" could come within the purview of Article 6 under its "civil" head if the outcome was decisive for private rights and obligations, in regard to such matters as, to give some examples, the sale of land, the running of a private clinic, property interests, the granting of administrative authorisations relating to the conditions of professional practice or of a licence to serve alcoholic beverages (see, among other authorities, the Ringeisen v. Austria judgment of 16 July 1971, Series A No. 13, p. 39, paragraph 94; the König judgment cited above, p. 32, paragraphs 94-95; the Sporrong and Lönnroth v. Sweden judgment of 23 September 1982, Series A No. 52, p. 19, paragraph 79; the Allan Jacobsson v. Sweden judgment of 25 October 1989, Series A No. 163, pp. 20-21, paragraph 73; the Benthem v. the Netherlands judgment of 23 October 1985, Series A No. 97, p. 16, paragraph 36; and the Tre Traktörer Aktiebolag v. Sweden judgment of 7 July 1989, Series A No. 159, p. 19, paragraph 43). Moreover, the State's increasing intervention in the individual's day-to-day life, in terms of welfare protection for example, has required the Court to evaluate features of public law and private law before concluding that the asserted right could be classified as "civil" (see, among other authorities, the Feldbrugge v. the Netherlands judgment of 29 May 1986, Series A No. 99, p. 16, paragraph 40; the Deumeland v. Germany judgment of 29 May 1986, Series A No. 100, p. 25, paragraph 74; the Salesi v. Italy judgment of 26 February 1993, Series A No. 257-E, pp. 59-60, paragraph 19; and the Schouten and Meldrum judgment cited above, p. 24, paragraph 60).

However, rights and obligations existing for an individual are not necessarily civil in nature. Thus, political rights and obligations, such as the right to stand for election to the National Assembly (see the Pierre-Bloch judgment cited above, p. 2223, paragraph 50), even though in those proceedings the applicant's pecuniary interests were at stake (ibid., paragraph 51), are not civil in nature, with the consequence that Article 6, paragraph 1, does not apply. Neither does that provision apply to disputes between administrative authorities and those of their employees who occupy posts involving participation in the exercise of powers conferred by public law (see Pellegrin v. France [GC], No. 28541/95, paragraphs 66-67, ECHR 1999-VIII). Similarly, the expulsion of aliens does not give rise to disputes (contestations) over civil rights for the purposes of Article 6, paragraph 1, of the Convention, which accordingly does not apply (see the Maaouia judgment cited above, paragraphs 37-38).

In the tax field, developments which might have occurred in democratic societies do not, however, affect the fundamental nature of the obligation on individuals or companies to pay tax. In comparison with the position when the Convention was adopted, those developments have not entailed a further intervention by the State into the "civil" sphere of the individual's life. The Court considers that tax matters still form part of the hard core of public-authority prerogatives, with the public nature of the relationship between the taxpayer and the tax authority remaining predominant. Bearing in mind that the Convention and its Protocols must be interpreted as a whole, the Court also observes that Article 1 of Protocol No. 1, which concerns the protection of property, reserves the right of States to enact such laws as they deem necessary for the purpose of securing the payment of taxes (see, *mutatis mutandis*, the Gasus Dosier- und Fördertechnik GmbH v. the Netherlands judgment of 23 February 1995, Series A No. 306-B, pp. 48-49, paragraph 60). Although the Court does not attach decisive importance to that factor, it does take it into account. It considers that tax disputes fall outside the scope of civil rights and obligations, despite the pecuniary effects which they necessarily produce for the taxpayer.

The principle according to which the autonomous concepts contained in the Convention must be interpreted in the light of present-day conditions in democratic societies does not give the Court power to interpret Article 6, paragraph 1, as though the adjective "civil" (with the restriction that that adjective necessarily places on the category of "rights and obligations" to which that Article applies) were not present in the text.

Accordingly, Article 6, paragraph 1, does not apply in the instant case.

That judgment appears to require a development (*idem* the Ferrazzini v. Italy judgment of 12 July 2001, Application No. 44759/98).

(For the application of Article 6, paragraph 1, to a claim for civil damages before the criminal courts, owing to the possible consequences for the civil claim, see the Callvelli and Ciglio v. Italy judgment of 17 January 2002, Application No. 32967/96, paragraph 62.)

Article 6 therefore applies to disputes concerning civil rights and obligations as defined above. It also applies to criminal charges (by way of reminder, decisions relating to the entry, residence and removal of aliens do not give rise to disputes over civil rights and obligations and are not concerned with criminal charges: the Maaouia v. France judgment of 5 October 2000).

The right to a tribunal in respect of "criminal charges"

The concept of a criminal "charge"

It is first of all necessary to consider the concept of "charge". In the Deweer v. Belgium case (judgment of 27 February 1980, Series A No. 35, pp. 22-24, paragraphs 42 and 44), the Court noted that this expression has an autonomous meaning in the Convention and that a substantive conception of the expression is to be preferred:

> The concept embodied in the French expression *"accusation en matière pénale"* is, however, "autonomous"; it has to be understood "within the meaning of the Convention" (see notably the König judgment of 28 June 1978, Series A No. 27, p. 29, paragraph 88).
>
> [...]
>
> [...] the prominent place held in a democratic society by the right to a fair trial (see especially the above-mentioned Airey judgment, pp. 12-13, paragraph 24) prompts the Court to prefer a "substantive", rather than a "formal", conception of the "charge" contemplated by Article 6, paragraph 1 (art. 6-1). The Court is compelled to look behind the appearances and investigate the realities of the procedure in question.

Accordingly, the Court stated (ibid., paragraph 46):

> The "charge" could, for the purposes of Article 6, paragraph 1 (art. 6-1), be defined as the official notification given to an individual by the competent authority of an allegation that he has committed a criminal offence. In several decisions and opinions the Commission has adopted a test that appears to be fairly closely related, namely whether "the situation of the [suspect] has been substantially affected" (the Neumeister case, Series B No. 6, p. 81; the case of Huber v. Austria, *Yearbook of the European Convention on Human Rights* 18, p. 356, paragraph 67); [...].

In that case, an order had been made for the provisional closure of the applicant's butcher's shop after he was alleged to have committed an offence against the legislation on prices. The closure would be terminated upon payment of a security in the form of a friendly settlement or, failing that, on the date on which the offence was determined by a court. The Court considered that from the time when that order was made, the applicant was facing a criminal charge within the meaning of the Convention.

It will be noted that in that judgment the Court already arrived at the idea of the "situation" of the person concerned being "substantially affected" (for example by searches, etc.). It was to establish that idea as a definition of "charge" in the Foti and Others v. Italy case (judgment of 10 December 1982, Series A No. 56, p. 18, paragraph 52) ; and in the Serves v. France judgment concerning the situation of a person in criminal proceedings where the document initiating the proceedings had been annulled (judgment of 20 October 1997, *Reports* 1997-VI, paragraph 42), the Court stated:

> It [the concept of charge] may thus be defined as "the official notification given to an individual by the competent authority of an allegation that he has committed a criminal offence", a definition that also corresponds to the test whether "the situation of the [suspect] has been substantially affected" (see, for example, the Deweer v. Belgium judgment of 27 February 1980, Series A No. 35, p. 22, paragraph 42, and p. 24, paragraph 46; and the Eckle v. Germany judgment of 15 July 1982, Series A No. 51, p. 33, paragraph 73).

In the Air Canada v. the United Kingdom case (judgment of 5 May 1995, Series A No. 316-A, paragraphs 52-55), the customs authorities had seized an aeroplane belonging to a company in which they had found a container without an airway bill containing cannabis. The plane had been released following payment of a pecuniary penalty. The Court declared:

> [...] the factors referred to above – the absence of a criminal charge or a provision which is "criminal" in nature and the lack of involvement of the criminal courts – taken together with the fact that there was no threat of any criminal proceedings in the event of non-compliance, are sufficient to distinguish the present case from that of Deweer v. Belgium (judgment of 27 February 1980, Series A No. 35) where the applicant was obliged to pay a sum of money under constraint of the provisional closure of his business in order to avoid criminal proceedings from being brought against him.

> It is further recalled that a similar argument had been made by the applicant in the AGOSI case (loc. cit.). On that occasion the Court held that the forfeiture of the goods in question by the national court were measures consequential upon the act of smuggling committed by another party and that criminal charges had not been brought against AGOSI in respect of that act. The fact that the property rights of AGOSI were adversely affected could not of itself lead to the conclusion that a "criminal charge" for the purposes of Article 6 (art. 6) could be considered as having been brought against the applicant company (loc. cit., p. 22, paragraphs 65-66).

> Bearing in mind that, unlike the AGOSI case, the applicant company had been required to pay a sum of money and that its property had not been confiscated, the Court proposes to follow the same approach.

Accordingly the matters complained of did not involve "the determination of [a] criminal charge".

It was important to define the expression "charge", because it is when the charge is brought that time begins to run for the purpose of a trial within a "reasonable time".

The notion of "criminal"

The charge referred to in Article 6 must relate to a criminal matter. In the Campbell and Fell v. the United Kingdom case (judgment of 28 June 1984, Series A No. 80, p. 35, paragraph 68), the Court recalled the principles laid down in the Engel case:

> The Court was confronted with a similar issue in the case of Engel and Others, which was cited in argument by those appearing before it in the present procee-dings. In its judgment of 8 June 1976 in that case (Series A No. 22, pp. 33-35, para-graphs 80-82), the Court, after drawing attention to the "autonomy" of the notion of "criminal charge" as conceived of under Article 6 (art. 6), set forth the following principles which it re-affirmed in its Öztürk judgment of 21 February 1984 (Series A No. 73, pp. 17-18, paragraphs 48-50).
>
> (a) The Convention is not opposed to the Contracting States creating or main-taining a distinction between criminal law and disciplinary law and drawing the dividing line, but it does not follow that the classification thus made is decisive for the purposes of the Convention.
>
> (b) If the Contracting States were able at their discretion, by classifying an offence as disciplinary instead of criminal, to exclude the operation of the fundamental clauses of Articles 6 and 7 (art. 6, art. 7), the application of these provisions would be subordinated to their sovereign will. A latitude exten-ding thus far might lead to results incompatible with the object and purpose of the Convention.

In seeking to ascertain the nature of an offence, the Court would then examine "the way in which it is described in domestic law, its nature, the degree of severity of the penalty and its purpose" (the Engel and Others v. the Netherlands judgment, 8 June 1976, Series A No. 22, pp. 34-35, para-graph 82). A similar choice of words may be found in the J.B. v. Switzerland judgment (3 May 2001, Application No. 31827/96, paragraph 44):

> In its earlier case-law the Court has established that there are three criteria to be taken into account when it is being decided whether a person was "charged with a criminal offence" for the purposes of Article 6. These are the classification of the offence under national law, the nature of the offence and the nature and degree of severity of the penalty that the person concerned risked incurring (see, among other authorities, the Öztürk v. Germany judgment of 21 February 1984, Series A No. 73, p. 18, paragraph 50). In the A.P., M.P. and T.P. v. Switzerland judg-ment, the Court moreover found that proceedings leading to the imposition of a fine on account of the criminal offence of tax evasion fall in principle to be examined under Article 6, paragraph 1, of the Convention (see the judgment cited above).

In the Weber v. Switzerland case (judgment of 22 May 1990, Series A No. 177, pp. 17-18, paragraphs 31-34), the Court reiterated that the classification of the offence according to the legal methods of the respondent State is of relative weight and serves only as a starting-point. The second and third tests – the nature of the offence and the nature and degree of severity of the penalty – have greater weight.

Generally, where the penalty entails deprivation of liberty, the Court considers that the offence is a criminal matter. In the Engel case, assignment to a disciplinary unit in the army was a criminal matter for the purposes of the Convention (see also the Joao José Brandao Ferreira v. Portugal case, Application No. 41921/98, decision of 28 September 2000, concerning "simple arrest" in the army). In the Weber case, the Court held that a fine – for breach of the confidential nature of a judicial investigation – of up to 500 Swiss francs, which could be converted into a short term of imprisonment on certain conditions, was sufficient for the matter to be classified as criminal for the purposes of the Convention.

In the Ravnsborg v. Sweden case (judgment of 23 March 1994, Series A No. 283-B, p. 31, paragraph 35), on the other hand, the offences in question, which were punished by fines, were not classified as "criminal" by the Court. On the basis of the third test – the nature and degree of severity of the penalty – the amount of each fine, which could be as much as 1 000 krona and which was convertible under Swedish law into a term of imprisonment, did not attain a level such as to make it a "criminal penalty" (see also the Inocêncio v. Portugal judgment of 11 January 2001, Application No. 43862/98).

It was necessary to define the concepts of "determination of [...] civil rights and obligations" and "criminal charge". It is the definition of these concepts that determines the scope of Article 6, paragraph 1, that is the situations in which there is a right to a "tribunal".

2. The scope of the "right to a tribunal"

Now that we have examined the sphere of application of the right to a tribunal, we must study its scope.

The right guaranteed by Article 6, paragraph 1, is the right of access to a tribunal

The Court has made one first, fundamental point concerning the scope of the right to have a case heard before a tribunal.

In a case involving a dispute over civil rights (the Golder v. the United Kingdom case, judgment of 21 February 1975, Series A No. 18, p. 12, paragraph 25, and pp. 17-18, paragraphs 35-36), the Court determined the question whether "Article 6, paragraph 1, is limited to guaranteeing in substance the right to a fair trial in legal proceedings which are already pending, or does it in addition secure a right of access to the courts for every person wishing to commence an action in order to have his civil rights and obligations determined":

> Were Article 6, paragraph 1 (art. 6-1), to be understood as concerning exclusively the conduct of an action which had already been initiated before a court, a Contracting State could, without acting in breach of that text, do away with its courts, or take away their jurisdiction to determine certain classes of civil actions and entrust it to organs dependent on the Government. Such assumptions, indissociable from a danger of arbitrary power, would have serious consequences which are repugnant to the aforementioned principles and which the Court cannot overlook (the Lawless judgment of 1 July 1961, Series A No. 3, p. 52, and the Delcourt judgment of 17 January 1970, Series A No. 11, pp. 14-15).
>
> [...]
>
> [...] it follows that the right of access constitutes an element which is inherent in the right stated by Article 6, paragraph 1 (art. 6-1). This is not an extensive interpretation forcing new obligations on the Contracting States: it is based on the very terms of the first sentence of Article 6, paragraph 1 (art. 6-1), read in its context and having regard to the object and purpose of the Convention, a law-making treaty (see the Wemhoff judgment of 27 June 1968, Series A No. 7, p. 23, paragraph 8), and to general principles of law.
>
> The Court thus reaches the conclusion [...] that Article 6, paragraph 1 (art. 6-1), secures to everyone the right to have any claim relating to his civil rights and obligations brought before a court or tribunal. In this way the Article embodies the "right to a court", of which the right of access, that is the right to institute proceedings before courts in civil matters, constitutes one aspect only.

(See also, for example, the Tsironis v. Greece judgment of 6 December 2001, Application No. 44584/98, paragraph 28.)

In the same vein, Article 6 is applicable to domestic remedies (appeals, appeals on points of law, etc.) as provided for in national legislation (see the Rodriguez Valin v. Spain judgment of 11 October 2001, Application No. 47792/99, paragraphs 23-28; the Tricard v. France judgment of 10 July 2001, Application No. 40472/98, paragraphs 25-34) and also to the rules on the time-barring of actions (the Stubbings and Others v. the United Kingdom judgment of 22 October 1996, *Reports* 1996-IV, paragraphs 50-57; and the Yagtzilar and Others v. Greece judgment of 6 December 2001, Application No. 41727/98, paragraphs 20-28) and to court fees (the Kreuz v. Poland judgment of 19 June 2001, Application No. 28249/95).

The right to a tribunal must be effective

The right to a tribunal must not only exist: it must also be effective. It is not enough that access to the tribunal is possible.

In the Airey v. Ireland decision (9 October 1979, Series A No. 32, pp. 12-14, paragraph 24), the Court took the opportunity to state that the member states must guarantee effective access to the courts. In that case the applicant, in the absence of legal aid and not being in a financial position to meet herself the costs involved, had been unable to find a solicitor willing to act for her. She could have appeared in person but the procedure was very complex. The Court found that there had been a violation of Article 6, paragraph 1:

> The Court does not regard this possibility (of going before the High Court without the assistance of a lawyer) of itself as conclusive of the matter. The Convention is intended to guarantee not rights that are theoretical or illusory but rights that are practical and effective (see, *mutatis mutandis*, the judgment of 23 July 1968 in the "Belgian linguistics" case, Series A No. 6, p. 31, paragraphs 3, in fine, and 4; the above-mentioned Golder judgment, p. 18, paragraph 35, in fine; the Luedicke, Belkacem and Koç judgment of 28 November 1978, Series A No. 29, pp. 17-18; paragraph 42; and the Marckx judgment of 13 June 1979, Series A No. 31, p. 15, paragraph 31). This is particularly so of the right of access to the courts in view of the prominent place held in a democratic society by the right to a fair trial (see, *mutatis mutandis*, the Delcourt judgment of 17 January 1970, Series A No. 11, p. 15, paragraph 25). It must therefore be ascertained whether Mrs Airey's appearance before the High Court without the assistance of a lawyer would be effective, in the sense of whether she would be able to present her case properly and satisfactorily.

> [...] the Court considers it most improbable that a person in Mrs Airey's position (see paragraph 8 above) can effectively present his or her own case.

> [...]

> The Court concludes from the foregoing that the possibility to appear in person before the High Court does not provide the applicant with an effective right of access. [...]

The Court explained the consequences of this finding on a State's obligation to institute a legal aid scheme (ibid., pp. 15-16, paragraph 26, in fine):

> The conclusion appearing at the end of paragraph 24 above does not therefore imply that the State must provide free legal aid for every dispute relating to a "civil right".

> To hold that so far-reaching an obligation exists would, the Court agrees, sit ill with the fact that the Convention contains no provision on legal aid for those disputes, Article 6, paragraph 3.*c* (art. 6-3-c), dealing only with criminal proceedings. However, despite the absence of a similar clause for civil litigation, Article 6, paragraph 1 (art. 6-1), may sometimes compel the State to provide for the assistance of a lawyer when such assistance proves indispensable for an effective access to court either because legal representation is rendered compulsory, as is done by the domestic law of certain Contracting States for various types of litigation, or by reason of the complexity of the procedure or of the case.

(See also the R.D. v. Poland judgment of 18 December 2001, Application No. 29692/96, paragraphs 43-52.)

The Bellet v. France judgment (4 December 1995, Series A No. 333-B, paragraphs 37-38) concerned compensation for haemophiliacs who had been infected by blood transfusions. The parties did not agree on whether by accepting compensation from the Compensation Fund the victims had waived any right of further action. The Paris Court of Appeal had declared the action inadmissible, in the absence of an interest in bringing proceedings. The Court declared:

> All in all, the system was not sufficiently clear or sufficiently attended by safeguards to prevent a misunderstanding as to the procedures for making use of the available remedies and the restrictions stemming from the simultaneous use of them.

> Having regard to all the circumstances of the case, the Court finds that the applicant did not have a practical, effective right of access to the courts in the proceedings before the Paris Court of Appeal. There has accordingly been a breach of Article 6, paragraph 1 (art. 6-1).

(See also the Dulaurans v. France judgment of 21 March 2000, Application No. 34553/97, concerning the dismissal of an appeal on a point of law arising from a manifest error of assessment (violation).)

The right of access does not entail an obligation to provide courts of further instance

In the Guérin v. France judgment (29 July 1998, *Reports* 1998-V, paragraph 44), the Court observed that Article 6 does not impose an obligation to provide remedies. It stated, however, that if such remedies exist, they must comply with the guarantees laid down in Article 6:

> Article 6, paragraph 1, of the Convention does not, it is true, compel the Contracting States to set up courts of appeal or of cassation. Nevertheless, a State which does institute such courts is required to ensure that persons amenable to the law shall enjoy before these courts the fundamental guarantees contained in Article 6 (see the Delcourt v. Belgium judgment of 17 January 1970, Series A No. 11, p. 14, paragraph 25).

Furthermore, in the De Cubber v. Belgium judgment (26 October 1984, Application No. 9186/80, Series A No. 86, paragraph 32), the Court made clear that the existence of courts of appeal or courts of cassation which comply with the guarantees flowing from Article 6 does not exempt the courts of first instance from the obligation to comply with them:

> Article 6, paragraph 1 (art. 6-1), concerns primarily courts of first instance; it does not require the existence of courts of further instance. It is true that its fundamental guarantees, including impartiality, must also be provided by any courts of appeal or courts of cassation which a Contracting State may have chosen to set up (see the above-mentioned Delcourt judgment, Series A No. 11, p. 14, in fine, and, as the most recent authority, the Sutter judgment of 22 February 1984, Series A No. 74, p. 13, paragraph 28). However, even when this is the case it does not follow that the lower courts do not have to provide the required guarantees. Such a result would be at variance with the intention underlying the creation of several levels of courts, namely to reinforce the protection afforded to litigants.

In that case, the dispute related to a criminal matter.

One point must be made. In reality, the Court adopts a flexible approach to applying those principles (while erecting safety barriers).

It adopts that approach in technical spheres such as the grant of patents (the British-American Tobacco Company Ltd v. the Netherlands judgment of 20 November 1996, Series A No. 331, paragraph 77) or town planning matters (the Chapman v. the United Kingdom judgment of 18 January 2001, Application No. 27238/95, paragraph 124) and disciplinary proceedings before professional disciplinary bodies (the Court has held that proceedings before the National Council of the Ordre des Médecins (Medical Association) gave rise to disputes over civil rights and obligations; see the Diennet v. France judgment of 26 September 1995, Series A No. 325-A, paragraph 27). In the Albert and Le Compte judgment (10 February 1983, Series A No. 58, p. 16, paragraph 29), the Court stated:

> In many member states of the Council of Europe, the duty of adjudicating on disciplinary offences is conferred on jurisdictional organs of professional associations. Even in instances where Article 6, paragraph 1 (art. 6-1), is applicable, conferring powers in this manner does not in itself infringe the Convention [...]. Nonetheless, in such circumstances the Convention calls at least for one of the two following systems: either the jurisdictional organs themselves comply with the requirements of Article 6, paragraph 1 (art. 6-1), or they do not so comply but are subject to subsequent control by a judicial body that has full jurisdiction and does provide the guarantees of Article 6, paragraph 1 (art. 6-1).

Therefore, where a judicial body responsible for dealing with disputes concerning "civil rights and obligations" does not satisfy all the requirements of Article 6, paragraph 1, there is no violation of the Convention if the proceedings before it were subject to "subsequent control by a judicial body that has full jurisdiction and does provide the guarantees of Article 6". Furthermore, in the Le Compte, Van Leuven and De Meyere judgment (23 June 1981, Series A No. 43, pp. 22-23, paragraphs 50-51), the Court had already stated:

> Whilst Article 6, paragraph 1 (art. 6-1), embodies the "right to a court" [...], it nevertheless does not oblige the Contracting States to submit "contestations" (disputes) over "civil rights and obligations" to a procedure conducted at each of its stages before "tribunals" meeting the Article's various requirements. Demands of flexibility and efficiency, which are fully compatible with the protection of human rights, may justify the prior intervention of administrative or professional bodies and, *a fortiori*, of judicial bodies which do not satisfy the said requirements in every respect; the legal tradition of many member states of the Council of Europe may be invoked in support of such a system.

Moreover, even in classic disputes such as criminal cases, the Court introduces the same flexibility when it applies Article 6, paragraph 1, to the various levels of court in a judicial order (see the Tolstoy Miloslavsky v. the United Kingdom judgment of 13 July 1995, Series A No. 316-B, paragraph 59). Thus, in the Botten v. Norway judgment (19 February 1996, *Reports* 1996-I, paragraph 39), the Court stated in respect of appeal proceedings:

> The Court reiterates that the manner of application of Article 6 (art. 6) to proceedings before courts of appeal depends on the special features of the proceedings involved; account must be taken of the entirety of the proceedings in

187

the domestic legal order and of the role of the appellate court therein. Where a public hearing has been held at first instance, the absence of such a hearing may be justified at the appeal stage by the special features of the proceedings at issue, having regard to the nature of the domestic appeal system, the scope of the appellate court's powers and to the manner in which the applicant's interests were actually presented and protected before the court of appeal, particularly in the light of the nature of the issues to be decided by it (see, *inter alia*, the Fejde v. Sweden judgment of 29 October 1991, Series A No. 212-C, pp. 67-69, paragraphs 27 and 31; and the Kremzow v. Austria judgment of 21 September 1993, Series A No. 268-B, p. 43, paragraphs 58-59).

According to the Court's case-law, leave-to-appeal proceedings and proceedings involving only questions of law, as opposed to questions of fact, may comply with the requirements of Article 6 (art. 6), although the appellant was not given an opportunity of being heard in person by the appeal or cassation court (see the Axen v. Germany judgment of 8 December 1983, Series A No. 72, pp. 12-13, paragraphs 27-28; and the Kremzow judgment cited above, pp. 43-44, paragraphs 60-61). Moreover, even if the court of appeal has full jurisdiction to examine both points of law and of fact, Article 6 (art. 6) does not always require a right to a public hearing or, if a hearing takes place, a right to be present in person (see, for instance, the Fejde judgment cited above, p. 69, paragraph 33).

(*Idem* the Haan v. the Netherlands judgment of 26 August 1997, Application No. 22839/93, *Reports* 1997-IV, paragraphs 51-55; and the Kerojärvi v. Finland judgment of 19 July 1995, Reports A322, paragraph 40.)

For the basis of the procedural requirements laid down by Article 6, paragraph 1, see below.

This right embodies implicit limits

It should be made clear that the Court considers that the "right of access to a court" is not absolute. It has observed (the above-mentioned Golder judgment, pp. 18-19, paragraph 38):

> The Court considers, accepting the views of the Commission and the alternative submission of the Government, that the right of access to the courts is not absolute. As this is a right which the Convention sets forth (see Articles 13, 14, 17 and 25) (art. 13, art. 14, art. 17, art. 25) without, in the narrower sense of the term, defining, there is room, apart from the bounds delimiting the very content of any right, for limitations permitted by implication.

As regards these "implicit limitations", the Court asserted in the Ashingdane v. the United Kingdom judgment (28 May 1985, Series A No. 93, pp. 24-25, paragraph 57) that:

> [...] the right of access to the courts [...] may be subject to limitations; these are permitted by implication since the right of access "by its very nature calls for regulation by the State, regulation which may vary in time and in place according to the needs and resources of the community and of individuals" (see the above-mentioned Golder judgment, p. 19, paragraph 38, quoting the "Belgian linguistics" judgment of 23 July 1968, Series A No. 6, p. 32, paragraph 5). In laying

down such regulation, the Contracting States enjoy a certain margin of appreciation. Whilst the final decision as to observance of the Convention's requirements rests with the Court, it is no part of the Court's function to substitute for the assessment of the national authorities any other assessment of what might be the best policy in this field (see, *mutatis mutandis*, the Klass and Others judgment of 6 September 1978, Series A No. 28, p. 23, paragraph 49).

Nonetheless, the limitations applied must not restrict or reduce the access left to the individual in such a way or to such an extent that the very essence of the right is impaired (see the above-mentioned Golder and "Belgian linguistics" judgments, ibid., and also the above-mentioned Winterwerp judgment, Series A No. 33, pp. 24 and 29, paragraphs 60 and 75). Furthermore, a limitation will not be compatible with Article 6, paragraph 1 (art. 6-1), if it does not pursue a legitimate aim and if there is not a reasonable relationship of proportionality between the means employed and the aim sought to be achieved.

Therefore (the Prince Hans-Adam II of Liechtenstein v. Germany judgment of 12 July 2001, Application No. 42527/98, paragraph 44):

> If the restriction is compatible with these principles, no violation of Article 6 will arise.

However, it is certain that the Court will prove demanding in accepting such restrictions or limitations. In the Ashingdane case, the ministerial authorisation which in English law was required before a prisoner could communicate with his lawyer could not be denied to Mr Golder, who sought to prove that he was not guilty of a charge relating to events which had occurred while he was in prison and which still had adverse consequences on his prison regime (*idem*, pp. 19-20, paragraph 40). That refusal of authorisation constituted a violation of Article 6, paragraph 1.

In the Fayed v. the United Kingdom judgment (21 September 1994, Series A No. 294-B, p. 56, paragraph 83), on the other hand, the Court considered (taking into account the margin of appreciation enjoyed by the States) that:

> [...] the limitation on the applicants' opportunity, before and after publication of the Inspectors' report, to take legal proceedings to challenge the Inspectors' findings damaging to their reputations did not involve an unjustified denial of their "right to a court" under Article 6, paragraph 1 (art. 6-1).

In the Al-Adsani v. the United Kingdom judgment (21 November 2001, Application No. 35763/97, paragraphs 56 and 66-67), the Court accepted that the immunity granted to States under international law, including in the present case immunity in respect of matters capable of falling within the ambit of Article 3, constituted a permissible limit of the right to a court deriving from Article 6:

> It follows that measures taken by a High Contracting Party which reflect generally recognised rules of public international law on State immunity cannot in principle be regarded as imposing a disproportionate restriction on the right of access to court as embodied in Article 6, paragraph 1. Just as the right of access to court is an inherent part of the fair trial guarantee in that Article, so some

restrictions on access must likewise be regarded as inherent, an example being those limitations generally accepted by the community of nations as part of the doctrine of State immunity.

[...]

The Court, while noting the growing recognition of the overriding importance of the prohibition of torture, does not accordingly find it established that there is yet acceptance in international law of the proposition that States are not entitled to immunity in respect of civil claims for damages for alleged torture committed outside the forum State. The 1978 Act, which grants immunity to States in respect of personal injury claims unless the damage was caused within the United Kingdom, is not inconsistent with those limitations generally accepted by the community of nations as part of the doctrine of State immunity.

In these circumstances, the application by the English courts of the provisions of the 1978 Act to uphold Kuwait's claim to immunity cannot be said to have amounted to an unjustified restriction on the applicant's access to court.

It follows that there has been no violation of Article 6, paragraph 1, in this case.

(*Idem* the Fogarty v. the United Kingdom judgment of 21 November 2001, Application No. 37112/97, paragraphs 32-39, concerning the dismissal of a member of staff of an embassy, and the McElhinney v. Ireland judgment of 21 November 2001, Application No. 31253/96, paragraphs 33-40; the Prince Hans-Adam II of Liechtenstein v. Germany judgment of 12 July 2001, Application No. 42527/98, paragraphs 51-70; and the Waite and Kennedy v. Germany judgment of 18 February 1999, Application No. 26083/94).

In addition, the implicit limitations may concern the statutory periods following which actions are time barred, orders for payment of security for costs or the rules concerning minors or the mentally handicapped (the Stubbings and Others v. the United Kingdom judgment of 22 October 1996, *Reports* 1996-IV, pp. 1502-1503, paragraphs 51-52; the Tolstoy Miloslavsky v. the United Kingdom judgment of 13 July 1995, Series A No. 316-B, pp. 80-81, paragraphs 62-67; and the above-mentioned Golder judgment, p. 19, paragraph 39), and other remedies.

The right to a court is also the right to enforcement of court decisions

The right of "access" to a court is one aspect of the "right to a court". In the Hornsby v. Greece judgment (19 March 1997, *Reports of Judgments and Decisions* 1997-II, pp. 510-511, paragraph 40), the Court stated that Article 6 concerns not only the right to bring proceedings before a court in civil matters. The "right" to secure enforcement of a judgment or decision forms an integral part of Article 6. In that judgment, the Court asserted:

> The Court reiterates that, according to its established case-law, Article 6, paragraph 1 (art. 6-1), secures to everyone the right to have any claim relating to his civil rights and obligations brought before a court or tribunal; in this way it embodies the "right to a court", of which the right of access, that is the right to institute proceedings before courts in civil matters, constitutes one aspect (see

the Philis v. Greece judgment of 27 August 1991, Series A No. 209, p. 20, paragraph 59). However, that right would be illusory if a Contracting State's domestic legal system allowed a final, binding judicial decision to remain inoperative to the detriment of one party. It would be inconceivable that Article 6, paragraph 1 (art. 6-1), should describe in detail procedural guarantees afforded to litigants – proceedings that are fair, public and expeditious – without protecting the implementation of judicial decisions; to construe Article 6 (art. 6) as being concerned exclusively with access to a court and the conduct of proceedings would be likely to lead to situations incompatible with the principle of the rule of law which the Contracting States undertook to respect when they ratified the Convention (see, *mutatis mutandis*, the Golder v. the United Kingdom judgment of 21 February 1975, Series A No. 18, pp. 16-18, paragraphs 34-36). Execution of a judgment given by any court must therefore be regarded as an integral part of the "trial" for the purposes of Article 6 (art. 6); moreover, the Court has already accepted this principle in cases concerning the length of proceedings (see, most recently, the Di Pede v. Italy and Zappia v. Italy judgments of 26 September 1996, *Reports of Judgments and Decisions* 1996-IV, pp. 1383-1384, paragraphs 20-24, and pp. 1410-1411, paragraphs 16-20 respectively.

To the same effect, see: the Logothetis v. Greece judgment (12 April 2001, Application No. 46352/99, paragraphs 11-16) or the Georgiadis v. Greece judgment of 28 March 2000 (Application No. 41209/98), concerning the failure to enforce a definitive judgment. See also the Scollo v. Italy judgment of 28 September 1995, Series A No. 315-C, paragraphs 41-45, concerning eviction proceedings and the Lunari v. Italy judgment of 11 January 2001 concerning a refusal to permit the use of the law enforcement agencies in an eviction pursuant to a court decision; the Comingersoll S.A. v. Portugal judgment of 6 April 2000, Application No. 35382/97, concerning the reasonable time for an enforcement procedure for recovery of sums payable under bills of exchange. See also the Antonakopoulos v. Greece judgment of 14 December 1999, Application No. 37098/97, concerning the refusal of the authorities to comply with a court decision.

It should further be noted that in enforcement matters, the court ordering enforcement must ensure that the earlier proceedings were in accordance with Article 6 when the decision to be enforced issues from a State which is not a Party to the Convention. Thus, in the Pellegrini v. Italy judgment (20 July 2001, Application No. 30882/96, paragraph 40), the Court stated:

> The Court notes at the outset that the applicant's marriage was annulled by a decision of the Vatican courts which was declared enforceable by the Italian courts. The Vatican has not ratified the Convention and, furthermore, the application was lodged against Italy. The Court's task therefore consists not in examining whether the proceedings before the ecclesiastical courts complied with Article 6 of the Convention, but whether the Italian courts, before authorising enforcement of the decision annulling the marriage, duly satisfied themselves that the relevant proceedings fulfilled the guarantees of Article 6. A review of that kind is required where a decision in respect of which enforcement is requested emanates from the courts of a country which does not apply the Convention. Such a review is especially necessary where the implications of a declaration of enforceability are of capital importance for the parties.

The right guaranteed by Article 6, paragraph 1, applies before the matter is brought before a court

In the Magee v. the United Kingdom judgment (6 June 2000, Application No. 28135/95, paragraph 41), the Court observed:

[...] even if the primary purpose of Article 6, as far as criminal matters are concerned, is to ensure a fair trial by a "tribunal" competent to determine "any criminal charge", it does not follow that the Article has no application to pre-trial proceedings. Thus, Article 6 – especially paragraph 3 – may be relevant before a case is sent for trial if and so far as the fairness of the trial is likely to be seriously prejudiced by an initial failure to comply with its provisions (see the Imbrioscia v. Switzerland judgment of 24 November 1993, Series A No. 275, p. 13, paragraph 36).

However, the Court has also had occasion to state (the Maillard Bous v. Portugal judgment of 28 June 2001, Application No. 41288/98, paragraph 19, available in French only – unofficial translation):

The Court recalls, however, that Article 6, paragraph 1, is not applicable to protective proceedings in which interim relief is sought. These proceedings are designed to govern a temporary situation pending a decision on the main action, and are therefore not intended to secure a decision on civil rights and obligations (see Moura Carreira and Lourenço Carreira v. Portugal (dec.), No. 41237/98, ECHR 2000-VIII).

3. The purpose of the "right to a court"

The purpose of the right to a court is to ensure a "decision" which settles the rights of the parties, taken by a body consisting of an "independent and impartial tribunal". We shall consider in turn the concepts of "independent and impartial tribunal" and "decision".

The concept of an "independent and impartial tribunal"

Examination of the concept of "independent and impartial tribunal" entails an examination of the expressions "tribunal", "impartial" and "independent".

The concept of "tribunal"

Of the various decisions on the concept of "tribunal", two are particularly deserving of attention. First of all, the Belilos v. Switzerland judgment (29 April 1988, Series A No. 132, p. 29, paragraph 64) sets out the criteria which the Court uses in order to determine whether the institution in question is a "tribunal" within the meaning of Article 6. The Court observed:

According to the Court's case-law, a "tribunal" is characterised in the substantive sense of the term by its judicial function, that is to say determining matters within its competence on the basis of rules of law and after proceedings conducted in a prescribed manner (see, as the most recent authority, the judgment of 30 November 1987 in the case of H. v Belgium, Series A No. 127, p. 34, paragraph 50). It must also satisfy a series of further requirements – independence, in particular of the executive; impartiality; duration of its members' terms of office; guarantees afforded by its procedure – several of which appear in the text of Article 6, paragraph 1 (art. 6-1), itself (see, *inter alia*, the Le Compte, Van Leuven and De Meyere judgment of 23 June 1981, Series A No. 43, p. 24, paragraph 55).

In the Campbell and Fell v. the United Kingdom judgment (28 June 1984, Series A No. 80, p. 39, paragraph 76) the Court stated:

> Again, the word "tribunal" in Article 6, paragraph 1 (art. 6-1), is not necessarily to be understood as signifying a court of law of the classic kind, integrated within the standard judicial machinery of the country (see, *mutatis mutandis*, the X. v. the United Kingdom judgment of 5 November 1981, Series A No. 46, p. 23, paragraph 53).

(See also the Coeme and Others v. Belgium judgment of 22 June 2000, Application No. 32492/96, on the concept of a tribunal "established by law".)

The concept of an "impartial tribunal"

As regards the "impartiality" which must characterise a tribunal, the Court described its approach in the Saraiva de Carvalho v. Portugal case (judgment of 22 April 1994, Series A No. 286-B, p. 38, paragraph 33):

> The Court points out that the existence of impartiality for the purposes of Article 6, paragraph 1 (art. 6-1), must be determined according to a subjective test, that is on the basis of the personal conviction of a particular judge in a given case, and also according to an objective test, that is ascertaining whether the judge offered guarantees sufficient to exclude any legitimate doubt in this respect (see, among other authorities, the Fey v. Austria judgment of 24 February 1993, Series A No. 255-A, p. 12, paragraph 28).

In this context, appearances have a role to play. In the Coeme and Others v. Belgium judgment (22 June 2000, Application No. 32492/96, paragraph 121), the Court recalled:

> In this respect [...] even appearances may be of a certain importance. What is at stake is the confidence which the courts in a democratic society must inspire in the public and above all, as far as criminal proceedings are concerned, in the accused (see, among other authorities, the Hauschildt v. Denmark judgment of 24 May 1989, Series A No. 154, p. 21, paragraph 48, and the Pullar v. the United Kingdom judgment of 10 June 1996, *Reports* 1996-III, p. 794, paragraph 38). In deciding whether there is a legitimate reason to fear that a court lacks independence or impartiality, the standpoint of the accused is important but not decisive. What is decisive is whether this fear can be held to be objectively justified (see, *mutatis mutandis*, the Hauschildt judgment cited above, p. 21, paragraph 48, and the Gautrin and Others judgment cited above, pp. 1030-1031, paragraph 58).

For various other situations, reference may be made to the following judgments:

– for a case where a judge presided over a court dealing with an opposition to a decision for which he himself was responsible: the De Haan v. the Netherlands judgment of 26 August 1997, Application No. 22839/93,

Reports 1997-IV, paragraphs 51-55: violation of Article 6, paragraph 1; for a case where a judge who had participated in a judgment at first instance had also taken part in examining an appeal against that judgment: the Oberschlick v. Austria (No. 1) judgment of 23 May 1991, Series A No. 204;

– for a case where the judge had already dealt with the same matter in the case of a person accused jointly with the applicants and when delivering his first judgment had referred to their participation: the Ferrantelli and Santangelo v. Italy judgment of 7 August 1996, *Reports* 1996-III, paragraphs 54-60; see also the Gregory v. the United Kingdom judgment of 25 February 1997, Application No. 22299/93, *Reports* 1997-I, paragraphs 48-50;

– the Kress v. France judgment of 7 June 2001, Application No. 39594/98, paragraphs 77-87, concerning the violation of Article 6 owing to the presence of the government law officer in the deliberations of the Council of State; the Procola v. Luxembourg judgment of 28 September 1995, Series A No. 326, paragraphs 40-45; the Wettstein v. Switzerland judgment of 21 December 2000, Application No. 33958/96, for a case where the lawyer representing the other side sat as a judge in related proceedings to which the applicant was a party: violation of Article 6, paragraph 1;

– the Morel v. France judgment of 6 June 2000, Application No. 34130/97, concerning the role of the insolvency judge in commercial matters; the Buscemi v. Italy judgment of 16 September 1999, Application No. 29569/95, concerning a judge dealing with a child custody case who conducted a dispute with the father in the press.

The concept of an "independent tribunal"

Last, as regards the independence of the tribunal within the meaning of Article 6, the Court has made a number of pronouncements. In the above-mentioned Campbell and Fell judgment (p. 40, paragraph 78), it laid down certain criteria:

> In determining whether a body can be considered to be "independent" – notably of the executive and of the parties to the case (see, *inter alia*, the Le Compte, Van Leuven and De Meyere judgment of 23 June 1981, Series A No. 43, p. 24, paragraph 55) – the Court has had regard to the manner of appointment of its members and the duration of their term of office (ibid., pp. 24-25, paragraph 57), the existence of guarantees against outside pressures (see the Piersack judgment of 1 October 1982, Series A No. 53, p. 13, paragraph 27) and the question whether the body presents an appearance of independence (see the Delcourt judgment of 17 January 1970, Series A No. 11, p. 17, paragraph 31).

From that aspect the Court has taken a position on the presence of officials within the courts. In the Sramek case (22 October 1984, Series A No. 84, paragraphs 41-42), the Court thus examined the concept of hierarchical subordination. After considering the situation of professional judges, it observed:

> There remain the three civil servants from the Office of the Land Government who, in accordance with the 1970/1973 Act (see paragraph 24 above), were, and had to be, included amongst the members of the Regional Authority.

In considering their position, it has to be recalled that it was held in the above-mentioned Ringeisen judgment that the presence of civil servants on the Upper Austrian Regional Commission was compatible with the Convention (Series A No. 13, pp. 39-40, paragraphs 95-97). Furthermore, in proceedings of the kind at issue the Government of the Tyrol are prevented by law from giving their civil servants instructions on carrying out their judicial functions.

However, the present case is distinguishable from the Ringeisen case in that the Land Government, represented by the Transactions Officer, acquired the status of a party when they appealed to the Regional Authority against the first-instance decision in Mrs Sramek's favour, and in that one of the three civil servants in question had the Transactions Officer as his hierarchical superior (see paragraph 12 above). That civil servant occupied a key position within the Authority.

[...]

Where, as in the present case, a tribunal's members include a person who is in a subordinate position, in terms of his duties and the organisation of his service, vis-à-vis one of the parties, litigants may entertain a legitimate doubt about that person's independence. Such a situation seriously affects the confidence which the courts must inspire in a democratic society (see, *mutatis mutandis*, the above-mentioned Piersack judgment, Series A No. 53, pp. 14-15, paragraph 30).

The Court therefore found that there had been a violation of Article 6, paragraph 1.

The Altay v. Turkey judgment (21 May 2001, Application No. 22279/93, paragraphs 72-75, available in French only – unofficial translation) concerned the fact that the National Security Courts include members of the armed forces in their composition, whereas the applicant was a civilian. The Court stated:

The Court recalls that, in the above-mentioned Incal judgment and in the Çiraklar v. Turkey judgment of 28 October 1998 (*Reports* 1998-VII), it considered arguments similar to those put forward by the Government in this case (see, as the most recent authority, the Gerger v. Turkey [GC] judgment, No. 24919/94, 8 July 1999, paragraph 61). In those judgments, the Court has noted that the status of military judges sitting as members of the National Security Courts does provide certain guarantees of independence and impartiality (see the above-mentioned Incal judgment, p. 1571, paragraph 65). However, it has also observed that certain aspects of these judges' status make their independence and impartiality questionable (ibid., paragraph 68), as the fact that they are servicemen who still belong to the army, which in turn takes its orders from the executive, and the fact that they remain subject to military discipline and their appointment and nomination to a great extent involve the administration and the army.

It is not the Court's task to determine *in abstracto* whether it was necessary to set up such courts in the light of the justification put forward by the Government, but to ascertain whether the manner in which the Istanbul National Security Court functioned infringed Mr Altay's right to a fair trial, and in particular whether Mr Altay objectively had legitimate grounds to fear a lack of independence and impartiality of the part of the court which tried him (the above-mentioned Incal judgment, p. 1572, paragraph 70).

In that regard, the Court sees no reason to depart from the conclusion which it reached in respect of Mr Incal and Mr Çiraklar, who, like the applicant, were both civilians. It is understandable that, when facing charges before a National Security Court of violating the constitutional order and national unity (paragraphs 25 and 27 above), Mr Altay should have had misgivings about appearing before judges whose number included a professional officer belonging to the military legal service. For that reason, he was entitled to fear that the Istanbul National Court would allow itself to be unduly influenced by considerations unrelated to the nature of his case. In other words, the applicant's fears regarding the lack of independence and impartiality of that court may be held to be objectively justified.

Accordingly, the Court concludes that there has been a violation of Article 6, paragraph 1, of the Convention.

(See also the Bryan v. the United Kingdom judgment of 22 November 1995, Series A No. 335-A, paragraph 38; the Hood v. the United Kingdom judgment of 18 February 1999, Application No. 27267/95; the Cyprus v. Turkey judgment of 10 May 2001, Application No. 25781/94, paragraphs 358-359; the Sadak and Others v. Turkey judgment of 10 July 2001, Applications Nos. 29900/96 and 29903/96, paragraphs 39-40; and the McGonnell v. the United Kingdom judgment of 8 February 2000, Application No. 28488/95.)

The concept of "decision"

An impartial and independent tribunal is therefore necessary in order to satisfy the purpose of Article 6. It is also necessary for that tribunal to take "decisions" within the meaning of that Article. In the Benthem v. the Netherlands case (judgment of 23 October 1985, Series A No. 97, p. 17, paragraph 40), the Court emphasised the importance of decision-making power as an attribute of a tribunal:

> [...] a power of decision is inherent in the very notion of "tribunal" within the meaning of the Convention (see the Sramek judgment of 22 October 1984, Series A No. 84, p. 17, paragraph 36).

In the Albert and Le Compte v. Belgium judgment (10 February 1983, Series A No. 58, p. 16, paragraph 29), the Court specified the extent of that decision-making power and stated that it must ensure that the applicants have the:

> [...] benefit of the "right to a court" (see the above-mentioned Golder judgment, Series A No. 18, p. 18, paragraph 36) and of a determination by a tribunal of the matters in dispute (see the above-mentioned König judgment, Series A No. 27, p. 34, paragraph 98, in fine), both for questions of fact and for questions of law.

It follows that a "tribunal" must therefore be at least competent to examine and settle questions of fact and of law.

Last, it should be made clear that the concept of "decision" presupposes a definitive settlement of the dispute before the tribunal. Thus, the Court stated in the Eckle v. Germany case (15 July 1982, Series A No. 51, p. 35, paragraph 77):

> In the event of conviction, there is no "determination [...] of any criminal charge", within the meaning of Article 6, paragraph 1 (art. 6-1), as long as the sentence is not definitively fixed. Thus, in the Ringeisen judgment of 16 July 1971 the Court took as the close of the proceedings the date on which the trial court had decided, following appeal proceedings, that the entire period spent by the applicant in detention on remand should be reckoned as part of the sentence (Series A No. 13, pp. 20 and 45, paragraphs 48 and 110).

Still on the subject of decisions, the Court recalled the following in the Hiro Balani v. Spain judgment (9 December 1994, Series A No. 303-B, pp. 29-30, paragraph 27):

> The Court reiterates that Article 6, paragraph 1 (art. 6-1), obliges the courts to give reasons for their judgments, but cannot be understood as requiring a detailed answer to every argument (see the Van de Hurk v. the Netherlands judgment of 19 April 1994, Series A No. 288, p. 20, paragraph 61). The extent to which this duty to give reasons applies may vary according to the nature of the decision.

Last, it should be stated that that does not preclude the principle of the secrecy of deliberations in criminal matters. Thus, in the Gregory v. the United Kingdom judgment (25 February 1997, Application No. 22299/93, *Reports* 1997-I, paragraph 44), the Court observed:

> The Court acknowledges that the rule governing the secrecy of jury deliberations is a crucial and legitimate feature of English trial law which serves to reinforce the jury's role as the ultimate arbiter of fact and to guarantee open and frank deliberations among jurors on the evidence which they have heard.

4. The nature of proceedings before the courts

Whatever the extent, the scope and the purpose of the "right to a tribunal", everything ultimately depends on the nature of the proceedings. The proceedings must be fair, they must take place within a reasonable time and they must satisfy certain criteria as regards the hearing and the pronouncement of judgments. That applies to civil proceedings and also in respect of criminal charges, concerning which the Court has had occasion to state (the Saunders v. the United Kingdom judgment of 17 December 1996, *Reports* 1996-VI, paragraph 74):

> [...] [the Court] considers that the general requirements of fairness contained in Article 6 (art. 6), including the right not to incriminate oneself, apply to criminal proceedings in respect of all types of criminal offences without distinction from the most simple to the most complex.

The requirement of fair proceedings

It should be noted that the requirements of Article 6, paragraph 3 (see above), may be broken down into particular elements of the right to a fair trial as flowing from Article 6, paragraph 1.

General aspects

The Court has emphasised that the proceedings provided for in paragraph 1 must be fair. In the Unterpertinger v. Austria case (24 November 1986, Series A No. 110, p. 14, paragraph 29), it recalled that:

> Those appearing before the Court made their submissions firstly in relation to paragraph 3.*d* of Article 6 (art. 6-3-d), and then in relation to paragraph 1 (art. 6-1). The Court recalls that the guarantees contained in paragraph 3 (art. 6-3) are specific aspects of the general concept of a fair trial set forth in paragraph 1 (art. 6-1) (see, as the most recent authority, the Bönisch judgment of 6 May 1985, Series A No. 92, pp. 14-15, paragraph 29).

In that case, the Court concluded that because the applicant had been convicted without being given the opportunity to question the witnesses (his wife and his stepdaughter), there had been an infringement of Article 6 (ibid., p. 15, paragraph 33).

Applying that approach, the Court has had occasion to deliver a number of interesting decisions. It has defined the limits on the use of anonymous witnesses from the aspect of the Convention. In the Kostovski case (20 October 1989, Series A No. 166, pp. 20-21, paragraphs 41 and 44), the following passages may be read:

> In principle, all the evidence must be produced in the presence of the accused at a public hearing with a view to adversarial argument (see the above-mentioned Barberà, Messegué and Jabardo judgment, Series A No. 146, p. 34, paragraph 78). This does not mean, however, that in order to be used as evidence statements of witnesses should always be made at a public hearing in court: to use as evidence such statements obtained at the pre-trial stage is not in itself inconsistent with paragraphs 3.*d* and 1 of Article 6 (art. 6-3-d, art. 6-1) provided the rights of the defence have been respected.
>
> As a rule, these rights require that an accused should be given an adequate and proper opportunity to challenge and question a witness against him, either at the time the witness was making his statement or at some later stage of the proceedings (see, *mutatis mutandis,* the Unterpertinger judgment of 24 November 1986, Series A No. 110, pp. 14-15, paragraph 31).
>
> Although the growth in organised crime doubtless demands the introduction of appropriate measures, the Government's submissions appear to the Court to lay insufficient weight on what the applicant's counsel described as "the interest of everybody in a civilised society in a controllable and fair judicial procedure". The right to a fair administration of justice holds so prominent a place in a democratic society (see the Delcourt judgment of 17 January 1970, Series A No. 11, p. 15, paragraph 25) that it cannot be sacrificed to expediency. The Convention does not preclude reliance, at the investigation stage of criminal proceedings, on sources such as anonymous informants. However, the subsequent use of anonymous statements as sufficient evidence to found a conviction, as in the present case, is a different matter. It involved limitations on the rights of the defence which were irreconcilable with the guarantees contained in Article 6 (art. 6). In fact, the Government accepted that the applicant's conviction was based "to a decisive extent" on the anonymous statements.

In the Van Mechelen and Others v. the Netherlands judgment (23 April 1997, *Reports of Judgments and Decisions* 1997-III, pp. 711-712, paragraphs 52-55), subsequent to the Doorson v. the Netherlands case (judgment of 26 April 1996, *Reports of Judgments and Decisions* 1996-II, p. 446), the Court again addressed the question of anonymous witnesses:

> As the Court had occasion to state in its Doorson judgment (ibid., p. 470, paragraph 69), the use of statements made by anonymous witnesses to found a conviction is not under all circumstances incompatible with the Convention.

In the same judgment, the Court continued:

> It is true that Article 6 (art. 6) does not explicitly require the interests of witnesses in general, and those of victims called upon to testify in particular, to be taken into consideration. However, their life, liberty or security of person may be at stake, as may interests coming generally within the ambit of Article 8 of the Convention (art. 8). Such interests of witnesses and victims are in principle protected by other, substantive provisions of the Convention, which imply that Contracting States should organise their criminal proceedings in such a way that those interests are not unjustifiably imperilled. Against this background, principles of fair trial also require that in appropriate cases the interests of the defence are balanced against those of witnesses or victims called upon to testify (see the above-mentioned Doorson judgment, p. 470, paragraph 70).
>
> However, if the anonymity of prosecution witnesses is maintained, the defence will be faced with difficulties which criminal proceedings should not normally involve. Accordingly, the Court has recognised that in such cases Article 6, paragraph 1, taken together with Article 6, paragraph 3.*d*, of the Convention (art. 6-1 + 6-3-d) requires that the handicaps under which the defence labours be sufficiently counterbalanced by the procedures followed by the judicial authorities (ibid., p. 471, paragraph 72).
>
> Finally, it should be recalled that a conviction should not be based either solely or to a decisive extent on anonymous statements (ibid., p. 472, paragraph 76).

(See the Luca v. Italy judgment of 27 February 2001, Application No. 33354/96, paragraph 41.)

The fair trial principle has other consequences. These include the prohibition on the legislature to influence a current case by promulgating a law one article of which "was an additional provision to that law and was in reality aimed at [the applicant] – although the latter was not mentioned by name" (the Stran Greek Refineries and Stratis Andreadis v. Greece judgment of 9 December 1994, Series A No. 301-B, p. 81, paragraph 47).

For other specific examples of the consequences which the principle of fairness entails, see:

– the Barberà, Messegué and Jabardo v. Spain judgment (6 December 1988, Series A No. 146), or the Coeme and Others v. Belgium judgment (22 June 2000, Application No. 32492/96, paragraphs 94-104);

– on surrender to custody in French law: the Khalfaoui v. France judgment of 14 December 1999, Application 34791/97, paragraphs 41-54; on the absence of the need to make recordings of proceedings during a period of custody: the Brennan v. the United Kingdom judgment of 16 October 2001, Application No. 39846/98, paragraphs 51-53; and the Eliazer v. the Netherlands judgment of 16 October 2001, Application No. 38055/97, concerning an appeal on a point of law.

Concerning evidence gathered illegally according to domestic law, the Court has described its approach to determining the fairness of a trial (the Schenk v. Switzerland judgment, 12 July 1988, Series A No. 140, p. 29, paragraph 46). It emphasises that its assessment forms part of an overall approach:

> While Article 6 (art. 6) of the Convention guarantees the right to a fair trial, it does not lay down any rules on the admissibility of evidence as such, which is therefore primarily a matter for regulation under national law.

> The Court therefore cannot exclude as a matter of principle and in the abstract that unlawfully obtained evidence of the present kind may be admissible. It has only to ascertain whether Mr Schenk's trial as a whole was fair.

In that case, the applicant's telephone conversations had been recorded without an order by the competent judge (see also the Khan v. the United Kingdom judgment of 12 May 2000 concerning the use in criminal proceedings of evidence obtained in breach of the Convention (Article 8): no violation of Article 6).

In fact, it is not within the Court's remit to evaluate evidence. In the above-mentioned Van Mechelen and Others judgment, it is again emphasised (paragraph 50) that:

> The Court reiterates that the admissibility of evidence is primarily a matter for regulation by national law and as a general rule it is for the national courts to assess the evidence before them. The Court's task under the Convention is not to give a ruling as to whether statements of witnesses were properly admitted as evidence, but rather to ascertain whether the proceedings as a whole, including the way in which evidence was taken, were fair (see, among other authorities, the above-mentioned Doorson judgment, p. 470, paragraph 67).

The principle of adversarial proceedings and equality of arms

In a number of recent judgments, the Court has expressed the view that the right to a "fair trial" entails, *inter alia*, the adversarial nature of the proceedings and equality of arms. This aspect deserves our attention.

In the F.R. v. Switzerland judgment, concerning documents which were not communicated to the applicant (28 June 2001, Application No. 37292/97, paragraph 36), the Court recalled:

> [...] the concept of fair trial also implies in principle the right for the parties to a trial to have knowledge of and comment on all evidence adduced or observations filed (see the Lobo Machado v. Portugal and Vermeulen v. Belgium judgments of 20 February 1996, *Reports* 1996-I, p. 206, paragraph 31, and p. 234, paragraph 33, respectively).

> [...]

What is particularly at stake here is litigants' confidence in the workings of justice, which is based on, *inter alia*, the knowledge that they have had the opportunity to express their views on every document in the file (see the Nideröst-Huber judgment cited above, p. 108, paragraph 29 [Nideröst-Huber v. Switzerland, 18 December 1997, *Reports* 1997-I, p. 108, paragraph 27]).

In the Mantovanelli v. France case (judgment of 18 March 1997, *Reports of Judgments and Decisions* 1997-II, p. 436, paragraph 33), the applicants complained that they had not been given the opportunity to participate in the preparation of an expert medical report or to comment on that document and on the evidence relating to the death of their daughter following a number of operations.

> The Court notes that one of the elements of a fair hearing within the meaning of Article 6, paragraph 1 (art. 6-1), is the right to adversarial proceedings; each party must in principle have the opportunity not only to make known any evidence needed for his claims to succeed, but also to have knowledge of and comment on all evidence adduced or observations filed with a view to influencing the court's decision (see, *mutatis mutandis*, the Lobo Machado v. Portugal and Vermeulen v. Belgium judgments of 20 February 1996, *Reports of Judgments and Decisions* 1996-I, pp. 206-207, paragraph 31, and p. 234, paragraph 33, respectively, and the Nideröst-Huber v. Switzerland judgment of 18 February 1997, *Reports* 1997-I, p. 108, paragraph 24).

> In this connection, the Court makes it clear at the outset that, just like observance of the other procedural safeguards enshrined in Article 6, paragraph 1 (art. 6-1), compliance with the adversarial principle relates to proceedings in a "tribunal"; no general, abstract principle may therefore be inferred from this provision (art. 6-1) that, where an expert has been appointed by a court, the parties must in all instances be able to attend the interviews held by him or to be shown the documents he has taken into account. What is essential is that the parties should be able to participate properly in the proceedings before the "tribunal" (see, *mutatis mutandis*, the Kerojärvi v. Finland judgment of 19 July 1995, Series A No. 322, p. 16, paragraph 42, in fine).

In that case, the Court continued (paragraph 36):

> However, while Mr and Mrs Mantovanelli could have made submissions to the administrative court on the content and findings of the report after receiving it, the Court is not convinced that this afforded them a real opportunity to comment effectively on it. The question the expert was instructed to answer was identical with the one that the court had to determine, namely whether the circumstances in which halothane had been administered to the applicants' daughter disclosed negligence on the part of the CHRN. It pertained to a technical field that was not within the judges' knowledge. Thus, although the administrative court was not in law bound by the expert's findings, his report was likely to have a preponderant influence on the assessment of the facts by that court.

> Under such circumstances, and in the light also of the administrative courts' refusal of their application for a fresh expert report at first instance and on appeal (see paragraphs 19-22 above), Mr and Mrs Mantovanelli could only have expressed their views effectively before the expert report was lodged. No

201

practical difficulty stood in the way of their being associated in the process of producing the report, as it consisted in interviewing witnesses and examining documents. Yet they were prevented from participating in the interviews, although the five people interviewed by the expert were employed by the CHRN and included the surgeon who had performed the last operation on Miss Mantovanelli, and the anaesthetist. The applicants were therefore not able to cross-examine these five people who could reasonably have been expected to give evidence along the same lines as the CHRN, the opposing side in the proceedings. As to the documents taken into consideration by the expert, the applicants only became aware of them once the report had been completed and transmitted.

Mr and Mrs Mantovanelli were thus not able to comment effectively on the main piece of evidence. The proceedings were therefore not fair as required by Article 6, paragraph 1, of the Convention (art. 6-1). There has accordingly been a breach of that provision (art. 6-1).

In the Voisine v. France judgment, the applicant, who was unrepresented, complained that – in the context of his appeal on a point of law to the Criminal Division of the Court of Cassation – he had not been able to consult the opinion of the Advocate-General and respond to it. The Court declared (judgment of 8 February 2000, Application No. 27362/95, paragraphs 30-34, available in French only – unofficial translation):

> The right to adversarial proceedings within the meaning of Article 6, paragraph 1, as interpreted by the case-law, "means in principle the right for the parties to a criminal or civil trial to have knowledge of and comment on all evidence adduced or observations filed, even by an independent member of the national legal service, with a view to influencing the court's decision (see, in relation to a criminal matter, the J.J. v. the Netherlands judgment of 27 March 1998, *Reports* 1998-II, p. 613, paragraph 43, in fine).

> In the present case, the applicant did not have access to the opinion of the Advocate-General. Accordingly, regard being had to "what was at stake for the applicant in the proceedings and to the nature of the advisory opinion of the Advocate-General, the fact that it was impossible for the applicant to reply to it before the Supreme Court [dismissed his appeal] infringed his right to adversarial proceedings" (ibid.).

> Although it is true that the applicant did not apply for legal aid so that he could be represented by a specialist lawyer, he did not waive the guarantees of adversarial proceedings, contrary to what the Government claim. It follows from a consistent line of decisions that waiver of the exercise of a right guaranteed by the Convention must be established in an unequivocal manner (the Colozza v. Italy judgment of 12 February 1985, Series A No. 89, pp. 14-15, paragraph 28).

> It is clear that the specific nature of proceedings before the Court of Cassation may justify reserving the right of audience solely to specialist lawyers. However, that specific nature does not justify an appellant on a point of law, who under domestic law is entitled to present his case in person, not being offered procedural means which will guarantee him the right to a fair trial before that court. The Court recalls that, according to its case-law, a State which provides itself with

a Court of Cassation is required to ensure that persons amenable to the law enjoy before it the fundamental guarantees contained in Article 6 (the Ekbatani v. Sweden judgment of 26 May 1988, Series A No. 134, p. 12, paragraph 24).

Thus, as the applicant was not offered a fair examination of his case before the Court of Cassation in an adversarial procedure, there has in this case been a violation of Article 6, paragraph 1.

(*Idem* the Adoud and Bosoni v. France judgment of 27 February 2001; see also the Coeme and Others v. Belgium judgment of 22 June 2000, Application No. 32492/96, paragraphs 128-130.)

The G.B. v. France judgment (2 October 2001, Application No. 44069/98) concerned the lodging of fresh documents by the prosecution at the beginning of a trial before the Assize Court involving morality. In that case, the applicant claimed that he had not been given a fair trial. His complaint was in three parts: first, the applicant claimed that there had been a violation of the principle of equality of arms and of the rights of the defence, owing to the circumstances in which the prosecution, at the beginning of the hearing before the Assize Court, had filed fresh documents and to the very brief time available to his lawyer to provide the applicant's defence following the filing of those documents; second, he complained that the expert had had only a quarter of an hour to peruse the new documents, which had resulted in him making a complete volte-face in his opinion; and, last, the applicant considered the refusal to grant his request to adduce expert evidence in rebuttal was unfair, even though the expert's reversal of opinion strongly influenced the jury against the applicant. The Court first considered the time allowed to the lawyer to prepare his defence in the light of the fresh documents. It declared (paragraphs 60-63):

> The Court notes that it was entirely lawful for the prosecution, at the beginning of the trial, to file new documents relating to the applicant's personality; these were communicated to the defence and subsequently examined adversarially. It also notes that the applicant himself did not criticise the production of those documents in itself. It finds therefore that this did not in itself give rise to any infringement of the principle of equality of arms between the parties.

> The Court has also carefully analysed the sequence of events described in the record of proceedings before the Assize Court, noting that it was at the beginning of the trial, at 10 a.m. on 13 March 1997, that the Deputy Public Prosecutor produced the new evidence, which the applicant's lawyer unsuccessfully asked the court to refuse to place in the file. On 13, 14 and 15 March there followed the examination of the defendants, the hearing of the witnesses and the expert, the civil parties' pleadings, the Deputy Public Prosecutor's submissions, the pleadings of the co-defendants' lawyers and finally the pleadings by the lawyer of the main defendant, namely the applicant, which were submitted from 7.05 to 8.45 p.m. on 15 March 1997 and brought the hearing to a close (the Court and the jury then retired to discuss the verdict, which they delivered some three hours later at 11.45 p.m.).

> In that connection, the Court would point out that it is not true that the applicant's lawyer had only half a day to read the new evidence (while following the continuing proceedings), as the applicant submitted. The half day in question

was only the time between the production of the evidence and the beginning of the expert's evidence, the importance of which must be examined separately (see paragraphs 68 *et seq.*, below).

In view of the foregoing, the Court considers that the applicant had adequate time and facilities to prepare his defence when faced with the new evidence and finds that in the instant case there has been no violation of Article 6, paragraph 1, of the Convention taken together with Article 6, paragraph 3.*b*, on that account.

As regards the time allowed to the expert to peruse the new documents and the refusal to allow expert evidence in rebuttal, the Court stated (paragraphs 65-70):

The Court further notes that in the middle of his evidence to the Assize Court Dr G. was granted a fifteen-minute adjournment to examine the new documents produced by the prosecution relating, in particular, to the applicant's sexual conduct at the age of sixteen and seventeen. The expert was thus able to study a statement dating from 1979 in which the applicant spontaneously admitted to having sexually interfered with young children of both sexes on a dozen or so occasions.

The applicant asserts that when the hearing resumed, the expert expressed a totally damning opinion about him that was entirely at odds with the written report he had prepared three and a half years earlier. The expert is alleged to have stated as follows:

"G.B. is a paedophile, for whom psychotherapy is necessary but would be ineffective because G.B. would have no feelings of guilt. The length of a prison sentence has no effect on an individual of this type and there is a high risk that he will reoffend."

The Court concedes that it is impossible to know exactly what the expert said in evidence since there are no written records of hearings before assize courts. However, it notes that the Government have never disputed that the expert had a brief opportunity to study the new documents in the middle of his evidence or that he made the comments attributed to him by the applicant; they have merely pointed out that the written report had already drawn attention to the defendant's psychopathic traits and signs of sexual perversion.

The Court would point out that the mere fact that an expert expresses a different opinion to that in his written statement when addressing an assize court is not in itself an infringement of the principle of a fair trial (see, *mutatis mutandis*, the Bernard v. France judgment cited above, paragraph 40). Similarly, the right to a fair trial does not require that a national court should appoint, at the request of the defence, a further expert even when the opinion of the expert appointed by the defence supports the prosecution case (see the Brandstetter v. Austria judgment of 28 August 1991, Series A No. 211, paragraph 46). Accordingly, the refusal to order a second opinion cannot in itself be regarded as unfair.

The Court notes, however, that in the instant case the expert not only expressed a different opinion when addressing the court from that set out in his written report – he completely changed his mind in the course of one and the same hearing (contrast the Bernard v. France judgment cited above). It also notes that the application for a second opinion lodged by the applicant followed this volte-face which the expert had effected having rapidly perused the new evidence, adopting a highly unfavourable stance towards the applicant. While it is difficult to ascertain what influence an expert's opinion may have had on the assessment of a jury, the Court considers it highly likely that such an abrupt turnaround would inevitably have lent the expert's opinion particular weight.

Having regard to these particular circumstances, namely the expert's volte-face, combined with the rejection of the application for a second opinion, the Court considers that the requirements of a fair trial were infringed and the rights of the defence were not respected. Accordingly, there has been a breach of Article 6, paragraphs 1 and 3.*b*, of the Convention taken together.

The right not to incriminate oneself

Although not expressly mentioned in Article 6, the right to remain silent and the right not to incriminate oneself are also guaranteed by the requirement for a fair trial.

That means, first of all, that a person cannot be convicted for having refused to answer questions. In the Heaney and McGuinness v. Ireland case (judgment of 21 December 2000), the domestic law (Section 52 of the Offences against the State Act 1939) on offences against the security of the State required suspects to account for their movements. Any suspect not doing so faced a prison sentence. The Court stated (Application No. 34720/97, paragraphs 55-59):

> [the Court] finds that the "degree of compulsion", imposed on the applicants by the application of Section 52 of the 1939 Act with a view to compelling them to provide information relating to charges against them under that act, in effect, destroyed the very essence of their privilege against self-incrimination and their right to remain silent.

> The Government contended that Section 52 of the 1939 Act is, nevertheless, a proportionate response to the subsisting terrorist and security threat given the need to ensure the proper administration of justice and the maintenance of public order and peace.

> The Court has taken judicial notice of the security and public order concerns detailed by the Government.

> However, it recalls that [...] the Court [...] found that the general requirements of fairness contained in Article 6, including the right not to incriminate oneself, "apply to criminal proceedings in respect of all types of criminal offences without distinction from the most simple to the most complex". It concluded that the public interest could not be invoked to justify the use of answers compulsorily obtained in a non-judicial investigation to incriminate the accused during the trial proceedings.

> Moreover, the Court also recalls that the Brogan case (Brogan and Others v. the United Kingdom judgment of 29 November 1988, Series A No. 145-B) concerned the arrest and detention, by virtue of powers granted under special legislation, of persons suspected of involvement in terrorism in Northern Ireland. The United

Kingdom Government had relied on the special security context of Northern Ireland to justify the length of the impugned detention periods under Article 5, paragraph 3. The Court found that even the shortest periods of detention at issue in that case would have entailed consequences impairing the very essence of the relevant right protected by Article 5, paragraph 3. It concluded that the fact that the arrest and detention of the applicants were inspired by the legitimate aim of protecting the community as a whole from terrorism was not, on its own, sufficient to ensure compliance with the specific requirements of Article 5, paragraph 3, of the Convention.

The Court, accordingly, finds that the security and public order concerns of the Government cannot justify a provision which extinguishes the very essence of the applicants' rights to silence and against self-incrimination guaranteed by Article 6, paragraph 1, of the Convention.

It concludes therefore that there has been a violation of the applicants' right to silence and their right not to incriminate themselves guaranteed by Article 6, paragraph 1, of the Convention.

The right not to incriminate oneself also prohibits the use of evidence given under constraint. In the Saunders v. the United Kingdom judgment (17 December 1996, *Reports of Judgments and Decisions* 1996-VI, pp. 2064-2065, paragraphs 68-69), the applicant had been compelled by law to make statements during a statutory investigation into company fraud. The investigation was conducted by independent inspectors pursuant to the Companies Act. The applicant's statements were subsequently used against him in criminal proceedings. The Court considered:

> The Court recalls that, although not specifically mentioned in Article 6 of the Convention (art. 6), the right to silence and the right not to incriminate oneself are generally recognised international standards which lie at the heart of the notion of a fair procedure under Article 6 (art. 6). Their rationale lies, *inter alia*, in the protection of the accused against improper compulsion by the authorities thereby contributing to the avoidance of miscarriages of justice and to the fulfilment of the aims of Article 6 (art. 6) (see the above-mentioned John Murray judgment, p. 49, paragraph 45, and the above-mentioned Funke judgment, p. 22, paragraph 44). The right not to incriminate oneself, in particular, presupposes that the prosecution in a criminal case seek to prove their case against the accused without resort to evidence obtained through methods of coercion or oppression in defiance of the will of the accused. In this sense the right is closely linked to the presumption of innocence contained in Article 6, paragraph 2, of the Convention (art. 6-2).

> The right not to incriminate oneself is primarily concerned, however, with respecting the will of an accused person to remain silent. As commonly understood in the legal systems of the Contracting Parties to the Convention and elsewhere, it does not extend to the use in criminal proceedings of material which may be obtained from the accused through the use of compulsory powers but which has an existence independent of the will of the suspect such as, *inter alia*, documents acquired pursuant to a warrant, breath, blood and urine samples and bodily tissue for the purpose of DNA testing.

It should also be noted that, in that judgment, the Court stated that the right not to incriminate oneself taken as the right to remain silent does not just cover admission of wrongdoing. In the judgment, the Court stated (paragraphs 71 and 74):

> In any event, bearing in mind the concept of fairness in Article 6 (art. 6), the right not to incriminate oneself cannot reasonably be confined to statements of admission of wrongdoing or to remarks which are directly incriminating. Testimony obtained under compulsion which appears on its face to be of a non-incriminating nature – such as exculpatory remarks or mere information on questions of fact – may later be deployed in criminal proceedings in support of the prosecution case, for example to contradict or cast doubt upon other statements of the accused or evidence given by him during the trial or to otherwise undermine his credibility.
>
> [...]
>
> The public interest cannot be invoked to justify the use of answers compulsorily obtained in a non-judicial investigation to incriminate the accused during the trial proceedings. It is noteworthy in this respect that under the relevant legislation statements obtained under compulsory powers by the Serious Fraud Office cannot, as a general rule, be adduced in evidence at the subsequent trial of the person concerned. Moreover the fact that statements were made by the applicant prior to his being charged does not prevent their later use in criminal proceedings from constituting an infringement of the right.

(To the same effect, see the I.J.L., G.M.R. and A.K.P. v. the United Kingdom judgment of 19 September 2000, Application No. 29522/95.)

For other situations, see the following judgments:

– the Ferrantelli and Santangelo v. Italy judgment of 7 August 1996, *Reports* 1996-III, paragraphs 45-50, concerning an allegation of extorted admissions; the Serves v. France judgment of 20 October 1997, *Reports* 1997-VI, paragraphs 43-47, no violation of Article 6 because of a financial criminal penalty imposed for having refused to take the oath as a witness;

– the J.B. v. Switzerland judgment of 3 May 2001, Application No. 31827/96, concerning the imposition of a fine on the applicant for having refused to provide certain information; the Court found that the applicant could not exclude that any additional income disclosed by the documents which he provided which came from untaxed sources could have constituted the offence of tax evasion. The Court concluded that those documents could not be obtained by coercion in defiance of the will of the person concerned: violation of Article 6, paragraph 1; and

– the Funke v. France judgment of 25 February 1993, Series A No. 256-A, paragraphs 43-44, where a criminal conviction for refusing to produce the information demanded by the customs authorities was held to constitute a violation of Article 6, paragraph 1; the Magee v. the United Kingdom judgment of 6 June 2000, Application No. 28135/95, paragraph 41, where the applicant complained that an oppressive environment had caused him to incriminate himself without the benefit of legal assistance.

At the same time, it should be noted that the Court does not rule out the possibility that conclusions may be drawn from an accused's silence. In the John Murray v. the United Kingdom judgment (8 February 1996, *Reports* 1996-I, paragraphs 51 and 54), the Court declared:

> The national court cannot conclude that the accused is guilty merely because he chooses to remain silent. It is only if the evidence against the accused "calls" for an explanation which the accused ought to be in a position to give that a failure to give any explanation "may as a matter of common sense allow the drawing of an inference that there is no explanation and that the accused is guilty". Conversely if the case presented by the prosecution had so little evidential value that it called for no answer, a failure to provide one could not justify an inference of guilt (ibid.).
>
> [...]
>
> As pointed out by the Delegate of the Commission, the courts in a considerable number of countries where evidence is freely assessed may have regard to all relevant circumstances, including the manner in which the accused has behaved or has conducted his defence.

In the same spirit, see also the Averill v. the United Kingdom judgment of 6 June 2000, Application No. 36408/97, and the Condron v. the United Kingdom judgment of 2 May 2000, Application No. 35718/97.

Access to a lawyer

A further aspect of the right to a fair trial is access to a lawyer by the accused as from the initial stage of the criminal proceedings. In the John Murray v. the United Kingdom judgment (8 February 1996, *Reports of Judgments and Decisions* 1996-I, pp. 54-55, paragraphs 62-63), the applicant was refused legal assistance during the first forty-eight hours of his detention by the police.

> The Court observes that it has not been disputed by the Government that Article 6 (art. 6) applies even at the stage of the preliminary investigation into an offence by the police. In this respect it recalls its finding in the Imbrioscia v. Switzerland judgment of 24 November 1993 that Article 6 (art. 6) – especially paragraph 3 (art. 6-3) – may be relevant before a case is sent for trial if and so far as the fairness of the trial is likely to be seriously prejudiced by an initial failure to comply with its provisions (art. 6-3) (Series A No. 275, p. 13, paragraph 36). As it pointed out in that judgment, the manner in which Article 6, paragraph 3.*c* (art. 6-3-c), is to be applied during the preliminary investigation depends on the special features of the proceedings involved and on the circumstances of the case (loc. cit., p. 14, paragraph 38).
>
> National laws may attach consequences to the attitude of an accused at the initial stages of police interrogation which are decisive for the prospects of the defence in any subsequent criminal proceedings. In such circumstances Article 6 (art. 6) will normally require that the accused be allowed to benefit from the assistance of a lawyer already at the initial stages of police interrogation. However, this right, which is not explicitly set out in the Convention, may be subject to restrictions for good cause. The question, in each case, is whether the restriction, in the light of the entirety of the proceedings, has deprived the accused of a fair hearing.

For a similar approach, see the Goedhart v. Belgium judgment (20 March 2001, Application No. 34989/97, paragraphs 31-33, available in French only – unofficial translation), where the Court stated:

> In the Omar and Guérin judgments, the Court considered that, "where an appeal on points of law is declared inadmissible solely because, as in the present case, the appellant has not surrendered to custody pursuant to the judicial decision challenged in the appeal, this ruling compels the appellant to subject himself in advance to the deprivation of liberty resulting from the impugned decision, although that decision cannot be considered final until the appeal has been decided or the time-limit for lodging an appeal has expired". The Court considered that this "impairs the very essence of the right of appeal, by imposing a disproportionate burden on the appellant, thus upsetting the fair balance that must be struck between the legitimate concern to ensure that judicial decisions are enforced, on the one hand, and the right of access to the Court of Cassation and exercise of the rights of the defence on the other (the above-mentioned Omar and Guérin judgments, p. 1841, paragraphs 40-41, and p. 1868, paragraph 43, respectively; also the Khalfoui v. France [Section III] judgment, Application No. 34791/97, ECHR 1999-IX, 14 December 1999, paragraph 40).

> In the present case, the Court observes that by a judgment of 10 December 1996, the Court of Cassation declared the appeal on a point of law inadmissible solely because the applicant had not surrendered to custody pursuant to the judicial decision challenged in the appeal (paragraph 18 above).

> In those circumstances, the Court sees no reason to arrive at a different conclusion from that adopted in the above-mentioned Omar and Guérin judgments.

> In the light of the circumstances of the case and in accordance with its case-law, the Court considers that the applicant suffered a disproportionate interference with his right of access to a court and, therefore, with his right to a fair trial. Accordingly, there has been a violation of Article 6, paragraph 1, of the Convention.

Requirement for judicial proceedings which take place "within a reasonable time"

For the purpose of determining fairness, proceedings are equally relevant if they do not take place "within a reasonable time". A great many judgments have been delivered on that point.

Reasonableness of the length of the proceedings

In the Zimmermann and Steiner v. Switzerland judgment (13 July 1983, Series A No. 66, p. 11, paragraph 24), the Court set out the criteria that serve to determine whether the length of proceedings is reasonable:

> The reasonableness of the length of proceedings coming within the scope of Article 6, paragraph 1 (art. 6-1), must be assessed in each case according to the particular circumstances (see the Buchholz judgment of 6 May 1981, Series A No. 42, p. 15, paragraph 49). The Court has to have regard, *inter alia*, to the complexity of the factual or legal issues raised by the case, to the conduct of the applicants and the competent authorities and to what was at stake for the

former; in addition, only delays attributable to the State may justify a finding of a failure to comply with the "reasonable time" requirement (see, *mutatis mutandis*, the König judgment of 28 June 1978, Series A No. 27, pp. 34-40, paragraphs 99, 102-105 and 107-111, and the above-mentioned Buchholz judgment, Series A No. 42, p. 16, paragraph 49).

The Court examines in turn the complexity or lack of complexity of the case before it, the conduct of the applicants (presence at or absence from the hearings, request for adjournment ...) and that of the judicial or administrative authorities. The Court recalled these criteria in the Vallée v. France case (26 April 1994, Series A No. 289-A, p. 17, paragraph 34). It drew the logical conclusion, to which it referred in the A.A.U. v. France judgment (19 June 2001, Application No. 44451/98, paragraph 29, available in French only – unofficial translation):

> The Court recalls that it is for the Contracting States to organise their judicial systems in such a way that their courts are able to guarantee everyone the right to secure a definitive decision in disputes over their civil rights and obligations within a reasonable time (the above-mentioned Frydlender judgment, paragraph 47).

Computation of time

Generally, a reasonable time includes examination of the proceedings, including before a constitutional court. Thus, in the Diaz Aparicio v. Spain judgment (11 October 2001, Application No. 49468/99, paragraph 21, available in French only – unofficial translation), the Court observed:

> [...] the Court has regard to the length of all the proceedings in issue, including the proceedings before the Constitutional Court (see, for example, the Ruiz-Mateos v. Spain judgment of 23 June 1993, Series A No. 262, p. 19, paragraph 35, and the Süssmann v. Germany judgment of 16 September 1996, *Reports of Judgments and Decisions* 1996-IV, paragraph 39).

Computation of time in criminal matters

In the Eckle v. Germany case (15 July 1982, Series A No. 51, p. 33, paragraph 73), the Court observed:

> In criminal matters, the "reasonable time" referred to in Article 6, paragraph 1 (art. 6-1), begins to run as soon as a person is "charged"; this may occur on a date prior to the case coming before the trial court (see, for example, the Deweer judgment of 27 February 1980, Series A No. 35, p. 22, paragraph 42), such as the date of arrest, the date when the person concerned was officially notified that he would be prosecuted or the date when preliminary investigations were opened [...].

(*Idem* the Metzger v. Germany judgment of 31 May 2001, Application No. 37591/97, paragraph 31.)

The Court continued (p. 34, paragraph 76):

> As regards the end of the "time", in criminal matters the period governed by Article 6, paragraph 1 (art. 6-1), covers the whole of the proceedings in issue,

including appeal proceedings (see the König judgment of 28 June 1978, Series A No. 27, p. 33, paragraph 98).

For an example where there was no violation, concerning an investigation in Corsica, see the Acquaviva v. France judgment of 21 November 1995, Application No. 19248/91, Series A No. 333-A, paragraph 46, where the Court took into account the particular circumstances of the case and the situation prevailing in Corsica at the time; concerning a case of medical responsibility investigated in the criminal courts following a complaint together with a claim for civil damages, see the Callvelli and Ciglio v. Italy judgment of 17 January 2002, Application No. 32967/96, paragraphs 63-67.

Computation of time in civil matters

As regards the civil sphere, the Court observed in the Erkner and Hofauer v. Austria judgment (23 April 1987, Series A No. 117, pp. 61-62, paragraphs 64-65):

> In civil proceedings, the "reasonable time" referred to in Article 6, paragraph 1 (art. 6-1), normally begins to run from the moment the action was instituted before the "tribunal" [...] it is conceivable, however, that in certain circumstances the time may begin to run earlier.

The König v. Germany case (28 June 1978, Series A No. 27, p. 33, paragraph 98) is an example of a case in which the reasonable time began to run "even before the issue of the writ commencing proceedings before the court".

As regards the end of the relevant period, the Court noted in the Erkner and Hofauer judgment (loc. cit.):

> [...] that the period whose reasonableness falls to be reviewed takes in the entirety of the proceedings in issue, including any appeals [...]. That period accordingly extends right up to the decision which disposes of the dispute ("contestation").

Furthermore, the Court has had occasion to make the following point: the length of enforcement proceedings following a judicial decision must be taken into account for the purpose of calculating the reasonable time where the dispute is only definitively settled during this second stage. In the Silva Pontes v. Portugal judgment (23 March 1994, Series A No. 286-A, p. 14, paragraphs 33-36) the Court made the following observation concerning a debt:

> The Court accordingly takes the view [...] that the "enforcement" proceedings were not intended solely to enforce an obligation to pay a fixed amount; they also served to determine important elements of the debt itself [...]. It follows that the dispute (contestation) over the applicant's right to damages would only have been resolved by the final decision in the enforcement proceedings.
>
> [...]
>
> There can be no doubt that Article 6 (art. 6) applies to [...] the second stage.

Public hearing and pronouncement of judgments

The final procedural requirements concern the public nature of the hearing and of the giving of judgments.

The importance of the public nature of the hearing

The Court stated in the Pretto and Others v. Italy judgment (8 December 1983, Series A No. 71, pp. 11-12, paragraphs 21-22) as regards the publicity of judicial proceedings:

> The public character of proceedings before the judicial bodies referred to in Article 6, paragraph 1 (art. 6-1), protects litigants against the administration of justice in secret with no public scrutiny; it is also one of the means whereby confidence in the courts, superior and inferior, can be maintained. By rendering the administration of justice visible, publicity contributes to the achievement of the aim of Article 6, paragraph 1 (art. 6-1), namely a fair trial, the guarantee of which is one of the fundamental principles of any democratic society, within the meaning of the Convention (see the Golder judgment of 21 February 1975, Series A No. 18, p. 18, paragraph 36, and also the Lawless judgment of 14 November 1960, Series A No. 1, p. 13).

> Whilst the member States of the Council of Europe all subscribe to this principle of publicity, their legislative systems and judicial practice reveal some diversity as to its scope and manner of implementation, as regards both the holding of hearings and the "pronouncement" of judgments. The formal aspect of the matter is, however, of secondary importance as compared with the purpose underlying the publicity required by Article 6, paragraph 1 (art. 6-1). The prominent place held in a democratic society by the right to a fair trial impels the Court, for the purposes of the review which it has to undertake in this area, to examine the realities of the procedure in question (see notably, *mutatis mutandis*, the Adolf judgment of 26 March 1982, Series A No. 49, p. 15, paragraph 30).

In the Diennet v. France judgment (26 September 1995, Series A No. 325-A, paragraph 33), the Court further stated:

> Admittedly, the Convention does not make this principle an absolute one, since by the very terms of Article 6, paragraph 1 (art. 6-1), "[...] the press and public may be excluded from all or part of the trial in the interests of morals [...], where the [...] protection of the private life of the parties so require[s], or to the extent strictly necessary in the opinion of the court in special circumstances where publicity would prejudice the interests of justice".

In that case, the Court held that the fact that proceedings before the disciplinary tribunal of the National Medical Association were not public constituted a violation of Article 6, paragraph 1.

See also:

– the Fischer v. Austria judgment (26 April 1995, Application No. 16922/90, Series A No. 312, paragraphs 43-44); the Malhous v. the Czech Republic judgment (12 July 2001, Application No. 33071/96, paragraphs 55-63); and the Asan Rushiti v. Austria judgment of 21 March 2000, Application No. 28389/95, on the lack of a hearing and public delivery of the decision in proceedings for compensation for provisional detention followed by acquittal; and

– the L. v. Finland judgment of 27 April 2000, Application No. 25651/94, for the lack of a hearing in proceedings concerning the right of access to children in the care of social services (violation); the Guisset v. France judgment of 26 September 2000, Application No. 33933/96, concerning the hearing in private before the Disciplinary Offences (Budget and Finance) Court adjudicating on an infringement of the rules on public accounting punishable by a fine; and the Riepan v. Austria judgment of 15 June 2000, Application No. 35115/97, for a trial held in prison (violation of Article 6).

Public "pronouncement" of judgments

In the same judgment the Court interpreted the requirement of Article 6, paragraph 1, that "Judgment shall be pronounced publicly". It held (p. 12, paragraph 26):

> The Court therefore does not feel bound to adopt a literal interpretation. It considers that in each case the form of publicity to be given to the "judgment" under the domestic law of the respondent State must be assessed in the light of the special features of the proceedings in question and by reference to the object and purpose of Article 6, paragraph 1 (art. 6-1).

In this case the judgments of the Court of Appeal and Court of Cassation had been made public by being deposited in the court registry, whereas anyone could consult or obtain copies of the judgments of the Court of Cassation. The absence of public pronouncement of the Court of Cassation's judgment did not contravene Article 6, paragraph 1.

In the Sutter v. Switzerland case (22 February 1984, Series A No. 74, p. 14-15, paragraphs 31-34) the judgment of the Military Court of Cassation was served on the parties and moreover anyone who could establish an interest could consult or obtain a full copy of judgments of this court. Therefore, the absence of public pronouncement of the judgment in this case did not violate Article 6, paragraph 1.

(See also the Lamanna v. Austria judgment of 10 July 2001, Application No. 28923/95, paragraphs 27-34; the B. v. the United Kingdom judgment of 24 April 2001, Application No. 36337/97; B. and P. v. the United Kingdom judgment of 24 April 2001, Application No. 36337/97 concerning child custody; and the Tierce and Others v. Saint-Marin judgment of 25 July 2000, Application No. 24954/94.)

Waiver of a public hearing

In the case of Håkansson and Sturesson v. Sweden (21 February 1990, Series A No. 171-A, p. 20, paragraph 66) the Court considered:

> The public character of court hearings constitutes a fundamental principle enshrined in paragraph 1 of Article 6 (art. 6-1). Admittedly neither the letter nor the spirit of this provision prevents a person from waiving of his own free will, either expressly or tacitly, the entitlement to have his case heard in public (see, *inter alia*, the Le Compte, Van Leuven and De Meyere judgment of 23 June 1981, Series A No. 43, p. 25, paragraph 59, and the H. v. Belgium judgment of 30 November 1987, Series A No. 127, p. 36, paragraph 54). However, a waiver must be made in an unequivocal manner and must not run counter to any important public interest.

Article 6, paragraph 2 – Presumption of innocence

Article 6, paragraph 2, is worded as follows:

---

2. Everyone charged with a criminal offence shall be presumed innocent until proved guilty according to law.

---

1. Sphere of application and scope of Article 6, paragraph 2

Definition of the expression "charged with a criminal offence"

Article 6, paragraph 2, is applicable to everyone "charged with a criminal offence".

The Court gave an interpretation, in the Lutz v. Germany judgment (25 August 1987, Series A No. 123, p. 22, paragraph 52), of, *inter alia*, the notion "charged with a criminal offence". It makes reference to the terms "criminal charge" and "charged with a criminal offence", which appear elsewhere in Article 6, and of which it had already given an interpretation:

> The Court thus proceeded on the basis that in using the terms "criminal charge" *(accusation en matière pénale)* and "charged with a criminal offence" *(accusé d'une infraction)* the three paragraphs of Article 6 (art. 6-1, art. 6-2, art. 6-3) referred to identical situations. It had previously adopted a similar approach to Article 6, paragraph 2 (art. 6-2), albeit in a context that was undeniably a criminal one under the domestic law (see the Adolf judgment of 26 March 1982, Series A No. 49, p. 15, paragraph 30, and the Minelli judgment of 25 March 1983, Series A No. 62, p. 15, paragraph 27).

Thus, the Court applies its usual principles to determine the criminal nature of the offence. In the Minelli v. Switzerland judgment (25 March 1983, Series A No. 62, p. 15, paragraph 28), the Court held, for example, that the proceedings of a private prosecution for defamation in an article in the newspaper in this case were of a criminal nature.

> The infringement of an individual's "civil" right sometimes also constitutes a criminal offence. To determine whether there is a "criminal charge"/*"accusation en matière pénale"*, one has, *inter alia*, to examine the situation of the accused – as it arises under the domestic legal rules in force – in the light of the object of Article 6 (art. 6), namely the protection of the rights of the defence (see the above-mentioned Adolf judgment, ibid.).

> In Switzerland, defamation is included amongst the offences defined by and punishable under the Federal Criminal Code (see paragraph 17 above). A prosecution for defamation may take place only if the victim has filed a complaint *(Strafantrag)*, but the conduct of the prosecution is governed by the Cantonal Codes of Criminal Procedure, in this case that of the Canton of Zürich; the proceedings may lead to penalties, in the shape of a fine or even of imprisonment, which will be entered in the judicial criminal records (see paragraph 18 above).

Scope

Article 6, paragraph 2, is applicable to the whole of the proceedings in the case of a criminal charge. In the Minelli case again, the Court considered (pp. 15-16, paragraph 30):

> Article 6, paragraph 2 (art. 6-2), governs criminal proceedings in their entirety, irrespective of the outcome of the prosecution, and not solely the examination of the merits of the charge (see, *mutatis mutandis,* the above-mentioned Adolf judgment, Series A No. 49, p. 16, paragraph 33, in fine).

Article 6, paragraph 2, applies to the different public authorities, as shown by the Court's judgment in the Allenet de Ribemont v. France case (judgment of 10 February 1995, Series A No. 308, pp. 16-17, paragraphs 36-37 and 41):

> The Court considers that the presumption of innocence may be infringed not only by a judge or court but also by other public authorities.

> At the time of the press conference of 29 December 1976, Mr Allenet de Ribemont had just been arrested by the police (see paragraph 9 above). Although he had not yet been charged with aiding and abetting intentional homicide (see paragraph 12 above), his arrest and detention in police custody formed part of the judicial investigation begun a few days earlier by a Paris investigating judge and made him a person "charged with a criminal offence" within the meaning of Article 6, paragraph 2 (art. 6-2).

> [...]

> The Court notes that (during the press conference) some of the highest-ranking officers in the French police referred to Mr Allenet de Ribemont, without any qualification or reservation, as one of the instigators of a murder and thus an accomplice in that murder. This was clearly a declaration of the applicant's guilt which, firstly, encouraged the public to believe him guilty and, secondly, prejudged the assessment of the facts by the competent judicial authority. There has therefore been a breach of Article 6, paragraph 2 (art. 6-2).

On the other hand, when the accused is pronounced guilty, Article 6, paragraph 2, ceases to apply in respect of all the allegations made in the sentencing proceedings (the Philips v. the United Kingdom judgment of 5 July 2001, Application No. 41087/98, paragraph 35):

> However, whilst it is clear that Article 6, paragraph 2, governs criminal proceedings in their entirety, and not solely the examination of the merits of the charge (see, for example, the Minelli v. Switzerland judgment of 25 March 1983, Series A No. 62, paragraph 30, the Sekanina v. Austria judgment of 25 August 1993, Series A No. 266-A, and the Allenet de Ribemont v. France judgment of 10 February 1995, Series A No. 308), the right to be presumed innocent under Article 6, paragraph 2, arises only in connection with the particular offence "charged". Once an accused has properly been proved guilty of that offence, Article 6, paragraph 2, can have no application in relation to allegations made about the accused's character and conduct as part of the sentencing process, unless such accusations are of such a nature and degree as to amount to the bringing of a new "charge" within the autonomous Convention meaning referred

to in paragraph 28 above (see the Engel and Others v. the Netherlands judgment of 8 June 1976, Series A No. 22, paragraph 90).

(See also the above-mentioned Heaney and McGuinness v. Ireland judgment of 21 December 2000.)

2. The force of Article 6, paragraph 2

Article 6, paragraph 2, conviction and lack of sufficient evidence, doubt in favour of the accused

In the Telfner v. Austria judgment of 20 March 2001 (Application No. 33501/96, paragraphs 15-20), the Court held that the courts had transferred the burden of proof to the defence by requiring the owner of a vehicle involved in an accident at night to provide an explanation; the owner refused to make a statement and was convicted on the basis of a police report stating that he was the main user of the vehicle and had not slept at home that evening. The Court noted:

> The Court recalls that, as a general rule, it is for the national courts to assess the evidence before them, while it is for the Court to ascertain that the proceedings considered as a whole were fair, which in case of criminal proceedings includes the observance of the presumption of innocence. Article 6, paragraph 2, requires, *inter alia*, that when carrying out their duties, the members of a court should not start with the preconceived idea that the accused has committed the offence charged; the burden of proof is on the prosecution, and any doubt should benefit the accused (see the Barberà, Messegué and Jabardo v. Spain judgment of 6 December 1988, Series A No. 146, pp. 31 and 33, paragraphs 67-68 and 77). Thus, the presumption of innocence will be infringed where the burden of proof is shifted from the prosecution to the defence (see the John Murray v. the United Kingdom judgment of 8 February 1996, *Reports of Judgments and Decisions* 1996-I, p. 52, paragraph 54).

> It is true, as the Government pointed out, that legal presumptions are not in principle incompatible with Article 6 (see for instance the Salabiaku v. France judgment of 7 October 1988, Series A No. 141-A, pp. 15-16, paragraph 28); nor is the drawing of inferences from the accused's silence (see the John Murray judgment, cited above, pp. 49-52, paragraphs 45-54).

> However, the present case does not concern the application of a legal presumption of fact or law, nor is the Court convinced by the Government's argument that the domestic courts could legitimately draw inferences from the applicant's silence. The Court recalls that the above-mentioned John Murray judgment concerned a case in which the law allowed for the drawing of common-sense inferences from the accused's silence, where the prosecution had established a case against him, which called for an explanation. Considering that the evidence adduced at the trial constituted a formidable case against the applicant, the Court found that the drawing of such inferences, which was moreover subject to important procedural safeguards, did not violate Article 6 in the circumstances of the case (ibid.). The Court considers that the drawing of inferences from an

accused's silence may also be permissible in a system like the Austrian one where the courts freely evaluate the evidence before them, provided that the evidence adduced is such that the only common-sense inference to be drawn from the accused's silence is that he had no answer to the case against him.

In the present case, both the District Court and the Regional Court relied in essence on a report of the local police station that the applicant was the main user of the car and had not been home on the night of the accident. However, the Court cannot find that these elements of evidence, which were moreover not corroborated by evidence taken at the trial in an adversarial manner, constituted a case against the applicant which would have called for an explanation from his part. In this context, the Court notes, in particular, that the victim of the accident had not been able to identify the driver, nor even to say whether the driver had been male or female, and that the Regional Court, after supplementing the proceedings, found that the car in question was also used by the applicant's sister. In requiring the applicant to provide an explanation although they had not been able to establish a convincing prima-facie case against him, the courts shifted the burden of proof from the prosecution to the defence.

In addition, the Court notes that both the District Court and the Regional Court speculated about the possibility of the applicant having been under the influence of alcohol which was, as they admitted themselves, not supported by any evidence. Although such speculation was not directly relevant to establishing the elements of the offence with which the applicant had been charged, it contributes to the impression that the courts had a preconceived view of the applicant's guilt.

In conclusion, the Court finds that there has been a violation of Article 6, paragraph 2, of the Convention.

Article 6, paragraph 2, presumption of guilt and of objective criminal responsibility

The Court was asked in the Salabiaku v. France case (7 October 1988, Series A No. 141-A, pp. 15-16, paragraphs 27-28) to give a judgment about certain presumptions laid down in the French Customs Code relating to the presumption of innocence.

As the Government and the Commission have pointed out, in principle the Contracting States remain free to apply the criminal law to an act where it is not carried out in the normal exercise of one of the rights protected under the Convention (the Engel and Others judgment of 8 June 1976, Series A No. 22, p. 34, paragraph 81) and, accordingly, to define the constituent elements of the resulting offence. In particular, and again in principle, the Contracting States may, under certain conditions, penalise a simple or objective fact as such, irrespective of whether it results from criminal intent or from negligence. Examples of such offences may be found in the laws of the Contracting States.

In this case the applicant was convicted for being liable for the possession of "smuggled goods" (narcotics) at Roissy airport. This offence appears under the heading "Criminal Liability". Under this provision a conclusion is drawn from a simple fact, which in itself does not necessarily constitute a petty or more serious offence, that the "criminal liability" for the unlawful importation of goods, whether they are prohibited or not, or the failure to declare them, lies with the person in whose possession they are found. The Court continued:

> This shift from the idea of accountability in criminal law to the notion of guilt shows the very relative nature of such a distinction. It raises a question with regard to Article 6, paragraph 2 (art. 6-2), of the Convention.
>
> Presumptions of fact or of law operate in every legal system. Clearly, the Convention does not prohibit such presumptions in principle. It does, however, require the Contracting States to remain within certain limits in this respect as regards criminal law. If, as the Commission would appear to consider (paragraph 64 of the report), paragraph 2 of Article 6 (art. 6-2) merely laid down a guarantee to be respected by the courts in the conduct of legal proceedings, its requirements would in practice overlap with the duty of impartiality imposed in paragraph 1 (art. 6-1). Above all, the national legislature would be free to strip the trial court of any genuine power of assessment and deprive the presumption of innocence of its substance, if the words "according to law" were construed exclusively with reference to domestic law. Such a situation could not be reconciled with the object and purpose of Article 6 (art. 6), which, by protecting the right to a fair trial and in particular the right to be presumed innocent, is intended to enshrine the fundamental principle of the rule of law (see, *inter alia,* the *Sunday Times* judgment of 26 April 1979, Series A No. 30, p. 34, paragraph 55).
>
> Article 6, paragraph 2 (art. 6-2), does not therefore regard presumptions of fact or of law provided for in the criminal law with indifference. It requires States to confine them within reasonable limits which take into account the importance of what is at stake and maintain the rights of the defence.

In this case the Court concluded that the French courts did not apply the Customs Code in a way which conflicted with the presumption of innocence.

Article 6, paragraph 2, content of judgments

In the above-mentioned Minelli judgment the Court stated the following (p. 18, paragraph 37):

> In the Court's judgment, the presumption of innocence will be violated if, without the accused's having previously been proved guilty according to law and, notably, without his having had the opportunity of exercising his rights of defence, a judicial decision concerning him reflects an opinion that he is guilty. This may be so even in the absence of any formal finding; it suffices that there is some reasoning suggesting that the court regards the accused as guilty.

In the Minelli case the applicant was ordered by the Swiss court to pay part of the costs of the proceedings, together with compensation to the victims in respect of their expenses, whilst terminating the prosecution on account of limitation to bring the case before the court. The Swiss Court had concluded in its judgment that, in the absence of limitation, the article in the newspaper complained of would "very probably have led to the conviction". The Court concluded that Article 6, paragraph 2, had been violated.

3. Particular instances

Presumption of innocence and compensation for lawful detention on remand

In the Englert v. Germany judgment (25 August 1987, Series A No. 123, pp. 34-35, paragraphs 36-37) the Court made some general remarks concerning claims for reimbursement of costs and compensation for lawful detention on remand after an acquittal or discontinuance of criminal proceedings:

> The Court points out [...] like the Commission and the Government, that neither Article 6, paragraph 2 (art. 6-2), nor any other provision of the Convention gives a person "charged with a criminal offence" a right to reimbursement of his costs or a right to compensation for lawful detention on remand where proceedings taken against him are discontinued.

In the same case, the Court also turned its attention to the motives behind a decision to reject such claims.

> Nevertheless, a decision whereby compensation for detention on remand and reimbursement of an accused's necessary costs and expenses are refused following termination of proceedings may raise an issue under Article 6, paragraph 2 (art. 6-2), if supporting reasoning which cannot be dissociated from the operative provisions (see the same judgment, p. 18, paragraph 38) amounts in substance to a determination of the accused's guilt without his having previously been proved guilty according to law and, in particular, without his having had an opportunity to exercise the rights of the defence (ibid., paragraph 37).

In this case the Court found that there was no breach of Article 6, paragraph 2. It took the view that the decisions of the German courts described "a state of suspicion" and did not amount to a finding of guilt.

On the other hand, in the case of Sekanina v. Austria (25 August 1993, Series A No. 266-A, p. 15-16, paragraphs 29-30) the applicant was acquitted by a judgment which became final. In their decisions rejecting the applicant's claim for compensation the Austrian courts undertook an assessment of the applicant's guilt, despite the fact that there had been a final acquittal. In this case Article 6, paragraph 2, had been violated.

(See also the Lamanna v. Austria judgment of 10 July 2001, Application No. 28923/95, paragraphs 35-40, and the Asan Rushiti v. Austria judgment of 21 March 2000, Application No. 28389/95, concerning a refusal to order compensation for provisional detention.)

Presumption of innocence and detention arrangements

For a situation where the lack of separate arrangements for prisoners in provisional detention did not give rise to a violation of Article 6, paragraph 2: the Peers v. Greece judgment of 19 April 2001, Application No. 28524/95.

Article 6, paragraph 3 – Precise rights of the accused

Article 6, paragraph 3, is worded as follows:

---

3. **Everyone charged with a criminal offence has the following minimum rights:**

a   to be informed promptly, in a language which he understands and in detail, of the nature and cause of the accusation against him;

b   to have adequate time and facilities for the preparation of his defence;

c   to defend himself in person or through legal assistance of his own choosing or, if he has not sufficient means to pay for legal assistance, to be given it free when the interests of justice so require;

d   to examine or have examined witnesses against him and to obtain the attendance and examination of witnesses on his behalf under the same conditions as witnesses against him;

e   to have the free assistance of an interpreter if he cannot understand or speak the language used in court.

The requirements of paragraph 3.*a, b, c, d* and *e* of Article 6 of the Convention are to be analysed as particular aspects of the right to a fair trial guaranteed by paragraph 1 (Art. 6-1) (see the Vacher v. France judgment of 17 December 1996, *Reports* 1996-VI, paragraph 22).

1. Article 6, paragraph 3.*a* – The right to be informed of the accusation

In the Kamasinski v. Austria case (19 December 1989, Series A No. 168, pp. 36-37, paragraph 79) the Court expressed its views on the translation to an alien of the charges against him. In that regard the Court observed that:

> Paragraph 3.*a* of Article 6 (art. 6-3-a) clarifies the extent of interpretation required in this context by securing to every defendant the right "to be informed promptly, in a language which he understands and in detail, of the nature and cause of the accusation against him". Whilst this provision does not specify that the relevant information should be given in writing or translated in written form for a foreign defendant, it does point to the need for special attention to be paid to the notification of the "accusation" to the defendant. An indictment plays a crucial role in the criminal process, in that it is from the moment of its service that the defendant is formally put on written notice of the factual and legal basis of the charges against him. A defendant not conversant with the court's language may in fact be put at a disadvantage if he is not also provided with a written translation of the indictment in a language he understands.

The question of the redefinition of charges also arises. The Sadak and Others v. Turkey judgment provides an example of such a case. The applicants complained, in particular, that the characterisation of the charges against them had been altered at the last hearing of their trial. They had initially been charged with separatism and undermining the integrity of the State. On the day on which judgment was delivered, however, the National Security Court asked them on the spot to prepare their defence to a new charge, namely belonging to an illegal armed organisation. The National Security Court then dismissed their application for further time to prepare their defence against the new charge. The applicants maintained that they had not been able to defend themselves properly and to adduce evidence against this new charge. The Court stated (judgment of 10 July 2001, Applications Nos. 29900/96 and 29903/96, paragraphs 48-52 and 56-59):

> [...] Article 6, paragraph 3.*a*, also affords the defendant the right to be informed not only of the cause of the accusation, that is to say the acts he is alleged to have committed and on which the accusation is based, but also, in detail, the legal characterisation given to those acts (see Pélissier and Sassi v. France [GC], No. 25444/94, paragraph 51, ECHR 1999-II).

> The scope of Article 6, paragraph 3.*a*, must in particular be assessed in the light of the more general right to a fair hearing guaranteed by the first paragraph of Article 6 of the Convention (see, *mutatis mutandis*, the following judgments: Deweer v. Belgium, 27 February 1980, Series A No. 35, pp. 30-31, paragraph 56; Artico v. Italy, 13 May 1980, Series A No. 37, p. 15, paragraph 32; Guddi v Italy, 9 April 1984, Series A No. 76, p. 11, paragraph 28; and Colozza v. Italy, 12 February 1985, Series A No. 89, p. 14, paragraph 26). The Court considers that in criminal matters the provision of full, detailed information to the defendant concerning the charges against him – and consequently the legal characterisation that the court might adopt in the matter – is an essential prerequisite for ensuring that the proceedings are fair (see Pélissier and Sassi, cited above, paragraph 52).

> Lastly, as regards the complaint under Article 6, paragraph 3.*b*, of the Convention, the Court considers that sub-paragraphs *a* and *b* of Article 6, paragraph 3, are connected and that the right to be informed of the nature and the cause of the accusation must be considered in the light of the accused's right to prepare his defence (see Pélissier and Sassi, cited above, paragraph 54).

> In the instant case, the Court notes first of all that in the bill of indictment filed by the prosecution on 21 June 1994 the applicants were accused solely of the crime of treason against the integrity of the State, as provided for by Article 125 of the Criminal Code. Although the applicants' links with PKK members were mentioned by the prosecution, the Court notes that throughout the investigation those links were examined only with a view to establishing the constituent elements of the offence of which the applicants were initially accused by the prosecution. It is not disputed that, up to the last day, the hearing before the National Security Court had related solely to the crime of treason against the integrity of the State.

> That being so, the Court must ascertain whether it was sufficiently foreseeable for the applicants that the characterisation of the offence could be changed from the one of treason against the integrity of the State of which they were initially

accused to that of belonging to an armed organisation set up for the purpose of destroying the integrity of the State.

[...]

In the light of the foregoing, the Court considers that belonging to an illegal armed organisation did not constitute an element intrinsic to the offence of which the applicants had been accused since the start of the proceedings.

The Court therefore considers that, in using the right which it unquestionably had to recharacterise facts over which it properly had jurisdiction, the Ankara National Security Court should have afforded the applicants the possibility of exercising their defence rights on that issue in a practical and effective manner, particularly by giving them the necessary time to do so. The case file shows that the National Security Court, which could, for example, have decided to adjourn the hearing once the facts had been recharacterised, did not give the applicants the opportunity to prepare their defence to the new charge, which they were not informed of until the last day of the trial, just before the judgment was delivered, which was patently too late. In addition, the applicants' lawyers were absent on the day of the last hearing. Whatever the reason for their absence, the fact is that the applicants could not consult their lawyers on the recharacterisation of the facts by the prosecution and the National Security Court.

Having regard to all the above considerations, the Court concludes that the applicants' right to be informed in detail of the nature and cause of the accusation against them and their right to have adequate time and facilities for the preparation of their defence were infringed (see, *mutatis mutandis*, Pélissier and Sassi, cited above, paragraphs 60-63, and Mattoccia v. Italy, Application No. 23969/94, paragraphs 62-72, ECHR 2000-IX).

Consequently, there has been a violation of paragraph 3.*a* and *b* of Article 6 of the Convention, taken together with paragraph 1 of that Article, which requires a fair trial.

(See also the Dallos v. Hungary judgment of 1 March 2001, Application No. 29082/95, paragraphs 47-53 ; and the Pélissier and Sassi v. France judgment of 25 March 1999, Application No. 25444/94.)

2. Article 6, paragraph 3.*b* – The right to adequate time and facilities to prepare the defence

The Court has also stated that Article 6, paragraph 3.*b*, did not entitle an accused to have access to the case-file if he was represented by a lawyer (the above-mentioned Kaminski v. Austria judgment, p. 39, paragraphs 87-88) :

By virtue of Section 45, paragraph 2, of the Austrian Code of Criminal Procedure, the right to inspect and make copies of the court file is restricted to the defendant's lawyer, the defendant himself only having such access if he is legally unrepresented (see paragraph 48 above).

[...]

The system provided for under Section 45, paragraph 2, of the Austrian Code of Criminal Procedure is not in itself incompatible with the right of the defence safeguarded under Article 6, paragraph 3.*b* (art. 6-3-b).

As regards the notion "adequate time" the Court observed in the Campbell and Fell judgment (28 June 1984, Series A No. 80, p. 45, paragraph 98):

> Mr Campbell was informed of the charges against him on 1 October 1976, five days before the Board sat (see paragraph 13 above). He also received "notices of report", those relative to the Board's adjudication having been given to him on the day before it met; the notices drew attention to the fact that he could reply to the charges in writing (ibid.).

> The Court considers that in all the circumstances the applicant was left with "adequate time" to prepare his defence; it notes that he apparently did not seek an adjournment of the hearing (ibid.).

(See also the above-mentioned Sadak and Others v. Turkey judgment of 10 July 2001, Applications Nos. 29900/96 and 29903/96, paragraphs 48-52 and 56-59.)

3. Article 6, paragraph 3.*c* – The right to defend oneself in person or the right to legal assistance

The right to legal assistance from the accused's point of view

The point at which the accused must have access to a lawyer

In the John Murray v. the United Kingdom judgment (8 February 1996, *Reports* 1996-I, paragraphs 62-64 and 66), the Court stated that this right may come into play at the beginning of the police investigation. It pointed out:

> The Court observes that it has not been disputed by the Government that Article 6 (art. 6) applies even at the stage of the preliminary investigation into an offence by the police. In this respect it recalls its finding in the Imbrioscia v. Switzerland judgment of 24 November 1993 that Article 6 (art. 6) – especially paragraph 3 (art. 6-3) – may be relevant before a case is sent for trial if and so far as the fairness of the trial is likely to be seriously prejudiced by an initial failure to comply with its provisions (art. 6-3) (Series A No. 275, p. 13, paragraph 36).

> As it pointed out in that judgment, the manner in which Article 6, paragraph 3.*c* (art. 6-3-c), is to be applied during the preliminary investigation depends on the special features of the proceedings involved and on the circumstances of the case (loc. cit., p. 14, paragraph 38). National laws may attach consequences to the attitude of an accused at the initial stages of police interrogation which are decisive for the prospects of the defence in any subsequent criminal proceedings. In such circumstances Article 6 (art. 6) will normally require that the accused be allowed to benefit from the assistance of a lawyer already at the initial stages of police interrogation. However, this right, which is not explicitly set out in the Convention, may be subject to restrictions for good cause. The question, in each case, is whether the restriction, in the light of the entirety of the proceedings, has deprived the accused of a fair hearing.

> In the present case, the applicant's right of access to a lawyer during the first forty-eight hours of police detention was restricted under Section 15 of the Northern Ireland (Emergency Provisions) Act 1987 on the basis that the police

had reasonable grounds to believe that the exercise of the right of access would, *inter alia*, interfere with the gathering of information about the commission of acts of terrorism or make it more difficult to prevent such an act.

[...]

The Court is of the opinion that the scheme contained in the Order is such that it is of paramount importance for the rights of the defence that an accused has access to a lawyer at the initial stages of police interrogation. It observes in this context that, under the Order, at the beginning of police interrogation, an accused is confronted with a fundamental dilemma relating to his defence. If he chooses to remain silent, adverse inferences may be drawn against him in accordance with the provisions of the Order. On the other hand, if the accused opts to break his silence during the course of interrogation, he runs the risk of prejudicing his defence without necessarily removing the possibility of inferences being drawn against him.

Under such conditions the concept of fairness enshrined in Article 6 (art. 6) requires that the accused has the benefit of the assistance of a lawyer already at the initial stages of police interrogation.

Contra, in the light of the circumstances of the case, in the Brennan v. the United Kingdom judgment (16 October 2001, Application No. 39846/98, paragraphs 45-48) for a period of twenty-four hours before access to a lawyer was allowed; but *idem* in the Averill v. the United Kingdom judgment of 6 June 2000, Application No. 36408/97, where the Court held that the applicant should have been granted legal assistance before being questioned (the Magee v. the United Kingdom judgment of 6 June 2000, Application No. 28135/95, paragraph 41).

Confidentiality of communications with a lawyer

In the S. v. Switzerland case (judgment of 28 November 1991, Series A No. 220, p. 16, paragraph 48), the applicant had been unable while in custody to communicate with his lawyer freely and without supervision.

The Court considers that an accused's right to communicate with his advocate out of hearing of a third person is part of the basic requirements of a fair trial in a democratic society and follows from Article 6, paragraph 3.*c* (art. 6-3-c), of the Convention. If a lawyer were unable to confer with his client and receive confidential instructions from him without such surveillance, his assistance would lose much of its usefulness, whereas the Convention is intended to guarantee rights that are practical and effective (see, *inter alia*, the Artico judgment of 13 May 1980, series A No. 37, p. 16, paragraph 33).

(*Idem* the Brennan v. the United Kingdom judgment of 16 October 2001, Application No. 39846/98, paragraphs 58-63; and the Lanz v. Austria judgment of 31 January 2002, Application No. 24430/94 , paragraphs 46-53.)

Assistance and representation at the hearing

In one case, Lala v. the Netherlands (22 September 1994, Series A No. 298-A, p. 13, paragraph 33), the Court had occasion to make another very important point concerning the possibility for persons being prosecuted to be represented by a lawyer during criminal trials. In the Lala case the applicant had voluntarily failed to appear at the appeal hearing and the Court of Appeal had "decided the case without his counsel, whom he had charged to conduct the defence and who attended the trial with the clear intention of doing so, being allowed to defend him". The government claimed, *mutatis mutandis*, that this encouraged those charged with a criminal offence to appear in person. The Court observed:

> As this Court pointed out in its Poitrimol judgment (loc. cit., p. 15, paragraph 35), in the interests of a fair and just criminal process it is of capital importance that the accused should appear at his trial. As a general rule, this is equally true for an appeal by way of rehearing. However, it is also of crucial importance for the fairness of the criminal justice system that the accused be adequately defended, both at first instance and on appeal, [...].

> In the Court's view the latter interest prevails. Consequently, the fact that the defendant, in spite of having been properly summoned, does not appear, cannot – even in the absence of an excuse – justify depriving him of his right under Article 6, paragraph 3 (art. 6-3), of the Convention to be defended by counsel.

It will be seen that the Court uses the word "assistance" in a broad sense: the purpose is not only to ensure that an accused who is present at the hearing can be assisted but also to ensure that an accused can be represented in his absence (see the Krombach v. France judgment of 13 February 2001, Application No. 29731/96, paragraphs 82-91, concerning criminal proceedings *in absentia* before the Assize Court):

> The Court cannot adopt the Government's narrow construction of the word "assistance" within the meaning of Article 6, paragraph 3.*c*, of the Convention. It sees no reason for departing from the opinion it expressed on that subject in the Poitrimol case (see the judgment cited above, paragraph 34), in which the Government had already suggested that a distinction should be drawn between "assistance" and "representation" for the purposes of proceedings in the criminal court.

(*Idem* the Goedhart v. Belgium judgment of 20 March 2001, Application No. 34989/97, paragraphs 24-28, concerning an opposition declared null and void because of the domestic criminal procedure, which requires an appearance in person; the court had refused to allow representation by a lawyer; the Magee v. the United Kingdom judgment of 6 June 2000, Application No. 28135/95, paragraph 41; and the Stroek v. Belgium judgment of 20 March 2001, Applications Nos. 36449/97 and 36467/97, paragraphs 21-25.)

On the conduct of the hearing and interruption of the lawyer, see the G. v. the United Kingdom judgment (19 December 2001, Application No. 43373/98, paragraphs 35-43).

The right to legal assistance from the State's point of view

The Kamasinski v. Austria case also provided the Court with the opportunity to define the scope of the obligations which Article 6, paragraph 3.*b*, imposes on the State. The Court stated (p. 33, paragraph 65) that:

> Certainly, in itself the appointment of a legal aid defence counsel does not necessarily settle the issue of compliance with the requirements of Article 6, paragraph 3.*c* (art. 6-3-c). As the Court stated in its Artico judgment of 13 May 1980: "The Convention is intended to guarantee not rights that are theoretical or illusory but rights that are practical and effective [...]. [M]ere nomination does not ensure effective assistance since the lawyer appointed for legal aid purposes may die, fall seriously ill, be prevented for a protracted period from acting or shirk his duties. If they are notified of the situation, the authorities must either replace him or cause him to fulfil his obligations" (Series A No. 37, p. 16, paragraph 33). Nevertheless, "a State cannot be held responsible for every short-coming on the part of a lawyer appointed for legal aid purposes" (ibid., p. 18, paragraph 36). It follows from the independence of the legal profession from the State that the conduct of the defence is essentially a matter between the defendant and his counsel, whether counsel be appointed under a legal aid scheme or be privately financed. [...] the competent national authorities are required under Article 6, paragraph 3.*c* (art. 6-3-c), to intervene only if a failure by legal aid counsel to provide effective representation is manifest or sufficiently brought to their attention in some other way.

It will have been noticed that Article 6, paragraph 3.*c*, lays down the right to free legal assistance "when the interests of justice so require". It remains to be determined in which cases "the interests of justice so require".

In the Quaranta v. Switzerland case (24 May 1991, Series A No. 205, p. 17, paragraphs 32-34), the Court stated:

> In order to determine whether the "interests of justice" required that the applicant receive free legal assistance, the Court will have regard to various criteria.
>
> [...]
>
> In the first place, consideration should be given to the seriousness of the offence of which Mr Quaranta was accused and the severity of the sentence which he risked. [...] An additional factor is the complexity of the case.

Reference may be made, by way of example, to the Biba v. Greece judgment of 26 September 2000, where an alien without resources was refused free legal assistance to bring an appeal on a point of law (Application No. 33170/96) and where the Court found that there had been a violation of Article 6, paragraph 3.*c*.

The right to defend oneself

For the right to defend oneself, see the Medenica v. Switzerland judgment of 14 June 2001, Application No. 20491/92, paragraphs 53-60; the Pobornikoff v. Austria judgment of 3 October 2000, Application No. 28501/95; the Cooke v. Austria judgment of 8 February 2000, Application No. 25878/94; and the Prinz v. Austria judgment of 8 February 2000, Application No. 23867/94.

4. Article 6, paragraph 3.*d* – The right to examine witnesses

The Court has had the opportunity to rule on the concept of "witness". In the Luca v. Italy judgment (27 February 2001, Application No. 33354/96, paragraph 41), it stated:

> [...] the fact that the depositions were, as here, made by a co-accused rather than by a witness is of no relevance. In that connection, the Court reiterates that the term "witness" has an "autonomous" meaning in the Convention system (see the Vidal v. Belgium judgment of 22 April 1992, Series A No. 235-B, paragraph 33). Thus, where a deposition may serve to a material degree as the basis for a conviction, then, irrespective of whether it was made by a witness in the strict sense or by a co-accused, it constitutes evidence for the prosecution to which the guarantees provided by Article 6, paragraphs 1 and 3.*d*, of the Convention apply (see, *mutatis mutandis*, the Ferrantelli and Santangelo v. Italy judgment of 7 August 1996, *Reports* 1996-III, paragraphs 51 and 52).

As regards witnesses, it is appropriate to refer to the fairness of the trial as required by Article 6, paragraph 1. See, however, by way of example, the Ferrantelli and Santangelo v. Italy judgment (7 August 1996, *Reports* 1996-III, paragraphs 51-52), concerning the lack of confrontation with a prosecution witness who had died.

A further example is the Sadak and Others v. Turkey judgment (judgment of 10 July 2001, Applications Nos. 29900/96 and 29903/96, paragraph 67), where the Court observed:

> [...] In any event, paragraph 1 of Article 6, taken together with paragraph 3, requires the Contracting States to take positive steps, in particular to enable the accused to examine or have examined witnesses against him (see the Barberà, Messegué and Jabardo v. Spain judgment of 6 December 1988, Series A No. 146, pp. 33-34, paragraph 78). Such measures form part of the diligence which the Contracting States must exercise in order to ensure that the rights guaranteed by Article 6 are enjoyed in an effective manner (see the Colozza v. Italy judgment of 12 February 1985, Series A No. 89, p. 15, paragraph 28).

Last, that extract should be supplemented by the following, more detailed extract from the Perna v. Italy judgment (25 July 2001, Application No. 48898/99, paragraph 26):

> The Court reiterates that the admissibility of evidence is primarily a matter for regulation by national law and as a general rule it is for the national courts to assess the evidence before them. The Court's task under the Convention is not to give a ruling as to whether statements of witnesses were properly admitted as evidence, but rather to ascertain whether the proceedings as a whole, including the way in which evidence was taken, were fair (see, among many other authorities, the Van Mechelen and Others v. the Netherlands judgment of 23 April 1997, *Reports of Judgments and Decisions* 1997-III, paragraph 50). In particular, "as a general rule, it is for the national courts to assess the evidence before them as well as the relevance of the evidence which defendants seek to adduce [...]. More specifically, Article 6, paragraph 3.*d*, leaves it to them, again as a general rule, to assess whether it is appropriate to call witnesses" (see the Vidal v. Belgium judgment of 22 April 1992, Series A No. 235-B, paragraph 33). Consequently, it is

not sufficient for an accused to complain that he was not permitted to examine certain witnesses; he must also support his request to call witnesses by explaining the importance of doing so and it must be necessary for the court to take evidence from the witnesses concerned in order to be able to establish the true facts (see Engel and Others v. the Netherlands, 8 June 1976, Series A No. 22, paragraph 91, and Bricmont v. Belgium, 7 July 1989, Series A No. 158, paragraph 89, and the European Commission of Human Rights, No. 29420/95, decision of 13 January 1997, *Decisions and Reports* 88-B, pp. 148 and 158-159). That principle also applies to the complainant in a defamation case where, as in the present case, it is requested that he be called as a witness of the facts asserted in the allegedly defamatory statements.

See also the P.S. v. Germany judgment of 20 December 2001, Application No. 33900/96, and the Solakov v. "the former Yugoslav Republic of Macedonia" judgment of 31 October 2001, Application No. 47023/99, concerning the use of testimony by persons detained abroad; and the Pisano v. Italy judgment of 27 July 2000, Application No. 36732/97, concerning the refusal to hear witnesses for the defence whose names had not been provided until after the opening of the trial (no violation). Last, the A.M. v. Italy judgment of 14 December 1999.

5. Article 6, paragraph 3.*e* – The right to an interpreter

Also in the Kamasinski v. Austria case, the Court recalled what it had previously said concerning the content of the right to the free assistance of an interpreter (ibid., p. 35, paragraph 74):

> The right, stated in paragraph 3.*e* of Article 6 (art. 6-3-e), to the free assistance of an interpreter applies not only to oral statements made at the trial hearing but also to documentary material and the pre-trial proceedings. Paragraph 3.*e* (art. 6-3-e) signifies that a person "charged with a criminal offence" who cannot understand or speak the language used in court has the right to the free assistance of an interpreter for the translation or interpretation of all those documents or statements in the proceedings instituted against him which it is necessary for him to understand or to have rendered into the court's language in order to have the benefit of a fair trial (see the Luedicke, Belkacem and Koç judgment of 28 November 1978, Series A No. 29, p. 20, paragraph 48).

> However, paragraph 3.*e* (art. 6-3-e) does not go so far as to require a written translation of all items of written evidence or official documents in the procedure. The interpretation assistance provided should be such as to enable the defendant to have knowledge of the case against him and to defend himself, notably by being able to put before the court his version of the events.

> In view of the need for the right guaranteed by paragraph 3.*e* (art. 6-3-e) to be practical and effective, the obligation of the competent authorities is not limited to the appointment of an interpreter but, if they are put on notice in the particular circumstances, may also extend to a degree of subsequent control over the adequacy of the interpretation provided (see, *mutatis mutandis*, the Artico judgment previously cited, Series A No. 37, pp. 16 and 18, paragraphs 33 and 36 – quoted above at paragraph 65).

Article 7 ECHR – No punishment without legislation

Article 7, paragraph 1 – Prohibition on retroactive application of the criminal law

Article 7, paragraph 1, is worded as follows:

> 1. No one shall be held guilty of any criminal offence on account of any act or omission which did not constitute a criminal offence under national or international law at the time when it was committed. Nor shall a heavier penalty be imposed than the one that was applicable at the time the criminal offence was committed.

1. The sphere of application of Article 7, paragraph 1

Article 7 does not apply to "preventive" legislation

In the Lawless v. Ireland case (judgment of 1 July 1961, Series A No. 3, p. 54, paragraph 19) the Court had occasion to explain the sphere of application of Article 7. The Court observed that it did not apply to legislation laying down preventive measures:

> Whereas the proceedings show that the Irish Government detained G.R. Lawless under the Offences against the State (Amendment) Act 1940, for the sole purpose of restraining him from engaging in activities prejudicial to the preservation of public peace and order or the security of the State; whereas his detention, being a preventive measure, cannot be deemed to be due to his having been held guilty of a criminal offence within the meaning of Article 7 (art. 7) of the Convention; whereas it follows that Article 7 (art. 7) has no bearing on the case of G.R. Lawless; whereas, therefore, the Irish Government, in detaining G.R. Lawless under the 1940 Act, did not violate their obligation under Article 7 (art. 7) of the Convention.

(To the same effect, see the De Wilde, Ooms and Versyp judgment of 18 June 1971, Series A No. 12, paragraph 87, concerning vagrancy.)

Article 7 applies to "punitive" legislation

The notion of punishment for the purposes of Article 7

The Court does not allow states to avoid the application of Article 7 by describing a measure as they see fit. In connection with the notion of "penalty" the Court held in the Welch v. the United Kingdom case (9 February 1995, Series A No. 307-A, paragraphs 27-28) that:

> The concept of a "penalty" in this provision is, like the notions of "civil rights and obligations" and "criminal charge" in Article 6, paragraph 1 (art. 6-1), an autonomous Convention concept (see, *inter alia*, as regards "civil rights", the X. v. France

judgment of 31 March 1992, Series A No. 234-C, p. 98, paragraph 28, and – as regards "criminal charge" – the Demicoli v. Malta judgment of 27 August 1991, Series A No. 210, pp. 15-16, paragraph 31). To render the protection offered by Article 7 (art. 7) effective, the Court must remain free to go behind appearances and assess for itself whether a particular measure amounts in substance to a "penalty" within the meaning of this provision (see, *mutatis mutandis*, the Van Droogenbroeck v. Belgium judgment of 24 June 1982, Series A No. 50, p. 20, paragraph 38, and the Duinhof and Duijf v. the Netherlands judgment of 22 May 1984, Series A No. 79, p. 15, paragraph 34).

The wording of Article 7, paragraph 1 (art. 7-1), second sentence, indicates that the starting-point in any assessment of the existence of a penalty is whether the measure in question is imposed following conviction for a "criminal offence". Other factors that may be taken into account as relevant in this connection are the nature and purpose of the measure in question; its characterisation under national law; the procedures involved in the making and implementation of the measure; and its severity.

In the Coeme and Others v. Belgium case (22 June 2000, Applications Nos. 32492/96, 32547/96, 32548/96, 33209/96 and 33210/96, paragraph 145), the Court further pointed out:

Having regard to the aim of the Convention, which is to protect rights that are practical and effective, [the Court] may also take into consideration the need to preserve a balance between the general interest and the fundamental rights of individuals and the notions currently prevailing in democratic States (see, among other authorities, the Airey v. Ireland judgment of 9 October 1979, Series A No. 32, pp. 14-15, paragraph 26, and the Guzzardi v. Italy judgment of 6 November 1980, Series A No. 39, pp. 34-35, paragraph 95).

Examples

Returning to the Welch v. the United Kingdom case, which concerned a confiscation order made in respect of assets acquired from the proceeds of drug trafficking, adopted on the basis of a provision enacted subsequent to the facts, the Court declared that that confiscation must be regarded as a penalty and that there had therefore been a violation of Article 7 by virtue of its retroactive application (ibid., paragraph 35):

Taking into consideration the combination of punitive elements outlined above [the fact that the confiscation order is directed to the proceeds involved in drug dealing and is not limited to actual enrichment or profit; the discretion of the trial judge, in fixing the amount of the order, to take into consideration the degree of culpability of the accused; and the possibility of imprisonment in default of payment by the offender – are all elements which, when considered together, provide a strong indication of, *inter alia*, a regime of punishment [...]], the confiscation order amounted, in the circumstances of the present case, to a penalty. Accordingly, there has been a breach of Article 7, paragraph 1 (art. 7-1).

In the case of Jamil v. France (8 June 1995, Series A No. 317-B, paragraph 32) the applicant complained of the prolongation of the term of imprisonment in default ordered by the Paris Court of Appeal pursuant to a law enacted after the offence was committed. With regard to the main question whether the imprisonment in default is a penalty within the meaning of the second sentence of Article 7, paragraph 1, the Court considered as follows.

> The Court notes that the sanction imposed on Mr Jamil was ordered in a criminal-law context – the prevention of drug trafficking. It observes, however, that in France imprisonment in default is not confined to this single, ordinary-law field. As it is a means of enforcing the payment of debts to the Treasury other than those partaking of the nature of civil damages, it can also be attached to penalties for customs or tax offences, among others.

> In order to determine how imprisonment in default should be classified for the purposes of Article 7 (art. 7), it is therefore necessary also to ascertain its purpose and the rules which govern it. The measure in question is intended to ensure payment of fines, *inter alia*, by enforcement directed at the person of a debtor who cannot prove his insolvency, and its object is to compel such payment by the threat of incarceration under a prison regime. This regime is harsher than for sentences of imprisonment under the ordinary criminal law, mainly because it is not attenuated as they are by such measures as parole or pardon. Imprisonment in default is a survival of the ancient system of imprisonment for debt; it now exists only in respect of debts to the State and does not absolve the debtor from the obligation to pay which led to his committal to prison. Although he can no longer thereafter be compelled to pay by means directed against his person, his goods are still subject to distraint. It is not a measure which can be likened to the seizure of movable or immovable property referred to by the Government.

> The sanction imposed on Mr Jamil was ordered by a criminal court, was intended to be deterrent and could have led to a punitive deprivation of liberty (see, *mutatis mutandis*, the Engel and Others v. the Netherlands judgment of 8 June 1976, Series A No. 22, p. 35, paragraph 82, and the Öztürk v. Germany judgment of 21 February 1984, Series A No. 7, p. 20, paragraph 53). It was therefore a penalty within the meaning of Article 7, paragraph 1 (art. 7-1), of the Convention.

2. The scope and content of Article 7, paragraph 1

General principles

In the Coeme and Others v. Belgium case (22 June 2000, Applications Nos. 32492/96, 32547/96, 32548/96, 33209/96 and 33210/96, paragraphs 146 and 149-151), the Court stated:

> The Court must [...] verify that at the time when an accused person performed the act which led to his being prosecuted and convicted there was in force a legal provision which made that act punishable, and that the punishment imposed did not exceed the limits fixed by that provision (see Murphy v. the United Kingdom, Application No. 4681/70, Commission decision of 3 and 4 October 1972, *Collection of Decisions* 43, p. 1).

In doing so, the Court applies a number of fundamental principles, which are summarised in the S.W. v. the United Kingdom and the R. v. the United

Kingdom judgments of 22 November 1995 (Series A No. 335-B and 335-C, pp. 41-42, paragraphs 34-36, and pp. 68-69, paragraphs 32-34, respectively):

> The guarantee enshrined in Article 7 (art. 7), which is an essential element of the rule of law, occupies a prominent place in the Convention system of protection, as is underlined by the fact that no derogation from it is permissible under Article 15 (art. 15) in time of war or other public emergency. It should be construed and applied, as follows from its object and purpose, in such a way as to provide effective safeguards against arbitrary prosecution, conviction and punishment.

> Accordingly, as the Court held in its Kokkinakis v. Greece judgment of 25 May 1993 (Series A No. 260-A, p. 22, paragraph 52), Article 7 (art. 7) is not confined to prohibiting the retrospective application of the criminal law to an accused's disadvantage: it also embodies, more generally, the principle that only the law can define a crime and prescribe a penalty *(nullum crimen, nulla poena sine lege)* and the principle that the criminal law must not be extensively construed to an accused's detriment, for instance by analogy. From these principles it follows that an offence must be clearly defined in the law. In its aforementioned judgment the Court added that this requirement is satisfied where the individual can know from the wording of the relevant provision and, if need be, with the assistance of the courts' interpretation of it, what acts and omissions will make him criminally liable. The Court thus indicated that when speaking of "law" Article 7 (art. 7) alludes to the very same concept as that to which the Convention refers elsewhere when using that term, a concept which comprises written as well as unwritten law and implies qualitative requirements, notably those of accessibility and foreseeability (see, as a recent authority, the Tolstoy Miloslavsky v. the United Kingdom judgment of 13 July 1995, Series A No. 316-B, pp. 71-72, paragraph 37).

> However clearly drafted a legal provision may be, in any system of law, including criminal law, there is an inevitable element of judicial interpretation. There will always be a need for elucidation of doubtful points and for adaptation to changing circumstances. Indeed, [...] in the [...] Convention States, the progressive development of the criminal law through judicial law-making is a well entrenched and necessary part of legal tradition. Article 7 (art. 7) of the Convention cannot be read as outlawing the gradual clarification of the rules of criminal liability through judicial interpretation from case to case, provided that the resultant development is consistent with the essence of the offence and could reasonably be foreseen.

Generally, in the cases before it, the Court is often led to examine, in order: the existence of a criminal measure prohibiting the applicant's conduct; the greater or lesser extent to which it is clear or straightforward; and the question of limitation.

Application

The existence of a legal text – Prohibition of reasoning by analogy

The requirement for a legal basis for a conviction is sometimes examined by means of its corollary, the prohibition of reasoning by analogy in criminal matters. Article 7, paragraph 1, prohibits such reasoning. In the Baskaya and

Okçuoglu v. Turkey judgment, the applicant had been prosecuted under Section 8 of the Turkish Prevention of Terrorism Act of April 1991. That section provided: "(1) Written and spoken propaganda, meetings, assemblies and demonstrations aimed at undermining the territorial integrity of the Republic of Turkey or the indivisible unity of the nation are prohibited, irrespective of the methods used and the intention. Any person who engages in such an activity shall be sentenced to not less than two and not more than five years' imprisonment and a fine of from 50 million to 100 million Turkish liras. (2) Where the crime of propaganda contemplated in the above paragraph is committed through the medium of periodicals within the meaning of Section 3 of the Press Act (Law No. 5680), the publisher shall also be liable to a fine equal to ninety per cent of the income from the average sales for the previous month if the periodical appears more frequently then monthly, or from the average sales for the previous month of the daily newspaper with the largest circulation if the offence involves printed matter other than periodicals or if the periodical has just been launched. However, the fine may not be less than 100 million Turkish liras. The editor of the periodical concerned shall be ordered to pay a sum equal to half the fine imposed on the publisher and sentenced to not less than six months' and not more than two years' imprisonment." The editor of that periodical was sentenced to pay half of the fine imposed on the publisher and also to six months' imprisonment. The applicant complained that there had been a violation of Article 7 on the ground that he had been given the penalty laid down for editors whereas he had been the publisher. The Court stated (8 July 1999, Applications Nos. 23536/94 and 24408/94, *Reports* 1999-IV, paragraphs 36 and 41-42):

> The Court recalls that, according to its case-law, Article 7 embodies, *inter alia*, the principle that only the law can define a crime and prescribe a penalty *(nullum crimen, nulla poena sine lege)* and the principle that the criminal law must not be extensively construed to an accused's detriment, for instance by analogy. [...]

> As regards sentencing [...] the [...] applicant complained that he had been sentenced to a term of imprisonment under a provision in Section 8, paragraph 2, which expressly applied to the sentencing of editors, while publishers could only be punished by a fine. In this connection, the Government stressed that the application of Section 8, paragraph 2, to publishers would normally entail a more favourable sentence than under Section 8, paragraph 1. Although this may be so, it rather appears that Section 8, paragraph 2, was a *lex specialis* on the sentencing of editors and publishers and that the sentence imposed on the applicant publisher in the present case was based on an extensive construction, by analogy, of the rule in the same sub-section on the sentencing of editors.

> In these circumstances, the Court considers that the imposition of a prison sentence on the second applicant was incompatible with the principle *"nulla poena sine lege"* embodied in Article 7.

The requirement of foreseeability

The Court is not satisfied with the mere existence of a criminal measure. It also requires that the measure be sufficiently clear. This is the requirement of foreseeability. The Court has interpreted that requirement in the

Cantoni v. France judgment in respect of the ban on the sale of medicinal products in supermarkets (15 November 1996, Application No. 17862/91, *Reports* 1996-V, paragraphs 29, 31 and 34-36). After noting a point already referred to in the S.W. v. the United Kingdom judgment, the Court stated:

> An offence must be clearly defined in the law. This requirement is satisfied where the individual can know from the wording of the relevant provision (art. 7) and, if need be, with the assistance of the courts' interpretation of it, what acts and omissions will make him criminally liable.
>
> [...]
>
> As the Court has already had occasion to note, it is a logical consequence of the principle that laws must be of general application that the wording of statutes is not always precise. One of the standard techniques of regulation by rules is to use general categorisations as opposed to exhaustive lists. The need to avoid excessive rigidity and to keep pace with changing circumstances means that many laws are inevitably couched in terms which, to a greater or lesser extent, are vague. The interpretation and application of such enactments depend on practice (see, among other authorities, the Kokkinakis v. Greece judgment of 25 May 1993, Series A No. 260-A, p. 19, paragraph 40).
>
> Like many statutory definitions, that of "medicinal product" contained in Article L. 511 of the Public Health Code is rather general (see paragraph 18 above). When the legislative technique of categorisation is used, there will often be grey areas at the fringes of the definition. This penumbra of doubt in relation to borderline facts does not in itself make a provision incompatible with Article 7 (art. 7), provided that it proves to be sufficiently clear in the large majority of cases. The role of adjudication vested in the courts is precisely to dissipate such interpretational doubts as remain, taking into account the changes in everyday practice.
>
> The Court must accordingly ascertain whether in the present case the text of the statutory rule read in the light of the accompanying interpretive case-law satisfied this test at the relevant time.
>
> [...] Thus, well before the events in the present case, the Court of Cassation had adopted a clear position on this matter, which with the passing of time became even more firmly established.
>
> The Court recalls that the scope of the notion of foreseeability depends to a considerable degree on the content of the text in issue, the field it is designed to cover and the number and status of those to whom it is addressed (see the Groppera Radio AG and Others v. Switzerland judgment of 28 March 1990, Series A No. 173, p. 26, paragraph 68). A law may still satisfy the requirement of foreseeability even if the person concerned has to take appropriate legal advice to assess, to a degree that is reasonable in the circumstances, the consequences which a given action may entail (see, among other authorities, the Tolstoy Miloslavsky v. the United Kingdom judgment of 13 July 1995, Series A No. 316-B, p. 71, paragraph 37).
>
> This is particularly true in relation to persons carrying on a professional activity, who are used to having to proceed with a high degree of caution when pursuing their occupation. They can on this account be expected to take special care in assessing the risks that such activity entails.

With the benefit of appropriate legal advice, Mr Cantoni, who was, moreover, the manager of a supermarket, should have appreciated at the material time that, in view of the line of case-law stemming from the Court of Cassation and from some of the lower courts, he ran a real risk of prosecution for unlawful sale of medicinal products.

There has accordingly been no breach of Article 7 (art. 7).

In the S.W. v. the United Kingdom judgment (22 November 1995, Series A No. 335-B, paragraphs 43-45), the applicant had been convicted of the rape of his wife. He complained that he had been convicted in respect of conduct which at the relevant time was not an offence. He claimed that the general common law principle that a husband could not be found guilty of raping his wife still applied on the date on which he committed the acts which led to his being accused of rape. He relied in particular on Section 1, paragraph 1, of the Sexual Offences (Amendment) Act 1976, worded as follows: "For the purposes of Section 1 of the Sexual Offences Act 1956 (which relates to rape) a man commits rape if (a) he has unlawful sexual intercourse with a woman who at the time of the intercourse does not consent to it [...]". The United Kingdom courts had considered that the word "unlawful" in the definition of rape was merely redundant and did not prevent "removing a common law fiction which had become anachronistic and offensive". The applicant's response was while that the Court of Appeal and the House of Lords had not established a new offence or altered the ingredients of the offence of rape, they had adapted an existing offence in such a way as to bring within it conduct which the common law had previously excluded from it. He therefore considered that the criterion of foreseeability had not been satisfied. The Court considered that there had been no violation of Article 7 of the Convention. In reaching that conclusion, it took into account the fact that:

> The decisions of the Court of Appeal and then the House of Lords did no more than continue a perceptible line of case-law development dismantling the immunity of a husband from prosecution for rape upon his wife (for a description of this development, see paragraphs 11 and 23-27 above). There was no doubt under the law as it stood on 18 September 1990 that a husband who forcibly had sexual intercourse with his wife could, in various circumstances, be found guilty of rape. Moreover, there was an evident evolution, which was consistent with the very essence of the offence, of the criminal law through judicial interpretation towards treating such conduct generally as within the scope of the offence of rape. This evolution had reached a stage where judicial recognition of the absence of immunity had become a reasonably foreseeable development of the law (see paragraph 36 above).

> The essentially debasing character of rape is so manifest that the result of the decisions of the Court of Appeal and the House of Lords – that the applicant could be convicted of attempted rape, irrespective of his relationship with the victim – cannot be said to be at variance with the object and purpose of Article 7 (art. 7) of the Convention, namely to ensure that no one should be subjected to arbitrary prosecution, conviction or punishment (see paragraph 34 above). What is more, the abandonment of the unacceptable idea of a husband being immune against prosecution for rape of his wife was in conformity not only with a

civilised concept of marriage but also, and above all, with the fundamental objectives of the Convention, the very essence of which is respect for human dignity and human freedom.

Consequently, by following the Court of Appeal's ruling in R. v. R. in the applicant's case, Mr Justice Rose did not render a decision permitting a finding of guilt incompatible with Article 7 (art. 7) of the Convention.

Furthermore, there is *de facto* compliance with the condition of foreseeability where the Court holds that that requirement is satisfied in relation to another Article of the Convention (see, for example, the Erdogdu and Ince v. Turkey judgment of 8 July 1999, Applications Nos. 25067/94 and 25068/94, *Reports* 1999-IV, paragraph 59):

> The Court recalls that when speaking of "law" Article 7 alludes to the very same concept as that to which the Convention refers elsewhere when using that term (see the S.W. v. the United Kingdom judgment of 22 November 1995, Series A No. 335-B, p. 42, paragraph 35). In view of its conclusion at paragraph 39 above in respect of the "prescribed by law" requirement under Article 10, paragraph 2, the Court finds that there has been no violation of Article 7 of the Convention.

Limitation

In the Coeme and Others v. Belgium case (22 June 2000, Applications Nos. 32492/96, 32547/96, 32548/96, 33209/96 and 33210/96, paragraphs 146 and 149-151), the Court stated that the extension by law of a limitation period is valid from the aspect of Article 7 provided that immunity from prosecution has not been acquired:

> Limitation may be defined as the statutory right of an offender not to be prosecuted or tried after the lapse of a certain period of time since the offence was committed. Limitation periods, which are a common feature of the domestic legal systems of the Contracting States, serve several purposes, which include ensuring legal certainty and finality and preventing infringements of the rights of defendants, which might be impaired if courts were required to decide on the basis of evidence which might have become incomplete because of the passage of time (see the Stubbings and Others v. the United Kingdom judgment of 22 October 1996, *Reports* 1996-IV, pp. 1502-1503, paragraph 51).
>
> [...]
>
> The extension of the limitation period brought about by the Law of 24 December 1993 and the immediate application of that statute by the Court of Cassation did, admittedly, prolong the period of time during which prosecutions could be brought in respect of the offences concerned, and they therefore detrimentally affected the applicants' situation, in particular by frustrating their expectations. However, this does not entail an infringement of the rights guaranteed by Article 7, since that provision cannot be interpreted as prohibiting an extension of limitation periods through the immediate application of a procedural law where the relevant offences have never become subject to limitation.
>
> The question whether Article 7 would be breached if a legal provision were to restore the possibility of punishing offenders for acts which were no longer punishable because they had already become subject to limitation is not pertinent to the present case and the Court is accordingly not required to examine it [...].

The Court notes that the applicants, who could not have been unaware that the conduct they were accused of might make them liable to prosecution, were convicted of offences in respect of which prosecution never became subject to limitation. The acts concerned constituted criminal offences at the time when they were committed and the penalties imposed were not heavier than those applicable at the material time. Nor did the applicants suffer, on account of the Law of 24 December 1993, greater detriment than they would have faced at the time when the offences were committed (see, *mutatis mutandis,* the Welch judgment cited above, p. 14, paragraph 34).

Consequently, the applicants' rights under Article 7 of the Convention were not infringed.

Non-retroactivity and the concept of continuous penalty

Article 7 does not prohibit the immediate application of the procedural laws (see the above-mentioned Coeme and Others judgment). Nor does it prevent the retroactive application of substantive laws more favourable to the accused. Thus, in the G. v. France judgment (27 September 1995, Application No. 15312/89, Series A No. 325-B, paragraphs 24 and 26-27), the Court declared:

According to the Court's case-law, Article 7, paragraph 1 (art. 7-1), of the Convention embodies generally the principle that only the law can define a crime and prescribe a penalty and prohibits in particular the retrospective application of the criminal law where it is to an accused's disadvantage (see the Kokkinakis v. Greece judgment of 25 May 1993, Series A No. 260-A, p. 22, paragraph 52).

[...]

The Court notes that the acts of which the applicant was accused also fell within the scope of the new legislation. On the basis of the principle that the more lenient law should apply both as regards the definition of the offence and the sanctions imposed, the national courts applied the new Article 333 of the Criminal Code for the imposition of sanctions as that provision downgraded the offence of which Mr G. was accused from serious offence (crime) to less serious offence *(délit)* (see paragraphs 13 and 14 above). Its application, admittedly retrospective, therefore operated in the applicant's favour.

In conclusion, there has been no violation of Article 7, paragraph 1 (art. 7-1), of the Convention.

The question of retroactivity may arise in respect of continuous offences. In the Ecer and Zeyrek v. Turkey case, the Court set out the precautions which the national authorities must take in regard to continuous offences in charges and in judgments. The applicants claimed that they had been given a prison sentence in application of a law of 1991 for offences committed in 1988 and 1989: they claimed that there had been a violation of Article 7 of the Convention. The government contended that the offences in question had continued until 1991. The Court held (27 February 2001, Applications Nos. 29295/95 and 29363/95, paragraphs 32-37):

[...] The only question to be determined is whether the 1991 Act was applied to offences committed before the Act came into force so that it constituted an *ex post facto* criminal penalty in breach of Article 7, paragraph 1, of the Convention.

The Court notes that the Government maintain that the offence of which the applicants were charged is to be considered a continuing offence under Article 169 of the Turkish Criminal Code (see paragraph 19). On that understanding, the Court observes that, by definition, a "continuing offence" is a type of crime committed over a period of time. In its view, when an accused is charged with a continuing offence, the principle of legal certainty requires that the acts which go to make up that offence, and which entail his criminal liability, be clearly set out in the bill of indictment (see, *mutatis mutandis*, Pélissier and Sassi v. France [GC], paragraph 51, No. 25444/94, ECHR 1999-II). Furthermore, the decision rendered by the domestic court must also make it clear that the accused's conviction and sentence result from a finding that the ingredients of a continuing offence have been made out by the prosecution.

In this connection, the Court observes that the Chief Public Prosecutor, in his indictment filed with the State Security Court, charged the applicants with offences committed "between 1988 and 1989". Furthermore, in its judgment of 12 May 1994 the State Security Court indicated that the applicants had been convicted on account of acts committed "in 1988 and 1989". Nowhere in its reasoned judgment did the State Security Court state that it had found the applicants guilty of any offences committed subsequent to 1989. For the European Court, it would appear to emerge from these considerations that the applicants stood trial in respect of offences allegedly committed by them in or between 1988 and 1989. Accordingly, and contrary to what was suggested by the Government, the Court considers that the years 1988 and 1989 cannot be taken to be the commencement dates of the offence at issue.

The Court further notes that, in seeking to substantiate the applicants' involvement in the PKK up until August 1993, the Government relied on their confession statements made in custody at the Sirnak Central Gendarme Command. Furthermore, with reference to the evidence given by a former PKK militant, the Government emphasised that the applicants had continued their activities even after 1989.

[...] in the Court's opinion, the introduction of such evidence of a continuing offence is inconsistent with the very terms of the indictment, which related to the years 1988 and 1989 only. [...] Furthermore, it does not appear from the State Security Court's judgment that any offences which they may have committed after 1989 constituted the basis of their conviction. Indeed, the focus of the trial court's decision would appear to have been on their activities carried out between 1988 and 1989. The Court must also take into account that, as regards other accused charged with continuing offences under the 1991 Act, the bills of indictment were carefully framed in order to indicate the dates of the incriminated acts [...].

In these circumstances, the Court concludes that the applicants were subject to the imposition of a heavier sentence under the 1991 Act than the sentence to which they were exposed at the time of the commission of the offence of which they were convicted.

Accordingly, there has been a violation of Article 7, paragraph 1, of the Convention.

Where one State is succeeded by another

In the K.-H.W. v. Germany case (22 March 2001, Application No. 37201/97, paragraphs 84-86), the Court examined the consequences to be drawn from

Article 7 from the aspect of the problem where one State succeeds another. In that case, proceedings had been initiated by the Federal German Republic on the basis of the laws of the former German Democratic Republic for the homicide of German citizens who had attempted to cross the border at the time of the wall. The Court stated:

> The Court considers that it is legitimate for a State governed by the rule of law to bring criminal proceedings against persons who have committed crimes under a former regime; similarly, the courts of such a State, having taken the place of those which existed previously, cannot be criticised for applying and interpreting the legal provisions in force at the material time in the light of the principles governing a State subject to the rule of law.

> Indeed, the Court reiterates that for the purposes of Article 7, paragraph 1, however clearly drafted a provision of criminal law may be, in any legal system, there is an inevitable element of judicial interpretation. There will always be a need for elucidation of doubtful points and for adaptation to changing circumstances (see the S.W. v. the United Kingdom and the R. v. the United Kingdom judgments of 22 November 1995, Series A Nos. 335-B and 335-C, pp. 41-42, paragraphs 34-36, and pp. 68-69, paragraphs 32-34 respectively – paragraph 45 above). Admittedly, that concept applies in principle to the gradual development of case-law in a given State subject to the rule of law and under a democratic regime, factors which constitute the cornerstones of the Convention, as its preamble states (see paragraph 86 below), but it remains wholly valid where, as in the present case, one State has succeeded another.

> Contrary reasoning would run counter to the very principles on which the whole system of protection put in place by the Convention is built. The framers of the Convention referred to those principles in the preamble to the Convention when they reaffirmed "their profound belief in those fundamental freedoms which are the foundation of justice and peace in the world and are best maintained on the one hand by an effective political democracy and on the other by a common understanding and observance of the human rights upon which they depend" and declared that they were "like-minded" and had "a common heritage of political traditions, ideals, freedom and the rule of law".

3. The penalty in the event of a violation of Article 7, paragraph 1

The first consequence is a violation of that Article. Thus, in the above-mentioned Jamil case, the Court concluded that there had been a violation of Article 6, paragraph 1, since Mr Jamil had been given a penalty that did not exist at the time of the facts and that the anti-drug trafficking law had been applied retroactively.

In the above-mentioned Welch judgment, the Court also concluded that there had been a violation of Article 7. It also made the following important point:

> [...] this conclusion concerns only the retrospective application of the relevant legislation and does not call into question in any respect the powers of confiscation conferred on the courts (for a non-retrospective application).

Article 7, paragraph 2 – Derogatory clause

Article 7, paragraph 2, is worded as follows:

> **2. This Article shall not prejudice the trial and punishment of any person for any act or omission which, at the time when it was omitted, was criminal according to the general principles of law recognised by civilised nations.**

The derogation in this provision refers to the Nuremberg principles in the event of war crimes and crimes against humanity.

Article 8 ECHR – The right to respect for private and family life

Article 8, paragraph 1

Article 8, paragraph 1, is worded as follows:

---
1. **Everyone has the right to respect for his private and family life, his home and his correspondence.**

---

1. The scope of Article 8, paragraph 1

Examination of the scope of Article 8 leads us to look at two aspects.

The first aspect is whether the obligation not to do something (the prohibition on interference with private life, etc.) must sometimes be accompanied by an obligation to do something (in order to ensure respect for private life, etc.).

The second aspect relates to the possible waiver of the rights recognised in Article 8.

Interference and inaction

The first consequence of Article 8, paragraph 1, is that the State must refrain from any interference. This follows from paragraph 2, which provides that "there shall be no interference by a public authority".

However, it is not only an "interference" that can entail a violation of Article 8. A simple failure to act on the part of the State may have the same effect. Member states must ensure effective respect for the rights established in the Convention. In that regard, the Court summarised in the Airey v. Ireland case (judgment of 9 October 1979, Series A No. 32, p. 17, paragraphs 32-33) the principles laid down in the earlier Marckx case. It will be recalled that in that case Mrs Airey had been unable to institute judicial separation proceedings in the absence of legal aid in Ireland. The Court stated that:

> The Court does not consider that Ireland can be said to have "interfered" with Mrs Airey's private or family life: the substance of her complaint is not that the State has acted but that it has failed to act. However, although the object of Article 8 (art. 8) is essentially that of protecting the individual against arbitrary interference by the public authorities, it does not merely compel the State to abstain from such interference: in addition to this primarily negative undertaking, there may be positive obligations inherent in an effective respect for private or family life (see the above-mentioned Marckx judgment, p. 15, paragraph 31).

> In Ireland, many aspects of private or family life are regulated by law. As regards marriage, husband and wife are in principle under a duty to cohabit but are entitled, in certain cases, to petition for a decree of judicial separation; this amounts to recognition of the fact that the protection of their private or family

life may sometimes necessitate their being relieved from the duty to live together.

Effective respect for private or family life obliges Ireland to make this means of protection effectively accessible, when appropriate, to anyone who may wish to have recourse thereto. However, it was not effectively accessible to the applicant: not having been put in a position in which she could apply to the High Court (see paragraphs 20-28 above), she was unable to seek recognition in law of her *de facto* separation from her husband. She has therefore been the victim of a violation of Article 8 (art. 8).

In the Rees v. the United Kingdom case (judgment of 17 October 1986, Series A No. 106, p. 15, paragraph 37) the Court explained how to determine whether or not a positive obligation exists.

In determining whether or not a positive obligation exists, regard must be had to the fair balance that has to be struck between the general interest of the community and the interests of the individual, the search for which balance is inherent in the whole of the Convention (see, *mutatis mutandis*, amongst others, the James and Others judgment of 21 February 1986, Series A No. 98, p. 34, paragraph 50, and the Sporrong and Lönnroth judgment of 23 September 1982, Series A No. 52, p. 26, paragraph 69). In striking this balance the aims mentioned in the second paragraph of Article 8 (art. 8-2) may be of a certain relevance, although this provision refers in terms only to "interferences" with the right protected by the first paragraph – in other words is concerned with the negative obligations flowing therefrom (see, *mutatis mutandis*, the Marckx judgment of 13 June 1979, Series A No. 31, p. 15, paragraph 31).

So the Court gives a useful indication of the difference between positive and negative obligations. However, in a more recent judgment it stressed the lack of precision attached to this distinction and the determination of the positive obligation of the State resulting from it (Keegan v. Ireland judgment of 26 May 1994, Series A No. 290, p. 19, paragraph 49):

The Court recalls that the essential object of Article 8 (art. 8) is to protect the individual against arbitrary action by the public authorities. There may in addition be positive obligations inherent in an effective "respect" for family life. However, the boundaries between the State's positive and negative obligations under this provision do not lend themselves to precise definition. The applicable principles are, none the less, similar. In both contexts regard must be had to the fair balance that has to be struck between the competing interests of the individual and of the community as a whole; and in both contexts the State enjoys a certain margin of appreciation (see, for example, the Powell and Rayner v. the United Kingdom judgment of 21 February 1990, Series A No. 172, p. 18, paragraph 41, and the above-mentioned Johnston and Others judgment, p. 25, paragraph 55).

Waiver of the right flowing from Article 8

In the M.S. v. Sweden judgment (27 August 1997, Application No. 20837/92, *Reports* 1997-IV, paragraphs 31-32), the Court agreed to examine the respondent government's argument that the applicant had waived her right under Article 8. It observed:

> In contesting the applicability of Article 8, paragraph 1, the Government submitted that, by having initiated the compensation proceedings, the applicant had waived her right to confidentiality with regard to the medical data which the clinic had communicated to the Office (see paragraph 11 above). The measure had constituted a foreseeable application of the relevant Swedish law, from which it clearly followed that the Office was under an obligation to request the information in issue, which the clinic had a corresponding duty to impart (see paragraphs 18-19 above). In this connection, they stressed that the data had not been made public but remained confidential in the Office (see paragraph 16 above).
>
> The Court observes that under the relevant Swedish law, the applicant's medical records at the clinic were governed by confidentiality (see paragraph 10 above). Communication of such data by the clinic to the Office would be permissible under the Insurance Act only if the latter authority had made a request and only to the extent that the information was deemed to be material to the application of the Insurance Act (see paragraph 18 above). This assessment was left exclusively to the competent authorities, the applicant having no right to be consulted or informed beforehand (see paragraph 21 above).
>
> It thus appears that the disclosure depended not only on the fact that the applicant had submitted her compensation claim to the Office but also on a number of factors beyond her control. It cannot therefore be inferred from her request that she had waived in an unequivocal manner her right under Article 8, paragraph 1, of the Convention to respect for private life with regard to the medical records at the clinic. Accordingly, the Court considers that this provision applies to the matters under consideration.

2. Article 8, paragraph 1, and protection of private life

It is appropriate to begin by defining the concept of "private life". The following are some illustrations of the protection afforded by Article 8.

The concept of private life

The concept of private life is not easy to define. The Court itself has said so. The limit between the public domain and the private domain varies from one case to another. The different judgments mentioned make it possible to form an idea of the Court's approach.

In the case of Niemietz v. Germany (judgment of 16 December 1992, Series A No. 251-B, pp. 33-34, paragraph 29) the law office of the applicant was searched by the Public Prosecutor's office and the police for documents which could reveal the identity of the person who had insulted a certain person. In its judgment the Court gave an elaborate statement of the notion "private life".

> The Court does not consider it possible or necessary to attempt an exhaustive definition of the notion of "private life". However, it would be too restrictive to limit the notion to an "inner circle" in which the individual may live his own

243

personal life as he chooses and to exclude therefrom entirely the outside world not encompassed within that circle. Respect for private life must also comprise to a certain degree the right to establish and develop relationships with other human beings.

There appears, furthermore, to be no reason of principle why this understanding of the notion of "private life" should be taken to exclude activities of a professional or business nature since it is, after all, in the course of their working lives that the majority of people have a significant, if not the greatest, opportunity of developing relationships with the outside world. This view is supported by the fact that, as was rightly pointed out by the Commission, it is not always possible to distinguish clearly which of an individual's activities form part of his professional or business life and which do not. Thus, especially in the case of a person exercising a liberal profession, his work in that context may form part and parcel of his life to such a degree that it becomes impossible to know in what capacity he is acting at a given moment of time.

To deny the protection of Article 8 (art. 8) on the ground that the measure complained of related only to professional activities – as the Government suggested should be done in the present case – could moreover lead to an inequality of treatment, in that such protection would remain available to a person whose professional and non-professional activities were so intermingled that there was no means of distinguishing between them. In fact, the Court has not heretofore drawn such distinctions: it concluded that there had been an interference with private life even where telephone tapping covered both business and private calls (see the Huvig v. France judgment of 24 April 1990, Series A No. 176-B, p. 41, paragraph 8, and p. 52, paragraph 25); and, where a search was directed solely against business activities, it did not rely on that fact as a ground for excluding the applicability of Article 8 (art. 8) under the head of "private life" (see the Chappell v. the United Kingdom judgment of 30 March 1989, Series A No. 152-A, pp. 12-13, paragraph 26, and pp. 21-22, paragraph 51.)

In the N.F. v. Italy case, disciplinary proceedings had been commenced against a number of judges who were members of the Freemasons and the list of those concerned was published, at least in part, in the press. The Court observed that the private sphere covers a person's physical and psychological integrity. However, it emphasised the easily accessible nature of the information disclosed (judgment of 2 August 2001, Application No. 37119/97) and concluded that there had been no interference:

The Court notes that, according to its case-law, private life, in the Court's view, encompasses a person's physical and psychological integrity; the guarantee afforded by Article 8 of the Convention is primarily intended to ensure the development, without outside interference, of the personality of each individual in his relations with other human beings (see the Botta v. Italy, judgment of 24 February 1998, *Reports of Judgments and Decisions* 1998-I, p. 422, paragraph 32). In the instant case the applicant has not proved that the disclosure by the press of his membership of the Freemasons caused him any injury in that regard. However, he acknowledged that "anyone could ascertain who was a member by consulting the register of members".

Accordingly, there has not been an interference.

In a recent case, Rotaru v. Romania, concerning the system of collecting and archiving information on persons (judgment of 4 May 2000, Application No. 28341/95, paragraphs 42-44), the Court established a number of nuances:

> The Government denied that Article 8 was applicable, arguing that the information in the RIS's letter of 19 December 1990 related not to the applicant's private life but to his public life. By deciding to engage in political activities and have pamphlets published, the applicant had implicitly waived his right to the "anonymity" inherent in private life. As to his questioning by the police and his criminal record, they were public information.

> The Court reiterates that the storing of information relating to an individual's private life in a secret register and the release of such information come within the scope of Article 8, paragraph 1 (see the Leander v. Sweden judgment of 26 March 1987, Series A No. 116, p. 22, paragraph 48).

> Respect for private life must also comprise to a certain degree the right to establish and develop relationships with other human beings: furthermore, there is no reason of principle to justify excluding activities of a professional or business nature from the notion of "private life" (see the Niemietz v. Germany judgment of 16 December 1992, Series A No. 251-B, pp. 33-34, paragraph 29, and the Halford v. the United Kingdom judgment of 25 June 1997, *Reports* 1997-III, pp. 1015-1016, paragraphs 42-46)

> The Court has already emphasised the correspondence of this broad interpretation with that of the Council of Europe's Convention of 28 January 1981 for the Protection of Individuals with regard to Automatic Processing of Personal Data, which came into force on 1 October 1985 and whose purpose is "to secure [...] for every individual [...] respect for his rights and fundamental freedoms, and in particular his right to privacy with regard to automatic processing of personal data relating to him" (Article 1), such personal data being defined in Article 2 as "any information relating to an identified or identifiable individual" (see Amann v. Switzerland [GC], No. 27798/95, paragraph 65, ECHR 2000-II).

> Moreover, public information can fall within the scope of private life where it is systematically collected and stored in files held by the authorities. That is all the truer where such information concerns a person's distant past.

> In the instant case the Court notes that the RIS's letter of 19 December 1990 contained various pieces of information about the applicant's life, in particular his studies, his political activities and his criminal record, some of which had been gathered more than fifty years earlier. In the Court's opinion, such information, when systematically collected and stored in a file held by agents of the State, falls within the scope of "private life" for the purposes of Article 8, paragraph 1, of the Convention. That is all the more so in the instant case as some of the information has been declared false and is likely to injure the applicant's reputation.

> Article 8 consequently applies.

In the P.G. and J.H. v. the United Kingdom judgment (25 September 2001, Application No. 44787/98, paragraphs 56-60), the Court provided a summary of its case-law. The case concerned the recording of the voices of persons who had been arrested, both in the custody cells and while the charges were being read to them by the police. These recordings, of which the persons concerned were not aware, were intended to be used for comparison with other voice recordings made in their apartments. The police hoped that they would thereby be able to impute to one or other of them the words recorded in the apartment. The Court held:

> Private life is a broad term not susceptible to exhaustive definition. The Court has already held that elements such as gender identification, name and sexual orientation and sexual life are important elements of the personal sphere protected by Article 8 (see, for example, the B. v. France judgment of 25 March 1992, Series A No. 232-C, paragraph 63; the Burghartz v. Switzerland judgment of 22 February 1994, Series A No. 280-B, paragraph 24; the Dudgeon v. the United Kingdom judgment of 22 October 1981, Series A No. 45, paragraph 41; and the Laskey, Jaggard and Brown v. the United Kingdom judgment of 19 February 1997, *Reports* 1997-I, paragraph 36). Article 8 also protects a right to identity and personal development, and the right to establish and develop relationships with other human beings and the outside world (see, for example, Burghartz v. Switzerland, Commission's report of 21 October 1992, op. cit., paragraph 47; and Friedl v. Austria, No. 15225/89, Commission's report of 19 May 1994, Series A No. 305-B, paragraph 45). It may include activities of a professional or business nature (see the Niemietz v. Germany judgment of 16 December 1992, Series A No. 251-B, paragraph 29; and the Halford v. the United Kingdom judgment of 25 June 1997, *Reports* 1997-III, paragraph 44). There is therefore a zone of interaction of a person with others, even in a public context, which may fall within the scope of "private life".
>
> There are a number of elements relevant to a consideration of whether a person's private life is concerned in measures effected outside a person's home or private premises. Since there are occasions when people knowingly or intentionally involve themselves in activities which are or may be recorded or reported in a public manner, a person's reasonable expectations as to privacy may be a significant, though not necessarily conclusive factor. A person who walks down the street will, inevitably, be visible to any member of the public who is also present. Monitoring by technological means of the same public scene (for example, a security guard viewing through close circuit television) is of a similar character. Private life considerations may arise however once any systematic or permanent record comes into existence of such material from the public domain. It is for this reason that files gathered by security services on a particular individual fall within the scope of Article 8 even where the information has not been gathered by any intrusive or covert method (see Rotaru v. Romania [GC], No. 28341/95, ECHR 2000-V, paragraphs 43-44). The Court has referred in this context to the Council of Europe's Convention of 28 January 1981 for the Protection of Individuals with regard to Automatic Processing of Personal Data, which came into force on 1 October 1985, whose purpose is "to secure in the territory of each Party for every individual [...] respect for his rights and fundamental freedoms, and in particular his right to privacy, with regard to the automatic processing of personal data relating to him" (Article 1), such data being defined as "any information relating to an identified or identifiable individual" (Article 2) (see Amman v. Switzerland [GC], No. 27798/95, ECHR 2000-II, paragraphs 65-67, where the

storing of information about the applicant on a card in a file was found to be an interference with private life, even though it contained no sensitive information and had probably never been consulted).

In the case of photographs, the Commission previously had regard, for the purpose of delimiting the scope of protection afforded by Article 8 against arbitrary interference by public authorities, to whether the taking of the photographs amounted to an intrusion into the individual's privacy, whether the photographs related to private matters or public incidents and whether the material obtained was envisaged for a limited use or was likely to be made available to the general public (see Friedl v. Austria, No. 15225/89, Commission's report of 19 May 1994, Series A No. 305-B, p. 21, paragraphs 49-52). Where photographs were taken of an applicant at a public demonstration in a public place and retained by the police in a file, the Commission found no interference with private life, giving weight to the fact that the photograph was taken and retained as a record of the demonstration and no action had been taken to identify the persons photographed on that occasion by means of data processing (see Friedl v. Austria above, paragraphs 51-52).

The Court's case-law has, on numerous occasions, found that the covert taping of telephone conversations falls within the scope of Article 8 in both aspects of the right guaranteed, namely, respect for private life and correspondence. While it is generally the case that the recordings were made for the purpose of using the content of the conversations in some way, the Court is not persuaded that recordings taken for use as voice samples can be regarded as falling outside the scope of the protection afforded by Article 8. A permanent record has none the less been made of the person's voice and it is subject to a process of analysis directly relevant to identifying that person in the context of other personal data. Though it is true that when being charged the applicants answered formal questions in a place where police officers were listening to them, the recording and analysis of their voices on this occasion must still be regarded as concerning the processing of personal data about the applicants.

The Court concludes therefore that the recording of the applicants' voices when being charged and when in their police cell discloses an interference with their right to respect for private life within the meaning of Article 8, paragraph 1, of the Convention.

It should further be noted that in the Stubbings and Others v. the United Kingdom judgment of 22 October 1996, *Reports* 1996-IV, paragraph 61), the Court recalled:

The Court observes, first, that Article 8 (art. 8) is clearly applicable to these complaints, which concern a matter of "private life", a concept which covers the physical and moral integrity of the person (see the X. and Y. v. the Netherlands judgment of 26 March 1985, Series A No. 91, p. 11, paragraph 22).

These examples are primarily concerned with cases of interference.

As regards cases of inactivity on the part of the State, reference may be made to the Botta v. Italy judgment, concerning a complaint by a handicap person that he was unable to gain proper access to the beaches. The Court gave a summary and a reminder of the principles which place a positive obligation on the State to ensure respect for private life (judgment of 24 February 1998, Application No. 21439/93, *Reports* 1998-I, paragraphs 32-35) and stated:

> Private life, in the Court's view, includes a person's physical and psychological integrity; the guarantee afforded by Article 8 of the Convention is primarily intended to ensure the development, without outside interference, of the personality of each individual in his relations with other human beings (see, *mutatis mutandis*, the Niemietz v. Germany judgment of 16 December 1992, Series A No. 251-B, p. 33, paragraph 29).

> In the instant case the applicant complained in substance not of action but of a lack of action by the State. While the essential object of Article 8 is to protect the individual against arbitrary interference by the public authorities, it does not merely compel the State to abstain from such interference: in addition to this negative undertaking, there may be positive obligations inherent in effective respect for private or family life. These obligations may involve the adoption of measures designed to secure respect for private life even in the sphere of the relations of individuals between themselves (see the X. and Y. v. the Netherlands judgment of 26 March 1985, Series A No. 91, p. 11, paragraph 23, and the Stjerna v. Finland judgment of 25 November 1994, Series A No. 299-B, p. 61, paragraph 38). However, the concept of respect is not precisely defined. In order to determine whether such obligations exist, regard must be had to the fair balance that has to be struck between the general interest and the interests of the individual, while the State has, in any event, a margin of appreciation.

> The Court has held that a State has obligations of this type where it has found a direct and immediate link between the measures sought by an applicant and the latter's private and/or family life.

> Thus, in the case of Airey v. Ireland (judgment of 9 October 1979, Series A No. 32), the Court held that the applicant had been the victim of a violation of Article 8 on the ground that under domestic law there was no system of legal aid in separation proceedings, which by denying access to court directly affected her private and family life.

> In the above-mentioned X. and Y. v. the Netherlands case, which concerned the rape of a mentally handicapped person and accordingly related to her physical and psychological integrity, the Court found that because of its shortcomings the Netherlands Criminal Code had not provided the person concerned with practical and effective protection (p. 14, paragraph 30).

> More recently, in the López Ostra v. Spain judgment (*mutatis mutandis*, 9 December 1994, Series A No. 303-C), in connection with the harmful effects of pollution caused by the activity of a waste-water treatment plant situated near the applicant's home, the Court held that the respondent State had not succeeded in striking a fair balance between the interest of the town of Lorca's economic well-being – that of having a waste-treatment plant – and the applicant's effective enjoyment of her right to respect for her home and her private and family life (p. 56, paragraph 58).

> Lastly, in the Guerra and Others v. Italy judgment of 19 February 1998 (*mutatis mutandis, Reports of Judgments and Decisions* 1998-I), the Court held that the

direct effect of the toxic emissions from the Enichem factory on the applicants' right to respect for their private and family life meant that Article 8 was applicable (p. 227, paragraph 57). It decided that Italy had breached that provision in that it had not communicated to the applicants essential information that would have enabled them to assess the risks they and their families might run if they continued to live in Manfredonia, a town particularly exposed to danger in the event of an accident within the confines of the factory (p. 228, paragraph 60).

In the instant case, however, the right asserted by Mr Botta, namely the right to gain access to the beach and the sea at a place distant from his normal place of residence during his holidays, concerns interpersonal relations of such broad and indeterminate scope that there can be no conceivable direct link between the measures the State was urged to take in order to make good the omissions of the private bathing establishments and the applicant's private life.

Accordingly, Article 8 is not applicable.

Examples of the application of Article 8 in relation to private life

The potentialities for the application of Article 8 are very important. They are by no means exhaustive, but they represent an attempt to illustrate the diversity of the situations in which that provision is used.

Article 8 and the right to a name

The Court has applied Article 8 to the patronymic name. In the Burghartz v. Switzerland case, the applicants "complained that the authorities had withheld from Mr Burghartz the right to put his own surname before their family name although Swiss law afforded that possibility to married women who had chosen their husbands' surname as their family name". In its judgment of 22 February 1994, Series A No. 280-B, p. 28, paragraph 24, the Court noted:

> Unlike some other international instruments, such as the International Covenant on Civil and Political Rights (Article 24, paragraph 2), the Convention on the Rights of the Child of 20 November 1989 (Articles 7 and 8) or the American Convention on Human Rights (Article 18), Article 8 (art. 8) of the Convention does not contain any explicit provisions on names. As a means of personal identification and of linking to a family, a person's name none the less concerns his or her private and family life. The fact that society and the State have an interest in regulating the use of names does not exclude this, since these public-law aspects are compatible with private life conceived of as including, to a certain degree, the right to establish and develop relationships with other human beings, in professional or business contexts as in others (see, *mutatis mutandis,* the Niemietz v. Germany judgment of 16 December 1992, Series A No. 251-B, p. 33, paragraph 29).

> In the instant case, the applicant's retention of the surname by which, according to him, he has become known in academic circles may significantly affect his career. Article 8 (art. 8) therefore applies.

Then, as concerned respect for Article 14 in conjunction with Article 8, the Court observed (pp. 28-29, paragraphs 25, 27 and 29):

> Mr and Mrs Burghartz complained that the authorities had withheld from Mr Burghartz the right to put his own surname before their family name although Swiss law afforded that possibility to married women who had chosen their husbands' surname as their family name. They said that this resulted in discrimination on the ground of sex, contrary to Articles 14 and 8 (art. 14 + 8) taken together.
>
> [...]
>
> The Court reiterates that the advancement of the equality of the sexes is today a major goal in the member States of the Council of Europe; this means that very weighty reasons would have to be put forward before a difference of treatment on the sole ground of sex could be regarded as compatible with the Convention (see, as the most recent authority, the Schuler-Zgraggen v. Switzerland judgment of 24 June 1993, Series A No. 263, pp. 21-22, paragraph 67).
>
> [...]
>
> The difference of treatment complained of lacks an objective and reasonable justification and accordingly contravenes Article 14 taken together with Article 8.

But the application of Article 8 to surnames is none the less limited. In the Stjerna v. Finland case (judgment of 25 November 1994, Series A No. 299-B, pp. 60-61, paragraphs 38-39), the Court considered that the requirements of public interest regarding the stability of the surname may be more important than the desire of the applicant to change his name:

> The refusal of the Finnish authorities to allow the applicant to adopt a specific new surname cannot, in the view of the Court, necessarily be considered an interference in the exercise of his right to respect for his private life, as would have been, for example, an obligation on him to change surname. [...]
>
> Despite the increased use of personal identity numbers in Finland and in other Contracting States, names retain a crucial role in the identification of people. Whilst therefore recognising that there may exist genuine reasons prompting an individual to wish to change his or her name, the Court accepts that legal restrictions on such a possibility may be justified in the public interest; for example in order to ensure accurate population registration or to safeguard the means of personal identification and of linking the bearers of a given name to a family.

In the instant case, the Court considered that the sources of inconvenience the applicant complained of – that is the difficulties in the spelling and pronunciation of his Swedish name in Finland and the possibility of turning his name into a pejorative nickname – were not sufficient to support the conclusion that the refusal of the Finnish authorities did constitute a lack of respect for his private life. Accordingly, Article 8 had not been violated.

In the Guillot v. France judgment (24 October 1996, *Reports of Judgments and Decisions* 1996-V, pp. 1602-1603, paragraphs 21-22), the Court considered that Article 8 also applies to forenames.

> The Court notes that Article 8 (art. 8) does not contain any explicit provisions on forenames. However, since they constitute a means of identifying persons within

their families and the community, forenames, like surnames (see, *mutatis mutandis*, the Burghartz v. Switzerland judgment of 22 February 1994, Series A No. 280-B, p. 28, paragraph 24, and the Stjerna v. Finland judgment of 25 November 1994, Series A No. 299-B, p. 60, paragraph 37), do concern private and family life.

Furthermore, the choice of a child's forename by its parents is a personal, emotional matter and therefore comes within their private sphere. The subject matter of the complaint thus falls within the ambit of Article 8 (art. 8), and indeed this was not contested.

The applicants wanted to give their daughter the name "Fleur de Marie". The registrar of births, deaths and marriages refused to register this name, since it did not appear in any calendar of saints' days. The Court concluded that Article 8 has not been violated. The child could regularly use the forename in issue without hindrance and the applicants were allowed by the French courts to register the forename as "Fleur-Marie".

Article 8 and sexual life

General observation

In the case of X. and Y. v. the Netherlands, judgment of 26 March 1985, Series A No. 91, p. 11, paragraph 22, the Court considered that the notion of "private life" is "a concept which covers the physical and moral integrity of the person, including his or her sexual life".

Homosexuality

The Court has held that the maintenance in force of legislation which has the effect of making homosexual acts between consulting adult males – that is over the age of 21 years – in private criminal offences constitutes a continuing – and in this case unjustified – interference with the applicants' right to respect for private life. (Dudgeon v. the United Kingdom, judgment of 22 October 1981, Series A No. 45, p. 24, paragraphs 60-61).

The A.D.T. v. the United Kingdom judgment (31 July 2000, Application No. 35765/97, paragraphs 32-34 and 38-39) concerns the criminalisation of homosexual relations between more than two consenting adults. The Court held:

> The Court recalls that in the case of Dudgeon, in which the Court was considering the existence of legislation, the Court (p. 24, paragraph 60) found no "pressing social need" for the criminalisation of homosexual acts between two consenting male adults over the age of 21 years, and that such justifications as there were for retaining the law were outweighed by the
>
> > "detrimental effects which the very existence of the legislative provisions in question can have on the life of a person of homosexual orientation like the applicant. Although members of the public who regard homosexuality as immoral may be shocked, offended or disturbed by the commission by others of private homosexual acts, this cannot on its own warrant the

application of penal sanctions when it is consenting adults alone who are involved."

Those principles were adopted and repeated in the subsequent cases of Norris v. Ireland (judgment of 26 October 1988, Series A No. 142, p. 20, paragraph 46), Modinos v. Cyprus (judgment of 22 April 1994, Series A No. 259, p. 12, paragraph 25) and Marangos v. Cyprus (No. 31106/96, Commission report of 3 December 1997).

There are differences between those decided cases and the present application. The principal point of distinction is that in the present case the sexual activities involved more than two men, and that the applicant was convicted for gross indecency as more than two men had been present.

[...]

Given the narrow margin of appreciation afforded to the national authorities in the case, the absence of any public health considerations and the purely private nature of the behaviour in the present case, the Court finds that the reasons submitted for the maintenance in force of legislation criminalising homosexual acts between men in private, and *a fortiori* the prosecution and conviction in the present case, are not sufficient to justify the legislation and the prosecution.

There has therefore been a violation of Article 8 of the Convention.

The case of Smith and Grady v. the United Kingdom (27 September 1999, Applications Nos. 33986/96 and 33986/96, paragraphs 71, 87-89 and 111-112) concerned investigations carried out by the military authorities into the homosexuality of members of the armed forces which led to their being excluded from the armed forces. The Court observed:

The Court notes that the Government have not claimed that the applicants waived their rights under Article 8 of the Convention when they initially joined the armed forces. It also notes that the applicants were not dismissed for failure to disclose their homosexuality on recruitment. Further, it finds from the evidence that Ms Smith only came to realise that she was homosexual after recruitment.

In these circumstances, the Court is of the view that the investigations by the military police into the applicants' homosexuality, which included detailed interviews with each of them and with third parties on matters relating to their sexual orientation and practices, together with the preparation of a final report for the armed forces' authorities on the investigations, constituted a direct interference with the applicants' right to respect for their private lives. Their consequent administrative discharge on the sole ground of their sexual orientation also constituted an interference with that right (see the Dudgeon v. the United Kingdom judgment of 22 October 1981, Series A No. 45, pp. 18-19, paragraph 41, and, *mutatis mutandis*, the Vogt v. Germany judgment of 26 September 1995, Series A No. 323, p. 23, paragraph 44).

[...]

An interference will be considered "necessary in a democratic society" for a legitimate aim if it answers a pressing social need and, in particular, is proportionate to the legitimate aim pursued (see the Norris judgment cited above, p. 18, paragraph 41).

Given the matters at issue in the present case, the Court would underline the link between the notion of "necessity" and that of a "democratic society", the hallmarks of the latter including pluralism, tolerance and broadmindedness (see the Vereinigung demokratischer Soldaten Österreichs and Gubi judgment cited above, p. 17, paragraph 36, and the Dudgeon judgment cited above, p. 21, paragraph 53).

The Court recognises that it is for the national authorities to make the initial assessment of necessity, though the final evaluation as to whether the reasons cited for the interference are relevant and sufficient is one for this Court. A margin of appreciation is left to Contracting States in the context of this assessment, which varies according to the nature of the activities restricted and of the aims pursued by the restrictions (see the Dudgeon judgment cited above, pp. 21 and 23, paragraphs 52 and 59).

Accordingly, when the relevant restrictions concern "a most intimate part of an individual's private life", there must exist "particularly serious reasons" before such interferences can satisfy the requirements of Article 8, paragraph 2, of the Convention (see the Dudgeon judgment cited above, p. 21, paragraph 52).

When the core of the national security aim pursued is the operational effectiveness of the armed forces, it is accepted that each State is competent to organise its own system of military discipline and enjoys a certain margin of appreciation in this respect (see the Engel and Others judgment cited above, p. 25, paragraph 59). The Court also considers that it is open to the State to impose restrictions on an individual's right to respect for his private life where there is a real threat to the armed forces' operational effectiveness, as the proper functioning of an army is hardly imaginable without legal rules designed to prevent service personnel from undermining it. However, the national authorities cannot rely on such rules to frustrate the exercise by individual members of the armed forces of their right to respect for their private lives, which right applies to service personnel as it does to others within the jurisdiction of the State. Moreover, assertions as to a risk to operational effectiveness must be "substantiated by specific examples" (see, *mutatis mutandis*, the Vereinigung demokratischer Soldaten Österreichs and Gubi judgment cited above, p. 17, paragraphs 36 and 38, and the Grigoriades judgment cited above, pp. 2589-2590, paragraph 45).

[...]

[...] the Court finds that neither the investigations conducted into the applicants' sexual orientation, nor their discharge on the grounds of their homosexuality in pursuance of the Ministry of Defence policy, were justified under Article 8, paragraph 2, of the Convention.

Accordingly, there has been a violation of Article 8 of the Convention.

(*Idem* the Lustig-Prean and Beckett v. the United Kingdom judgment of 27 September 1999.)

Transsexualism

The Court has also dealt with the question of transsexualism. In the B. v. France case (25 March 1992, Series A No. 232-C, p. 52, paragraph 58) it took the view that there had been a breach of Article 8 with regard to a transsexual who had not succeeded in having his masculine civil status altered on his official documents. In that case the Court first of all stated that:

> The judgments supplied to the Court by the Government do indeed show that non-recognition of the change of sex does not necessarily prevent the person in question from obtaining a new forename which will better reflect his or her physical appearance (see paragraph 23 above).

> However, this case-law was not settled at the time when the Libourne and Bordeaux courts gave their rulings. Indeed, it does not appear to be settled even today, as the Court of Cassation has apparently never had an occasion to confirm it.

The Court thus accepted the applicant's argument that the indication of her – original – sex in official documents, administrative documents (INSEE number),[1] etc., was the source of daily problems in her private life. While reaching its conclusion, the Court observed (pp. 53-54, paragraphs 62-63) that:

> [...] the inconveniences complained of by the applicant in this field reach a sufficient degree of seriousness to be taken into account for the purposes of Article 8 (art. 8).

> [...]

> The Court [...] reaches the conclusion, on the basis of the above-mentioned factors which distinguish the present case from the Rees and Cossey cases and without it being necessary to consider the applicant's other arguments, that she finds herself daily in a situation which, taken as a whole, is not compatible with the respect due to her private life. Consequently, even having regard to the State's margin of appreciation, the fair balance which has to be struck between the general interest and the interests of the individual (see paragraph 44 above) has not been attained, and there has thus been a violation of Article 8 (art. 8).

> The respondent State has several means to choose from for remedying this state of affairs. It is not the Court's function to indicate which is the most appropriate [...].

Thus, the Court does not impose on the State the obligation to accept a change of sex in official documents. The State must, however, take measures of its choosing to remedy the violation of Article 8 that results from the situation the applicant finds herself in.

------

1. Translator's note: the number allocated to each person by the Institut national de la statistique et des études économiques (National Institute for Statistics and Economic Studies); the first digit indicates the person's sex and the number is widely used, being, *inter alia*, the basis of the social security number.

In the case of X. Y. and Z. v. the United Kingdom (22 April 1997, *Reports of Judgments and Decisions* 1997-II, pp. 632 and 635, paragraphs 42 and 52), the applicant, X., who is a female-to-male transsexual, was not permitted to be registered as father of the child that was born to his partner, Y., by artificial insemination with sperm from an anonymous donor. After having established that in this case there is "family life" within the meaning of Article 8 of the Convention, the Court considered:

> The present case is distinguishable from the previous cases concerning transsexuals which have been brought before the Court (see the above-mentioned Rees judgment, the above-mentioned Cossey judgment and the B. v. France judgment of 25 March 1992, Series A No. 232-C), because here the applicants' complaint is not that the domestic law makes no provision for the recognition of the transsexual's change of identity, but rather that it is not possible for such a person to be registered as the father of a child; indeed, it is for this reason that the Court is examining this case in relation to family, rather than private, life (see paragraph 37 above).

> It is true that the Court has held in the past that where the existence of a family tie with a child has been established, the State must act in a manner calculated to enable that tie to be developed and legal safeguards must be established that render possible, from the moment of birth or as soon as practicable thereafter, the child's integration in his family (see for example the above-mentioned Marckx judgment, p. 15, paragraph 31; the Johnston and Others v. Ireland judgment of 18 December 1986, Series A No. 112, p. 29, paragraph 72; the above-mentioned Keegan judgment, p. 19, paragraph 50; and the above-mentioned Kroon and Others judgment, p. 56, paragraph 32). However, hitherto in this context it has been called upon to consider only family ties existing between biological parents and their offspring. The present case raises different issues, since Z. was conceived by AID and is not related, in the biological sense, to X., who is a transsexual.

In the instant case, the Court held that there was no common standard in the member states with regard to the granting of parental rights to transsexuals and that they must be afforded a wide margin of appreciation (paragraph 44). It concluded:

> In conclusion, given that transsexuality raises complex scientific, legal, moral and social issues, in respect of which there is no generally shared approach among the Contracting States, the Court is of the opinion that Article 8 (art. 8) cannot, in this context, be taken to imply an obligation for the respondent State formally to recognise as the father of a child a person who is not the biological father. That being so, the fact that the law of the United Kingdom does not allow special legal recognition of the relationship between X. and Z. does not amount to a failure to respect family life within the meaning of that provision (art. 8).

See also the Sheffield and Horsham v. the United Kingdom judgment (30 July 1998, Applications Nos. 22885/93 and 23390/94, *Reports* 1998-V, paragraph 60), where the Court stated:

> [...] it is nevertheless the case that there is an increased social acceptance of transsexualism and an increased recognition of the problems which post-

operative transsexuals encounter. Even if it finds no breach of Article 8 in this case, the Court reiterates that this area needs to be kept under review by Contracting States.

Sado-masochistic acts

Although the Court has stated that the sexual life of a person is protected by Article 8 of the Convention, it observed in the Laskey, Jaggard and Brown v. the United Kingdom judgment (19 February 1997, *Reports of Judgments and Decisions* 1997-I, pp. 131-133, paragraphs 36, 43, 44, 45, 46 and 49) that:

> [...] not every sexual activity carried out behind closed doors necessarily falls within the scope of Article 8 (art. 8). In the present case, the applicants were involved in consensual sado-masochistic activities for purposes of sexual gratification. There can be no doubt that sexual orientation and activity concern an intimate aspect of private life (see, *mutatis mutandis*, the Dudgeon v. the United Kingdom judgment of 22 October 1981, Series A No. 45, p. 21, paragraph 52). However, a considerable number of people were involved in the activities in question which included, *inter alia*, the recruitment of new "members", the provision of several specially equipped "chambers" and the shooting of many videotapes which were distributed among the "members" (see paragraphs 8 and 9 above). It may thus be open to question whether the sexual activities of the applicants fell entirely within the notion of "private life" in the particular circumstances of the case.

> However, since this point has not been disputed by those appearing before it, the Court sees no reason to examine it of its own motion in the present case. Assuming, therefore, that the prosecution and conviction of the applicants amounted to an interference with their private life, the question arises whether such an interference was "necessary in a democratic society" within the meaning of the second paragraph of Article 8 (art. 8-2).

> [...]

> The applicants maintained that the interference in issue could not be regarded as "necessary in a democratic society". This submission was contested by the Government and by a majority of the Commission.

> In support of their submission, the applicants alleged that all those involved in the sado-masochistic encounters were willing adult participants; that participation in the acts complained of was carefully restricted and controlled and was limited to persons with like-minded sado-masochistic proclivities; that the acts were not witnessed by the public at large and that there was no danger or likelihood that they would ever be so witnessed; that no serious or permanent injury had been sustained, no infection had been caused to the wounds, and that no medical treatment had been required. Furthermore, no complaint was ever made to the police – who learnt about the applicants' activities by chance (see paragraph 8 above).

> The potential for severe injury or for moral corruption was regarded by the applicants as a matter of speculation. [...]

> According to the Court's established case-law, the notion of necessity implies that the interference corresponds to a pressing social need and, in particular, that

it is proportionate to the legitimate aim pursued; in determining whether an interference is "necessary in a democratic society", the Court will take into account that a margin of appreciation is left to the national authorities (see, *inter alia*, the Olsson v. Sweden (No. 1) judgment of 24 March 1988, Series A No. 130, pp. 31-32, paragraph 67), whose decision remains subject to review by the Court for conformity with the requirements of the Convention.

The scope of this margin of appreciation is not identical in each case but will vary according to the context. Relevant factors include the nature of the Convention right in issue, its importance for the individual and the nature of the activities concerned (see the Buckley v. the United Kingdom judgment of 25 September 1996, *Reports of Judgments and Decisions* 1996-IV, pp. 1291-1292, paragraph 74).

The Court considers that one of the roles which the State is unquestionably entitled to undertake is to seek to regulate, through the operation of the criminal law, activities which involve the infliction of physical harm. This is so whether the activities in question occur in the course of sexual conduct or otherwise.

The determination of the level of harm that should be tolerated by the law in situations where the victim consents is in the first instance a matter for the State concerned since what is at stake is related, on the one hand, to public health considerations and to the general deterrent effect of the criminal law and, on the other, to the personal autonomy of the individual.

The applicants have contended that, in the circumstances of the case, the behaviour in question formed part of private morality which is not the State's business to regulate. In their submission the matters for which they were prosecuted and convicted concerned only private sexual behaviour.

The Court is not persuaded by this submission. It is evident from the facts established by the national courts that the applicants' sado-masochistic activities involved a significant degree of injury or wounding which could not be characterised as trifling or transient. This, in itself, suffices to distinguish the present case from those applications which have previously been examined by the Court concerning consensual homosexual behaviour in private between adults where no such feature was present (see the Dudgeon judgment cited above, the Norris v. Ireland judgment of 26 October 1988, Series A No. 142, and the Modinos v. Cyprus judgment of 22 April 1993, Series A No. 259).

Nor does the Court accept the applicants' submission that no prosecution should have been brought against them since their injuries were not severe and since no medical treatment had been required.

In deciding whether or not to prosecute, the State authorities were entitled to have regard not only to the actual seriousness of the harm caused – which as noted above was considered to be significant – but also, as stated by Lord Jauncey of Tullichettle (see paragraph 21 above), to the potential for harm inherent in the acts in question. In this respect it is recalled that the activities were considered by Lord Templeman to be "unpredictably dangerous" (see paragraph 20 above).

The Court held in that case that there had been no violation of Article 8 of the Convention. It observed that:

[...] the charges of assault were numerous and referred to illegal activities which had taken place over more than ten years. However, only a few charges were selected for inclusion in the prosecution case. It further notes that, in recognition of the fact that the applicants did not appreciate their actions to be criminal, reduced sentences were imposed on appeal (see paragraphs 15-17 above). In these circumstances, bearing in mind the degree of organisation involved in the offences, the measures taken against the applicants cannot be regarded as disproportionate.

Surveillance of persons

Physical surveillance

In the Cyprus v. Turkey judgment, the Court observed (judgment of 10 May 2001, Application No. 25781/94, paragraphs 300-301):

> In this connection the Court cannot but endorse the Commission's conclusion at paragraph 489 of its report that the restrictions which beset the daily lives of the enclaved Greek Cypriots create a feeling among them "of being compelled to live in a hostile environment in which it is hardly possible to lead a normal private and family life". The Commission noted in support of this conclusion that the adverse circumstances to which the population concerned was subjected included: the absence of normal means of communication (see paragraph 45 above); the unavailability in practice of the Greek-Cypriot press (see paragraph 45 above); the insufficient number of priests (see paragraph 47 above); the difficult choice with which parents and schoolchildren were faced regarding secondary education (see paragraphs 43-44 above); the restrictions and formalities applied to freedom of movement, including, the Court would add, for the purposes of seeking medical treatment and participation in bi- or inter-communal events; and the impossibility of preserving property rights upon departure or on death (see paragraph 40 above).

> The Court, like the Commission, considers that these restrictions are factors which aggravate the violations which it has found in respect of the right of the enclaved Greek Cypriots to respect for private and family life (see paragraph 296) [...].

Surveillance by listening

In the P.G. and J.H. v. the United Kingdom judgment (25 September 2001, Application No. 44787/98, paragraphs 9-14 and 35-38), the Court held that the installation of a covert listening device in a sofa in the applicant's flat in the context of an investigation in order to capture the conversations of the various occupants constituted an interference with the right to respect for private life. In this case, it held that the interference did not comply with the conditions of Article 8, paragraph 2.

The problem of listening arises most frequently in the case of telephone tapping.

It should be noted, first of all, that the mere existence of a law authorising telephone tapping may entail a violation of Article 8 provided that that law makes no provision for control on the part of the users. In the Halford v. the United Kingdom judgment (25 June 1997, Application No. 20605/92, *Reports* 1997-III, paragraph 56), the Court recalled this solution, which was put forward in the Klass judgment:

> The Court recalls that in the above-mentioned Klass and Others case it was called upon to decide, *inter alia*, whether legislation which empowered the authorities secretly to monitor the correspondence and telephone conversations of the applicants, who were unable to establish whether such measures had in fact been applied to them, amounted to an interference with their Article 8 rights (art. 8). The Court held in that case that "in the mere existence of the legislation itself there is involved, for all those to whom the legislation could be applied, a menace of surveillance; this menace necessarily strikes at freedom of communication between users of the postal and telecommunication services and thereby constitutes an 'interference by a public authority' with the exercise of the applicants' right to respect for private and family life and for correspondence" (p. 21, paragraph 41).

According to established case-law, the tapping of business telephone lines comes within the scope of Article 8. Thus, in the case of Kopp v. Switzerland (25 March 1998, Application No. 23224/94, *Reports* 1998-II, paragraphs 50 and 53), the Court observed:

> In the Court's view, it is clear from its case-law that telephone calls made from or to business premises, such as those of a law firm, may be covered by the notions of "private life" and "correspondence" within the meaning of Article 8, paragraph 1 (see, among other authorities, the Halford v. the United Kingdom judgment of 25 June 1997, *Reports* 1997-III, p. 1016, paragraph 44, and, *mutatis mutandis*, the Niemietz v. Germany judgment of 16 December 1992, Series A No. 251-B, pp. 33-35, paragraphs 28-33). This point was in fact not disputed.
>
> [...]
>
> The subsequent use of the recordings made has no bearing on that finding.

The same solution was reached in the Halford v. the United Kingdom judgment (25 June 1997, Application No. 20605/92, *Reports* 1997-III, paragraph 42). In that judgment, moreover, the Court found that a reasonable probability that the applicant's business line had been tapped was sufficient to establish an interference. It noted (paragraph 48):

> The Court agrees. The evidence justifies the conclusion that there was a reasonable likelihood that calls made by Ms Halford from her office were intercepted by the Merseyside police with the primary aim of gathering material to assist in the defence of the sex-discrimination proceedings brought against them (see paragraph 17 above). This interception constituted an "interference by a public authority", within the meaning of Article 8, paragraph 2 (art. 8-2), with the exercise of Ms Halford's right to respect for her private life and correspondence.

The case of Malone v. the United Kingdom (2 August 1984, Series A No. 82, pp. 30-33, paragraphs 64-68) provided the Court with a new opportunity to rule on the conditions which a law-making provision for telephone tapping must satisfy for the purpose of Article 8, paragraph 2, which authorises interferences with private life. It stated, first of all, that there had been interferences with the applicant's rights as guaranteed by Article 8. It then described the characteristics of the law on which the respondent State relied:

> It was common ground that one telephone conversation to which the applicant was a party was intercepted at the request of the police under a warrant issued by the Home Secretary (see paragraph 14 above). As telephone conversations are covered by the notions of "private life" and "correspondence" within the meaning of Article 8 (art. 8) (see the Klass and Others judgment of 6 September 1978, Series A No. 28, p. 21, paragraph 41), the admitted measure of interception involved an "interference by a public authority" with the exercise of a right guaranteed to the applicant under paragraph 1 of Article 8 (art. 8-1).

> [...]

> The principal issue of contention was whether the interferences found were justified under the terms of paragraph 2 of Article 8 (art. 8-2), notably whether they were "in accordance with the law" and "necessary in a democratic society" for one of the purposes enumerated in that paragraph.

> The first such principle was that the word "law/*loi*" is to be interpreted as covering not only written law but also unwritten law (see the above-mentioned *Sunday Times* judgment, p. 30, paragraph 47). A second principle, recognised by Commission, Government and applicant as being applicable in the present case, was that "the interference in question must have some basis in domestic law" (see the above-mentioned Silver and Others judgment, p. 33, paragraph 86). The expressions in question were, however, also taken to include requirements over and above compliance with the domestic law. [...]

> The Court would reiterate its opinion that the phrase "in accordance with the law" does not merely refer back to domestic law but also relates to the quality of the law, requiring it to be compatible with the rule of law, which is expressly mentioned in the preamble to the Convention (see, *mutatis mutandis*, the above-mentioned Silver and Others judgment, p. 34, paragraph 90, and the Golder judgment of 21 February 1975, Series A No. 18, p. 17, paragraph 34). The phrase thus implies – and this follows from the object and purpose of Article 8 (art. 8) – that there must be a measure of legal protection in domestic law against arbitrary interferences by public authorities with the rights safeguarded by paragraph 1 (art. 8-1) (see the report of the Commission, paragraph 121). Especially where a power of the executive is exercised in secret, the risks of arbitrariness are evident (see the above-mentioned Klass and Others judgment, Series A No. 28, pp. 21 and 23, paragraphs 42 and 49). [...] Nevertheless, the law must be sufficiently clear in its terms to give citizens an adequate indication as to the circumstances in which and the conditions on which public authorities are empowered to resort to this secret and potentially dangerous interference with the right to respect for private life and correspondence.

In that case, the Court considered that the law in issue was not sufficiently precise, in that it did not set out with sufficient precision the scope of the authorities' discretion and the rules governing its exercise. The Court did not deem it necessary to consider the other conditions of paragraph 2 in order to find that there had been a violation of Article 8, paragraph 1 (the same solution was reached in the Khan v. the United Kingdom judgment of 12 May 2000, Application No. 35394/97, paragraphs 22-28; see also the P.G. and J.H. v. the United Kingdom judgment of 25 September 2001, Application No. 44787/98, paragraphs 35-38).

In the Lambert v. France judgment, the Court also examined the law authorising telephone interceptions in France. While it accepted that this law provided sufficient guarantees for the person whose telephone line it was, it found that there was insufficient protection of third parties holding conversations on those lines. In this case, an individual's telephone line had been tapped. Following the tapping of the telephone and the interception of a number of his conversations, the applicant, who was not the owner of the telephone line but had called the individual in question, was charged with aggravated handling of stolen goods. He had then claimed that the tapping of the telephone was void. His appeals were dismissed on the ground that he lacked standing to criticise the conditions in which the tapping of a line allocated to a third party had been ordered. That decision was upheld by the Court of Cassation. The Court held (judgment of 24 August 1998, Application No. 23618/94, paragraphs 21, 28 and 38-41):

> The Court points out that as telephone conversations are covered by the notions of "private life" and "correspondence" within the meaning of Article 8, the admitted measure of interception amounted to "interference by a public authority" with the exercise of a right secured to the applicant in paragraph 1 of that Article (see, among other authorities, the following judgments: Malone v. the United Kingdom, 2 August 1984, Series A No. 82, p. 30, paragraph 64; Kruslin v. France and Huvig v. France, 24 April 1990, Series A No. 176-A and B, p. 20, paragraph 26, and p. 52, paragraph 25; Halford v. the United Kingdom, 25 June 1997, *Reports of Judgments and Decisions* 1997-III, pp. 1016–1017, paragraph 48; and Kopp v. Switzerland, 25 March 1998, *Reports* 1998-II, p. 540, paragraph 53). In this connection, it is of little importance that the telephone tapping in question was carried out on the line of a third party.
>
> [...]
>
> The Court considers, as the Commission did, that Articles 100 *et seq.* of the Code of Criminal Procedure, inserted by the Law of 10 July 1991 on the confidentiality of telecommunications messages, lay down clear, detailed rules and specify with sufficient clarity the scope and manner of exercise of the relevant discretion conferred on the public authorities (see the Kruslin and Huvig judgments cited above, pp. 24-25, paragraphs 35-36, and p. 56, paragraphs 34-35, respectively, and, as the most recent authority and, *mutatis mutandis*, the Kopp judgment cited above, pp. 541-543, paragraphs 62-75).
>
> [...] However, it has to be recognised that the Court of Cassation's reason' could lead to decisions whereby a very large number of people are depriv the protection of the law, namely all those who have conversations on phone line other than their own. That would in practice render the pr machinery largely devoid of substance.

That was the case with the applicant, who did not enjoy the effective protection of national law, which does not make any distinction according to whose line is being tapped (Articles 100 *et seq.* of the Code of Criminal Procedure – see paragraph 15 above).

The Court therefore considers, like the Commission, that the applicant did not have available to him the "effective control" to which citizens are entitled under the rule of law and which would have been capable of restricting the interference in question to what was "necessary in a democratic society".

There has consequently been a violation of Article 8 of the Convention.

On investigations of this type, and their justification under Article 8, paragraph 2, the following passage from the P.G. and J.H. v. the United Kingdom judgment (25 September 2001, Application No. 44787/98, paragraph 62) is relevant:

It recalls that the Government relied as the legal basis for the measure on the general powers of the police to store and gather evidence. While it may be permissible to rely on the implied powers of police officers to note evidence and collect and store exhibits for steps taken in the course of an investigation, it is trite law that specific statutory or other express legal authority is required for more invasive measures, whether searching private property or taking personal body samples. The Court has found that the lack of any express basis in law for the interception of telephone calls on public and private telephone systems and for using covert surveillance devices on private premises does not conform with the requirement of lawfulness (see the Malone, Halford and Khan judgments cited above). It considers that no material difference arises where the recording device is operated, without the knowledge or consent of the individual concerned, on police premises. The underlying principle that domestic law should provide protection against arbitrariness and abuse in the use of covert surveillance techniques applies equally in that situation.

Surveillance by metering

In the above-mentioned case of Malone (judgment of 2 August 1984), the Court considered that metering also infringes a right laid down in Article 8 (ibid., pp. 37-38, paragraphs 83-84):

The process known as "metering" involves the use of a device (a meter check printer) which registers the numbers dialled on a particular telephone and the time and duration of each call (see paragraph 56 above).

[...]

A meter check printer registers information that a supplier of a telephone service may in principle legitimately obtain, notably in order to ensure that the subscriber is correctly charged or to investigate complaints or possible abuses of the service. By its very nature, metering is therefore to be distinguished from interception of communications, which is undesirable and illegitimate in a democratic society unless justified. The Court does not accept, however, that the use of data obtained from metering, whatever the circumstances and purposes, ∩nnot give rise to an issue under Article 8 (art. 8). The records of metering ⸱ain information, in particular the numbers dialled, which is an integral element in the communications made by telephone. Consequently, release of that information to the police without the consent of the subscriber also amounts, in the opinion of the Court, to an interference with a right guaranteed by Article 8 (art. 8).

The Court held that practice not "in accordance with the law", within the meaning of paragraph 2 of Article 8. In the P.G. and J.H. v. the United Kingdom judgment (25 September 2001, Application No. 44787/98, paragraphs 42-51), the Court examined a similar case but concluded that the interference was in accordance with a law meeting the requirements of Article 8, paragraph 2.

Information-gathering activities

The Court has also ruled on information-gathering activities. In the Leander v. Sweden judgment (26 March 1987, Series A No. 116, pp. 22 and 25-27, paragraphs 48, 60, 65 and 67) the Court held that the impugned information-gathering activities constituted a violation of Article 8, paragraph 1. In that case Mr Leander had been refused a post in a naval base in the light of information obtained about him by the State services. The information-gathering activity in question was held to be necessary in a democratic society for the maintenance of national security. The Court observed that.

> It is uncontested that the secret police register contained information relating to Mr Leander's private life.

> Both the storing and the release of such information, which were coupled with a refusal to allow Mr Leander an opportunity to refute it, amounted to an interference with his right to respect for private life as guaranteed by Article 8, paragraph 1 (art. 8-1).

But in developing its reasoning, the Court ruled that this interference was justified under paragraph 2. The Swedish Government claimed that the register in question was intended to assist in appointing candidates to a post on a naval base and argued security considerations. The Court accepted this position, judging that the holding of information concerning Mr Leander was necessary for maintaining national security in a democratic society. Nevertheless, the Court insisted that the existence and use of such a register should be subject to safeguards:

> Nevertheless, in view of the risk that a system of secret surveillance for the protection of national security poses of undermining or even destroying democracy on the ground of defending it, the Court must be satisfied that there exist adequate and effective guarantees against abuse (see the Klass and Others judgment of 6 September 1978, Series A No. 28, pp. 23-24, paragraphs 49-50).

> [...]

> The Court attaches particular importance to the presence of parliamentarians on the National Police Board and to the supervision effected by the Chancellor of Justice and the Parliamentary Ombudsman as well as the Parliamentary Committee on Justice (see paragraph 62 above, Nos. v, x, xi and xii).

The Court, like the Commission, thus reaches the conclusion that the safeguards contained in the Swedish personnel control system meet the requirements of paragraph 2 of Article 8 (art. 8-2). Having regard to the wide margin of appreciation available to it, the respondent State was entitled to consider that in the present case the interests of national security prevailed over the individual interests of the applicant (see paragraph 59 above). The interference to which Mr Leander was subjected cannot therefore be said to have been disproportionate to the legitimate aim pursued.

Personal data

Medical secrecy

Article 8 of the Convention is also particularly relevant for the protection of personal data. In the Z. v. Finland judgment (25 February 1997, *Reports of Judgments and Decisions* 1997-I, p. 347-348, paragraphs 95-99) the Court gave some general guidelines with regard to its assessment of cases in which the disclosure of personal data is at stake. In the case of Z. v. Finland confidential medical information of the applicant was disclosed without her prior consent for the benefit of criminal proceedings concerning the husband of the applicant.

In this connection, the Court will take into account that the protection of personal data, not least medical data, is of fundamental importance to a person's enjoyment of his or her right to respect for private and family life as guaranteed by Article 8 of the Convention (art. 8). Respecting the confidentiality of health data is a vital principle in the legal systems of all the Contracting Parties to the Convention. It is crucial not only to respect the sense of privacy of a patient but also to preserve his or her confidence in the medical profession and in the health services in general.

Without such protection, those in need of medical assistance may be deterred from revealing such information of a personal and intimate nature as may be necessary in order to receive appropriate treatment and, even, from seeking such assistance, thereby endangering their own health and, in the case of transmissible diseases, that of the community (see Recommendation No. R (89) 14 on the ethical issues of HIV infection in the health care and social settings, adopted by the Committee of Ministers of the Council of Europe on 24 October 1989, in particular the general observations on confidentiality of medical data in paragraph 165 of the explanatory memorandum).

The domestic law must therefore afford appropriate safeguards to prevent any such communication or disclosure of personal health data as may be inconsistent with the guarantees in Article 8 of the Convention (art. 8) (see, *mutatis mutandis*, Articles 3, paragraph 2.c, 5, 6 and 9 of the Convention for the Protection of Individuals with regard to Automatic Processing of Personal Data, European Treaty Series No. 108, Strasbourg, 1981).

The above considerations are especially valid as regards protection of the confidentiality of information about a person's HIV infection. The disclosure of such data may dramatically affect his or her private and family life, as well as social and employment situation, by exposing him or her to opprobrium and the risk of ostracism. For this reason it may also discourage persons from seeking diagnosis or treatment and thus undermine any preventive efforts by the community to contain the pandemic (see the above-mentioned explanatory memorandum to Recommendation No. R (89) 14, paragraphs 166-68). The interests in protecting the confidentiality of such information will therefore weigh heavily in the balance in determining whether the interference was proportionate to the legitimate aim pursued. Such interference cannot be compatible with Article 8 of the Convention (art. 8) unless it is justified by an overriding requirement in the public interest.

In view of the highly intimate and sensitive nature of information concerning a person's HIV status, any State measures compelling communication or disclosure of such information without the consent of the patient call for the most careful scrutiny on the part of the Court, as do the safeguards designed to secure an effective protection (see, *mutatis mutandis*, the Dudgeon v. the United Kingdom judgment of 22 October 1981, Series A No. 45, p. 21, paragraph 52; and the Johansen v. Norway judgment of 7 August 1996, *Reports of Judgments and Decisions* 1996-III, pp. 1003-1004, paragraph 64).

At the same time, the Court accepts that the interests of a patient and the community as a whole in protecting the confidentiality of medical data may be outweighed by the interest in investigation and prosecution of crime and in the publicity of court proceedings (see, *mutatis mutandis*, Article 9 of the above-mentioned 1981 data protection convention), where such interests are shown to be of even greater importance.

It must be borne in mind in the context of the investigative measures in issue that it is not for the Court to substitute its views for those of the national authorities as to the relevance of evidence used in the judicial proceedings (see, for instance, the above-mentioned Johansen judgment, pp. 1006-1007, paragraph 73).

As to the issues regarding access by the public to personal data, the Court recognises that a margin of appreciation should be left to the competent national authorities in striking a fair balance between the interest of publicity of court proceedings, on the one hand, and the interests of a party or a third person in maintaining the confidentiality of such data, on the other hand. The scope of this margin will depend on such factors as the nature and seriousness of the interests at stake and the gravity of the interference (see, for instance, the Leander v. Sweden judgment of 26 March 1987, Series A No. 116, p. 25, paragraph 58; and, *mutatis mutandis*, the Manoussakis and Others v. Greece judgment of 26 September 1996, *Reports* 1996-IV, p. 1364, paragraph 44).

In that case, court orders had been served on the applicant's medical advisers forcing them to give evidence. The Court continued:

As regards the orders requiring the applicant's doctors and psychiatrist to give evidence, the Court notes that the measures were taken in the context of Z. availing herself of her right under Finnish law not to give evidence against her husband (see paragraphs 14, 17 and 21 above). The object was exclusively to ascertain from her medical advisers when X. had become aware of or had reason to suspect his HIV infection. Their evidence had the possibility of being at the material time decisive for the question whether X. was guilty of sexual offences only or in addition of the more serious offence of attempted manslaughter in relation to two offences committed prior to 19 March 1992, when the positive results of the HIV test had become available. There can be no doubt that the competent national authorities were entitled to think that very weighty public interests militated in favour of the investigation and prosecution of X. for attempted manslaughter in respect of all of the five offences concerned and not just three of them.

The Court further notes that, under the relevant Finnish law, the applicant's medical advisers could be ordered to give evidence concerning her without her informed consent only in very limited circumstances, namely in connection with the investigation and the bringing of charges for serious criminal offences for which a sentence of at least six years' imprisonment was prescribed (see paragraph 46 above). Since they had refused to give evidence to the police, the latter had to obtain authorisation from a judicial body – the City Court – to hear them as witnesses (see paragraph 28 above). The questioning took place in camera before the City Court, which had ordered in advance that its file, including transcripts of witness statements, be kept confidential (see paragraphs 19 and 23 above). All those involved in the proceedings were under a duty to treat the information as confidential. Breach of their duty in this respect could lead to civil and/or criminal liability under Finnish law (see paragraphs 53-56 above).

The Court concluded that the interference in issue was justified under Article 8, paragraph 2.

For another case involving medical secrecy, see the M.S. v. Sweden judgment (27 August 1997, Application No. 20837/92, *Reports* 1997-IV, paragraphs 31-44), concerning communication of a medical file to the social security office (no violation of Article 8 in this case).

Physical integrity

In the Bensaid v. the United Kingdom judgment (6 February 2001, Application No. 44599/98, paragraphs 47-49), the Court responded to the applicant's argument that his expulsion to Algeria violated his right to private life, given the consequences that it could have on his mental health as a result of the different medical treatment he would receive in that country. The Court considered that it was not proved that appropriate medical treatment was impossible to the extent of aggravating his situation.

In the Matter v. Slovakia judgment (5 July 1999, Application No. 31534/96, paragraphs 62-71), the Court held that an individual was forcibly taken to a psychiatric hospital for a mental health check was not disproportionate and complied with Article 8, paragraph 2. The applicant suffered from paranoid psychosis.

In the case of Raninen v. Finland, the Court set out this criteria concerning the wearing of handcuffs:

> According to the Court's case-law, the notion of "private life" is a broad one and is not susceptible to exhaustive definition; it may, depending on the circumstances, cover the moral and physical integrity of the person (see the X. and Y. v. the Netherlands judgment of 26 March 1985, Series A No. 91, p. 11,

paragraph 22; the Niemietz v. Germany judgment of 16 December 1992, Series A No. 215-B, p. 11, paragraph 29; and the Costello-Roberts v. the United Kingdom judgment of 25 March 1993, Series A No. 247-C, pp. 60-61, paragraphs 34 and 36). The Court further recognises that these aspects of the concept extend to situations of deprivation of liberty. Moreover, it does not exclude the possibility that there might be circumstances in which Article 8 could be regarded as affording a protection in relation to conditions during detention which do not attain the level of severity required by Article 3.

In the case under consideration, as noted above, the applicant based his complaint under Article 8 on the same facts as that under Article 3, which the Court has considered and found not to have been established in essential aspects. In particular, it had not been shown that the handcuffing had affected the applicant physically or mentally or had been aimed at humiliating him (see paragraph 58 above). In these circumstances, the Court does not consider that there are sufficient elements enabling it to find that the treatment complained of entailed such adverse effects on his physical or moral integrity as to constitute an interference with the applicant's right to respect for private life as guaranteed by Article 8 of the Convention.

Accordingly, the Court does not find any violation of this provision either.

(See also the Stubbings and Others v. the United Kingdom judgment of 22 October 1996, *Reports* 1996-IV, paragraphs 59-67.)

Various hypotheses

In the Hatton judgment, the Court held that the additional noise caused by an increase in night-time air traffic lent itself to examination under Article 8 as being capable of impinging on the right to a home and the right to private life (the Hatton and Others v. the United Kingdom judgment of 2 October 2001, Application No. 36022/97, paragraphs 94-99). The Court held:

> The Court considers that it is not possible to make a sensible comparison between the situation of the present applicants and that of the applicants in the previous cases referred to by the Government because, first, the present applicants complain specifically about night noise, whereas the earlier applicants complained generally about aircraft noise and, secondly, the present applicants complain largely about the increase in night noise which they say has occurred since the Government altered the restrictions on night noise in 1993, whereas the previous applications concerned noise levels prior to 1993. The Court concludes, therefore, that the outcome of previous applications is not relevant to the present case.

> The Court notes that Heathrow airport and the aircraft which use it are not owned, controlled or operated by the Government or by any agency of the Government. The Court considers that, accordingly, the United Kingdom cannot be said to have "interfered" with the applicants' private or family life. Instead, the applicants' complaints fall to be analysed in terms of a positive duty on the State to take reasonable and appropriate measures to secure the applicants' rights under Article 8, paragraph 1, of the Convention (see the Powell and Rayner v. the United Kingdom judgment of 21 February 1990, Series A No. 172, paragraph 41, and the Guerra v. Italy judgment of 19 February 1998, *Reports* 1998-I, paragraph 58).

In that case, the Court considered that Article 8 had been violated in the absence of detailed studies on the advantages and disadvantages of increased air traffic in the face of the two opposing stakes: the expected economic advantage and the interest of the neighbourhood. Last, we should note the McGinley and Egan v. the United Kingdom judgment (9 June 1998, Applications Nos. 21825/93 and 23414/94, *Reports* 1998-II, paragraphs 96-104), concerning the problem of the communication of information on the levels of radiation to which the applicants had been exposed (Article 8 applicable, no violation owing to a procedure which had made it possible to obtain the information).

3. Article 8, paragraph 1, and the protection of family life

The concept of family life

By way of introduction, the concept of "family" is a question of fact. In the K. and T. v. Finland judgment (12 July 2001, Application No. 25702/94, paragraph 150), the Court observed:

> The Court would point out, in accordance with its previous case-law (see, amongst others, the Marckx v. Belgium judgment of 13 June 1979, Series A No. 31, paragraph 31), that the existence or non-existence of "family life" is essentially a question of fact depending upon the real existence in practice of close personal ties.

Article 8 applies to families no matter what their status

In the Marckx v. Belgium judgment (13 June 1979, Series A No. 31, p. 14, paragraph 31), the Court noted that no distinction must be drawn on the basis of the "legitimate" or "illegitimate" nature of the family for the purpose of applying Article 8:

> The Court concurs entirely with the Commission's established case-law on a crucial point, namely that Article 8 (art. 8) makes no distinction between the "legitimate" and the "illegitimate" family. Such a distinction would not be consonant with the word "everyone", and this is confirmed by Article 14 (art. 14) with its prohibition, in the enjoyment of the rights and freedoms enshrined in the Convention, of discrimination grounded on "birth". In addition, the Court notes that the Committee of Ministers of the Council of Europe regards the single woman and her child as one form of family no less than others (Resolution (70) 15 of 15 May 1970 on the social protection of unmarried mothers and their children, paragraph I-10, paragraph II-5, etc.).

> This decision deserves approval. As the Court emphasises, there must be a family life already in existence.

Article 8 applies to families already in existence

Article 8 protects family life only as an existing state. It does not cover the freedom to found a family – which comes under Article 12. In the

Marckx v. Belgium case quoted above (13 June 1979, Series A No. 31, p. 14, paragraph 31) the Court notes clearly:

> By guaranteeing the right to respect for family life, Article 8 (art. 8) presupposes the existence of a family.

In the Abdulaziz, Cabales and Balkandali v. the United Kingdom judgment (28 May 1985, Series A No. 94, p. 32, paragraph 62), the Court explained the meaning of the "existence of a family" as a precondition of the application of Article 8. In that case, the applicants' spouses were not permitted to remain with or join their wives, who were lawfully and permanently settled in the United Kingdom. The Court accepted the proposed family life of persons who are already married as being sufficient to entail the application of Article 8:

> [This] does not mean that all intended family life falls entirely outside its ambit. Whatever else the word "family" may mean, it must at any rate include the relationship that arises from a lawful and genuine marriage, such as that contracted by Mr and Mrs Abdulaziz and Mr and Mrs Balkandali, even if a family life of the kind referred to by the Government has not yet been fully established. Those marriages must be considered sufficient to attract such respect as may be due under Article 8 (art. 8).

> Furthermore, the expression "family life", in the case of a married couple, normally comprises cohabitation. The latter proposition is reinforced by the existence of Article 12 (art. 12), for it is scarcely conceivable that the right to found a family should not encompass the right to live together.

In the Berrehab v. the Netherlands judgment of 21 June 1988, Series A No. 138, p. 14, paragraph 21, the Court extended that case-law and held that cohabitation is not always necessary for "family life" within the meaning of Article 8. The case concerned a family with a child, where the parents were no longer living together. The Court stated:

> The Court likewise does not see cohabitation as a *sine qua non* of family life between parents and minor children. It has held that the relationship created between the spouses by a lawful and genuine marriage – such as that contracted by Mr and Mrs Berrehab – has to be regarded as "family life" (see the Abdulaziz, Cabales and Balkandali judgment of 28 May 1985, Series A No. 94, p. 32, paragraph 62). It follows from the concept of family on which Article 8 (art. 8) is based that a child born of such a union is *ipso jure* part of that relationship; hence, from the moment of the child's birth and by the very fact of it, there exists between him and his parents a bond amounting to "family life", even if the parents are not then living together.

> Subsequent events, of course, may break that tie, but this was not so in the instant case.

In that regard, it will be recalled that, according to the Court, the family tie between a child born of a marital union and its parents can be broken only in exceptional conditions. Thus, in the Sen v. the Netherlands judgment, where both parents lived apart from their child, who lived in another country (21 December 2001, Application No. 31465/96, paragraph 28, available in French only – unofficial translation), the Court noted:

> [...] The Court recalls that a child born of a marital union is *ipso jure* part of that relationship; hence, from the moment of the child's birth and by the very fact of it, there exists between him and his parents a bond amounting to "family life" (the Gül v. Switzerland judgment of 19 February 1996, *Reports of Judgments and Decisions* 1996-I, pp. 173-174, paragraph 32, and the Boughanemi v. France judgment of 24 April 1996, *Reports* 1996-I, p. 608, paragraph 35) that subsequent events many break only in exceptional circumstances (the Berrehab v. the Netherlands judgment of 21 June 1988, Series A No. 138, p. 14, paragraph 21 and the Ahmut v. the Netherlands judgment of 28 November 1996, *Reports* 1996-VI, p. 2030, paragraph 60).

The McMichael v. the United Kingdom judgment (24 February 1995, Series A No. 307-B) concerns a natural child. Two applicants had brought proceedings before the Court: the natural father and mother of a child who had been placed in an institution. In this case, the mother's parental rights had been withdrawn on account of her mental state and the fact that she had (previously) been compulsorily admitted to psychiatric hospitals. The natural father had sought right of access and then parental authority by using the channels of appeal available before the British panels with jurisdiction in child placement matters. As the child had been born out of wedlock the Scottish legal system did not automatically grant the natural father parental rights; nor had the father made an application to the court for an order for parental rights, as he could have done.

Faced with that situation, the Court had no alternative but to find that Article 6 did not apply in his case with regard to the father:

> The care proceedings in question did not involve the determination of any of those rights, since he had not taken the requisite prior step of seeking to obtain legal recognition of his status as a father.

However, the Court none the less held that Article 8 was applicable (ibid., paragraph 91). The Court held that there was no contradiction between the existence of a "family life" protected by Article 8 and the absence of a right to be protected by Article 6:

> [...] the Court would point to the difference in the nature of the interests protected by Articles 6, paragraph 1, and 8 (art. 6-1, art. 8). Thus, Article 6, paragraph 1 (art. 6-1), affords a procedural safeguard, namely the "right to a court" in the determination of one's "civil rights and obligations" (see the Golder v. the United Kingdom judgment of 21 February 1975, Series A No. 18, p. 18, paragraph 36); whereas not only does the procedural requirement inherent in Article 8 (art. 8) cover administrative procedures as well as judicial proceedings, but it is ancillary to the wider purpose of ensuring proper respect for, *inter alia*, family life (see, for example, the B. v. the United Kingdom judgment of 8 July 1987, Series A No. 121-B, pp. 72-75, paragraphs 63-65 and 68). The difference between the purpose pursued by the respective safeguards afforded by Articles 6, paragraph 1, and 8 (art. 6-1, art. 8) may, in the light of the particular circumstances, justify the examination of the same set of facts under both Articles

(art. 6, art. 8) (compare, for example, the above-mentioned Golder judgment, pp. 20-22, paragraphs 41-45, and the O. v. the United Kingdom judgment of 8 July 1987, Series A No. 120-A, pp. 28-29, paragraphs 65-67).

The Court therefore took account of the reality, rather than the legality, of the situation. Nonetheless, it should be pointed out that the father married the mother while the case was pending, a factor which the Court necessarily took into account in determining the existence of family life:

> [...] it is true that at the outset, in late 1987 and early 1988, the second applicant denied the first applicant's paternity of A. and that the initial relevant instance of non-disclosure of documents at a children's hearing occurred two weeks before the first applicant's name had been added to A.'s birth certificate (4 and 18 February 1988 respectively) (see paragraphs 7, 11, 14, 15 and 18 above). However, the first applicant had claimed paternity on 27 January 1988; and even at the time of this initial children's hearing he was living with the second applicant and was, especially in his capacity as her representative, closely associated in the attempt to obtain access to A. (see paragraphs 7, 13, 14 and 15 above). Thereafter the two applicants acted very much in concert in their endeavour to recover the custody of and have access to A., not only in the framework of the legal proceedings before the children's hearing and the Sheriff Court but also in their dealings with the social work department of the local authority (see paragraphs 18 and 20-25 above). During the relevant period taken as a whole they were living together and leading a joint "family life", to the extent that that was possible in the light of the second applicant's periodic hospitalisation (see paragraphs 16 and 30 above).

More recently, the Court has recalled (the Elsholz v. Germany judgment of 13 July 2000, Application No. 25735/94, paragraph 43) that:

> [...] the notion of family under this provision is not confined to marriage-based relationships and may encompass other *de facto* "family" ties where the parties are living together out of wedlock. A child born out of such a relationship is *ipso jure* part of that "family" unit from the moment and by the very fact of his birth. Thus there exists between the child and his parents a bond amounting to family life (see the Keegan judgment cited above, pp. 17-18, paragraph 44).

Recomposed families

The Court has had the opportunity to rule on the position regarding recomposed families, in the K. and T. v. Finland judgment (12 July 2001, Application No. 25702/94, paragraphs 149-150). In that case, the applicant T. was not the father of child M. but lived with K., M.'s mother. Child J. was born of the relationship between K. and T. The Court stated:

> [...] In the instant case, both the applicants had lived together with M. until he was voluntarily placed in a children's home and later taken into public care (see paragraph 12 above). Prior to the birth of J. the applicants and M. had formed a family with a clear intention of continuing their life together. The same intention existed as regards the new-born baby J., for whom T. actually cared during some time soon after her birth and before he became her custodian in law (see paragraphs 35 and 38 above). In these circumstances the Court cannot but find that at the time when the authorities intervened there existed between the applicants

271

an actual family life, within the meaning of Article 8, paragraph 1, of the Convention, which extended to both children, M. and J. The Court accordingly will not draw any distinction between the applicants K. and T. as regards the scope of the "family life" which they jointly enjoyed with the two children.

Family, collateral ties, ties with grandparents

It should also be mentioned that relationships with brothers or sisters or with grandparents characterise the existence of a "family life" and are therefore protected by Article 8. In the Marckx judgment (ibid., paragraph 45), the Court observed that:

> [...] "family life", within the meaning of Article 8 (art. 8), includes at least the ties between near relatives, for instance those between grandparents and grandchildren, since such relatives may play a considerable part in family life.

Examples of the application of Article 8 in family matters

Educational assistance

The case-law on educational assistance is relatively abundant.

In the Johansen v. Norway judgment (*Reports of Judgments and Decisions* 1996-III, pp. 1008-1009, paragraph 52), the Court stated:

> The Court recalls that the mutual enjoyment by parent and child of each other's company constitutes a fundamental element of family life and that domestic measures hindering such enjoyment amount to an interference with the right protected by Article 8 (art. 8) (see, amongst others, the McMichael v. the United Kingdom judgment of 24 February 1995, Series A No. 307-B, p. 55, paragraph 86).

Measures relating to the care of minors therefore undoubtedly constitute interferences with respect for the right to family life. In the Scozzari and Giunta v. Italy judgment (13 July 2000, Applications Nos. 39221/98 and 41963/98, paragraph 148), the Court stated:

> The Court reiterates that "[...] it is an interference of a very serious order to split up a family. Such a step must be supported by sufficiently sound and weighty considerations in the interests of the child [...]" (see the Olsson v. Sweden (No. 1) judgment of 24 March 1988, Series A No. 130, pp. 33-34, paragraph 72). Therefore, "[...] regard must be had to the fair balance that has to be struck between the competing interests of the individual and the community as a whole, and in both contexts the State [...] enjoy[s] a certain margin of appreciation [...]" (see the Hokkanen v. Finland judgment of 23 September 1994, Series A 299-A, p. 20, paragraph 55). In this sphere, "[...] the Court['s] [...] review is not limited to ascertaining whether a respondent State exercised its discretion reasonably, carefully and in good faith [...]. In the second place, in exercising its supervisory jurisdiction, the Court cannot confine itself to considering the impugned decisions in isolation, but must look at them in the light of the case as a whole; it must determine whether the reasons adduced to justify the interferences at issue are 'relevant and sufficient [...]'" (see the Olsson (No. 1) judgment cited above, p. 32, paragraph 68, and, *mutatis mutandis*, the Vogt v. Germany judgment of 26 September 1995, Series A No. 323, pp. 25-26, paragraph 52).

In the above-mentioned K. and T. v. Finland judgment (12 July 2001, Application No. 25702/94, paragraph 165), the Court, sitting as a Grand Chamber, indicated its approach to examining situations involving minors being taken into care. For each child, emergency care decisions and then normal care decisions must be examined separately:

> The Grand Chamber [...] considers it appropriate to examine the emergency care order and the normal care order for each child separately as they were different kinds of decision, which had different consequences – an emergency care order being of short, limited duration and a normal care order being of a more permanent nature – and which were the product of separate decision-making processes, even though one measure followed immediately after the other. In the Grand Chamber's view there are substantive and procedural differences to be taken into account which warrant examining the two sets of decisions separately.

Later, it continued (paragraph 178):

> The Grand Chamber, like the Chamber, would first recall the guiding principle whereby a care order should in principle be regarded as a temporary measure, to be discontinued as soon as circumstances permit, and that any measures implementing temporary care should be consistent with the ultimate aim of reuniting the natural parents and the child (see, in particular, the above-mentioned Olsson (No. 1) judgment, paragraph 81). The positive duty to take measures to facilitate family reunification as soon as reasonably feasible will begin to weigh on the responsible authorities with progressively increasing force as from the commencement of the period of care, subject always to its being balanced against the duty to consider the best interests of the child.

Thus, the Court examines, in turn, emergency care orders, normal care orders, the efforts made by the State to reunite the family and restrictions on parental visits while the care order is in force (see the L. v. Finland judgment of 27 April 2000, Application No. 25651/94).

Sill on the subject of care orders, in the above-mentioned K. and T. v. Finland judgment, the Court stated (paragraph 173):

> The fact that a child could be placed in a more beneficial environment for his or her upbringing will not on its own justify a compulsory measure of removal from the care of the biological parents; there must exist other circumstances pointing to the "necessity" for such an interference with the parents' right under Article 8 of the Convention to enjoy a family life with their child.

In various cases, the Court has set out the principles applicable in order to determine whether the interference consisting in placing a minor in care was necessary in a democratic society. In the T.P. and K.M. v. the United Kingdom judgment (10 May 2001, Application No. 28945/95, paragraphs 70-73), the Court stated:

> In determining whether the impugned measures were "necessary in a democratic society", the Court will consider whether, in the light of the case as a whole, the reasons adduced to justify them were relevant and sufficient for the purposes of paragraph 2 of Article 8 of the Convention. Undoubtedly, consideration of what lies in the best interest of the child is of crucial importance in every case of this kind. Moreover, it must be borne in mind that the national authorities have the

benefit of direct contact with all the persons concerned. It follows from these considerations that the Court's task is not to substitute itself for the domestic authorities in the exercise of their responsibilities regarding custody and access issues, but rather to review, in the light of the Convention, the decisions taken by those authorities in the exercise of their power of appreciation (see the Hokkanen v. Finland judgment of 23 September 1994, Series A No. 299-A, p. 20, paragraph 55, and, *mutatis mutandis*, the Bronda v. Italy judgment of 9 June 1998, *Reports of Judgments and Decisions* 1998-IV, p. 1491, paragraph 59).

The margin of appreciation to be accorded to the competent national authorities will vary in accordance with the nature of the issues and the importance of the interests at stake. Thus, the Court recognises that the authorities enjoy a wide margin of appreciation, in particular when assessing the necessity of taking a child into care. However, a stricter scrutiny is called for in respect of any further limitations, such as restrictions placed by those authorities on parental rights of access, and of any legal safeguards designed to secure an effective protection of the right of parents and children to respect for their family life. Such further limitations entail the danger that the family relations between the parents and a young child would be effectively curtailed (see, amongst other authorities, the Johansen v. Norway judgment of 7 August 1996, *Reports* 1996-III, p. 1003, paragraph 64).

The Court further recalls that whilst Article 8 contains no explicit procedural requirements, the decision-making process involved in measures of interference must be fair and such as to afford due respect to the interests safeguarded by Article 8:

> "[W]hat has to be determined is whether, having regard to the particular circumstances of the case and notably the serious nature of the decisions to be taken, the parents have been involved in the decision-making process, seen as a whole, to a degree sufficient to provide them with the requisite protection of their interests. If they have not, there will have been a failure to respect their family life and the interference resulting from the decision will not be capable of being regarded as 'necessary' within the meaning of Article 8" (see the W. v. the United Kingdom judgment of 8 July 1987, Series A No. 121-A, pp. 28-29, paragraphs 62 and 64).

It has previously found that the failure to disclose relevant documents to parents during the procedures instituted by the authorities in placing and maintaining a child in care meant that the decision-making process determining the custody and access arrangements did not afford the requisite protection of the parents' interests as safeguarded by Article 8 (see the McMichael v. the United Kingdom judgment of 24 February 1995, Series A No. 307-B, p. 57, paragraph 92).

(See also the K. and T. v. Finland judgment of 12 July 2001, Application No. 25702/94, paragraphs 154-155.)

The substantive conditions are accompanied by procedural obligations. That requirement is by no means new. Thus, in the W. v. the United Kingdom judgment (8 July 1987, Series A No. 121, p. 29, paragraph 64), the Court observed:

> What [...] has to be determined is whether [...] the parents have been involved in the decision-making process, seen as a whole, to a degree sufficient to provide

them with the requisite protection of their interests. If they have not, there will have been a failure to respect their family life and the interference resulting from the decision will not be capable of being regarded as "necessary" within the meaning of Article 8 (art. 8).

It should be noted in that regard, however, that the Court has accepted emergency measures taken without the parents being informed when circumstances appear to justify it; but it has correctly proved to be very demanding where babies have been taken from their mothers immediately after birth.

(On a child placed by preference in the care of its grandmother, see the above-mentioned Scozzari and Giunta v. Italy judgment, paragraphs 221-227; on the preference shown to the host family with whom the child in care wished to remain, see the Bronda v. Italy judgment of 9 June 1998, *Reports* 1998-V, paragraphs 61-62; on the involvement of the parents in the care decision, see the Buscemi v. Italy judgment of 16 September 1999, Application No. 29569/95, paragraphs 57-63, or the Buchberger v. Austria judgment of 20 December 2001, Application No. 32899/96, paragraphs 41-43, the Sommerfeld v. Germany judgment of 11 October 2001, Application No. 31871/96, paragraphs 41-45, and the Elsholz v. Germany judgment of 13 July 2000, Application No. 25735/94, paragraphs 51-53; see the Sahin v. Germany judgment of 11 October 2001, Application No. 30943/96, paragraphs 46-49, concerning the hearing of the child's views; on the restriction of the right to visit of a grandfather suspected of sexual abuse, see the L. v. Finland judgment of 27 April 2000, Application No. 25651/94, paragraphs 127-128.)

Family rights

In the Camp and Bourimi v. the Netherlands judgment of 3 October 2000 (Application No. 28369/95, paragraphs 26-28), the Court considered that the absence of retroactivity of an act of legitimation in respect of a child did not entail a violation of Article 8 in the sense claimed by the applicant, that is, that it was impossible to create ties with the father's family. The Court considered that the fact that no family ties had developed between the child and its father's family was not due to an interference or failure to act on the part of the State but referred implicitly to a question of fact. However, the Court found in that case that there had been a violation of Article 14.

In that judgment, the Court reasserted (paragraph 35):

> Despite the fact that Article 8 does not as such guarantee a right to inherit, the Court has previously accepted that matters of intestate succession between near relatives nevertheless fall within the scope of that provision as they represent a feature of family life (see the aforementioned Marckx judgment, loc. cit., pp. 23-24, paragraphs 52-53). The fact that Mr Abbie Bourimi's death occurred before Sofian was born is no reason for the Court to adopt a different approach in the present case.

In the matter of adoption, we should note the Söderbäck v. Sweden judgment (28 October 1998, Application No. 24484/97, *Reports* 1998-VII,

275

paragraphs 30-35) for a case where a child was adopted by the mother's cohabitee, the natural father being the applicant.

The question of the implementation by a parent of a right of access or staying access recognised by law or ordered by a court where the other parent is opposed to such access has given rise to various decisions. In the Ignaccolo-Zenide v. Romania judgment (25 January 2000, Application No. 31679/96, paragraphs 94 and 96), the Court stated:

> [...] the national authorities' obligation to take measures to facilitate reunion is not absolute, since the reunion of a parent with children who have lived for some time with the other parent may not be able to take place immediately and may require preparatory measures to be taken. The nature and extent of such preparation will depend on the circumstances of each case, but the understanding and co-operation of all concerned are always an important ingredient. Whilst national authorities must do their utmost to facilitate such co-operation, any obligation to apply coercion in this area must be limited since the interests as well as the rights and freedoms of all concerned must be taken into account, and more particularly the best interests of the child and his or her rights under Article 8 of the Convention. Where contacts with the parent might appear to threaten those interests or interfere with those rights, it is for the national authorities to strike a fair balance between them (see the Hokkanen judgment cited above, p. 22, paragraph 58).
>
> [...]
>
> What is decisive in the present case is therefore whether the national authorities did take all steps to facilitate execution of the order of 14 December 1994 that could reasonably be demanded (Hokkanen judgment, ibid.).

(See also the Glaser judgment of 19 September 2000 and the Nuutinen judgment of 27 June 2000.)

Article 8 also covers a number of more specific aspects such as the right to recover the body of a deceased close relative. In the Pannullo and Forte v. France judgment of 30 October 2001 (Application No. 37794/97, paragraphs 38-40, available in French only – unofficial translation), the applicants complained that the body of their child had not been returned to them following an autopsy carried out in connection with an investigation into the causes of death. The autopsy ordered by the investigating judge had taken place on 9 July 1996 and permission to bury was not issued until 14 February 1997. The Court declared:

> The Court considers that the requirements of the investigation meant that the French authorities should retain Erika's body for the time necessary for the autopsy, that is until 9 July 1996. As regards the subsequent period, on the other hand, Professor L.'s letter to the State Prosecutor clearly showed that the child's body could have been returned to the parents immediately after the autopsy, as the necessary samples had been taken and the preparation of the report did not require that the body be kept at the forensic institution. It is also clear from that letter that the investigating judge was immediately informed of the position and that the forensic institution made a number of approaches to the judge in that regard.

In those circumstances, whether the delay was caused, as the Government state, either by inertia on the part of the experts or by a "misunderstanding of the medical matters" on the part of the judge, the Court considers, regard being had to the circumstances of the case and to the tragic nature, for the parents, of the loss of their child, that the French authorities did not strike a fair balance between the applicants' right to respect for their private and family life and the legitimate aim pursued.

Accordingly, the Court concludes that there has been a violation of Article 8 of the Convention.

Expulsion, removal, prohibition on entering the territory, non-renewal of a residence permit

Depending on the case, it may be an interference (expulsion, removal, prohibition on entering the territory) or a failure to act (failure to grant a residence permit, etc.) that may give rise to a question of the existence of positive obligations.

Where the applicant has had to leave the State against which he has brought an action before the Court, the Court takes into account his age, his knowledge of the languages, his nationality, the existence of relatives in the country of destination, the existence of obstacles to his return or to contacts, etc., and weighs up the situation in which he will be placed with the objective pursued by the State. As regards the respondent State, it generally relies on economic grounds or grounds associated with the prevention of disorder.

Economic or public-interest grounds

In one case (the Berrehab v. the Netherlands case, 21 June 1988, Series A No. 138, p. 16, paragraph 29), the Court considered that the expulsion of an alien by the Netherlands following his divorce from a Dutch national by whom he had a child did not satisfy the criterion of proportionality required by Article 8, paragraph 2. The Netherlands defended the expulsion as being necessary for the protection of the employment market and the economic welfare of the country [...]. In the Court's view, the aim pursued by that interference with family life did not sufficiently justify that expulsion where the alien in question had close ties with his daughter. The Court observed that:

> As to the aim pursued, it must be emphasised that the instant case did not concern an alien seeking admission to the Netherlands for the first time but a person who had already lawfully lived there for several years, who had a home and a job there, and against whom the Government did not claim to have any complaint. Furthermore, Mr Berrehab already had real family ties there – he had married a Dutch woman, and a child had been born of the marriage.

> As to the extent of the interference, it is to be noted that there had been very close ties between Mr Berrehab and his daughter for several years (see paragraphs 9 and 21 above) and that the refusal of an independent residence permit and the ensuing expulsion threatened to break those ties. That effect of

the interferences in issue was the more serious as Rebecca needed to remain in contact with her father, seeing especially that she was very young.

Having regard to these particular circumstances, the Court considers that a proper balance was not achieved between the interests involved and that there was therefore a disproportion between the means employed and the legitimate aim pursued. That being so, the Court cannot consider the disputed measures as being necessary in a democratic society. It thus concludes that there was a violation of Article 8 (art. 8).

As regards immigration and the right of immigrants to have their families with them, mention may be made of the Ahmut v. the Netherlands judgment (28 November 1996, Application No. 21702/93, *Reports* 1996-VI, paragraph 67), where the Court observed:

> The applicable principles have been stated by the Court in its Gül judgment as follows (loc. cit., paragraph 38):
>
> (a) The extent of a State's obligation to admit to its territory relatives of settled immigrants will vary according to the particular circumstances of the persons involved and the general interest.
>
> (b) As a matter of well-established international law and subject to its treaty obligations, a State has the right to control the entry of non-nationals into its territory.
>
> (c) Where immigration is concerned, Article 8 (art. 8) cannot be considered to impose on a State a general obligation to respect immigrants' choice of the country of their matrimonial residence and to authorise family reunion in its territory.

In this case, the Court held that the applicant had chosen to settle in the Netherlands rather than in Morocco, to which he could return unhindered. The fact that he had a separate residence from his son, who had remained in Morocco, was therefore the result of a conscious decision. His son had been placed in a boarding school and he had family in Morocco. The Court held that the refusal of a residence permit for the son in question could not be regarded as a failure to strike a fair balance between the applicant's interests, on the one hand, and the interest in controlling immigration, on the other. For another case of the same type, see also the above-mentioned case of Gül v. Switzerland (judgment of 19 February 1996, *Reports* 1996-I, paragraphs 39-43), where the Court held that the parents' separation from their child was the result of the parents' choice and where it set out its approach quite restrictively, stating (paragraphs 39 and 42-43):

> In this case, therefore, the Court's task is to determine to what extent it is true that Ersin's move to Switzerland would be the only way for Mr Gül to develop family life with his son.
>
> [...]
>
> In view of the length of time Mr and Mrs Gül have lived in Switzerland, it would admittedly not be easy for them to return to Turkey, but there are, strictly speaking, no obstacles preventing them from developing family life in Turkey.
>
> [...]

Having regard to all these considerations, and while acknowledging that the Gül family's situation is very difficult from the human point of view, the Court finds that Switzerland has not failed to fulfil [its] obligations.

For an example of removal, it is useful to consult the case of Nsona v. the Netherlands, 28 November 1996 (Application No. 23366/94, *Reports* 1996-V, paragraphs 112-114), concerning the arrival of a minor of Zairean origin bearing a false identity, where the Court held that the State could not for that reason be criticised for having failed to respect family life.

Grounds connected with public order

In the Boujlifa v. France judgment (21 October 1997, Application No. 25404/94, *Reports* 1997-VI, paragraphs 36 and 44-45), the Court stated:

> The question whether the applicant had a private and family life within the mean-
> ing of Article 8 must be determined by the Court in the light of the position at
> the time when the impugned measure was adopted (see, *mutatis mutandis*, the
> Bouchelkia v. France judgment of 29 January 1997, *Reports* 1997-I, p. 63, para-
> graph 41). That means on 8 April 1991, but the applicant had been informed on
> 21 November 1990 that deportation proceedings had been commenced against
> him (see paragraph 10 above). Mr Boujlifa was not therefore entitled to claim at
> that time to be involved in a relationship with Miss V.
>
> However, the Court observes that he arrived in France in 1967 at the age of 5
> and has lived there since then, except while he was imprisoned in Switzerland.
> He received his schooling there (partly in prison), and his parents and his eight
> brothers and sisters – with whom he seems to have remained in touch – live
> there (see paragraph 8 above). Consequently, the Court is in no doubt that the
> measure complained of amounts to interference with the applicant's right to
> respect for his private and family life.
>
> [...]
>
> The Court reiterates that it is for the Contracting States to maintain public order,
> in particular by exercising their right, as a matter of well-established inter-
> national law and subject to their treaty obligations, to control the entry and
> residence of aliens. To that end they have the power to deport aliens convicted
> of criminal offences.
>
> However, their decisions in this field must, in so far as they may interfere with a
> right protected under paragraph 1 of Article 8, be necessary in a democratic
> society, that is to say, justified by a pressing social need and, in particular, pro-
> portionate to the legitimate aim pursued (see, as the most recent authority, the
> Bouchelkia judgment cited above, p. 65, paragraph 48).
>
> The Court's task accordingly consists in ascertaining whether the measure in
> issue struck a fair balance between the relevant interests, namely the applicant's
> right to respect for his private and family life, on the one hand, and the preven-
> tion of disorder or crime, on the other.
>
> On the other hand, it seems that he did not show any desire to acquire French
> nationality at the time when he was entitled to do so.

The Court notes that the offences committed (armed robbery and robbery), by their seriousness and the severity of the penalties they attracted, constituted a particularly serious violation of the security of persons and property and of public order.

It considers that in the instant case the requirements of public order outweighed the personal considerations which prompted the application.

Having regard to the foregoing, the Court considers that the making of the order for the applicant's deportation cannot be regarded as disproportionate to the legitimate aims pursued. There has accordingly been no breach of Article 8.

(*Idem* in the case of Bouchelkia v. France, judgment of 29 January 1997, Application No. 23078/93, *Reports* 1997-I, paragraphs 52-53, concerning the expulsion of a young man who had committed a rape while a minor to his place of origin, whose nationality he possessed and where he had close relatives living; *idem* the V. v. Belgium judgment of 7 August 1996, Application No. 21794/93, *Reports* 1996-III, paragraph 36.)

The case of Nasri v. France concerned the expulsion of a deaf and dumb person who had been convicted of gang rape. The Court observed (judgment of 13 July 1995, Application No. 19465/92, Series A No. 320-B, paragraph 48):

> In view of this accumulation of special circumstances, notably his situation as a deaf and dumb person, capable of achieving a minimum psychological and social equilibrium only within his family, the majority of whose members are French nationals with no close ties with Algeria, the decision to deport the applicant, if executed, would not be proportionate to the legitimate aim pursued. It would infringe the right to respect for family life and therefore constitute a breach of Article 8 (art. 8).

In the case of Boultif v. Switzerland (2 August 2001, Application No. 54273/2000, paragraphs 53-56), the Court was required to consider the refusal to renew the residence permit of a man married to a Swiss national who had committed an offence. The circumstances were less exceptional than in the case of Nasri v. France. However, the Court noted:

> The Court has considered, first, whether the applicant and his wife could live together in Algeria. The applicant's wife is a Swiss national. It is true that the applicant's wife can speak French and has had contacts by telephone with her mother-in-law in Algeria. However, the applicant's wife has never lived in Algeria, she has no other ties with that country, and indeed she does not speak Arabic. In these circumstances she cannot, in the Court's opinion, be expected to follow her husband, the applicant, to Algeria.
>
> There remains the question of establishing family life elsewhere and notably in Italy. In this respect the Court notes that the applicant lawfully resided in Italy from 1989 until 1992 when he left for Switzerland, and it appears that he is now again residing with friends in Italy, albeit without regular status. In the Court's opinion, it has not been established that both the applicant and his wife could obtain the authorisation to reside lawfully and, as a result, to lead their family life in Italy. In that context, the Court has noted that the Government have argued that the applicant's current whereabouts are irrelevant in view of the nature of the offence which he had committed.

The Court considers that the applicant has been subjected to a serious impediment to establish family life, since it is practically impossible for him to live his family life outside Switzerland. On the other hand, when the Swiss authorities decided to refuse his continuing stay in Switzerland, the applicant only presented a comparatively limited danger to public order. The Court is therefore of the opinion that the interference was not proportionate to the aim pursued.

There has accordingly been a breach of Article 8 of the Convention.

In the case of Baghli v. France, the Court examined the penalty of prohibition from entering the territory imposed on those convicted of certain offences. The prohibition may be imposed definitively or for a certain time. In this case, the prohibition had been ordered for ten years. The Court acknowledged that this measure was an interference with the applicant's private and family life, but considered that it was compatible with paragraph 2 of Article 8. It stated (judgment of 30 November 1999, Application No. 34374/97, paragraphs 36-37 and 48-49):

> It is with regard to the position at the time the exclusion order became final that the Court must examine the question whether the applicant had a family life within the meaning of Article 8 of the Convention (see the Bouchelkia v. France judgment of 29 January 1997, *Reports of Judgments and Decisions* 1997-I, p. 63, paragraph 41, and the El Boujaïdi v. France judgment of 26 September 1997, *Reports* 1997-VI, pp. 1990-1991, paragraph 33). In the instant case, the exclusion order became final in September 1993 when the Court of Cassation dismissed the appeal against the Court of Appeal's judgment of 23 January 1992. The applicant may therefore rely on his relationship with Miss I., which had begun earlier.

> The Court observes that the applicant entered France in 1967 at the age of 2 and, with the exception of the period he spent doing his military service in Algeria, lived there until the exclusion order was enforced in May 1994. He did all his schooling in France and worked there for several years. In addition, his parents and brothers and sisters live in France. Consequently, the Court has no doubt that the temporary exclusion order amounts to an interference with the applicant's right to respect for both his private and his family life.

> [...]

> However, the applicant, who is single and has no children, has not shown that he has close ties with either his parents or his brothers and sisters living in France. In addition, it should be noted that when the applicant's relationship with Miss I. began in December 1992 the exclusion order had already been imposed; accordingly he must have been aware of the precariousness of his position.

> Furthermore, he retained his Algerian nationality and has never suggested that he cannot speak Arabic. He performed his military service in his country of origin and went there on holiday several times. It appears, too, that he never evinced a desire to become French when he was entitled to do so. Thus, even though his main family and social ties are in France, there is evidence, as the Government submitted, that the applicant has preserved ties, going beyond mere nationality, with his native country.

> As regards the seriousness of the offence, the Court notes that the Lyons Court of Appeal sentenced the applicant to three years' imprisonment, two of which

were suspended, for dealing in heroin, part of which was for his own and his companion's use and the remainder for sale to finance further purchases, after being adulterated in a way that made it particularly hazardous for buyers. The offence indisputably constituted a serious breach of public order and undermined the protection of the health of others. In view of the devastating effects of drugs on people's lives, the Court understands why the authorities show great firmness with regard to those who actively contribute to the spread of this scourge (see the Dalia v. France judgment of 19 February 1998, *Reports* 1998-I, p. 92, paragraph 54).

In the light of the foregoing, the Court considers that the ten-year exclusion order was not disproportionate to the legitimate aims pursued. There has therefore been no violation of Article 8.

(*Idem* the Dalia v. France judgment of 19 February 1998, Application No. 26102/95, *Reports* 1998-I, paragraphs 39, 45 and 52-54; and the El Boujaïdi v. France judgment of 26 September 1997, *Reports* 1997-VI, Application No. 25613/94.)

Various hypotheses

Prison visits

The Messina v. Italy (No. 2) judgment (28 September 2000, Application No. 25498/94, paragraphs 61-63, 66-70 and 72-74) dealt with restrictions on family visits to a detained person in respect of whom a warrant for immediate production before an investigating judge had been made for murder of a judge; who had been sentenced to seventeen years' imprisonment; and in respect of whom other proceedings were pending on charges of Mafia association. The Court observed:

> The Court observes that any detention which is lawful for the purposes of Article 5 of the Convention entails by its nature a limitation on private and family life. However, it is an essential part of a prisoner's right to respect for family life that the prison authorities assist him in maintaining contact with his close family (see Ouinas v. France, Application No. 13756/88, Commission decision of 12 March 1990, *Decisions and Reports* 65, p. 265).

> In the present case the applicant was subject to a special prison regime which involved restrictions on the number of family visits (not more than two per month) and imposed measures for the supervision of such visits (prisoners were separated from visitors by a glass partition).

> The Court considers that these restrictions constitute interference with the exercise of the applicant's right to respect for his family life, guaranteed by Article 8, paragraph 1, of the Convention (see X. v. the United Kingdom, Application No. 8065/77, Commission decision of 3 May 1978, *Decisions and Reports* 14, p. 246).

> Such interference is not in breach of the Convention if it is "in accordance with the law", pursues one or more of the legitimate aims contemplated in paragraph 2 of Article 8 and may be regarded as a measure which is "necessary in a democratic society".

[...]

[...] the Court takes into account the specific nature of the phenomenon of organised crime, particularly of the Mafia type, in which family relations often play a crucial role. Moreover, numerous States Party to the Convention have high-security regimes for dangerous prisoners. These regimes are also based on separation from the prison community, accompanied by tighter supervision.

That being the case, the Court considers that the Italian legislature could reasonably consider, in the critical circumstances of the investigations of the Mafia being conducted by the Italian authorities, that the measures complained of were necessary in order to achieve the legitimate aim.

The Court still has to consider whether the extended application of the special regime to the applicant infringed his rights under Article 8 of the Convention.

It observes in the first place that the applicant was subject to the special regime for approximately four and a half years, from 26 November 1993 (see paragraph 13 above) to 21 May 1998 (see paragraph 38 above), on account of the very serious offences of which he had been convicted and of which in some cases he still stood accused, particularly crimes linked to the Mafia.

The Government submitted that the necessity of extending application of the special regime was on each occasion assessed with the greatest care by the relevant authorities.

[...]

Moreover, the Court notes that the applicant was not subject to the restrictions on family visits laid down by Section 41 *bis* for the whole of the period during which the special regime was applied to him. By two decisions of the President of the Trapani Assize Court of 9 and 20 December 1993 (see paragraphs 15 and 19 above) he was authorised for the first time to receive extra visits from his wife and daughters [...].

The Court considers that these decisions attest to the Italian authorities' concern to help the applicant maintain contact with his close family, in so far as that was possible, and thus strike a fair balance between the applicant's rights and the aims it was sought to achieve through the special regime.

In the light of the above considerations, the Court considers that the restrictions of the applicant's right to respect for his family life did not go beyond what is necessary in a democratic society for the protection of public safety and the prevention of disorder or crime, within the meaning of Article 8, paragraph 2, of the Convention.

There has therefore been no violation of Article 8 of the Convention in this respect.

Travelling people

In the Chapman v. the United Kingdom judgment (18 January 2001), the Court considered that life in a caravan was an integral part of the applicant's Gypsy identity as it formed part of the long tradition of travelling followed by that minority. Measures relating to the stationing of the applicant's caravans not only had consequences for her right to respect for her home but also affected her ability to retain her Gypsy identity and to pursue a private and family life in keeping with that tradition.

That naturally leads to an examination of the protection of the home.

4. Article 8, paragraph 1, and protection of the home

The concept of "home"

Article 8 and the future home

In the case of Loizidou v. Turkey, the Court considered whether undeveloped land on which the applicant intended to have a home built was covered by the protection afforded by Article 8. In this case, the applicant claimed to be the owner of a plot in northern Cyprus. Before the Turkish invasion of that region, the construction of flats, one of which was to serve as the home of the applicant's family, was begun on a plot. According to the applicant, the Turkish forces had prevented her and continued to prevent her from returning there and enjoying her possessions. The Court stated (judgment of 18 December 1996, Application No. 15318/89, *Reports* 1996-VI, paragraph 66) :

> The Court observes that the applicant did not have her home on the land in question. In its opinion it would strain the meaning of the notion "home" in Article 8 (art. 8) to extend it to comprise property on which it is planned to build a house for residential purposes. Nor can that term be interpreted to cover an area of a State where one has grown up and where the family has its roots but where one no longer lives.

> Accordingly, there has been no interference with the applicant's rights under Article 8 (art. 8).

Home and business premises

In the above-mentioned Niemietz v. Germany judgment, the Court shed light on the concept of "home" and its application to business premises (p. 34, paragraphs 30-31).

> As regards the word "home", appearing in the English text of Article 8 (art. 8), the Court observes that in certain Contracting States, notably Germany (see paragraph 18 above), it has been accepted as extending to business premises. Such an interpretation is, moreover, fully consonant with the French text, since the word *"domicile"* has a broader connotation than the word "home" and may extend, for example, to a professional person's office.

> In this context also, it may not always be possible to draw precise distinctions, since activities which are related to a profession or business may well be conducted from a person's private residence and activities which are not so related may well be carried on in an office or commercial premises. A narrow interpretation of the words "home" and *"domicile"* could therefore give rise to the same risk of inequality of treatment as a narrow interpretation of the notion of "private life" (see paragraph 29 above).

> More generally, to interpret the words "private life" and "home" as including certain professional or business activities or premises would be consonant with the essential object and purpose of Article 8 (art. 8), namely to protect the individual against arbitrary interference by the public authorities (see, for example, the Marckx v. Belgium judgment of 13 June 1979, Series A No. 31, p. 15, paragraph 31). Such an interpretation would not unduly hamper the Contracting

States, for they would retain their entitlement to "interfere" to the extent permitted by paragraph 2 of Article 8 (art. 8-2); that entitlement might well be more far-reaching where professional or business activities or premises were involved than would otherwise be the case.

Legal tie between the inhabitant and his home

In the Mentes and Others v. Turkey judgment, the Court made clear that there is no need for the complainant to be the owner of a house or for his presence there to be permanent in order for it to be regarded as his home, provided that the occupation was regular (judgment of 28 November 1997, Application No. 23186/94, *Reports* 1997-VIII, paragraph 73).

> The Court sees no reason to distinguish between the first applicant, Ms Azize Mentes, and the second and third applicants. While it was in all probability her father-in-law and not she who owned the house in question, the first applicant did live there for significant periods on an annual basis when she visited the village (see paragraph 34 above). Given her strong family connection and the nature of her residence, her occupation of the house on 25 June 1993 falls within the scope of the protection guaranteed by Article 8 of the Convention.

The case of Buckley v. the United Kingdom gave the Court the opportunity to examine the application of Article 8 to illegally established homes. In this case, the applicant, a Gypsy, was refused the planning permission that would have allowed her to live in a caravan on the land she owned with her family. Following the Gillow judgment, the Court observed, with respect to the applicability of Article 8 of the Convention (25 September 1996, *Reports of Judgments and Decisions* 1996-IV, No. 16, pp. 1287-1288, paragraphs 52-54):

> The Government disputed that any of the applicant's rights under Article 8 (art. 8) was in issue. In its contention, only a "home" legally established could attract the protection of that provision (art. 8).

> In the submission of the applicant and the Commission there was nothing in the wording of Article 8 (art. 8) or in the case-law of the Court or Commission to suggest that the concept of "home" was limited to residences which had been lawfully established.

> The Court, in its Gillow v. the United Kingdom judgment of 24 November 1986 (Series A No. 109), noted that the applicants had established the property in question as their home, had retained ownership of it intending to return there, had lived in it with a view to taking up permanent residence, had relinquished their other home and had not established any other in the United Kingdom. That property was therefore to be considered their "home" for the purposes of Article 8 (art. 8) (loc. cit., p. 19, paragraph 46).

> Although in the Gillow case the applicant's home had initially been established legally, similar considerations apply in the present case. The Court is satisfied that the applicant bought the land to establish her residence there. She has lived there almost continuously since 1988 – save for an absence of two weeks, for family reasons, in 1993 (see paragraphs 11 and 13 above) – and it has not been suggested that she has established, or intends to establish, another residence elsewhere. The case therefore concerns the applicant's right to respect for her "home".

Examples of the application of Article 8 in relation to the home

In the Selçuk and Asker v. Turkey judgment, the applicants maintained that the destruction of their houses and of Mrs Selçuk's mill by the law-enforcement agencies, and their eviction from their village, were to be analysed as violations of Article 8. The Court stated (judgment of 20 April 1998, Applications Nos. 23184/94 and 23185/94, *Reports* 1998-II, paragraphs 86-87):

> The Court recalls that it finds it established that security forces deliberately destroyed the applicants' homes and household property, and the mill partly owned by Mrs Selçuk, obliging them to leave Islamköy (see paragraph 77 above). There can be no doubt that these acts, in addition to giving rise to violations of Article 3, constituted particularly grave and unjustified interferences with the applicants' rights to respect for their private and family lives and homes, and to the peaceful enjoyment of their possessions.

> It follows that the Court finds violations of Article 8 of the Convention and Article 1 of Protocol No. 1.

(See, to the same effect, the Dulas v. Turkey judgment of 30 January 2001, Application No. 25801/94, paragraphs 57-61; the Bilgin v. Turkey judgment of 16 November 2001, Application No. 23819/94, paragraphs 105-109; or the Akdivar and Others v. Turkey judgment of 16 September 1996, *Reports* 1996-IV, Application No. 21893/93, paragraph 88, concerning the burning down of houses.)

In the McLeod v. the United Kingdom judgment (23 September 1998, Application No. 24755/94, *Reports* 1998-VII, paragraphs 36 and 57), the Court naturally pointed out that the entry into a home by police officers constitutes an interference with the right to respect for the home. Such an entry may be justified by law if it is proportionate to the aim pursued and carried out in the circumstances defined in paragraph 2 of Article 8. In this case, the police had accompanied the applicant's former husband, who wished to retrieve various possessions. The Court stated:

> The Court considers further that, upon being informed that the applicant was not present, the police officers should not have entered her house, as it should have been clear to them that there was little or no risk of disorder or crime occurring. It notes in this regard that the police officers remained outside the property for some of the time, suggesting a belief on their part that a breach of the peace was not likely to occur in the absence of the applicant (see paragraph 14 above). The fact that an altercation did occur upon her return (see paragraph 15 above) is, in its opinion, immaterial in ascertaining whether the police officers were justified in entering the property initially.

> For the above reasons, the Court finds that the means employed by the police officers were disproportionate to the legitimate aim pursued. Accordingly, there has been a violation of Article 8 of the Convention.

Concerning searches, the Camenzind v. Switzerland judgment shows that they clearly constitute an interference with respect for the right to the home. Searches, too, may be justified under paragraph 2 of Article 8. The

Court stated (judgment of 16 December 1997, Application No. 21353/93, *Reports* 1997-VIII, paragraphs 45-47):

> The Contracting States may consider it necessary to resort to measures such as searches of residential premises and seizures in order to obtain physical evidence of certain offences. The Court will assess whether the reasons adduced to justify such measures were relevant and sufficient and whether the aforementioned proportionality principle has been adhered to (see the Funke v. France, Crémieux v. France and Miailhe v. France judgments of 25 February 1993, Series A No. 256-A, pp. 24-25, paragraphs 55-57, Series A No. 256-B, pp. 62-63, paragraphs 38-40, and Series A No. 256-C, pp. 89-90, paragraphs 36-38, respectively; and, *mutatis mutandis*, the Z. v. Finland judgment of 25 February 1997, *Reports of Judgments and Decisions* 1997-I, p. 347, paragraph 94). As regards the latter point, the Court must firstly ensure that the relevant legislation and practice afford individuals "adequate and effective safeguards against abuse" (ibid.); notwithstanding the margin of appreciation which the Court recognises the Contracting States have in this sphere, it must be particularly vigilant where, as in the present case, the authorities are empowered under national law to order and effect searches without a judicial warrant. If individuals are to be protected from arbitrary interference by the authorities with the rights guaranteed under Article 8, a legal framework and very strict limits on such powers are called for. Secondly, the Court must consider the particular circumstances of each case in order to determine whether, in the concrete case, the interference in question was proportionate to the aim pursued.

> In the present case the purpose of the search was to seize an unauthorised cordless telephone that Mr Camenzind was suspected of having used contrary to Section 42 of the Federal Act of 1922 "regulating telegraph and telephone communications" (see paragraphs 7-9 above). Admittedly, the authorities already had some evidence of the offence as the radio communications surveillance unit of the Head Office of the PTT had recorded the applicant's conversation and Mr Camenzind had admitted using the telephone (see paragraphs 7 and 10 above). Nevertheless, the Court accepts that the competent authorities were justified in thinking that the seizure of the *corpus delicti* – and, consequently, the search – were necessary to provide evidence of the relevant offence.

> With regard to the safeguards provided by Swiss law, the Court notes that under the Federal Administrative Criminal Law Act of 22 March 1974, as amended (see paragraphs 17-25 above), a search may, subject to exceptions, only be effected under a written warrant issued by a limited number of designated senior public servants (Section 48) and carried out by officials specially trained for the purpose (Section 20); they each have an obligation to stand down if circumstances exist which could affect their impartiality (Section 29). Searches can only be carried out in "dwellings and other premises [...] if it is likely that a suspect is in hiding there or if objects or valuables liable to seizure or evidence of the commission of an offence are to be found there" (Section 48); they cannot be conducted on Sundays, public holidays or at night "except in important cases or where there is imminent danger" (Section 49). At the beginning of a search the investigating official must produce evidence of identity and inform the occupier of the premises of the purpose of the search. That person or, if he is absent, a relative or a member of the household must be asked to attend. In principle, there will

also be a public officer present to ensure that "[the search] does not deviate from its purpose". A record of the search is drawn up immediately in the presence of the persons who attended; if they so request, they must be provided with a copy of the search warrant and of the record (Section 49). Furthermore, searches for documents are subject to special restrictions (Section 50). In addition, suspects are entitled, whatever the circumstances, to representation (Section 32); anyone affected by an "investigative measure" who has "an interest worthy of protection in having the measure [...] quashed or varied" may complain to the Indictment Division of the Federal Court (Sections 26 and 28). Lastly, a "suspect" who is found to have no case to answer may seek compensation for the losses he has sustained (Sections 99-100).

As regards the manner in which the search was conducted, the Court notes that it was at Mr Camenzind's request that it was carried out by a single official (see paragraph 11 above). It took place in the applicant's presence after he had been allowed to consult the file on his case and telephone a lawyer (see paragraph 10 above). Admittedly, it lasted almost two hours and covered the entire house, but the investigating official did no more than check the telephones and television sets; he did not search in any furniture, examine any documents or seize any-thing (see paragraph 11 above).

Having regard to the safeguards provided by Swiss legislation and especially to the limited scope of the search, the Court accepts that the interference with the applicant's right to respect for his home can be considered to have been propor-tionate to the aim pursued and thus "necessary in a democratic society" within the meaning of Article 8. Consequently, there has not been a violation of that provision.

5. Article 8, paragraph 1, and the protection of correspondence

On various occasions, the Court has held that the control of correspondence constituted an interference with the right protected by Article 8. It has so stated in cases involving prisoners' correspondence with their lawyers or with the Convention institutions.

In the case of Campbell v. the United Kingdom, the applicant complained that his correspondence with has lawyer and with the European Commission of Human Rights had been opened and read by the prison authorities, contrary to Article 8. In its judgment of 25 March 1992, Series A No. 233, p. 16, paragraph 33, the Court observed:

> [...] from the outset in his application to the Commission of 14 January 1986 the applicant complained that "his correspondence with his solicitors and the European Commission of Human Rights has regularly been subjected to inter-ference in so far as it has been opened, perused, scrutinised and censored by the prison authorities". He added that he was restricted in his contacts with his so-licitor and the Commission because he knew that "this correspondence will be read [...] and noted by the prison authorities". The Court further observes that the Government did not dispute that the applicant's incoming and outgoing cor-respondence with his solicitor, other than that concerning a petition to the Commission, could be examined under the prison rules. Indeed, the SHHD had informed the applicant and his solicitor that this correspondence was subject to

the existing rules which provided for the opening and reading of such letters (see paragraphs 13-14 above). In these circumstances, the applicant can claim to be a victim of an interference with his right to respect for correspondence under Article 8 (art. 8).

The Court considered, in this case, that the opening and reading of the applicant's correspondence with his solicitor and the opening of letters from the Commission did not meet any pressing social need and were therefore not "necessary in a democratic society" within the meaning of Article 8, paragraph 2.

Such an interference may be justified, however, if it satisfies the three conditions set forth in paragraph 2 of Article 8. In the Rinzivillo v. Italy judgment (21 December 2000, Application No. 31543/96, paragraph 28, available in French only – unofficial translation), the Court stated:

> Such an interference entails a violation of [Article 8] unless it is "in accordance with the law" and pursues one or more of the aims recognised as legitimate by paragraph 2 and, in addition, is "necessary in a democratic society" to attain such aims (the Silver and Others v. the United Kingdom judgment of 25 March 1983, Series A No. 61, p. 32, paragraph 84, the Campbell v. the United Kingdom judgment of 25 March 1992, Series A No. 233, p. 16, paragraph 34, the above-mentioned Calogero Diana judgment, p. 1775, paragraph 28, the above-mentioned Domenichini judgment, p. 1799, paragraph 28, and the Petra v. Romania judgment of 23 September 1998, *Reports* 1998-VII, p. 2853, paragraph 36).

The first condition is that the control of the correspondence must be provided for by a legal measure. The Court has held that the legal measure must be sufficiently precise. In the Calogero Diana v. Italy judgment, concerning the control of prisoner's post ordered by the judge responsible for the enforcement of sentences, the Court stated (15 November 1996, Application No. 15211/89, *Reports* 1996-V, paragraph 32):

> The Court reiterates that while a law which confers a discretion must indicate the scope of that discretion, it is impossible to attain absolute certainty in the framing of the law, and the likely outcome of any search for certainty would be excessive rigidity (see, among many other authorities, the Silver and Others judgment previously cited, p. 33, paragraph 88). In this instance, however, Law No. 354 leaves the authorities too much latitude. In particular, it goes no further than identifying the category of persons whose correspondence may be censored and the competent court, without saying anything about the length of the measure or the reasons that may warrant it. The gaps in Section 18 of the law weigh in favour of rejecting the Government's argument.

> In sum, the Italian law does not indicate with reasonable clarity the scope and manner of exercise of the relevant discretion conferred on the public authorities, so that Mr Diana did not enjoy the minimum degree of protection to which citizens are entitled under the rule of law in a democratic society (see the Kruslin judgment previously cited, pp. 24-25, paragraph 36). There has therefore been breach of Article 8 (art. 8).

See, to the same effect, the Petra v. Romania judgment (23 September 1998, Application No. 27273/95, *Reports* 1998-VII, paragraph 37), where the Court held that the law left the national authorities too much latitude, being restricted, in particular, to stating in very generally terms that convicted prisoners were entitled to receive and send correspondence and authorising the prison authorities to keep any letter or any newspaper, book or magazine not appropriate for the rehabilitation of the convicted prisoner, so that the control of correspondence seemed to be automatic, irrespective of any decision by a judicial authority, and not amenable to any remedy (*idem* the Di Giovine v. Italy judgment of 26 July 2001, Application No. 39920/98, paragraphs 25-27; and the Nidbala v. Poland judgment of 4 July 2000, Application No. 27915/95, paragraphs 78-81).

In general, the second condition does not cause any problems. The Court is quite ready to recognise that the aims pursued by the control of correspondence, such as the desire to protect "national security" and/or the "prevention of disorder" or the "prevention of crime", are legitimate aims for the purposes of Article 8, paragraph 2.

Third condition: is the control of correspondence none the less necessary? In the Campbell v. the United Kingdom judgment of 25 March 1992 (Series A No. 233, pp. 18-19, paragraphs 44-48), the Court examined the question of the need to monitor correspondence with a lawyer:

> [...] the notion of necessity implies that the interference corresponds to a pressing social need and, in particular, that it is proportionate to the legitimate aim pursued. In determining whether an interference is "necessary in a democratic society" regard may be had to the State's margin of appreciation (see, amongst other authorities, the *Sunday Times* v. the United Kingdom (No. 2) judgment of 26 November 1991, Series A No. 217, pp. 28-29, paragraph 50).

> It has also been recognised that some measure of control over prisoners' correspondence is called for and is not of itself incompatible with the Convention, regard being paid to the ordinary and reasonable requirements of imprisonment (see the Silver and Others v. the United Kingdom judgment of 25 March 1983, Series A No. 61, p. 38, paragraph 98). In assessing the permissible extent of such control in general, the fact that the opportunity to write and to receive letters is sometimes the prisoner's only link with the outside world should, however, not be overlooked.

> It is clearly in the general interest that any person who wishes to consult a lawyer should be free to do so under conditions which favour full and uninhibited discussion. It is for this reason that the lawyer-client relationship is, in principle, privileged. Indeed, in its S. v. Switzerland judgment of 28 November 1991 the Court stressed the importance of a prisoner's right to communicate with counsel out of earshot of the prison authorities. It was considered, in the context of Article 6 (art. 6), that if a lawyer were unable to confer with his client without such surveillance and receive confidential instructions from him his assistance would lose much of its usefulness, whereas the Convention is intended to guarantee rights that are practical and effective (Series A No. 220, pp. 15-16, paragraph 48; see also, in this context, the Campbell and Fell v. the United Kingdom judgment of 28 June 1984, Series A No. 80, p. 49, paragraphs 111-113).

In the Court's view, similar considerations apply to a prisoner's correspondence with a lawyer concerning contemplated or pending proceedings where the need for confidentiality is equally pressing, particularly where such correspondence relates, as in the present case, to claims and complaints against the prison authorities. That such correspondence be susceptible to routine scrutiny, particularly by individuals or authorities who may have a direct interest in the subject matter contained therein, is not in keeping with the principles of confidentiality and professional privilege attaching to relations between a lawyer and his client.

Admittedly, as the Government pointed out, the borderline between mail concerning contemplated litigation and that of a general nature is especially difficult to draw and correspondence with a lawyer may concern matters which have little or nothing to do with litigation. Nevertheless, the Court sees no reason to distinguish between the different categories of correspondence with lawyers which, whatever their purpose, concern matters of a private and confidential character. In principle, such letters are privileged under Article 8 (art. 8). This means that the prison authorities may open a letter from a lawyer to a prisoner when they have reasonable cause to believe that it contains an illicit enclosure which the normal means of detection have failed to disclose. The letter should, however, only be opened and should not be read. Suitable guarantees preventing the reading of the letter should be provided, for example opening the letter in the presence of the prisoner. The reading of a prisoner's mail to and from a lawyer, on the other hand, should only be permitted in exceptional circumstances when the authorities have reasonable cause to believe that the privilege is being abused in that the contents of the letter endanger prison security or the safety of others or are otherwise of a criminal nature. What may be regarded as "reasonable cause" will depend on all the circumstances but it presupposes the existence of facts or information which would satisfy an objective observer that the privileged channel of communication was being abused (see, *mutatis mutandis*, the Fox, Campbell and Hartley v. the United Kingdom judgment of 30 August 1990, Series A No. 182, p. 16, paragraph 32).

The question arose, in particular, in respect of detained persons suspected of terrorism. In the Erdem v. Germany judgment, concerning the trial of members of the PKK (of 5 July 2001, Application No. 38321/97, paragraphs 64-66, available in French only – unofficial translation), the Court stated:

In the Klass and Others v. Germany judgment of 18 November 1978 (Series A No. 78, p. 23, paragraph 48), concerning a law which authorised restrictions on the secrecy of correspondence, mail and telecommunications, the Court had laid down the following principles regarding the fight against terrorism:

"[...] Democratic societies nowadays find themselves threatened by highly sophisticated forms of espionage and by terrorism, with the result that the State must be able, in order effectively to counter such threats, to undertake the secret surveillance of subversive elements operating within its jurisdiction. The Court has therefore to accept that the existence of some legislation granting powers of secret surveillance over the mail, post and telecommunications is, under exceptional conditions, necessary in a democratic society in the interests of national security and/or for the prevention of crime."

It none the less remains that the confidentiality of correspondence between a detained person and his legal representative constitutes a fundamental right for an individual and directly affects the rights of the defence. It is for that reason that, as the Court has stated above, a derogation from that principle may be authorised in exceptional cases and must be accompanied with appropriate and sufficient guarantees against abuse (see also, *mutatis mutandis*, the above-mentioned Klass judgment, ibid.).

The proceedings against the senior members of the PKK come within the exceptional context of the fight against terrorism in all its forms. Furthermore, it appeared to be lawful for the German authorities to ensure that the proceedings would take place in the best conditions of security, having regard to the large Turkish community, many of whose members are of Kurdish origin, living in Germany.

Next, the Court observes that the provision in question is drafted very precisely, since it specifies the category of persons whose correspondence must be monitored, namely detained persons suspected of belonging to a terrorist organisation within the meaning of Article 129.a of the Criminal Code. Furthermore, that measure, which is exceptional in nature since it derogates from the general rule that correspondence between a detained person and his legal representative is confidential, is accompanied with a number of guarantees: unlike other cases before the Court, where mail was opened by the prison authorities (see, in particular, the above-mentioned Campbell and Fell and the Campbell judgments), in this case the power of control is exercised by an independent judge, who must have no connection with the investigation and who must keep secret the information of which he thus has knowledge. Last, the control in question is restricted, since the detained person is free to communicate orally with his legal representative; admittedly, the latter cannot give him written documents or other items, but he can inform the detained person of the content of the written documents.

Moreover, the Court recalls that some compromise between the requirements for defending democratic society and those of protecting individual rights is inherent in the system of the Convention (see, *mutatis mutandis*, the above-mentioned Klass judgment, p. 28, paragraph 59).

Regard being had to the threat presented by terrorism in all its forms (see the decision of the Commission in the case of Bader, Meins, Meinhof and Grundmann v. Germany, 30 May 1975, Application No. 6166/75), to the guarantees surrounding the control of correspondence in this case and of the margin of appreciation of the State, the Court concludes that the contested interference was not disproportionate to the legitimate aims pursued.

Accordingly, there has been no violation of Article 8 of the Convention.

Mention should also be made of the Silver and Others v. the United Kingdom judgment (25 March 1983, Series A No. 61, p. 40, paragraph 103), where the Court accepted the exception to Article 8, paragraph 2. It considered that the prison authorities could retain the letters of one of the detained persons in order to ensure the continuing prevention of disorder. It noted, *inter alia*:

> Mr Cooper's letters Nos. 28-31 were stopped not only for employing grossly improper language but also for containing threats of violence (see paragraphs 45.*a*.iv, and 65 above). His counsel contested the Commission's view that the interference was "necessary" on the second ground.

> The Court agrees with the Commission. Letters Nos. 28-30 contained clear threats and letter No. 31 can be regarded as a continuation thereof. In the Court's judgment, the authorities had sufficient reason for concluding that the stopping of these letters was necessary "for the prevention of disorder or crime", within the meaning of Article 8, paragraph 2 (art. 8-2).

In the Valasinas v. Lithuania judgment, on the other hand (24 July 2001, Application No. 44558/98, paragraphs 129-130), the Court stated that the control did not satisfy the requirement of necessity within the meaning of Article 8, paragraph 2 (*idem* the case of Peers v. Greece, 19 April 2001, Application No. 28524/95, paragraphs 82-83; the Rehbock v. Slovenia judgment of 28 November 2000, Application No. 29462/95, paragraphs 97-101; or the Messina v. Italy (No. 2) judgment of 28 September 2000; the Foxley v. the United Kingdom judgment of 20 June 2000, Application No. 33274/96, paragraphs 38-47).

Article 8, paragraph 2 – Derogatory clause

Article 8, paragraph 2, is worded as follows:

> **2. There shall be no interference by a public authority with the exercise of this right except such as is in accordance with the law and is necessary in a democratic society in the interests of national security, public safety or the economic well-being of the country, for the prevention of disorder or crime, for the protection of health or morals, or for the protection of the rights and freedoms of others.**

We shall deal here with the restrictive clauses found in Article 8 and in other Articles such as Articles 9, 10 and 11. Their wording is often very similar. They will not be examined in future in as much detail as here.

Examination of the case-law on telephone tapping and correspondence provided an initial approach to this provision.

1. Interference "in accordance with the law"

In order to be justified, the interference must first of all be "in accordance with the law". In the *Sunday Times* v. the United Kingdom (No. 1) judgment the Court explained the meaning of that expression (26 April 1979, Series A No. 30, pp. 30-31, paragraphs 47 and 49):

> [in the expression] "prescribed by law" the word "law" covers not only statute but also unwritten law. Accordingly, the Court does not attach importance here to the fact that contempt of court is a creature of the common law and not of legislation. It would clearly be contrary to the intention of the drafters of the Convention to hold that a restriction imposed by virtue of the common law is not "prescribed by law" on the sole ground that it is not enunciated in legislation: this would deprive a common-law State which is Party to the Convention of the protection of Article 10, paragraph 2 (art. 10-2), and strike at the very roots of that State's legal system.
>
> [...]
>
> In the Court's opinion, the following are two of the requirements that flow from the expression "prescribed by law". Firstly, the law must be adequately accessible: the citizen must be able to have an indication that is adequate in the circumstances of the legal rules applicable to a given case. Secondly, a norm cannot be regarded as a "law" unless it is formulated with sufficient precision to enable the citizen to regulate his conduct: he must be able – if need be with appropriate advice – to foresee, to a degree that is reasonable in the circumstances, the consequences which a given action may entail. Those consequences need not be foreseeable with absolute certainty: experience shows this to be unattainable. Again, whilst certainty is highly desirable, it may bring in its train excessive rigidity and the law must be able to keep pace with changing circumstances.

Accordingly, many laws are inevitably couched in terms which, to a greater or lesser extent, are vague and whose interpretation and application are questions of practice.

In the Silver and Others judgment of 25 March 1983, Series A No. 61, p. 33, paragraph 88, the Court recognised that there may be limits to the requirement of precision. It stated:

A law which confers a discretion must indicate the scope of that discretion. However, the Court has already recognised the impossibility of attaining absolute certainty in the framing of laws and the risk that the search for certainty may entail excessive rigidity.

As concerns the concept of "law", see the above-mentioned Malone judgment under the heading "surveillance by telephone tapping".

2. Interference following a "legitimate aim"

The next condition is that the interference must pursue one of the legitimate aims referred to in paragraph 2 (prevention of disorder, protection of morals, etc.). As a general rule that condition does not cause any serious problems, other than where a State has clearly acted in bad faith.

3. Interference "necessary in a democratic society"

The interference must still satisfy one final condition. This is the condition of "necessity", which is more difficult to satisfy – all the more so because the necessity must be evaluated within the context of "a democratic society". On this point, the above-mentioned Silver and Others judgment (ibid., pp. 37-38, paragraph 97) provides a useful summary of the Court's case-law:

On a number of occasions, the Court has stated its understanding of the phrase "necessary in a democratic society", the nature of its functions in the examination of issues turning on that phrase and the manner in which it will perform those functions. It suffices here to summarise certain principles:

(a) The adjective "necessary" is not synonymous with "indispensable", neither has it the flexibility of such expressions as "admissible", "ordinary", "useful", "reasonable" or "desirable" (see the Handyside judgment of 7 December 1976, Series A No. 24, p. 22, paragraph 48).

(b) The Contracting States enjoy a certain but not unlimited margin of appreciation in the matter of the imposition of restrictions, but it is for the Court to give the final ruling on whether they are compatible with the Convention (ibid., p. 23, paragraph 49).

(c) The phrase "necessary in a democratic society" means that, to be compatible with the Convention, the interference must, *inter alia,* correspond to a "pressing social need" and be "proportionate to the legitimate aim pursued" (ibid., pp. 22-23, paragraphs 48-49).

(d) Those paragraphs of Articles of the Convention which provide for an exception to a right guaranteed are to be narrowly interpreted (see the above-mentioned Klass and Others judgment, Series A No. 28, p. 21, paragraph 42).

A specific reference to the Klass v. Germany judgment is appropriate. That judgment sets out a number of important points concerning the principles derived from the concept of "democratic society" in the light of which the Court intended to examine the necessity for the interference (6 September 1978, Series A No. 28, pp. 25-26, paragraph 55):

> One of the fundamental principles of a democratic society is the rule of law, which is expressly referred to in the Preamble to the Convention (see the Golder judgment of 21 February 1975, Series A No. 18, pp. 16-17, paragraph 34). The rule of law implies, *inter alia*, that an interference by the executive authorities with an individual's rights should be subject to an effective control which should normally be assured by the judiciary, at least in the last resort, judicial control offering the best guarantees of independence, impartiality and a proper procedure.

> In the Handyside v. the United Kingdom judgment of 7 December 1976, Series A No. 24, p. 23, paragraph 49, the Court has stated that a "democratic society" is characterised by "pluralism, tolerance and broadmindedness".

In reality, it all depends on the particular circumstances. The Court will seek above all to ascertain whether the interference is proportionate to the legitimate aim relied on by the State. In so doing, the Court will pay particular attention to the principles proper to a "democratic society" (Silver judgment, paragraphs 97 *et seq.*).

Article 9 ECHR – Freedom of thought, conscience and religion

Article 9, paragraph 1

Article 9, paragraph 1, is worded as follows:

> 1. **Everyone has the right to freedom of thought, conscience and religion; this right includes freedom to change his religion or belief and freedom, either alone or in community with others and in public or private, to manifest his religion or belief, in worship, teaching, practice and observance.**

On this subject, for a long time more decisions have been taken by the Commission than by the Court.

The first part of Article 9, paragraph 1, protects freedom of thought, conscience and religion in general. The second part of Article 9, paragraph 1, protects, more specifically, freedom to change religion or belief. This second part also guarantees freedom to manifest one's "religion" or "belief", each of which has a different scope; and particular information is given on the various ways of manifesting one's "religion" in the form of "rites" [...].

Furthermore, Article 9 is logically invoked by applicants in conjunction with Article 2 of Protocol No. 1, which provides that "No person shall be denied the right to education. In the exercise of any functions which it assumes in relation to education and to teaching, the State shall respect the right of parents to ensure such education and teaching in conformity with their own religious and philosophical convictions" (for example: the Efstratiou v. Greece judgment of 18 December 1996, *Reports* 1996-VI).

1. Importance and content of freedom of thought, conscience and religion

It is appropriate to cite, principally, the Kokkinakis v. Greece judgment (25 May 1993, Series A No. 260-A, p.17, paragraph 31), according to which:

> As enshrined in Article 9 (art. 9), freedom of thought, conscience and religion is one of the foundations of a "democratic society" within the meaning of the Convention. It is, in its religious dimension, one of the most vital elements that go to make up the identity of believers and their conception of life, but it is also a precious asset for atheists, agnostics, sceptics and the unconcerned. The pluralism indissociable from a democratic society, which has been dearly won over the centuries, depends on it.
>
> While religious freedom is primarily a matter of individual conscience, it also implies, *inter alia*, freedom to "manifest [one's] religion". Bearing witness in words and deeds is bound up with the existence of religious convictions.
>
> According to Article 9 (art. 9), freedom to manifest one's religion is not only exercisable in community with others, "in public" and within the circle of those

whose faith one shares, but can also be asserted "alone" and "in private"; furthermore, it includes in principle the right to try to convince one's neighbour, for example through "teaching", failing which, moreover, "freedom to change [one's] religion or belief", enshrined in Article 9 (art. 9), would be likely to remain a dead letter.

2. Freedom of thought and conscience

In the case of X. v. the Federal Republic of Germany (Application No. 7705/76, *Decisions and Reports* 9, pp. 199 *et seq.*, paragraph 1), the Commission interpreted Article 9 in the light of Article 4 and decided that the sanctions taken by a state against conscientious objectors who refused to perform civilian service in place of military service do no violate their freedom of conscience :

> Article 9 of the Convention relied on by the applicant guarantees everyone the right to freedom of thought, conscience and religion.

> When interpreting this provision in similar cases the Commission has taken into consideration Article 4, paragraph 3.*b*, of the Convention, which provides that the term "forced or compulsory labour" within the meaning of that Article shall not include "any service of a military character or, in the case of conscientious objectors in countries where they are recognised, service exacted instead of compulsory military service".

> Since this text expressly recognises that conscientious objectors may be required to perform civilian service in substitution for compulsory military service it must be inferred that according to the Convention conscientious objection does not imply a right to be exempted from substitute civilian service (see the Commission's opinion in Application No. 2299/66, Grandrath v. the Federal Republic of Germany – report dated 12 December 1968, paragraph 32). It does not prevent a State from imposing sanctions on those who refuse such service (see, *mutatis mutandis*, decision on Application No. 5591/72 v. Austria, *Collection* 43, p. 161).

In the case of Thlimmenos v. Greece (6 April 2000, Application No. 34639/97, paragraphs 39, 41-42 and 44-49), the Court ruled on the refusal to allow access to the profession of chartered accountant to a person formerly convicted of having refused to serve in the armed forces owing to his religious convictions. The Court examined the question from the aspect of Article 9 in conjunction with Article 14 and indicated :

> The Court considers that the applicant's complaint falls to be examined under Article 14 of the Convention taken in conjunction with Article 9 for the following reasons.

> [...]

> The Court notes that the applicant was not appointed a chartered accountant as a result of his past conviction for insubordination consisting in his refusal to wear the military uniform. He was thus treated differently from the other persons who had applied for that post on the ground of his status as a convicted person. The Court considers that such difference of treatment does not generally come

within the scope of Article 14 in so far as it relates to access to a particular profession, the right to freedom of profession not being guaranteed by the Convention.

However, the applicant does not complain of the distinction that the rules governing access to the profession make between convicted persons and others. His complaint rather concerns the fact that in the application of the relevant law no distinction is made between persons convicted of offences committed exclusively because of their religious beliefs and persons convicted of other offences. In this context the Court notes that the applicant is a member of the Jehovah's Witnesses, a religious group committed to pacifism, and that there is nothing in the file to disprove the applicant's claim that he refused to wear the military uniform only because he considered that his religion prevented him from doing so. In essence, the applicant's argument amounts to saying that he is discriminated against in the exercise of his freedom of religion, as guaranteed by Article 9 of the Convention, in that he was treated like any other person convicted of a serious crime although his own conviction resulted from the very exercise of this freedom. Seen in this perspective, the Court accepts that the "set of facts" complained of by the applicant – his being treated as a person convicted of a serious crime for the purposes of an appointment to a chartered accountant's post despite the fact that the offence for which he had been convicted was prompted by his religious beliefs – "falls within the ambit of a Convention provision", namely Article 9.

[...]

The Court has so far considered that the right under Article 14 not to be discriminated against in the enjoyment of the rights guaranteed under the Convention is violated when States treat differently persons in analogous situations without providing an objective and reasonable justification (see the Inze judgment cited above, p. 18, paragraph 41). However, the Court considers that this is not the only facet of the prohibition of discrimination in Article 14. The right not to be discriminated against in the enjoyment of the rights guaranteed under the Convention is also violated when States without an objective and reasonable justification fail to treat differently persons whose situations are significantly different.

It follows that Article 14 of the Convention is of relevance to the applicant's complaint and applies in the circumstances of this case in conjunction with Article 9 thereof.

The next question to be addressed is whether Article 14 of the Convention has been complied with. According to its case-law, the Court will have to examine whether the failure to treat the applicant differently from other persons convicted of a serious crime pursued a legitimate aim. If it did the Court will have to examine whether there was a reasonable relationship of proportionality between the means employed and the aim sought to be realised (see the Inze judgment cited above, ibid.).

The Court [...] notes that the applicant did serve a prison sentence for his refusal to wear the military uniform. In these circumstances, the Court considers that imposing a further sanction on the applicant was disproportionate. It follows that the applicant's exclusion from the profession of chartered accountants did not pursue a legitimate aim. As a result, the Court finds that there existed no objective and reasonable justification for not treating the applicant differently from other persons convicted of a serious crime.

[...] The Court has never excluded that legislation may be found to be in direct breach of the Convention (see, *inter alia*, Chassagnou and Others v. France [GC], Nos. 25088/94, 28331/95 and 28443/95, ECHR 1999-III). In the present case the Court considers that it was the State having enacted the relevant legislation which violated the applicant's right not to be discriminated against in the enjoyment of his right under Article 9 of the Convention. That State did so by failing to introduce appropriate exceptions to the rule barring persons convicted of a serious crime from the profession of chartered accountants.

The Court concludes, therefore, that there has been a violation of Article 14 of the Convention taken in conjunction with Article 9.

In the Arrowsmith v. the United Kingdom case the applicant had been prosecuted for distributing "pacifist" pamphlets concerning the activities of the British Army in Northern Ireland to members of the armed forces. It was declared inadmissible by the Commission on the ground that the activities at issue did not constitute a "manifestation" of beliefs in the proper sense. The Commission observed (Application No. 7805/77, *Decisions and Reports* 19, pp. 19 *et seq.*, paragraphs 71-72):

> [...] the term "practice" as employed in Article 9, paragraph 1, does not cover each act which is motivated or influenced by a religion or a belief.

> It is true that public declarations proclaiming generally the idea of pacifism and urging the acceptance of a commitment to non-violence may be considered as a normal and recognised manifestation of pacifist belief. However, when the actions of individuals do not actually express the belief concerned they cannot be considered to be as such protected by Article 9, paragraph 1, even when they are motivated or influenced by it.

> The leaflet here in question starts with the citation of the statements of two ex-soldiers one of whom says: "I'm not against being a soldier. I would be willing to fight to defend this country against an invader – I'd be willing to fight for a cause I can believe in. But what is happening in Ireland is all wrong." Although this is an individual opinion of a person who is not necessarily linked to the organisation which edited the leaflet its citation nevertheless indicates that the authors consider it recommendable. It can therefore not be found that the leaflet conveys the idea that one should under no circumstances, even not in response to the threat of or the use of force, secure one's political or other objectives by violent means. It only follows from the contents of the leaflet that its authors were opposed to British policy in Northern Ireland.

The Commission concluded that there had been no "manifestation of a belief" and that, accordingly, Article 9 had not been violated. Only Article 10, concerning freedom of expression, could be taken into account.

3. Freedom of religion

General observations

Once again, it is appropriate to refer to the Kokkinakis v. Greece judgment (25 May 1993, Series A No. 260-A, p. 17, paragraph 31), where the Court expands upon the content of religious freedom:

> While religious freedom is primarily a matter of individual conscience, it also implies, *inter alia*, freedom to "manifest [one's] religion". Bearing witness in words and deeds is bound up with the existence of religious convictions.
>
> According to Article 9 (art. 9), freedom to manifest one's religion is not only exercisable in community with others, "in public" and within the circle of those whose faith one shares, but can also be asserted "alone" and "in private"; furthermore, it includes in principle the right to try to convince one's neighbour, for example through "teaching", failing which, moreover, "freedom to change [one's] religion or belief", enshrined in Article 9 (art. 9), would be likely to remain a dead letter.

Clearly, the freedom enshrined in Article 9 also covers the right not to belong to and not to practise a religion. In the case of Buscarini and Others v. San Marino, two Members of Parliament were obliged to take the oath on the Gospels, failing which they would lose the mandate (judgment of 18 February 1999, Application No. 24645/94, *Reports* 1999-I, paragraph 34). Before concluding that there had been a violation of Article 9, the Court referred to the Kokkinakis judgment, stating:

> The Court reiterates that: "As enshrined in Article 9, freedom of thought, conscience and religion is one of the foundations of a 'democratic society' within the meaning of the Convention. It is, in its religious dimension, one of the most vital elements that go to make up the identity of believers and their conception of life, but it is also a precious asset for atheists, agnostics, sceptics and the unconcerned. The pluralism indissociable from a democratic society, which has been dearly won over the centuries, depends on it" (see the Kokkinakis v. Greece judgment of 25 May 1993, Series A No. 260-A, p. 17, paragraph 31). That freedom entails, *inter alia*, freedom to hold or not to hold religious beliefs and to practise or not to practise a religion.
>
> In the instant case, requiring Mr Buscarini and Mr Della Balda to take an oath on the Gospels did indeed constitute a limitation within the meaning of the second paragraph of Article 9, since it required them to swear allegiance to a particular religion on pain of forfeiting their parliamentary seats. Such interference will be contrary to Article 9 unless it is "prescribed by law", pursues one or more of the legitimate aims set out in paragraph 2 and is "necessary in a democratic society".

However, not all conduct can be classified as a "manifestation" of religion.

In the Kalaç v. Turkey judgment (1 July 1997, *Reports* 1997-IV, paragraphs 27-31), a Turkish military judge had been retired from the army. The decision to retire him had been based, more specifically, on the fact that the applicant's conduct and actions "showed that he had adopted illegal integrationist opinions". The respondent government contended that the applicant had provided legal assistance to and participated in training meetings of an integrationist organisation and had on several occasions been involved in the appointment of military members of the sect. On the basis of those documents, a committee of five members of the military representing the senior ranks of the armed forces concluded that in receiving and applying instructions from the directors of that organisation, Colonel Kalaç had acted in breach of military discipline and must therefore be retired. The Court declared:

> The Court reiterates that while religious freedom is primarily a matter of individual conscience, it also implies, *inter alia*, freedom to manifest one's religion not only in community with others, in public and within the circle of those whose faith one shares, but also alone and in private (see the Kokkinakis v. Greece judgment of 25 May 1993, Series A No. 260-A, p. 17, paragraph 31). Article 9 (art. 9) lists a number of forms which manifestation of one's religion or belief may take, namely worship, teaching, practice and observance. Nevertheless, Article 9 (art. 9) does not protect every act motivated or inspired by a religion or belief. Moreover, in exercising his freedom to manifest his religion, an individual may need to take his specific situation into account.

> In choosing to pursue a military career Mr Kalaç was accepting of his own accord a system of military discipline that by its very nature implied the possibility of placing on certain of the rights and freedoms of members of the armed forces limitations incapable of being imposed on civilians (see the Engel and Others v. the Netherlands judgment of 8 June 1976, Series A No. 22, p. 24, paragraph 57). States may adopt for their armies disciplinary regulations forbidding this or that type of conduct, in particular an attitude inimical to an established order reflecting the requirements of military service.

> It is not contested that the applicant, within the limits imposed by the requirements of military life, was able to fulfil the obligations which constitute the normal forms through which a Muslim practises his religion. For example, he was in particular permitted to pray five times a day and to perform his other religious duties, such as keeping the fast of Ramadan and attending Friday prayers at the mosque.

> The Supreme Military Council's order was, moreover, not based on Colonel Kalaç's religious opinions and beliefs or the way he had performed his religious duties but on his conduct and attitude (see paragraphs 8 and 25 above). According to the Turkish authorities, this conduct breached military discipline and infringed the principle of secularism.

> The Court accordingly concludes that the applicant's compulsory retirement did not amount to an interference with the right guaranteed by Article 9 (art. 9) since it was not prompted by the way the applicant manifested his religion.

> There has therefore been no breach of Article 9 (art. 9).

(*Idem* the Hassan and Tchaouch v. Bulgaria judgment of 26 October 2000, Application No. 30985/96, paragraph 60.)

The Commission had ruled some time before on an advertisement in which the Church of Scientology extolled, using arguments of a religious nature, the merits of a device for measuring the state of the soul. The Commission considered that the decision of a tribunal to exclude from that advertisement the use of certain religious terms was not contrary to Article 9 (Application No. 7805/77, *Decisions and Reports* 16, p. 72, paragraph 4). The Commission did not regard that advertisement as constituting the "manifestation" of a religious belief, and observed:

> The Commission is of the opinion that the concept, contained in the first paragraph of Article 9, concerning the manifestation of a belief in practice does not confer protection on statements of purported religious belief which appear as selling "arguments" in advertisements of a purely commercial nature by a religious group. In this connection the Commission would draw a distinction, however, between advertisements which are merely "informational" or "descriptive" in character and commercial advertisements offering objects for sale. Once an advertisement enters into the latter sphere, although it may concern religious objects central to a particular need, statements of religious content represent, in the Commission's view, more the manifestation of a desire to market goods for profit than the manifestation of a belief in practice, within the proper sense of that term. Consequently the Commission considers that the works used in the advertisement under scrutiny fall outside the proper scope of Article 9, paragraph 1, and that therefore there has been no interference with the applicants' right to manifest their religion or beliefs in practice under that Article.

(See also the case of Efstratiou v. Greece, 18 December 1996, *Reports* 1996-VI, where the Court held that an obligation for schoolchildren to take part in a procession on the national holiday, in which the armed forces participated, was not susceptible of offending the religious convictions of the applicants, who were Jehovah's Witnesses.)

Practical examples

The Metropolitan Church of Bessarabia and Others v. Moldova judgment (13 December 2001, Application No. 45701/99) concerned the refusal to recognise a Church. The Court observed (paragraph 105):

> [...] not being recognised, the applicant Church cannot operate. In particular, its priests may not conduct divine service, its members may not meet to practise their religion and, not having legal personality, it is not entitled to judicial protection of its assets.

> The Court therefore considers that the Moldovan Government's refusal to recognise the applicant Church, upheld by the Supreme Court of Justice's decision of 9 December 1997, constituted interference with the right of the applicant Church and the other applicants to freedom of religion, as guaranteed by Article 9, paragraph 1, of the Convention.

In that case, the Court stated (paragraphs 129-130):

> [...] the Court notes that in the absence of recognition the applicant Church may neither organise itself nor operate. Lacking legal personality, it cannot bring legal proceedings to protect its assets, which are indispensable for worship, while its members cannot meet to carry on religious activities without contravening the legislation on religious denominations.

As regards the tolerance allegedly shown by the Government towards the applicant Church and its members, the Court cannot regard such tolerance as a substitute for recognition, since recognition alone is capable of conferring rights on those concerned.

The Court further notes that on occasion the applicants have not been able to defend themselves against acts of intimidation, since the authorities have fallen back on the excuse that only legal activities are entitled to legal protection (see paragraphs 56-57 and 84 above).

Lastly, it notes that when the authorities recognised other liturgical associations they did not apply the criteria which they used in order to refuse to recognise the applicant Church and that no justification has been put forward by the Moldovan Government for this difference in treatment.

In conclusion, the Court considers that the refusal to recognise the applicant Church has such consequences for the applicants' freedom of religion that it cannot be regarded as proportionate to the legitimate aim pursued or, accordingly, as necessary in a democratic society, and that there has been a violation of Article 9.

The Hassan and Tchaouch v. Bulgaria judgment (26 October 2000, Application No. 30985/96, paragraphs 61-65) dealt with the organisation of Churches and the involvement of the State in their organisation. The Court noted:

In the present case the parties differ on the question whether or not the events under consideration, which all relate to the organisation and leadership of the Muslim community in Bulgaria, concern the right of the individual applicants to freedom to manifest their religion and, consequently, whether or not Article 9 of the Convention applies. The applicants maintained that their religious liberties were at stake, whereas the Government analysed the complaints mainly from the angle of Article 11 of the Convention.

The Court recalls that religious communities traditionally and universally exist in the form of organised structures. They abide by rules which are often seen by followers as being of a divine origin. Religious ceremonies have their meaning and sacred value for the believers if they have been conducted by ministers empowered for that purpose in compliance with these rules. The personality of the religious ministers is undoubtedly of importance to every member of the community. Participation in the life of the community is thus a manifestation of one's religion, protected by Article 9 of the Convention.

Where the organisation of the religious community is at issue, Article 9 of the Convention must be interpreted in the light of Article 11, which safeguards associative life against unjustified State interference. Seen in this perspective, the believers' right to freedom of religion encompasses the expectation that the community will be allowed to function peacefully, free from arbitrary State intervention. Indeed, the autonomous existence of religious communities is indispensable for pluralism in a democratic society and is thus an issue at the very heart of the protection which Article 9 affords. It directly concerns not only the organisation of the community as such but also the effective enjoyment of the right to freedom of religion by all its active members. Were the organisational life of the community not protected by Article 9 of the Convention, all other aspects of the individual's freedom of religion would become vulnerable.

There is no doubt, in the present case, that the applicants are active members of the religious community. The first applicant was an elected Chief Mufti of the Bulgarian Muslims. The Court need not establish whether the second applicant, who used to work as an Islamic teacher, was also employed as a secretary to the Chief Mufti's Office, it being undisputed that Mr Chaush is a Muslim believer who actively participated in religious life at the relevant time.

It follows that the events complained of concerned both applicants' right to freedom of religion, as enshrined in Article 9 of the Convention. That provision is therefore applicable.

Further, the Court does not consider that the case is better dealt with solely under Article 11 of the Convention, as suggested by the Government. Such an approach would take the applicants' complaints out of their context and disregard their substance.

The Court finds, therefore, that the applicants' complaints fall to be examined under Article 9 of the Convention. In so far as they touch upon the organisation of the religious community, the Court reiterates that Article 9 must be interpreted in the light of the protection afforded by Article 11 of the Convention.

In this case, the Court stated that the interference in issue was not prescribed by law (paragraph 86):

> The Court finds, therefore, that the interference with the internal organisation of the Muslim community and the applicants' freedom of religion was not "prescribed by law" in that it was arbitrary and was based on legal provisions which allowed an unfettered discretion to the executive and did not meet the required standards of clarity and foreseeability.

Still on the matter of organisation, in the Serif v. Greece judgment of 14 December 1999, Application No. 38178/97, *Reports* 1999-IX, paragraph 52, the Court stated:

> [...] the Court does not consider that, in democratic societies, the State needs to take measures to ensure that religious communities remain or are brought under a unified leadership.

In the case of Manoussakis and Others v. Greece (26 September 1996, *Reports of Judgments and Decisions* 1996, pp. 1362 and 1365, paragraphs 40 and 47), the applicants were convicted for having established and operated a place of worship for religious ceremonies and meetings for followers of the Jehovah's Witnesses' denomination without first obtaining the authorisation of the Minister of Education and Religious Affairs and of the bishop. With regard to the authorisation requirement the Court observed:

> Like the applicants, the Court recognises that the States are entitled to verify whether a movement or association carries on, ostensibly in pursuit of religious aims, activities which are harmful to the population. Nevertheless, it recalls that

Jehovah's Witnesses come within the definition of "known religion" as provided for under Greek law (see the Kokkinakis v. Greece judgment of 25 May 1993, Series A No. 260-A, p. 15, paragraph 23). This was moreover conceded by the Government.

However, this power of the State is not unlimited. The Court stated furthermore:

The right to freedom of religion as guaranteed under the Convention excludes any discretion on the part of the State to determine whether religious beliefs or the means used to express such beliefs are legitimate.

The Court held in this judgment that the conviction of the applicants was not "necessary in a democratic society". It considered that the prosecution and the Heraklion Criminal Court sitting on appeal, in its judgment of 15 February 1990, relied expressly on the lack of the bishop's authorisation as well as the lack of an authorisation from the Minister of Education and Religious Affairs.

(See also the Cha'are Shalom Ve Tsedek v. France judgment of 27 June 2000, Application No. 27417/95, paragraphs 64, 73-74 and 80-85, concerning the authorisation of establishments to carry out the ritual slaughter required by the Jewish religion.)

Article 9, paragraph 2 – Derogatory clause

Article 9, paragraph 2, is worded as follows:

> 2. **Freedom to manifest one's religion or beliefs shall be subject only to such limitations as are prescribed by law and are necessary in a democratic society in the interests of public safety, for the protection of public order, health or morals, or for the protection of the rights and freedoms of others.**

1. Limits to the application of the derogatory clause

In the above-mentioned Kokkinakis v. Greece case the Court observed (paragraph 33):

> The fundamental nature of the rights guaranteed in Article 9, paragraph 1 (art. 9-1), is also reflected in the wording of the paragraph providing for limitations on them. Unlike the second paragraphs of Articles 8, 10 and 11 (art. 8-2, art. 10-2, art 11-2) which cover all the rights mentioned in the first paragraphs of those Articles (art. 8-1, art. 10-1, art. 11-1), that of Article 9 (art. 9-1) refers only to "freedom to manifest one's religion or belief". In so doing, it recognises that in democratic societies, in which several religions coexist within one and the same population, it may be necessary to place restrictions on this freedom in order to reconcile the interests of the various groups and ensure that everyone's beliefs are respected.

In that case, however, the Court decided that Mr Kokkinakis's conviction for "proselytism" (Article 4 of the Greek statute) violated Article 9 in view of the failure to state the actual reasons on which the judgment convicting him was based (paragraph 49):

> The Court notes [...] that in their reasoning the Greek courts established the applicant's liability by merely reproducing the wording of Section 4 and did not sufficiently specify in what way the accused had attempted to convince his neighbour by improper means. None of the facts they set out warrants that finding.

> That being so, it has not been shown that the applicant's conviction was justified in the circumstances of the case by a pressing social need. The contested measure therefore does not appear to have been proportionate to the legitimate aim pursued or, consequently, "necessary in a democratic society [...] for the protection of the rights and freedoms of others".

The case of Larissis and Others v. Greece (24 February 1998, Applications Nos. 23372/94, 26377/94 and 26378/94, *Reports* 1998-I, paragraphs 55 and 61) concerned three officers convicted of proselytism with regard to both members of the military and civilians. The Court held that the convictions for proselytism with regard to the members of the military were justified under Article 9, paragraph 2, but maintained the stance taken in the Kokkinakis judgment in respect of the civilians.

2. Considerations as regards the requirement of limitations "prescribed by law"

As regards the principle of the legality of restrictions on the freedom enshrined in Article 9, the Court refers to its case-law in respect of Articles 8 and 11 (see the Hassan and Tchaouch v. Bulgaria judgment of 26 October 2000, Application No. 30985/96, paragraph 84).

> The Court reiterates its settled case-law according to which the expressions "prescribed by law" and "in accordance with the law" in Articles 8 to 11 of the Convention not only require that the impugned measure should have some basis in domestic law, but also refer to the quality of the law in question. The law should be both adequately accessible and foreseeable, that is, formulated with sufficient precision to enable the individual – if need be with appropriate advice – to regulate his conduct (see the *Sunday Times* v. the United Kingdom (No. 1) judgment of 26 April 1979, Series A No. 30, p. 31, paragraph 49; the Larissis and Others v. Greece judgment of 24 February 1998, *Reports* 1998-I, p. 378, paragraph 40; Hashman and Harrup v. the United Kingdom [GC], No. 25594/94, paragraph 31, ECHR 1999-VIII; and Rotaru v. Romania [GC], No. 28341/95, paragraph 52, ECHR 2000-V).

> For domestic law to meet these requirements it must afford a measure of legal protection against arbitrary interferences by public authorities with the rights safeguarded by the Convention. In matters affecting fundamental rights it would be contrary to the rule of law, one of the basic principles of a democratic society enshrined in the Convention, for a legal discretion granted to the executive to be expressed in terms of an unfettered power. Consequently, the law must indicate with sufficient clarity the scope of any such discretion conferred on the competent authorities and the manner of its exercise (see Rotaru, cited above, paragraph 55).

> The level of precision required of domestic legislation – which cannot in any case provide for every eventuality – depends to a considerable degree on the content of the instrument in question, the field it is designed to cover and the number and status of those to whom it is addressed (see Hashman and Harrup, cited above, paragraph 31, and the Groppera Radio AG and Others v. Switzerland judgment of 28 March 1990, Series A No. 173, p. 26, paragraph 68).

3. Considerations relating to the requirement that these limitations be "necessary"

In the case of the Metropolitan Church of Bessarabia and Others v. Moldova (3 December 2001, Application No. 45701/99, paragraphs 115-119), the Court set out the principles, concerning the requirement for "necessity", that must influence the action of the member states where they set limits to the life of the various religions:

> The Court has [...] said that, in a democratic society, in which several religions coexist within one and the same population, it may be necessary to place restrictions on this freedom in order to reconcile the interests of the various groups and ensure that everyone's beliefs are respected (see the previously cited Kokkinakis judgment, p. 18, paragraph 33).

However, in exercising its regulatory power in this sphere and in its relations with the various religions, denominations and beliefs, the State has a duty to remain neutral and impartial (see the previously cited Hasan and Chaush judgment, paragraph 78). What is at stake here is the preservation of pluralism and the proper functioning of democracy, one of the principle characteristics of which is the possibility it offers of resolving a country's problems through dialogue, without recourse to violence, even when they are irksome (see the United Communist Party of Turkey and Others v. Turkey judgment of 30 January 1998, *Reports* 1998-I, p. 27, paragraph 57). Accordingly, the role of the authorities in such circumstances is not to remove the cause of tension by eliminating pluralism, but to ensure that the competing groups tolerate each other (see Serif v. Greece, No. 38178/97, paragraph 53, ECHR 1999).

The Court further observes that in principle the right to freedom of religion for the purposes of the Convention excludes assessment by the State of the legitimacy of religious beliefs or the ways in which those beliefs are expressed. State measures favouring a particular leader or specific organs of a divided religious community or seeking to compel the community or part of it to place itself, against its will, under a single leadership would also constitute an infringement of the freedom of religion. In democratic societies the State does not need to take measures to ensure that religious communities remain or are brought under a unified leadership (see Serif v. Greece, cited above, paragraph 52). Similarly, where the exercise of the right to freedom of religion or of one of its aspects is subject under domestic law to a system of prior authorisation, involvement in the procedure for granting authorisation of a recognised ecclesiastical authority cannot be reconciled with the requirements of paragraph 2 of Article 9 (see, *mutatis mutandis,* Pentidis and Others v. Greece, No. 23238/94, Commission's report of 27 February 1996, paragraph 46).

Moreover, since religious communities traditionally exist in the form of organised structures, Article 9 must be interpreted in the light of Article 11 of the Convention, which safeguards associative life against unjustified State interference. Seen in that perspective, the right of believers to freedom of religion, which includes the right to manifest one's religion in community with others, encompasses the expectation that believers will be allowed to associate freely, without arbitrary State intervention. Indeed, the autonomous existence of religious communities is indispensable for pluralism in a democratic society and is thus an issue at the very heart of the protection which Article 9 affords (see Hasan and Caush, cited above, paragraph 62).

In addition, one of the means of exercising the right to manifest one's religion, especially for a religious community, in its collective dimension, is the possibility of ensuring judicial protection of the community, its members and its assets, so that Article 9 must be seen not only in the light of Article 11, but also in the light of Article 6 (see, *mutatis mutandis,* the Sidiropoulos and Others v. Greece judgment of 10 July 1998, *Reports* 1998-IV, p. 1614, paragraph 40, and the Canea Catholic Church v. Greece judgment of 16 December 1997, *Reports* 1997-VIII, p. 2857, paragraphs 33 and 40-41 and Commission's report, p. 2867, paragraphs 48-49).

According to its settled case-law, the Court leaves to States Party to the Convention a certain margin of appreciation in deciding whether and to what extent an interference is necessary, but that goes hand in hand with European supervision of both the relevant legislation and the decisions applying it. The Court's task is to ascertain whether the measures taken at national level are justified in principle and proportionate.

In order to determine the scope of the margin of appreciation in the present case the Court must take into account what is at stake, namely the need to maintain true religious pluralism, which is inherent in the concept of a democratic society (see the previously cited Kokkinakis v. Greece judgment, p. 17, paragraph 31). Similarly, a good deal of weight must be given to that need when determining, as paragraph 2 of Article 9 requires, whether the interference corresponds to a "pressing social need" and is "proportionate to the legitimate aim pursued" (see, *mutatis mutandis*, among many other authorities, the Wingrove v. the United Kingdom judgment of 25 November 1996, *Reports* 1996-V, p. 1956, paragraph 53). In exercising its supervision, the Court must consider the interference complained of on the basis of the file as a whole (see the previously cited Kokkinakis v. Greece judgment, p. 21, paragraph 47).

Article 10 ECHR – Freedom of expression

Article 10 is worded as follows:

---

1. Everyone has the right to freedom of expression. This right shall include freedom to hold opinions and to receive and impart information and ideas without interference by public authority and regardless of frontiers. This Article shall not prevent States from requiring the licensing of broadcasting, television or cinema enterprises.

2. The exercise of these freedoms, since it carries with it duties and responsibilities, may be subject to such formalities, conditions, restrictions or penalties as are prescribed by law and are necessary in a democratic society, in the interests of national security, territorial integrity or public safety, for the prevention of disorder or crime, for the protection of health or morals, for the protection of the reputation or rights of others, for preventing the disclosure of information received in confidence, or for maintaining the authority and impartiality of the judiciary.

---

1. The fundamental nature of freedom of expression

In the Handyside v. the United Kingdom case the Court emphasised the fundamental nature of the freedom enshrined in Article 10 (7 December 1976, Series A No. 24, p. 23, paragraph 49). The Court stated that:

> Freedom of expression constitutes one of the essential foundations of [a democratic society], one of the basic conditions for its progress and for development of every man. Subject to paragraph 2 of Article 10, it is applicable not only to "information" or "ideas" that are favourably received or regarded as inoffensive or as a matter of indifference, but also to those that offend, shock or disturb the State or any sector of the population. Such are the demands of that pluralism, tolerance and broadmindedness without which there is no "democratic society".

It is no doubt for that reason that the Court emphasised in the Autronic AG v. Switzerland case (22 May 1990, Series A No. 178, p. 23, paragraph 47) that:

> Article 10 [...] applies to "everyone", whether natural or legal persons. The Court has, moreover, already held on three occasions that it is applicable to profit-making corporate bodies (see the *Sunday Times* judgment of 26 April 1979, Series A No. 30, the Markt Intern Verlag GmbH and Klaus Beermann judgment of 20 November 1989, Series A No. 165, and the Groppera Radio AG and Others judgment of 28 March 1990, Series A No. 173). [...] Indeed the Article expressly mentions in the last sentence of its first paragraph certain enterprises essentially concerned with [Article 10].

2. Content of freedom of expression

The second sentence of Article 10, paragraph 1, gives some indication of the content of freedom of expression. It covers both "freedom of expression" properly so-called and freedom "to receive and impart information and ideas". The decisions of the Court and the Commission have made it possible to identify the various elements of that definition.

Freedom of opinion as an ingredient of freedom of expression

In the case of Lingens v. Austria, the applicant had been convicted for having used certain expressions ("basest opportunism", "immoral" and "undignified") towards the Federal Chancellor in two newspaper articles. The Court declared (judgment of 8 July 1986, Series A No. 103, paragraphs 46-47):

> In the Court's view, a careful distinction needs to be made between facts and value-judgments. The existence of facts can be demonstrated, whereas the truth of value-judgments is not susceptible of proof. The Court notes in this connection that the facts on which Mr Lingens founded his value-judgment were undisputed, as was also his good faith (see paragraph 21 above).

> Under paragraph 3 of Article 111 of the Criminal Code, read in conjunction with paragraph 2, journalists in a case such as this cannot escape conviction for the matters specified in paragraph 1 unless they can prove the truth of their statements (see paragraph 20 above).

> As regards value-judgments this requirement is impossible of fulfilment and it infringes freedom of opinion itself, which is a fundamental part of the right secured by Article 10 (art. 10) of the Convention.

> From the various foregoing considerations it appears that the interference with Mr Lingens' exercise of the freedom of expression was not "necessary in a democratic society [...] for the protection of the reputation [...] of others"; it was disproportionate to the legitimate aim pursued. There was accordingly a breach of Article 10 (art. 10) of the Convention.

Freedom of expression as freedom to receive information

In the Leander v. Sweden case (judgment of 26 March 1987, Series A No. 116, p. 29, paragraphs 74-75) the Court indicated what is covered by freedom to receive information, recognising it as the right to receive information which the holder of that information wishes to communicate. It is not a right of access to information which the holder wishes to keep for his or her own use. In the words of the judgment:

> The Court observes that the right to freedom to receive information basically prohibits a Government from restricting a person from receiving information that others wish or may be willing to impart to him. Article 10 does not, in circumstances such as those of the present case, confer on the individual a right of access to a register containing information on his personal position, nor does it embody an obligation on the Government to impart such information to the individual.

There has thus been no interference with Mr Leander's freedom to receive information, as protected by Article 10.

However, this does not mean that every complainant is without resources. In the Gaskin v. the United Kingdom case (7 July 1989, Series A No. 160, p. 20, paragraph 49) the Court held that although a refusal to give access to personal information did not constitute a violation of Article 10 it might none the less amount to a violation of Article 8. In this case the applicant sought access to a file held by a City Council concerning his care as a minor by the Social Services with a view to bringing legal proceedings against the local authority. Without expressing any opinion on whether general rights of access to personal data and information may be derived from Article 8, the Court explicitly stated that in this case access to the applicant's file came within the application of Article 8, paragraph 1, of the Convention (ibid., p. 15, paragraph 37).

For an example of censoring of school textbooks, see the Cyprus v. Turkey judgment of 10 May 2001, Application No. 25781/94, paragraphs 248-254.

Freedom of expression as freedom to impart information and ideas

Freedom of expression implies also the freedom to impart information. The Müller and Others v. Switzerland judgment (24 May 1988, Series A No. 133, p. 19, paragraph 27) contains an example concerning artistic expression (24 May 1988, Series A No. 133, p. 19, paragraph 27). The Court observed that Article 10:

> [...] includes freedom of artistic expression – notably within freedom to receive and impart information and ideas – which affords the opportunity to take part in the public exchange of cultural, political and social information and ideas of all kinds.

> The question of advertising may also arise in relation to freedom to impart information. On that point, the Court initially avoided adopting a position. This was in the Barthold v. the Federal Republic of Germany judgment (25 March 1985, Series A No. 90, p. 20, paragraph 42), where the applicant had been accused of making statements to a journalist which constituted publicity for his professional activity. The Court declared that in the statements at issue the "opinions" and "information" on a topic of general interest (the activity in question) overlapped to such an extent that there was nothing to justify dissociating the elements from the statements. It thus held that Article 10 was applicable in a general way, without having to distinguish between whether or not the statements constituted advertising.

However, the Commission clearly stated its views in connection with an advertisement by the Church of Scientology in Sweden. Certain passages of a religious nature had been suppressed by a court. On that point, the Commission observed (application cited above under Article 9, *Decisions and Reports* No. 16, p. 72, paragraph 5):

> The restrictions imposed on the applicants' advertisements rather fall to be considered under Article 10. Article 10, paragraph 1, secures to everyone the

right to freedom of expression. This right includes freedom to hold opinions and to receive and impart information and ideas without interference by a public authority.

More recently (the Casado Coca v. Spain judgment of 24 February 1994, Series A No. 285, p. 16, paragraph 35), the Court adopted a more definite approach to the application of Article 10 to commercial advertising. In the passage, it also provides some general examples of freedom to impart ideas:

> In its Barthold v. Germany judgment [...] the Court left open the question whether commercial advertising as such came within the scope of the guarantees under Article 10, but its later case-law provides guidance on this matter. Article 10 does not apply solely to certain types of information or ideas or forms of expression (see the Markt Intern Verlag GmbH and Klaus Beermann v. Germany judgment of 20 November 1989, Series A No. 165, p. 17, paragraph 26), in particular those of a political nature; it also encompasses artistic expression (see the Müller and Others v. Switzerland judgment of 24 May 1988, Series A No. 133, p. 19, paragraph 27), information of a commercial nature (see the Markt Intern Verlag GmbH [...] judgment previously cited, ibid.) – as the Commission rightly pointed out – and even light music and commercials transmitted by cable (see the Groppera Radio AG and Others v. Switzerland judgment of 28 March 1990, Series A No. 173, p. 22, paragraphs 54-55).

Freedom of expression taking the form of freedom of means of communication

It is not enough to be free to receive and impart information. Access to the necessary technical means is also important. In the above-mentioned Autronic AG case (ibid., p. 23, paragraph 47) the Court clearly stated that Article 10:

> [...] applies not only to the content of information but also to the means of transmission or reception since any restriction imposed on the means necessarily interferes with the right to receive and impart information.

Generally, communication by press, radio, television, etc., falls within the scope of Article 10. The same applies to the distribution of pamphlets (see under Article 9 in the above-mentioned Arrowsmith report). That leads us directly to examine some cases where Article 10 has applied.

3. Examples of the application of Article 10

The examples of the application of Article 10 are numerous. Clearly, they systematically involve Article 10, paragraph 2, which provides that the exercise of the freedoms provided for in paragraph 1 of Article 10, since it carries with it duties and responsibilities, may be subject to certain formalities, conditions, restrictions or penalties as are prescribed by law and are necessary in a democratic society, in the interests of national security, territorial integrity or public safety, for the prevention of disorder or crime, for the protection of health or morals, for the protection of the reputation or rights of others, for preventing the disclosure of information received in confidence, or for maintaining the authority and impartiality of the judiciary.

Restrictions must therefore be "prescribed by law", they must be "necessary" and they must pursue one of the "legitimate aims" mentioned: prevention of crime, etc.

As regards the requirement for a legal basis, reference may be made to the Vgt VereinGegen Tierfabriken v. Switzerland judgment (28 June 2001, Application No. 24699/94, paragraph 52), where the Court stated:

> The Court recalls its case-law according to which the expression "in accordance with the law" requires not only that the impugned measure should have some basis in domestic law, but also refers to the quality of the law in question, requiring that it should be accessible to the person concerned and foreseeable as to its effects (see Amann v. Switzerland [GC], No. 27798/95, ECHR 1999-II). However, it is primarily for the national authorities, notably the courts, to interpret and apply domestic law (see the Kopp v. Switzerland judgment of 25 March 1998, *Reports* 1998-II, p. 541, paragraph 59; and the Kruslin v. France judgment of 24 April 1990, Series A No. 176-A, pp. 21 *et seq.*, paragraph 29).

On the "foreseeability" of the law, see the Hashman and Harrup v. the United Kingdom judgment (25 November 1999, *Reports* 1999-VIII, paragraphs 31 and 34), where the Court noted:

> The Court recalls that one of the requirements flowing from the expression "prescribed by law" is foreseeability. A norm cannot be regarded as a "law" unless it is formulated with sufficient precision to enable the citizen to regulate his conduct. At the same time, whilst certainty in the law is highly desirable, it may bring in its train excessive rigidity and the law must be able to keep pace with changing circumstances. The level of precision required of domestic legislation – which cannot in any case provide for every eventuality – depends to a considerable degree on the content of the instrument in question, the field it is designed to cover and the number and status of those to whom it is addressed (see generally in this connection, Rekvényi v. Hungary [GC], No. 25390/94, paragraph 34, ECHR 1999-III).
>
> [...]
>
> The Court also noted that the requirement under Article 10, paragraph 2, that an interference with the exercise of freedom of expression be "prescribed by law" is similar to that under Article 5, paragraph 1, that any deprivation of liberty be "lawful" (ibid., p. 2742, paragraph 94).

(See also the Öztürk v. Turkey judgment of 28 September 1999, *Reports* 1999-VI, paragraphs 51-57.)

When examining the "necessity" for the restrictions or interferences on which it is required to adjudicate, the Court adopts the following approach (see, for example, the Janowski v. Poland judgment of 21 January 1999, *Reports* 1999-I, paragraph 30):

> As set forth in Article 10, this freedom is subject to exceptions, which must, however, be construed strictly, and the need for any restrictions must be established convincingly (see the following judgments: Handyside v. the United

Kingdom, 7 December 1976, Series A No. 24, p. 23, paragraph 49; Lingens v. Austria, 8 July 1986, Series A No. 103, p. 26, paragraph 41; and Jersild v. Denmark, 23 September 1994, Series A No. 298, p. 23, paragraph 31).

(ii) The adjective "necessary", within the meaning of Article 10, paragraph 2, implies the existence of a "pressing social need". The Contracting States have a certain margin of appreciation in assessing whether such a need exists, but it goes hand in hand with a European supervision, embracing both the legislation and the decisions applying it, even those given by an independent court. The Court is therefore empowered to give the final ruling on whether a "restriction" is reconcilable with freedom of expression as protected by Article 10 (see the above-mentioned Lingens judgment, p. 25, paragraph 39).

(iii) In exercising its supervisory jurisdiction, the Court must look at the impugned interference in the light of the case as a whole, including the content of the remarks held against the applicant and the context in which he made them. In particular, it must determine whether the interference in issue was "proportionate to the legitimate aims pursued" and whether the reasons adduced by the national authorities to justify it are "relevant and sufficient" (see the above-mentioned Lingens judgment, pp. 25-26, paragraph 40, and the Barfod v. Denmark judgment of 22 February 1989, Series A No. 149, p. 12, paragraph 28). In doing so, the Court has to satisfy itself that the national authorities applied standards which were in conformity with the principles embodied in Article 10 and, moreover, that they based themselves on an acceptable assessment of the relevant facts (see the above-mentioned Jersild judgment, p. 24, paragraph 31).

That said, it is possible to look at various cases.

Freedom of political expression, criticism in political matters or of officials

In the Ibrahim Aksoy v. Turkey judgment (10 October 2000, Application No. 28635/95, paragraphs 51-80), the Court held that the applicant's conviction for making separatist propaganda violated Article 10. As regards, more generally, the dissemination of general or political information by advertising spots, see the Vgt VereinGegen Tierfabriken v. Switzerland judgment of 28 June 2001, Application No. 24699/94, paragraphs 70-71 (see also the Andreas Wabl v. Austria judgment of 21 March 2000, and the Jerusalem v. Austria judgment of 27 February 2001, Application No. 26958/95).

Criticism in political matters formed the subject-matter of the Castells v. Spain judgment (23 April 1992, Series A No. 236, pp. 23-24, paragraphs 46-50). In that case a Member of Parliament had criticised the government for not taking positive action to investigate a number of attacks which in his view had been perpetrated by persons who continued to occupy positions of responsibility. He was convicted and the courts refused to allow him to prove the truth of his words. The Court declared generally – and this is the most significant aspect of the judgment – that the limits to criticism are broader when the target is the government than when it is aimed at an individual.

The Court then concluded that there had been a violation of Article 10 because the applicant was not allowed to adduce evidence:

> The limits of permissible criticism are wider with regard to the Government than in relation to a private citizen, or even a politician. In a democratic system the actions or omissions of the Government must be subject to the close scrutiny not only of the legislative and judicial authorities but also of the press and public opinion. Furthermore, the dominant position which the Government occupies makes it necessary for it to display restraint in resorting to criminal proceedings, particularly where other means are available for replying to the unjustified attacks and criticisms of its adversaries or the media. Nevertheless it remains open to the competent State authorities to adopt, in their capacity as guarantors of public order, measures, even of a criminal law nature, intended to react appropriately and without excess to defamatory accusations devoid of foundation or formulated in bad faith.

> The article which appeared in *Punto y Hora de Euskalherria* (see paragraph 7 above) must be considered as a whole. The applicant began by drawing up a long list of murders and attacks perpetrated in the Basque Country, then stressed that they had remained unpunished; he continued by alleging the involvement of various extremist organisations, which he named, and finally attributed to the Government the responsibility for the situation. In fact, many of these assertions were susceptible to an attempt to establish their truth, just as Mr Castells could reasonably have tried to demonstrate his good faith.

> It is impossible to state what the outcome of the proceedings would have been had the Supreme Court admitted the evidence which the applicant sought to adduce; but the Court attaches decisive importance to the fact that it declared such evidence inadmissible for the offence in question (see paragraph 12 above). It considers that such an interference in the exercise of the applicant's freedom of expression was not necessary in a democratic society.

For other examples relating to the same topic, reference should be made to the above-mentioned Lingens v. Austria judgment of 8 December 1986, Series A No. 103. Reference may also be made to the Lopes Gomes da Silva v. Portugal judgment of 28 September 2000, Application No. 37698/97, paragraphs 34-36. In that case, the applicant had been convicted for using in a newspaper words such as "grotesque", "buffoonish" and "coarse", deemed to be plain insults which exceeded the limits of freedom of expression. The Court declared:

> [...] the applicant's article and, in particular, the expressions used could be considered to be polemical. They do not, however, convey a gratuitous personal attack because the author supports them with an objective explanation. The Court points out in that connection that, in this field, political invective often spills over into the personal sphere; such are the hazards of politics and the free debate of ideas, which are the guarantees of a democratic society. Accordingly, the applicant expressed an opinion shaped by the political persuasions of Mr Silva Resende, who is himself a regular commentator in the press. Were there no factual basis, such an opinion could, admittedly, appear excessive, but in the light of the established facts that is not so here. Lastly, it should be reiterated that journalistic freedom also covers possible recourse to a degree of exaggeration, or

even provocation (see the Prager and Oberschlick v. Austria judgment of 26 April 1995, Series A No. 313, p. 19, paragraph 38).

[...]

Furthermore, in printing alongside the editorial in question numerous extracts from recent articles by Mr Silva Resende, the applicant, who was the manager of the daily *Público* at the time, acted in accordance with the rules governing the journalistic profession. Thus, while reacting to those articles, he allowed readers to form their own opinion by placing the editorial in question alongside the declarations of the person referred to in that editorial. The Court attaches great importance to that fact.

Contrary to the Government's affirmations, what matters is not the fact that the applicant was sentenced to the minimum penalty, but that he was convicted at all (see the above-mentioned Jersild judgment, p. 25, paragraph 35). The journalist's conviction was not therefore reasonably proportionate to the pursuit of the legitimate aim, having regard to the interest of a democratic society in ensuring and maintaining the freedom of the press.

(See also the Tammer v. Estonia judgment of 6 February 2001, the Feldek v. Slovakia judgment of 12 July 2001, Application No. 29032/95, paragraphs 77-90, and see below: proceedings against journalists.)

The Janowski v. Poland judgment (21 January 1999, *Reports* 1999-I, paragraphs 33-35) concerned insults towards municipal guards in respect of which the applicant had first been sentenced to a term of imprisonment plus a fine and then, on appeal, to a fine. The Court noted and concluded:

The Court [...] notes the Commission's reasoning that civil servants acting in an official capacity are, like politicians, subject to the wider limits of acceptable criticism (see paragraph 28 above). Admittedly those limits may in some circumstances be wider with regard to civil servants exercising their powers than in relation to private individuals. However, it cannot be said that civil servants knowingly lay themselves open to close scrutiny of their every word and deed to the extent to which politicians do and should therefore be treated on an equal footing with the latter when it comes to the criticism of their actions (see the Oberschlick v. Austria (No. 2) judgment of 1 July 1997, *Reports* 1997-IV, p. 1275, paragraph 29).

What is more, civil servants must enjoy public confidence in conditions free of undue perturbation if they are to be successful in performing their tasks and it may therefore prove necessary to protect them from offensive and abusive verbal attacks when on duty. In the present case the requirements of such protection do not have to be weighed in relation to the interests of the freedom of the press or of open discussion of matters of public concern since the applicant's remarks were not uttered in such a context (see paragraph 32 above; and the above-mentioned Lingens judgment, p. 26, paragraph 42, in fine).

In the Court's view, the reasons prompting the applicant's conviction were relevant ones in terms of the legitimate aim pursued. It is true that the applicant resorted to abusive language out of genuine concern for the well-being of fellow citizens in the course of a heated discussion. This language was directed at law-enforcement officers who were trained how to respond to it. However, he insulted the guards in a public place, in front of a group of bystanders, while they were carrying out their duties. The actions of the guards, even though they were not based on the explicit regulations of the municipal council but on sanitary and traffic considerations, did not warrant resort to offensive and abusive verbal attacks (see paragraph 8 above). Consequently, even if there were some circumstances arguing the other way, sufficient grounds existed for the decision ultimately arrived at by the national courts.

Having regard to the foregoing, the Court is satisfied that the reasons adduced by the national authorities were "relevant and sufficient" for the purposes of paragraph 2 of Article 10. The Court further finds that, in the particular circumstances of the instant case, the resultant interference was proportionate to the legitimate aim pursued. In this connection, it is noteworthy that the applicant's sentence was substantially reduced on appeal and, most significantly, his prison sentence was quashed by the Sieradz Regional Court (see paragraph 12 above). In sum, it cannot be said that the national authorities overstepped the margin of appreciation available to them in assessing the necessity of the contested measure.

There has consequently been no breach of Article 10 of the Convention.

(See also the Thoma v. Luxembourg judgment of 29 March 2001.)

Freedom of expression and the publication of secret information

In a 1995 judgment the Court applied the principles which it established previously. This was in the Vereniging Weekblad *Bluf!* v. the Netherlands case (9 February 1995, Series A No. 306-A, pp. 15-16, paragraphs 43-46). The editorial staff of the newspaper *Bluf!* came into possession of what was already an old report of the internal security service (BVD). They published the report but the copies of the newspaper were seized by the authorities. However, since the police had forgotten to confiscate the printing plates, new copies were produced and sold. The authorities did not intervene to prevent the copies from being sold: it was the Queen's birthday and the authorities did not want to cause any public disorder. Subsequently the Public Prosecutor had the copies withdrawn from circulation.

The Court held that the withdrawal of the copies constituted an interference in freedom of expression, and went on to state that although that interference was in accordance with the law and pursued the legitimate aim of protecting national security, it was not necessary in a democratic society in order to achieve that purpose. In considering the case, the Court relied essentially on the criteria of the "publicity" of information. It observed:

> The withdrawal from circulation [...] must be considered in the light of the events as a whole. After the newspaper had been seized, the publishers reprinted a large number of copies and sold them in the streets of Amsterdam, which were very crowded (see paragraphs 11 and 38 above).

> Consequently, the information in question had already been widely distributed when the journal was withdrawn from circulation. Admittedly, the figure of 2 500 copies advanced by the applicant association was disputed by the

Government. Nevertheless, the Court sees no reason to doubt that, at all events, a large number were sold and that the BVD's report was made widely known.

In this latter connection, the Court points out that it has already held that it was unnecessary to prevent the disclosure of certain information seeing that it had already been made public (see the Weber judgment previously cited, pp. 22-23, paragraph 49) or had ceased to be confidential (see the *Observer* and *Guardian* v. the United Kingdom judgment of 26 November 1991, Series A No. 216, pp. 33-35, paragraphs 66-70, and the *Sunday Times* (No. 2) judgment previously cited, pp. 30-31, paragraphs 52-56).

Admittedly, in the instant case the extent of publicity was different. However, the information in question was made accessible to a large number of people, who were able in their turn to communicate it to others. Furthermore, the events were commented on by the media. That being so, the protection of the information as a State secret was no longer justified and the withdrawal of issue No. 267 of *Bluf!* no longer appeared necessary to achieve the legitimate aim pursued. It would have been quite possible, however, to prosecute the offenders.

In short, as the measure was not necessary in a democratic society, there has been a breach of Article 10 (art. 10).

Freedom of expression in the context of the public service

Article 10, paragraph 2, states that freedom of expression carries with it duties and responsibilities. This means that there are limits to freedom of expression for certain occupations, such as the posts of judges, civil servants, etc. The Court has dealt with these issues, and has recently stated that disciplinary measures imposed on a lawyer for infringing a ban on professional advertising were in accordance with Article 10, paragraph 2.

It is impossible to deal with everything in the present document, and for that reason only one particular aspect will be examined, namely the situation where persons who have made use of their freedom of expression have been dismissed from or refused a post in the civil service. In that regard, it is appropriate to cite the Glasenapp v. Germany judgment (28 August 1986, Series A No. 104, p. 26, paragraphs 49-50). In Germany it is necessary to take an oath of allegiance to the Constitution and its values in order to be admitted to the civil service and the authorities exclude probationers who belong to the extreme left or the extreme right. The Court pointed out first of all:

> While [...] the Contracting States did not want to commit themselves to the recognition in the Convention or its Protocols of a right of recruitment to the civil service, it does not follow that in other respects civil servants fall outside the scope of the Convention (see, *mutatis mutandis*, the Abdulaziz, Cabales and Balkandali judgment of 28 May 1985, Series A No. 94, pp. 31-32, paragraph 60).

The Court then qualified its reasoning somewhat:

> The status of probationary civil servant that Mrs Glasenapp had acquired through her appointment as a secondary-school teacher accordingly did not deprive her of the protection afforded by Article 10. This provision is certainly a material one in the present case, but in order to determine whether it was

infringed it must first be ascertained whether the disputed measure amounted to an interference with the exercise of freedom of expression – in the form, for example, of a "formality, condition, restriction or penalty" – or whether the measure lay within the sphere of the right of access to the civil service, a right that is not secured in the Convention.

After examining the circumstances of the case, the Court observed (paragraph 53) that:

> Access to the civil service lies at the heart of the issue submitted to the Court. In refusing Mrs Glasenapp such access, the Land authority took account of her opinions and attitude merely in order to satisfy itself as to whether she possessed one of the necessary personal qualifications for the post in question.

> That being so, there has been no interference with the exercise of the right protected under paragraph 1 of Article 10.

In another case the Court took the opposite view (Vogt v. Germany, judgment of 26 September 1995, Series A No. 323, paragraph 44). In that case the applicant was not a probationer but was already a permanent civil servant. Before finding that there had been a violation of Article 10 which was not necessary in a democratic State, the Court observed that Article 10, paragraph 1, was indeed applicable:

> The Court considers, like the Commission, that the present case is to be distinguished from the cases of Glasenapp and Kosiek. In those cases the Court analysed the authorities' action as a refusal to grant the applicants access to the civil service on the ground that they did not possess one of the necessary qualifications. Access to the civil service had therefore been at the heart of the issue submitted to the Court, which accordingly concluded that there had been no interference with the right protected under paragraph 1 of Article 10 (see the previously cited Glasenapp judgment, p. 27, paragraph 53).

> Mrs Vogt for her part, had been a permanent civil servant since February 1979. She was suspended in August 1986 and dismissed in 1987 (see paragraphs 16 and 20 above), as a disciplinary penalty, for allegedly having failed to comply with the duty owed by every civil servant to uphold the free democratic system within the meaning of the Basic Law. According to the authorities, she had by her activities on behalf of the DKP and by her refusal to dissociate herself from that party expressed views inimical to the above-mentioned system. It follows that there was indeed an interference with the exercise of the right protected by Article 10 of the Convention.

> [...] Although it is legitimate for a State to impose on civil servants, on account of their status, a duty of discretion, civil servants are individuals and, as such, qualify for the protection of Article 10 (art. 10) of the Convention. It therefore falls to the Court, having regard to the circumstances of each case, to determine whether a fair balance has been struck between the fundamental right of the individual to freedom of expression and the legitimate interest of a democratic State in ensuring that its civil service properly furthers the purposes enumerated in Article 10, paragraph 2 (art. 10-2). In carrying out this review, the Court will bear in mind that whenever civil servants' right to freedom of expression is in issue the "duties and responsibilities" referred to in Article 10, paragraph 2 (art. 10-2), assume a special significance, which justifies leaving to the national

authorities a certain margin of appreciation in determining whether the impugned interference is proportionate to the above aim (see also the judgment of Ahmed and Others v. the United Kingdom, 2 September 1998, *Reports of Judgments and Decisions* 1998-VI, p. 2378, paragraph 56).

(See also the Wille v. Liechtenstein judgment of 28 October 1999, *Reports* 1999-VII, paragraphs 36-51.)

Freedom of expression in radio and television broadcasting, cinema and video

Radio and television broadcasting

In the Groppera v. Switzerland case the Court set forth the conditions for the application of Article 10, paragraph 1, third sentence, in relation to the licensing systems which the States may introduce in this sphere. The Court observed that the provisions of paragraph 2 covering freedom of expression apply also to such regulations (the Groppera Radio AG and Others judgment, 28 March 1990, Series A No. 173, p. 24, paragraph 61):

> [...] the purpose of the third sentence of Article 10, paragraph 1, of the Convention is to make it clear that States are permitted to control by a licensing system the way in which broadcasting is organised in their territories, particularly in its technical aspects. It does not, however, provide that licensing measures shall not otherwise be subject to the requirements of paragraph 2, for that would lead to a result contrary to the object and purpose of Article 10 taken as a whole.

In another case, Informationsverein Lentia and Others v. Austria, the Court applied these principles. In that case the applicants had been refused the right to set up an internal cable television network. The relevant Austrian statute vested in the federal authorities power to regulate broadcasting activities and no special licences had been granted to the applicants, since there was no statutory basis for such licences. The Austrian State declared that its intention was to guarantee the objectivity and impartiality of news, pluralism, etc., by maintaining the existing public monopoly. The Court held (Informationsverein Lentia and Others v. Austria, 24 November 1993, Series A No. 276, pp. 16-17, paragraphs 38-39 and 42) that the refusal to grant a licence undoubtedly constituted an interference "in accordance with the law", but that it was not necessary in a democratic society. First of all the Court observed:

> The Court has frequently stressed the fundamental role of freedom of expression in a democratic society, in particular where, through the press, it serves to impart information and ideas of general interest, which the public is moreover entitled to receive (see, for example, *mutatis mutandis*, the *Observer* and *Guardian* v. the United Kingdom judgment of 26 November 1991, Series A No. 216, pp. 29-30, paragraph 59). Such an undertaking cannot be successfully accomplished unless it is grounded in the principle of pluralism, of which the State is the ultimate guarantor. This observation is especially valid in relation to audio-visual media, whose programmes are often broadcast very widely.

Of all the means of ensuring that these values are respected, a public monopoly is the one which imposes the greatest restrictions on the freedom of expression, namely the total impossibility of broadcasting otherwise than through a national station and, in some cases, to a very limited extent through a local cable station. The far-reaching character of such restrictions means that they can only be justified where they correspond to a pressing need.

After examining the government's argument mentioned above, the Court stated:

> The Court is not persuaded by the Government's arguments. Their assertions are contradicted by the experience of several European States, of a comparable size to Austria, in which the coexistence of private and public stations, according to rules which vary from country to country and accompanied by measures preventing the development of private monopolies, shows the fears expressed to be groundless.

> For other examples of decisions relating to televisual communications, reference may be made to the above-mentioned Autronic judgment, cited at the beginning of the examination of Article 10, or to the Tele 1 Privatfernseh GmbH v. Austria judgment of 21 September 2000, Application No. 32240/96.

Cinema

As regards the cinema, the Otto-Preminger-Institut v. Austria case should be mentioned (22 September 1994, Series A No. 295-A, p. 19, paragraph 49). In that case a film had been seized by the State authorities because of the provocation which it constituted for Catholics. The Court found no violation of Article 10. Interestingly, it lays down principles which may be applied when a work of art causes offence to religious beliefs:

> As is borne out by the wording itself of Article 10, paragraph 2, whoever exercises the rights and freedoms enshrined in the first paragraph of that Article undertakes "duties and responsibilities". Amongst them – in the context of religious opinions and beliefs – may legitimately be included an obligation to avoid as far as possible expressions that are gratuitously offensive to others and thus an infringement of their rights, and which therefore do not contribute to any form of public debate capable of furthering progress in human affairs.

> This being so, as a matter of principle it may be considered necessary in certain democratic societies to sanction or even prevent improper attacks on objects of religious veneration, provided always that any "formality", "condition", "restriction" or "penalty" imposed be proportionate to the legitimate aim pursued (see the Handyside v. the United Kingdom judgment of 7 December 1976, Series A No. 24, p. 23, paragraph 49).

The Court concluded:

> The Court cannot disregard the fact that the Roman Catholic religion is the religion of the overwhelming majority of Tyroleans. In seizing the film, the Austrian authorities acted to ensure religious peace in that region and to prevent that some people should feel the object of attacks on their religious beliefs in an unwarranted and offensive manner. It is in the first place for the national authorities, who are better placed than the international judge, to assess the need for

such a measure in the light of the situation obtaining locally at a given time. In all the circumstances of the present case, the Court does not consider that the Austrian authorities can be regarded as having overstepped their margin of appreciation in this respect (ibid., p. 21, paragraph 56).

Video

In the case of Wingrove v. the United Kingdom (25 November 1996, *Reports of Judgments and Decisions* 1996-V, pp. 1957-1960, paragraphs 58 and 63) the applicant had directed and made a video work entitled *Visions of Ecstasy*. The British Board of Film Classification refused to grant a distribution certificate in respect for this video work because it was considered to be blasphemous. In the judgment the Court reiterates the applicable principles with regard to the margin of appreciation of the Contracting States in political speech cases and in so-called "artistic expression" cases in relation to "morals":

> [...] the fact remains that there is as yet not sufficient common ground in the legal and social orders of the member States of the Council of Europe to conclude that a system whereby a State can impose restrictions on the propagation of material on the basis that it is blasphemous is, in itself, unnecessary in a democratic society and thus incompatible with the Convention (see, *mutatis mutandis*, the Otto-Preminger-Institut judgment cited above at paragraph 46, p. 19, paragraph 49).
>
> Whereas there is little scope under Article 10, paragraph 2, of the Convention for restrictions on political speech or on debate of questions of public interest (see, *mutatis mutandis*, among many other authorities, the Lingens v. Austria judgment of 8 July 1986, Series A No. 103, p. 26, paragraph 42; the Castells v. Spain judgment of 23 April 1992, Series A No. 236, p. 23, paragraph 43; and the Thorgeir Thorgeirson v. Iceland judgment of 25 June 1992, Series A No. 239, p. 27, paragraph 63), a wider margin of appreciation is generally available to the Contracting States when regulating freedom of expression in relation to matters liable to offend intimate personal convictions within the sphere of morals or, especially, religion. Moreover, as in the field of morals, and perhaps to an even greater degree, there is no uniform European conception of the requirements of "the protection of the rights of others" in relation to attacks on their religious convictions. What is likely to cause substantial offence to persons of a particular religious persuasion will vary significantly from time to time and from place to place, especially in an era characterised by an ever growing array of faiths and denominations. By reason of their direct and continuous contact with the vital forces of their countries, State authorities are in principle in a better position than the international judge to give an opinion on the exact content of these requirements with regard to the rights of others as well as on the "necessity" of a "restriction" intended to protect from such material those whose deepest feelings and convictions would be seriously offended (see, *mutatis mutandis*, the Müller and Others v. Switzerland judgment of 24 May 1988, Series A No. 133, p. 22, paragraph 35).
>
> This does not of course exclude final European supervision. Such supervision is all the more necessary given the breadth and open-endedness of the notion of

blasphemy and the risks of arbitrary or excessive interferences with freedom of expression under the guise of action taken against allegedly blasphemous material. In this regard the scope of the offence of blasphemy and the safeguards inherent in the legislation are especially important. Moreover the fact that the present case involves prior restraint calls for special scrutiny by the Court (see, *mutatis mutandis*, the *Observer* and *Guardian* v. the United Kingdom judgment of 26 November 1991, Series A No. 216, p. 30, paragraph 60).

The Court's task in this case is to determine whether the reasons relied on by the national authorities to justify the measures interfering with the applicant's freedom of expression are relevant and sufficient for the purposes of Article 10, paragraph 2, of the Convention (art. 10-2).

[…]

It was submitted by both the applicant and the Delegate of the Commission that a short experimental video work would reach a smaller audience than a major feature film, such as the one at issue in the Otto-Preminger-Institut case. [...]

Furthermore, this risk could have been reduced further by restricting the distribution of the film to licensed sex shops.

In this case the British Board of Film Classification refused to grant a classification at all. As result of this refusal the applicant was not allowed to distribute the video work. With regard to these submissions the Court responded as follows (paragraph 63):

The Court notes, however, that it is in the nature of video works that once they become available on the market they can, in practice, be copied, lent, rented, sold and viewed in different homes, thereby easily escaping any form of control by the authorities.

In these circumstances, it was not unreasonable for the national authorities, bearing in mind the development of the video industry in the United Kingdom (see paragraph 22 above), to consider that the film could have reached a public to whom it would have caused offence. The use of a box including a warning as to the film's content (see paragraph 62 above) would have had only limited efficiency given the varied forms of transmission of video works mentioned above. In any event, here too the national authorities are in a better position than the European Court to make an assessment as to the likely impact of such a video, taking into account the difficulties in protecting the public.

Conclusion: no violation of Article 10.

Freedom of expression and freedom of the press and of publication

Banning of publications

Obscene publications

Upon publication of a book (called here a "Schoolbook" or a "small book") the United Kingdom authorities had brought proceedings on the ground that it was obscene. The court convicted the person concerned and ordered that the work be confiscated and destroyed (the Handyside v. the United

Kingdom judgment, 7 December 1976, Series A No. 24). On the question of the necessity for that interference with the author's freedom of expression, the Court examined the pleadings of the parties in turn.

The Court began by rejecting the applicant's plea that obscene revues were permitted in the United Kingdom, and noted (paragraph 56):

> The treatment meted out to the Schoolbook and its publisher in 1971 was, according to the applicant and the minority of the Commission, all the less "necessary" in that a host of publications dedicated to hard core pornography and devoid of intellectual or artistic merit allegedly profit by an extreme degree of tolerance in the United Kingdom. They are exposed to the gaze of passers-by and especially of young people and are said generally to enjoy complete impunity, the rare criminal prosecutions launched against them proving, it was asserted, more often than not abortive due to the great liberalism shown by juries. The same was claimed to apply to sex shops and much public entertainment.

> In principle it is not the Court's function to compare different decisions taken, even in apparently similar circumstances, by prosecuting authorities and courts; and it must, just like the respondent Government, respect the independence of the courts. Furthermore and above all, the Court is not faced with really analogous situations: as the Government pointed out, the documents in the file do not show that the publications and entertainment in question were aimed, to the same extent as the Schoolbook (paragraph 52 above), at children and adolescents having ready access thereto.

Then, as regards the fact that the work had been published in other member states of the Council of Europe, the Court observed (paragraph 57):

> The applicant and the minority of the Commission laid stress on the further point that, in addition to the original Danish edition, translations of the "small book" appeared and circulated freely in the majority of the member States of the Council of Europe.

> Here again, the national margin of appreciation and the optional nature of the "restrictions" and "penalties" referred to in Article 10, paragraph 2 (art. 10-2), prevent the Court from accepting the argument. The fact that most of (the Contracting States) decided to allow the work to be distributed does not mean that the contrary decision of the Inner London Quarter Sessions was a breach of Article 10 (art. 10).

Last, with regard to the gravity of the interference with freedom of expression, the Court set out the following argument (paragraphs 58-59):

> [...] at the hearing on 5 June 1976, the delegate expounding the opinion of the minority of the Commission maintained that in any event the respondent State need not have taken measures as Draconian as the initiation of criminal proceedings leading to the conviction of Mr Handyside and to the forfeiture and subsequent destruction of the Schoolbook. The United Kingdom was said to have violated the principle of proportionality, inherent in the adjective "necessary", by not limiting itself either to a request to the applicant to expurgate the book or to restrictions on its sale and advertisement.

Concerning the request to expurgate the book [...], the Court merely stated that Article 10 "certainly does not oblige the Contracting States to introduce such prior censorship".

As regards the request to limit its sale, the Court considered that the Schoolbook would have thereby lost the substance regarded by the applicant as its *raison d'être*.

> On the strength of the data before it, the Court thus reaches the conclusion that no breach of the requirements of Article 10 (art. 10) has been established in the circumstances of the present case.

It will have been noted that a large margin of discretion is left to the member states in restrictions on freedom of expression based on the protection of morals.

Political publications

A further example of a prohibition may be illustrated by the Association Ekin v. France judgment of 10 July 2001, Application No. 39288/98, paragraph 63, concerning a decree prohibiting the circulation, distribution and offer for sale throughout France of a publication alleged to represent a threat to public order, which was subsequently annulled by the Council of State. The Court agreed with the Council of State that, regard being had in particular to security and to public order, the content of the publication was not such as to justify the gravity of the interference with the applicant's freedom of expression represented by the prohibition ordered by the Minister of the Interior. In short, the Court considered that the decree of the Minister of the Interior did not meet a pressing social need and was not proportionate to the legitimate aim pursued (see also the Öztürk v. Turkey judgment of 28 September 1999, *Reports* 1999-VI, paragraphs 64-74).

Seizure and confiscation of newspapers

In the case of the *Observer* and *Guardian* v. the United Kingdom (26 November 1991, Series A No. 216, pp. 29-30, paragraphs 59-60), the Court presented a summary of the fundamental principles resulting for the press from freedom of expression:

> (a) Freedom of expression constitutes one of the essential foundations of a democratic society; subject to paragraph 2 of Article 10 (art. 10-2), it is applicable not only to "information" or "ideas" that are favourably received or regarded as inoffensive or as a matter of indifference, but also to those that offend, shock or disturb. Freedom of expression, as enshrined in Article 10 (art. 10), is subject to a number of exceptions which, however, must be narrowly interpreted and the necessity for any restrictions must be convincingly established.
>
> (b) These principles are of particular importance as far as the press is concerned. Whilst it must not overstep the bounds set, *inter alia*, in the "interests of national security" or for "maintaining the authority of the judiciary", it is nevertheless incumbent on it to impart information and ideas on matters of public interest. Not only does the press have the task of imparting such

information and ideas: the public also has a right to receive them. Were it otherwise, the press would be unable to play its vital role of "public watchdog".

(c) The adjective "necessary", within the meaning of Article 10, paragraph 2 (art. 10-2), implies the existence of a "pressing social need". The Contracting States have a certain margin of appreciation in assessing whether such a need exists, but it goes hand in hand with a European supervision, embracing both the law and the decisions applying it, even those given by independent courts. The Court is therefore empowered to give the final ruling on whether a "restriction" is reconcilable with freedom of expression as protected by Article 10 (art. 10).

(d) The Court's task, in exercising its supervisory jurisdiction, is not to take the place of the competent national authorities but rather to review under Article 10 (art. 10) the decisions they delivered pursuant to their power of appreciation. This does not mean that the supervision is limited to ascertaining whether the respondent State exercised its discretion reasonably, carefully and in good faith; what the Court has to do is to look at the interference complained of in the light of the case as a whole and determine whether it was "proportionate to the legitimate aim pursued" and whether the reasons adduced by the national authorities to justify it are "relevant and sufficient".

[...] Article 10 (art. 10) of the Convention does not in terms prohibit the imposition of prior restraints on publication, as such. This is evidenced not only by the words "conditions", "restrictions", "preventing" and "prevention" which appear in that provision, but also by the Court's *Sunday Times* judgment of 26 April 1979 and its Markt Intern Verlag GmbH and Klaus Beermann judgment of 20 November 1989 (Series A No. 165). On the other hand, the dangers inherent in prior restraints are such that they call for the most careful scrutiny on the part of the Court. This is especially so as far as the press is concerned, for news is a perishable commodity and to delay its publication, even for a short period, may well deprive it of all its value and interest.

(*Idem* the Association Ekin v. France judgment of 10 July 2001, Application No. 39288/98, paragraphs 56-57, or the Fressoz and Roire v. France judgment of 21 January 1999, *Reports* 1999-I, paragraph 45.)

The *Sunday Times* v. the United Kingdom (No. 1) judgment of 26 April 1979, Series A No. 30, is one of the leading cases on which the Court based its summary in the *Observer* and *Guardian* case. In that case the applicants wished to publish an article about the way in which a company had tested a medicine (Thalidomide) before putting it on the market. The medicine had produced harmful effects and the victims had instituted legal proceedings. The pharmaceutical company succeeded in obtaining an injunction against the publication of the article in question on the ground that it constituted a contempt of court. Concerning the injunction, the Court said (paragraph 65):

There is general recognition of the fact that the courts cannot operate in a vacuum. Whilst they are the forum for the settlement of disputes, this does not mean that there can be no prior discussion of disputes elsewhere, be it in specialised journals, in the general press or amongst the public at large.

Furthermore, whilst the mass media must not overstep the bounds imposed in the interests of the proper administration of justice, it is incumbent on them to impart information and ideas concerning matters that come before the courts just as in other areas of public interest. Not only do the media have the task of imparting such information and ideas: the public also has a right to receive them.

The Court then pointed out that the victims' families had a right to information, that in fact they (paragraph 66):

> [...] had a vital interest in knowing all the underlying facts and the various possible solutions. They could be deprived of this information, which was crucially important for them, only if it appeared absolutely certain that its diffusion would have presented a threat to the "authority of the judiciary".

For a complete ban on the publication of a photograph of a suspect while criminal proceedings were pending, see the News Verlag GmbH & CoKG v. Austria judgment of 11 January 2000.

As regards the combination of State measures which force a newspaper to cease to appear, see the Özgür Gündem v. Turkey judgment of 16 March 2000, Application No. 23144/93. In that case the Court concluded that the respondent State had not taken the appropriate protective and investigative measures to preserve Özgür Gündem's right to freedom of expression and that it had imposed certain measures on the newspaper, namely search and arrest and also numerous prosecutions and convictions in respect of certain editions of the newspaper, which were disproportionate and unjustified as a means of attaining any legitimate aim whatsoever. As the combined effect of these factors was to force the newspaper to cease to appear, there had been a violation of Article 10 of the Convention.

Proceedings against journalists: defamation, receiving documents, etc.

The Court is generally extremely vigilant in its supervision of Article 10 in relation to the press and to proceedings against journalists. Frequently such proceedings are brought for defamation, but not always.

The Court has had the opportunity to declare (the Bergens Tidende and Others v. Norway judgment of 2 May 2000, paragraphs 49-50):

> The Court further recalls the essential function the press fulfils in a democratic society. Although the press must not overstep certain bounds, particularly as regards the reputation and rights of others and the need to prevent the disclosure of confidential information, its duty is nevertheless to impart – in a manner consistent with its obligations and responsibilities – information and ideas on all matters of public interest (see the Jersild v. Denmark judgment of 23 September 1994, Series A No. 298, pp. 23-24, paragraph 31, the De Haes and Gijsels v. Belgium judgment of 24 February 1997, *Reports of Judgments and Decisions* 1997-I, pp. 233-34, paragraph 37, and the Bladet Tromsø and *Stensaas* judgment cited above, paragraph 59). In addition, the Court is mindful of the fact that journalistic freedom also covers possible recourse to a degree of exaggeration, or

even provocation (see the Prager and Oberschlick v. Austria judgment of 26 April 1995, Series A No. 313, p. 19, paragraph 38, and the Bladet Tromsø and *Stensaas* judgment cited above, paragraph 59). In cases such as the present one, the national margin of appreciation is circumscribed by the interests of a democratic society in enabling the press to exercise its vital role of "public watchdog" by imparting information of serious public concern (ibid., paragraph 59).

The Court's task in exercising its supervisory function is not to take the place of the national authorities, but rather to review under Article 10, in the light of the case as a whole, the decisions they have taken pursuant to their power of appreciation (ibid., paragraph 60).

[...]

[...] the Court further observes that Article 10 of the Convention does not guarantee a wholly unrestricted freedom of expression even with respect to press coverage of matters of serious public concern. Under the terms of paragraph 2 of the Article, the exercise of this freedom carries with it "duties and responsibilities" which also apply to the press. As the Court pointed out in the Bladet Tromsø and *Stensaas* judgment cited above, paragraph 65, these "duties and responsibilities" assume significance when, as in the present case, there is question of attacking the reputation of private individuals and undermining the "rights of others". By reason of the "duties and responsibilities" inherent in the exercise of freedom of expression, the safeguard afforded by Article 10 to journalists in relation to reporting on issues of general interest is subject to the proviso that they are acting in good faith in order to provide accurate and reliable information in accordance with the ethics of journalism (see the Goodwin v. the United Kingdom judgment of 27 March 1996, *Reports* 1996-II, p. 500, paragraph 39, and Fressoz and Roire v. France [GC], No. 29183/95, paragraph 54, ECHR 1999-I).

In this case, the Court held that the applicants' conviction for publishing the unfortunate experiences of the patients of a cosmetic surgeon, who following the appearance of those accounts experienced financial problems and had to close his surgery, entailed a violation of Article 10 (paragraphs 56-57 and 60):

The Court attaches considerable weight to the fact that in the present case the women's accounts of their treatment by Dr R. were found not only to have been essentially correct but also to have been accurately recorded by the newspaper. It is true that, as pointed out by the national courts, the women had expressed themselves in graphic and strong terms and that it was these terms which were highlighted in the newspaper articles. However, the expressions used reflected the women's own understandable perception of the appearance of their breasts after the unsuccessful cosmetic surgery, as shown in the accompanying photographs. Moreover, in none of the articles was it stated that the unsatisfactory results were attributable to negligent surgery on the part of Dr R. This meaning was one derived by the Supreme Court, not from the express terms but from the general tenor of the articles, whose common sting, however, lay in the true allegation that Dr R. had failed in his duties as a cosmetic surgeon in not providing proper or adequate post-surgical treatment to remedy the results of unsuccessful operations. Reading the articles as a whole, the Court cannot find that the statements were excessive or misleading.

The Court is further unable to accept that the reporting of the accounts of the women showed a lack of any proper balance. Admittedly, the applicant newspaper did not make it explicitly clear in the articles themselves that the accounts given by the women were not to be taken as suggesting a lack of surgical skills on the part of Dr R. However, the Court recalls that news reporting based on interviews constitutes one of the most important means whereby the press is able to play its vital role of "public watchdog".

[...]

In the light of the above, the Court cannot find that the undoubted interest of Dr R. in protecting his professional reputation was sufficient to outweigh the important public interest in the freedom of the press to impart information on matters of legitimate public concern. In short, the reasons relied on by the respondent State, although relevant, are not sufficient to show that the interference complained of was "necessary in a democratic society". The Court considers that there was no reasonable relationship of proportionality between the restrictions placed by the measures applied by the Supreme Court on the applicants' right to freedom of expression and the legitimate aim pursued.

Accordingly, there has been a violation of Article 10 of the Convention.

Mention should also be made of the Thorgeir Thorgeirson v. Iceland judgment of 25 June 1992, Series A No. 239, where it was held that the conviction and sentence of a writer for defamation constituted a violation of Article 10. In this case, he was prosecuted for having published two articles on police brutality in a newspaper.

In the Prager and Oberschlick v. Austria case, on the other hand (26 April 1995, Series A No. 313), the conviction of a journalist and a publisher for defamation of a judge was not considered a violation of Article 10. The Court observed :

> that the allegations levelled against the judge "were extremely serious" (paragraph 36) ;

> that "the excessive breadth of the accusations [...], in the absence of a sufficient factual basis, appeared unnecessarily prejudicial" (paragraph 37) ;

> and that the applicant "could [not] invoke his good faith or compliance with the ethics of journalism. The research that he had undertaken does not appear adequate to substantiate such serious allegations" (paragraph 37).

Having regard to these factors and to "the special role of the judiciary in society", the Court found that the imposition of a fine and the confiscation of the remaining copies of the offending periodical did not constitute a violation of Article 10 (paragraph 38). Another example concerning the defamation of – lay – judges may be found in the Barfod v. Denmark judgment of 22 February 1989, Series A No. 149. See also the Perna v. Italy judgment of 25 July 2001, Application No. 48898/99, paragraphs 38-48), where the Court stated, in particular (paragraph 38) :

> [...] an opinion, by definition, is not susceptible of proof. It may, however, be excessive, in particular in the absence of any factual basis (see the De Haes and

Gijsels v. Belgium judgment of 24 February 1997, *Reports of Judgments and Decisions* 1997-I, paragraph 47).

(v) The matters of public interest on which the press has the right to impart information and ideas, in a way consistent with its duties and responsibilities, include questions concerning the functioning of the judiciary. However, the work of the courts, which are the guarantors of justice and which have a fundamental role in a State governed by the rule of law, needs to enjoy public confidence. It should therefore be protected against unfounded attacks, especially in view of the fact that judges are subject to a duty of discretion that precludes them from replying (see the Prager and Oberschlick v. Austria judgment of 26 April 1995, Series A No. 313, paragraph 34).

See also the Du Roy and Malaurie v. France judgment (3 October 2000, Application No. 34000/96, paragraphs 28-37) concerning the prohibition prescribed by law of the publication of information on criminal complaints accompanied by claims for civil damages (violation of Article 10) (breach of the prohibition was a criminal offence).

The Court has also held that the conviction of a television journalist for being involved in spreading racist statements made by the so-called "Greenjackets" was contrary to Article 10. The Court observed (the Jersild v. Denmark case, 23 September 1994, Series A No. 298, pp. 23 and 25-26, paragraphs 31 and 35):

> A significant feature of the present case is that the applicant did not make the objectionable statements himself but assisted in their dissemination in his capacity of television journalist responsible for a news programme of Danmarks Radio (see paragraphs 9 to 11 above). In assessing whether his conviction and sentence were "necessary" the Court will therefore have regard to the principles established in its case-law relating to the role of the press (as summarised in for instance the *Observer* and *Guardian* v. the United Kingdom judgment of 26 November 1991, Series A No. 216, pp. 29-30, paragraph 59).
>
> [...]
>
> News reporting based on interviews, whether edited or not, constitutes one of the most important means whereby the press is able to play its vital role of "public watchdog" (see for instance, the above-mentioned *Observer* and *Guardian* judgment, pp. 29-30, paragraph 59). The punishment of a journalist for assisting in the dissemination of statements made by another person in an interview would seriously hamper the contribution of the press to discussion of matters of public interest and should not be envisaged unless there are particularly strong reasons for doing so. In this regard the Court does not accept the Government's argument that the limited nature of the fine is relevant; what matters is that the journalist was convicted.
>
> There can be no doubt that the remarks in respect of which the Greenjackets were convicted (see paragraph 14 above) were more than insulting to members of the targeted groups and did not enjoy the protection of Article 10 (see, for example, the Commission's admissibility decisions in Applications Nos. 8948/78 and 8406/78, Glimmerveen and Hagenbeek v. the Netherlands, *Decisions and Reports* 18, p. 187, and No. 9235/81, Künen v. the Federal Republic of Germany,

Decisions and Reports 29, p. 194). However, even having regard to the manner in which the applicant prepared the Greenjackets item (see paragraph 32 above), it has not been shown that, considered as a whole, the feature was such as to justify also his conviction of, and punishment for, a criminal offence under the Penal Code.

Protection of journalistic sources

Article 10 of the Convention protects journalists in principle against the compulsion or an order to reveal his sources. In the Goodwin v. the United Kingdom judgment (27 March 1996, *Reports of Judgments and Decisions* 1996-II, pp. 500 and 502, paragraphs 39 and 45) the applicant was telephoned by a person who supplied him with information about the financial problems of Tetra Ltd company. This information derived from a confidential corporate plan which appeared to have been stolen. The applicant maintained that he did not know that the information derived from a stolen or confidential document. Tetra asked for an injunction restraining the publishers from publishing any information derived from the corporate plan. The High Court granted this application. After the granting of the injunction the High Court ordered the applicant to disclose the source's identity. With regard to the disclose order the Court considers:

Protection of journalistic sources is one of the basic conditions for press freedom, as is reflected in the laws and the professional codes of conduct in a number of Contracting States and is affirmed in several international instruments on journalistic freedoms (see, amongst others, the Resolution on Journalistic Freedom and Human Rights, adopted at the 4th European Ministerial Conference on Mass Media Policy (Prague, 7-8 December 1994) and the Resolution on the Confidentiality of Journalists' Sources by the European Parliament, 18 January 1994, *Official Journal of the European Communities* No. C 44/34). Without such protection, sources may be deterred from assisting the press in informing the public on matters of public interest. As a result the public-watchdog role of the press may be undermined and the ability of the press to provide accurate and reliable information may be adversely affected. Having regard to the importance of the protection of journalistic sources for press freedom in a democratic society and the potentially chilling effect an order of source disclosure has on the exercise of that freedom, such a measure cannot be compatible with Article 10 of the Convention unless it is justified by an overriding requirement in the public interest.

In that case, the Court concluded that:

On the facts of the present case, the Court cannot find that Tetra's interests in eliminating, by proceedings against the source, the residual threat of damage through dissemination of the confidential information otherwise than by the press, in obtaining compensation and in unmasking a disloyal employee or collaborator were, even if considered cumulatively, sufficient to outweigh the vital public interest in the protection of the applicant journalist's source. The Court does not therefore consider that the further purposes served by the disclosure order, when measured against the standards imposed by the Convention, amount to an overriding requirement in the public interest.

[...]

Accordingly, the Court concludes that both the order requiring the applicant to reveal his source and the fine imposed upon him for having refused to do so gave rise to a violation of his right to freedom of expression under Article 10.

Concerning the conviction of journalists for receiving photocopies of tax assessments obtained in breach of professional secrecy from an unidentified tax official and published in a newspaper, reference may be made to the Fressoz and Roire v. France [GC] judgment (21 January 1999, No. 29183/95, paragraph 54, ECHR 1999-I, paragraphs 54-56), where the Court stated:

If, as the Government accepted, the information about Mr Calvet's annual income was lawful and its disclosure permitted, the applicants' conviction merely for having published the documents in which that information was contained, namely the tax assessments, cannot be justified under Article 10. In essence, that Article leaves it for journalists to decide whether or not it is necessary to reproduce such documents to ensure credibility. It protects journalists' right to divulge information on issues of general interest provided that they are acting in good faith and on an accurate factual basis and provide "reliable and precise" information in accordance with the ethics of journalism (see, in particular, the Goodwin judgment cited above, p. 500, paragraph 39; the Schwabe v. Austria judgment of 28 August 1992, Series A No. 242-B, p. 34, paragraph 34; and, as an example of a finding to the contrary on the facts, the Prager and Oberschlick judgment cited above, p. 18, paragraph 37).

In the instant case, the Court notes that neither Mr Fressoz and Mr Roire's account of the events nor their good faith has been called into question. Mr Roire, who verified the authenticity of the tax assessments, acted in accordance with the standards governing his profession as a journalist. The extracts from each document were intended to corroborate the terms of the article in question. The publication of the tax assessments was thus relevant not only to the subject matter but also to the credibility of the information supplied.

In sum, there was not, in the Court's view, a reasonable relationship of proportionality between the legitimate aim pursued by the journalists' conviction and the means deployed to achieve that aim, given the interest a democratic society has in ensuring and preserving freedom of the press. There has therefore been a violation of Article 10 of the Convention.

Article 11 ECHR – Freedom of assembly and association

Article 11, paragraph 1

Article 11, paragraph 1, is worded as follows:

---

1. Everyone has the right to freedom of peaceful assembly and to freedom of association with others, including the right to form and to join trade unions for the protection of his interests.

As stated, this Article deals with both freedom of assembly and freedom of association.

1. Freedom of assembly

As regards freedom of assembly, mention should be made of a number of decisions relating to its fundamental character, to its content and to certain limitations that are applicable.

The fundamental nature of freedom of assembly

In the Rassemblement jurassien v. Switzerland case (Application No. 8191/78, decision of 10 October 1979, *Decisions and Reports* 17, p. 119, paragraph 3) the Commission stated:

> The Commission wishes to state at the outset that the right of peaceful assembly stated in this Article is a fundamental right in a democratic society and, like the right to freedom of expression, is one of the foundations of such a society (the Handyside case, judgment of 7 December 1976, Series A, paragraph 49). As such this right covers both private meetings and meetings in public thoroughfares.

Content of freedom of assembly

In its decision of 16 July 1980 in the Christians against Racism and Fascism v. the United Kingdom case (Application No. 8840/78, *Decisions and Reports* 21, p. 148, paragraph 4) the Commission stated that:

> [...] the freedom of peaceful assembly covers not only static meetings, but also public processions. It is moreover a freedom capable of being exercised not only by the individual participants of such demonstration, but also by those organising it, including a corporate body such as the applicant association.

On the other hand, the desire of prisoners to share the same cell is not part of freedom of assembly (the McFeeley v. the United Kingdom case, Application No. 8317/78, decision of 15 May 1980, *Decisions and Reports* 20, p. 98, paragraphs 114-115). The Commission stated:

> As the language of Article 11 suggests, the concept of freedom of association, of which the right to form and join trade unions is a special aspect, is concerned with the right to form or be affiliated with a group or organisation pursuing

particular aims. It does not concern the right of prisoners to share the company of other prisoners or to "associate" with other prisoners in this sense.

Consequently the Commission considers that this complaint must be rejected under Article 27, paragraph 2, as incompatible *ratione materiae* with the provisions of the Convention.

Restrictions and limitations by the State on freedom of assembly

In the above-mentioned Rassemblement jurassien v. Switzerland case (ibid., p. 119, paragraph 3, in fine) the Commission ruled on the lawfulness of a system which subjected demonstrations to prior authorisation:

> Where [meetings in public thoroughfares] are concerned, their subjection to an authorisation procedure does not normally encroach upon the essence of the right. Such a procedure is in keeping with the requirements of Article 11, paragraph 1, if only in order that the authorities may be in a position to ensure the peaceful nature of a meeting, and accordingly does not as such constitute interference with the exercise of the right.

The Christians against Racism and Fascism v. the United Kingdom case (the above-mentioned case, p. 150, paragraph 5) shows the circumstances in which a general prohibition on demonstrations for a specific period is lawful under Article 11. The Commission stated:

> A general ban on demonstrations can only be justified if there is a real danger of their resulting in disorder which cannot be prevented by other less stringent measures. In this connection, the authority must also take into account the effect of a ban on processions which do not by themselves constitute a danger for the public order. Only if the disadvantage of such processions being caught by the ban is clearly outweighed by the security considerations justifying the issue of the ban, and if there is no possibility of avoiding such undesirable side effects of the ban by a narrow circumscription of its scope in terms of territorial application and duration, can the ban be regarded as being necessary within the meaning of Article 11, paragraph 2, of the Convention.

By way of a counterpart to the possibility of suppressing or restricting freedom of assembly, the State is under a positive obligation to permit its effective exercise. This is especially the case when demonstrators come into conflict with their opponents. In the Plattform "Ärzte für das Leben" v. Austria case (21 June 1988, Series A No. 139, p. 12, paragraphs 32 and 34) the Court observed that:

> A demonstration may annoy or give offence to persons opposed to the ideas or claims that it is seeking to promote. The participants must, however, be able to hold the demonstration without having to fear that they will be subjected to physical violence by their opponents; such a fear would be liable to deter associations or other groups supporting common ideas or interests from openly expressing their opinions on highly controversial issues affecting the community. In a democracy the right to counter-demonstrate cannot extend to inhibiting the exercise of the right to demonstrate.
>
> Genuine, effective freedom of peaceful assembly cannot, therefore, be reduced to a mere duty on the part of the State not to interfere: a purely negative

conception would not be compatible with the object and purpose of Article 11. Like Article 8, Article 11 sometimes requires positive measures to be taken, even in the sphere of relations between individuals, if need be (see, *mutatis mutandis*, the X. and Y. v. the Netherlands judgment of 26 March 1985, Series A No. 91, p. 11, paragraph 23).

The Court went on to point out:

> While it is the duty of Contracting States to take reasonable and appropriate measures to enable lawful demonstrations to proceed peacefully, they cannot guarantee this absolutely and they have a wide discretion in the choice of the means to be used (see, *mutatis mutandis*, the Abdulaziz, Cabales and Balkandali judgment of 28 May 1985, Series A No. 94, pp. 33-34, paragraph 67, and the Rees judgment of 17 October 1986, Series A No. 106, pp. 14-15, paragraphs 35-37). In this area the obligation they enter into under Article 11 of the Convention is an obligation as to measures to be taken and not as to results to be achieved.

In that case, the Court found that the Austrian State had taken "reasonable and appropriate measures" (see also the Stankov and the United Macedonian Organisation Inlinden v. Bulgaria judgment of 2 October 2001, Application No. 29221/95, paragraphs 76-112).

2. Freedom of association

General observations

As well as the freedom of assembly, Article 11 deals also with freedom of association.

In the National Union of Belgian Police case (27 October 1975, Series A No. 19, p. 17, paragraph 38) the Court observed trade union freedom is a particular feature of freedom of association:

> Article 11, paragraph 1 (art. 11-1), presents trade union freedom as one form or a special aspect of freedom of association.

It was for that reason that in the Sigurður A. Sigurjónsson v. Iceland case (30 June 1993, Series A No. 264, p. 14, paragraph 32) the Court merely found that the organisation at issue on the nature of which the Court was to rule was an association and that there was no need, for the purposes of Article 11, to ascertain whether it was also a trade union.

> It is not necessary to decide whether Frami can also be regarded as a trade union within the meaning of Article 11, since the right to form and join trade unions in that provision is an aspect of the wider right to freedom of association, rather than a separate right (see, amongst other authorities, the Schmidt and Dahlström v. Sweden judgment of 6 February 1976, Series A No. 21, p. 15, paragraph 34).

The Court has also stated that freedom of association applies to political parties. In the United Communist Party of Turkey and Others v. Turkey judgment (30 January 1998, *Reports* 1998-I, paragraphs 24-25 and 27), it stated:

> The Court considers that the wording of Article 11 provides an initial indication as to whether political parties may rely on that provision. It notes that although

Article 11 refers to "freedom of association with others, including the right to form [...] trade unions [...]", the conjunction "including" clearly shows that trade unions are but one example among others of the form in which the right to freedom of association may be exercised. It is therefore not possible to conclude, as the Government did, that by referring to trade unions – for reasons related mainly to issues that were current at the time – those who drafted the Convention intended to exclude political parties from the scope of Article 11.

However, even more persuasive than the wording of Article 11, in the Court's view, is the fact that political parties are a form of association essential to the proper functioning of democracy. In view of the importance of democracy in the Convention system (see paragraph 45 below), there can be no doubt that political parties come within the scope of Article 11.

[...]

The Court notes [...] that an association, including a political party, is not excluded from the protection afforded by the Convention simply because its activities are regarded by the national authorities as undermining the constitutional structures of the State and calling for the imposition of restrictions. As the Court has said in the past, while it is in principle open to the national authorities to take such action as they consider necessary to respect the rule of law or to give effect to constitutional rights, they must do so in a manner which is compatible with their obligations under the Convention and subject to review by the Convention institutions (see the Open Door and Dublin Well Woman v. Ireland judgment of 29 October 1992, Series A No. 246-A, p. 29, paragraph 69).

This section will therefore include judgments on freedom of association in the strict sense and trade union freedom in that they provide general information on freedom of association. For questions relating solely to trade union freedom, see the following section.

Notion of association

In the case of Chassagnou and Others v. France (judgment of 29 April 1999, *Reports* 1999-III), the Court stated that the notion of association has an autonomous scope and does not depend on the classification of "public" or "para-administrative" resulting from national law. This case concerned hunting associations (ACCA) in French law. The Court declared (paragraph 100):

However, the question is not so much whether in French law ACCAs are private associations, public or para-public associations, or mixed associations, but whether they are associations for the purposes of Article 11 of the Convention.

If Contracting States were able, at their discretion, by classifying an association as "public" or "para-administrative", to remove it from the scope of Article 11, that would give them such latitude that it might lead to results incompatible with the object and purpose of the Convention, which is to protect rights that are not theoretical or illusory but practical and effective (see the Artico v. Italy judgment of 13 May 1980, Series A No. 37, pp. 15-16, paragraph 33, and, more recently, the United Communist Party of Turkey and Others v. Turkey judgment of 30 January 1998, *Reports of Judgments and Decisions* 1998-I, pp. 18-19, paragraph 33).

Freedom of thought and opinion and freedom of expression, guaranteed by Articles 9 and 10 of the Convention respectively, would thus be of very limited scope if they were not accompanied by a guarantee of being able to share one's beliefs or ideas in community with others, particularly through associations of individuals having the same beliefs, ideas or interests.

The term "association" therefore possesses an autonomous meaning; the classification in national law has only relative value and constitutes no more than a starting-point.

The criteria which enable a group as an "association" were examined in the Le Compte, Van Leuven and De Meyere v. Belgium judgment (23 June 1981, Series A No. 43, pp. 26-27, paragraphs 64-65). Called upon in that case to determine whether the organisation in question had the nature of an association or not, the Court used three criteria: the origin, the objective and the means of organisation of the body concerned. In this case it was the Ordre des Médecins:

> The Court notes first that the Belgian Ordre des Médecins is a public-law institution. It was founded not by individuals but by the legislature; it remains integrated within the structures of the State and judges are appointed to most of its organs by the Crown. It pursues an aim which is in the general interest, namely the protection of health, by exercising under the relevant legislation a form of public control over the practice of medicine. Within the context of this latter function, the Ordre is required in particular to keep the register of medical practitioners. For the performance of the tasks conferred on it by the Belgian State, it is legally invested with administrative as well as rule-making and disciplinary prerogatives out of the orbit of the ordinary law *(prérogatives exorbitantes du droit commun)* and, in this capacity, employs processes of a public authority (see paragraphs 20-34 above).

> Having regard to these various factors taken together, the Ordre cannot be considered as an association within the meaning of Article 11.

It is all a question of degree, however. In a recent case (the above-mentioned Sigurđur A. Sigurjónsson v. Iceland case, 30 June 1993, pp. 13-14, paragraphs 30-31) the Icelandic Government contended that Frami – an association of taxicab drivers – was not a "trade union", nor even an association within the meaning of Article 11, but a professional organisation of a public-law character. In support of its argument, it claimed that Frami was not an employees' organisation representing its members in conflict with their employer or engaging in collective bargaining. Furthermore, Frami performed certain functions which were provided by law or had evolved through practice and served the public interest no less than the interests of its members. The Court considered that the above-mentioned elements are not sufficient for Frami to be regarded as a public-law association outside the ambit of Article 11. Admittedly, Frami performed certain functions which were to some extent provided for in the applicable legislation and which served not only its members but also the public at large (see paragraphs 22-23 above). However, the role of supervision of the implementation of the relevant rules was entrusted primarily to another institution, namely the Committee, which in addition had the power to issue licences and to decide on their suspension and revocation (see paragraphs 20 and 25 above). Frami was established under private law and enjoyed full autonomy in determining its own aims, organisation and procedure. According to its Articles, admittedly old and currently under revision, the purpose of Frami was to protect the professional interests of its members and promote solidarity among professional taxicab drivers; to determine, negotiate and present demands relating to the working hours, wages and rates of its members; to seek to maintain limitations on the number of taxicabs and to represent its members before the public authorities (see paragraph 21 above). Frami was therefore predominantly a private-law organisation and must thus be considered an "association" for the purposes of Article 11.

(See also the above-mentioned Chassagnou and Others v. France judgment of 29 April 1999, *Reports* 1999-III, paragraph 101: Article 11 applicable.)

Content of freedom of association

There are two aspects to freedom of association: the first, negative one, is the right not to associate; it concerns the question of compulsory membership of an association. The second, positive, aspect is the right to associate or belong to an association. There is also the question of the creation and dissolution of associations.

Creation and dissolution of associations

In the United Communist Party of Turkey and Others v. Turkey judgment (30 January 1998, *Reports* 1998-I, paragraphs 32-34, 46 and 61), concerning the dissolution of a political party, the Court stated:

> It does not, however, follow that the authorities of a State in which an association, through its activities, jeopardises that State's institutions are deprived of the right to protect those institutions. In this connection, the Court points out that it has previously held that some compromise between the requirements of defending democratic society and individual rights is inherent in the system of the Convention (see, *mutatis mutandis*, the Klass and Others v. Germany judgment of 6 September 1978, Series A No. 28, p. 28, paragraph 59). For there to be a compromise of that sort any intervention by the authorities must be in accordance with paragraph 2 of Article 11, which the Court considers below (see paragraphs 37 *et seq.*). Only when that review is complete will the Court be in a position to decide, in the light of all the circumstances of the case, whether Article 17 of the Convention should be applied.
>
> Before the Commission the Government also submitted, in the alternative, that while Article 11 guaranteed freedom to form an association, it did not on that account prevent one from being dissolved.
>
> The Commission took the view that freedom of association not only concerned the right to form a political party but also guaranteed the right of such a party, once formed, to carry on its political activities freely.
>
> The Court reiterates that the Convention is intended to guarantee rights that are not theoretical or illusory, but practical and effective (see, among other authorities, the Artico v. Italy judgment of 13 May 1980, Series A No. 37, p. 16,

paragraph 33, and the Loizidou judgment cited above, p. 27, paragraph 72). The right guaranteed by Article 11 would be largely theoretical and illusory if it were limited to the founding of an association, since the national authorities could immediately disband the association without having to comply with the Convention. It follows that the protection afforded by Article 11 lasts for an association's entire life and that dissolution of an association by a country's authorities must accordingly satisfy the requirements of paragraph 2 of that provision (see paragraphs 35-47 below).

In conclusion Article 11 is applicable to the facts of the case.

[...]

[...] the exceptions set out in Article 11 are, where political parties are concerned, to be construed strictly; only convincing and compelling reasons can justify restrictions on such parties' freedom of association. In determining whether a necessity within the meaning of Article 11, paragraph 2, exists, the Contracting States have only a limited margin of appreciation, which goes hand in hand with rigorous European supervision embracing both the law and the decisions applying it, including those given by independent courts. The Court has already held that such scrutiny was necessary in a case concerning a Member of Parliament who had been convicted of proffering insults (see the Castells judgment cited above, pp. 22-23, paragraph 42); such scrutiny is all the more necessary where an entire political party is dissolved and its leaders banned from carrying on any similar activity in the future.

[...]

[...] a measure as drastic as the immediate and permanent dissolution of the TBKP, ordered before its activities had even started and coupled with a ban barring its leaders from discharging any other political responsibility, is disproportionate to the aim pursued and consequently unnecessary in a democratic society. It follows that the measure infringed Article 11 of the Convention.

(See also the Freedom and Democracy Party (Özdep) v. Turkey judgment of 8 December 1999, *Reports* 1999-VIII, paragraphs 37-48; the Socialist Party and Others v. Turkey judgment of 25 May 1998, *Reports* 1998-III, paragraphs 41-54; and for a case where the dissolution of a political party was not held to be contrary to Article 11, see the Refah Partisi (Prosperity Party) and Others v. Turkey judgment of 31 July 2001, Application No. 41340/98, paragraphs 43-53 and 64-84, where the senior party officials had stated their intention of establishing a multi-legal system based on discrimination on grounds of beliefs and of introducing Islamic law.)

Freedom not to associate

The main controversy has turned on freedom not to associate. In that regard, a distinction is drawn according to whether the body of which membership is compulsory is or is not an association within the meaning of the Convention. Where it is not an association within the meaning of the Convention, the law may provide for compulsory membership, but subject to the condition that this does not preclude freedom to establish associations which coexist with such an organisation. Thus in the above-mentioned

Le Compte, Van Leuven and de Meyere v. Belgium judgment (p. 27, paragraph 65) the Court, after observing that the Belgian Ordre des Médecins was not an association and that compulsory membership did not violate Article 11, paragraph 1, which referred solely to associations, observed:

> [...] if there is not to be a violation, the setting up of the Ordre by the Belgian State must not prevent practitioners from forming together or joining professional associations. Totalitarian regimes have resorted – and resort – to the compulsory regimentation of the professions by means of closed and exclusive organisations taking the place of the professional associations and the traditional trade unions. The authors of the Convention intended to prevent such abuses (see the Collected Edition of the *"Travaux Préparatoires"* of the *European Convention on Human Rights*, vol. II, pp. 116-118).
>
> The Court notes that in Belgium there are several associations formed to protect the professional interests of medical practitioners and which they are completely free to join or not (see paragraph 22 above).
>
> In these circumstances, the existence of the Ordre and its attendant consequence – that is to say, the obligation on practitioners to be entered on the register of the Ordre and to be subject to the authority of its organs – clearly have neither the object nor the effect of limiting, even less suppressing, the right guaranteed by Article 11, paragraph 1.

Where the organisation in question is an association, the question of compulsory membership is more delicate. The Court initially adopted a prudent approach. In the Young, James and Webster v. the United Kingdom (13 August 1981, Series A No. 44, pp. 21-23, paragraphs 52-55), it stated that a system which forced someone to join a trade union was not necessarily always contrary to Article 11; and although in this case it found that the obligation to belong to a particular trade union was contrary to that provision, it emphasised that the refusal to join had had a very serious consequence: the applicants had been dismissed. The Court observed:

> Assuming for the sake of argument that [...] a general rule such as that in Article 20, paragraph 2, of the Universal Declaration of Human Rights was deliberately omitted from, and so cannot be regarded as itself enshrined in, the Convention, it does not follow that the negative aspect of a person's freedom of association falls completely outside the ambit of Article 11 and that each and every compulsion to join a particular trade union is compatible with the intention of that provision. To construe Article 11 as permitting every kind of compulsion in the field of trade union membership would strike at the very substance of the freedom it is designed to guarantee (see, *mutatis mutandis*, the judgment of 23 July 1968 on the merits of the "Belgian linguistics" case, Series A No. 6, p. 32, paragraph 5, the Golder judgment of 21 February 1975, Series A No. 18, p. 19, paragraph 38, and the Winterwerp judgment of 23 October 1979, Series A No. 33, p. 24, paragraph 60).
>
> The Court emphasises once again that, in proceedings originating in an individual application, it has, without losing sight of the general context, to confine its attention as far as possible to the issues raised by the concrete case before it (see,

inter alia, the Guzzardi judgment of 6 November 1980, Series A No. 39, pp. 31-32, paragraph 88). Accordingly, in the present case, it is not called upon to review the closed shop system as such in relation to the Convention or to express an opinion on every consequence or form of compulsion which it may engender; it will limit its examination to the effects of that system on the applicants.

[...]

Assuming that Article 11 does not guarantee the negative aspect of that freedom on the same footing as the positive aspect, compulsion to join a particular trade union may not always be contrary to the Convention.

However, a threat of dismissal involving loss of livelihood is a most serious form of compulsion and, in the present instance, it was directed against persons engaged by British Rail before the introduction of any obligation to join a particular trade union

In the Court's opinion, such a form of compulsion, in the circumstances of the case, strikes at the very substance of the freedom guaranteed by Article 11.

The Court adopted a distinctly firmer approach in the Sigurður A. Sigurjónsson v. Iceland judgment (cited above, p. 16, paragraph 35). Before stating that there had been a violation of Article 11, it observed:

[...] it should be recalled that the Convention is a living instrument which must be interpreted in the light of present-day living conditions (see, amongst other authorities, the Soering v. the United Kingdom judgment of 7 July 1989, Series A No. 161, p. 40, paragraph 102). Accordingly, Article 11 must be viewed as encompassing a negative right of association. It is not necessary for the Court to determine in this instance whether this right is to be considered on an equal footing with the positive right.

More recently, in the Chassagnou and Others v. France case (29 April 1999, *Reports* 1999-III, paragraph 101) the law provided that owners of land of less than a certain area, which varied from one *département* to another, were required to become members of the local ACCA and to make their land available in order to create a hunting ground for the local community. The Court found that there had been a violation of Article 11.

The right to join

Alongside the issue of compulsory membership, the right to belong to an association has been the subject of a number of points. In the Cheall v. the United Kingdom case (Application No. 10550/83, decision of 13 May 1985, *Decisions and Reports* 42, p. 185) the Commission ruled on the internal regulations and decisions of associations on the admission and expulsion of their members:

In the Commission's view the right to form trade unions involves, for example, the right of trade unions to draw up their own rules, to administer their own affairs and to establish and join trade union federations. Such trade union rights are explicitly recognised in Articles 3 and 5 of ILO Convention No. 87 which must be taken into account in the present context [...].

Accordingly, trade union decisions in these domains must not be subject to restrictions and control by the State except on the basis of Article 11, paragraph 2. As a corollary, such decisions must be regarded as private activity for which, in principle, the State cannot be responsible under the Convention.

The right to join a union "for the protection of his interests" cannot be interpreted as conferring a general right to join the union of one's choice irrespective of the rules of the union. In the exercise of their rights under Article 11, paragraph 1, unions must remain free to decide, in accordance with union rules, questions concerning admission to and expulsion from the union. The protection afforded by the provision is primarily against interference by the State.

The right to join also concerns the right not to state whether or not one is a member of an organisation. In the Grande Oriente d'Italia di Palazzo Giustiniani v. Italy judgment (2 August 2001, Application No. 35972/97), the applicant association complained in respect of the adoption by the Region of the Marches of a law requiring candidates for a public post to declare that they did not belong to the society of Freemasons. Before declaring that that measure was not necessary in a democratic society, the Court stated (paragraphs 15-16):

> The Court reiterates that Article 11 applies to associations, such as political parties (see the United Communist Party of Turkey and Others v. Turkey, judgment of 30 January 1998, *Reports of Judgments and Decisions* 1998-I, and the Socialist Party and Others v. Turkey, judgment of 25 May 1998, *Reports* 1998-III). It has indicated in general that "an association, including a political party, is not excluded from the protection afforded by the Convention simply because its activities are regarded by the national authorities as undermining the constitutional structures of the State and calling for the imposition of restrictions" (see the United Communist Party of Turkey and Others, cited above, p. 17, paragraph 27). The Court is of the opinion that this reasoning applies all the more to an association which, like the applicant association, is not suspected of undermining the constitutional structures. Additionally, and above all, the Court accepts that the measure in question may injure the applicant association – as it submits – in terms of loss of members and prestige.

> The Court therefore concludes that there has been interference. It follows that the applicant association can claim to be a victim of the alleged violation and that, accordingly, the Government's objection must be dismissed.

Further on, the Court continued (paragraphs 25-26):

> The proportionality principle demands that a balance be struck between the requirements of the purposes listed in Article 11, paragraph 2, of the Convention and those of the free exercise of freedom of association. The pursuit of a just balance must not result in individuals being discouraged, for fear of having their applications for office rejected, from exercising their right of association on such occasions.

> [...] The Court considers [...] that freedom of association is of such importance that it cannot be restricted in any way, even in respect of a candidate for public office, so long as the person concerned does not himself commit, by reason of his membership of the association, any reprehensible act. It is also clear that the association will suffer the consequences of its members' decisions. In short, the

prohibition complained of, however minimal it might be for the applicant association, does not appear "necessary in a democratic society".

3. Questions particularly applicable to trade unions

The Court has examined a number of aspects peculiar to trade union freedom.

What is not covered by trade union freedom

In the National Union of Belgian Police case the Court observed (p. 17, paragraph 38) that:

> [...] while Article 11, paragraph 1, presents trade union freedom as one form or a special aspect of freedom of association, the Article does not guarantee any particular treatment of trade unions, or their members by the State.

Then (same judgment, p. 18, paragraph 38) the Court went on to state that Article 11 did not lay down:

> [...] the right to be consulted by [the State]. Not only is this latter right not mentioned in Article 11, paragraph 1, but neither can it be said that all the Contracting States in general incorporate it in their national law or practice, or that it is indispensable for the effective enjoyment of trade union freedom. It is thus not an element necessarily inherent in a right guaranteed by the Convention.

From the same aspect (the Schmidt and Dahlström v. Sweden case, 6 February 1975, Series A No. 21, pp. 15-16, paragraphs 34 and 36) the Court established two further points:

> Article 11 does not secure [for] trade union members [...] the right to retroactivity of benefits, for instance salary increases, resulting from a new collective agreement. Such a right, which is enunciated neither in Article 11, paragraph 1, nor even in the Social Charter of 18 October 1961, is not indispensable for the effective enjoyment of trade union freedom and in no way constitutes an element necessarily inherent in a right guaranteed by the Convention.
>
> [...]
>
> [The right to strike] which is not expressly enshrined in Article 11, may be subject under national law to regulation of a kind that limits its exercise in certain instances.

What is meant by trade union freedom

The Court does not deprive trade union freedom of all its content; in the National Union of Belgian Police case (judgment cited above, p. 18, paragraph 39) the Court observed, in relation to the right to be consulted:

> [...] the Convention safeguards freedom to protect the occupational interests of trade union members by trade union action, the conduct and development of which the Contracting States must both permit and make possible. In the opinion of the Court, it follows that the members of a trade union have a right, in order to protect their interests, that the trade union should be heard. Article 11,

paragraph 1, certainly leaves each State a free choice of the means to be used towards this end. While consultation is one of these means, there are others. What the Convention requires is that under national law trade unions should be enabled, in conditions not at variance with Article 11, to strive for the protection of their members' interests.

A distinction is thus made between the right to be heard and its possible implementation by means of consultation It appears that the State may choose whatever means it considers most appropriate.

Thus, trade union freedom was seen in terms of union organisation. As far as trade union freedom from the aspect of individuals is concerned, reference should be made to the above-mentioned Cheall v. the United Kingdom case, where the Commission observed (*Decisions and Reports* 42, p. 186):

> [...] for the right to join a union to be effective the State must protect the individual against any abuse of a dominant position by trade unions (see the European Court of Human Rights, Young, James and Webster judgment of 13 August 1981, Series A No. 44, p. 25, paragraph 63). Such abuse might occur, for example, where exclusion or expulsion was not in accordance with union rules or where the rules were wholly unreasonable or arbitrary or where the consequences of exclusion or expulsion resulted in exceptional hardship such as job loss because of a closed shop.

Article 11, paragraph 2 – Derogatory clause

Article 11, paragraph 2, is worded as follows:

> **2. No restrictions shall be placed on the exercise of these rights other than such as are prescribed by law and necessary in a democratic society in the interests of national security or public safety, for the prevention of disorder or crime, for the protection of health or morals or for the protection of the rights and freedoms of others. This Article shall not prevent the imposition of lawful restrictions on the exercise of these rights by members of the armed forces, of the police or of the administration of the State.**

Article 11, paragraph 2, provides for two types of restriction: restrictions that apply to everybody, or ordinary restrictions, and restrictions that apply especially to administrations.

1. Article 11, paragraph 2, first sentence: ordinary restrictions

Concerning that first category of restrictive clauses, it must be observed that restrictions on freedom of association must be "prescribed by law", "pursue "a legitimate aim" and be "necessary".

As regards the requirement for legality (and foreseeability, according to the habitual case-law of the Court), mention may be made of the N.F. v. Italy judgment of 2 August 2001, Application No. 37119/97, paragraphs 24-34, concerning disciplinary measures taken against judges belonging to the society of Freemasons (violation of Article 11, in the absence of foreseeability).

As regards the criterion of necessity, the Ezelin v. France judgment of 26 April 1991 should be mentioned (Series A No. 202, paragraph 53). In that case a lawyer had been reprimanded for taking part in a demonstration against the adoption of the "security and liberty" act. The Court observed:

> Admittedly, the penalty imposed on Mr Ezelin was at the lower end of the scale of disciplinary penalties given in Article 107 of the Decree of 9 June 1972 (see paragraph 25 above); it had mainly moral force, since it did not entail any ban, even a temporary one, on practising the profession or on sitting as a member of the Bar Council. The Court considers, however, that the freedom to take part in a peaceful assembly – in this instance a demonstration that had not been prohibited – is of such importance that it cannot be restricted in any way, even for an *avocat*, so long as the person concerned does not himself commit any reprehensible act on such an occasion.

> In short, the sanction complained of, however minimal, does not appear to have been "necessary in a democratic society". It accordingly contravened Article 11.

2. Article 11, paragraph 2, second sentence: legitimate restrictions involving the administration

On this point, the decision of the Commission in the Council of Civil Service Unions v. the United Kingdom case should be mentioned (Application No. 11603/85, decision of 20 January 1987, *Decisions and Reports* 50, p. 239, paragraph 1, and p. 241, paragraph 1, in fine). In this case the applicants complain that the respondent government have removed the right of individual employees at GCHQ (Government Communications Headquarters, responsible for monitoring military and official communications) to belong to a trade union. The Commission made a number of points concerning the applicability and scope of the second sentence of Article 11, paragraph 2:

> The Commission has examined whether the staff serving at GCHQ fall under the term "members [...] of the administration of the State". To a certain extent, the meaning and scope of these terms is uncertain and the Commission will not attempt to define them in detail. Nevertheless, the Commission notes that the terms are mentioned in the same sentence in Article 11, paragraph 2, together with "members of the armed forces [and] of the police". In the present case, the Commission is confronted with a special institution, namely GCHQ, whose purpose resembles to a large extent that of the armed forces and the police insofar as GCHQ staff directly or indirectly, by ensuring the security of the respondent Government's military and official communications, fulfil vital functions in protecting national security.
>
> The Commission is therefore satisfied that the staff serving at GCHQ can be considered as "members [...] of the administration of the State" within the meaning of the second sentence of Article 11, paragraph 2, of the Convention. It must therefore examine whether the further conditions of the second sentence of Article 11, paragraph 2, have been met, in particular whether the restrictions at issue were "lawful" within the meaning of that provision.
>
> [...]
>
> The Commission has examined first the applicants' submission that the term "restrictions" in the second sentence of Article 11, paragraph 2, cannot imply complete suppression of the exercise of the right in Article 11. However, the Commission recalls that the same term is also employed in the first sentence of Article 11, paragraph 2. This provision has been interpreted by the Commission as also covering a complete prohibition of the exercise of the rights in Article 11 (see, for example, Application No. 8191/78, Rassemblement jurassien and Unité jurassienne v. Switzerland, decision of 10 October 1979, *Decisions and Reports* 17, p. 93). Accordingly, the term "restrictions" in the second sentence of Article 11, paragraph 2, is sufficiently broad also to cover the measures at issue.
>
> [...] the Commission notes the applicants' submissions that the term "lawful" in the second sentence of Article 11, paragraph 2, includes the principle of proportionality. In this respect, the Commission finds that, even if the term "lawful" *("légitime")* should require something more than a basis in national law, in particular a prohibition of arbitrariness, there can be no doubt that this condition was in any event also observed in the present case.

The Commission recalls its case-law according to which States must be given a wide discretion when ensuring the protection of their national security (see Leander v. Sweden, Commission's report of 17 May 1985, paragraph 68, Series A No. 116, p. 43).

The case of Grande Oriente d'Italia di Palazzo Giustiniani v. Italy (2 August 2001, Application No. 35972/97, paragraphs 30-33), cited above, provides an illustration of the application of the second sentence of Article 11, paragraph 2 :

> The Court reiterates that the term "lawful" in this sentence alludes to the same concept of lawfulness as that to which the Convention refers elsewhere when using the same or similar expressions, notably the expression "prescribed by law" found in the second paragraphs of Articles 9 to 11. The concept of lawfulness used in the Convention, apart from positing conformity with domestic law, also implies qualitative requirements in the domestic law such as foreseeability and, generally, an absence of arbitrariness (see Rekvényi v. Hungary [GC], No. 25390/94, paragraph 59, ECHR 1999-III).
>
> [...]
>
> As to whether the offices covered by Section 5 of the 1996 Law fall within the scope of "the administration of the State", the Court notes that the offices listed in schedules A and B to the 1992 Law were not part of the organisational structure of the region, but fell into two other categories : regional organisations and nominations and appointments for which the Regional Council was responsible. According to the Court's case-law, "the concept of administration of the State should be interpreted narrowly, in the light of the post held by the official concerned" (see Vogt v. Germany, judgment of 26 September 1995, *Reports of Judgments and Decisions* 1995-II, p. 31, paragraph 67). The Court reiterates that in Vogt it did not consider it necessary to determine the issue whether a teacher – a permanent civil servant – was part of the administration of the State (ibid., paragraph 68). In the present case it notes on the basis of the evidence before it that the link between the offices referred to in schedules A and B to the 1995 Law and the Marches Region is undoubtedly looser than the link which existed between Mrs Vogt, a permanent teacher, and her employer.
>
> Accordingly, the interference in question cannot be justified under the second sentence of Article 11, paragraph 2, either.
>
> In conclusion, there has been a breach of Article 11 of the Convention.

Article 12 ECHR – Freedom to marry

Article 12 is worded as follows:

> **Men and women of marriageable age have the right to marry and to found a family, according to the national laws governing the exercise of this right.**

1. The persons concerned by the right to marry

In the Rees v. the United Kingdom case (17 October 1986, Series A No. 106, p. 19, paragraphs 49-51) the Court considered that Article 12 could apply only between persons of the opposite sexes. In that case there had been no violation of Article 12 where marriage with a transsexual was refused. It will be observed that the Court based its decision on the concept of biological sex rather than that of apparent sex:

> In the Court's opinion, the right to marry guaranteed by Article 12 refers to the traditional marriage between persons of opposite biological sex. This appears also from the wording of the Article which makes it clear that Article 12 is mainly concerned to protect marriage as the basis of the family.

> Furthermore, Article 12 lays down that the exercise of this right shall be subject to the national laws of the Contracting States. The limitations thereby introduced must not restrict or reduce the right in such a way or to such an extent that the very essence of the right is impaired. However, the legal impediment in the United Kingdom on the marriage of persons who are not of the opposite biological sex cannot be said to have an effect of this kind.

> There is accordingly no violation in the instant case of Article 12 of the Convention.

See for another example the Cossey v. the United Kingdom judgment of 27 September 1990, Series A No. 184, pp. 17-18, paragraphs 43-46, or the Sheffield and Horsham v. the United Kingdom judgment of 30 July 1998, *Reports* 1998-V, paragraphs 62-70.

2. The force of the right to marry

In the F. v. Switzerland case (18 December 1987, Series A No. 128, p. 16, paragraphs 32-33) the Court considered that a temporary prohibition on remarrying imposed on a person following his third divorce constituted a violation of Article 12. The Court recalled its decision in the Rees case and observed:

> Article 12 secures the fundamental right of a man and a woman to marry and to found a family. The exercise of this right gives rise to personal, social and legal consequences. It is "subject to the national laws of the Contracting States", but "the limitations thereby introduced must not restrict or reduce the right in such a way or to such an extent that the very essence of the right is impaired" (see the Rees judgment of 17 October 1986, Series A No. 106, p. 19, paragraph 50). In all

the Council of Europe's member States, these "limitations" appear as conditions and are embodied in procedural or substantive rules. The former relate mainly to publicity and the solemnisation of marriage, while the latter relate primarily to capacity, consent and certain impediments.

The prohibition imposed on F. was applied under rules governing the exercise of the right to marry, as Article 12 does not distinguish between marriage and remarriage.

After considering the government's arguments concerning the protection of the stability of marriage, the interest of the children, etc., the Court came to the conclusion (p. 19, paragraph 40) that:

> The disputed measure, which affected the very essence of the right to marry, was disproportionate to the legitimate aim pursued. There was, therefore, a violation of Article 12.

3. The right to marry and the right to divorce

In the Johnston and Others v. Ireland case (18 December 1986, Series A No. 112, p. 24, paragraphs 52 and 54) the Court took the view that Article 12 did not contain a right to divorce. The Court stated that:

> [...] the ordinary meaning of the words "right to marry" is clear, in the sense that they cover the formation of marital relationships but not their dissolution. Furthermore, these words are found in a context that includes and express reference to "national laws"; even if, as the applicants would have it, the prohibition on divorce is to be seen as a restriction on capacity to marry, the Court does not consider that, in a society adhering to the principle of monogamy, such a restriction can be regarded as injuring the substance of the right guaranteed by Article 12.
>
> [...]
>
> [...] the applicants cannot derive a right to divorce from Article 12.

Article 13 ECHR – The right to an effective remedy

Article 13 is worded as follows:

> Everyone whose rights and freedoms as set forth in this Convention are violated shall have an effective remedy before a national authority notwithstanding that the violation has been committed by persons acting in an official capacity.

1. General principles flowing from Article 13

With the passing of time, the Court has identified a certain number of general principles flowing from Article 13. Generally, it has noted that Article 13 provides a procedural guarantee. This is what it did in the Iatridis v. Greece judgment (25 March 1999, *Reports* 1999-II, paragraph 65), where it drew a parallel with Article 1 of Protocol No. 1:

> The Court notes that the complaint under Article 13 arises out of the same facts as those it examined when dealing with the objection of non-exhaustion and the complaints under Article 1 of Protocol No. 1. However, there is a difference in the nature of the interests protected by Article 13 of the Convention and Article 1 of Protocol No. 1: the former affords a procedural safeguard, namely the "right to an effective remedy", whereas the procedural requirement inherent in the latter is ancillary to the wider purpose of ensuring respect for the right to the peaceful enjoyment of possessions.

(*Idem* the Aksoy v. Turkey judgment of 18 December 1996, *Reports* 1996-VI, p. 2286, paragraph 95; the Aydin v. Turkey judgment of 25 September 1997, *Reports* 1997-VI, pp. 1895-1896, paragraph 103; and the Kaya v. Turkey judgment of 19 February 1998, *Reports* 1998-I, pp. 329-330, paragraph 106.)

In the Büyükdag v. Turkey judgment of 21 December 2000, Application No. 28340/95, paragraph 64, available in French only – unofficial translation, concerning the lacunae in an investigation into ill-treatment, the Court described the scope of Article 13:

> The scope of the obligation flowing from Article 13 varies according to the nature of the complaint which the applicant bases on the Convention. However, the action required by Article 13 must be "effective" in practice as well as in law, particularly in so far as its exercise must not be unjustifiably hindered by the acts or omissions of the authorities of the respondent State (the above-mentioned Aksoy judgment, p. 2286, paragraph 95, the Aydin v. Turkey judgment of 25 September 1997, pp. 1895-1896, paragraph 103, and the Kaya v. Turkey judgment of 19 February 1998, *Reports* 1998-I, pp. 329-330, paragraph 106).

In the case of Leander v. Sweden, the Court observed (26 March 1987, Series A No. 116, pp. 29-30, paragraph 77) that:

> For the interpretation of Article 13, the following general principles are of relevance:
>
> (a) Where an individual has an arguable claim to be the victim of a violation of the rights set forth in the Convention, he should have a remedy before a national authority in order both to have his claim decided and, if appropriate, to obtain redress (see, *inter alia*, the above-mentioned Silver and Others judgment, Series A No. 61, p. 42, paragraph 113).
>
> (b) The authority referred to in Article 13 need not be a judicial authority but, if it is not, the powers and the guarantees which it affords are relevant in determining whether the remedy before it is effective (ibid.).
>
> (c) Although no single remedy may itself entirely satisfy the requirements of Article 13, the aggregate of remedies provided for under domestic law may do so (ibid.).
>
> (d) Article 13 does not guarantee a remedy allowing a Contracting State's laws as such to be challenged before a national authority on the ground of being contrary to the Convention or equivalent domestic norms (see the James and Others judgment of 21 February 1986, Series A No. 98, p. 47, paragraph 85).

The last point may be explained by the fact that there is no "obligation to incorporate the Convention into domestic law" (ibid., see also the James and Others judgment). Here one can see the Court taking into account different States' individualities when it comes to implementing international law (to be noted especially in the case of the United Kingdom). One can also detect a desire to avoid offending the sensibilities of States desirous to retain their sovereignty in legislative matters. It is enough that an appeal system exists to decide on the applicant's complaint, it does not require that there be a remedy allowing the laws of a Contracting State to be challenged before a national authority on the grounds of being contrary to the Convention.

Another fundamental principle is recalled in the Boyle and Rice v. the United Kingdom judgment (27 April 1988, Series A No. 131, pp. 23-24, paragraphs 52 and 55). Article 13, which is intended to ensure that a remedy before a national court is available to anyone whose Convention rights have been violated, is applicable even in the absence of a violation of one of these rights. It is sufficient to be able to make an arguable case for the violation of a right:

> Notwithstanding the terms of Article 13 read literally, the existence of an actual breach of another provision of the Convention (a "substantive" provision) is not a prerequisite for the application of the Article (see the Klass and Others judgment of 6 September 1978, Series A No. 28, p. 29, paragraph 64). Article 13 guarantees the availability of a remedy at a national level to enforce – and hence to allege non-compliance with – the substance of the Convention rights and freedoms in whatever form they may happen to be secured in the domestic legal order (see the Lithgow and Others judgment of 8 July 1986, Series A No. 102, p. 74, paragraph 205, and the authorities cited there).

However, Article 13 cannot reasonably be interpreted so as to require a remedy in domestic law in respect of any supposed grievance under the Convention that an individual may have, no matter how unmeritorious his complaint may be: the grievance must be an arguable one in terms of the Convention (see, as the most recent authority, the Leander judgment of 26 March 1987, Series A No. 116, p. 29, paragraph 77, sub-paragraph *a*).

[...]

The Court does not think that it should give an abstract definition of the notion of arguability. Rather it must be determined, in the light of the particular facts and the nature of the legal issue or issues raised, whether each individual claim of violation forming the basis of a complaint under Article 13 was arguable and, if so, whether the requirements of Article 13 were met in relation thereto.

In the Powell and Rayner v. the United Kingdom judgment of 12 February 1990, Series A No. 172, pp. 14-15, paragraph 33, the Court gave an elucidation about the relation between the notions "arguable" (Article 13, remedy in domestic law) and "manifestly ill-founded" (Article 27, paragraph 2, procedural law of the Convention). It proposed that the two notions should be aligned:

As the Court stated in the Boyle and Rice judgment, "on the ordinary meaning of the words, it is difficult to conceive how a claim that is 'manifestly ill-founded' can nevertheless be 'arguable' and vice versa" (loc. cit., p. 24, paragraph 54). Furthermore, Article 13 and Article 27 are concerned within their respective spheres, with the availability of remedies for the enforcement of the same Convention rights and freedoms. The coherence of this dual system of enforcement is at risk of being undermined if Article 13 is interpreted as requiring national law to make available an "effective remedy" for a grievance classified under Article 27, paragraph 2, as being so weak as not to warrant examination on its merits at international level. Whatever threshold the Commission has set in its case-law for declaring claims "manifestly ill-founded" under Article 27, paragraph 2, in principle it should set the same threshold in regard to the parallel notion of "arguability" under Article 13.

2. Limits to the application of Article 13

It should be noted that the Court does not regard it as appropriate to examine a complaint based on Article 13 where it has already considered the question of a remedy under another Article. In the Foti and Others v. Italy case (10 December 1982, Series A No. 56, p. 24, paragraph 78) the Court observed:

Like the Commission (see paragraph 151 of the report), the Court considers it superfluous to decide on the application of Article 13 in the instant case in view of the fact that the parties have not pursued the matter and in view of its own conclusion that there has been a breach of Article 6, paragraph 1.

See for another example the Hentrich v. France judgment of 22 September 1994 Series A No. 296-A, p. 24, paragraph 65:

In view of its decision in respect of Article 6, paragraph 1, the Court considers it unnecessary to look at the case under Article 13 of the Convention; this is because the requirements of that provision are less strict than, and are here absorbed by, those of Article 6, paragraph 1 (see, among other authorities, the Pudas v. Sweden judgment of 27 October 1987, Series A No. 125-A, p. 17, paragraph 43).

Similarly, in the X. and Y. v. the Netherlands judgment (26 March 1985, Series A No. 91, p. 15, paragraph 36) the Court stated that:

> The Court has already considered, in the context of Article 8, whether an adequate means of obtaining a remedy was available to Miss Y. Its finding that there was no such means was one of the factors which led it to conclude that Article 8 had been violated.

> This being so, the Court does not have to examine the same issue under Article 13.

However, it may be seen from the Kudła v. Poland judgment (26 October 2000, Application No. 30210/96, paragraphs 146-149, 152 and 156) that the Court's approach has changed somewhat:

> In many previous cases in which the Court has found a violation of Article 6, paragraph 1, it did not consider it necessary also to rule on an accompanying complaint made under Article 13. More often than not this was because in the circumstances Article 6, paragraph 1, was deemed to constitute a *lex specialis* in relation to Article 13.

> Thus, where the Convention right asserted by the individual is a "civil right" recognised under domestic law – such as the right of property – the protection afforded by Article 6, paragraph 1, will also be available (see, for example, the Sporrong and Lönnroth v. Sweden judgment of 23 September 1982, Series A No. 52, pp. 31-32, paragraph 88). In such circumstances the safeguards of Article 6, paragraph 1, implying the full panoply of a judicial procedure, are stricter than, and absorb, those of Article 13 (see, for example, the Brualla Gómez de la Torre judgment cited above, p. 2957, paragraph 41).

> The Court has applied a similar logic in cases where the applicant's grievance has been directed at the adequacy of an existing appellate or cassation procedure coming within the ambit of both Article 6, paragraph 1, under its "criminal" head and Article 13 (see the Kamasinski v. Austria judgment of 19 December 1989, Series A No. 168, pp. 45-46, paragraph 110 – in relation to nullity proceedings before the Supreme Court).

> In such cases there is no legal interest in re-examining the same subject matter of complaint under the less stringent requirements of Article 13.

> There is, however, no overlap and hence no absorption where, as in the present case, the alleged Convention violation that the individual wishes to bring before a "national authority" is a violation of the right to trial within a reasonable time, contrary to Article 6, paragraph 1. The question of whether the applicant in a given case did benefit from trial within a reasonable time in the determination of civil rights and obligations or a criminal charge is a separate legal issue from that of whether there was available to the applicant under domestic law an effective remedy to ventilate a complaint on that ground. In the present case the issue to be determined before the Article 6, paragraph 1, "tribunals" was the criminal

charges brought against the applicant, whereas the complaint that he wanted to have examined by a "national authority" for the purposes of Article 13 was the separate one of the unreasonable length of the proceedings.

In comparable cases in the past, the Court has none the less declined to rule on an accompanying complaint of the absence of an effective remedy as guaranteed by Article 13, considering it unnecessary in view of its prior finding of a breach of the "reasonable time" requirement laid down in Article 6, paragraph 1 (see, among other examples, the judgments cited above: Pizzetti, p. 37, paragraph 21; Bouilly, paragraph 27; and Giuseppe Tripodi, paragraph 15).

In the Court's view, the time has come to review its case-law in the light of the continuing accumulation of applications before it in which the only, or principal, allegation is that of a failure to ensure a hearing within a reasonable time in breach of Article 6, paragraph 1.

The growing frequency with which violations in this regard are being found has recently led the Court to draw attention to "the important danger" that exists for the rule of law within national legal orders when "excessive delays in the administration of justice" occur "in respect of which litigants have no domestic remedy" (see, for example, Bottazzi v. Italy [GC], No. 34884/97, paragraph 22, ECHR 1999-V; Di Mauro v. Italy [GC], No. 34256/96, paragraph 23, ECHR 1999-V; A.P. v. Italy [GC], No. 35265/97, paragraph 18, 28 July 1999, unreported; and Ferrari v. Italy [GC], No. 33440/96, paragraph 21, 28 July 1999, unreported).

Against this background, the Court now perceives the need to examine the applicant's complaint under Article 13 taken separately, notwithstanding its earlier finding of a violation of Article 6, paragraph 1, for failure to try him within a reasonable time.

[...]

The object of Article 13, as emerges from the *travaux préparatoires* (see the *Collected Edition of the "Travaux Préparatoires" of the European Convention on Human Rights*, vol. II, pp. 485 and 490, and vol. III, p. 651), is to provide a means whereby individuals can obtain relief at national level for violations of their Convention rights before having to set in motion the international machinery of complaint before the Court. From this perspective, the right of an individual to trial within a reasonable time will be less effective if there exists no opportunity to submit the Convention claim first to a national authority; and the requirements of Article 13 are to be seen as reinforcing those of Article 6, paragraph 1, rather than being absorbed by the general obligation imposed by that Article not to subject individuals to inordinate delays in legal proceedings.

[...]

In view of the foregoing considerations, the Court considers that the correct interpretation of Article 13 is that that provision guarantees an effective remedy before a national authority for an alleged breach of the requirement under Article 6, paragraph 1, to hear a case within a reasonable time.

Article 14 ECHR – Prohibition of discrimination

Article 14 is worded as follows:

> The enjoyment of the rights and freedoms set forth in this Convention shall be secured without discrimination on any ground such as sex, race, colour, language, religion, political or other opinion, national or social origin, association with a national minority, property, birth or other status.

As it reads, Article 14 does not have an autonomous character. The Court has stated that it does not have an absolute scope.

There are, however, numerous examples of its application.

1. The characteristics of Article 14

Non-autonomous nature of Article 14

First of all, it is appropriate to point out the non-autonomous nature of Article 14: it cannot be applied unless it is taken together with another Article of the Convention. In the Rasmussen v. Denmark case (28 November 1984, Series A No. 87, p. 12, paragraph 29) it is clearly stated that:

> Article 14 complements the other substantive provisions of the Convention and the Protocols. It has no independent existence since it has effect solely in relation to "the enjoyment of the rights and freedoms" safeguarded by those provisions. [...] there can be no room for its application unless the facts at issue fall within the ambit of one or more of the latter (see, *inter alia*, the Van der Mussele judgment of 23 November 1983, Series A No. 70, p. 22, paragraph 43).

However, Article 14 comes into play when it is relied on together with another Article of the Convention. The Court refers to this in the Petrovic v. Austria judgment (27 March 1998, Application No. 20458/92, *Reports* 1998-I, paragraph 28):

> The Court has said on many occasions that Article 14 comes into play whenever "the subject-matter of the disadvantage [...] constitutes one of the modalities of the exercise of a right guaranteed" (see the National Union of Belgian Police v. Belgium judgment of 27 October 1975, Series A No. 19, p. 20, paragraph 45), or the measures complained of are "linked to the exercise of a right guaranteed" (see the Schmidt and Dahlström v. Sweden judgment of 6 February 1976, Series A No. 21, p. 17, paragraph 39).

However, the following point must be made: for the purpose of relying on Article 14, there is no requirement that the impugned measure submitted to the Court violates in itself one of the rights guaranteed by the Convention. Even if such a measure is consistent with one or other Article of the Convention, Article 14 may be pleaded together with that Article provided that discrimination can be detected. It is enough that a violation of Article 14 in conjunction with one of those provisions is possible. The Court had already indicated this in the "Belgian linguistics" case. In the National Union of Belgian Police judgment it repeated the terms more explicitly (judgment of 27 October 1975, Series A No. 19, p. 19, paragraph 44):

> Although the Court has found no violation of Article 11, paragraph 1, it has to be ascertained whether the differences in treatment complained of by the applicant union contravene Articles 11 and 14 taken together. Although Article 14 has no independent existence, it is complementary to the other normative provisions of the Convention and Protocols: it safeguards individuals, or groups of individuals, placed in comparable situations, from all discrimination in the enjoyment of the rights and freedoms set forth in those provisions. A measure which in itself is in conformity with the requirements of the Article enshrining the right or freedom in question may therefore infringe this Article when read in conjunction with Article 14 for the reason that it is of a discriminatory nature. It is as though Article 14 formed an integral part of each of the articles laying down rights and freedoms whatever their nature (the case relating to certain aspects of the laws on the use of languages in education in Belgium, judgment of 23 July 1968, Series A No. 6, pp. 33-34, paragraph 9).

> These considerations apply in particular where a right embodied in the Convention and the corresponding obligation on the part of the State are not defined precisely, and consequently the State has a wide choice of the means for making the exercise of the right possible and effective.

The non-absolute nature of Article 14

In the above-mentioned "Belgian linguistics" case the Court indicated that Article 14 did not preclude all differences in treatment (23 July 1968, Series A No. 6, pp. 33-34, paragraph 10 of the section headed "Interpretation adopted by the Court"):

> In spite of the very general wording of the French version *("sans distinction aucune")*, Article 14 does not forbid every difference in treatment in the exercise of the rights and freedoms recognised. This version must be read in the light of the more restrictive text of the English version ("without discrimination"). In addition, and in particular, one would reach absurd results were one to give Article 14 an interpretation as wide as that which the French version seems to imply. One would, in effect, be led to judge as contrary to the Convention every one of the many legal or administrative provisions which do not secure to everyone complete equality of treatment in the enjoyment of the rights and freedoms recognised. The competent national authorities are frequently confronted with situations and problems which, on account of differences inherent therein, call for different legal solutions; moreover, certain legal inequalities tend only to correct factual inequalities. The extensive interpretation mentioned above cannot consequently be accepted.

In the Lithgow and Others v. the United Kingdom judgment (8 July 1986, Series A No. 102, pp. 66-67, paragraph 177) the Court recalled the criteria which it uses and the steps which it takes when it considers whether or not a measure is discriminatory:

> [Article 14] safeguards persons (including legal persons) who are "placed in analogous situations" against discriminatory differences of treatment; and, for the purposes of Article 14, a difference of treatment is discriminatory if it "has no objective and reasonable justification", that is, if it does not pursue a "legitimate aim" or if there is not a "reasonable relationship of proportionality between the means employed and the aim sought to be realised" (see, amongst many authorities, the Rasmussen judgment of 28 November 1984, Series A No. 87, p. 13, paragraph 35, and p. 14, paragraph 38). Furthermore, the Contracting States enjoy a certain margin of appreciation in assessing whether and to what extent differences in otherwise similar situations justify a different treatment in law; the scope of this margin will vary according to the circumstances, the subject-matter and its background (ibid., p. 15, paragraph 40).

(See also the Cha'are Shalom ve Tsedek v. France judgment of 27 June 2000, Application No. 27417/95, paragraphs 85-88; and the Larkos v. Cyprus judgment of 18 February 1999, *Reports* 1999-I, paragraphs 22-32.)

Mention should also be made of the case of Magee v. the United Kingdom (6 June 2000, Application No. 28135/95, paragraph 50), where the applicant claimed that suspects arrested and detained in England and Wales under the anti-terrorism legislation were able to consult a lawyer immediately and to have a lawyer present while being interviewed. Furthermore, at the material time, no adverse inferences could be drawn where a person who had been arrested refused to speak while being interviewed, unlike the position in Northern Ireland under the 1988 Order. The Court stated:

> The Court recalls that Article 14 of the Convention protects against a discriminatory difference in treatment of persons in analogous positions in the exercise of the rights and freedoms recognised by the Convention and its Protocols. It observes in this connection that in the constituent parts of the United Kingdom there is not always a uniform approach to legislation in particular areas. Whether or not an individual can assert a right derived from legislation may accordingly depend on the geographical reach of the legislation at issue and the individual's location at the time. For the Court, in so far as there exists a difference in treatment of detained suspects under the 1988 Order and the legislation of England and Wales on the matters referred to by the applicant, that difference is not to be explained in terms of personal characteristics, such as national origin or association with a national minority, but on the geographical location where the individual is arrested and detained. This permits legislation to take account of regional differences and characteristics of an objective and reasonable nature. In the present case, such a difference does not amount to discriminatory treatment within the meaning of Article 14 of the Convention.

Article 14 and "positive discrimination"

In the case of Thlimmenos v. Greece (6 April 2000, Application No. 34639/97, paragraphs 39, 41-42 and 44-49), the Court rules on the refusal to permit access to the profession of chartered accountant to a person who had previously been convicted for having refused to do military service on account of his religious beliefs. The Court examined the question under Article 9 taken together with Article 14 and stated:

> The Court notes that the applicant was not appointed a chartered accountant as a result of his past conviction for insubordination consisting in his refusal to wear the military uniform. He was thus treated differently from the other persons who had applied for that post on the ground of his status as a convicted person. The Court considers that such difference of treatment does not generally come within the scope of Article 14 in so far as it relates to access to a particular profession, the right to freedom of profession not being guaranteed by the Convention.

> However, the applicant does not complain of the distinction that the rules governing access to the profession make between convicted persons and others. His complaint rather concerns the fact that in the application of the relevant law no distinction is made between persons convicted of offences committed exclusively because of their religious beliefs and persons convicted of other offences. In this context the Court notes that the applicant is a member of the Jehovah's Witnesses, a religious group committed to pacifism, and that there is nothing in the file to disprove the applicant's claim that he refused to wear the military uniform only because he considered that his religion prevented him from doing so. In essence, the applicant's argument amounts to saying that he is discriminated against in the exercise of his freedom of religion, as guaranteed by Article 9 of the Convention, in that he was treated like any other person convicted of a serious crime although his own conviction resulted from the very exercise of this freedom. Seen in this perspective, the Court accepts that the "set of facts" complained of by the applicant – his being treated as a person convicted of a serious crime for the purposes of an appointment to a chartered accountant's post despite the fact that the offence for which he had been convicted was prompted by his religious beliefs – "falls within the ambit of a Convention provision", namely Article 9.

> The Court has so far considered that the right under Article 14 not to be discriminated against in the enjoyment of the rights guaranteed under the Convention is violated when States treat differently persons in analogous situations without providing an objective and reasonable justification (see the Inze judgment cited above, p. 18, paragraph 41). However, the Court considers that this is not the only facet of the prohibition of discrimination in Article 14. The right not to be discriminated against in the enjoyment of the rights guaranteed under the Convention is also violated when States without an objective and reasonable justification fail to treat differently persons whose situations are significantly different.

> It follows that Article 14 of the Convention is of relevance to the applicant's complaint and applies in the circumstances of this case in conjunction with Article 9 thereof.

> The next question to be addressed is whether Article 14 of the Convention has been complied with. According to its case-law, the Court will have to examine whether the failure to treat the applicant differently from other persons convicted of a serious crime pursued a legitimate aim. If it did the Court will have

to examine whether there was a reasonable relationship of proportionality between the means employed and the aim sought to be realised (see the Inze judgment cited above, ibid.).

The Court [...] notes that the applicant did serve a prison sentence for his refusal to wear the military uniform. In these circumstances, the Court considers that imposing a further sanction on the applicant was disproportionate. It follows that the applicant's exclusion from the profession of chartered accountants did not pursue a legitimate aim. As a result, the Court finds that there existed no objective and reasonable justification for not treating the applicant differently from other persons convicted of a serious crime.

[...] The Court has never excluded that legislation may be found to be in direct breach of the Convention (see, *inter alia*, Chassagnou and Others v. France [GC], Nos. 25088/94, 28331/95 and 28443/95, ECHR 1999-III). In the present case the Court considers that it was the State having enacted the relevant legislation which violated the applicant's right not to be discriminated against in the enjoyment of his right under Article 9 of the Convention.

The Court concludes, therefore, that there has been a violation of Article 14 of the Convention taken in conjunction with Article 9.

2. Examples of the application of Article 14

There are cases where the Court, after finding that there has been a violation of a clause of the Convention, does not consider it appropriate to consider the problem from the viewpoint of Article 14. Apart from those cases, two categories of decisions can be distinguished: those where the difference in treatment is found to be discriminatory and those where it is acceptable.

Discriminatory differences in treatment

In family matters

In the Hoffmann v. Austria judgment (23 June 1993, Series A No. 255-C, pp. 59-60, paragraphs 33 and 36) the Court found that there had been a violation of Article 14 in the form of the decision of the Austrian Supreme Court refusing to confer parental authority on a mother essentially on the fact that she was a Jehovah's Witness. The Court observed:

[...] there has been a difference in treatment and [...] this difference was on the ground of religion; this conclusion is supported by the tone and phrasing of the Supreme Court's considerations regarding the practical consequences of the applicant's religion.

[...]

In the present context, reference may be made to Article 5 of Protocol No. 7, which entered into force for Austria on 1 November 1988; although it was not prayed in aid in the present proceedings, it provides for the fundamental equality of spouses, *inter alia*, as regards parental rights and makes it clear that in cases of this nature the interests of the children are paramount.

Where the Austrian Supreme Court did not rely on the Federal Act on the Religious Education of Children, it weighed the facts differently from the courts below, whose reasoning was moreover supported by psychological expert opinion. Notwithstanding any possible arguments to the contrary, a distinction based essentially on a difference in religion alone is not acceptable.

The Court therefore cannot find that a reasonable relationship of proportionality existed between the means employed and the aim pursued; there has accordingly been a violation of Article 8 taken in conjunction with Article 14.

In the case of Salgueiro Da Silva Mouta v. Portugal (21 December 1999, Application No. 33290/96, paragraphs 34-36), the applicant claimed to have suffered discrimination based on his sexual orientation when the national court reached a decision on parental authority. The Court stated:

> [...] The Court of Appeal [...] took account of the fact that the applicant was a homosexual and was living with another man in observing that "The child should live in [...] a traditional Portuguese family" and that "It is not our task here to determine whether homosexuality is or is not an illness or whether it is a sexual orientation towards persons of the same sex. In both cases it is an abnormality and children should not grow up in the shadow of abnormal situations" (ibid.).

> It is the Court's view that the above passages from the judgment in question, far from being merely clumsy or unfortunate as the Government maintained, or mere *obiter dicta*, suggest, quite to the contrary, that the applicant's homosexuality was a factor which was decisive in the final decision. That conclusion is supported by the fact that the Court of Appeal, when ruling on the applicant's right to contact, warned him not to adopt conduct which might make the child realise that her father was living with another man "in conditions resembling those of man and wife" (ibid.).

> The Court is therefore forced to find, in the light of the foregoing, that the Court of Appeal made a distinction based on considerations regarding the applicant's sexual orientation, a distinction which is not acceptable under the Convention (see, *mutatis mutandis*, the Hoffmann judgment cited above, p. 60, paragraph 36).

The Court cannot therefore find that a reasonable relationship of proportionality existed between the means employed and the aim pursued; there has accordingly been a violation of Article 8 taken in conjunction with Article 14.

For a difference in treatment between natural fathers and divorced fathers in regard to the right of access, see the Sommerfeld v. Germany judgment of 11 October 2001, Application No. 31871/96.

In the case of Burghartz v. Switzerland (22 February 1994, Series A No. 280-B, pp. 29-30, paragraphs 27-29, the facts of which are described under Article 8 above), the Court condemned the difference drawn between husbands and wives regarding the possibility of combining their own name with the chosen family name:

> [...] the advancement of the equality of the sexes is today a major goal in the member States of the Council of Europe; this means that very weighty reasons would have to be put forward before a difference of treatment on the sole ground

of sex could be regarded as compatible with the Convention (see, as the most recent authority, the Schuler-Zgraggen v. Switzerland judgment of 24 June 1993, Series A No. 263, pp. 21-22, paragraph 67).

In support of the system complained of, the Government relied, firstly, on the Swiss legislature's concern that family unity should be reflected in a single joint surname. The Court is not persuaded by this argument, since family unity would be no less reflected if the husband added his own surname to his wife's, adopted as the joint family name, than it is by the converse argument allowed by the Civil Code.

In the second place, it cannot be said that a genuine tradition is at issue here. Married women have enjoyed the right from which the applicant seeks to benefit only since 1984. In any event, the Convention must be interpreted in the light of present-day conditions, especially the importance of the principle of non-discrimination.

Nor is there any distinction to be derived from the spouses' choice of one of their surnames as the family name in preference to the other. Contrary to what the Government contended, it cannot be said to represent greater deliberateness on the part of the husband than on the part of the wife. It is therefore unjustified to provide for different consequences in each case.

As to the other types of surname, such as a double-barrelled name or any other informal manner of use, the Federal Court itself distinguished them from the legal family name, which is the only one that may appear in a person's official papers. They therefore cannot be regarded as equivalent to it.

In sum, the difference of treatment complained of lacks an objective and reasonable justification and accordingly contravenes Article 14 taken together with Article 8.

For questions of succession, reference should be made to the following judgments: the Marckx v. Belgium judgment of 13 June 1979, Series A No. 31, p. 24, paragraph 54; the Vermeire v. Belgium judgment of 29 November 1991, Series A No. 214-C, p. 83, paragraph 28; the Camp and Bourimi v. the Netherlands judgment of 3 October 2000, Application No. 28369/95, paragraphs 30-39. For a case involving the different treatment of two children, one born out of wedlock and the other born of an adulterous relationship, see the Mazurek v. France judgment (1 February 2000, Application No. 34406/97, paragraphs 54-55):

The only issue submitted to the Court concerns the question of inheritance from the mother by her two children, one born out of wedlock and the other adulterine. The Court does not find any ground in the instant case on which to justify discrimination based on birth out of wedlock. In any event, an adulterine child cannot be blamed for circumstances for which he or she is not responsible. It is an inescapable finding that the applicant was penalised, on account of his status as an adulterine child, in the division of the assets of the estate.

Having regard to all the foregoing, the Court concludes that there was not a reasonable relationship of proportionality between the means employed and the aim pursued.

> There has therefore been a violation of Article 1 of Protocol No. 1 taken in conjunction with Article 14 of the Convention.

Concerning the institution of parental leave, see the Petrovic v. Austria judgment (27 March 1998, Application No. 20458/92, *Reports* 1998-I, paragraphs 30-43).

Other matters

In the case of Karlheinz-Schmidt v. Germany (18 July 1994, Series A No. 291-B, p. 33, paragraph 28) concerning the obligation imposed solely on men to serve in the fire brigade or pay a financial contribution in lieu the Court considers:

> Irrespective of whether or not there can nowadays exist any justification for treating men and women differently as regards compulsory service in the fire brigade, what is finally decisive in the present case is that the obligation to perform such service is exclusively one of law and theory. In view of the continuing existence of a sufficient number of volunteers, no male person is in practice obliged to serve in a fire brigade. The financial contribution has – not in law but in fact – lost its compensatory character and has become the only effective duty. In the imposition of a financial burden such as this, a difference of treatment on the ground of sex can hardly be justified.

In the Gaygusuz v. Austria case (16 September 1996, *Reports of Judgments and Decisions* 1996-IV, pp. 1142-1143, paragraphs 42 and 46-50), the applicant was denied emergency assistance under the Unemployment Insurance Act on account of his nationality. The Court first recalled that "very weighty reasons would have to be put forward before the Court could regard a difference of treatment based exclusively on the ground of nationality as compatible with the Convention":

> The Court notes in the first place that Mr Gaygusuz was legally resident in Austria, worked there at certain times (see paragraph 10 above), paying contributions to the unemployment insurance fund in the same capacity and on the same basis as Austrian nationals.

> It observes that the authorities' refusal to grant him emergency assistance was based exclusively on the fact that he did not have Austrian nationality as required by Section 33, paragraph 2.*a*, of the 1977 Unemployment Insurance Act (see paragraph 20 above).

> In addition, it has not been argued that the applicant failed to satisfy the other statutory conditions for the award of the social benefit in question. He was accordingly in a like situation to Austrian nationals as regards his entitlement thereto.

> Admittedly, Sections 33 and 34 of the 1977 Unemployment Insurance Act (see paragraph 20 above) lay down certain exceptions to the nationality condition, but the applicant did not fall into any of the relevant categories.

> The Court therefore finds the arguments put forward by the Austrian Government unpersuasive. It considers, like the Commission, that the difference of treatment between Austrians and non-Austrians as regards entitlement to emergency assistance, of which Mr Gaygusuz was a victim, is not based on any "objective and reasonable justification".

The Austrian Government had submitted that "the difference of treatment was based on the idea that the State has special responsibility for its own nationals and must take care of them and provide for their essential needs". Furthermore, the government argued that "the Unemployment Insurance Act laid down certain exceptions to the nationality condition and that Austria was not bound by any contractual obligation to grant emergency assistance to Turkish nationals".

Lastly, in the Darby v. Sweden case the Court condemned the fact that the applicant had found it impossible to secure a reduction in the special tax for the Church of Sweden granted to persons who did not belong to that Church on the sole ground that he was not officially registered as a resident (the Darby case, 23 October 1990, Series A No. 187, p. 13, paragraphs 32-34):

> It appears first that Dr Darby can claim to have been, as regards his right to an exemption under the Dissenters Tax Act, in a situation similar to that of other non-members of the Church who were formally registered as residents of Sweden.
>
> As regards the aim of this difference in the treatment of residents and non-residents, it is worth noting the following. According to the Government Bill (1951: 175) which gave raise to the Dissenters Tax Act, the reason why the right to exemption was reserved for persons formally registered as residents was that the case for reduction could not be argued with the same force in regard to persons who were not so registered as it could be in regard to those who were, and that the procedure would be more complicated if the reduction was to apply to non-residents (see paragraph 22 above) The Government Bill (1978/79: 58) containing the tax-law amendments that brought about this complaint did not mention the special situation which the amendments would create for non-residents under the Dissenters Tax Act (see paragraph 20 above). In fact, the Government stated at the hearing before the Court that they did not argue that the distinction in treatment had a legitimate aim.
>
> In view of the above, the measure complained of cannot be seen as having had any legitimate aim under the Convention. Accordingly, there has been a violation of Article 14 of the Convention.

Non-discriminatory differences in treatment

In the Abdulaziz, Cabales and Balkandali v. the United Kingdom case (28 May 1985, Series A No. 94, pp. 39-40, paragraphs 84-85) the Court ruled on the immigration policy in the United Kingdom. The following passage refers to the conclusions of the Commission:

> A majority of the Commission concluded that there had been no violation of Article 14 under this head. Most immigration policies – restricting, as they do, free entry – differentiated on the basis of people's nationality, and indirectly their race, ethnic origin and possibly their colour. Whilst a Contracting State could not implement "policies of a purely racist nature", to give preferential treatment to its nationals or to persons from countries with which it had the closest links did not constitute "racial discrimination". The effect in practice of the United Kingdom

rules did not mean that they were abhorrent on the grounds of racial discrimination, there being no evidence of an actual difference of treatment on grounds of race.

A minority of the Commission, on the other hand, noted that the main effect of the rules was to prevent immigration from the New Commonwealth and Pakistan. This was not coincidental: the legislative history showed that the intention was to "lower the number of coloured immigrants". By their effect and purpose, the rules were indirectly racist and there had thus been a violation of Article 14 under this head in the cases of Mrs Abdulaziz and Mrs Cabales.

The Court agrees in this respect with the majority of the Commission.

In the Rasmussen case the applicant complained that the Danish legislation imposed a time-limit on his right to disown a child born during the marriage although it allowed his ex-wife to take action to challenge paternity at any time. The Court stated (Rasmussen v. Sweden, 28 November 1984, Series A No. 87, pp. 15-16, paragraphs 41-42) that:

> The Court has had close regard to the circumstances and the general background and has borne in mind the margin of appreciation which must be allowed to the authorities in the matter. In its view, they were entitled to think that the introduction of time-limits for the institution of paternity proceedings was justified by the desire to ensure legal certainty and to protect the interests of the child. In this respect, the legislation complained of did not differ substantially from that of most other Contracting States or from that currently in force in Denmark. The difference of treatment established on this point between husbands and wives was based on the notion that such time-limits were less necessary for wives than for husbands since the mother's interests usually coincided with those of the child, she being awarded custody in most cases of divorce or separation.
>
> [...]
>
> The Court thus concludes that the difference of treatment complained of was not discriminatory, within the meaning of Article 14.

In the National Union of Belgian Police judgment (27 October 1975, Series A No. 19, pp. 21-22, paragraph 49), the Court observed that the absence of consultation of certain trade unions under a decree adopted for the purpose of restricting the number of organisations to be consulted did not constitute a violation of Article 14 (the above-mentioned case, paragraph 49):

> The Court is of the opinion that the uniform nature [of the criterion employed in the Decree] does not justify the conclusion that the Government has exceeded the limits of its freedom to lay down the measures it deems appropriate in its relations with the trade unions. The Court considers that it has not been clearly established that the disadvantage suffered by the applicant is excessive in relation to the legitimate aim pursued by the Government. The principle of proportionality has therefore not been offended.

In the "Belgian linguistics" case the question arose whether the government could object, in the unilingual regions, to the establishment and subsidy by the State of schools which did not comply with the general linguistic requirements. The Court stated (the "Belgian linguistics" case, 23 July 1968, Series A No. 6, p. 44, paragraph 7, first question, in fine):

> On this point the Court observes that the provisions which are challenged concern only official or subsidised education. They in no way prevent, in the Dutch-unilingual region, the organisation of independent French-language education, which in any case still exists there to a certain extent. The Court, therefore, does not consider that the measures adopted in this matter by the Belgian legislature are so disproportionate [in comparison] to the requirements of the public interest which is being pursued as to constitute a discrimination contrary to Article 14 of the Convention, read in conjunction (with other Articles of the Convention).

Article 15 ECHR – General derogatory clause

Article 15 is worded as follows:

1. In time of war or other public emergency threatening the life of the nation any High Contracting Party may take measures derogating from its obligations under this Convention to the extent strictly required by the exigencies of the situation, provided that such measures are not inconsistent with its other obligations under international law.

2. No derogation from Article 2, except in respect of deaths resulting from lawful acts of war, or from Articles 3, 4 (paragraph 1) and 7 shall be made under this provision.

3. Any High Contracting Party availing itself of this right of derogation shall keep the Secretary General of the Council of Europe fully informed of the measures which it has taken and the reasons therefor. It shall also inform the Secretary General of the Council of Europe when such measures have ceased to operate and the provisions of the Convention are again being fully executed

1. Conditions for the implementation of Article 15

Basic conditions

There are three basic conditions.

"War" or "public emergency threatening the life of the nation"

The Court has qualified the role of the States in determining a "public emergency" (the Aksoy v. Turkey judgment of 18 December 1996, *Reports* 1996-VI, paragraph 68-70):

> The Court recalls that it falls to each Contracting State, with its responsibility for "the life of [its] nation", to determine whether that life is threatened by a "public emergency" and, if so, how far it is necessary to go in attempting to overcome the emergency. By reason of their direct and continuous contact with the pressing needs of the moment, the national authorities are in principle better placed than the international judge to decide both on the presence of such an emergency and on the nature and scope of the derogations necessary to avert it. Accordingly, in this matter a wide margin of appreciation should be left to the national authorities.

> Nonetheless, Contracting Parties do not enjoy an unlimited discretion. It is for the Court to rule whether, *inter alia*, the States have gone beyond the "extent strictly required by the exigencies" of the crisis. The domestic margin of appreciation is thus accompanied by a European supervision. In exercising this supervision, the Court must give appropriate weight to such relevant factors as the nature of the rights affected by the derogation and the circumstances leading to, and the duration of, the emergency situation (see the Brannigan and McBride v. the United Kingdom judgment of 26 May 1993, Series A No. 258-B, pp. 49-50, paragraph 43).

The Court has therefore made an attempt at defining the concept of "public emergency threatening the life of the nation". In the Lawless v. Ireland judgment (1 July 1961, Series A No. 3, p. 56, paragraph 28), which concerned special legislation on terrorism connected with Northern Ireland, the Court observed that:

> In the general context of Article 15 of the Convention, the natural and customary meaning of the words "other public emergency threatening the life of the nation" is sufficiently clear; they refer to an exceptional situation of crisis or emergency which affects the whole population and constitutes a threat to the organised life of the community of which the State is composed. Having thus established the natural and customary meaning of this conception, the Court must determine whether the facts and circumstances which led the Irish Government to make their Proclamation of 5 July 1957 [relating to a special Act on administrative detention] come within this conception. The Court, after an examination, finds this to be the case; the existence at the time of a "public emergency threatening the life of the nation" was reasonably deduced by the Irish Government from a combination of several factors, namely: in the first place, the existence in the territory of the Republic of Ireland of a secret army engaged in unconstitutional activities and using violence to attain its purposes; secondly, the fact that this army was also operating outside the territory of the State, thus seriously jeopardising the relations of the Republic of Ireland with its neighbour; thirdly the steady and alarming increase in terrorist activities from the autumn of 1956 and throughout the first half of 1957.

More specifically, in order for there to be a "public emergency" within the meaning of Article 15, the following criteria must be present (the Greek case, *Yearbook of the European Convention on Human Rights*, 1969, p. 72):

1. [The danger] must be actual or imminent.
2. Its effects must involve the whole nation.
3. The continuance of the organised life of the community must be threatened.
4. The crisis or danger must be exceptional, in that the normal measures or restrictions, permitted by the Convention for the maintenance of public safety, health and order, are plainly inadequate.

The requirement that the measures be appropriate to the situation

If the "public emergency" is characterised, any measures derogating from the Convention must have been taken only "to the extent strictly required by the exigencies of the situation". In the Ireland v. the United Kingdom judgment, the Court indicated (18 January 1978, Series A No. 25, pp. 78-79, paragraph 207) the nature of its power of review in that regard:

> It falls in the first place to each Contracting State, with its responsibility for "the life of [its] nation", to determine whether that life is threatened by a "public emergency" and, if so, how far it is necessary to go in attempting to overcome the emergency. By reason of their direct and continuous contact with the pressing needs of the moment, the national authorities are in principle in a better position than the international judge to decide both on the presence of such an emergency and on the nature and scope of derogations necessary to avert it. In this matter Article 15, paragraph 1, leaves those authorities a wide margin of appreciation.

Nevertheless, the States do not enjoy an unlimited power in this respect. The Court, which, with the Commission, is responsible for ensuring the observance of the States' engagements (Article 19), is empowered to rule on whether the States have gone beyond the "extent strictly required by the exigencies" of the crisis (the Lawless judgment of 1 July 1961, Series A No. 3, p. 55, paragraph 22, and pp. 57-59, paragraphs 36-38). The domestic margin of appreciation is thus accompanied by a European supervision.

In the above-mentioned Lawless case, the Court carried out such supervision. Concerning a special law on administrative detention in derogation from Article 15 of the Convention, the Court observed (pp. 57-58, paragraph 36) :

> However, considering, in the judgment of the Court, that in 1957 the application of the ordinary law had proved unable to check the growing danger which threatened the Republic of Ireland. The ordinary criminal courts, or even the special criminal courts or military courts, could not suffice to restore peace and order ; in particular, the amassing of the necessary evidence to convict persons involved in activities of the IRA and its splinter groups was meeting with great difficulties caused by the military, secret and terrorist character of those groups and the fear they created among the population. The fact that these groups operated mainly in Northern Ireland, their activities in the Republic of Ireland being virtually limited to the preparation of armed raids across the border, was an additional impediment to the gathering of sufficient evidence. The sealing of the border would have had extremely serious repercussions on the population as a whole, beyond the extent required by the exigencies of the emergency.

> It follows from the foregoing that none of the above-mentioned means would have made it possible to deal with the situation existing in Ireland in 1957. Therefore, the administrative detention – as instituted under the (Amendment) Act of 1940 – of individuals suspected of intending to take part in terrorist activities, appeared, despite its gravity, to be a measure required by the circumstances.

In the case of Brannigan and McBride v. the United Kingdom (26 May 1993, Series A No. 258-B, pp. 51-52 and 56, paragraphs 49, 51-54 and 66) the applicants claimed that the impugned derogation giving the government wider powers in the face of the terrorist threat was not a necessary response to any new or altered state of affairs but was the government's reaction to the decision in Brogan and Others (judgment of 29 November 1988, Series A No. 145) and was lodged merely to circumvent the consequences of this judgment.

> The Court first observes that the power of arrest and extended detention has been considered necessary by the Government since 1974 in dealing with the threat of terrorism. Following the Brogan and Others judgment the Government were then faced with the option of either introducing judicial control of the decision to detain under Section 12 of the 1984 Act or lodging a derogation from their Convention obligations in this respect. The adoption of the view by the Government that judicial control compatible with Article 5, paragraph 3, was not feasible because of the special difficulties associated with the investigation and prosecution of terrorist crime rendered derogation inevitable. Accordingly, the power of extended detention without such judicial control and the derogation of

23 December 1988 being clearly linked to the persistence of the emergency situation, there is no indication that the derogation was other than a genuine response.

The applicants cited the government's declared intention to abide more closely by the Convention in future, and further contended that the derogation was an interim measure not provided for by Article 15, and was thus premature.

The Court does not accept the applicant's argument that the derogation was premature.

While it is true that Article 15 does not envisage an interim suspension of Convention guarantees pending consideration of the necessity to derogate, it is clear from the notice of derogation that "against the background of the terrorist campaign, and the overriding need to bring terrorists to justice, the Government did not believe that the maximum period of detention should be reduced". However, it remained the Government's wish "to find a judicial process under which extended detention might be reviewed and, where appropriate, authorised by a judge or other judicial officer" (see paragraph 31 above).

The validity of the derogation cannot be called into question for the sole reason that the Government had decided to examine whether in the future a way could be found for ensuring greater conformity with Convention obligations. Indeed, such a process of continued reflection is not only in keeping with Article 15, paragraph 3, which requires permanent review of the need for emergency measures but is also implicit in the very notion of proportionality.

The Court concluded:

Having regard to the nature of the terrorist threat in Northern Ireland, the limited scope of the derogation and the reasons advanced in support of it, as well as the existence of basic safeguards against abuse, the Court takes the view that the Government have not exceeded their margin of appreciation in considering that the derogation was strictly required by the exigencies of the situation.

In the Aksoy v. Turkey judgment of 18 December 1996, *Reports* 1996-VI, paragraphs 77-84, on the other hand, the Court reached a different conclusion:

In the Brannigan and McBride judgment (cited at paragraph 68 above), the Court held that the United Kingdom Government had not exceeded their margin of appreciation by derogating from their obligations under Article 5 of the Convention (art. 5) to the extent that individuals suspected of terrorist offences were allowed to be held for up to seven days without judicial control.

The Court has taken account of the unquestionably serious problem of terrorism in south-east Turkey and the difficulties faced by the State in taking effective measures against it. However, it is not persuaded that the exigencies of the situation necessitated the holding of the applicant on suspicion of involvement in terrorist offences for fourteen days or more in incommunicado detention without access to a judge or other judicial officer.

Absence of inconsistency with other obligations under international law

The last basic condition is that the measures derogating from the Convention must not be "inconsistent with [the State's] other obligations under international law". This seems never to have caused problems. The Court habitually observes that (the above-mentioned Lawless judgment, p. 60, paragraph 41):

> No facts have come to the knowledge of the Court which give it cause to hold that the measures taken by the Irish Government derogating from the Convention may have conflicted with the said Government's other obligations under international law.

Still on the subject of "other obligations under international law", some applicants have relied on the 1966 United Nations International Covenant on Civil and Political Rights. In the above-mentioned Brannigan and McBride v. the United Kingdom judgment, the applicants contended that a public emergency has not been "officially proclaimed", as required by Article 4 of that Covenant (pp. 56-57, paragraphs 68 and 72-73). The Court stated:

> The Court observes that it is not its role to seek to define authoritatively the meaning of the terms "officially proclaimed" in Article 4 of the Covenant. Nevertheless it must examine whether there is any plausible basis for the applicant's argument in this respect.

> In his statement of 22 December 1988 to the House of Commons the Secretary of State for the Home Department explained in detail the reasons underlying the Government's decision to derogate and announced that steps were being taken to give notice of derogation under both Article 15 of the European Convention and Article 4 of the Covenant. He added that there was "a public emergency within the meaning of these provisions in respect of terrorism connected with the affairs of Northern Ireland in the United Kingdom [...]" (see paragraph 30 above).

> In the Court's view the above statement, which was formal in character and made public the Government's intentions as regards derogation, was well in keeping with the notion of an official proclamation. It therefore considers that there is no basis for the applicant's arguments in this respect.

That leads to an examination of the formal conditions required by Article 15.

Formal conditions of derogations from Article 15

Article 15, paragraph 3, concerns the formal conditions required for the implementation of measures derogating from the Convention. In the Lawless case the Court considered whether those conditions had been met. It also provided some information on their content (1 July 1961, Series A No. 3, pp. 61-62, paragraph 47):

> The Court is called upon in the first instance to examine whether, in pursuance of paragraph 3 of Article 15 of the Convention, the Secretary-General of the Council of Europe was duly informed both of the measures taken and of the reasons therefor. The Court notes that a copy of the Offences against the State (Amendment) Act 1940 and a copy of the Proclamation of 5 July, published on 8 July 1957, bringing into force Part II of the aforesaid Act, were attached to the letter of 20 July; that it was explained in the letter of 20 July that the measures had been taken in order "to prevent the commission of offences against public peace and order and to prevent the maintaining of military or armed forces other than those authorised by the Constitution"; that the Irish Government thereby

gave the Secretary-General sufficient information of the measures taken and the reasons therefor; that, in the second place, the Irish Government brought this information to the Secretary-General's attention only twelve days after the entry into force of the measures derogating from their obligations under the Convention; and that the notification was therefore made without delay. In conclusion, the Convention does not contain any special provision to the effect that the Contracting State concerned must promulgate in its territory the notice of derogation addressed to the Secretary General of the Council of Europe.

The Court accordingly finds that, in the present case, the Irish Government fulfilled their obligations as Party to the Convention under Article 15, paragraph 3, of the Convention.

The formalities required by Article 15 are strict. In the Sakik and Others v. Turkey judgment of 26 November 1997, *Reports* 1997-VII, the Court observed:

The Court notes that Legislative Decrees Nos. 424, 425 and 430, which are referred to in the derogation of 6 August 1990 and the letter of 3 January 1991, apply, according to the descriptive summary of their content, only to the region where a state of emergency has been proclaimed, which, according to the derogation, does not include the city of Ankara (see paragraphs 25 and 28 above). However, the applicants' arrest and detention took place in Ankara on the orders first of the Public Prosecutor attached to the Ankara National Security Court and later of the judges of that court (see paragraphs 7-11 above).

The Government submitted that this was no bar to the derogation's applicability. The facts of the case constituted only the prolongation of a terrorist campaign being conducted from inside the area where the state of emergency had been proclaimed, in south-east Turkey.

[...]

It should be noted, however, that Article 15 authorises derogations from the obligations arising from the Convention only "to the extent strictly required by the exigencies of the situation".

In the present case the Court would be working against the object and purpose of that provision if, when assessing the territorial scope of the derogation concerned, it were to extend its effects to a part of Turkish territory not explicitly named in the notice of derogation. It follows that the derogation in question is inapplicable *ratione loci* to the facts of the case.

Consequently, it is not necessary to determine whether it satisfies the requirements of Article 15.

2. Scope of Article 15

As stated in paragraph 1 of Article 15, clauses derogating from the Convention can concern "[a State's] obligations under this Convention". However, this general statement is limited by paragraph 2. Thus there can be no derogation from Articles 3, 4, paragraph 1, or 7. The same applies to Article 2, except in respect of deaths resulting from "lawful" acts of war. It will be observed, however, that everything depends on the definition of "lawful".

Article 16 ECHR – Restrictions on the political activities of aliens

Article 16 is worded as follows:

> Nothing in Articles 10, 11 and 14 shall be regarded as preventing the High Contracting Parties from imposing restrictions on the political activity of aliens.

The Court has not often had occasion to rule on the application of this provision.

Nonetheless, in the Piermont v. France judgment of 27 April 1995, Series A No. 314, paragraphs 62-64, an expulsion order from French Polynesia and an exclusion order from New Caledonia had been adopted against a German national who was a Member of the European Parliament and who had taken part in a demonstration in Polynesian territory condemning nuclear tests and the French presence in the Pacific. The applicant claimed that there had been a violation of Article 10, while the Government pleaded justification under Article 16. In the following extract, the Court examines the applicant's counter-argument:

> The applicant replied that the restrictions in Article 16 did not apply in her case because of her dual status as a European citizen and an MEP. To object that she was an alien when the nature of her functions entailed taking an interest in the whole of the Community's territory seemed to her to be beside the point.
>
> [...]
>
> The Commission accepted the applicant's submissions in substance.
>
> The Court cannot accept the argument based on European citizenship, since the Community treaties did not at the time recognise any such citizenship. Nevertheless, it considers that Mrs Piermont's possession of the nationality of a member State of the European Union and, in addition to that, her status as a Member of the European Parliament do not allow Article 16 of the Convention to be raised against her, especially as the people of the Ots take part in the European Parliament elections.

In conclusion, this provision did not authorise the State to restrict the applicant's exercise of the right guaranteed in Article 10.

Article 17 ECHR – Prohibition on the abuse of rights

Article 17 is worded as follows:

> **Nothing in this Convention may be interpreted as implying for any State, group or person any right to engage in any activity or perform any act aimed at the destruction of any of the rights and freedoms set forth herein or at their limitation to a greater extent than is provided for in the Convention.**

Article 17 prohibits the use of any provision of the Convention for the purpose of undermining the rights established by it. In the same way, its provisions may not be used in order to limit those rights to a greater extent than the Convention itself permits.

1. Scope of Article 17 in relation to activities aimed at the destruction of the rights recognised in the Convention

Article 17 prohibits a right being inferred from the Convention to use the Convention against itself. For example, in the case of Glimmerveen and Hagenbeek v. the Netherlands the applicants were convicted for having possessed with a view to distribution of leaflets considered to be inciting to racial discrimination. They were also prevented from participating in the municipal elections. Their candidature in these elections could reasonably be considered as the disguised participation of a prohibited racist political party. The applicants invoked Article 10 of the Convention. In its decision (11 October 1979, *Decisions and Reports* 18, p. 196) the Commission considered as follows:

> [...] the Government have drawn the attention of the Commission in particular in the light of Article 60 of the Convention, to the Netherlands international obligations under the International Convention on the Elimination of all Forms of Racial Discrimination of 1965, to which the Netherlands acceded in 1971.

> The Netherlands' authorities in allowing the applicants to proclaim freely and without penalty their ideas would certainly encourage the discrimination prohibited by the European Convention on Human Rights referred to above and the above-mentioned Convention of New York of 1965.

> The Commission holds the view that the expression of the political ideas of the applicants clearly constitutes an activity within the meaning of Article 17 of the Convention.

> The applicants are essentially seeking to use Article 10 to provide a basis under the Convention for a right to engage in these activities which are, as shown above, contrary to the text and spirit of the Convention and which right, if granted, would contribute to the destruction of the rights and freedoms referred to above.

> Consequently, the Commission finds that the applicants cannot, by reason of the provisions of Article 17 of the Convention, rely on Article 10 of the Convention.

The Commission did also not find it necessary to determine the questions about violation of Article 3 of Protocol No. 1:

> [...] as it considers that the applicants intended to participate in these elections and to avail themselves of the above right for a purpose which the Commission has just found to be unacceptable under Article 17 in relation to the complaints under Article 10 of the Convention.

Article 17 also prohibits the deprivation of the rights guaranteed by Articles 5 and 6.

In the Lawless v. Ireland case (1 July 1961, Series A No. 3, pp. 44-45, paragraphs 5-7) the Irish Government had supported a very broad interpretation of Article 17 which the Court did not accept. It declared Article 17 only prohibited the inference from the Convention of a right to perform acts aimed at destroying the rights and freedoms protected by the Convention. And it asserted that that provision may not be interpreted *a contrario* as depriving a physical person of the fundamental individual rights guaranteed by Articles 5 and 6 of the Convention. The Court stated:

> The Irish Government submitted to the Commission and reaffirmed before the Court (i) that G.R. Lawless, at the time of his arrest in July 1957, was engaged in IRA activities; (ii) that the Commission, in paragraph 138 of its report, had already observed that his conduct was "such as to draw upon the applicant the gravest suspicion that, whether or not he was any longer a member, he was still concerned with the activities of the IRA at the time of his arrest in July 1957"; (iii) that the IRA was banned on account of its activity aimed at the destruction of the rights and freedoms set forth in the Convention; that, in July 1957, G.R. Lawless was thus concerned in activities falling within the terms of Article 17 of the Convention; that he therefore no longer had a right to rely on Articles 5, 6, 7 or any other Article of the Convention; that no State, group or person engaged in activities falling within the terms of Article 17 of the Convention may rely on any of the provisions of the Convention; and that this construction was supported by the Commission's decision on the admissibility of the application submitted to it in 1957 by the German Communist Party;
>
> [...]
>
> In the opinion of the Court the purpose of Article 17, in so far as it refers to groups or to individuals, is to make it impossible for them to derive from the Convention a right to engage or perform any act aimed at destroying in any activity any of the rights and freedoms set forth in the Convention. Therefore, no person may be able to take advantage of the provisions of the Convention to perform acts aimed at destroying the aforesaid rights and freedoms. This provision, which is negative in scope, cannot be construed *a contrario* as depriving a physical person of the fundamental individual rights guaranteed by Articles 5 and 6 of the Convention. In the present instance G.R. Lawless has not relied on the Convention in order to justify or perform acts contrary to the rights and freedoms recognised therein but has complained of having been deprived of the guarantees granted in Articles 5 and 6 of the Convention. Accordingly, the Court cannot, on this ground, accept the submissions of the Irish Government.

The case of Lehideux and Isorni v. France (judgment of 23 September 1998, *Reports* 1998-VII), concerned a publication about Pétain. The respondent government submitted that the eulogy for which the applicants were responsible in their publication was the result of the use of two different techniques: the authors had sometimes tried to justify Philippe Pétain's decisions by endeavouring to give them a different meaning and at other times simply omitted to mention historical facts which were a matter of common knowledge, and were inescapable and essential for any objective account of that policy. The first technique was used in presenting Philippe Pétain's policy at Montoire. By describing this policy in the text as "supremely skilful", the applicants lent credence to the "double game" theory, although they knew that by 1984 all historians, both French and non-French, refuted that theory. The Court stated (paragraph 47):

> The Court considers that it is not its task to settle this point, which is part of an ongoing debate among historians about the events in question and their inter pretation. As such, it does not belong to the category of clearly established historical facts – such as the Holocaust – whose negation or revision would be removed from the protection of Article 10 by Article 17. In the present case, it does not appear that the applicants attempted to deny or revise what they themselves referred to in their publication as "Nazi atrocities and persecutions" or "German omnipotence and barbarism". In describing Philippe Pétain's policy as "supremely skilful", the authors of the text were rather supporting one of the conflicting theories in the debate about the role of the head of the Vichy Government, the so-called "double game" theory.

2. The prohibition of limitation of the rights and freedoms to a greater extent than is provided for in the Convention

There are few examples of the treatment of this provision by the Court.

In the Engel and Others v. the Netherlands case (8 June 1976, Series A No. 22, pp. 42-43, paragraph 104) the Court declared that if these limitations are justified in the light of the derogating clauses specific to the various articles there is no need to consider whether there had been a violation of Article 17. Thus the Court observed:

> Mr Dona and Mr Schul further claim that, contrary to Articles 17 and 18, the exercise of their freedom of expression was subject to "limitation to a greater extent than is provided for" in Article 10 and for a "purpose" not mentioned therein.

> The complaint does not support examination since the Court has already concluded that the said limitation was justified under paragraph 2 of Article 10 (see paragraphs 96-101 above).

> In the Sporrong and Lönnroth v. Sweden case (23 September 1982, Series A No. 52, p. 28, paragraph 76) the Court also held that there was no need to consider whether there had been a violation of Article 17 because it had already found that there had been a violation of another Article:

> The applicants also relied on Articles 17 and 18 of the Convention. They claimed that the exercise of their right to the peaceful enjoyment of their possessions was

subjected to "restrictions that were more far-reaching than those contemplated" by Article 1 of Protocol No. 1 and had a "purpose" that is not mentioned in that Article.

The Commission concluded unanimously that there had been no violation.

Having found that there was a breach of Article 1 of Protocol No. 1, the Court does not consider it necessary also to examine the case under Articles 17 and 18 of the Convention.

Article 18 ECHR – Limitation on use of restrictions on rights

Article 18 is worded as follows:

> **The restrictions permitted under this Convention to the said rights and freedoms shall not be applied for any purpose other than those for which they have been prescribed.**

As regards this Article, reference should be made to the last two extracts cited under Article 17.

Part 2. The additional protocols

The additional protocols contain numerous provisions, but only certain of these are regularly invoked by litigants. We shall therefore deal only with those which are of general interest.

Protocol No. 1

Article 1 of Protocol No. 1

Article 1 of Protocol No. 1 is worded as follows:

> **Every natural or legal person is entitled to the peaceful enjoyment of his possessions. No one shall be deprived of his possessions except in the public interest and subject to the conditions provided for by law and by the general principles of international law.**
>
> **The preceding provisions shall not, however, in any way impair the right of a State to enforce such laws as it deems necessary to control the use of property in accordance with the general interest or to secure the payment of taxes or other contributions or penalties.**

The Sporrong and Lönnroth judgment (23 September 1982, Series A No. 52) provides an analysis of this Article. In the James and Others v. the United Kingdom case (21 February 1986, Series A No. 98, pp. 29-30, paragraph 37) the Court gave a summary of the main lines of its earlier analysis:

> Article 1 in substance guarantees the right of property (see the Marckx judgment of 13 June 1979, Series A No. 31, pp. 27-28, paragraph 63). In its judgment of 23 September 1982 in the case of Sporrong and Lönnroth, the Court analysed Article 1 as comprising "three distinct rules": the first rule, set out in the first sentence of the first paragraph, is of a general nature and enunciates the principle of the peaceful enjoyment of property; the second rule, contained in the second sentence of the first paragraph, covers deprivation of possessions and subjects it to certain conditions; the third rule, stated in the second paragraph, recognises that the Contracting States are entitled, amongst other things, to control the use of property in accordance with the general interest (Series A No. 52, p. 24, paragraph 61). The Court further observed that, before inquiring whether the first general rule has been complied with, it must determine whether the last two are applicable (ibid.). The three rules are not, however, "distinct" in the sense of being unconnected. The second and third rules are concerned with particular instances of interference with the right to peaceful enjoyment of property and should therefore be construed in the light of the general principle enunciated in the first rule.

As may be seen, Article 1 sets forth three distinct guarantees presented respectively in its three sentences. We shall look first at the last two, and afterwards at the first, which plays only a subsidiary role. But before this, we must examine the scope of application of Article 1 and the meaning of the term "possessions", as well as the extent of the legal protection guaranteed.

1. Scope of Article 1 of Protocol No. 1

As the first sentence states, Article 1 protects "possessions". The concept of "possessions" has been defined, so that it is possible to cast light on the application of this Article.

In the Gasus Dosier- und Födertechnik GmbH v. the Netherlands case, the applicant had sold a concrete-mixer with a retention of title clause. The Court held that this right of retention of title constituted a possession within the meaning of that Article (23 February 1995, Series A No. 306-B, p. 46, paragraph 53). It also set out a number of general principles concerning the nature of the possessions referred to in Article 1 :

> The Court recalls that the notion "possessions" (in French "*biens*") in Article 1 of Protocol No. 1 has an autonomous meaning which is certainly not limited to ownership of physical goods: certain other rights and interests constituting assets can also be regarded as "property rights", and thus as "possessions", for the purposes of this provision. In the present context it is therefore immaterial whether Gasus's right to the concrete-mixer is to be considered as a right of ownership or as a security right *in rem*. In any event, the seizure and sale of the concrete-mixer constituted an "interference" with the applicant company's right "to the peaceful enjoyment" of a "possession" within the meaning of Article 1 of Protocol No. 1.

In the Van Marle and Others v. the Netherlands case, moreover, the Court treated a clientele in the same way as a "possession" (26 June 1986, Series A No. 101, p. 13, paragraphs 41-42) :

> The Court agrees with the Commission that the right relied upon by the applicants may be likened to the right of property embodied in Article 1: by dint of their own work, the applicants had built up a clientele; this had in many respects the nature of a private right and constituted an asset and, hence, a possession within the meaning of the first sentence of Article 1. This provision was accordingly applicable in the present case.

In the Van der Mussele v. Belgium judgment, on the other hand, the Court considered that the obligation imposed on a lawyer who was officially assigned to provide services without remuneration did not deprive him of "possessions" within the meaning of Article 1. It also considered that the costs which he incurred in performing his obligation were also outside the scope of Article 1 (23 November 1983, Series A No. 70, pp. 23-24, paragraphs 47-49) :

> Mr Van der Mussele finally relied on Article 1 of Protocol No. 1.

[...]

His arguments do not bear examination in so far as they relate to the absence of remuneration. The text set out above is limited to enshrining the right of everyone to the peaceful enjoyment of "his" possessions; it thus applies only to existing possessions (see, *mutatis mutandis*, the above-mentioned Marckx judgment, Series A No. 31, p. 23, paragraph 50). In the instant case, however, the Legal Advice and Defence Office of the Antwerp Bar decided on 18 December 1979 that no assessment of fees could be made, because of Mr Ebrima's lack of means (see paragraph 12 above). It follows, as the Commission unanimously inferred, that no debt in favour of the applicant ever arose in this respect.

Consequently, under this head, there is no scope for the application of Article 1 of Protocol No. 1, whether taken on its own or together with Article 14 of the Convention; moreover, Mr Van der Mussele invoked the latter Article solely in conjunction with Article 4

The matter cannot be put in the same terms as far as the non-reimbursement of expenses is concerned, since Mr Van der Mussele was required to pay certain sums out of his own pocket in this connection (see paragraph 12 above).

That does not suffice, however, to warrant the conclusion that Article 1 of Protocol No. 1 is applicable.

In many cases, a duty prescribed by law involves a certain outlay for the person bound to perform it. To regard the imposition of such a duty as constituting in itself an interference with possessions for the purposes of Article 1 of Protocol No. 1 would be giving the Article a far-reaching interpretation going beyond its object and purpose.

The Court sees no valid cause to think otherwise in the instant case.

The expenses in question were incurred by Mr Van der Mussele in acting for his *pro Deo* clients. Although in no wise derisory (the epithet bestowed on them by the Government), these expenses were relatively small and resulted from the obligation to perform work compatible with Article 4 of the Convention.

Article 1 of Protocol No. 1, whether taken alone or in conjunction with Article 14 of the Convention, is thus not applicable in this connection.

This case may be linked, rather, to the nature of the possessions referred to.

The question has just been referred to in the above-mentioned Van der Mussele judgment: in order for there to be a "possession", within the meaning of Article 1, there must be a present or existing possession.

This is also stated in the Marckx v. Belgium judgment (13 June 1979, Series A No. 31, p. 23, paragraph 50). In this case, the applicant complained that Belgian law prevented her from acquiring goods on inheritance, and claimed that there had been a violation of Article 1 of Protocol No. 1. The Court stated:

> As concerns the second applicant, the Court has taken its stand solely on Article 8 of the Convention, taken both alone and in conjunction with Article 14. The Court in fact excludes Article 1 of Protocol No. 1: like the Commission and the Government, it notes that this Article does no more than enshrine the right of everyone to the peaceful enjoyment of "his" possessions, that consequently it applies only to a person's existing possessions and that it does not guarantee the

right to acquire possessions whether on intestacy or through voluntary disposi-tions. Besides, the applicants do not appear to have relied on this provision in support of Alexandra's claims. Since Article 1 of the Protocol proves to be inapplicable, Article 14 of the Convention cannot be combined with it on the point now being considered.

In the Stran Greek Refineries and Stratis Andreadis v. Greece judgment (9 December 1994, Series A No. 301-B, pp. 84-85, paragraphs 58-62), the Court considered that the existence of a claim was sufficiently established by the various judicial and arbitration proceedings of which it had formed the subject-matter. It thus refuted the Greek Government's argument that "neither [the] judgment [...] nor the arbitration award was sufficient to estab-lish the existence of a claim" and therefore the existence of a possession. The Court therefore upheld the classification of the claim as a "possession" within the meaning of Article 1, stating that:

> The principal thrust of the Government's argument was that no "possession" of the applicants, within the meaning of Article 1 of Protocol No. 1, had been subject to interference through the operation of Law No. 1701/1987.

> In their view, neither judgment No. 13910/79 nor the arbitration award was sufficient to establish the existence of a claim against the State. A judicial decision that had not yet become final, or an arbitration award, could not be equated to the right which might be recognised by such decision or award.

> In order to determine whether the applicants had a "possession" for the purpose of Article 1 of Protocol No. 1, the Court must ascertain whether judgment No. 13910/79 of the Athens Court of First Instance and the arbitration award had given rise to a debt in their favour that was sufficiently established to be enforceable.

> In the nature of things, a preliminary decision prejudges the merits of a dispute by ordering an investigative measure. Although the Athens Court of First Instance would appear to have accepted the principle that the State owed a debt to the applicants – as the Commission likewise noted – it nevertheless ordered that witnesses be heard (see paragraph 11 above) before ruling on the existence and extent of the alleged damage. The effect of such a decision was merely to furnish the applicants with the hope that they would secure recognition of the claim put forward. Whether the resulting debt was enforceable would depend on any review by two superior courts.

> This is not the case with regard to the arbitration award, which clearly recognised the State's liability up to a maximum of specified amounts in three different currencies (see paragraph 13 above).

> The Court agrees with the Government that it is not its task to approve or disapprove the substance of that award. It is, however, under a duty to take note of the legal position established by that decision in relation to the parties.

> According to its wording, the award was final and binding; it did not require any further enforcement measure and no ordinary or special appeal lay against it (see paragraph 10 above). Under Greek legislation arbitration awards have the force of final decisions and are deemed to be enforceable. The grounds for appealing against them are exhaustively listed in Article 897 of the Code of Civil Procedure (see paragraph 25 above); no provision is made for an appeal on the merits.

At the moment when Law No. 1701/1987 was passed the arbitration award of 27 February 1984 therefore conferred on the applicants a right in the sums awarded. Admittedly, that right was revocable, since the award could still be annulled, but the ordinary courts had by then already twice held – at first instance and on appeal – that there was no ground for such annulment. Accordingly, in the Court's view, that right constituted a "possession" within the meaning of Article 1 of Protocol No. 1.

In the case of Matos e Silva, Lda and Others v. Portugal (16 September 1996, *Collection of Judgments and Decisions* 1996-IV, p. 1111, paragraph 75) the Court had to consider whether the applicants had a "possession" in the sense of Article 1 of Protocol No. 1. Matos e Silva is a private limited company involved in land cultivation, fish-farming and salt extraction. Of the land it works, some is owned by the company and the remainder is held as a concession. The Court stated:

> Like the Commission, the Court notes that the ownership of part of the land is not contested.

> As to the other part [...] the Court agrees with the Government that it is not for the Court to decide whether or not a right of property exists under domestic law. However, it recalls that the notion "possessions" (in French *"biens"*) in Article 1 of Protocol No. 1 has an autonomous meaning (see the Gasus Dosier- und Fördertechnik GmbH v. the Netherlands judgment of 23 February 1995, Series A No. 306-B, p. 46, paragraph 53). In the present case the applicants' unchallenged rights over the disputed land for almost a century and the revenue they derive from working it may qualify as "possessions" for the purposes of Article 1.

2. Extent of the legal guarantees covering possessions established by Article 1

In the Marckx v. Belgium judgment (13 June 1979, Series A No. 31, p. 27, paragraph 63) the Court made clear that Article 1 of Protocol No. 1 protects the right to property. The following passage is taken from that judgment:

> The Court takes the same view as the Commission. By recognising that everyone has the right to the peaceful enjoyment of his possessions, Article 1 is in substance guaranteeing the right of property. This is the clear impression left by the words "possessions" and "use of property" (in French *"biens"*, *"propriété"*, *"usage des biens"*); the *travaux préparatoires*, for their part, confirm this unequivocally: the drafters continually spoke of "right of property" or "right to property" to describe the subject-matter of the successive drafts which were the forerunners of the present Article 1.

The Marckx judgment also states (ibid., p. 27, paragraph 63) that the right to dispose of one's possessions is protected by Article 1, in the light of the fact that:

> Indeed, the right to dispose of one's property constitutes a traditional and fundamental aspect of the right of property (see the Handyside judgment of 7 December 1976, Series A No. 24, p. 29, paragraph 62).

It follows from that judgment, therefore, that Article 1 affords protection not only against an interference with the right of property taken as a whole (for example an expropriation), but also against interferences with the various constituent elements of that right, taken individually.

In another case (the Sporrong and Lönnroth v. Sweden judgment of 23 September 1982, Series A No. 52, pp. 23-24, paragraph 60), the Court upheld that principle. In that case permits had been issued to the town of Stockholm allowing it to expropriate specific properties for several years. Those permits were accompanied by prohibitions on construction for the owners. The Court stated that:

> Although the expropriation left intact in law the owners' right to use and dispose of their possessions, they nevertheless in practice significantly reduced the possibility of its exercise. They also affected the very substance of ownership in that they recognised before the event that any expropriation would be lawful and authorised the city of Stockholm to expropriate whenever it found it expedient to do so. The applicants' right of property thus became precarious and defensible.
>
> The prohibitions on construction, for their part, undoubtedly restricted the applicants' right to use their possessions.
>
> There was therefore an interference with the applicants' right of property and, as the Commission rightly pointed out, the consequences of that interference were undoubtedly rendered more serious by the combined use, over a long period of time, of expropriation permits and prohibitions on construction.

In that judgment, the Court therefore applied the third sentence of Article 1. This leads us directly to the examination of the conditions laid down by Article 1 for any interference with property and possessions.

3. Article 1 of Protocol No. 1, second sentence: deprivation of property

The second sentence of Article 1 is worded as follows:

> **No one shall be deprived of his possessions except in the public interest and subject to the conditions provided for by law and by the general principles of international law.**

Before beginning to examine the conditions laid down by the second sentence of Article 1 in relation to "deprivation of possessions", it is appropriate to define what is to be meant by those terms. The second sentence of Article 1 refers to "deprivation of possessions" to the exclusion of other interferences with possessions, which are covered by the third sentence.

The concept of "deprivation of possessions"

Expropriation is naturally a "deprivation of possessions", but is only one of the ways of depriving a person of his possessions.

Expropriation

There is no expropriation where the prerogatives flowing from the right of property are preserved. Thus in the Sporrong and Lönnroth case (the facts of which are set out above) the Court observed (p. 24, paragraph 62):

> It should be recalled first of all that the Swedish authorities did not proceed to an expropriation of the applicants' properties. The applicants were therefore not formally "deprived" of their possessions at any time: they were entitled to use, sell, devise, donate or mortgage their properties.

However, it is still essential that those prerogatives are actually preserved. In the same case, the Court went on to state (pp. 24-25, paragraph 63):

> In the absence of a formal expropriation, that is to say a transfer of ownership, the Court considers that it must look behind the appearances and investigate the realities of the situation complained of (see, *mutatis mutandis*, the Van Droogen-broeck judgment of 24 June 1982, Series A No. 50, p. 20, paragraph 38). Since the Convention is intended to guarantee rights that are "practical and effective" (the Airey judgment of 9 October 1979, Series A No. 32, p. 12, paragraph 24), it has to be ascertained whether that situation amounted to a *de facto* expropriation, as was argued by the applicants.
>
> In the Court's opinion, all the effects complained of (see paragraph 58 above) stemmed from the reduction of the possibility of disposing of the properties concerned. Those effects were occasioned by limitations imposed on the right of property, which right had become precarious, and from the consequences of those limitations on the value of the premises. However, although the right in question lost some of its substance, it did not disappear. The effects of the measures involved are not such that they can be assimilated to a deprivation of possessions. The Court observes in this connection that the applicants could continue to utilise their possessions and that, although it became more difficult to sell properties in Stockholm affected by expropriation permits and prohibitions on construction, the possibility of selling subsisted; according to information supplied by the Government, several dozen sales were effected (see paragraph 30 above).

The second sentence of the first paragraph was therefore not applicable in that case.

However, the Court recognised the existence of such a *de facto* expropriation in the Papamichalopoulos and Others v. Greece judgment (24 June 1993, Series A No. 260-B, pp. 69-70, paragraphs 41-46). In that case the army had occupied land on the basis of Law No. 109/1967. The Court observed:

> The occupation of the land in issue by the Navy Fund represented a clear inter-ference with the applicants' exercise of their right to the peaceful enjoyment of their possessions. The interference was not for the purpose of controlling the use of property within the meaning of the second paragraph of Article 1 of Protocol No. 1. Moreover, the applicants were never formally expropriated: Law No. 109/67 did not transfer ownership of the land in question to the Navy Fund.

Since the Convention is intended to safeguard rights that are "practical and effective", it has to be ascertained whether the situation complained of amounted nevertheless to a *de facto* expropriation, as was argued by the applicants (see, among other authorities, the Sporrong and Lönnroth v. Sweden judgment of 23 September 1982, Series A No. 52, paragraph 63).

It must be remembered that in 1967, under a law enacted by the military government of the time, the Navy Fund took possession of a large area of land which included the applicants' land; it established a naval base there and a holiday resort for officers and their families.

From that date the applicants were unable either to make use of their property or to sell, bequeath, mortgage or make a gift of it; Mr Petros Papamichalopoulos, the only one who obtained a final court decision ordering the navy to return his property to him, was even refused access to it (see paragraphs 11-12 above).

[...]

The Court considers that the loss of all ability to dispose of the land in issue, taken together with the failure of the attempts made so far to remedy the situation complained of, entailed sufficiently serious consequences for the applicants *de facto* to have been expropriated in a manner incompatible with their right to the peaceful enjoyment of their possessions.

There had therefore been, and there continued to be, a violation of Article 1 of Protocol No. 1.

In addition to cases of expropriation such as those illustrated by these extracts, there are other types of deprivation of possessions within the meaning of the second sentence of Article 1.

Other cases of deprivation of possessions

There is a deprivation of possessions where possessions are pre-empted. An example is provided by the Hentrich v. France case (22 September 1994, Series A No. 296-A, p. 18, paragraph 35), where the tax authorities had used the statutory right of pre-emption available where the price paid on the sale of immovable property between individuals is insufficient. The Court observed:

Because the right of pre-emption was exercised, Mrs Hentrich was deprived of her property within the meaning of the second sentence of the first subparagraph of Article 1; the Government did not contest that.

There may also be a deprivation where possessions are confiscated, as in the Handyside case (the Handyside v. the United Kingdom judgment of 7 December 1976, Series A No. 24, p. 30, paragraph 63).

The forfeiture and destruction of the Schoolbook, on the other hand, permanently deprived the applicant of the ownership of certain possessions. However, these measures were authorised by the second paragraph of Article 1 of Protocol No. 1, interpreted in the light of the principle of law, common to the Contracting States, whereunder items whose use has been lawfully adjudged illicit and dangerous to the general interest are forfeited with a view to destruction.

The AGOSI v. the United Kingdom judgment of 24 October 1986, Series A No. 108, concerning the seizure and confiscation of smuggled Krugerrands, provides a novel example.

In the Raimondo v. Italy case, however, the Court observed (22 February 1994, Series A No. 281-A, p. 16, paragraph 29) that confiscation does not necessarily fall within the scope of the second sentence. The Court stated:

> Although it involves a deprivation of possessions, confiscation of property does not necessarily come within the scope of the second sentence of the first paragraph of Article 1 of Protocol No. 1 (see the Handyside v. the United Kingdom judgment of 7 December 1976, Series A No. 24, p. 30, paragraph 63, and the AGOSI v. the United Kingdom judgment of 24 October 1986, Series A No. 108, p. 17, paragraph 51).

That leads directly to the definitive character of the deprivation of possessions.

Requirement that the deprivation be definitive

In order for the second sentence of Article 1 to enter into play, it is not enough for there to be a deprivation: it is also necessary for the deprivation to be definitive. If not, it is the third sentence that will apply, as in the case of Raimondo v. Italy, concerning a confiscation (ibid, pp. 16-17, paragraph 29):

> According to Italian case-law, confiscation of the kind which is in issue in this case could not moreover have the effect of transferring ownership to the State until there had been an irrevocable decision (see paragraph 20 above). There was no such decision in this instance because Mr Raimondo had challenged the order of the Catanzaro District Court of 16 October 1985 (see paragraph 13 above). Here too therefore it is the second paragraph of Article 1 which applies.

The Court has also applied this principle in relation to expropriation. Thus, in the Poiss v. Austria case (23 April 1987, Series A No. 117) the following can be read (p. 108, paragraph 64):

> The Court notes first of all that the Austrian authorities did not effect either a formal expropriation or a *de facto* expropriation (see the Sporrong and Lönnroth judgment of 23 September 1982, Series A No. 52, p. 24, paragraphs 62-63). The transfer carried out in April 1963 was a provisional one; only the entry into force of a consolidation plan will make it irrevocable (see paragraph 32 above). The applicants may therefore recover their land if the final plan does not confirm the distribution made at the earlier stage of the proceedings. Accordingly, it cannot be said that the applicants have been definitively "deprived of their possessions" within the meaning of the second sentence of the first paragraph of Article 1.

Conditions for the application of Article 1, second sentence

There are three conditions which the deprivation of possessions must satisfy: the deprivation must be "in the public interest", the conditions provided for by law must be respected and the "general principles of international law" must be observed.

The requirement that the deprivation be "in the public interest"

In the James and Others v. the United Kingdom case (22 February 1986, Series A No. 98, p. 32, paragraph 46) the Court described its approach when examining the "public interest" condition:

> Because of their direct knowledge of their society and its needs, the national authorities are in principle better placed than the international judge to appreciate what is "in the public interest". Under the system of protection established by the Convention, it is thus for the national authorities to make the initial assessment both of the existence of a problem of public concern warranting measures of deprivation of property and of the remedial action to be taken (see, *mutatis mutandis*, the Handyside judgment of 7 December 1976, Series A No. 24, p. 22, paragraph 48). Here, as in other fields to which the safeguards of the Convention extend, the national authorities accordingly enjoy a certain margin of appreciation.

> Furthermore, the notion of "public interest" is necessarily extensive. In particular, as the Commission noted, the decision to enact laws expropriating property will commonly involve consideration of political, economic and social issues on which opinions within a democratic society may reasonably differ widely. The Court, finding it natural that the margin of appreciation available to the legislature in implementing social and economic policies should be a wide one, will respect the legislature's judgment as to what is "in the public interest" unless that judgment be manifestly without reasonable foundation. In other words, although the Court cannot substitute its own assessment for that of the national authorities, it is bound to review the contested measures under Article 1 of Protocol No. 1 and, in so doing, to make an inquiry into the facts with reference to which the national authorities acted.

The Court therefore merely ascertains whether the "public interest" aim claimed is lawful, or rather that it is not "manifestly unreasonable". In this case, it observed (ibid., p. 34, paragraph 49):

> The Court therefore agrees with the Commission's conclusion: the United Kingdom Parliament's belief in the existence of a [reason in the public interest] was not such as could be characterised as manifestly unreasonable.

However, the "public interest" condition requires more than a lawful, or not unreasonable, aim. The public interest implies a fair balance between the aim alleged to be in the public interest and the means used (the deprivation of possessions), as the Court went on to say (ibid., p. 34, paragraph 50):

> This, however, does not settle the issue. Not only must a measure depriving a person of his property pursue, on the facts as well as in principle, a legitimate aim "in the public interest", but there must also be a reasonable relationship of proportionality between the means employed and the aim sought to be realised (see, amongst others, and, *mutatis mutandis*, the above-mentioned Ashingdane judgment, Series A No. 93, pp. 24-25, paragraph 57). This latter requirement was expressed in other terms in the Sporrong and Lönnroth judgment by the notion of the "fair balance" that must be struck between the demands of the general interest of the community and the requirements of the protection of the individual's fundamental rights (Series A No. 52, p. 26, paragraph 69). The requisite balance

will not be found if the person concerned has had to bear "an individual and excessive burden" (ibid., p. 28, paragraph 73). Although the Court was speaking in that judgment in the context of the general rule of peaceful enjoyment of property enunciated in the first sentence of the first paragraph, it pointed out that "the search for this balance is [...] reflected in the structure of Article 1" as a whole (ibid., p. 26, paragraph 69).

In the same spirit, the Court has been led to establish an implied right to compensation (the Holy Monasteries v. Greece case, 9 December 1994, Series A No. 301-A, p. 35, paragraph 71):

> Compensation terms under the relevant legislation are material to the assessment whether the contested measure respects the requisite fair balance and, notably, whether it does not impose a disproportionate burden on the applicants. In this connection, the taking of property without payment of an amount reasonably related to its value will normally constitute a disproportionate interference and a total lack of compensation can be considered justifiable under Article 1 only in exceptional circumstances. Article 1 does not, however, guarantee a right to full compensation in all circumstances, since legitimate objectives of "public interest" may call for less than reimbursement of the full market value (see the Lithgow and Others v. the United Kingdom judgment of 8 July 1986, Series A No. 102, pp. 50-51, paragraph 121).

Lastly, the Court had the opportunity in the James and Others judgment to determine the following point: the fact that the interference with the ownership of possessions is of advantage only to certain persons does not necessarily mean that the deprivation is not in the "public interest" (the above-mentioned James and Others judgment, pp. 31-32, paragraphs 41 and 45).

> Neither can it be read into the English expression "in the public interest" that the transferred property should be put into use for the general public or that the community generally, or even a substantial proportion of it, should directly benefit from the taking. The taking of property in pursuance of a policy calculated to enhance social justice within the community can properly be described as being "in the public interest". In particular, the fairness of a system of law governing the contractual or property rights of private parties is a matter of public concern and therefore legislative measures intended to bring about such fairness are capable of being "in the public interest", even if they involve the compulsory transfer of property from one individual to another.

> For these reasons, the Court comes to the same conclusion as the Commission: a taking of property effected in pursuance of legitimate social, economic or other policies may be "in the public interest", even if the community at large has no direct use or enjoyment of the property taken. The leasehold reform legislation is not therefore *ipso facto* an infringement of Article 1 (P1-1) on this ground. Accordingly, it is necessary to inquire whether in other respects the legislation satisfied the "public interest" test and the remaining requirements laid down in the second sentence of Article 1 (P1-1).

The requirement that the interference be lawful

The existence of a reason in the public interest is not enough. Article 1 also requires that the deprivation has a lawful basis. In that regard, the Court requires two things: the law must not be applied unfairly; and it must be sufficiently clear to allow individuals to be aware of possible interference with their possessions. In the Hentrich v. France judgment (22 September 1994, Series A No. 296-A, p. 19, paragraph 42) the Court observed in connection with a pre-emption measure:

> In the instant case the pre-emption operated arbitrarily and selectively and was scarcely foreseeable, and it was not attended by the basic procedural safeguards. In particular, Article 668 of the General Tax Code, as interpreted up to that time by the Court of Cassation and as applied to the applicant, did not sufficiently satisfy the requirements of precision and foreseeability implied by the concept of law within the meaning of the Convention.

The need to observe the general principles of international law

In regard to this third and final condition, the Court had the opportunity to state (the above-mentioned James and Others judgment, p. 40, paragraph 66):

> For all these reasons, the Court concludes that the general principles of international law are not applicable to a taking by a state of the property of its own nationals.

4. Article 1 of Protocol No. 1, third sentence (second paragraph)

The third sentence of Article 1 constitutes the second paragraph. It is worded as follows:

> **The preceding provisions shall not, however, in any way impair the right of a State to enforce such laws as it deems necessary to control the use of property in accordance with the general interest or to secure the payment of taxes or other contributions or penalties.**

Conditions for the application of Article 1, third sentence (second paragraph

In the Handyside judgment (7 December 1976, Series A No. 24, p. 29, paragraph 62, in fine) the Court stated:

> Unlike Article 10, paragraph 2, of the Convention, [the second] paragraph sets the Contracting States up as sole judges of the "necessity" for an interference. Consequently, the Court must restrict itself to supervising the lawfulness and the purpose of the restriction in question.

Even so, it does not follow that every interference is permissible. More generally, the Court recalled in the Gasus Dosier- und Fördertechnik GmbH v. the Netherlands case (22 February 1995, Series A No. 306-B, p. 49, paragraph 62) that:

> According to the Court's well-established case-law, the second paragraph of Article 1 of Protocol No. 1 must be construed in the light of the principle laid down in the Article's first sentence (see, among many other authorities, the AGOSI judgment, ibid.). Consequently, an interference must achieve a "fair

balance" between the demands of the general interest of the community and the requirements of the protection of the individual's fundamental rights. The concern to achieve this balance is reflected in the structure of Article 1 as a whole, including the second paragraph: there must therefore be a reasonable relationship of proportionality between the means employed and the aim pursued.

The final part of the previous extract also means that the Court will verify the aim and proportionality of the interference.

Examples of the application of Article 1, third sentence (second paragraph)

Measures taken in the social interest

The third sentence applies, for example, in cases of rent control. In that regard, the Court stated in the Mellacher and Others judgment (19 December 1989, Series A No. 169, p. 25, paragraph 44):

> The Court finds that the measures taken did not amount either to a formal or to a *de facto* expropriation. There was no transfer of the applicants' property nor were they deprived of their right to use, let or sell it. The contested measures which, admittedly, deprived them of part of their income from the property amounted in the circumstances merely to a control of the use of property Accordingly, the second paragraph of Article 1 applies in this case.

The Court concluded (ibid., p. 30, paragraph 57):

> The Court thus reaches the conclusion that when enacting the 1981 Rent Act the Austrian legislature, having regard to the need to strike a fair balance between the general interests of the community and the right of property of landlords in general and of the applicants in particular, could reasonably hold that the means chosen were suited to achieving the legitimate aim pursued. The Court finds that the requirements of the second paragraph of Article 1 of Protocol No. 1 were satisfied in relation to the reductions of rent suffered by the applicants pursuant to the 1981 Rent Act.

> Concerning measures controlling the use of land, see the Coster v. the United Kingdom judgment of 18 January 2001, Application No. 24876/94, paragraphs 130-133.

Punitive and preventive measures

The third sentence (second paragraph) also applies to sequestration. On that point the Court observed (the Vendittelli v. Italy case, 18 July 1994, Series A No. 293-A, p. 12, paragraph 38):

> Like the Commission, the Court finds that the impugned measure was provided for by law and was designed not to deprive the applicant of his property but only to prevent him from using it. Consequently, the second paragraph of Article 1 of Protocol No. 1 applies in this instance.

The Court also applies the third sentence (second paragraph) to seizure. In the Raimondo v. Italy case (22 February 1994, Series A No. 281-A, p. 16, paragraph 27) it observed:

> Like the Commission, the Court finds that the seizure was provided for in Section 2 *ter* of the 1965 Act (see paragraph 18 above) and did not purport to deprive the applicant of his possessions but only to prevent him from using them. It is therefore the second paragraph of Article 1 of Protocol No. 1 which is relevant here.

As regards confiscation, reference should be made to Article 1, second sentence.

Other cases

The third sentence is also applicable to prohibitions on construction (Sporrong and Lönnroth v. Sweden, 23 September 1982, Series A No. 52, p. 25, paragraph 64).

In fact the third sentence applies to every type of regulation provided for by law.

5. Article 1 of Protocol No. 1, first sentence

The first sentence of Article 1 is worded as follows:

> **Every natural or legal person is entitled to the peaceful enjoyment of his possessions.**

The subsidiary nature of the first sentence

The first sentence plays a subsidiary role and determines whether there has been an interference by the State where, strictly speaking, there has been no deprivation of possessions (second sentence) or control of the use of property (third sentence). Thus, in the Sporrong and Lönnroth v. Sweden judgment (23 September 1982, Series A No. 152, p. 25, paragraph 65), the Court observed in relation to an expropriation permit:

> [...] the expropriation permits were not intended to limit or control [the use of possessions]. Since they were an initial step in a procedure leading to deprivation of possessions, they did not fall within the ambit of the second paragraph. They must be examined under the first sentence of the first paragraph.

Thus, in the Poiss v. Austria case (23 April 1987, Series A No. 117, pp. 107-108, paragraphs 62 and 64) the Court stated in connection with the provisional transfer of land:

> There has indisputably been an interference with the applicants' right of property as guaranteed in Article 1 of the Protocol (see the Marckx judgment of 13 June 1979, Series A No. 31, p. 27, paragraph 63): on 22 April 1963, their land was allocated to other landowners, who were parties to the consolidation scheme, or else used for communal measures or facilities, and they have not so

far secured, by a final decision, the compensation in kind stipulated by the provincial legislation.

[...]

The Court notes first of all that the Austrian authorities did not effect either a formal expropriation or a *de facto* expropriation (see the Sporrong and Lönnroth judgment of 23 September 1982, Series A No. 52, p. 24, paragraph 62-63). The transfer carried out in April 1963 was a provisional one; only the entry into force of a consolidation plan will make it irrevocable (see paragraph 32 above). The applicants may therefore recover their land if the final plan does not confirm the distribution made at the earlier stage of the proceedings. Accordingly, it cannot be said that the applicants have been definitively "deprived of their possessions" within the meaning of the second sentence of the first paragraph of Article 1.

Nor was the provisional transfer essentially designed to restrict or control the "use" of the land (second paragraph of Article 1), but to achieve an early restructuring of the consolidation area with a view to improved, rational farming by the "provisional owners" (see paragraph 32 above). The transfer must therefore be considered under the first sentence of the first paragraph of Article 1 (the Poiss case, Series A No. 117, paragraph 64).

The Court again stated this principle in the Stran Greek Refineries and Stratis Andreadis v. Greece judgment (9 December 1994, Series A No. 301-B, p. 86, paragraphs 67-68):

[...] it was impossible for the applicants to secure enforcement of an arbitration award having final effect and under which the State was required to pay them specified sums in respect of expenditure that they had incurred in seeking to fulfil their contractual obligations or even for them to take further action to recover the sums in question through the courts.

In conclusion, there was an interference with the applicants' property right.

The interference in question was neither an expropriation nor a measure to control the use of property; it falls to be dealt with under the first sentence of the first paragraph of Article 1.

The implementation of Article 1

The relationship between observance of the second and third sentences and observance of the first sentence

The James and Others v. the United Kingdom judgment (21 February 1986, Series A No. 98, p. 43, paragraph 71) relates to this question.

Alternatively and additionally, the applicants asserted a violation of their rights of peaceful enjoyment of property as guaranteed by the first sentence of Article 1.

The rule (in the second sentence) subjecting deprivation of possessions to certain conditions concerns a particular category, indeed the most radical kind, of interference with the right to peaceful enjoyment of property (see paragraph 37, in fine, above); the second sentence supplements and qualifies the general principle enunciated in the first sentence. This being so, it is inconceivable that application of that general principle to the present case should lead to any conclusion different from that already arrived at by the Court in application of the second sentence.

The implementation of the first sentence

In the Sporrong and Lönnroth v. Sweden case (23 September 1982, Series A No. 52, p. 26, paragraph 69) the Court observed:

> The fact that the permits fell within the ambit neither of the second sentence of the first paragraph nor of the second paragraph does not mean that the interference with the said right violated the rule contained in the first sentence of the first paragraph.
>
> For the purposes of the latter provision, the Court must determine whether a fair balance was struck between the demands of the general interest of the community and the requirements of the protection of the individual's fundamental rights (see, *mutatis mutandis*, the judgment of 23 July 1968 in the "Belgian linguistics" case, Series A No. 6, p. 32, paragraph 5). The search for this balance is inherent in the whole of the Convention and is also reflected in the structure of Article 1.

Article 2 of Protocol No. 1 – The right to an education

Article 2 of Protocol No. 1 is worded as follows:

No person shall be denied the right to education. In the exercise of any functions which it assumes in relation to education and to teaching, the State shall respect the right of parents to ensure such education and teaching in conformity with their own religious and philosophical convictions.

The Kjeldsen, Busk Madsen and Pedersen v. Denmark judgment (2 December 1976, Series A No. 23, p. 25-26, paragraphs 51-52) contains an analysis of this Article:

> As is shown by its very structure, Article 2 constitutes a whole that is dominated by its first sentence. By binding themselves not to "deny the right to education", the Contracting States guarantee to anyone within their jurisdiction "a right of access to educational institutions existing at a given time" and "the possibility of drawing", by "official recognition of the studies which he has completed", "profit from the education received" (judgment of 23 July 1968 on the merits of the "Belgian linguistics" case, Series A No. 6, pp. 30-32, paragraphs 3-5).
>
> The right set out in the second sentence of Article 2 is an adjunct of this fundamental right to education (paragraph 50 above). It is in the discharge of a natural duty towards their children – parents being primarily responsible for the "education and teaching" of their children – that parents may require the State

to respect their religious and philosophical conviction. Their right thus corresponds to a responsibility closely linked to the enjoyment and the exercise of the right to education.

On the other hand, "the provisions of the Convention and Protocol must be read as a whole" (the above-mentioned judgment of 23 July 1968, ibid., p. 30, paragraph 1). Accordingly, the two sentences of Article 2 must be read not only in the light of each other but also, in particular, of Articles 8, 9 and 10 of the Convention [...].

After this introduction to the subject, it is appropriate to examine in turn the two sentences which make up Article 2.

1. Article 2 of Protocol No. 1, first sentence – The right to an education

The first sentence of Article 2 is worded as follows:

> **No person shall be denied the right to education.**

The "Belgian linguistics" case provided the first indication of the meaning of this sentence (judgment of 23 July 1968, Series A No. 6, pp. 31-32, paragraphs 3-5):

> The first sentence of Article 2 of the Protocol [...] guarantees, in the first place, a right of access to educational institutions existing at a given time, but such access constitutes only a part of the right to education. For the "right to education" to be effective, it is further necessary that, *inter alia,* the individual who is the beneficiary should have the possibility of drawing profit from the education received, that is to say, the right to obtain, in conformity with the rules in force in each State, and in one form or another, official recognition of the studies which he has completed.

In the same case, the Court stated that (pp. 42-43, paragraph 7):

> [The problem] principally concerns the State's refusal to establish or subsidise, in the Dutch-unilingual region, primary school education (which is compulsory in Belgium) in which French is employed as the language of instruction.

> Such a refusal is not compatible with the requirements of the first sentence of Article 2 of the Protocol. In interpreting this provision, the Court has already held that it does not enshrine the right to the establishment or subsidising of schools in which education is provided in a given language. The first sentence of Article 2 contains in itself no linguistic requirement. It guarantees the right of access to educational establishments existing at a given time and the right to obtain, in conformity with the rules in force in each State and in one form or another, the official recognition of studies which have been completed, this last right not being relevant to the point which is being dealt with here. In the unilingual regions, both French-speaking and Dutch-speaking children have access to public or subsidised education, that is to say to education conducted in the language of the region.

In the Campbell and Cosans v. the United Kingdom case the Court held that the suspension of a child from school violated the "right to education" (judgment of 25 February 1982, Series A No. 48, p. 19, paragraph 41). The child had been suspended because both he and his parents were opposed to corporal punishment. The Court took the view that this punishment was contrary to the second sentence of Article 2 of the Protocol. It therefore decided that this ground could not justify the suspension and that, accordingly, the "right to education" had not been observed:

> The right to education guaranteed by the first sentence of Article 2 by its very nature calls for regulation by the State, but such regulation must never injure the substance of the right nor conflict with other rights enshrined in the Convention or its Protocols (see the judgment of 23 July 1968 on the merits of the "Belgian linguistics" case, Series A No. 6, p. 32, paragraph 5).

> The suspension of Jeffrey Cosans – which remained in force for nearly a whole school year – was motivated by his and his parents' refusal to accept that he receive or be liable to corporal chastisement (see paragraphs 10-11 above). His return to school could have been secured only if his parents had acted contrary to their convictions, convictions which the United Kingdom is obliged to respect under the second sentence of Article 2 (see paragraphs 35-36 above). A condition of access to an educational establishment that conflicts in this way with another right enshrined in Protocol No. 1 cannot be described as reasonable and in any event falls outside the State's power of regulation under Article 2.

> There has accordingly also been, as regards Jeffrey Cosans, breach of the first sentence of that Article.

It will have been noted that it was the ground for the suspension that was seen as most important in that case.

2. Article 2 of Protocol No. 1, second sentence – Respect for the parents' religious and philosophical convictions

The second sentence of Article 2 is worded as follows:

> **In the exercise of any functions which it assumes in relation to education and to teaching, the State shall respect the right of parents to ensure such education and teaching in conformity with their own religious and philosophical convictions.**

The meaning of "religious and philosophical convictions"

In the Campbell and Cosans v. the United Kingdom case (25 February 1982, Series A No. 48, p. 16, paragraph 36) the Court gave an explanation of the words "philosophical convictions" within the meaning of the second sentence of Article 2:

> In its ordinary meaning the word "convictions", taken on its own, is not synonymous with the words "opinions" and "ideas", such as are utilised in Article 10 of the Convention, which guarantees freedom of expression; it is more akin to the

term "beliefs" (in the French text *"convictions"*) appearing in Article 9 – which guarantees freedom of thought, conscience and religion – and denotes views that attain a certain level of cogency, seriousness, cohesion and importance.

As regards the adjective "philosophical", it is not capable of exhaustive definition and little assistance as to its precise significance is to be gleaned from the *travaux préparatoires*. The Commission pointed out that the word "philosophy" bears numerous meanings: it is used to allude to a fully-fledged system of thought or, rather loosely, to views on more or less trivial matters. The Court agrees with the Commission that neither of these two extremes can be adopted for the purposes of interpreting Article 2: the former would too narrowly restrict the scope of a right that is guaranteed to all parents and the latter might result in the inclusion of matters of insufficient weight or substance.

Having regard to the Convention as a whole, including Article 17, the expression "philosophical convictions" in the present content denotes, in the Court's opinion, such convictions as are worthy of respect in a "democratic society" (see, most recently, the Young, James and Webster judgment of 13 August 1981, Series A No. 44, p. 25, paragraph 63) and are not incompatible with human dignity; in addition, they must not conflict with the fundamental right of the child to education, the whole of Article 2 being dominated by its first sentence (see the Kjeldsen, Busk Madsen and Pedersen judgment of 7 December 1976, Series A No. 23, pp. 25-26, paragraph 52).

In its judgment in the "Belgian linguistics" case the Court stated (p 32, paragraph 6) that the parents' linguistic preferences could not be considered to be of a philosophical or religious nature, but fell within the ambit of the content of the education, which the second sentence does not guarantee:

> The second sentence of Article 2 of the Protocol does not guarantee a right to education; this is clearly shown by its wording: [...] This provision does not require of States that they should, in the sphere of education or teaching, respect parents' linguistic preferences, but only their religious and philosophical convictions. To interpret the terms "religious" and "philosophical" as covering linguistic preferences would amount to a distortion of their ordinary and usual meaning and to read into the Convention something which is not there.

Scope and consequences of the second sentence of Article 2

Scope of the second sentence from the State's point of view

The Kjeldsen, Busk Madsen and Pedersen v. Denmark judgment (2 December 1976, Series A No. 23, pp. 25-26, paragraphs 51-52) indicates the approach which the State must take in reading Article 2 in order to respect the "convictions" of the parents:

> [...] "the provisions of the Convention and Protocol must be read as a whole" (the above-mentioned judgment of 23 July 1968, ibid., p. 30, paragraph 1). Accordingly, the two sentences of Article 2 must be read not only in the light of each other but also, in particular, of Articles 8, 9 and 10 of the Convention, which proclaim the right of everyone, including parents and children, "to respect for his private and family life", to "freedom of thought, conscience and religion", and to "freedom [...] to receive and impart information and ideas".

More precisely, it indicates that Article 2 applies to all educational subjects (ibid.):

> Article 2, which applies to each of the State's functions in relation to education and to teaching, does not permit a distinction to be drawn between religious instruction and other subjects. It enjoins the State to respect the parent's convictions, be they religious or philosophical, throughout the entire State education programme.

Going into greater detail, the Kjeldsen case also made it possible to cast light on the State's role in defining school curricula (ibid., pp. 26-27, paragraph 53). The Court observed that:

> [...] the setting and planning of the curriculum fall in principle within the competence of the Contracting States. This mainly involves questions of expediency on which it is not for the Court to rule and whose solution may legitimately vary according to the country and the era. In particular, the second sentence of Article 2 of the Protocol does not prevent States from imparting through teaching or education information or knowledge of a directly or indirectly religious or philosophical kind. It does not even permit parents to object to the integration of such teaching or education in the school curriculum, for otherwise all institutionalised teaching would run the risk of proving impracticable. In fact, it seems very difficult for many subjects taught at school not to have, to a greater or lesser extent, some philosophical complexion or implications. The same is true of religious affinities if one remembers the existence of religions forming a very broad dogmatic and moral entity which has or may have answers to every question of a philosophical, cosmological or moral nature.

> The second sentence of Article 2 implies on the other hand that the State, in fulfilling the functions assumed by it in regard to education and teaching, must take care that information or knowledge included in the curriculum is conveyed in an objective, critical and pluralistic manner. The State is forbidden to pursue an aim of indoctrination that might be considered as not respecting parents' religious and philosophical convictions. That is the limit that must not be exceeded.

> Such an interpretation is consistent at one and the same time with the first sentence of Article 2 of the Protocol, with Articles 8 to 10 of the Convention and with the general spirit of the Convention itself, an instrument designed to maintain and promote the ideals and values of a democratic society.

In this case the applicants claimed that sex education was contrary to their beliefs. The Court stated (p. 28, paragraph 54):

> [...] the disputed legislation in itself in no way offends the applicants' religious and philosophical convictions to the extent forbidden by the second sentence of Article 2 of the Protocol, interpreted in the light of its first sentence and of the whole of the Convention.

Lastly, the Kjeldsen case (ibid., p. 24, paragraph 50) defines the role of the State in the organisation of education. The Court stated:

> The second sentence of Article 2 is binding upon the Contracting States in the exercise of each and every function – it speaks of "any functions" – that they undertake in the sphere of education and teaching, including that consisting of the organisation and financing of public education.

It was in application of this principle that the Court considered that disciplinary matters fell within the scope of Article 2, second sentence, and made the State responsible for them (the aforementioned Campbell and Cosans case, pp. 15-16, paragraph 35):

> The functions assumed by the respondent State [in the] area [of education] extend to the supervision of the [...] educational system in general, which must include questions of discipline (see paragraph 34 above).

In the Cambell and Cosans case the Court therefore found that the government had violated Article 2 by failing to respect the parents' beliefs on the use of corporal punishment (p. 18, paragraph 38):

> Mrs Campbell and Mrs Cosans have accordingly been victims of a violation of the second sentence of Article 2 of Protocol No 1,

The scope of the second sentence of Article 2 from the parents' point of view

In the face of all the obligations thus borne by the State, the Court has emphasised that the parents' rights in the matter of their convictions are accompanied by a duty (ibid., pp. 25-26, paragraphs 51-52):

> It is in the discharge of a natural duty towards their children – parents being primarily responsible for the "education and teaching" of their children – that parents may require the State to respect their religious and philosophical conviction. Their right thus corresponds to a responsibility closely linked to the enjoyment and the exercise of the right to education.

In the Olsson v. Sweden case, it was held that parents do not lose their rights under Article 2 while their children are in the care of the public authority. The following passage may be read (the Olsson case, 24 March 1988, Series A No. 130, p. 40, paragraphs 95-96):

> The Court agrees with the Commission that the fact that the children were taken into public care did not cause the applicants to lose all their rights under Article 2 of Protocol No. 1.

In this case, however, the Court considered that there had not been a violation of Article 2:

> It notes, however, as did the Commission, that Mr and Mrs Olsson, though describing themselves as atheists, have not left the Church of Sweden (see paragraph 8 above) and that there is no serious indication of their being particularly concerned, except at a rather late stage, with giving the children a non-religious upbringing.

> Neither have Mr and Mrs Olsson shown that in practice the general education of the children whilst in public care diverged from what they would have wished.

> In these circumstances, no violation of Article 2 of Protocol No. 1 has been established.

Lastly, the Court has stressed that the second sentence of Article 2 guarantees a right only to parents, not to under-age children. In Eriksson v. Sweden (22 June 1989, Series A No. 156, p. 31, paragraph 93) Mrs Eriksson's daughter, Lisa, was taken into care by the public authority. In the Court's opinion:

> The complaint under Article 2 of Protocol No. 1 is based only on its second sentence, which guarantees a right of parents, and not on the first, which states that "no person shall be denied the right to education". Lisa therefore cannot claim to be the victim of the alleged violation of Article 2, taken alone or together with Article 13 of the Convention.

Article 3 of Protocol No. 1 – Right to elections

Article 3 of Protocol No. 1 is worded as follows:

> **The High Contracting Parties undertake to hold free elections at reasonable intervals by secret ballot, under conditions which will ensure the free expression of the opinion of the people in the choice of the legislature.**

In the Mathieu-Mohin and Clerfayt v. Belgium case (2 March 1987, Series A No. 113, pp. 22-24, paragraphs 48-54) the Court gave an interpretation of this provision:

> Where nearly all the other substantive clauses in the Convention and in Protocols Nos. 1, 4, 6 and 7 use the words "Everyone has the right" or "No one shall" Article 3 uses the phrase "The High Contracting Parties undertake". It has sometimes been inferred from this that the Article does not give rise to individual rights and freedoms "directly secured to anyone" within the jurisdiction of these Parties (see the Ireland v. the United Kingdom judgment of 18 January 1978, Series A No. 25, p. 91, paragraph 239), but solely to obligations between States.
>
> [...]
>
> Such a restrictive interpretation does not stand up to scrutiny.
>
> [...]
>
> Accordingly – and those appearing before the Court were agreed on this point – the inter-state colouring of the wording of Article 3 does not reflect any difference of substance from the other substantive clauses in the Convention and Protocols. The reason for it would seem to lie rather in the desire to give greater solemnity to the commitment undertaken and in the fact that the primary obligation in the field concerned is not one of abstention or non-interference, as with the majority of the civil and political rights, but one of adoption by the State of positive measures to "hold" democratic elections.

It will have been noted that this Article is one of the rare provisions to impose a positive obligation on the State; and although it protects a fundamental right, it does not seem to have formed the subject of any significant judgments. The Court has merely stated that it leaves each State a wide margin of appreciation in the choice of the electoral system adopted (same judgment):

> The rights in question are not absolute. Since Article 3 recognises them without setting them forth in express terms, let alone defining them, there is room for implied limitations (see, *mutatis mutandis*, the Golder judgment of 21 February 1975, Series A No. 18, pp. 18-19, paragraph 38).
>
> [...]
>
> Article 3 applies only to the election of the "legislature", or at least of one of its chambers if it has two or more (*Collected Edition of the "Travaux Préparatoires" of the European Convention on Human Rights*, vol. VIII, pp. 46, 50 and 52). The word "legislature" does not necessarily mean only the national parliament, however; it has to be interpreted in the light of the constitutional structure of the State in question.
>
> [...]
>
> As regards the method of appointing the "legislature", Article 3 provides only for "free" elections "at reasonable intervals", "by secret ballot" and "under conditions which will ensure the free expression of the opinion of the people". Subject to that, it does not create any "obligation to introduce a specific system" (*Collected Edition of the "Travaux Préparatoires" of the European Convention on Human Rights*, vol. VII, pp. 130, 202 and 210, and vol. VIII, p. 14) such as proportional representation or majority voting with one or two ballots.
>
> Here too the Court recognises that the Contracting States have a wide margin of appreciation, given that their legislation on the matter varies from place to place and from time to time.
>
> Electoral systems seek to fulfil objectives which are sometimes scarcely compatible with each other: on the one hand, to reflect fairly faithfully the opinions of the people, and on the other, to channel currents of thought so as to promote the emergence of a sufficiently clear and coherent political will. In these circumstances the phrase "conditions which will ensure the free expression of the opinion of the people in the choice of the legislature" implies essentially – apart from freedom of expression (already protected under Article 10 of the Convention) – the principle of equality of treatment of all citizens in the exercise of their right to vote and their right to stand for election.
>
> It does not follow, however, that all votes must necessarily have equal weight as regards the outcome of the election or that all candidates must have equal chances of victory. Thus no electoral system can eliminate "wasted votes".
>
> For the purpose of Article 3 of Protocol No. 1, any electoral system must be assessed in the light of the political evolution of the country concerned; features that would be unacceptable in the context of one system may accordingly be justified in the context of another, at least so long as the chosen system provides for conditions which will ensure the "free expression of the opinion of the people in the choice of the legislature".

The Gitonas and Others v. Greece case (1 July 1997, *Reports of Judgments and Decisions* 1997-IV, pp. 1233-1238, paragraphs 39-40 and 44) concerns the disqualification of certain persons from standing for election as Members of

Parliament. In this case the election of five Members of Parliament was annulled. The applicants were disqualified from standing for election because, in accordance with Article 56 of the Greek Constitution, they had held posts in public office for more than three months during the three years preceding the elections:

> The Court reiterates that Article 3 of Protocol No. 1 implies subjective rights to vote and to stand for election. As important as those rights are, they are not, however, absolute. Since Article 3 recognises them without setting them forth in express terms, let alone defining them, there is room for "implied limitations" (see the Mathieu-Mohin and Clerfayt v. Belgium judgment of 2 March 1987, Series A No. 113, p. 23, paragraph 52). In their internal legal orders the Contracting States make the rights to vote and to stand for election subject to conditions which are not in principle precluded under Article 3. They have a wide margin of appreciation in this sphere, but it is for the Court to determine in the last resort whether the requirements of Protocol No. 1 have been complied with; it has to satisfy itself that the conditions do not curtail the rights in question to such an extent as to impair their very essence and deprive them of their effectiveness; that they are imposed in pursuit of a legitimate aim; and that the means employed are not disproportionate (ibid., p. 23, paragraph 52).

> More particularly, the States enjoy considerable latitude to establish in their constitutional order rules governing the status of parliamentarians, including criteria for disqualification. Though originating from a common concern – ensuring the independence of Members of Parliament, but also the electorate's freedom of choice – the criteria vary according to the historical and political factors peculiar to each State. The number of situations provided for in the constitutions and the legislation on elections in many member States of the Council of Europe shows the diversity of possible choice on the subject. None of these criteria should, however, be considered more valid than any other provided that it guarantees the expression of the will of the people through free, fair and regular elections.

> The Court notes that paragraph 3 of Article 56 of the Constitution, which was applied in the applicants' case, establishes grounds for disqualification that are both relative and final in that certain categories of holders of public office – including salaried public servants and members of staff of public-law entities and public undertakings – are precluded from standing for election and being elected in any constituency where they have performed their duties for more than three months in the three years preceding the elections; the disqualification will moreover stand notwithstanding a candidate's prior resignation, unlike the position with certain other categories of public servant under paragraph 1 of that Article (see paragraph 29 above).

> Such disqualification, for which equivalent provisions exist in several member States of the Council of Europe, serves a dual purpose that is essential for the proper functioning and upholding of democratic regimes, namely ensuring that candidates of different political persuasions enjoy equal means of influence (since holders of public office may on occasion have an unfair advantage over other candidates) and protecting the electorate from pressure from such officials who, because of their position, are called upon to take many – and sometimes

important – decisions and enjoy substantial prestige in the eyes of the ordinary citizen, whose choice of candidate might be influenced.

[...]

The Court points out that it is primarily for the national authorities, and in particular the courts of first-instance and of appeal, which are specially qualified for the task, to construe and apply domestic law.

It notes that the positions held by the applicants were not among those expressly referred to in Article 56, paragraph 3. However, that did not guarantee them a right to be elected. The Special Supreme Court has sole jurisdiction under Article 58 of the Constitution (see paragraph 29 above) to decide any dispute over disqualifications and, as in any judicial order where such a system exists, anyone elected in breach of the applicable rules will forfeit his position as a Member of Parliament.

In the instant case the Special Supreme Court, after analysing the nature of the posts held by the applicants and the applicable legislation, held that the posts were similar to the ones described in paragraph 3 of Article 56; it further found that the conditions relating to when the position was held, and the duration and extent of the duties, were met in the case of each of the applicants. On reasonable grounds it considered it necessary to annul their election (see paragraphs 10, 14, 18, 22 and 27 above).

The Court cannot reach any other conclusion; there is nothing in the judgments of the Special Supreme Court to suggest that the annulments were contrary to Greek legislation, arbitrary or disproportionate, or thwarted "the free expression of the opinion of the people in the choice of the legislature" (see, *mutatis mutandis*, the aforementioned Mathieu-Mohin and Clerfayt v. Belgium judgment, p. 25, paragraph 57).

Consequently, there has been no violation of Article 3 of Protocol No. 1.

As regards the removal of a person from the electoral register, see the Labita v. Italy judgment (6 April 2000, Application No. 26772/95, paragraphs 201-203), where the Court held:

The Court points out that implicit in Article 3 of Protocol No. 1, which provides for "free" elections at "reasonable intervals" "by secret ballot" and "under conditions which will ensure the free expression of the opinion of the people", are the subjective rights to vote and to stand for election. Although those rights are important, they are not absolute. Since Article 3 recognises them without setting them forth in express terms, let alone defining them, there is room for implied limitations (see the Mathieu-Mohin and Clerfayt v. Belgium judgment of 2 March 1987, Series A No. 113, p. 23, paragraph 52). In their internal legal orders the Contracting States make the rights to vote and to stand for election subject to conditions which are not in principle precluded under Article 3. They have a wide margin of appreciation in this sphere, but it is for the Court to determine in the last resort whether the requirements of Protocol No. 1 have been complied with; it has to satisfy itself that the conditions do not curtail the rights in question to such an extent as to impair their very essence and deprive them of their effectiveness; that they are imposed in pursuit of a legitimate aim; and that the means employed are not disproportionate (see the Gitonas and Others v. Greece

405

judgment of 1 July 1997, *Reports* 1997-IV, pp. 1233-1234, paragraph 39, and Matthews v. the United Kingdom [GC], No. 24833/94, paragraph 63, ECHR 1999-I).

The Court observes that persons who are subject to special police supervision are automatically struck off the electoral register as they forfeit their civil rights because they represent "a danger to society" or, as in the instant case, are suspected of belonging to the Mafia (see paragraphs 107 and 110 above). The Government pointed to the risk that persons "suspected of belonging to the Mafia" might exercise their right of vote in favour of other members of the Mafia.

The Court has no doubt that temporarily suspending the voting rights of persons against whom there is evidence of Mafia membership pursues a legitimate aim. It observes, however, that although the special police supervision measure against the applicant was in the instant case imposed during the course of the trial, it was not applied until the trial was over, once the applicant had been acquitted on the ground that "he had not committed the offence". The Court does not accept the view expressed by the Government that the serious evidence of the applicant's guilt was not rebutted during the trial. That affirmation is in contradiction with the tenor of the judgments of the Trapani District Court (see paragraph 23 above) and the Palermo Court of Appeal (see paragraph 26 above). When his name was removed from the electoral register, therefore, there was no concrete evidence on which a "suspicion" that the applicant belonged to the Mafia could be based (see, *mutatis mutandis*, paragraph 196 above).

In the circumstances, the Court cannot regard the measure in question as proportionate.

There has therefore been a violation of Article 3 of Protocol No. 1.

Protocol No. 4

Article 1 of Protocol No. 4

Article 1 of Protocol No. 4 is worded as follows:

> **No one shall be deprived of his liberty merely on the ground of inability to fulfil a contractual obligation.**

This Article complements Article 5 of the Convention. It refers to the notion of "deprivation of liberty" which was examined under Article 5. It also contains the expression "contractual obligation", which, like a number of other Convention concepts, has an autonomous meaning.

Articles 2, 3 and 4 of Protocol No. 4 concern freedom of movement.

Article 2 of Protocol No. 4

Article 2 of Protocol No. 4 is worded as follows:

> 1. **Everyone lawfully within the territory of a State shall, within that territory, have the right to liberty of movement and freedom to choose his residence.**
>
> 2. **Everyone shall be free to leave any country, including his own.**
>
> 3. **No restrictions shall be placed on the exercise of these rights other than such as are in accordance with law and are necessary in a democratic society in the interests of national security or public safety, for the maintenance of *ordre public*, for the prevention of crime, for the protection of health or morals, or for the protection of the rights and freedoms of others.**
>
> 4. **The rights set forth in paragraph 1 may also be subject, in particular areas, to restrictions imposed in accordance with law and justified by the public interest in a democratic society.**

1. Article 2, paragraph 1, of Protocol No. 4

Article 2, paragraph 1, of Protocol 4 applies above all to aliens lawfully on the territory of a State even though it is formulated in general terms. In the case of A. v. San Marino (9 July 1993, *Decisions and Reports* 75, p. 249, paragraph 1) the Commission notes that this provision:

> [...] cannot be interpreted as recognising the right of an alien to reside or continue to reside in a country of which he is not a national. Its sole purpose is to guarantee those lawfully resident within the territory of a State, whether they are nationals of that State or not, the freedom to come and go within the territory and the freedom to choose their place of residence there without interference.

The Commission, of course, had the opportunity to rule on the notion of "lawful" presence on the territory of a State in the Paramanathan v. the Federal Republic of Germany case (Application No. 12068/86, decision of 1 December 1986, *Decisions and Reports* 51, p. 240, paragraph 1).

> The Commission observes that Article 2, paragraph 1, of Protocol No. 4 secures the freedom of movement to persons "lawfully within the territory of a State". This condition refers to the domestic law of the State concerned. It is for the domestic law and organs to lay down the conditions which must be fulfilled for a person's presence in the territory to be considered "lawful". The Commission, in this respect, recalls its constant case-law according to which there is no right of an alien to enter, reside or remain in a particular country, as such, guaranteed by the Convention (see Applications Nos. 9214/80, 9473/81 and 9474/81, decision of 11 May 1982, *Decisions and Reports* 29, p. 176). The Commission is of the opinion that aliens provisionally admitted to a certain district of the territory of a State, pending proceedings to determine whether or not they are entitled to a residence permit under the relevant provisions of domestic law, can only be regarded as "lawfully" in the territory as long as they comply with the conditions to which their admission and stay are subjected.

The interesting Raimondo v. Italy judgment (22 February 1994, Series A No. 281-A, p. 19, paragraphs 39-40) provides an example of the application of Article 2, paragraph 1, to an Italian national whose movements in his own country were restricted by a supervision measure (he was suspected of belonging to a Mafia-type criminal association). In this case, the Court held that there was a violation of Article 2.

> The Court considers in the first place that, notwithstanding the applicant's assertion to the contrary, the measure in issue did not amount to a deprivation of liberty within the meaning of Article 5, paragraph 1, of the Convention. The mere restrictions on the liberty of movement resulting from special supervision fall to be dealt with under Article 2 of Protocol No. 2 (see the Guzzardi judgment, cited above, p. 33, paragraph 92).

> In view of the threat posed by the Mafia to "democratic society", the measure was in addition necessary "for the maintenance of *ordre public*" and "for the prevention of crime". It was in particular proportionate to the aim pursued, up to the moment at which the Catanzaro Court of Appeal decided, on 4 July 1986, to revoke it (see paragraph 14 above).

> It remains to consider the period between 4 July and 20 December 1986, when the decision was notified to the applicant (see the same paragraph). Even if it is accepted that this decision, taken in private session, could not acquire legal force until it was filed with the registry, the Court finds it hard to understand why there should have been a delay of nearly five months in drafting the grounds for a decision which was immediately enforceable and concerned a fundamental right, namely the applicant's freedom to come and go as he pleased; the latter was moreover not informed of the revocation for eighteen days.

> The Court concludes that at least from 2 to 20 December 1986 the interference in issue was neither provided for by law nor necessary. There has accordingly been a violation of Article 2 of Protocol No. 4.

Idem in the case of Labita v. Italy (judgment of 6 April 2000, Application No. 26772/95, paragraphs 189-197), where the applicant was placed under special police supervision in spite of being acquitted.

In the case of Denizci and Others v. Cyprus (23 May 2001, Application No. 25316/94, paragraphs 404-406), the Cypriot authorities were closely monitoring the applicants' movements both between the northern part and the southern part of the island and within the southern part. The applicants could not move freely in the south and had to advise the police whenever they wished to go to the north to visit their families or their friends and do likewise when they arrived in the south. The Court stated:

> The Court recalls that mere restrictions on liberty of movement resulting from special supervision fall to be dealt with under Article 2 of Protocol No. 4 (see the Raimondo v. Italy judgment of 22 February 1994, Series A No. 281, p. 19, paragraph 39, and the Labita v. Italy [GC] judgment, No. 26772/95, ECHR 2000).

> In the present case, the Court considers that the restrictions to the applicants' movements as described above also fall under the provision of Article 2 of Protocol No. 4 and constitute an interference with their freedom of movement protected by that provision.

> Such interference breaches Article 2 of Protocol No. 4 unless it is "in accordance with law", pursues one of the legitimate aims set out in Article 2, paragraphs 3 and 4, of Protocol No. 4 and is, in addition, necessary in a democratic society to achieve the aim or aims in question.

> The Court notes that no lawful basis for the applicants' restrictions of movements was advanced by the respondent Government. Moreover, the respondent Government did not claim that the measure was necessary in a democratic society to achieve one of the legitimate aims set forth in paragraphs 3 and 4 of Article 2 of Protocol No. 4.

> The Court concludes that the restrictions on the applicants' freedom of movement were neither provided for by law nor necessary. There has accordingly been a violation of Article 2 of Protocol No. 4.

In the case of Piermont v. France (27 April 1995, Series A No. 314) the applicant, a German citizen who was at the material time a Member of the European Parliament, maintained that, having entered French Polynesia lawfully, she had the right to liberty of movement there. The applicant had taken part in a public meeting, had joined a demonstration and denounced during the demonstration the continuation of nuclear testing and the French presence in the Pacific, whereas the High Commissioner of the French Republic in French Polynesia had requested her to show some discretion in any comments she made on French internal matters, failing which she risked being expelled. The day after the demonstration – that is 2 March 1986 – the High Commissioner made an order expelling the applicant and prohibiting her from re-entering the territory. In its judgment (paragraph 44):

> The Court notes that the expulsion order of 2 March 1986 was served on Mrs Piermont next day when she had already taken her seat in the aircraft (see paragraph 13 above). The applicant, who was not travelling on business for the European Parliament, had been able to move around Polynesia as she wished

from 24 February to 3 March 1986 and during that period had suffered no interference with the exercise of her right to liberty of movement within the meaning of Article 2 of Protocol No. 4.

[...]

Article 5, paragraph 4, of the Protocol[1] (see paragraph 28 above) requires that Polynesia should be regarded as a separate territory for the purposes of the references in Article 2 to the territory of the State. At all events, the Aliens (Conditions of Entry and Residence) Ordinance 1945 had not been promulgated there (see paragraph 29 above). As a result, once the expulsion order had been served, the applicant was no longer lawfully on Polynesian territory and in those circumstances did not suffer any interference with the exercise of her right to liberty of movement, as secured by the provision in question, at that point either.

After her visit to French Polynesia the applicant went to New Caledonia. The applicant submitted that having entered New Caledonia lawfully, she should have been able to move there freely. According to the applicant, an expulsion measure had been taken against her that had incorrectly been described as an exclusion. The Conseil d'État had described the order as a decision "excluding Mrs Piermont from the territory of New Caledonia" (paragraph 49).

In the instant case the Court considers that the applicant's argument that the mere fact of going through immigration control regularises a person's position in a territory is too formalistic. At an airport such as Nouméa's a passenger remains liable to checks for as long as he remains within the perimeter. In this instance Mrs Piermont was stopped just after her passport had been stamped and the impugned order was served on her before she had left the airport, since she was still held in an office under police guard.

The order made by the High Commissioner of the Republic is headed "Order prohibiting an alien from entering the territory" and Article 1 of it embodies that prohibition. The Conseil d'État in its decision of 12 May 1989 did not question the nature of the order. That being so, the applicant was never lawfully within the territory, a requirement if Article 2 of Protocol No. 4 is to apply. There has therefore been no breach of that provision.

2. Article 2, paragraph 2, of Protocol No. 4

In the case of Peltonen v. Finland (20 February 1995, *Decisions and Reports* 80-A, p. 43, paragraph 1) the Commission interpreted the provisions of Article 2, paragraph 2, of Protocol No. 4. In this case the applicant had permanently resided in Sweden since December 1986. In reply to his request

---

1. Article 5, paragraph 4, of Protocol No. 4 provides: "The territory of any State to which this Protocol applies by virtue of ratification or acceptance by that State, and each territory to which this Protocol is applied by virtue of a declaration by that State under this article, shall be treated as separate territories for the purpose of the references in Article 2 and 3 to the territory of a State."

Article 5, paragraph 1, of Protocol No. 4 provides: "Any High Contracting Party may, at the time of signature or ratification of this Protocol, or at any time thereafter, communicate to the Secretary General of the Council of Europe a declaration stating the extent to which it undertakes that the provisions of this Protocol shall apply to such of the territories for the international relations of which it is responsible as are named therein."

for a ten-year passport at the Finnish Embassy in Stockholm, the embassy informed the applicant that he could not be issued with a passport, as he had failed to attend the call-up for military service.

> The Commission observes that the refusal to issue the applicant with a Finnish passport has not prevented him from leaving that country, nor is it preventing him from leaving a Nordic country for another Nordic country. Article 2, paragraph 2, of Protocol No. 4 provides, however, that everyone shall be free to leave "any country", which implies a right to leave for such a country of the person's choice to which he may be admitted. The Commission therefore considers that the passport refusal interfered with this freedom of the applicant. It remains to be examined whether the interference was justified under paragraph 3 of Article 2.

The Commission decided that the refusal to issue the applicant with the requested ten-year passport could reasonably be considered necessary in a democratic society for the purposes of pursuing the legitimate aims of maintaining *ordre public* and ensuring national security.

3. Article 2, paragraphs 3 and 4, of Protocol No. 4

Article 2, paragraph 3, provides for derogations from the rights provided for in paragraphs 1 and 2 of that Article.

It should be recalled that also under Article 2, paragraph 4, the rights set forth in paragraph 1 of this Article can be restricted.

Articles 3 and 4 of Protocol No. 4

Articles 3 and 4 of Protocol No. 4 are worded as follows:

Article 3

1. No one shall be expelled, by means either of an individual or of a collective measure, from the territory of the State of which he is a national.

2. No one shall be deprived of the right to enter the territory of the State of which he is a national.

Article 4

Collective expulsion of aliens is prohibited.

Article 3 of Protocol No. 4 ensures that a person is allowed to remain in the country of which he is a national. Article 4 prohibits the collective expulsion of aliens. In connection with the notion of collective expulsion, reference should be made to the A. and Others v. the Netherlands case (Application

No. 14209/88, decision of 16 December 1988, *Decisions and Reports* 59, p. 277), where the Commission stated:

> The Commission recalls its decision in Application No. 7011/75 (decision of 3 December 1975, *Yearbook of the European Convention on Human Rights* 19, pp. 416 and 454) wherein it defined collective expulsion as follows:
>
> " [...] any measure of the competent authorities compelling aliens as a group to leave the country, except where such a measure is taken after and on the basis of a reasonable and objective examination of the particular cases of each individual alien of the group."

See Protocol No. 7.

Protocol No. 6 – Abolition of the death penalty

Articles 1 to 4 of Protocol No. 6

Articles 1 to 4 are worded as follows:

Article 1

The death penalty shall be abolished. No one shall be condemned to such penalty or executed.

Article 2

A State may make provision in its law for the death penalty in respect of acts committed in time of war or of imminent threat of war; such penalty shall be applied only in the instances laid down in the law and in accordance with its provisions. The State shall communicate to the Secretary General of the Council of Europe the relevant provisions of that law.

Article 3

No derogation from the provisions of this Protocol shall be made under Article 15 of the Convention

Article 4

No reservation may be made under Article 64 of the Convention in respect of the provisions of this Protocol.

In the absence of relevant case-law, it must suffice to refer to the study of Article 2 of the Convention (Part 1).

Protocol No. 7

Article 1 of Protocol No. 7

Article 1 of Protocol No. 7 is worded as follows:

---

1. An alien lawfully resident in the territory of a State shall not be expelled therefrom except in pursuance of a decision reached in accordance with law and shall be allowed:

a. to submit reasons against his expulsion;

b. to have his case reviewed; and

c. to be represented for these purposes before the competent authority or a person or persons designated by that authority.

2. An alien may be expelled before the exercise of his rights under paragraph 1.*a*, *b* and *c* of this Article, when such expulsion is necessary in the interests of public order or is grounded on reasons of national security.

In the case of Voulfovitch and Oulianova v. Sweden (13 January 1993, *Decisions and Reports* 74, p. 209, paragraph 3) the Commission interpreted the term "lawfully resident".

> In the context of an instrument which, like the Convention, does not guarantee a right to asylum or other residence authorisation, the term "lawfully resident" used in Article 1 of Protocol No. 7 must be interpreted to refer basically to lawfulness of the presence according to national law. Thus, an alien whose visa or residence permit has expired cannot, at least normally, be regarded as being "lawfully resident" in the country.

> Whatever the exact scope of the term "lawfully resident", it clearly does not comprise aliens in the applicant's situation. The applicants only had a transit visa for a one-day visit to Sweden and have remained, after the expiry of the visa, in the country solely in order to await, first, a decision on their request for political asylum or residence permit and, subsequently, the enforcement of the expulsion order.

Articles 2, 3 and 4 of Protocol No. 7

Articles 2, 3 and 4 of Protocol No. 7 contain procedural provisions concerning criminal matters which complement the requirements of Article 6 of the Convention. They enshrine the principle of an appeal, the principle of compensation in the event of error by the courts and the principle *ne bis in idem*.

Article 2 of Protocol No. 7

Article 2 is worded as follows:

> 1. Everyone convicted of a criminal offence by a tribunal shall have the right to have his conviction or sentence reviewed by a higher tribunal. The exercise of this right, including the grounds on which it may be exercised, shall be governed by law.
>
> 2. This right may be subject to exceptions in regard to offences of a minor character, as prescribed by law, or in cases in which the person concerned was tried in the first instance by the highest tribunal or was convicted following an appeal against acquittal.

1. Article 2, paragraph 1, of Protocol No. 7

The first thing is to determine whether the applicant has been "convicted of a criminal offence". In the case of Borrelli v. Switzerland (2 September 1993, *Decisions and Reports* 75, p. 165, paragraph 3), the Commission stated:

> The Commission has just found that the proceedings instituted against the applicant did not constitute the "determination of [... a] criminal charge against him" within the meaning of Article 6, paragraph 1, of the Convention. The Commission considers that for the same reasons it cannot be said that the applicant was "convicted of a criminal offence" within the meaning of Article 2 of Protocol No. 7. This provision was therefore also not applicable to the proceedings instituted against the applicant.

Where the applicant has indeed been "convicted of a criminal offence", the State retains a certain margin of appreciation as regards the detailed implementation of Article 2 of Protocol No. 7. In the case of Krombach v. France (13 February 2001, Application No. 29731/96, paragraph 96), the Court declared, in respect of the fact that he was not permitted to appeal on a point of law against a judgment delivered *in absentia*:

> The Court reiterates that the Contracting States dispose in principle of a wide margin of appreciation to determine how the right secured by Article 2 of Protocol No. 7 to the Convention is to be exercised. Thus, the review by a higher court of a conviction or sentence may concern both points of fact and points of law or be confined solely to points of law. Furthermore, in certain countries, a defendant wishing to appeal may sometimes be required to seek permission to do so. However, any restrictions contained in domestic legislation on the right to a review mentioned in that provision must, by analogy with the right of access to a court embodied in Article 6, paragraph 1, of the Convention, pursue a legitimate aim and not infringe the very essence of that right (see the Haser v. Switzerland [Section II] decision, No. 33050/96, 27 April 2000). This rule is in itself consistent with the exception authorised by paragraph 2 of Article 2 and is backed up by the French declaration regarding the interpretation of the Article, which reads: "[...] in accordance with the meaning of Article 2, paragraph 1, the review by a higher court may be limited to a control of the application of the law, such as an appeal to the Supreme Court".

In the case in point, the Court continued (paragraph 100):

> In the present case the applicant wished both to defend the charges on the merits and to raise a preliminary procedural objection. The Court attaches weight to the fact that the applicant was unable to obtain a review, at least by the Court of Cassation, of the lawfulness of the Assize Court's refusal to allow the defence lawyers to plead (see, mutatis mutandis, the Poitrimol judgment cited above, paragraph 38, in fine; the Van Geyseghem judgment cited above, paragraph 35; and, *a contrario,* the Haser decision cited above).
>
> By virtue of Articles 630 and 639 of the Code of Criminal Procedure taken together (see paragraph 59 above) the applicant, on the one hand, could not be and was not represented in the Assize Court by a lawyer (see paragraph 46 above), and, on the other, was unable to appeal to the Court of Cassation as he was a defendant *in absentia*. He therefore had no real possibility of being defended at first instance or of having his conviction reviewed by a higher court.
>
> Consequently, there has also been a violation of Article 2 of Protocol No. 7 to the Convention.

However, in the case of Näss v. Sweden (6 April 1994, *Decisions and Reports* 77-A, p. 40, paragraph 2), where the applicant complained that he had been deprived of his right to have his conviction by the Court of Appeal reviewed by a higher tribunal, since his request for leave to appeal to the Supreme Court had been refused, the Commission stated:

> The Commission notes that different rules govern review by a higher tribunal in the various member States of the Council of Europe. In some member States, like Sweden, a person wishing to appeal to the highest tribunal must apply for leave to appeal. The Commission considers that the procedure on the right to apply to the Supreme Court in the present case is in itself to be regarded as a review within the meaning of Article 2 of Protocol No. 7.

Last, in the case of Ekbatani v. Sweden (26 May 1988, Series A No. 134, p. 13, paragraph 26), the Court held:

> Taking both Articles into account – that is Article 7 of Protocol No. 7 and Article 60 of the Convention – the Court can find no warrant for the view that the addition of this Protocol was intended to limit, at the appellate level, the scope of the guarantees contained in Article 6 of the Convention.

2. Article 2, paragraph 2, of Protocol No. 7

In the case of Putz v. Austria (3 December 1993, *Decisions and Reports* 76-A, p. 61, paragraph 2) a fine of 5 000 Austrian schillings was imposed upon the applicant for an "offence against the order in court", in view of insulting remarks towards the court in his submissions.

> The Commission, assuming that the above court decisions imposing fines upon the applicant for "offences against the order in court" related to a criminal offence within the meaning of Article 2 of Protocol No. 7, had regard to paragraph 2 of this provision, which subjects the right to review by a higher tribunal to "exceptions in regard to offences of a minor character, as prescribed by law".

[...]

The Commission finds that an "offence against the order in court" within the meaning of the Austrian Court Organisation Act, in conjunction with the Code of Civil Procedure, and the Code of Criminal Procedure respectively, constitutes a less serious offence both as to its nature and to the severity of the punishment involved. The Commission therefore considers that an "offence against the order in court" as being of a minor character. The exception to the right to a review by a higher tribunal, pursuant to Article 2, paragraph 2, of Protocol No. 7, thus applies.

As regards the notion of "criminal offence" a reference should be made to the Ravnsborg v. Sweden judgment (23 March 1994, Series A No. 283-B, mentioned above under Article 6, paragraph 1, the notion of "criminal charge").

Article 3 of Protocol No. 7

Article 3 is worded as follows:

> When a person has by a final decision been convicted of a criminal offence and when subsequently his conviction has been reversed, or he has been pardoned, on the ground that a new or newly discovered fact shows conclusively that there has been a miscarriage of justice, the person who has suffered punishment as a result of such conviction shall be compensated according to the law or the practice of the State concerned, unless it is proved that the non-disclosure of the unknown fact in time is wholly or partly attributable to him.

No relevant case-law has yet been published as regards Article 3 of Protocol No. 7.

Article 4 of Protocol No. 7

Article 4 is worded as follows:

> 1. No one shall be liable to be tried or punished again in criminal proceedings under the jurisdiction of the same State for an offence for which he has already been finally acquitted or convicted in accordance with the law and penal procedure of that State.
>
> 2. The provisions of the preceding paragraph shall not prevent the reopening of the case in accordance with the law and penal procedure of the State concerned, if there is evidence of new or newly discovered facts, or if there has been a fundamental defect in the previous proceedings, which could affect the outcome of the case.
>
> 3. No derogation from this Article shall be made under Article 15 of the Convention

1. The scope of Article 4

In the case of Baragiola v. Switzerland (21 October 1993, *Decisions and Reports* 75, p. 127, paragraph 3) the Commission stated:

> [...] it is clear from the express terms of this provision, that it upholds the *"ne bis in idem"* principle only in respect of cases where a person has been tried or punished twice for the same offence by the courts of a single State. But the applicant was first convicted in Italy, whereas the second conviction, in respect of the same acts, was pronounced by a Swiss court.

2. Applicability *ratione temporis* of Article 4

In the Gradinger v. Austria case (23 October 1995, Series A No. 328-C, paragraph 53) the Court ruled upon the applicability *ratione temporis* of this provision. It indicates that Article 4 is applicable if the new proceedings are concluded after the entry into force of that Article. The date on which these proceedings were begun is irrelevant.

> Like the Commission, the Court observes that the aim of Article 4 of Protocol No. 7 is to prohibit the repetition of criminal proceedings that have been concluded by a final decision. That provision does not therefore apply before new proceedings have been opened. In the present case, inasmuch the new proceedings reached their conclusion in a decision later in date then the entry into force of Protocol No. 7, namely the Administrative Court's judgment of 29 March 1989, the conditions for applicability *ratione temporis* are satisfied.

3. Compliance with Article 4

In that case, the applicant, while driving a car, caused an accident which led to the death of a cyclist. The applicant was convicted on 15 May 1987 by the criminal judge of causing death by negligence and sentenced to 200 day-fines of 160 Austrian schillings with 100 days' imprisonment in default of payment pursuant to the Criminal Code. He was acquitted for driving under the influence of alcohol which exceeded the prescribed limit. The district authority issued on 16 July 1987 for the same conduct a sentence order imposing a fine of 12 000 schillings on the applicant for driving under the influence of alcohol, with two weeks' imprisonment in default pursuant to the Road Traffic Act. Unlike the criminal judge, the district authority found that the blood alcohol level exceeded the prescribed limit. This – administrative – procedure ended with the judgment of the Administrative Court of 29 March 1989.

> The Court notes that, according to the St Pölten Regional Court, the aggravating circumstance referred to in Article 81, paragraph 2, of the Criminal Code, namely a blood alcohol level of 0.8 grams per litre or higher, was not made out with regard to the applicant. On the other hand, the administrative authorities found, in order to bring the applicant's case within the ambit of Section 5 of the Road Traffic Act, that that alcohol level had been attained. The Court is fully aware that the provisions in question differ not only as regards the designation of the offences but also, more importantly, as regards their nature and purpose. It further observes that the offence provided for in Section 5 of the Road Traffic Act

represents only one aspect of the offence punished under Article 81, paragraph 2, of the Criminal Code. Nevertheless, both impugned decisions were based on the same conduct. Accordingly, there has been a breach of Article 4 of Protocol No. 7 (ibid., paragraph 55).

See also the Franz Fischer v. Austria judgment of 29 May 2001, Application No. 37950/97, paragraphs 20-32.

Article 5 of Protocol No. 7

Article 5 of Protocol No. 7 is worded as follows:

> **Spouses shall enjoy equality of rights and responsibilities of a private law character between them, and in their relations with their children, as to marriage, during marriage and in the event of its dissolution. This Article shall not prevent States from taking such measures as are necessary in the interests of the children.**

As regards this provision, a reference should be made to Articles 8 and 14 of the Convention, which were examined in Part 1. In the Burghartz v. Switzerland judgment of 22 February 1994, Series A No. 280-B, p. 28, paragraph 23, the Court points out that:

> [...] under Article 7 of Protocol No. 7, Article 5 is to be regarded as an addition to the Convention, including Articles 8 and 60. Consequently, it cannot replace Article 8 or reduce its scope (see, *mutatis mutandis*, the Ekbatani v. Sweden judgment of 26 May 1988, Series A No. 134, pp. 12-13, paragraph 26).

Index of principal cases and of states

A

A. and Others v. the Netherlands, 411

A. v. San Marino, 407

Abdulaziz, Cabales and Balkandali v. the United Kingdom, 22, 73, 269, 320, 337, 365-366

Adolf v. Austria, 212, 214-215

AGOSI v. the United Kingdom, 181, 389, 392

Ahmed v. Austria, 75-77

Airey v. Ireland, 180, 184-185, 230, 241-242, 248, 387

Aksoy v. Turkey, 60, 132, 352, 368, 371

Albert and Le Compte v. Belgium, 58, 170, 187, 196

Allenet de Ribemont v. France, 215

Amuur v. France, 90-92, 96

Arrowsmith v. the United Kingdom, 300, 314

Artico v. Italy, 156, 221, 224, 226, 228, 338, 340

Ashingdane v. the United Kingdom, 98, 159, 188-189, 390

Austria, 39, 52-53, 72-73, 75, 77, 137-140, 143, 147, 162, 165-166, 175-176, 178, 180, 188, 193-195, 198, 204, 211-213, 215-217, 219-220, 222, 224, 226, 228, 246-247, 275, 298, 312, 316-318, 322-324, 329-332, 334, 336-337, 355, 357, 361-362, 364-365, 389, 393-395, 416-419

Autronic AG v. Switzerland, 311, 314, 323

B

B. v. France, 57, 246, 254-255

Baragiola v. Switzerland, 418

Barberà, Messegué and Jabardo v. Spain, 198-199, 216, 227

Barfod v. Denmark, 316, 331

Barthold v. Germany, 313-314

Beaumartin v. France, 176

"Belgian linguistics" case, 185, 188-189, 342, 358, 366-367, 396-399

Belgium, 25, 58, 70, 72-73, 82, 84-88, 92-93, 100, 115-116, 121-123, 149-152, 160-162, 165, 171, 177, 180-181, 186, 192-193, 196, 199-201, 203, 209, 213, 221, 225, 227-228, 230-231, 236-237, 268-269, 280, 284, 329, 332, 339, 342, 357-358, 363, 382-383, 395, 397, 402, 404-405

Belilos v. Switzerland, 192

Benham v. the United Kingdom, 93-94, 104

Benthem v. the Netherlands, 169-170, 174-175, 179, 196

Berrehab v. the Netherlands, 269-270, 277

Bönisch v. Austria, 198

Borrelli v. Switzerland, 415

Bouamar v. Belgium, 93, 96, 115-116

Boyle and Rice v. the United Kingdom, 353-354

Bozano v. France, 94, 97-99, 127

Brannigan and McBride v. the United Kingdom, 368, 370-372

Brogan and Others v. the United Kingdom, 105, 112, 127-129, 131, 159-160, 167, 205, 370

Brüggemann and Scheuten v. the Federal Republic of Germany, 39

Buchholz v. Germany, 209-210

Buckley v. the United Kingdom, 257, 285

Burghartz v. Switzerland, 246, 249-251, 362-363, 419

C

Campbell v. the United Kingdom, 56, 288-290, 292

Sales agents for publications of the Council of Europe
Agents de vente des publications du Conseil de l'Europe